JI

COMMENTARY ON ROMANS

COMMENTARY
on
ROMANS

by

WM. S. PLUMER

KREGEL PUBLICATIONS
Grand Rapids, Michigan 49501

Published by Kregel Publications, a Division of Kregel, Inc.,
P.O. Box 2607, Grand Rapids, Michigan 49501. All rights
reserved. Formerly published by Anson D. F. Randolph &
Co., New York, 1870, under the title *Commentary on
Paul's Epistle to the Romans with an Introduction on the
Life, Times, Writings and Character of Paul.*

Library of Congress Catalog Card Number 73 - 155251

ISBN: 0-8254-3501-3

First Kregel Publications edition 1971
Reprinted 1979

Printed in the United States of America

CONTENTS

AN

INTRODUCTION

TO THE

LIFE, TIMES, WRITINGS

AND CHARACTER

OF PAUL

INTRODUCTION

I. THE VARIETY OF SCRIPTURE

IN his unerring wisdom God did not give us the Scriptures in one connected treatise, but in sixty-six distinct books. Of these *thirty-nine* are in the Old Testament, and *twenty-seven* in the New. The word of God contains a number of historical books. Others are poetical. Some are didactic; others, polemic. Some are marked with the best style of proverb; others, with the best kind of parable and allegory. All Scripture is inspired by God, and is profitable.

The first *three* books of the New Testament contain sketches of the life of Jesus Christ. The *fourth* is evidently written chiefly to establish his divinity, and show forth his glory. The *fifth* records the early labors, successes and sufferings of the apostles in planting churches throughout the world. The *last* book of Scripture is chiefly prophetical. Many things in it foretold are yet to be accomplished. The remaining *twenty-one* books of the New Testament are strictly in the form of Epistles. Of these one is written by James, the son of Alpheus, often (from his stature) called the Less; one by Jude (Judas not Iscariot); two by Simon Peter, son of Jonas; and three by John. The remaining *fourteen* are written by Paul. Of these some are addressed to churches, and some to particular persons; some are mainly doctrinal and some chiefly practical; some are specially designed to instruct Jews; and some, Gentiles; some teach the laity their duties and some give good counsels and precepts to pastors and evangelists.

It is worthy of notice that while the Old Testament does not contain one entire book, but at the most a few verses in an epistolary form, yet of the two hundred and fifty-six chapters in the New Testament one hundred and seventeen are in that form. Of these Paul wrote eighty-seven chapters, containing two thousand and nine verses. Of the Pauline epistles the first three contain more matter than the remaining eleven. On the other hand, the New Testament has in it but little poetry, and that quoted from heathen

3

poets or from Christian hymns. Various reasons are assigned for this abounding of epistles in the New Testament. The Holy Ghost, who inspired the writers, chose this form of communication, and that will satisfy the pious mind. But the state of literature throughout the world about the time of the first propagation of the Gospel greatly favored this style of communication. Long treatises were written in the *epistles* of learned men. We might cite those of Cicero, Seneca, Symmachus and Pliny, the Younger. In fact both ancients and moderns have in this way handled a great variety of topics, friendship, art, science, politics, literature and religion. There are a thousand ways of writing a good letter. All the peculiarities of the writer's genius may have full scope in that kind of composition. If he does not rise to the sublime, or the beautiful, he did not promise to do so. If he dwells on very familiar topics, that well agrees with this kind of composition. The best letters on moral subjects are marked with clearness, brevity and plainness, and with constant allusions to things well understood between the writer and his friends. Because a letter is long, it is not necessarily tedious. Many a good letter has not in it an epigram or an antithesis. While epistles should not be set lectures, they may be solid, weighty, and even argumentative. Easy and familiar as epistles may certainly be, we have a right to expect that they be courteous, giving no just cause of offence. No greater influence is exerted among men than that of epistolary correspondence. Lord Bacon says: " Such letters, as are written from wise men, are of all the words of man, in my judgment, the best; for they are more natural than orations and public speeches, and more advised than conferences or private ones." Over other kinds of writing epistles have one advantage : they are always read, sometimes often read. If Paul ever wrote anything but epistles, we neither have it nor any reliable account of it.

II. What we know of Paul's early life

Our knowledge of Paul is derived chiefly from the account we have of him in the Acts of the Apostles, written by his companion, Luke, and from his own epistles. By comparing " what Paul says of Paul " with what Luke says of him, we gain a sufficient insight into his history. Most of the unwritten traditions respecting him are wholly unreliable, some are probable, and a few are apparently countenanced by hints in the Scriptures.

In Hebrew he was called *Saul*. The precise import of this name is uncertain. Some think it signifies a *pit*, the *sepulchre or death;* others, that it signifies *lent* or *demanded,* as if he had been given to his parents in answer to prayer. It is of the less importance to look into this matter, as he entirely dropped this cognomen soon after his conversion, and ever after bore the name of *Paul*. Some think this word means a *worker;* but others think it is taken from the Latin, *Paulus*, which means *little*. This is the more probable opinion, and well coincides with the lowliness of this apostle often expressed, and particularly where he says, "I am less than the least of all saints," Eph. 3 : 8. This is a better explanation than that which makes the apostle take his name from Sergius Paulus, one of his converts, Acts 8 : 7. But Origen, Tholuck and others think that along with his Jewish name, this apostle in common with many Israelites, who lived among the Romans, had a Latin name, and that there is no special significancy in his change of name.

Both of Paul's parents were of the seed of Jacob. So that phrase, "a Hebrew of the Hebrews," clearly teaches. Like king Saul, our apostle was of the tribe of Benjamin. He was a native of Tarsus, in Cilicia, "no mean city." To all its freemen Augustus had given the freedom of Roman citizens, because of their fidelity to his interests. The time of Paul's birth is uncertain. From something said by Chrysostom, in one of his homilies, some have inferred that Paul was born two years before our Lord. But this is pretty certainly a mistake; for he was still "a young man" at Stephen's martyrdom, which occurred certainly as late as A. D. 33. And a man from thirty-five to thirty-seven years old would not be so spoken of. It is therefore highly probable that Paul was considerably younger than Jesus of Nazareth.

In religious persuasion and profession before his conversion Paul was a Pharisee of "the most straitest sect." He had remarkable advantages for 'profiting' in his knowledge of his national religion and in the learning of his times. The school at Tarsus was well known in the Roman empire. It furnished professors for other famous seats of learning in those days. At an early age Paul was placed under the tuition of that renowned doctor of the law of Moses, Gamaliel, Acts 22 : 3. This school was at Jerusalem. In his outward observance of the ritual and morals of his religion, Paul was "blameless," Phil. 3 : 6. But he was grossly ignorant of the holy and spiritual character of the decalogue. Rom. 7 : 7. Nor had he any knowledge of the great truth that equal love to man and supreme love to God were the sum of the law. Consequently when a mere youth, from a wretched wrong-headedness of conscience, he became a persecutor of the most malignant type. He held the clothes of the men, who stoned Stephen, and consented to his cruel death. From that time he was like a ravening wolf in the flock of Christ. He had no mercy, and seems to have had no remorse, unless that phrase—" It is hard for thee to kick against the pricks,"—teaches that he had compunctions. He verily thought he ought to do many things contrary to the name of Jesus of Nazareth. He therefore "made havoc" of the church. He was "exceeding mad" against the Christians. His very breath stank of blood. He "breathed out threatenings and slaughter." How long he pursued this flagitious course is not certain; but it was probably for fifteen or twenty months. His zeal and bitterness at length knew no bounds. He went unto "strange cities" in quest of prey. But the prayer of dying Stephen and of other holy martyrs for their enemy and murderer, and especially the intercession of our great High Priest, prevailed, and next we read of

III. THE CONVERSION OF PAUL

This great moral change in his character is thrice recorded in the Acts of the Apostles. It is commonly, and with reason, supposed to have occurred about two years after Christ's ascension from Olivet. It was attended with remarkable circumstances, yet produced in him no permanent effects but such as were necessary to fit him for his work, sufferings and triumphs. Luke, who wrote the Acts of the Apostles, thus narrates this great event:

"And Saul, yet breathing out threatenings and slaughter against the disciples of the Lord, went unto the high priest, and desired of him letters to Damascus to the synagogues, that if he found any of this way, whether they were men or women, he might bring them bound unto Jerusalem. And as he journeyed, he came near Damascus: and suddenly there shined round about him a light from heaven, and he fell to the earth, and heard a voice saying unto him, Saul, Saul, why persecutest thou me? And he said, Who art thou, Lord? And the Lord said, I am Jesus whom thou persecutest: it is hard for thee to kick against the pricks. And he trembling and astonished, said, Lord, what wilt thou have me to do? And the Lord said unto him, Arise, and go into the city, and it shall be told thee what thou must do. And the men which journeyed with him stood speechless, hearing a voice, but seeing no man. And Saul arose from the earth, and when his eyes were opened, he saw no man ; but they led him by the hand, and brought him into Damascus. And he was three days without sight, and neither did eat nor drink. And there was a certain disciple at Damascus named Ananias ; and to him said the Lord in a vision, Ananias. And he said, Behold, I am here, Lord. And the Lord said unto him, Arise, and go into the street which is called Straight, and inquire in the house of Judas for one called Saul of Tarsus: for behold, he prayeth, and hath seen in a vision a man named Ananias, coming in, and putting his hand on him, that he might receive his sight. Then Ananias answered, Lord, I have heard by many of this man, how much evil he hath done to thy saints at Jerusalem : and here he hath authority from the chief priests, to bind all that call on thy name. But the Lord said unto him, Go thy way: for he is a chosen vessel unto me, to bear my name before the Gentiles and Kings, and the children of Israel. For I will show him how great things he must suffer for my name's sake. And Ananias went his way, and entered into the house : and putting his hands on him, said, Brother Saul, the Lord (even Jesus that appeared unto thee in the way as thou camest) hath sent me, that thou mightest receive thy sight, and be filled with the Holy Ghost. And immediately there fell from his eyes as it had been scales : and he received sight forthwith, and arose, and was baptized. And when he had received meat, he was strengthened. Then was Saul certain days with the disciples which were at Damascus. And straightway he preached Christ in the synagogues, that he is the Son of God. But all that heard him were amazed, and said, Is not this he that destroyed them which called on this name in Jerusalem, and came hither for that intent,. that he might bring them bound unto the chief priests? But Saul increased the more in strength, and confounded the Jews which dwelt at Damascus, proving that this is·very Christ." Acts 9 : 1–22. This is Luke's account of Paul's conversion. But in his history of Paul's life he records two accounts, which Paul publicly gave of the same great event. The first of these is found in Acts 22 : 3–21 ; the other, in Acts 26 : 9–20. These narratives from the lips of Paul mention some incidents not given in Acts 9. But there is no disagreement with that narrative, with one apparent exception. In Luke's narrative he says : " The men which journeyed with him stood speechless, hearing a voice, but seeing no man," Acts 9 : 7; while in Paul's defence made before the chief captain he says : " They that were with me saw indeed the light, and were afraid ; but they heard not the voice of him that spoke to me." Acts 22 : 9. This difficulty is only apparent, not real. It arises from the fact that the word rendered *voice* is used in two different senses. Often it signifies any *noise* or *sound* though it be wholly inarticulate; as in these cases : " The wind bloweth where it listeth, and thou hearest the *sound* thereof," John 3 : 8. In 1 Cor. 14 : 7, 8 it is thrice rendered *sound.* In Rev. 1 : 15 ; 9 : 9 ; 18 : 22 it is four times rendered *sound ;* in Rev. 6 : 1 it is rendered *noise.* In many places it might be rendered sound or noise, as where we read of " the *voice* of many waters," and " the *voice* of mighty thunderings." In this sense of the word Paul's attendants heard the voice, that is the *sound* or *noise*. But the same word is used for an articulate voice, as where it is said, " The *voice* of one crying in the wilderness, Prepare ye the way of the Lord ;" and " Lo a *voice* from heaven, saying, This is my beloved Son, in whom I am well pleased," and in many other places. So that in this sense Paul's companions did not hear the voice, the articulate sound. That Paul used it in this sense is manifest from the very words: " they heard not *the voice of him that spake to me.*" They heard not the *word* spoken to me.

It is evident that Paul always regarded his conversion as a demonstration of the truth of Christianity. Nor was this a fallacy. Every effect must have an adequate cause. When we see a lion turned into a lamb, a bird of prey into a gentle dove, a blasphemer into a devout man, a bitter persecutor into an incomparable preacher, we ask for a cause. We find none but that assigned by Paul himself. Lord Lyttleton was right when he concluded that Paul's conversion was an unanswerable proof of the truth of the Christian religion. He has given his argument to the world. No flaw in it has yet been detected. As an event Paul's conversion cannot be easily overestimated. Adolphe Monod: " Grace came, omnipotent grace, and the rampart of that great soul fell like the walls of Jericho; the impregnable citadel was carried in an hour, and all its ample magazines were redeemed for the service of the Lord."

IV. THE PUBLIC LIFE OF PAUL THE APOSTLE

Many attempts have been made to settle the chronological order of the leading events in the life of the great apostle to the Gentiles. The following brief view is probably nearly correct. Paul was engaged in persecution a part of A. D. 34 and the whole of 35. In the year 36 he was converted and went into Arabia, where he received abundance of direct visions and revelations. In 38 his life was sought at Damascus, but he was let down by the wall in a basket, and came to Jerusalem and " essayed to join himself to the disciples, but they were afraid of him," and avoided him till Barnabas introduced him. In 39 Paul preached in Cilicia the faith, which he had destroyed. He was not as yet known in person to the churches in Judea. In 40 he preached in Syria, not going to Antioch however. About 41 a door of access to the Gentiles was opened, and Paul entered, and labored and suffered much for two or three years. In 43 the persecution of Herod

(Agrippa) began. In 44 Paul and Barnabas carried relief to the suffering Christians in Jerusalem, and Mark joined Paul and Barnabas, and these last were fully set apart to preach to the Gentiles. In 45 Paul preached extensively in Cyprus and in Pamphylia; in 46, in Pisidia and Lycaonia. The next year he and his companions visited the same churches, "confirming the souls of the disciples." In 48 Paul had his first great conflict with the judaizing teachers. In 49 he and his companions labored much in Phœnicia and Samaria. The same year he reported the progress of the Gospel among the Gentiles to the brethren at Jerusalem, where the first general council was held. In 50 Paul and Barnabas separated, and Paul took to him Silas (or Silvanus) and Timothy. He travelled extensively this year. He spent the year 51 at Philippi, going also to Amphipolis, Apollonia, Thessalonica and Berea. The next year the Jews were expelled from Rome by Claudius, and Paul visited Athens and Corinth, and had a great desire to visit the church at Rome. In 54 Paul went to Ephesus and Cæsarea. This year his personal acquaintance with Apollos probably began. In 54 or 55 Paul began his reasonings in the school of Tyrannus in Ephesus. These lasted two years. In 57 he left Asia and, passing through Troy, came into Macedonia, and thence into Greece. In 58 he was also at Philippi, visited Jerusalem, and made his address before Ananias, and in Cæsarea before Felix, who kept him a prisoner, hoping to receive a bribe for his release. In the year 60 Paul stood before Festus and Agrippa, and, by appeal, was sent to Rome. On his way he was shipwrecked, but reached Rome pretty early in 61. He remained a prisoner for at least two years, yet having considerable privileges. In 63 he went as far as Spain. In 64 he went to Crete, thence to Judea, thence to Colosse, thence to Macedonia. He spent the winter of 65 at Nicopolis; thence he went to Corinth, and in 66 to Troy. In 67 he came to Miletus, and thence voluntarily to Rome. There he was imprisoned. He continued a prisoner till some time in 68, when he suffered martyrdom. This general outline is as nearly correct, according to our best lights, as any that has been given. It is sober and avoids wild conjectures.

Paul began his public life under Tiberius, who was emperor eighteen years before Christ's death, and died in 37, three years after Paul came on the stage. Tiberius was succeeded by Caligula, who died in 41, and was succeeded by Claudius, who died by poison in 54, and was succeeded by Nero, who killed himself in 68. So that Paul acted a conspicuous part under four Roman Emperors.

V. The order and time of writing Paul's epistles

It is generally known that in no edition of the Bible are Paul's epistles arranged according to the chronological order, in which they were written. J. D. Michaelis says their present order is agreed on "according to the supposed rank and importance of the communities, or persons, to which they were addressed." This remark may indicate the state of mind in those that made up the canon, but if such a notion prevailed there was certainly some misapplication of it. The order in which the books of Scripture are bound up in no way affects the doctrines they teach, and is at best a mere matter of taste, or personal preference, or general convenience. It may be satisfactory to the reader, and it may hereafter save time now to state that Marcion and Michaelis make Paul's epistle to the Galatians the earliest, the latter author dating it A. D. 49; while the authorized version, Eichhorn, Lardner, Lloyd, Tomline, Horne, Pearson, Hug and Scott all make his 1st epistle to the Thessalonians the earliest, and his 2nd Epistle to the Thessalonians the next in order. But they are not agreed as to the dates of these epistles, some making them as early as 52, and some two years later. While Michaelis regards the epistle to the Galatians as Paul's first, most of those writers just quoted regard it as the third; Lardner, Tomline, Horne and Bagster's Comprehensive Bible dating it as early as 52 or 53; Scott, in 56; Pearson, in 57; our authorized version and Lloyd as late as 58.

The 1st epistle to the Corinthians is pretty confidently supposed to come next in order, though Schrader makes it the earliest and Marcion makes it the second; Lardner fixes it at 53; Tomline, at 56; Michaelis, Pearson, Horne and Bagster, at 57; Lloyd, at 59, and the authorized version and Scott, at 60. Though Marcion regards the 2nd epistle to the Corinthians as the third of Paul's writing, and Hug as the sixth, yet neither of these gives the common view. Eichhorn makes it the fifth. So does Schrader. Pearson, Lardner, Tomline and Bagster date it in 57; Michaelis and Horne, in 58; the authorized version and Lloyd, in 60; and Scott, in 61. The epistle to the Romans was probably the sixth in order, though Schrader makes it the third; Marcion, the fourth; and Hug, the eighth. Pearson, Dupin and Tomline date it in 57; Horne, in 57 or 58; Lord Barrington, Benson, Michaelis and Lardner, in 58; the authorized version, Usher, Eichhorn and Lloyd, in 60, and Scott, in 61. Schrader makes the epistle to the Ephesians the sixth of Paul's writing; Pearson, the eighth; Marcion and Eichhorn, the seventh. Lardner, Horne, Tomline and Bagster date it in 61; the authorized version, Lloyd and Scott, in

64; and Michaelis, in 64 or 65. It is, however, generally agreed that the epistles to the Philippians, Colossians and Philemon were written the same year (at least about the same time) as that to the Ephesians, though Scott dates Philippians a year later than the other three. The epistle to the Hebrews probably comes next, though Hug makes it the last of all. Horne and Bagster date it in 62 or 63; Pearson, Lardner and Tomline, in 63; the authorized version and Lloyd, in 64; Michaelis, in 64 or 65, and Scott, in 65. The 1st epistle to Timothy is very generally regarded as the twelfth in order. Lardner dates it as early as 56, and Michaelis in 58; but Pearson, Horne and Tomline date it in 64; Le Clerc, L'Enfant, Cave, Fabricius, Mill, Macknight, Paley, Lloyd, Scott and our authorized version, in 65. The epistle to Titus is the thirteenth in order, though Hug makes it the third, and Michaelis dates it in 51 or 52, and Lardner, in 56; but Horne, Tomline and Bagster date it in 64; and the authorized version, Pearson and Lloyd, in 65; and Scott, in 66. The last thing Paul ever wrote was his 2nd epistle to Timothy, though Lardner dates it in 61; but Horne and Tomline, in 65; the authorized version, Michaelis and Lloyd, in 66; Benson, Macknight, Paley, Clarke and Rosenmuller, not long before he suffered martyrdom. Nero died in June 68, and Paul was beheaded under that emperor. It is probable the later dates given are nearer the truth than the earlier. Scott dates it in 67 and Pearson in 68.

VI. THE PLACES WHERE PAUL'S EPISTLES WERE WRITTEN

It seems to be pretty generally agreed that the epistles to the Ephesians, Philippians, Colossians, Philemon and the 2nd to Timothy were written from Rome. The subscriptions to those epistles say so, and there seems to be no countervailing evidence of any considerable force. The authorized version admits that all these were written from the imperial city. To the above some add the epistle to the Hebrews. Horne thinks this is perhaps true. With him agrees Slade. The subscription says it was from Italy. So does the authorized version. The following epistles are commonly supposed to have been written from Corinth, viz: Romans, 1st Thessalonians and 2nd Thessalonians. So say Horne and Slade. But the subscriptions to both epistles to the Thessalonians say they were written from Athens, and the authorized version adopts that statement. The subscription to the epistle to the Galatians dates it from Rome. The authorized version follows this. But Horne dates it from Corinth, and Slade from Corinth or Macedonia. The subscription to the 1st epistle to the Corinthians says it was written from Philippi. With this agrees the authorized version; but Horne and Slade correctly think it was written at Ephesus, as is proven by what Paul himself says: " I will tarry at Ephesus until Pentecost," 1 Cor. 16 : 8. The subscription to the 2nd epistle to the Corinthians says it was written at Philippi. With this agrees our authorized version. But Horne and Slade date it from Macedonia, without fixing the particular city. It is generally agreed that the epistle to Titus was probably written from Macedonia; the subscription and the authorized version say from Nicopolis, which was in Macedonia. Horne and Slade date the 1st epistle to Timothy from Macedonia, though the subscription and authorized version date it from Laodicea, which was the capital of Phrygia Pacotiana in Asia Minor.

All Paul's epistles in our authorized version and in many other versions and editions have *subscriptions*, that is, a few words or lines purporting to tell where they were written, and sometimes by whom they were sent. Having already referred to these, it is convenient here, once for all, to say respecting them: 1. They are not Scripture They were not written by Paul, nor by any one under his direction. They were written by some later writer unknown to us. 2. Some of them may and perhaps do correctly give the date of place; but we cannot rely on them unless supported by evidence drawn from some other source. 3. The Doway Bible, Guyse, the continuators of Henry, Scott and others pay no regard to them, dropping them altogether. 4. It is certain that some of them are erroneous as that to the 1st epistle to the Corinthians, which the Doway Bible and respectable scholars generally admit was written from Ephesus, not from Philippi, as stated in the subscription. 5. Several of them are awkward and impertinent.

For these reasons they might well be unnoticed in any concise work on Paul's epistles. It may be observed that the doctrinal and practical truths of Paul's writings are just the same wherever or whenever written; that no duty is affected by our views on these points; and that the chief importance attached to the date of time or place in any epistle arises from the use that may be made of it in an argument with gainsayers on questions of criticism. In some cases possibly there may be more point in some things said; if dated at one time or place rather than another, but this is doubtful.

VII. The excellence of Paul's writings

From the death of Paul to this day there has not been a Sabbath when he was not read, recited or quoted in the public ministrations of God's house; and so it will be to the end of time. Devils and wicked men, as well as saints and angels still say, "Jesus I know and Paul I know." The power of Jesus as a teacher arose from the fact that he was the author of truth, and the embodiment of truth, and knew what was in man, and spoke as man never spoke. The secret of Paul's power as a teacher is found, not merely or chiefly in his genius, though that was prodigious, nor in his acquaintance with Hebrew and Grecian lore, though that was vast, but in his thorough instruction by the abundance of visions and revelations, which he had from the Lord Jesus and from the large measure of God's Spirit granted him during his whole Christian life. Thus he was able with great clearness, directness, pungency and tenderness to address men orally and by writing. Lord Shaftesbury says that "the concealment of order and method in this manner of writing (epistolary) makes the chief beauty of the work." If this is a just observation, one entire class of objection to Paul's epistles falls to the ground.

Augustine expressed the wish that he could have seen "Christ in the flesh and Paul in the pulpit." Among mere men Paul was probably the prince of preachers. Was Paul eloquent? The answer to this question depends on our definition of eloquence. If with Cecil we regard eloquence as "animated simplicity" in the treatment of great themes; or with Webster, as "forcible language, which gives utterance to deep emotion;" or with Worcester, as "the art of clothing thoughts in such language, and of uttering them in such a manner, as is adapted to produce conviction or persuasion;" then was Paul eloquent in a high degree—a master of the art. But if by eloquence is meant what some understand thereby, "elegant language uttered with fluency," or pleasing the ears and fancy of men by high-wrought but imaginary scenes of woe or bliss, then was Paul not eloquent. He intentionally and avowedly rejected all flashy and meretricious ornaments both in speaking and in writing. 1 Cor. 1 : 17; 2 : 1, 4, 13.

Surely Beza spoke well : " When I more narrowly consider the whole genius and character of Paul's style, I must confess I have found no such sublimity of speaking in Plato himself; as often as the apostle is pleased to thunder out the mysteries of God : no exquisiteness of vehemence in Demosthenes equal to his, as often as he had a mind to terrify men with a dread of the Divine judgments, or to admonish them concerning their conduct, òr to allure them to the contemplation of the Divine benignity, or to excite them to the duties of piety and morality. In a word, not even in Aristotle, nor in Galen, though most excellent artists, do I find a more exact method of teaching." The 'method' here referred to is not that of the rhetoricians, but that natural method, by which great truths are conveyed in simple terms, and truths, unwelcome to the natural heart, are tenderly and ingeniously insinuated into the mind, nothing in the manner of communicating them naturally irritating or justly offending the weak or the prejudiced.

Let it not be forgotten that Paul had much higher aims than ever entered the mind of any Grecian orator, moralist or poet; that his views penetrated the veil of endless duration; that he lived as seeing him who is invisible; that "the sacred oracles were not designed as works of genius, to. attract the admiration of the learned, nor to set before them a finished model of fine writing for their imitation; but to turn mankind from sin to God;" and that every thing foreign from this great object was a grand impertinence.

That Paul had a high order of eloquence was admitted by the great critic, Dionysius Longinus: "Demosthenes, Lysias, Aeschines, Hyperides, Isocrates, Antiphon are the glory of all eloquence and of Greek genius; to whom may be added Paul of Tarsus, who, so far as I know, was the first who did not make use of demonstration." It is true that Fabricius and Ruhnken have questioned the genuineness of this passage; but the reasons they have given are insufficient. All the usual signs of interpolation are wanting. We may, therefore, fairly receive the testimony of this important critic, who belonged to a school pretty well acquainted with the writings in use among the Christians. Yet no one would think the less of Paul if he should regard the sentence as spurious; just as no one thinks the better of Paul when he esteems it genuine.

In 1588 there was born at Saumur, Claudius Saumaise, afterwards known to the learned world by the Latin name of Salmasius. Casaubon spoke of him as 'learned to a wonder' — "ad miraculum doctus." He was admired over all Europe. At Leyden he was successor to Scaliger. Richelieu offered him 12,000 livres a year, if he would but live in France. The judgment of no literary man on the Continent of Europe in the 17th century carried with it such weight as did that of Salmasius. On his death-bed (at the age of 65), this giant in every species of solid and polite learning said: " O, I have lost a world of time. If one year more were added to my life, it should be spent in reading David's Psalms and Paul's epistles." Of the epistle to the Ephesians Grotius says it expresses the grand matters of which it treats in words " more sublime than are to be found in any human language." John Locke says: " Paul is full of the matter he treats . and writes with warmth, which usually neglects method, and those partitions and pauses, which men educated in the school of rhetoricians usually observe." Macknight says: " All who wish to understand true Christianity ought to study the epistles of this great apostle with the utmost care." Pages might easily be filled with high commendations of Paul's writings, gathered from all sorts of respectable writers for the last sixteen hundred years. What doctrine did he ever handle but with great profit to the humble ? What hard question did he ever blink or fail therein to give repose to honest hearts and tender consciences? What duty did he fail to make plain and show the urgent reasons for its performance ? What case of distress did he overlook or slight ? When did he come short of presenting adequate considerations to sustain the meek and lowly believer? Then all he says is so practical, so wisely presented and so tenderly urged, that simple-hearted men feel that Paul understood their case, while the greatest minds have felt no need of lessons more elevating than they found in his writings. Above most men Paul was thoroughly practical. Of him Chrysostom well says: " Like a wall of adamant, his writings form a bulwark around all the churches of the world, while himself, as some mighty champion stands even now in the midst, casting down every high thing that exalteth itself against the knowledge of God, and bringing into captivity every thought to the obedience of Christ." Adolphe Monod says: " Should any one ask me to name the man, who, of all others, has been the greatest benefactor of our race, I should say, without hesitation, the *Apostle Paul*. His name is the type of human activity, the most endless, and at the same time, the most useful that history has cared to preserve."

VIII. Is Paul hard to be understood ?

The correct answer to this question is given by Peter: " In all his [Paul's] epistles speaking in them of these things; in which are some things hard to be understood, which they that are unlearned and unstable wrest, as they do also the other Scriptures, unto their own destruction." 2 Pet. 3 : 16. In this language of the Apostle of the circumcision there is both caution and candor. 1. He says that before men can get harm from Paul's epistles, they must '*wrest*,' wrench, turn awry, violently pervert things. Whose language can bear unfair dealing, uncandid distorting?

We know who, and whose type he was that said: "Every day they wrest my words." "The Scripture is so penned that they, who have a mind to know, may know; they who have a mind to wrangle may take occasion enough of offence, and justly perish by the rebellion of their own minds; for God never intended to satisfy men of stubborn and perverse spirits." All this is but saying that the Bible is profitable to those only who have candor, humility, docility and the love of the truth. 2. Peter tells us who they are, that thus pervert things. First, they are '*unlearned*,' or uninstructed, those who are unsettled in the elements of truth. Then they are '*unstable*,' not steadfast. They have no true and fixed first principles, but are driven like waves by every wind. Such people are ever bewildered, and liable to be 'bewitched,' as the Galatians were. 3. The obscurity is not so much in Paul's manner of discussing these subjects, as in the subjects themselves; for the 'which' refers not to the epistles but to 'these things,' of which he had been speaking. No writer can overcome difficulties inherent in a subject itself. Paul by the Spirit was led to discuss the sublimest mysteries in the nature and providence of God, and in the experience of men, as well as the knottiest questions in casuistry. The Christian world has ever been thankful for the light thus given, but the unlearned and unstable, who have no spiritual wisdom, abuse such discussions. The fault is their own. 4. This is proven by the fact that the same men 'wrest also the other Scriptures.' No part of God's word is duly received by them. 5. They are bad men on their way to "destruction."

It is freely admitted also that to us the ancient Greek, in which Paul wrote, is a dead language; that Paul's education led him to use many forms of speech borrowed rom the Hebrew; that he did not always use pure classical Greek, but that which is often called Alexandrian, the Greek of the Septuagint, then somewhat modified and modernized. Cornelius a Lapide says: "The apostle wrote in Greek and often grecianized; but because he was a Hebrew, he often hebraized." When we add to this that the language of mortals is very inadequate to convey heavenly ideas; that all men are naturally blind in spiritual things, and that in conveying spiritual conceptions it is necessary to use terms in a sense very different from that which they have when our discourse is of carnal things, the reader will not wonder that it is not easy for us at this distance of time and place from the apostle's age and country always, even after careful study, to tell certainly what is the precise shade of idea which he would convey to us. It is therefore for a joy that God hears prayer, and opens his ear to the cry of all who search for knowledge·as for hid treasure. The devout mind makes most progress in discovering the true nature and uses of all the teachings of God's word. "If any man lack wisdom, let him ask of God, who giveth to all men liberally and upbraideth not."

IX. THE STATE OF THE WORLD DURING PAUL'S PUBLIC LIFE

Paul was acting a public part, as early as some time in A. D. 34. He was converted in 36. If he was beheaded in 68, he was a Christian teacher for thirty-two years, and lived till within (about) two years of the destruction of Jerusalem. That is, he was a prominent and stirring actor thirty-four out of the last thirty-six years of the national existence of the Jews. In the Roman empire he was cotemporary with Tiberius, Caligula, Claudius and Nero. The liberties of the Jews were gone, they being lorded over by Roman governors and other officials. The liberties of Greece had very much perished in the same way, as also by factions. And the liberties of Roman citizens had well nigh become extinct through the cruelties of the emperors, and the rapacity of their subordinates. The state of religion was low. The Jews, who still adhered to their ritual, were to a fearful extent heartless hypocrites, utterly denying the power of godliness, and greatly given to forms and fables. By their unbelief they justified their nation in crucifying the Redeemer, and were anew crying: 'His blood be upon us and upon our children.' Upon them was soon to be visited the blood of all the holy prophets, from the blood of Abel to that of Zecharias, that perished between the altar and the temple. The Greeks had long been steeped in abominable idolatries. Devil worship (such is all idolatry, 1 Cor. 10 : 20, 21) never did elevate a people; though some forms and stages of it are more debasing than others. The Athenians were worshipping all the gods of which their poets had sung, or their fathers had told; and then, lest there should be some failure, they had erected an altar to THE UNKNOWN GOD. At Rome the Pantheon was crowded with representations of the idols worshipped in the provinces. But with all this show, religious obligation was every where despised. Venality, cruelty, meanness, hypocrisy and corruption terribly prevailed. Skepticism swayed large masses of men. The schools of philosophy, never potential for real good, now taught frivolities, or brutal coarseness, or chilling insensibility, or senseless refinements. An oath by any god had very much lost its sacredness. There was not a ray of hope for the world but that emanating from the cross of Calvary; and to the great mass of the Jews that cross was an offence, and to the great mass of pagans it was foolishness. Men bitterly scorned or with curled lip smiled at the idea of being saved by one, who, they said, was not able to save himself from the ignominy of crucifixion.

Yet there were present advantages for spreading the truth. The Greek language was spoken by many, and read and understood by more. The Greek schoolmasters had been abroad, and vast numbers of their pupils in Italy and elsewhere were capable of enjoying any thing written in the original language of the New Testament. This is abundantly proven by Juvenal, Ovid and Tacitus. This was true in many parts of Africa, as well as in Europe and Asia. Then the Romans by their conquests had made the most populous portions of Western Asia, Northern Africa and Southern and Central Europe accessible to travellers on any errand of commerce, philosophy or religion. Had the Christian doctrine only asked for a place among sister systems of religion; had it tolerated idols and bad morals; had it merely told of the miracles of Jesus without stating what they proved; and had it humbly asked that the statue of Jesus might be placed in the Pantheon alongside of almost any of the many gods there represented; it is not probable it would have awakened either considerable notice or violent opposition. But when it came condemning all the darling vices of mankind, uprooting hoary systems of superstition, denouncing heaven's wrath against all ungodliness and unrighteousness, and commanding men, on pain of eternal damnation, to cease from idols, from human wisdom, from self-will, self-esteem and self-righteousness, and to rest all their hopes of happiness for the next world on the person, the sacrifice, the intercession and the authority of him, who bled and died in the midst of malefactors; Jew and Gentile, Stoic and Platonist rose up in a rage, and said, Away with so unsocial and accursed a form of superstition; and they soon began to persecute it.

X. PAUL THE VERY SORT OF MAN FOR THIS STATE OF THINGS

In Greek and Hebrew learning, in an acquaintance with Jewish prophets and heathen poets, in acuteness and discrimination, in power of reasoning and persuasion, in address and intrepidity Paul was the very sort of man to enter into this state of things, and fight a great battle for the truth. Naturally inclined to extremes, his conversion and subsequent discipline had taught him all the rules of a just moderation. Hug: "Formerly hasty and irritable, now only spirited and resolved; formerly violent, now full of energy and enterprising: once ungovernably refractory against every thing which obstructed him, now only persevering; once fanatical and morose, now only serious; once cruel, now only severe; once a harsh zealot, now fearing God; formerly unrelenting, deaf to sympathy and commiseration, now himself acquainted with tears, which he had seen without effect in others. Formerly the friend of none, now the brother of mankind, well-meaning, compassionate, sympathizing; yet never weak, always great, in the midst of sadness and sorrow manly and noble; . . in the midst of pain full of dignity." He was as bold as Peter, as tender as John, as seraphic as Isaiah. He gave all; he suffered all; he sacrificed all; he gained all. He was meek, never tame; humble, never mean; giving no needless offence, yet never yielding Christian liberty; averse to strife, yet never forgetting that he was set for the defence of the Gospel; bold when the truth was in peril, yet gentle as a nurse among her children; not counting his own life dear, yet tenderly regarding the feelings and comfort of others; writing epistles full of just and terrible rebuke to the heady, and as full of tenderness to the penitent and sorrowful; despising all the arts of effeminacy, yet in the best sense an honorable gentleman; detesting voluntary humility and all affectation, yet working at his trade, tent-making; carrying about in his body the dying of the Lord Jesus, but finally winning and eternally wearing a martyr's crown. Blessed, incomparable man! raised up by the adorable head of the church to be to the end of the world a pattern of what grace, and courage, and diligence, and faith, and gentleness can do.

XI. IN WRITING HIS FOURTEEN EPISTLES PAUL WAS DIVINELY INSPIRED

It is proof of the intense jealousy of the early church in admitting to the canon of Scripture any book, that at first some of the epistles, which bear Paul's name were doubted, and their genuineness suspected. It is no less proof of the abundant evidence of their divine inspiration that long since all hesitancy in receiving them was removed, and that for ages the Christian world, divided on many other matters, has been harmonious in receiving all he has written, not as the word of man, but, as it is indeed, the word of God. And all but neologists and semi-infidels as freely admit that his inspiration was plenary, infallibly preserving him from error, and verbal, leading him to use " words which the Holy Ghost teacheth." The apocryphal books of the New Testament are peculiarly unworthy of respect. Even the church of Rome rejects them from the canon. Hodge: " A comparison of the genuine apostolic writings with the spurious productions of the first and second centuries, affords one of the strongest collateral evidences of the authenticity and inspiration of the former." But it is not intended here to argue at length, but only to declare the inspiration of Paul's epistles. They are and ought to be received and treated as the words of Jehovah. They bind and ought to bind the conscience. The scope for criticism and interpretation is and ought to be strictly limited to finding out the true text and the true meaning of these writings; the very words used and the sense in which they were used. But the highest claim of divine inspiration neither denies nor discourages the idea that the Lord employed the turn of mind and mode of thinking peculiar to any sacred penman, and made use of them for the instruction of mankind. Inspiration did not metamorphose the mind, but it divinely guided it into the way of truth. Holy men of God spake as they were moved by the Holy Ghost.

XII. TRANSLATIONS OR VERSIONS OF PAUL'S EPISTLES

These are almost countless. Besides such as are parts of the entire word of God, large numbers of persons, scholiasts or commentators on particular epistles, have given us amended, improved or new translations. Some of these were obviously made for strictly sectarian or heretical purposes. Such have almost uniformly fallen into disuse or oblivion after a short and ignoble notoriety. They claim no special notice from us. Others having no marked merits, have yet cast light on some few texts. Others have been in a high degree scholarly and refreshing. Some of the older English versions from quaintness, if not from elegance, do often give the sense in a striking way. But none have, as a whole, been comparable to the authorized English version. Its amazing mastery of our mother tongue, its pure Anglo-Saxon diction and its very careful rendering of the true idea of the author still place it far above all competition. The reader will therefore expect no new translation in this work. Where a reference to the original will aid us in getting the sense, it will be freely made, and where other versions, than that in common use, give a good hint, it will be freely used. But in interpreting any one of Paul's epistles, besides being governed as in other books by the meaning of words, the context, the grammatical construction of sentences and the analogy of faith, we must look very much to what he has said in other epistles, and particularly to what we learn from the Acts of the Apostles. This has been so justly and so fully illustrated in many particulars by Paley in his *Horae Paulinae*, that a simple reference to that work renders unnecessary extended remarks. It should never be forgotten that Paul's apostleship was entirely independent of that of others. So he often asserts, and so the history shows. 1 Cor. 11 : 23 ; 2 Cor. 12 : 1–7; Gal. 1 : 12, 17.

XIII. Did Paul write all the epistles ascribed to him?

Much time need not here be spent in discussing this matter, because there is at present and for a long time has been so general an agreement on the subject among all that class of persons, to whom the religious world looks with deference; and because the subject has been so fully and ably discussed by learned men. There has been more doubt respecting Paul's writing the epistle to the Hebrews than any other ascribed to him. That he was the author of that book has been now almost universally conceded. The argument on the subject is very conclusive ; but it is inconsistent with the design of this work to encumber it with so long a disquisition as would be necessary in order fully and fairly to state it here. It may be gathered from Carpzov, Bengel, Whitby, Hales, Rosenmuller, Horne, Townsend, Macknight and many others. Very few, if any, who admit that Paul wrote the epistle to the Hebrews, deny his authorship of any of the other thirteen epistles commonly ascribed to him. And here the general question of authorship may rest. But nothing here said is intended to deny that Paul often employed an amanuensis, as Tertius in writing Romans (Rom. 16 : 22); Timothy in writing more than one epistle, etc., etc.

XIV. Did Paul write epistles, which are not now extant?

Paul was a man of loving heart, formed warm friendships and had very tender affection for those, whom he had begotten in the Gospel, and for all the churches. It would be very remarkable that such a man, with his literary tastes, should have written, during a ministry of such length, nothing but the fourteen epistles now in our hands. This does not concede that any of his epistles designed for the edification of the church in all coming ages have been lost.

Nor would it at all impair the authenticity and canonical authority of the books we have, if it could be proven that some given by divine inspiration have perished. It is not absurd to say that some of Paul's writings may have been designed to answer a purpose, like that of the apostolic office, and then pass away. Michaelis: "As Divine Providence has thought proper, that only fourteen [of Paul's epistles] should descend to posterity, we have no more reason to complain of the loss of his other epistles, than that several of Christ's speeches, all of which contained the words of God, were not committed to writing." That may all be so. But when we are asked to believe that some portions of God's word, designed for the edification of believers in all coming time, have not been preserved, we solemnly pause and ask for more weighty reasons than are drawn from 1 Cor. 5 : 9, or from 2 Pet. 3 : 15. The view of F. Stosch and Lardner is far more probable, and is sustained by far better considerations. They maintain that we have all Paul's epistles ever written for the churches. Indeed, their language is even stronger than that. On this matter Lardner is very forcible ; perhaps the reader will say, conclusive : " We have only four genuine Gospels, and only one history of the Acts of the Apostles : and we have no reason to suppose that more Gospels, or more ecclesiastical histories were written by apostles, or apostolic men." Why then should we suppose that more epistles, besides the twenty-one now in the canon, were designed to have a place there? This argument is fair and very powerful. Again : " If more epistles had been written, the apostle or apostles, who wrote them, would have taken care that they should be preserved, and transmitted to posterity, as well as those which have actually descended to us." The whole history of the formation of the canon of Scripture clearly evinces two things— great caution in admitting any writing to a place among the sacred books, and great care to preserve and perpetuate those which had been thus received. Moreover, such has been the wonderful providence of God in preserving for our use the sacred books we have, notwithstanding the efforts made to destroy them, that no more vigilance of the all-seeing eye was necessary to preserve any others, had they been written by inspired men, and designed for our use. The church of God, especially the more pious and intelligent part of it, will never yield the point that God's care in preserving to us entire his holy word is one of the most illustrious proofs of his providence and of his love for Zion. On this matter the faith of the better sort of Christians is very settled. Again : " No Christian community, which had received an epistle from an apostle, would have suffered that epistle to be lost." Why should they? Piety would have perpetuated it. Even lower considerations than *ought* to govern men, would not have been without their power to dispose the early Christians to hold fast their sacred books. Josephus, though with the Roman army besieging the holy city, made a successful effort to save the writings of the prophets. It has been estimated that at the close of the I. Century there were some thousands of copies (some say as many as five thousand copies) of God's word in the world; and all these were most probably in the hands of the friends of Christ. It is hardly credible that any part of the canon of Scripture has perished. And it is wholly incredible that any sacred book of the Christians should have ceased to be found on earth; and yet we have no respectable history or credible tradition of such a disaster. Moreover, all serious and intelligent Christians admit that there is no duty or sin, of which we have not full information, or warning in the books now found in the canon of Scripture.

XV. THE NEW TESTAMENT WAS ALL ORIGINALLY WRITTEN IN GREEK

Judicious writers regard the evidence as conclusive that the original of the entire New Testament was Greek. Where doubt has been expressed, it has commonly been unsupported by evidence. Bellarmine goes so far as to hold that the epistle to the Romans was first written in Latin. But the Doway Bible says it was written in Greek. Bertholdt says that all Paul's epistles were written in Hebrew, popularly so called, Aramaic as scholars usually call it. But there is no evidence to support these opinions. There has been more doubt respecting the original of the Gospel of Matthew and of the epistle to the Hebrews. Some have contended that our Greek copy of Matthew is only a translation from the Hebrew. It may, without any prejudice to the argument, be admitted that Matthew or some one under his direction early gave to those who spoke the vernacular of his country a version of his Gospel. That is all that has as yet been made probable. But that the original was in Greek has been made very clear by many. A sufficient statement of the proof will be found in Whitby.

We are more immediately concerned with the epistle to the Hebrews. Clement of Alexandria, Origen, Jerome, J. D. Michaelis and others have decidedly favored the opinion that it was originally written in Hebrew. Those, who thus maintain, suppose, or leave us to suppose, that it was afterwards translated into Greek by Luke, Barnabas, or Clement. But this hypothesis is encumbered with difficulties. The quotations from the Old Testament found in the epistle to the Hebrews are generally made from the Septuagint, not from the Hebrew, even when they widely differ from the Hebrew. This would surely not be done in writing to those who were most familiar with the Jewish Scriptures in the original. If it were written in Hebrew, why should the words *Melchisedek* and *Salem* be translated? No Hebrew needed to be

told that the latter signified *peace;* the former, *king of righteousness.*
In it many things of this kind are found. There are also in it
several paronomasias on Greek words, which would not be possi-
ble in a translation from Hebrew. Then it reads like an original.
It is free, flowing, not cramped, not strained. Moreover the
Greek was well known in Judea, as might be argued from Luke
23 : 38, and as is proven by much historical evidence. That the
Greek was much esteemed by the Jews in the first century is
established by the fact that Josephus and Philo both wrote in
Greek. Philo was sometimes called the Jewish Plato. He
adopted his philosophy and wrote elegantly in his language.
There were probably more Hebrews residing elsewhere than in
Judea. Nor is this all. There is extant no copy of the epistle to
the Hebrews in the mother tongue of the Hebrews of the first
century, which can be shown to have existed at that time. Nor is
there any history or tradition, on which we can at all rely, to the
contrary of the views here maintained.

If neither the Gospel of Matthew nor the epistle to the Hebrews was originally written in Hebrew, it is unnecessary to
prove that no other book of the New Testament, and in particular that none of the remaining thirteen epistles of Paul were originally written in any other language than the Greek. On this
matter the learned reader will find very lucid discussion in
Carpzov.

XVI. QUOTATIONS IN THIS WORK

Any remark or sentence in this work, which the author has
found to be the literary property of any one person, has been fully
credited. But nearly all pious and sensible writers of any one
class of commentators on God's word say things which have been
said by many others. Thousands of such truths lie on the very
surface of Scripture. In such cases a formal quotation would be
mere pedantry. It would make a false impression, ascribing to
one what was common to many. There is a very large range of
thought, which is fairly common. property to all learned and
devout students of Paul's writings. Let every man avail himself
of it. It is as fairly his, as the light or air of heaven. It is the
setting up of an exclusive or original claim to this great and common fund, that makes some sciolists both ridiculous and odious.
The annotator of Bagster's Comprehensive Bible speaking of his
labors says: "From the alteration, abridgment and condensation,
and frequently from the blending together of the observations of
two or more writers, as well as from want of room, it was foun-

impossible to specify the name of the author or authors from which they (the remarks) are derived." He truthfully adds: "No class of writers borrow from each other more freely without acknowledgment than Biblical critics and commentators, and, in many instances, the substance of the information belongs to the common stock of Biblical criticism, and could not, with propriety, be assigned as the property of any individual." Nevertheless every thing due to any author is in this work carefully acknowledged, so far as known. If there is any exception, it is by mistake or oversight, and not willingly. Yet where an author's name is given, and a word, a phrase, or a sentence immediately follows, quotation marks are not used, giving the name of the author being thought sufficient. But this never extends beyond a single sentence.

XVII. Syriac, Arabic and Ethiopic versions

The author has no acquaintance with Syriac. His quotations from the Peshito version are made chiefly on the authority of Murdock's translation of that venerable monument of antiquity. Nor does he know either Arabic or Ethiopic, but relies on the Latin translation in Walton's Polyglot as giving the sense of those versions. In other cases he has generally resorted to the original versions, from which he has quoted.

XVIII. Some notice of commentators on Paul's epistles

The authors who have attempted to elucidate Paul's writings are almost countless. No complete catalogue of them has yet been given to the world. In the III. century we have Origen; in the IV. Chrysostom; in the V. Augustine, Theodoret and Pelagius; in the X. Œcumenius; in the XI. Theophylact; in the XII. Hugo a Sancto Victore; in the XIII. Thomas Aquinas; in the XVI. Luther, Zwingle, Melancthon, Erasmus, Salmeron, Bellarmine, Calvin, Bugenhagen and Bucer; in the XVII. Beza, Hunnius, the Assembly's Annotations, the Dutch Annotations, Ferme, Melville, Justinian, Diodati, Baldwin, Schlichting, Burkitt, Cornelius a Lapide, Grotius, Piscator, Fabricius, Calov, S. Schmidt, Cocceius, Hammond, John Brown of Wamphray, Pool and Henry's continuators; in the XVIII. Limborch, Wetstein, J. Alphonsus Turrettin, Bengel, Rosenmuller, Guyse, Benson, Baumgarten, C. Schmidt, Wolf, Heumann, Carpzov, Koppe, Gill, Doddridge, John Brown of Haddington, Macknight; in the XIX. J. F. Flatt, Tholuck, Hawker, Haldane, Scott, Clarke, Stuart, Hodge, Williams, Cobbin,

Barnes, Sampson, Slade, Olshausen, Conybeare and Howson, Chalmers, and many others. Some of these have written on all Paul's epistles, some on several, some on two, a few on one and no more. A large number of authors have written Introductions to the New Testament, in which they give much attention to Paul's epistles. Then we have many disquisitions on particular parts of these epistles either in separate treatises or embodied in works on Systematic Divinity. We might name the writings of T. Adam, Kohlbrugge, Dickinson, Wardlaw and many others. In this work where a sentence or more is credited to "Brown," it means John Brown of Wamphray, unless otherwise stated.

XIX. Reasons for Writing This Book

The author with pleasure acknowledges the goodness of God in giving to the church many valuable expositions of his word—of Paul's writings in particular. Of these some are very costly, some are in Latin, some abound in discussions of no special interest to the masses of this generation, and some are so voluminous that but few have time to read them. Yet in most of them are thoughts, which ought to be perpetuated. The author of this work undertook it for many reasons: 1. He knew no law against it. The field was open to enter in and reap. It is open to all. No man can forbid. 2. Many judicious persons, learned and plain, having read the author's work on the Psalms, have greatly encouraged him to write on other portions of Scripture. This has been done in public print and in private letters, especially by such persons, as never had given him bad counsel. 3. He hoped that many would find in it things which the press of business would not allow them to search for in large and rare works. 4. This work fell in with the author's course of studies. Paul's epistles in Greek, Latin, and English have long been his delight. For years he seldom took a journey without some volume on the epistles in his hand. For some time he has been teaching classes in some of these epistles, and often referring to all of them, and expounding large portions of them. 5. All evangelical people put a high estimate on Paul's writings. In them they find great refreshment. Their spiritual life is not a little supported by the doctrines and encouragements found in them. The author would fain aid such in their attempts to know the mind of God as here revealed. 6. He found his heart drawn to this work. He loved the study of these epistles of truth and love. Except when preaching the Gospel to the perishing, or teaching candidates for the ministry, he never was happier than when searching to find out what the Spirit of Christ did sig-

nify when he spoke by Paul. 7. He found hims confined, during most of the year, to his duties a theology, commonly with a few hours each day and remembered that he was accountable for the this precious time. He dared not waste it. He price put into his hands to glorify God. He hope in preparing this volume. 8. He remembered cometh when no man can work, and that blessed is beside all water courses, and so does all the go well-intentioned publication of saving truth sha divine reward.

XX. Recent Works on Roman

Since the plan of this work was formed, of it executed, several commentaries on this epist No notice of them appears in this volume, and reasons: 1. The author wished these works to s merits before the public without any unfriendl 2. He did not wish to impart to this work any spirit of controversy with his cotemporaries, as if he had quoted freely from some of them. 3. extended notice of them would have somewha of this volume, and he thought it best to ma change in that respect. 4. So far as he has l thinks the main objects contemplated in this secured without dwelling on the new forms o sion introduced by these authors, as in any ot

COMMENTARY ON

ROMANS

FOR date of time and place of this Epistle see Introduction §§ V. & VI. Of the state of the world at the time when it was written see Introduction § IX.

On the day of Pentecost among Peter's hearers were *strangers of Rome.* Acts 2 : 10. Some of these at once embraced the Gospel. Acts 2 : 41. It is highly probable that some of them very soon returned to the imperial city, and, being full of zeal, persuaded others to embrace Christ, and thus the nucleus of a Christian church was formed. It early became a famous church, so that its " faith was spoken of throughout the world." Rom. 1 : 8. There is not the slightest evidence that it was founded by Peter and Paul, or by either of them. Paul had not even visited them when he wrote this epistle, though he had long desired to do so. Rom. 15 : 23. It cannot be proven beyond doubt that Peter was ever in Rome, though the tradition that he was there long after the formation of the Roman church amounts to a reasonable historic probability. But it is entirely clear that he was not there and had not been there when this epistle was written.

From all we can learn of the church at Rome it was at an early day composed both of Jews and Gentiles. This is evident from many things in this epistle itself, chap. 1 : 13; 4 : 1; 7 : 1; 11 : 1; 15 : 15, 16, as well as from other sources of information, especially from the book of Acts. How persistent and urgent the Judaizers were is proclaimed by the united voice of antiquity. Indeed not a few of them boldly said : " Except ye be circumcised after the manner of Moses, ye cannot be saved." Acts 15 : 1. As a class they were very troublesome.

The epistle, which we are now to study, is excelled by no portion of God's word in the weight and excellence of its matter.

Macknight calls it " a writing, which, for sublimity and truth of sentiment, for brevity and strength of expression, for regularity in its structure, but above all, for the unspeakable importance of the discoveries which it contains, stands unrivalled by any mere human composition, and as far exceeds the most celebrated productions of the learned Greeks and Romans, as the shining of the sun exceedeth the twinkling of the stars." Scott : " The epistle itself is one of the longest, and most comprehensive, of all that were written by the apostle." Olshausen : " Every thing in the epistle wears strongly the impress of the greatest originality, liveliness, and freshness of experience." The Dutch Annotations : " This epistle is rightly accounted a key for the right understanding of all the Holy Scriptures ; and especially for the right understanding of the fulfilling of the promise made to the people of Israel by Moses and the prophets, for salvation both of Jews and Gentiles." Hodge : " There is no book in the Bible, and there is no ancient book in the world, of which the authenticity is more certain than that of this epistle."

Chapter 1

ROMANS 1
VERSES 1–7

THE INSCRIPTION AND SALUTATION

P AUL, a servant of Jesus Christ, called *to be* an apostle, separated unto the gospel of God.

2 (Which he had promised afore by his prophets in the holy Scriptures,)

3 Concerning his Son Jesus Christ our Lord, which was made of the seed of David according to the flesh ;

4 And declared *to be* the Son of God with power, according to the Spirit of holiness, by the resurrection from the dead :

5 By whom we have received grace and apostleship, for obedience to the faith among all nations, for his name :

6 Among whom are ye also the called of Jesus Christ ·

7 To all that be in Rome, beloved of God, called *to be* saints : Grace to you, and peace, from God our Father and the Lord Jesus Christ.

1. PAUL, *a servant of Jesus Christ, called* to be *an apostle, separated unto the gospel of God. Paul*, on this name see Introduction § 1. Paul practised no concealment; he boldly gave his name. *A servant*, not the word rendered hired servant, Luke ·15 : 17, 19, but a word, which when referring to the civil condition of men, means the opposite of *free ;* in Eph. 6 : 8, Col. 3 : 11, Rev. 13 : 16 rendered *bond.* Conybeare and Howson : a bondsman. Macknight : The original word properly signifies *a slave.* Taylor : The word may be taken in its strict and primary sense, as signifying a servant who is the absolute property of the master and bound to him for life. Wetstein : But as a servant of a king is a name of dignity ; so also is a servant of Messias. It is a favorite title of Christian ministers, Gal. 1 : 10; 4 : 12; Phil. 1 : 1 ; 2 Tim. 2 : 24; Jas. 1 : 1; 2 Pet. 1 : 1; Jude 1; Rev. 1 : 1. In both Testaments it often denotes any true friend of God. Hodge : It is a general official designation. Paul is a servant of no common master, but of *Jesus Christ. Jesus* is the proper name of our Saviour, the Greek form of the Hebrew Joshua. Heb. 4 : 8. Yet this name was not given him without reference to the salvation he should effect for

his people. Matt. 1 : 21. *Christ*, corresponding to the Hebrew Messias, meaning *anointed*, the official name of our Lord. His anointing was by the Holy Ghost. He had the spirit without measure, John 3 : 34. *Called* to be *an apostle.* Here the authorised version follows that of Tyndale, Geneva, and Rheims. Cranmer: called to the office of an apostle; Peshito: called and sent; Wiclif: clepid an apostle; Dutch Annotations and Macknight: a called apostle; Stuart: a chosen apostle; Turrettin: an apostle by divine vocation; Beza: an apostle by the call of God. The word is often found in the New Testament, and is not once in the authorized version rendered *chosen*, but always called, or a few times *bidden* in the sense of called. It is more than once found in the same verse as the word chosen, and in a sense different from it. Many are *called*, but few chosen, Matt. 20 : 16; 22 : 14. They that are with him are *called*, and chosen, and faithful, Rev. 17 : 14. In Rom. 8 : 30 it is carefully distinguished from the purpose of God: Whom he did predestinate, them he also *called*, and whom he *called*, them he also justified. We have the same word in vs. 6, 7. As many questioned Paul's right to teach and act with apostolic authority, he often alleged his divine call to that office. *An apostle*, one sent; in 1 Cor. 8 : 23, rendered *messenger*; the Peshito here and elsewhere has *legate*. In Heb. 3 : 1 it is applied to Christ; but in almost every other case where the title is conceded, it designates the office of those thirteen men, who had seen the Lord Jesus, were witnesses that he had risen from the dead, and had authority from Him to reveal his will to the churches. If any man has not been an eye-witness of Christ's resurrection, he cannot be an apostle, so say the Scriptures; they no less declare that Paul had seen him. Acts 1 : 8, 22 ; 2 : 32; 3 : 15; 4 : 33; 22 : 14, 15 ; 26 : 16 ; 1 Cor. 9 : 1 ; 15 : 8, 15. Whateley justly says: Successors to the apostles there are none. There never has been an apostle on earth since the death of John. Paul was *separated unto the Gospel. Separated*, Tyndale, Cranmer and Genevan: put *apart*; Stewart, Conybeare and Howson: set apart; Beza, Doddridge, Macknight: separated. The word may mean chosen, selected, as Hesychius shows. In some of its forms the word occurs ten times in the New Testament and always has the sense of *separate*, though in Matt. 13 : 49 we read the angels shall " *sever* the wicked from among the just." In Matt. 25 : 32 it is for euphony variously rendered: "He shall *separate* them from one another, as a shepherd *divideth* his sheep from the goats." There are several interpretations. One is that Paul *alludes* to his having been a pharisee, which means *separatist*, when he had been separated from all ceremonial defilement and from the mass of the common people; so now he was separated, distinguished from the mass of men to preach the gospel. This is the view taken by Drusius and Whitby. Olshausen wholly rejects this as a mere play upon words. Others think it finds its best interpretation in Acts 13 : 2. "The Holy Ghost said, *Separate* me Barnabas and Saul, for the work whereunto I have called them." This is the view of Theodoret, Turrettin and Olshausen. The same word is used in Acts 13 : 2, as in our verse. But Paul is here asserting his plenary apostolic power, and not that he in common with Barnabas had a special designation to go to the heathen. Another interpretation refers the separation to the divine purpose. This is the sense given to the word by Luther in Gal. 1 : 15, by the Dutch Annotations, by Guyse and Stuart. This word in no instance has the sense of sanctified or consecrated. Some make it explanatory of the word *called*. All that can fairly be gotten from the two words *called* and *separated* is that Paul was selected, effectually called and divinely appointed to his work. Ferme : The calling is the separation of the person called. Calvin : I cannot agree with those who refer the call of which he speaks to the eternal election of God. He was separated

Unto the gospel of God. Gospel; Conybeare & Howson, Glad tidings. The word is derived from *God*, good, and *spel*, or *spell*, word or speech. Gospel very precisely conveys the sense of the Greek. It is called the gospel of salvation, because it shows that salvation is possible, and in what way. It is called the gospel of Christ, because it is the fruit of Christ's grace and compassion to men, and because Christ's person, work, sufferings, death, exaltation and glory constitute the sum of it. Without Christ there would have been no good news to sinners. It is called here the *gospel of God*, because God is its author. It is the ' good tidings ' sent by God.

2. *Which he had promised afore by his prophets in the holy Scriptures.* This verse is clearly parenthetical, and is so put in most editions of the English version. How fully the gospel was promised in the Old Testament appears more and more as we piously study it. It was preached in Eden, Gen. 3 : 15 ; and to Abraham, Gal. 3 : 8. When we read David, Isaiah and Zechariah it sometimes seems as if we were reading one of the Gospels. Both Jesus and his apostles often insisted that they proposed nothing contrary to the teachings of the prophets, and nothing which the prophets had not led the church to expect. John 1 : 45 ; 5 : 46 ; 8 : 56 ; 12 : 16 ; Luke 24 : 27, 44 ; Acts 3 : 21-24 ; 10 : 43 ; and often in this epistle. *In the holy Scriptures ;* literally in holy writings ; the article is wanting ; Wiclif : in holi scripturis. There was

but one set of holy writings, received by the Jewish church. To those, to whom Paul wrote, this designation was clear. The New Testament writers use *scripture* or *scriptures*, singular or plural, indiscriminately to designate the word of God; so Paul in this epistle. God is the author of the gospel, yet the great subject matter of it is

3. *Concerning his son Jesus Christ our Lord, which was made of the seed of David according to the flesh.* He, who is substantially right respecting the person, work and glory of Christ, has the substance of the gospel; he, who here errs fundamentally, errs fatally. If Jesus Christ is truly *the Son of God*, equal with God, having the same nature with the Father, the only begotten of the Father, then he is fit to be *our Lord*, the absolute proprietor of our persons, worthy to receive all the homage and service we can possibly offer. The word here rendered *Lord* has a long history and interesting. It is the word used in the Septuagint to translate the words Jehovah and Adonai; the former denoting the self-existent, independent, eternal and unchangeable I AM; the latter expressing his authority and sovereignty over us. It is a title given in the New Testament to our Saviour hundreds of times. In a few cases it is rendered Master, as " Your Master also is in heaven." Eph. 6 : 9. No man in the true sense of terms can say that Jesus Christ is Lord but by the Holy Ghost, 1 Cor. 12 : 3. He is Lord and we should so confess; it is to the glory of the Father, and not in derogation of it. Phil. 2 : 11. He is no less the Son of God and our Lord because he *was made of the seed of David according to the flesh.* For *made* Tyndale has begotten; Peshito, Cranmer, Macknight, Hodge, Conybeare and Howson, born; Dutch Annotations, became. In Rom. 3 : 19; 4 : 18; 7 : 13 it is rendered become; in Rom. 2 : 25; 10 : 20; 11 : 9 made, and often was, hath been, etc. *Seed*, a word rendered with absolute uniformity in the authorized version. When Christ is said to be of the seed of David, the meaning is, he is of the house and lineage of David, he is of David's posterity, he is of that royal line. *According to the flesh*, as to his human nature, or so far as he was a man. Had he not been the son of man and the seed of David he would not have met the demands of prophecy. 2 Sam. 7 : 16; Isa. 11 : 1. One evangelist fitly traces his genealogy to the first pair to prove that he was the seed of the woman ; another to David, thus shewing how completely he met the requirements of the Old Testament And all this was settled by a legal process before his birth—by the very process by which the titles to the lands of the country were determined.

4. *And declared* to be *the Son of God with power, according to the*

spirit of holiness, by the resurrection from the dead. *Declared*, this word is preferred by Chrysostom, Theodoret, Tyndalé, Cranmer, the Genevan, Calvin, Beza, Diodati, Brown of Wamphray, Tholuck and Hodge. The Assembly's Annotations and J. Owen follow the margin and read, determined ; Le Clerc, Elsner, Dodd-ridge, Conybeare and Howson, marked out ; Origen, Cyril and Boothroyd, proved ; Macknight, made to appear what he is ; Ferme, Burkitt, Whitby and Cox, demonstrated ; Peshito, made known as. All these substantially agree. There is no good rea-son for rendering the word predestinated, as do Irenæus, Epi-phanius, Augustine, Vulgate, Doway and Rheims. It is mourn-ful to find Stuart rendering it constituted, and contending for it at great length. The verb signifies to mark off, bound, define, and so to declare, or determine. He was declared to be the *Son of God with power.* On the phrase *Son of God* see on v. 3. The phrase *with power* [or *in power*] has been variously explained. The larger number connect it with declared. Guyse paraphrases the whole thus—determinately avowed, openly proclaimed and convincingly demonstrated ; Burkitt, mightily and powerfully demonstrated ; Doddridge, determinately, and in the most con-vincing manner marked out as the Son of God, with the most astonishing display of divine power ; Macknight, declared, with great power of evidence ; Genevan, declared mightily ; Hodge, clearly declared. It is best to connect the words declared and with power. All this was done *according to the spirit of holiness.* Wiclif : bi the spirit of halowynge ; Tyndale : with power of the holy goost that sanctifieth ; Cranmer : after the sprete that sanctyfyeth ; Genevan : touching the Spirite that sanctifieth ; Rheims : according to the spirit of sanctification ; Peshito : by the Holy Spirit ; Beza agrees with the authorized version ; Ferme : his own sanctifying spirit ; Stuart : as to his holy spiritual nature· Three methods have been adopted for explaining this phrase. 1. Some think it points to our Lord's personal sanctity as a man. This was indeed perfect ; but where do we learn that the phrase *spirit of holiness* simply denotes personal purity ? 2. Others ex-plain it of the Holy Spirit, the third person of the Trinity. This is admissible ; as Paul often uses such Hebrew forms of speech. This gives a good sense, according to the teachings of other parts of God's word. Christ said that the Comforter, the Spirit of truth, should testify of him. John 15 : 26. He did so on the day of Pentecost. The same truth is elsewhere declared, Heb. 2 : 3, 4. In creation, in providence, in raising Jesus from the dead, and in the resurrection of the saints at the last day, the Scriptures teach a concurrence of all the persons of the Godhead. Speaking of our Lord, Paul once says God the Father raised him up, Gal. I : I. Jesus claimed and exercised the power to raise his own body, John 2 : 19; 10 : 18. The Scriptures no less clearly say that the body of Christ was raised, and that the bodies of the saints shall be raised by the power of the Holy Ghost. Rom. 8 : 11. Just so we acknowledge God the Father Almighty as Maker of heaven and earth, yet without the Word was not any thing made that was made, and God's Spirit garnished the heavens, moved upon the face of the deep, and filled it with living things. 3. Others explain the phrase of the divine nature of our Lord.

In favor of the *second* of these explanations we have Calvin, Burkitt, Doddridge, Scott, Williams and others; in favor of the *third*, Diodati, Beza, Pool, Hammond, Ferme, Guyse, the Dutch Annotations, the Assembly's Annotations, Locke, Alford, Olshausen, Stuart, Haldane and Hodge. Several of these cite in proof I Tim. 3 : 16; Heb. 9 : 14; and I Pet. 3 : 18; and Haldane quotes I Cor. 15 : 45, and 2 Cor. 3 : 17 to show that Christ is explicitly called a Spirit. Gill regards either the second or the third view as admissible. The great argument for the *third* view is taken from the apparent antithesis between the *flesh* and the *spirit* in vs. 3, 4. If this contrast was intended by the apostle, the argument is conclusive. Certainly in some other places the same form of words indicates intended antithesis. Matt. 12 : 32; Rom. 4 : 4; 8: 1, 4, 5. This view is therefore preferred. *By the resurrection from the dead;* Peshito : who rose from the dead, Jesus Messiah, our Lord ; Coverdale, Tyndale, and Cranmer render the clause, since the time that he rose, &c. Theodoret, Luther, Grotius : from and after ; Stuart : after ; Hammond : after, and through, and by. The great mass of commentators agree with the authorized version. The latter phrase in the clause is literally *the resurrection of the dead ;* but this phrase more than once means the resurrection from the dead. I Cor. 15 : 42; Heb. 6 : 2. The resurrection of Jesus Christ settles his divine sonship in the clearest manner. 1. It was a very remarkable display of the power of God, and so the Scriptures speak of it. Eph. 1 : 19, 20. 2. Jesus Christ had foretold that he would arise by his own power; so that his omnipotence is the same as that of the Father. 3. Jesus Christ was the surety of his people, and eternal justice would not have released him till his humiliation was completed. 4. During his ministry our Lord had said and done many things contrary to the notions of the masses of men, and had set up the highest claims to reverence, worship and obedience from men. If he were not truly and properly divine, all these claims were those of a deceiver. But his resurrection confirmed them every one. 5. So great was the import-

ance of the event and such was its connection with all that is vital
in religion that our justification and indeed our whole hope of
salvation are in Scripture made to depend upon it. Rom. 4 : 25 ;
1 Pet. 1 : 3.

5. *By whom we have received grace and apostleship, for obedience to
the faith among all nations, for his name.* Whom refers to Jesus Christ,
and *we*, to the apostles, his ministers. *Grace*, a word of frequent
occurrence in the Scriptures. It may relate to disposition, speech
or act, and means favor, good-will, kindness undeserved, unbought
love. It is often used very much in the sense of *mercy;* yet is
perhaps the stronger word. Both words imply compassion to the
miserable ; but mercy may be to the unfortunate, whereas, strictly
speaking, grace is to the guilty, favor to the undeserving. The
gospel is itself a grace—an undeserved favor—to men. 2 Cor. 6:
1, Titus 2: 11. So the authority to preach the gospel is an unmerited privilege, and is so confessed by Paul himself. Eph. 3 : 8.
No man deserves to be a minister of Christ. Salvation from first
to last is of grace. No man deserves pardon, acceptance, renewal
or eternal life. 1 Cor. 15 : 10; Eph. 1 : 7; 2 : 5; Rom. 4 : 16. On
apostleship see v. 1. Grace and apostleship point to more than a
'gracious apostleship.' They include not only the office and its
miraculous gifts but all the work of God's Spirit necessary to prepare the apostle for his office and for salvation. The rest of the
verse is more difficult. Wiclif: to obeie to the faith in all folkis
for his name ; Coverdale : amonge all heythen, to set up the obedience of faith under his name ; Tyndale : to bring all maner
hethen people unto obedience of the faith that is in his name ;
Cranmer: that obedience might be geven unto the faith in his
name among all heithen ; Stuart: in order to promote the obedience of faith among all nations, for his name's sake ; Alford: in
order to bring about obedience to the faith among all (the) nations.
For obedience is best understood as unto obedience, i. e. to the end
that obedience may be secured. *The faith* may mean either the
grace of saving faith in the Redeemer, as often it does ; or it may
mean the essential creed of the saints, the gospel, the sum of the
things necessary to be believed. In this case the result reached
is the same whichsoever explanation be given. But see Acts 6: 7 ;
Rom. 16: 26 and many parallel passages. *For his name* is best
understood to the glory of his name, so Turrettin ; or for the purpose of magnifying his name, as Chalmers, though some connect
it with apostleship, and some with faith.

6. *Among whom are ye also the called of Jesus Christ.* Whom refers to nations [or Gentiles, as we often render the word.] On the
other words of this clause see above on v. 1. *The called of Jesus*

Christ means more than that they were invited by Jesus Christ. It declares that they had been effectually called, and were now the friends of the Redeemer, and joint heirs with him. The pertinency of this verse is to let the Roman Christians know that Paul's commission embraced them, first as they were among the Gentiles to whom the gospel was sent, and then as they were God's people by effectual calling.

7. *To all that be in Rome, beloved of God, called to be saints: Grace to you and peace from God our Father, and the Lord Jesus Christ.* *All* includes Jew and Gentile, established Christians and young converts. The mind and heart of the apostle delighted in overleaping all personal, sectional and national distinctions, and embracing all believers. His affectionate regards extended to all classes and conditions of God's people. And well they might, for they were *beloved of God.* No word in the New Testament expresses more kindness than *beloved,* sometimes rendered *well-*beloved, Mark 12 : 6; Rom. 16 : 5; 3 John 1; and sometimes *dearly beloved,* 1 Cor. 10 : 14; 2 Cor. 7 : 1; 1 Tim. 1 : 2; Philemon 1. Wiclif: derlyngis [darlings] of God. And then they were *called* to be *saints,* the same form of expression as in v. 1. *Called,* not merely denominated, but effectually called and so made to be *saints,* or *holy ones,* holy unto the Lord, in heart and life devoted to God. Coverdale: sayntes by callynge; Tyndale: sanctes by callinge; Genevan: sanctes by callyng; Cranmer: called sayntes; Peshito: called and sanctified; Arabic: called saints; Syriac: called and holy; Stuart: chosen saints. *Grace;* see on v. 5. The cognate verb was commonly employed by the Greeks in salutation. *Peace;* the Latin form of salutation. In Hebrew we have the same word for *peace* and for *prosperity.* Those, to whom Paul was writing were familiar with both forms of address. Both were expressions of good-will. In each the speaker, if sincere, desired his friend to receive all good things for time and eternity. Paul would go beyond what good manners required. Civility he would convert into hearty Christian love, and he would tell them whence he desired grace and peace to come—even *from God our Father, and the Lord Jesus Christ,* who were able to make all good things abound to them, and who had unsearchable riches to bestow on the faithful. This form of salutation without change (except that in Galatians we have God the Father instead of God our Father) is found in eleven out of Paul's fourteen epistles. In the pastoral epistles—1st Timothy, 2d Timothy and Titus—there is added the Hebrew form of salutation—Mercy be unto you; q. d. Whatever form of expressing good-will and hearty kindness you are familiar with, I adopt toward you; and I tell you

whence alone I expect so great blessings on you, even from God
our Father and from our Lord Jesus Christ.

DOCTRINAL AND PRACTICAL REMARKS

1. We can never too much admire and adore the wisdom and
mercy of God in taking the gifted, learned, bitter persecutor of
Tarsus, changing his heart, sending him to preach to the nations,
and inspiring him to write for the edification of the church in all
future ages the epistles he has left us, and in particular this great
doctrinal discussion, which more lucidly and logically than any
other one book of Scripture shows to men the way of salvation.

2. The greatest honor to which any man can attain on earth is
to be a *servant of Jesus Christ.* v. 1.   Such is every one that loves
the Saviour, and lives for him.   He may be poor, despised, forsaken of men; but he shall reign with Christ.

3. Approved ministers of the Gospel are Christ's *servants* in
the best senses. v. 1.   They act and suffer from a pure regard to
the honor of their Master.   They think it a small matter whether
they are sick or well, applauded or despised, provided he is duly
honored.   They hope to glorify him even in reproaches, and in
the fiery furnace.   They dare not preach themselves but Christ
Jesus the Lord, nor deliver any message but that which they have
received from him.   They expect to give account to him.   Nor
do they serve and suffer for him grudgingly.   They glory in
tribulations for his·sake and in his cause.   They think it honor
enough to serve in his house.   They know they serve a good
Master.   Their reward is sure.

4. But then all Christ's ministers must be *called* of God. v. 1.
They must be effectually called, soundly converted. Ps. 50 : 16.
Then they must be divinely called to the work of the ministry.
All the ecclesiastics on earth cannot give authority to minister in
God's house.   The utmost the church can do is to recognize a
call given by her Divine Head.   God's real servants in the ministry get their commission from heaven, not from men; from Jesus
Christ, not from the church,   Nor is it wrong for such to avow
and defend their call.   Nor is it assumptive in God's people to examine the call of any and all, who say they are sent of God. 1 John
4 : 1 ; Rev. 2 : 2.

5. It is no small grace in God to send us his servants; and
therefore when we find such duly called of God, we ought gravely
to consider our relation to them, and their's to us.   The people
owe a solemn duty to God's.ministers, to hear the word of God

which they preach, candidly to compare their discourses with Scripture, and heartily to receive and practise all the truth, which they deliver. Mal. 2 : 7; Acts 17 : 11; Ezek. 33 : 32.   The people owe to Christ's servants high esteem, temporal support, hearty prayer for their success, and obedience to them in the Lord. 1 Thess. 5 : 13; Gal. 6 : 6; 2 Thess. 3 : 1; Heb. 13 : 7.

6. Since the death of John there have been no apostles on earth.   Paul was the last, whom Jesus invested with that office. His personal call was necessary. John 20 : 21.   To all the apostles was promised plenary inspiration. John 16 : 13.   They had all seen the Lord.   They all were miraculously endowed, and had the signs of an apostle.   Although a man might have some of these things and not be an apostle; yet he could not be an apostle without having all these things.   All the pretences of moderns to the apostolic office are both absurd and wicked.

7. As all genuine ministers of the Gospel are *separated* by God to their good work, they ought to bestir themselves in it, be instant in season and out of season, and give themselves wholly to it. Acts 6 : 4; 1 Tim. 4 : 15; 2 Tim. 2 : 4.   No calling is so honorable; none is so important; none is so responsible.

8. When ministers so present religious truth as to make it appear sad tidings to meek and penitent souls, they mightily distort and pervert it; for they are sent to preach the *gospel*, glad news, good tidings unto the meek, to bind up the broken-hearted, to proclaim liberty to the captives, and the opening of the prison to them that are bound.   We do as sadly err when we smite and wound those whom God would comfort, as when we comfort those whom the Lord condemns.

9. Yet no man may forget that the message which ministers bear to men is of awful authority—it is the gospel *of God*. v. 1. It is not glad tidings, which we may hear or not, consider or not, obey or not, and still be safe.   It may be preached by a very modest, humble, ordinary man; yet even then it is accompanied with awful sanctions and responsibilities. Matt. 11 : 15; 10 : 40; John 10 : 20; 12 : 48; 1 Thess. 2 : 13.

10. Nor is the gospel any novelty. v. 2.   It was preached in Eden.   A long line of righteous men from Abel down to Simeon by faith received it.   Take from the types, promises and prophecies of the Old Testament their evangelical character, and there is nothing left in them to light the soul to God or happiness.   True, the light was not bright, for the sufferings of Christ and the glory that is now revealed were but dimly shadowed forth; but they were shadowed forth, and faith did receive them.   Rom. 3 : 21; Gal. 3 : 8, 23; Heb. 11 : 2; 1 Pet. 10 : 11.   It is great folly and

wickedness lightly to esteem Moses and the prophets.   If they
speak not the truth, neither do the evangelists and apostles.

11. For thousands of years there have been in the world rolls,
or parchments, or books, which have been known by various
names as the law, the Psalms and the prophets, the word of the
Lord, the Scripture, the Scriptures and the *holy Scriptures*, v. 2.
These contain a vast store of divine knowledge.   They have long
been the rejoicing of good men's hearts.   They sufficiently account
for the vast differences discovered between men and nations.
These books claim to be and they are God's word to men.   They
claim to be and they are a revelation from heaven.   They claim
to be and they are holy writings; for they teach holiness, encourage holiness, and abound in holy doctrines and precepts.   It is one
of God s great mercies to men that they have his written word.

12. Those best read both Testaments, who most happily find
Christ in each of them. v. 2.   He is the way, the truth and the
life.   He is all and in all.   Take from any book of Scripture the
portion that *concerns Jesus Christ*, and the residue is of no value to
men as sinners.   He has no names or titles, he fills no offices, sus-
tains no characters and teaches no lessons that are not dear and
of priceless value to his people.   He is their Lord, the absolute
proprietor of their persons.

13. The Scripture cannot be broken.   All that was written in
the prophets has been or shall be surely accomplished. v. 2.

14. There is nothing in the plan of redemption and in the sufferings of Christ that may not well fill us with wonder.   But which
part of the amazing history is the most astonishing, none can say.
Yet many sober writers speak as if they regarded Christ's being
made of the seed of David as unsurpassed in condescension. v. 3.
Perhaps it is.   Surely the Incarnation was an expression of infinite
love and pity.

15. He, who slights Jesus Christ, slights the Son of God; and
only he, who hopes in him as the Son of God, has any interest in
his salvation. v. 4.   God is indeed one in essence, but he is not
one in person.   We adore the Father, Son and Holy Ghost.   The
Father is of none, neither begotten nor proceeding.   The Holy
Ghost proceeds.   The Son is begotten, the only begotten of the
Father.   The Father doth eternally communicate to the Son his
own divine essence, though in a manner to us inconceivable and
ineffable.   So that although the Son was for us incarnate, yet is
he the brightness of the Father's glory and the express image of
his person.   The Son of God becoming man did not become two
persons, but in his two natures is one person for ever, the two
natures being united, not confused, nor mixed, but united, neither

nature being absorbed, so that we have one Christ, and not two, one Lord Jesus and but one Lord Jesus.

16. Christians seldom, perhaps never, lay too much stress on the fact and the doctrine of Christ's resurrection. The Scriptures fully admit that it is essential, fundamental, v. 4. I Cor. 15 : 14–18. Without it, Christ's servants are of all men most miserable. Without it, they would all go sadly through life, like the two disciples, saying, "We trusted that it had been he, which should have redeemed Israel." Luke 24 : 21. If Christ rose not, then his people will not rise, and so it is all over with them, and their pleasing anticipations. Christ's resurrection is here introduced to establish his Sonship with God. It makes one sad to find Stuart saying: "How could the *resurrection* declare, in any special manner, that Christ was the Son of God? Was not Lazarus raised from the dead? Were not others raised from the dead, by Christ, by the apostles, by Elijah, and by the bones of Elisha? And yet was their resurrection proof that they were the Sons of God?" The answer to these vain questions is obvious and simple, and has been given a thousand times. Slade: "Jesus having been put to death as a blasphemer for calling himself 'Christ the Son of the blessed,' God would not have raised him from the dead, if he had been an impostor: His resurrection therefore was a public testimony, borne by God himself, to the truth of our Lord's pretensions." The same is found almost verbatim in Macknight. Nor is this all. So truly did the fulness of the Godhead dwell in him bodily that incontestably and gloriously the power of his own divinity, his own omnipotence, appeared not only during his life in raising the dead, in his own name, but after he was dead he raised his own body by the same irresistible energy according to his own predictions. If such great facts do not establish all claims set forth by the Saviour, nothing can.

17. Blessed gospel! blessed ministry. vs. 1, 5. O how men ought to preach. O how they ought to hear. The stupor, with which many proclaim and listen to the word of God, is strong proof that by nature they are dead in trespasses and sins. The most animated preaching falls far below the zeal, which the glory of our theme would warrant. Often the best preaching is but shouting in dead men's ears.

18. The great end of the ministry of the Gospel is not gained until men yield the *obedience* of faith. v. 5. The mercy shown to us poor sinners of the Gentiles, in making known to us the word of life, deserves perpetual eucharistic offerings. Who loves as he ought? Paul claims special interest in all Gentiles, and they ought to respond to his kind calls.

19. Missions ought to find favor with all converted men, v. 5. The man, who has no desire to see *all nations* brought to a saving acquaintance with Christ, does not love either Christ or his neighbor.   Scott: " The end of the gospel-ministry is to bring sinners, of all nations, to obey the commands of God, by believing in his Son, and submitting to his authority ; that his name may be glorified in their salvation, and that they may become a peculiar people to shew forth his praises." Men *must* know and believe the truth. There is no way by which Christ may receive his promised reward but by the wide propagation and hearty reception of his gospel. Isa. 49 : 6; 53 : 10–12.

20. It is a great thing for us to get a true apprehension of *grace*, and to remember that every good and perfect gift comes down from God.   Let us hold fast the doctrine of divine gratuity, especially in the whole matter of salvation, in the conversion of the soul, the establishment of a church, and the ordination of the ministry.

21. The whole scheme of the gospel supposes that Christ is glorified by the salvation of men, so that all the progress of the saving truth is *for his name*, i. e. to his honor, and therefore we are bound to receive that gospel ourselves, and make it known to others.   Haldane: " Men are very unwilling to admit that God should have any end with respect to them greater than their happiness.   But his own glory is everywhere in the Scripture represented as the chief end of man's existence, and of the existence of all things."

22. If men are ever to know the saving power of Christ's grace, it must be by a holy and effectual calling, vs. 6, 7.   Something quite beyond a mere outward invitation or persuasion is necessary to move the dead soul.   To some, such a doctrine is discouraging. To those taught from heaven, it gives all the encouragement they have, and all they need.   If Ezekiel must prophesy over the dry bones, let him go at it in good earnest, for God is able to make them stand up a great army.

23. What a sad change has come over the church of Rome. " The Lord's beginning a good work in any place will not tye him to keep up the candlestick there in all time coming ; for Rome, that then was famous for saints in it, is now become the seat of the beast."

24. It far more than compensates the saints for all the ill will and ill treatment they receive from men that they are *beloved of God*, v. 7.   God loved them with compassion and good will even when they were his enemies by wicked works.   " It is the greatest love that God can show to man, being everlasting love, which originates

with himself." It is because God thus loves his people that he brings them to a saving knowledge of himself. Jer. 31 : 3.

25. Men are never the servants of God indeed and in truth, so as to secure to them the divine favor, until they are *saints*, or holy ones, v. 7. Without holiness no man shall see the Lord. Only that which is born of the Spirit is spirit. God hath not called us to uncleanness, but to holiness. This is the will of God, even your sanctification.

26. The best manners flow from pious affections. " True politeness is genuine kindness, kindly expressed." Even in saluting people that he never saw, Paul uses endearing terms, and sends to them the best wishes respecting both their souls and bodies. Dutch Annotations: " By the word *grace* is understood the original or fountain of all God's benefits towards us, and by the word *peace*, the fruits and sense thereof." It is much to be lamented that some good people, who really feel kindly, seem to have so strange an aversion to any proper expression of the real state of their hearts. Beyond cold civility, you get little or nothing from them. Such follow neither apostolic example, nor apostolic precept.

27. God's people are abundantly provided with all good things. They have *grace* and *peace*. Scott: " Without grace there can be no substantial peace: in proportion as grace is communicated, peace may be expected ; and when grace shall ripen into perfect holiness, peace will become complete fruition."

28. All believers have one God and *Father*, as well as one *Lord Jesus Christ*, v. 7.

29. It is impossible to give a satisfactory explanation to even the forms of apostolic salutation without admitting that there is more than one person in the Godhead. The form of baptism given in the Gospel, and the form of benediction in 2 Cor. 13 : 14, determine the number of persons in the Godhead to be three ; but verse 7 as clearly determines that there is more than one person, from whom grace and mercy may be sought by prayer and supplication for ourselves and our friends.

Chapter 2

ROMANS 1

VERSES 8–17

THE INTRODUCTION AND THEME

8 First, I thank my God through Jesus Christ for you all, that your faith is spoken of throughout the whole world.

9 For God is my witness, whom I serve with my spirit in the gospel of his Son, that without ceasing I make mention of you always in my prayers;

10 Making request, if by any means now at length I might have a prosperous journey by the will of God to come unto you.

11 For I long to see you, that I may impart unto you some spiritual gift, to the end ye may be established;

12 That is, that I may be comforted together with you by the mutual faith both of you and me.

13 Now I would not have you ignorant, brethren, that oftentimes I purposed to come unto you, (but was let hitherto,) that I might have some fruit among you also, even as among other Gentiles.

14 I am debtor both to the Greeks, and to the Barbarians; both to the wise, and to the unwise.

15 So, as much as in me is, I am ready to preach the gospel to you that are at Rome also.

16 For I am not ashamed of the gospel of Christ: for it is the power of God unto salvation to every one that believeth; to the Jew first, and also to the Greek.

17 For therein is the righteousness of God revealed from faith to faith: as it is written, The just shall live by faith.

8. *FIRST, I thank my God through Jesus Christ for you all, that your faith is spoken of throughout the whole world. First:* Peshito and Ferme: In the first place. It ordinarily marks the order of time, though in Matt. 6 : 33 and in not a few other cases it includes the order of importance. In Rom. 3 : 2 it is rendered *chiefly.* Here it is equivalent to, I begin by saying; Tholuck: Before I proceed to other matters. *I thank my God through Jesus Christ for you all.* In this as in many other places the authorized version and most versions take no notice of the Greek particle, often rendered *truly, indeed.* Yet Tyndale, Cranmer and the Genevan read, Verely I thanke etc. *My God.* It is a

declaration of an appropriating faith. *Through Jesus Christ* may qualify either part of the clause, so as to make the apostle say that Jehovah is his God through Jesus Christ, or that he offers his thanks through Jesus Christ. *For you all*, because of you all, on account of you all; Rheims: for al you. *That your faith is spoken of.* It is a meager exposition given by Macknight: " The faith of the Romans, which occasioned so much discourse, was their turning from idols." He might as well have said it was their turning from theft, or lying, or uncleanness. The faith of the Romans was a mighty principle. It turned them from all sorts of sin. It made them love all the commandments. It specially regarded Jesus Christ, and there in the imperial city set up the banner of the cross, and in so public and fearless a manner that the church of Rome was already a city set on a hill that could not be hid, but her faith was spoken of over the Roman empire, which now embraced Western Asia and Northern Africa, as well as nearly all Europe. In Luke 2 : 1 the phrase *all the world* is so used, though the Greek terms are not the same in the two places ; but they mean the same thing. Beza paraphrases these words: Every where by all the churches.

9. *For God is my witness, whom I serve with my spirit in the Gospel of his Son, that without ceasing I make mention of you always in my prayers.* Paul justly felt the importance of fully gaining the confidence of the brethren at Rome, and therefore uses all fair means to accomplish his object. He had before asserted his divine mission and his thanks for the grace granted to the church of Rome. He now avows in the strongest terms his lively and affectionate interest in them. *God is my witness.* Alford: There could be no other witness to his practice in his secret prayer, but God. This was no vain use of God's name. The occasion justified a solemn appeal to the searcher of hearts, involving the nature of an oath. Paul often makes such, but never frivolously. 2 Cor. 1 : 23 ; 11 : 31 ; Gal. 1 : 20 ; Phil. 1 : 8 ; 1 Thess. 2 : 5, 10. *Serve ;* we have the cognate noun in Rom. 9 : 4 ; 12 : 1. The verb is rendered *worship ;* Acts 7 : 42 ; 24 : 14 ; Phil. 3 : 3 ; and even where rendered *serve*, it commonly denotes worship, or religious service. We have it again in v. 25, where it denotes religious service offered to idols. Paul's service unto God was not only outward but with his *spirit ;* not merely by rites but with his heart. Ferme reads : cheerfully, with my whole soul, and unfeignedly. Compare John 4 : 23, 24. This service was rendered *in the gospel*, either in publishing the gospel, or in accordance with its requirements. The former is the better ; each gives a good sense, and both are true. In v. 1 the gospel is called the gospel

of God; in this verse it is called the gospel *of his Son.* Both phrases are just and true. Each explains the other. Christ is the substance of the gospel, as well as its revealer and author. *That without ceasing;* in the Greek one word, an adverb. It occurs also in 1 Thess. 1 : 3 ; 2 : 13 ; 5 : 17; and is uniformly rendered, as, Pray *without ceasing.* It is of course not to be taken literally, but as a hyperbole. Bretschneider renders it, assiduously ; Ferme : always ; Macknight : continually ; Cobbin : constantly ; equivalent to *day and night* among the Hebrews. Ps. 1 : 2. *I make mention of you always in my prayers.* Wiclif: I make mynde of you ever in my preiers, Paul had given thanks for the grace granted them. He had long and earnestly prayed for them.

10. *Making request, if by any means now at length I might have a prosperous journey by the will of God to come unto you. Now at length ;* Tyndale : at one tyme or another ; Peshito : hereafter ; i. e. at last, after so long time, or, at some time. *I might have a prosperous journey;* the Greek is one word. Wiclif: I haue a spedi way ; Peshito : a door may be opened to me. The word occurs in 1 Cor. 16 : 2 and twice in 3 John 2 ; in those cases it is rendered prosper. *The will of God;* is a phrase of frequent occurrence in the New Testament, and has a uniform significance. See Matt. 6 : 10; 12 : 50; Rom. 2 : 18 ; 12 : 2 ; 15 : 32; in Rev. 4 : 11 it is rendered pleasure.

11. *For I long to see you, that I may impart unto you some spiritual gift, to the end ye may be established. Long ;* elsewhere rendered earnestly desire, greatly desire, 2 Cor. 5 : 2 ; 2 Tim. 1 : 4. The cognate noun occurs twice and is rendered earnest desire, vehement desire, 2 Cor. 7 : 7, 11. This desire did not spring from vanity, curiosity or any fleeting cause, but from permanent and pure good will to them. *Impart,* twice rendered give, and thrice impart. *Gift;* in Rom. 5 : 15, 16 rendered free gift, that is a pure or unbought gift. This idea always belongs to the word whether it is expressed or not. Wiclif reads *grace. Spiritual* gifts are gifts from the Spirit of God, and are of two kinds, extraordinary, or miraculous, and ordinary, or such as are granted to the church from age to age. There is nothing in this verse or in the context to confine our ideas exclusively to either class of spiritual endowments. Verses 12, 13 show that the ordinary gifts of the Spirit were not out of the mind of the apostle, and the fact that up to this time no apostle had, so far as we know, visited Rome makes it probable that few extraordinary gifts had been as yet received by the church of that city. Yet chapter 12 : 6–8 shows that even then this church had gifts. Paul would impart both kinds of these gifts. The words rendered *spiritual gifts* are not found together in any other verse of the

Greek Testament, though it is pretty certain the word *gifts* is understood in 1 Cor. 12 : 1 ; 14 : 1. The authorized version, Tyndale, Cranmer and Genevan in each of those cases supply the word gifts, and so do the Peshito and Doway in 1 Cor. 14 : 1 ; though the Vulgate, Wiclif and others read spiritual things. The end sought by Paul was that the church at Rome *might be established*, or strengthened, fixed, or set steadfastly. Luke 9 : 51 ; 16 : 26 ; 22 : 32.

12. *That is, that I may be comforted together with you by the mutual faith both of you and me.* All the old English versions retain *that is,* but the Peshito, Ethiopic and Stuart have *and* or *also.* This verse is an amplification of the preceding. *That I may be comforted together* is the rendering of one Greek verb, found here only in the New Testament; Castelio: That we may be together refreshed ; Bēza : In order to receive common exhortation. The verb of which this is compounded often occurs, and is rendered comforted, besought, exhorted, intreated, and is cognate to the noun, which we render comforter in John 14 : 16–26 and elsewhere. Paul very modestly and justly expected to receive as well as to communicate comfort and edification. He was not above the humblest disciple. He condescended to men of low estate. If they but had *faith*, they were dear to him. In all the Scriptures there is not a word, which it more behooves us to understand than the word faith, yet we never learn its true nature by metaphysical refinements. See above on v. 8. True faith consists in taking God at his word ; it is such a persuasion of the truth as enables us heartily to embrace it and obey it ; it is a fruit of the Spirit, disposing us to receive Christ and rest on him alone as our Mediator ; it includes the assent of the mind and the consent of the heart to the testimony God has given, particularly that respecting his Son. Reliance on the testimony of God and on the person of Christ is of the very essence of faith ; and though we are bound to labor for full assurance of faith, yet the feeblest faith may be as genuine as the strongest.

13. *Now I would not have you ignorant, brethren, that oftentimes I purposed to come unto you, (but was let hitherto,) that I might have some fruit among you also, even as among other Gentiles.* The rendering of these words in the various English versions is remarkably uniform. Indeed the translations of it are very harmonious. *Purposed*, a verb quite expressive of a settled determination. It is found twice more in the New Testament; once in Rom. 3 : 25, where it is rendered *set forth*, and in Eph. 1 : 9, where it is applied to the unalterable plan of God, and is rendered *hath purposed*. It is cognate to the noun rendered *purpose* in Acts 11 : 23 ; Rom.

8 : 28 ; 9 : 11 ; Eph. 1 : 11 ; 3 : 11 ; 2 Tim. 1 : 9. *Was let ;* Wiclif,
lettid ; Peshito & Ferme : prevented ; Macknight, Stuart, Conybeare & Howson : hindered. The intelligent reader need not be
told that the best old English classics often use *let* in the sense of
hinder. In Luke 11 : 52 and Acts 8 : 36, the same word is rendered
hindered. The more common rendering of the verb however is
forbidden. This probably gives the true meaning here, viz. that
the Holy Ghost bound his spirit hitherto to labor elsewhere. It
is another word rendered hindered in Rom. 15 : 22, and in 1 Thess.
2 : 18. He desired to visit this church that he might have *some
fruit* among them. This is a favorite conception of Paul. The
Greek word is the same so often found in the sermons of our Lord.
In this place the word does not, as in Rom. 6 : 22, signify profit or
advantage to one's self, but fruit of his ministry, fruit unto God.
Calvin : " He no doubt speaks of that fruit, for the gathering of
which the Lord sent his apostles." John 15 : 16. Doddridge :
" Some fruit of my ministerial and apostolic labors." *Among you
also, even as among other Gentiles.* A large part of the world had
already been visited by the apostle. Almost everywhere he had
planted or visited churches ; but as yet Italy was an exception.
Abundant had been the fruit he had gathered in many places.

14. *I am debtor both to the Greeks, and to the Barbarians ; both to
the wise, and to the unwise.* A *debtor* is one who is truly and firmly
bound. Gal. 5 : 3. So was Paul bound by the love Christ had
showed him, by the commission he held, by the revelations he had
received and by the law of love to perishing men to do all he could
for all classes of men, however esteemed or denominated. The
Peshito, Arabic and Ethiopic render these words just as the
authorized version ; but Tyndale : To the Grekes and to them
which are no Grekes, unto the learned and also unto the unlearned. This is virtually followed by Cranmer and Genevan.
Erasmus and Doddridge have, learned and ignorant. Macknight's
paraphrase is *" to the Greeks,* however intelligent, *and to the barbarians, both to the philosophers, and to the common people.* All these
terms denote or describe the people who are in v. 13 called *Gentiles.* Stuart : " In classic usage, *barbarians* means all who spoke
a language foreign to the Greek." Hodge : " Properly it means
a foreigner, one of another language." In 1 Cor. 14 : 11 it is twice
used in this sense. Wise and unwise do not correspond to Greeks
and barbarians, but describe persons found both in and out of
Greece.

15. *So, as much as in me is, I am ready to preach the gospel to you
that are at Rome also.* *Ready,* in Matt. 26 : 41 willing ; the cognate
noun is rendered readiness, readiness of mind, ready mind, willing

mind, forwardness of mind, Acts 17 : 11 ; 2 Cor. 8 : 11, 12, 19 ; 9 : 2. *To preach the gospel,* in the Greek one word. There are several words in the Greek Testament, all of which are sometimes rendered *preach.* One means to tell or to speak, Acts 8 : 25 ; 11 : 19 ; 13 : 42. Another means to declare or announce fully, Luke 9 : 60. Another, cognate to the last preceding, means to publish, or bring a message, Acts 4 : 12 ; 13 : 5 ; Phil. 1 : 16. In Rom. 1 : 8 it is rendered spoken of. Another means to herald, as a crier, to announce publicly, Matt. 3 : 1 ; Acts 8 : 5 ; Rom. 2 : 21. The other is that used in our verse and means to bring good news, to publish glad tidings, Acts 13 : 32 ; Rom. 10 : 15 ; 1 Thess. 3 : 6. It is the verb from which our word evangelize comes, and is found in the New Testament more than fifty times. Paul's necessary delay had not extinguished his desire to visit and serve the church at Rome.

16. *For I am not ashamed of the gospel of Christ : for it is the power of God unto salvation to every one that believeth ; to the Jew first, and also to the Greek. Ashamed,* a word uniformly rendered in the New Testament. It is the same word used by our Lord in Mark 8 : 38 ; Luke 9 : 26. He says less than he means—I am not ashamed, i. e. I glory. *Gospel of Christ ;* see on v. 1. *It is the power of God.* We have several Greek words which in the New Testament are rendered power. One of these signifies authority and is often so rendered ; in Luke 23 : 7 it is rendered jurisdiction ; in John 1 : 10, power ; in Rev. 22 : 14, right. Then we have another word from which we get our word energy ; in Eph. 1 : 19 rendered working ; in Col. 2 : 12 operation ; in Eph. 3 : 7 effectual working. We have also a word, which in Mark 12 : 30 is rendered strength ; in Eph. 6 : 10 might ; in 2 Thess. 1 : 9 power ; in 1 Pet. 4 : 11 ability. But we have yet another word rendered power. It is that from which our word dynamics comes. We had it in v. 4. It occurs again in v. 20 and often elsewhere. In Col. 1 : 11 it is rendered might ; in Eph. 3 : 20 power ; in Matt. 25 : 15 ability ; in 2 Cor. 1 : 8 strength ; in Heb. 11 : 34 violence. Because it is very expressive of might, it is in the plural rendered miracles, mighty deeds, etc. 1 Cor. 12 : 10, 28 ; 2 Cor. 12 : 12. This is the word found in our verse. Alford : " Not only is the gospel the great example of divine Power ; it is the field of agency of the power of God, working in it, and interpenetrating it throughout." Compare 1 Cor. 1 : 18, 24. So mighty is the power of the gospel that it is *unto salvation.* As to us nothing can go beyond salvation. Nor does worship ever rise higher than when it ascribes salvation unto God. Ps. 37 : 39 ; Luke 1 : 46, 47, 68–71 ; Rev. 7 : 10 ; 19 : 1. The original word primarily means safety, then wel-

fare, then deliverance and eternal blessedness by a Reedeemer.
The word is uniformly rendered, except in Acts 27 : 34, where it
is health ; and in Acts 7 : 25, where it is applied to the deliverance
of Israel from Egypt.   Except the names given to God and our
Saviour, there is no sweeter word than salvation.   The rendering
of the verse by Wiclif is : For I schame not the gospel, for it is
the vertu of god into heelthe to eche man that belieued, etc.   The
Gospel is thus ' the highest and holiest vehicle of the divine
Power ' *to every one that believeth.*   Hodge : " Emphasis must be
laid upon both members of this clause.   The gospel is thus efficacious *to every one*, without distinction between Jew and Gentile ; and
to every one *that believeth*, not who is circumcised, or who obeys
the law, or who does this or that, or any other thing, but who
believes, i. e. receives and confides in Jesus Christ in all the characters, and for all the purposes in which he is represented in the
gospel."   *To the Jew first, and also to the Greek.*   *First*, see above
on v. 8.   Nothing beyond the order of naming these people, or
the order of time can here be intended.   Thus much the Scriptures teach.   Luke 24 : 47 ; Acts 3 : 26 ; 13 : 46.   The same particu-
larity and order are observed in Rom. 2 : 9, 10.   But the Scriptures are careful to let us know that there is no adaptation of the
gospel peculiar to any one people or nation ; and that in Christ
one tribe of men is as welcome and as well provided for as another.
Simeon, who was divinely inspired, named the Gentiles first and
Israel afterwards.   Luke 2 : 27–32.   A child of Abraham as much
needs salvation by Jesus Christ as a sinner of the Gentiles.

   17. *For therein is the righteousness of God revealed from faith to
faith : as it is written, The just shall live by faith.*   The preceding
verse speaks of *believing ;* this, of *faith.*   The noun and verb are
cognate.   See above on vs. 5, 8, 12.   The doctrine of faith is thus
urged upon our attention, and with it the doctrine of righteousness.   The faith in Christ and the gospel method of becoming
righteous are the great themes of this epistle.   They are here so
introduced to us.   Faith and righteousness are here and elsewhere fitly joined together.   Several kinds of faith are not saving—
do not secure to us righteousness.   Devils have an awful and fixed
persuasion of the truths of religion, so that they believe and tremble, but are neither made pure nor just thereby.   Jas. 2 : 19.   The
stony ground hearers had a temporary faith, which led them for a
time to receive the word of God with joy, but all passed away
without any thorough change of heart.   Matt. 13 : 20, 21.   Some
have a historical faith, by which they are so far persuaded of the
truths of God's word, that they have not an intellectual doubt of
them.   Still they obey them not, nor are changed by them.   Such

was the faith of Agrippa. Acts 26 : 27. Then there is the faith of miracles, whereby one is persuaded that by him or for him God will suspend the laws of nature, Acts 14 : 9 ; 1 Cor. 13 : 2. One may have any or all of these kinds of faith, and yet remain under condemnation. But saving faith not only historically credits the truths of God, but with the heart believes them. Rom. 10 : 10. Such faith receives God's witness concerning the divine nature and law, concerning man's sinful and guilty condition, and especially concerning Jesus Christ as the sole author of eternal salvation, and so it receives and rests upon Christ, as the way, the truth and the life, the one blessed Mediator between God and man. By this faith we are engrafted into Christ, and derive our fatness and fruitfulness from him. This is the faith of God's elect. It purifies the heart, Acts 15 : 9 ; it works by love, Gal. 5 : 9 ; it overcomes the world, 1 John 5 : 4, 5 ; it successfully resists temptation, Eph. 6 : 16. This faith abides in God's children, Eph. 3 : 17 ; it justifies all who have it, Rom. 5 : 1 ; and it is a mighty operative principle, James 2 : 22. This is the faith spoken of in our verse.

The term *righteousness* is also one of great importance in the right understanding of this verse and of this and other epistles of Paul. The word so rendered occurs more than ninety times in the Greek Testament, and in the authorized version is uniformly rendered righteousness ; so also in the old English versions ; but in the Doway it is uniformly rendered justice. Our English Bible employs the terms just and righteous interchangeably. Justice and righteousness are the same thing. The only advantage in the word righteousness is that its theological meaning is better understood than that of justice. The righteousness of God sometimes in the Old Testament, though never in the New, seems to be put by metonymy for the whole moral excellence of God, including his goodness, mercy and faithfulness. Isa. 41 : 8 ; 42 : 6. Then in both Testaments it points to that attribute of his nature whereby he is infallibly led to give to every one his due, Ps. 9 : 8 ; Rom. 3 : 5 ; Rev. 19 : 11. This is the strict sense of the word, out of which the fitness of the use of the term in other senses grows. Besides these two meanings of the phrase, the righteousness of God means the righteousness which God has provided ; the Father having devised and demanded it ; the Son having fulfilled it, and the Holy Ghost applying it. It may also be called the righteousness of God because it is pleasing and acceptable to God, the only righteousness which God will own as the ground of a sinner's acceptance. So the sacrifices of God in Ps. 51 : 17 are the sacrifices which please God, the sacrifices which he prefers above all others.

Sometimes in *Hebrew* the addition *of God* denotes the greatness of anything, as the trees of God are the great trees ; the river of God the great river, etc. And as Paul's writings abound in Hebraisms, this idea may not have been wholly out of his mind. The righteousness of God is the great righteousness. It is a glorious righteousness. This righteousness, so highly approved of God, is that which makes a believing sinner righteous in the eyes of the Judge of all the earth. It is called the righteousness of the law, because it is fully commensurate with all the demands of the law, Rom. 8 : 4. It is called the righteousness of faith, or by faith, because it is received by faith and not wrought out by personal obedience to law, Rom. 3 : 22 ; 4 : 13. It is called the righteousness of Christ because it consists of his merits, is made up of what he did and suffered for us; so that he is the Lord our Righteousness, Jer. 23 : 6. It is called imputed righteousness because it is ours, not by our own deserving, nor by being imparted to us, but by being reckoned, counted, imputed to us by God. Rom. 4 : 5, 6. So that when we believe in Jesus we are righteous before God or in the sight of God. It avails to all the ends and purposes of a complete justification. This is so manifestly the meaning of the term righteousness, that some have proposed to render it in this and some other places justification, or method of justification. But this makes confusion.

Christ's righteousness made ours is God's plan of salvation for lost men. It is righteousness without merit in the creature. It is righteousness without the deeds of the law. This sense might be powerfully argued from the cognate verb, rendered in the authorized version and even in the Doway justify. See Stuart on this place. Whitby : " This phrase (*the righteousness of God*) in St. Paul's stile, doth always signifie the *Righteousness of Faith in Christ Jesus*, dying, or shedding his blood for us."

In our verse this righteousness is said to be *revealed;* a word uniformly rendered in the authorized version. It is cognate to the noun given as a name to the last book of Scripture and means manifested, made known, made clear, brought to light.

And this righteousness is revealed *from faith to faith.* The various versions and translations cast no light on this clause. The two prepositions *of* and *to* are evidently in antithesis. The best explanation of the former in this place is by, or by means of. It has this sense in the last clause of this verse, and often. Luke 16 : 9 ; John 3 : 5; 9 : 6; Heb. 11 : 35 ; Rev. 3 : 18. The best rendering of the latter is that of the authorized version to, or unto, for, in order to, for the purpose of. In gaining the true sense we have no right to separate the words rendered faith further than is required. It cannot be

denied that there is difficulty in obtaining the exact meaning of
Paul.   The opinions presented are very various.   Augustine gives
two interpretations.   One is that God's righteousness is revealed
from the faith of preachers to the faith of hearers; the other, from
an obscure faith to a clear vision in the heavens.   Origen,
Theodoret and others make the first relate to faith in the
Old Testament; the second to faith in the New Testament.
Others explain the first as referring to a general belief of the
gospel out of which comes a special faith.   But none of these
views are admissible.   It will not do to use the word faith in two
senses so different as in this last case, nor does the phrase *from
faith to faith* denote things so separate as the faith of preachers and
that of hearers, or a weak faith and the beatific vision, or faith in
different portions of Scripture.   Others explain it of the gradual
apprehension of the truth first by a weak and afterwards by a
strong faith.   So says Theophylact: " It does not suffice to have
at first believed; we must rise from an incipient to a more finished
faith."   This is evidently the substance of the interpretation of
Beza, Tholuck and others.   Gill seems to prefer it.   Diodati mentions it approvingly.   The Dutch Annotations also explain the
phrase as equivalent to daily increase and strengthening in faith.
But this method of explaining like phrases would hardly be approved.   Compare Rom. 6 : 19; 2 Cor. 2 : 16; 3 : 18; 4 : 17.   It
should be remembered too that the least genuine faith because it
really unites the soul to Christ, does as truly receive the righteousness of God, as the strongest possible faith; and that the weak
believer is as fully justified as the strong.   Some have thought
that the apostle teaches that the righteousness of God is revealed
from the *faithfulness* of God in his word, to the *faith* of the
believer.   Although the doctrine thus taught is true, yet surely
the word *faith* is not here used in senses so different.   Whitby:
" The righteousness of God, which is by faith, is revealed in the
gospel to beget faith in men."   Barnes: " God's plan of justifying
men is revealed in the gospel, which plan is by faith, and the
benefits of which plan shall be extended to all that have faith or
believe."   Haldane: " The meaning is, the righteousness, which
is by faith, is revealed to faith, or in order to be believed."   Chalmers gives the weight of his judgment in the same direction.
Conybeare & Howson: " Therein God's righteousness is revealed,
a righteousness which springs from Faith, and which Faith receives."   Others take the same view, nor is there any doctrinal
error in the sense thus given.
    There is still another way of explaining these words.   Locke
thinks that the meaning of the apostle is that in the gospel the

righteousness of God is " all through, from one end to the other, founded in faith." Mace also says it is " wholly by faith." Scott: " This righteousness is altogether of faith, from first to last, and without any respect to other distinctions." Pool : " He saith not, from faith to works, or from works to faith ; but *from faith to faith*, i. e. only by faith." Hodge : " The most natural interpretation of these words is that, which makes the repetition entirely intensive— from faith to faith—entirely of faith, in which works have no part." Either of the last two explanations is to be preferred to any of those that preceded them, and the very last is incumbered with fewer difficulties than any that preceded it, though either of the last two teaches doctrine according to the analogy of faith, and is admissible.

As it is written, The just shall live by faith. This passage is found in four places : Hab. 2 : 4 ; Rom. 1 : 17 ; Gal. 3 : 11 ; Heb. 10 : 38. Various renderings and punctuations of it are given : Cobbin : The righteous by faith shall live ; Hodge : The just by faith, shall live, or, The just, by faith shall live ; Peshito : The righteous by faith, shall live ; The Hebrew in Habakkuk is liter- ally : The just, by his faith shall live ; Knapp and Macknight : The just by faith, shall live ; Ferme : The righteous from faith shall live ; Conbyeare & Howson : By faith shall the righteous live. These variations do not change the doctrine or materially modify the sense. The quotation contains a general truth, per- vading God's kingdom in all ages. All true faith is one and not many. One of the peculiarities of a Scriptural principle is its wide scope and unexpected applicability to new cases and princi- ples. *Shall live ;* live, and not be under sentence of death ; live, and enjoy the favor of God ; live, and not fall into spiritual decay ending in spiritual death ; live, and be happy ; wearing the divine image, quickened by the Divine Spirit, greatly refreshed and com- forted, having grace here and a sure pledge of glory hereafter.

DOCTRINAL AND PRACTICAL REMARKS

1. It is not sinful adulation to acknowledge the gifts or graces of God to men or in men. We ought with pleasure to own the worth of others. v. 8. The truth itself is always sufficiently dis- pleasing to the carnal or to the partially sanctified heart, without our making it more so by our manner of presenting it. Rudeness and harshness are not fidelity.

2. We ought to *thank* God a great deal, for we have a great deal to thank him for. v. 8. We are as truly bound to give thanks for God's goodness to our brethren as to ourselves ; and lively

saints are ready to say so. Every good gift is from the Father of lights. To him let our praises ascend.

3. It is a blessed attainment to be able in all boldness and humility to claim covenant relations with Jehovah, and to say *my God.* v. 8. He is the God of particular saints. He is the God of Abraham, of Isaac and of Jacob, Matt. 22 : 32; the God of Elijah, 2 Ki. 2 : 14; the God of Daniel, Dan. 6 : 26; and he is frequently called the God of Israel. Often do individual saints call him *my God,* and bodies of believers, *our God.* Let each man pray that his appropriating faith may be so strengthened, that he may be able to say, my Lord and my God.

4. All religious worship, thanksgiving in particular, should be offered to God through Jesus Christ. v. 8. It is as great an error to have many mediators as to have many gods. 1 Tim. 2 : 5. Some, who fail not to mention that blessed name in supplication, seem to forget that eucharistic services are never accepted but through a Mediator. On this point the Scripture is both full and explicit. Col. 3 : 17; Heb. 13 : 15.

5. We are specially bound to give thanks to God through Jesus Christ for grace manifested to others in saving their souls, and granting them large measures of strength and courage. v. 8. Our Lord gives two reasons for joy in abundant fruitfulness—1. it glorifies God; 2. it establishes discipleship. John 15 : 8. Elsewhere our apostle expresses like gratitude for similar blessings bestowed on other churches. Phil. 1 : 3–5; Col. 1 : 3–6; 1 Thess. 1 : 2, 3; 2 Thess. 1 : 3.

6. How can any deny that faith is the gift of God, since Paul gives thanks to God for it? v. 8. The same thing is elsewhere taught abundantly, Matt. 16 : 17; Lu. 17 : 5; Acts 11 : 21; 13 : 48; 16: 14; Rom. 12: 3; Gal. 5 : 22; Eph. 2 : 8; Phil. 1 : 29; Col. 2 : 13.

7. It is impossible so to conceal the good works and lively graces of God's people that they shall not be known and spoken of. v. 8. A good tree will bring forth good fruit. They in whom Christ is formed will show it. See Matt. 5 : 14, 15; 1 Tim. 5 : 25, and many other places. The hypocrite acts his part to be seen of men. The righteous acts his part to please God; but sooner or later his course will be known to men.

8. Loving ministers of Christ should be loved, listened to, and confided in, v. 9. Paul truly declared his tender affection for this church of Rome. He would fain win them more fully to his message and his Master. Their reputation as Christians bound them to receive him kindly. Brown: "Folks profession should lay bonds on them to welcome truths from the hands of God's messengers."

9. In a world of deception, suspicion and falsehood, the best men may find it necessary and useful, in a solemn manner, to call God to witness the truth of their declarations, v. 9. An oath for confirmation is to men an end of all strife. Heb. 6 : 17. Calvin: "An oath is a needful remedy, whenever a declaration, which ought to be received as true and indubitable, vacillates through uncertainty." The oath should in all cases be solemnly and not lightly taken. It is against profane oaths or oaths in common conversation that Christ and his kinsman apostle speak, Matt. 5 : 34–37; James 5 : 12. Against such we cannot be too guarded.

10. When men, the tenor of whose lives proves them sincere and upright, offer us their oath or affirmation, we should receive their statement, and act upon it as true. Even, if such may possibly be deceived, or, if in some cases those of good repute may speak untruly, we ought so far to credit what is said as not to be filled with suspicion. It is better to be deceived sometimes than to suspect every body. Brown: "When men dare hazard their souls, in calling God to witness in any particular, it is our duty to believe it as truth, and not to question it any more."

11. It is most reasonably required of us that we should *serve* and *worship* God, v. 9. He is a fit object of such obedience and adoration as we can render, even the highest. Reader, dost thou live to please God?

12. Then do we serve God aright, when we serve him in our hearts, and in the way pointed out by the gospel of his Son. v. 9. Compare Phil. 3 : 3. Doddridge: "Happy is the church of Christ, when its ministers are thus conscious of the excellency of the gospel, and thus earnestly desirous, in the midst of reproach, persecution and danger, to extend its triumphs." In Christ's people and ministers there is no substitute for godly sincerity. Lacking that, men serve themselves, not the Lord.

13. Good men ought to pray for each other, v. 9—ministers for the people, and the people for ministers. Compare 2 Thess. 3 : 3. The great want of the church in our day is the want of more, fervent, persevering prayer. Inconstancy is our great error. Luke 18 : 1; 21 : 36; Rom. 12 : 12; 1 Thess. 5 : 17.

14. It is a privilege, worth praying for with earnestness, to be allowed to extend our Christian acquaintance and our ministerial usefulness in the church of the Lord Jesus. Blessed is he that soweth beside all watercourses. He that reapeth receiveth wages and gathereth fruit unto life eternal.

15. Like other things, journeys are prosperous or adverse, as the Lord vouchsafes or withholds his favor and blessing, v. 10. And we should acknowledge his hand in the commonest affairs

of life.   One of the most mischievous practical errors among
even real Christians is that when the duty is comparatively easy,
and the burden comparatively light, they attempt to go on in
their own strength.   Thus they often fail—sadly fail.   Whereas,
if they had humbly looked to God, they would have found favor
and good success.

16. Ministers and Christians ought to seek to make their journeys and visits useful, imparting some useful hint, example, instruction or encouragement to others, v. 11.   Let men go about,
but let them go about doing good.

17. Doing good is one of the best ways of getting good.   And
it is mere vanity and intolerable pride in any man, however great
his acquiremements, to think that plain, humble, private Christians
cannot add anything to his strength and *comfort*, v. 12.   Calvin:
"There is no one so void of gifts in the church of Christ, as not
to be able to contribute something to our benefit."   Brown: "The
best way for pastors, or others, to prevent the discouragement
that young beginners are obnoxious unto, is not to harp too much
upon their weakness and infirmities, but rather to be putting
themselves in the same case and condition with them, as needing
the same supply and help that they stand in need of."

18. It is a great thing to *be established*, v. 11.   We all need it.
The strongest follower of Christ is as weak as water, except as
his ways and principles are confirmed and strengthened by divine
truth and all-sufficient grace constantly ministered to him.   Let
no man glory in his wisdom, or strength, or sufficiency, but only
in the Lord.

19. Preachers of the gospel must obey the directions of Providence respecting their fields of labor, and not consult their ease,
their pleasure or their emolument, in deciding where they shall
exercise their ministry, v. 13.   Compare Acts 19:21.   Even
Satan and wicked men are often let loose upon us by the Lord to
hinder us from carrying out our plans respecting the field we
seek or occupy, 1 Thess. 2:18.

20. The end of sowing is reaping, v. 13.   "*Fruit!*" what a
blessed word.   How rich is the grace that allows us poor creatures to gather *fruit unto life eternal.*   Let us be intent on our
work and give ourselves wholly to it.   Brown: "All such, whom
the Lord employeth in the work of the ministry, are not to look
upon the preaching of the gospel, and thereby the gaining of
souls, as an arbitrary and indifferent thing, which they may set
about, when and how they please, and leave off again, as they
think good."

21. Insatiable is the holy desire of a right-minded man to do

good and lead souls to Christ, v. 13. Already had Paul planted or visited and edified numerous and famous churches; but he would not rest till he could do something for Rome also. It is mentioned in the life of Rev. William Graham that when the great revival began in his church, he thought if some few precious youths were brought in, he would be satisfied. But when the Lord was pleased to bring them to hope in Christ, his desires increased indefinitely. Because insatiable, desires are not necessarily wicked.

22. Ministers and Christians are bound to do good to all *classes of men*, v. 14. They have no right to except any. Differences in nation, in origin, in politics, in social ideas, can never release us from the obligation to convey to men a knowledge of God's greatest blessing to man—a pure gospel. Such is the deplorable condition of man by nature, that without the salvation of Christ he is for ever undone. All men need the gospel. It suits the wants of all. We are commanded to preach it to every creature. Some slight the poor. Some avoid the rich. Some neglect the ignorant. Some are afraid of the learned. Some are offended with splendor. Some are driven away by squalid wretchedness. But in all these cases we err.

23. Let the measure of our ability be the measure of our duty, v. 15.

24. Godly and industrious ministers need not fear that they will ever run out of work. If all the *wise* are wise unto salvation, there are still the *unwise*. If the Greeks know God, the Barbarians are perhaps still ignorant. If Jerusalem, and Antioch, and Ephesus, and Corinth have embraced Christ, *Rome* may still need a more full instruction and discipline in the Gospel, vs. 14, 15.

25. It is incontestable proof of the deep depravity of man that he should be *ashamed* of the most glorious things—the gospel and the Saviour, v. 16. Could a greater perversion exist? Can any thing be more absurd than that men should blush to own their greatest and most needful blessings? It is true the taunts of ungodly men are very bitter and very scornful; but they are wholly harmless, except as we yield to them. Yet many do yield to them, and will finally and awfully perish. Mark 8 : 38 ; Luke 9 : 26 ; compared with Matt. 10 : 33 ; Luke 12 : 9 ; 2 Tim. 1 : 8 ; 2 : 12.

26. There have been many good discourses and essays written on the power of the gospel to bless and save and comfort mankind; but none of them have exhausted the subject or even risen to the full height of the argument. Paul calls it the *power of God*, v. 16; and in 1 Cor. 1 : 24 he says that Christ, who is the substance of the gospel is both "the power of God and the wisdom

of God." Calvin : " That the gospel is the savor of death to the ungodly, does not proceed from what it is, but from their own wickedness." The annals of this world tell us not of one instance where a sinner was converted, sanctified, filled with pious hopes, made willing to suffer in the cause of God, and enabled mightily to triumph over the world, the flesh and the devil; over fears, temptations and death itself, except by the gospel of Christ. It alone is mighty to the pulling down of strongholds. 2 Cor. 10 : 4. This word of God is quick and powerful. Heb. 4 : 12. Nothing should dishearten or discourage God's people and particularly his ministers from making known the blessed truths of salvation. All those are ashamed of the gospel, who, as Gill says ," hide and conceal it, who have abilities to preach it, and do not; or who preach, but not the gospel; or who preach the gospel only in part, who own in private that which they will not preach in public, and use ambiguous words, of doubtful signification, to cover themselves; who blend the gospel with their own inventions, seek to please men, and live upon popular applause, regard their own interest, and not Christ's, and can't bear the reproach of his gospel." I have known a man ashamed of his mother, because she spoke bad grammar; and another, of his father because he wore coarse clothing; and they gained no credit thereby. But he, who is ashamed of Christ and his gospel, is a sure candidate for shame and everlasting contempt. While he, who owns and obeys the gospel of Christ, shall infallibly experience its power to raise him even from the lowest depths of guilt, ignorance and pollution *unto salvation,* beyond which creatures cannot rise.

27. There is no limit to the power and adaptation of the gospel to men, v. 16. It suits the Jew; it suits the Greek; it meets the wants of the wise and of the unwise. It suits us poor sinners of the Gentiles. Compare Rom. 10 : 11, 12. It brings to men all they need.

28. The doctrine of faith is a great doctrine, which it behooves us so to understand as to make no fatal mistakes, vs. 8, 16, 17. The wicked may pour out their most cruel venom against it; but whether men shall be saved will in the last day turn, as God says it will, upon the fact, whether they had genuine living faith in the Redeemer. Nor can God more richly bless us in this life, than by granting us, not fewer sorrows, not lighter trials, but stronger faith.

29. The excellence of the true doctrine of faith is its simplicity and equal adaptation to all nations and classes of men, v. 16.

30. Of equal importance is the Scriptural doctrine in answer to the great question, How shall man be just with God? It is the

doctrine of righteousness, v. 17. There is no light on the way of a sinner's salvation but in the gospel of Jesus Christ. It tells of hope for the perishing, pardon for the guilty. It tells of God's method of justifying *the ungodly*. Rom. 4 : 5. It speaks of justification by faith without the deeds of the law. There never was but one way of justifying sinful men before God. The opposition to the true scriptural doctrine is strange, malignant and sometimes blasphemous; but we cannot give it up. Paul says, *It is written*. Yes it is written all over God's word, in the law, the prophets and the Psalms; in the Gospels, the Acts, the Epistles and the Apocalypse. Righteousness, perfect and spotless, must be secured at the very commencement of a religious life. Whoever is without it is under wrath, and receives nothing in a covenant way. Let no man deceive himself with forms, ceremonies, professions, self-inflicted sufferings, a hereditary creed, a sound creed, or any thing else. The only good hope of eternal life for any man is to be found in the righteousness by faith. Oh that men believed this truth, and held it fast. It is their life. The Lord is of purer eyes than to behold evil, and cannot look on iniquity. Hab. 1 : 13. Know ye not that the unrighteous shall not inherit the kingdom of God? 1 Cor. 6 : 9. If there is no way of making sinners perfectly righteous in the sight of God and of his law, there is no possibility of saving them. All this is the more striking and impressive when we duly consider the sinfulness of man. The apostle at once cites us to a survey of the state of the world.

Chapter 3

ROMANS 1
VERSES 18–32

THE HORRIBLE CORRUPTION, FATAL ERRORS AND DOLEFUL PROSPECTS OF THE HEATHEN

18 For the wrath of God is revealed from heaven against all ungodliness and unrighteousness of men, who hold the truth in unrighteousness;

19 Because that which may be known of God is manifest in them; for God hath shewed *it* unto them.

20 For the invisible things of him from the creation of the world are clearly seen, being understood by the things that are made, *even* his eternal power and Godhead; so that they are without excuse:

21 Because that, when they knew God, they glorified *him* not as God, neither were thankful; but became vain in their imaginations, and their foolish heart was darkened.

22 Professing themselves to be wise, they became fools,

23 And changed the glory of the uncorruptible God into an image made like to corruptible man, and to birds, and fourfooted beasts, and creeping things.

24 Wherefore God also gave them up to uncleanness, through the lusts of their own hearts, to dishonour their own bodies between themselves:

25 Who changed the truth of God into a lie, and worshipped and served the creature more than the Creator, who is blessed for ever.   Amen.

26 For this cause God gave them up unto vile affections: for even their women did change the natural use into that which is against nature:

27 And likewise also the men, leaving the natural use of the woman, burned in their lust one toward another; men with men working that which is unseemly, and receiving in themselves that recompense of their error which was meet.

28 And even as they did not like to retain God in *their* knowledge, God gave them over to a reprobate mind, to do those things which are not convenient;

29 Being filled with all unrighteousness, fornication, wickedness, covetousness, maliciousness; full of envy, murder, debate, deceit, malignity; whisperers,

30 Backbiters, haters of God, despiteful, proud, boasters, inventors of evil things, disobedient to parents,

31 Without understanding, covenant-breakers, without natural affection, implacable, unmerciful:

32 Who, knowing the judgment of God, that they which commit such things are worthy of death, not only do the same, but have pleasure in them that do them.

18. *FOR the wrath of God is revealed from heaven against all un-godliness and unrighteousness of men, who hold the truth in unrighteousness.* *For* notes the connection with the preceding. There was great need of a gospel of *a righteousness by faith.* God cannot but reject all who have not perfect righteousness, either in their own persons or in the person of the Redeemer. He is spotlessly holy and perfectly just. God's *wrath is revealed* against the wicked. The word rendered *wrath* occurs in the New Testament more than thirty times; in this epistle twelve times. It is commonly rendered as here, once indignation Rev. 14 : 10; once vengeance Rom. 3 : 5; and thrice anger. In six or seven cases it is applied to human anger; but commonly it is used to express the punitive displeasure of God. There is not necessarily (though there may be commonly) malignity in anger as felt by man. Mark 3 : 5. But God's wrath is his inflexible purpose to visit unatoned sin with condign punishment. *Revealed*, the same form of the same verb so rendered in v. 17, on which see above. There is no necessity for varying the signification in these two verses. Wrath is revealed in the whole course of providence in all ages. *From heaven*, we have the same words in Mark 8 : 11; Luke 9 : 54; 17 : 29; Acts 9 : 3; 1 Pet. 1 : 12. The two ideas, that seem to belong to the phrase are, 1. that the revelation is from God himself, and 2. that it is very clear. The wrath of God, breaking forth sometimes in terrible judgments, sometimes in punitive justice executed by law and by society, sometimes infallibly foretokened by remorse of conscience, and everywhere threatened in God's word, even in the gospel itself, against those, who abuse mercy and slight offered grace, no less than against those, who break the commandments and despise the authority of God, may fitly be said to be revealed from heaven. That the gospel comes with awful sanctions, imposing obligations of a kind more solemn than were ever before known to men, is a scriptural doctrine. Acts 14 : 16; 17 : 30, 31; Heb. 10 : 28, 29. The gospel offers more; it threatens louder; its promises are larger; its curses are heavier than those of any other dispensation of God to his creatures. It gives no countenance to wickedness; it never intimates that God will clear the guilty, or accept the sinner without a satisfaction to the retributive justice of God. Beyond the gospel nothing can go in opposing all sin, whether it be in the form of *ungodliness*—sin in violation of our duty to God; or in the form of *unrighteousness*, injustice, or iniquity—sin against our neighbor. Not only is God displeased with fallen angels, but with *men ;* and not only with some grossly ignorant men, but with many who *hold the truth*, but hold it *in unrighteousness.* The truth here referred to is the truth in regard to the

nature and will of God, however made known; in particular as manifest in the works of nature and in the government of the world.   Calvin: "The truth is the true knowledge of God;" Pool: " All the light, which is left in man since the fall."   The word, rendered *hold*, is in 1 Cor. 7 : 30 and 2 Cor. 6 : 10 rendered possess; in 1 Cor. 15 : 2 keep in memory; in 1 Thess. 5 : 21 ; Heb. 3 : 6; 10 : 23, hold fast; it has also the sense of hinder or restrain, 2 Thess 2 : 6, 7; in Luke 8 : 15; Heb. 3 14 it means to keep or steadfastly retain in a good sense.   Here it seems to mean possess, though some fine scholars prefer imprison, suppress, hinder, detain, confine, or oppose; Chalmers has stifle.   *Unrighteousness*, the same word as before.   When any truth is possessed without a corresponding practice it is held wickedly, hurtfully, wrongfully. Then men do not obey it; they are not made better by it.   Dutch Annotations: "Contrary to all right and equity, which requires that men give God that which belongs to him."   Other meanings have been gathered from the clause; but they are far-fetched; while this is obvious, is very important, grows out of the common use of the terms, and agrees with the context, v. 21.

19. *Because that which may be known of God is manifest in them ; for God hath showed* it *unto* them.   Peshito : Because a knowledge of God is manifest in them; for God hath manifested it in them. There have always been among men the means of knowing something of the existence and glory of God.   *Them* clearly refers to *men* in v. 18.   *In* here means among as in vs. 5, 6, 13 of our chapter, also Rom. 2 : 24; 1 Cor. 1 : 10, 11; 2 : 2, 6 and often; though not a few commentators refer it to the knowledge of God in men, making the clause parallel to one in Rom. 2 : 15.   They had some knowledge of God.

20. *For the invisible things of him from the creation of the world are clearly seen, being understood by the things that are made,* even *his eternal power and godhead ; so that they are without excuse.*   Tyndale, Coverdale, Cranmer and Genevan collocate the words better than in our authorized version : His invisible things, that is to say, his eternal power and Godhead, are understood, etc.   The external world has always, even *from the creation*, taught lessons concerning its Maker.   The heavens *declare* his glory ; the firmament *sheweth* his handy work, Ps. 19 : 1.   All his works praise him. The reason, why a miracle was never wrought to prove the existence and power of God, was that creation fully evinced both.   If men will not believe the things *that are made*, they would not believe the things that God might do.   The divine existence, power, majesty, wisdom, goodness and sincerity are wondrously demonstrated by the works of nature.   These things are seen " by

the intellect," as the Peshito has it.   This leaves all atheists and
all idolaters *without excuse*.   Nothing can shield from just reprehension men who shut their eyes to the clear manifestations
of truth.   If there is a Maker of heaven and earth, he is to be both
loved and feared.   Wiclif : So that thei maun not be excused.
Compare Acts 14 : 17.   Before men can yield themselves up to
atheism, polytheism, idolatry or ungodliness they must resist clear
and strong convictions, even if they live in heathen lands.   " Every
one that doeth evil hateth the light," wherever may be his home.
All ungodliness and unrighteousness are the fruit of a depraved
nature.   The light has shined on men *from the creation*.   This is
better than *by the creation*.

    21. *Because that, when they knew God, they glorified* him *not as*
God, neither were thankful ; but became vain in their imaginations,
and their foolish heart was darkened.   Several of the old versions
are striking.   Tyndale : In as moche as when they knewe God,
they glorified him not as God, nether were thankfull, but wexed
full of vanities in their imaginacions, and their folisshe hertes were
blynded.   The object of the apostle in this verse and in all this
context is to show that salvation by human merits is impossible,
inasmuch as men were both impious and unjust, having no righteousness whatever, even perverting and abusing the plainest and
chiefest truths in religion, such as the existence and excellence of
God.   To this they added ingratitude, the sum of all wickedness.
Well-bred people thank even another man's servant for a small
favor, such as a cup of cold water.   How vile must be the heart
that warms not with gratitude to him, who lavishes on us innumerable blessings, all wholly unmerited.   Often do heathen writers
acknowledge that God is the author of their benefits.   The
famous words—

Deus hæc otia nobis fecit—

are but a sample.   Yet how they forsake his worship and turn to
idols !   Even Socrates, condemned for rejecting polytheism, at his
death ordered a cock to be offered to Æsculapius.   And Seneca,
a cotemporary of Paul, wrote with great spirit and pungency
against the foolish and wicked idolatry of his times.   Yet he says
that a wise man will conform to such rites, as required by law, and
not at all as pleasing to God.   He adds : " All this ignoble rabble
of gods, which ancient superstition has now of a long time been
heaping up, we will so adore as to remember that the worship of
them is due rather to custom than material in itself."   So that as
Augustin says, " He worshipped what he found fault with, he practised what he reproved, and he adored what he blamed."   It is gen-

erally agreed that light and knowledge enhance guilt. These people not only might have known God, but did actually know much concerning him, and then refused to honor him as he deserved. To this they were led by one gross, master sin, ingratitude, to which their wicked hearts naturally and powerfully inclined them. The same depravity made them *vain in their imaginations.* The word rendered *imaginations* is elsewhere nine times rendered thoughts, once doubting, once doubtful, once disputings, once reasoning, here only imaginations. The cognate verb is eleven times rendered reasoned, once disputed, once consider, once mused and once cast in her mind. Wiclif and the Doway read thoughts; Rheims, cogitations; Chrysostom, Dutch Annotations, Adam, Doddridge, Pareus, Beza, Turrettin, Guyse, Pool, Macknight, and Conybeare and Howson have reasonings. Tholuck correctly refers the whole to man's mind, his inward being, and adds " religious and moral error is always the consequence of religious and moral perversity." Calvin : " They quickly choked by their own depravity the seed of right knowledge, before it grew to ripeness." *And their foolish heart was darkened.* For foolish Wiclif has unwise; Macknight, imprudent; Stuart, inconsiderate; Hodge, senseless and wicked. This dreadful perversity led to terrible folly and darkness. *Heart* sometimes designates the intellectual powers, Matt. 13 : 15; Acts 28 : 27; sometimes the conscience, 1 John 3 : 20, 21 ; sometimes the seat of the affections, Mark 16 : 14; Luke 8 : 15 ; Rom. 6 : 17, and sometimes the whole inner man, Matt. 15 : 19; Heb. 4 : 12. In our verse the word may be taken in each or in all of these senses, for they are all true. Wicked men are as foolish as they are perverse. They are awfully left to themselves. They are benighted. They are lost.

22. *Professing themselves to be wise, they became fools.* For *professing* Wiclif and Rheims have saying; Tyndale, Cranmer and Genevan, when they counted; Peshito, while they thought within themselves; Conybeare and Howson, calling themselves; Calvin, while they were thinking. In Acts 25 : 19 the same word is rendered, affirmed. Tholuck : The word most frequently in Greek denotes the vaunting of a pretender. The pretensions of the heathen to wisdom and piety have always been great. The Greeks and Romans were not exceptions. In particular the Greeks boasted prodigiously of their attainments in philosophy. But their claims were idle and delusive. In their wisdom they were, if possible, further from the truth than in their acknowledged ignorance. The philosophers were as far from the truth as the common people. They all together *became fools;* Guyse, were really stupid and senseless, like perfect idiots; Doddridge, they

became fools and idiots, degrading, in the lowest and most infamous manner, the reason which they so arrogantly pretended to improve, and almost to engross. But in the Scriptures a fool denotes either one, who is an idiot or a very weak man, Prov. 10 : 8; 13 : 20; 2 Cor. 12 : 6; or one who is vile and wicked, Ps. 14 : 1; Pr. 14 : 16; Luke 24 : 25. As all sin is folly, and in particular as high conceits of our own attainments in religion are proof both of the vanity and wickedness of our minds, so the apostle declares these Gentiles to be both unwise and vile. Such, beyond a doubt, was their real character. Nor is it possible to determine which was the more monstrous, their folly or their sinfulness, nor which of these had the greater tendency to produce the other, for wickedness leads to folly and folly to wickedness, yea, wickedness is folly, and folly in divine things is wickedness. So that the Bible is right in not carefully preserving the distinction between fools and sinners. Macknight thinks the language of this verse the more pungent, as it is put into a writing addressed to the Romans, who were great admirers of the Greeks.

23. *And changed the glory of the uncorruptible God into an image made like to corruptible man, and to birds, and four-footed beasts, and creeping things.* For *changed* many read turned. The substitution of any creature for Jehovah is vile perversion, but most of the forms of idolatry are so gross that we wonder every mind is not shocked. *Glory* here means honor, or majesty, or excellence. *Uncorruptible;* Tyndale and Cranmer, immortal; so rendered also in 1 Tim. 1 : 17; the opposite of corruptible or mortal in this verse, which applied to inanimate things means perishable, 1 Cor. 9 : 26; to man, mortal. The cognate noun is rendered sincerity, Eph. 6 : 24; Tit. 2 : 7; in 1 Cor. 15 four times incorruption, and elsewhere immortality, Rom. 2 : 7; 1 Tim. 1 : 10. Robinson renders it exemption from decay. The heathen vainly talked of their immortal gods, while they were mere vanities. The minds of the heathen being blinded and perverted, they freely consented to gross and wicked conceptions of the Almighty, such as could be set forth by some kind of image, often drawn from low and perishable things. The likeness of man or angel, of the sun or moon no more adequately or justly shows forth the true nature of God than does the similitude of an ox, or ass, an owl, a bat, a toad, a lizard or an anaconda. Therefore we need not marvel that when men become worshippers of any but Jehovah, they soon sink to the lowest depths of idolatry, or are ready to do so. Such wickedness could not pass unpunished.

24. *Wherefore God also gave them up to uncleanness, through the lusts of their own hearts, to dishonor their own bodies between themselves*

Gave them up, delivered them over, committed them, (abandoned says Ferme,) in a bad sense betrayed, found also in vs. 26, 28; in Rom. 4 : 25 ; 8 : 32 delivered. Chrysostom : " Not only was their doctrine satanical, but their life too was diabolical." *To uncleanness,* always so rendered in the authorized version, and commonly in most others. The cognate adjective *unclean* is the word applied to the possessions of devils, Matt. 10 : 1, and often. In Rev. 18 : 21 we have every *foul* spirit. The word here used often denotes wickedness in general, always impurity of some kind. God gave them not over to their hateful course without a cause. This was found in the *lusts of their own hearts. Lusts,* commonly used in a bad sense, then rendered as here or concupiscence, Rom. 7 : 8 ; Col. 3 : 5 ; but sometimes in a good sense, then rendered *desire,* Luke 22 : 15 ; 1 Thess. 2 : 15. Being given over of God, they sank into debasement, disgraceful to their whole natures. The word rendered dishonor is in Luke 20 : 11 entreat shamefully ; in James 2 : 6, despise ; Wiclif: Punysche with wrongis ; Tyndale, Cranmer and Genevan: defyle ; Rheims: abuse. By their *bodies* we are to understand their whole persons, preeminently their animal natures.

25. *Who changed the truth of God into a lie, and worshipped and served the creature, more than the Creator, who is blessed for ever. Amen.* This verse both in Greek and English closely resembles v. 23d. Cranmer: Which have turned hys truthe unto a lye, and worshypped and serued the thynges that be made, more than him that made them, &c.; Peshito: And they changed the truth of God into a lie ; and worshipped and served the created things much more than the Creator of them, to whom belong glory and blessing, for ever and ever: Amen ; Stuart: Who exchanged the true God for a false one, &c. *Changed,* the Greek occurs but twice in the N. T. here and in v. 26. It strictly means to exchange one thing for another. This is just what Gentilism does. It not merely mars right thoughts and the pure worship of God ; it wholly subverts all true religion. It changes not merely the manner but also the very object of worship. By *the truth of God* some understand the true God. No doubt that idea is included, but there is no necessity for so limiting the sense. The whole of religion is by paganism subverted, changed *into a lie,* or *lying.* The word is in the N. T. uniformly rendered. Whoever is pleased with idolatry under any form or pretence, shows that he is not of God nor of the truth, for no lie is of the truth, and no lie is of God. All false worship is a deception, a falsehood, a lying vanity. How could it be otherwise? It disowns Jehovah, and leaves the poor soul without a God, who can help, or hear, or see, or save. *Wor-*

shipped, i. e. venerated, reverenced, offered their devotions to. *Served*, primarily equivalent to rendered bodily service; but in the new Testament generally, gave religious homage. Matt. 4 : 10; Rom. 7 : 15. See above on v. 9. The two words include every thing rightly called religious worship. *The creature*, any thing made, often used collectively, once applied to a law *made* by man, 1 Pet. 2 : 13, and once to a building, Heb. 4 : 11. If worship is offered to any thing *made* by God or man, it matters little whether in created eyes it be great or small. One may as well worship a toad as the sun, an onion as an archangel, an atom as the whole creation. Each and all of these are infinitely below God. *More than*, in the Greek a preposition, which may be rendered more than, above, beyond, against or contrary to. In v. 26, also in Rom. 4 : 18 and elsewhere it is rendered against. Luther: Rather than the Creator; Erasmus: Above the Creator; Grotius: In the place of the Creator; Beza and Doddridge: To the neglect of the Creator. Whoever pays religious homage to any creature insults the divine majesty, honors something rather than God, more than God, against God, contrary to God, his being, his glory, his law, his government. *Blessed*, not the word signifying happy, rendered blessed in Matt. 5 : 3–11; in 1 Tim. 1 : 11; 6 : 15; but the word signifying praised, adored, extolled, i. e. worthy to be praised, &c. In the N. T. this word is applied to none but to God only; though the cognate verb is used to express the good wishes and hearty prayers of one creature for another, as well as praise to God. Compare Heb. 11 : 20, 21; Jas. 3 : 9. *For ever*, the precise form of words found in the Lord's prayer, Matt. 6 : 13. *Amen*, a word often transferred to various languages. It is Hebrew and means faithfulness, truth, or faithful, true. Jehovah early revealed himself as a God of *Amen*, Deut. 32 : 4. At the beginning of a sentence or speech Amen is a solemn mode of averring, as in Matt. 18 : 3; John 3 : 3. At the close of a speech from one, it is a response from others, or an expressed concurrence in a prayer offered in behalf of others or in communion with them.

26. *For this cause God gave them up unto vile affections: for even their women did change the natural use into that which is against nature.* *Gave up*, the same verb and in the same form as in v. 24. *Vile affections*, dishonorable lusts, shameful longings; Peshito: Vile passions; Stuart: base passions; Rheims: passions of ignominy; Locke: shameful and infamous lusts and passions. The corruption went so far that it invaded all the privacies of life, and debased the characters of the more delicate sex and stung men with the reflection that they could neither believe the innocence, nor trust the purity of their own wives, daughters, sisters or

mothers, and inspired jealousy, which is the rage of a man, to consume them with coals of juniper.

27. *And likewise also the men, leaving the natural use of the
woman, burned in their lust one toward another, men with men working
that which is unseemly, and receiving in themselves that recompense
of their error which was meet.* Such wickedness met with punishment, *recompense*, retribution, even in this life. The heathen
were led into it by *error*, the *deceit* that is in sin, the *fraud* practised
by the devil, all resulting from their *wandering* from God. Whoever has any familiarity with Greek and Roman classics cannot
lack proof of the horrible baseness and degrading practices referred to in vs. 24, 26, 27. See the testimonies of Petronius, Sueto-
nius, Martial, Seneca, Virgil, Juvenal and Lucian. Many such
are collected by Bos, Grotius, Wetstein, Cox, Macknight, Tholuck, Stuart and others. The destruction of domestic love, the
brutality consequent upon the basest vices, and the hideous forms
of loathsome disease thus induced constituted a *meet*, appropriate
reward of forsaking God.

28. *And even as they did not like to retain God in* their *knowledge, God gave them over to a reprobate mind, to do those things
which are not convenient.* Peshito has the first clause: And as
they did not determine with themselves to know God; Clarke:
They did not search to retain God in their knowledge; Tyndale: It seemed not good unto them to be aknowen of God.
The Doway and many others substantially agree with the authorized version. The first verb is well translated. They *did*
not *like*, i. e. it did not seem good to them, it was not their pleasure, they did not determine, as they would have done had they
been right minded. In Rom. 2 : 18 the same word is rendered
approve; in 14 : 22 allow. *To retain*, literally to have or to hold.
Gave over, the same in vs. 24, 26 is rendered gave up. See on v.
24. It is used both in a good and bad sense. *Reprobate*, always so
rendered in the N. T. except twice; in 1 Cor. 9 : 27, a castaway;
and in Heb. 6 : 8, rejected. It means rejected after trial, castaway
after being proved. Some render it undiscerning or unsearching;
but this is feeble and unsupported. The heathen did not like or
approve God, and God did not like or approve them. *Those
things which are not convenient*, not fit, right or becoming. For not
convenient Tyndale, Cranmer and Genevan, have not comly:
Stuart, base. More is implied than is expressed. It means they
were left to do odious and abominable things, such as are at once
mentioned :

29. *Being filled with all unrighteousness, fornication, wickedness,
covetousness, maliciousness ; full of envy, murder, debate, deceit, malig-*

nity; whisperers. Being filled and full, words in Greek, not even cognate. Perhaps one word is as strong as the other. The latter may mean *stuffed*. Conybeare and Howson render the latter, They overflow with. The first noun, *unrighteousness*, means injustice, iniquity, wrong. Wiclif has wickidness. It here refers to wrong committed by one man against another. It is preceded by *all*, which also qualifies the nouns following; all, i. e. every kind of injustice. When men rob and wrong God, you need not be surprised to hear of their practising the grossest injustice to each other. The second noun includes all violations of the seventh commandment, whether by adultery, fornication, whoredom, harlotry, concubinage, incest or any other form of lewdness. The Peshito and Doddridge render it lewdness; Macknight and Stuart, uncleanness. Clarke correctly says it includes "all commerce between the sexes out of the bounds of lawful marriage." The third noun, *wickedness*, is very comprehensive. Conybeare and Howson have depravity. It includes all acts of hurtfulness, grievousness, malignancy or badness; in our version always rendered as here, except once in the plural iniquities, Acts 3 : 26. Calvin cites Ammonius in favor of rendering this word wickedness, and thinks it means "practised wickedness, or licentiousness in doing mischief." Stuart has malice. The word points out all acts of oppression, which give men labor and sorrow. The fourth term, *covetousnsss*, points out the sin of grasping after more worldly possessions than one has, without due regard to the will of· God or the rights of men. It is the love of the world, particularly of wealth. By *maliciousness* we may understand that state of mind, which makes one a wrong-doer without provocation, a wanton, injurious person; one having a love of mischief. Stuart has mischief; Clarke, ill-will. In the common version it is also rendered evil, malice, wickedness and naughtiness. *Envy* is a malignant, restless, devilish, tormenting passion. It sickens at the worth, success, or good name of others, especially neighbors and competitors. It is the great instigator of strife and of bloodshedding. It caused the first fratricide, 1 John 3 : 12. Very appositely therefore does the apostle next mention *murder*, or the slaying of men. To this crime the propensity of men without the restraints of God's word and providence is so strong that society soon becomes intolerable. In ancient Rome the wicked and violent destruction of human life was truly fearful. But over most of the heathen world infanticide alone would justify the charge here made. Many murders spring from strife or *debate* as the word is according to an old usage rendered here and in 2 Cor. 12 : 20. Low quarrelling, bloody broils, perpetual contentions, cruel contests embitter life in all

heathen countries. Of course candor, fairness, truth are sadly
wanting, and *deceit*, guile, craft, subtilty (for the world has all
these renderings in the N. T.) sadly abound. The original word
means *bait*. The figure is drawn from hunting. Lying is so
common in heathen countries that in India it is a saying, Open the
mouth, and the lie will come out. All these things flow from and
promote malignity; Wiclif has yuel wille; Doddridge, inveteracy
of evil habits; Macknight, bad disposition; Genevan, takyng all
things in the euyl part. For the last rendering we have the best
classical authority, and no other word in this chapter expresses
that precise idea. The Peshito has evil machinations. Some
think the word denotes rudeness of manners; but the Genevan
translation gives the best interpretation. Wherever iniquity thus
abounds the tongue will be sure to be set on fire of hell; and next
we read of *whisperers*, a word found no where else in the N. T.
though we once have its cognate whisperings, 2 Cor. 12 : 20. It
points out those mischief-makers, secret slanderers, whose arts are
innumerable, and the evil consequences of whose conduct are felt
every where. Doddridge and Macknight think it designates only
secret slanderers of persons who are present. No doubt such are
included, but there is no authority for thus confining its meaning.
Locke and Stuart have backbiters; and Wiclif, prying backbiters.
But when without God's word wickedness is in the ascendant, it
knows no bounds, and the unregenerate are also,

30. *Backbiters, haters of God, despiteful, proud, boasters, inventors
of evil things, disobedient to parents.* Most English versions have
backbiters; Wiclif, Rheims and Doway, detractors; Macknight,
revilers; Tholuck and Stuart, open slanderers. *Haters of God*,
from the form of the Greek some would render it hated of God;
but in many cases words in that form have an active sense. Paul
is speaking of the sins of the heathen, not of their punishment.
That wicked men do hate God is proved by their daily conduct
and by many Scriptures. Ps. 81 : 15 : John 7 : 7; 15 : 23–25; Rom.
8 : 7. This language is not too strong. *Despiteful*, Peshito, scoffers; Wiclif, debaters; Tyndale, Cranmer and Genevan, doers of
wronge; Rheims, contumelious. In 1 Tim. 1 : 13 the same word
is by Paul applied to himself before his conversion, and is rendered
injurious. Doddridge has *violent* and overbearing. Locke, insult-
ers of men; Macknight, insolent towards inferiors; Conybeare
and Howson, outrageous. *Proud*, haughty, arrogant, in the N. T.
always rendered as here. Cicero, Juvenal and Horace all claim
that virtue is from ourselves, not from God. The cognate noun
occurs but once and is rendered pride, Mark 7 : 22. Conybeare
and Howson have overweening. *Boasters,* an excellent rendering,

the same as in 2 Tim. 3 : 2.   The Peshito has vain-glorious.   This
does not materially vary the sense.   All such assume to themselves more than is their due.   It is a sin full of evil to the world
that men should be assumptive in their hearts or manners.   *In-*
ventors of evil things, Wiclif, fynders of yuel thingis; Tyndale and
Cranmer, bringers vp of evyll thinges; Peshito, devisers of evil
things; Macknight, inventors of unlawful pleasures; Locke, inventors of new arts of debauchery; Doddridge has much the same.
These last authors doubtless point to the characters intended.
Disobedient to parents, Peshito, disregardful of parents.   The Doway
exactly agrees with the authorized version.   Several old English
versions for parents have fadir and modir.   The common version
is literal; but the phrase doubtless designates all violators of the
fifth commandment.   In heathen countries these abound, being
encouraged by the very principles of false religions.   Such persons
are naturally enough

31. *Without understanding, covenant-breakers, without natural*
affection, implacable, unmerciful.   Without understanding, the word
occurs in the N. T. five times and is in our version always rendered
as here, or foolish.   Wiclif has unwise; the Doway, foolish; Tholuck,
stupid about things divine; Macknight, imprudent; Stuart, inconsiderate or foolish; Conybeare & Howson, bereft of wisdom.   No
word could better describe the superstitions, follies, fancies,
frenzies and senseless rites and observances of Pagans, who are
also *covenant-breakers.*   This word does not here refer so much to
breaking covenant with God as with man, faithless persons, who
feel themselves free to act in disregard of their word, their promise,
their bond, and even their oath.   If such find that they have sworn
to their own hurt, or made a hard bargain, they will change, with
or without pretext.   Hesychius: "They adhere not to compacts."
The heathen are also to a fearful extent *without natural affection,*
parents sadly regardless of the lives and wants of their offspring;
children not being tender of the feelings, honor, or comfort of
their parents, especially of their mothers, and particulary when
they become infirm or helpless, etc.   This natural affection is
much celebrated in ancient writings, especially as it is displayed
in irrational creatures.   But sin often sinks men below the brutes.
Implacable, literally, without truce, declining reconciliation, refusing to be on peaceable terms.   Wiclif: with outen bonde of pees.
The word occurs in one other place, 2 Tim. 3 : 3; and is there
perhaps erroneously rendered truce-breakers.   If some men have
disagreements with neighbors, they are never afterwards reconciled.   Conybeare & Howson read ruthless.   Of course such men
are *unmerciful,* Peshito: in whom is no compassion; Wiclif,

Rheims and Doway: without mercy; Tyndale and Genevan: merciles; Stuart: without compassion. The Greek words of this verse all begin with the privative equal to our *un*, and Owen of Thrussington attempts to preserve something of that form— *Unintelligent, unfaithful, unnatural, unappeasable, unmerciful.*

32. *Who, knowing the judgment' of God, that they which commit such things are worthy of death, not only do the same, but have pleasure in them that do them.* For *judgment* some have erroneously read justice or righteousness. So Calvin, the Doway, and several old English versions. In this verse *judgment* is evidently equivalent to purpose, determination, decision. In Luke 1 : 6; Heb. 2 : 1, 10 the same word in the plural is rendered ordinances. The term is equivalent to the law of God, which law is written on the hearts of men. The heathen, therefore, knew this statute of God. Many of them inveighed against the things here condemned. Many laws were at various times enacted and sometimes enforced against them, even to the taking of life. But the death here mentioned is that of the soul, an endurance of the anger of God. For although in Luke 23 : 15 ; Acts 23 : 29 ; 25 : 11, 25 ; 26 : 31 the phrase refers to the death of the body, yet in each of those cases it is of human laws that the terms are employed. Peshito: They know the judgment of God, that he condemneth to death those, etc. But to be worthy of death at God's tribunal is an awful thing. It is to be under the curse of his law, under his wrath. Though the heathen knew God's law in these matters, they sinned on, and knowingly persisted in disregarding the divine will. They did more: they had pleasure in those who thus sinned. That is, they thought well of them, sympathized with them and encouraged them by being their boon companions.

DOCTRINAL AND PRACTICAL REMARKS

1. It is clear that God is angry with the wicked, v. 18. It cannot be otherwise. God is holy, and hates sin, and from the uprightness of his nature he must punish sin. His wrath is revealed in the human conscience and in the whole course of his providence. It is revealed in the clearest manner. Experience, history and observation thus teach.

2. Men seek in vain for justification by the deeds of the law, for in them are found ungodliness and unrighteousness, and over them impends the curse of a violated law, which is holy, just and good, both in its precept and in its penalty, v. 18.

3. Amazing is the self-righteousness of men, that hesitates and even refuses to regard the gospel scheme necessary to our salva-

tion, until we are stricken with a sense of the holiness and terrors of the Lord, v. 18.

4. Nothing can excuse much less justify our rebellion against God. It deserves all the divine displeasure revealed against it, v. 18. Its nature is hideous, frightful, so that in comparison of it nothing else is to be dreaded. God and all good beings abhor it.

5. Wicked as men are, and wild as is the confusion that sometimes seems to reign in human affairs, God still governs the world, and will sway his sceptre over it to the consummation, vs. 18, 19. And although time is not the part of duration, nor earth the theatre, where and when full justice is displayed; yet enough is done to enable a wise man to see that if these things be done in the green tree, that which shall be done in the dry will be very terrible.

6. Nor should godly men ever find fault with the dealings of the Lord with them in the way of chastisement, for the best of men are but men at the best, and in many things we all offend. Judgment may be expected to begin at the house of God. Wherefore doth a living man complain, a man for the punishment of his sins? Shall we, who deserve no favor, receive good at the hand of the Lord, and shall we, who deserve all disfavor, not receive evil also? Job 2 : 10; Lam. 3 : 39; 1 Pet. 4 : 17. Sin must be punished, will be punished.

7. It is very remarkable how slow men are to believe in their sinfulness. Though *all ungodliness and unrighteousness* abound in the world; though we see the best of men afflicted, and some bad men made examples and beacons to warn the world, yet after all how few have a deep or any just and lasting sense of their sinfulness in the sight of a holy God; yet all men esteem the gospel as good news only in proportion as they see their lost condition, and are burdened with a consciousness of personal ill-desert. There is no greater folly than to cry, All is well, when our state is one of ruin.

8. It is highly dangerous to hold the truth in unrighteousness; to know what is right, and refuse to do it; to see its fitness, and not feel its binding force; while to pervert it, stifle it, suppress it, and disobey it will surely lead to the saddest results. v. 18. That heathen was right, who said: " There is nothing more common for the gods to do than to pervert the minds of wicked men." Of all the aggravations of sin none is mentioned in Scripture in a more alarming manner than that of knowingly acting wickedly. To him that knoweth to do good, and doeth it not, to him it is sin, Jas. 4 : 17.

9. However much the light of nature may shine upon us, and

by sinning against it we may bring down upon us the wrath of heaven, yet on many accounts a revelation is necessary to our salvation. A revelation of wrath may terrify and convict, v. 18. It is a revelation of grace and mercy that saves. This is made clear in many ways. If the light of nature is enough, why did it never save even one man from sin and wretchedness? And why did it never lead at least one nation to adopt a code of pure morals? And why did it never inspire solid and animating hopes of a blessed eternity? Natural religion does indeed declare that God is, that he is almighty, good, wise, sincere, the patron of virtue; but it tells not how sinners may serve and please him.

10. So that on many accounts pity to our fallen race should lead us to make known the unsearchable riches of Christ to the nations that sit in darkness. No stronger, or sounder argument can be made out of God's word than that in favor of spreading the gospel over the whole earth. The heathen are in a sense a law to themselves; but they are not a gospel to themselves. No one of them can tell his brother how he may have a saving knowledge of God, though all of them have more light than they make a good use of. Though the light of nature cannot save, it is sufficient to condemn, vs. 19, 20. Well does Aristotle say: "God, who is invisible to mortal eyes, is to be seen by his works." In like manner Cicero: "Though thou seest him not, yet thou knowest God by his works." So clear is the light of nature that were men honest they would confess that the Most High alone is to be religiously worshipped, supremely loved, held in godly reverence, or implicitly obeyed.

11. Were men by nature irrational, idiotic, lunatic, or utterly beyond the possibility of knowing God, or of learning his will, the case would be vastly different. Where there is no law, there is no transgression. But because men have reason, and conscience, and many things to draw them to God, they are without excuse, v. 20. If men were right-minded, they would glory in this, that they understood and knew God. And were they rightly affected, they would inquire after him as for hid treasure; and as many as thought and felt aright would seek until they gained that knowledge of God and of Christ, which is eternal life. Light hated or abused has no saving tendency. Truth rejected and disobeyed has a damning power.

12. Reason suggests that the creature should honor the Creator. Scripture asserts in the clearest manner that we are bound to glorify God, v. 21. Compare Ps. 22 : 23; Isa. 49 : 3; Mat. 5 : 16; Rom. 15 : 6; 1 Pet. 4 : 16; Rev. 15 : 4. This is the capital point, in which most fail. Calvin: "He, who has a right notion of God,

ought to give him the praise due to his eternity, wisdom, goodness and justice." Yet where is the nation without God's word,
that puts any honor upon him? The great mass of teaching, of
rite and of fable among the heathen is precisely adapted to bring
into contempt all that is divine. Among both ancients and
moderns, many deny the divine existence, as Epicurus and Democ-
ritus, and the devotees of Boodh and Fo. Not a few are Panthe-
ists, as Orpheus. Even Aristotle avowed principles which fairly
led to Pantheism. So many held, as some modern mimics of
heathenism hold, that a dog, a cat, an onion, the mountains, the
ocean, all things material were a part of God. Numbers of the
heathen made it a part of their philosophy to doubt all truth concerning God, even his existence, as Protagoras and Diagoras and
their followers. Great masses of them held and taught that there
were many gods. In Rome thirty thousand were acknowledged,
and in China for a long time they have counted their gods by the
hundred million. If Jehovah is a father, where is his honor? if
he is a master, where is his fear?

13. How important then is it to possess the true knowledge of
God, v. 21. To some extent this may be had, and yet men be
corrupt and profane. But nothing short of the truth concerning
God can ever hinder a people from falling into deep debasement
in vice and impiety; for superstition is one of the worst forms of
irreligion. Theophylact uttered a truth confirmed by the annals
of all times, when he said: "He that will not know God, soon becomes corrupt in his life." Tholuck: "It is always found, that the
want of a sense of religion blunts the sense for general morality."

14. Revelation is well sustained by reason in asserting the obligations of gratitude. Until the human heart is changed by
divine grace, all men fail in this matter towards God, v. 21. Calvin: "There is no one, who is not indebted to him for numberless
benefits." But when did a heathen people ever make a meet
return? And can any plead for the virtue or piety of a man or
a people, who are not *grateful?* "Call me," said a heathen, "ungrateful, and after that you can say no evil of me."

15. Vain imaginings and mental darkness belong to sin in all
its stages and workings, v. 21. This has always been so. The
leaven of iniquity no sooner began to work than our first parents
had vain dreams about being as gods. The great source of evil
among the antediluvians was found in their sinful and unreasonable conceptions of things, Gen. 6:5. So prevalent is this evil
among men, that were it closely observed and condignly punished,
no flesh would be spared. Corrupt affections and false reasonings
are the great pillars of Satan's kingdom in this world. Nor is

there any cure for this blindness and falsehood and perversity without the gospel. Hodge: "The higher the advancement of the nations in refinement and philosophy, the greater, as a general rule, the degradation and folly of their systems of religion." Haldane: "What they deemed to be their wisdom was truly their folly." No man is so blind as he who will not see. Jesus taught: "Every one that doeth evil hateth the light, neither cometh to the light," John 3 : 20.

16. Beware of vain pretensions, v. 22. The greatest pretenders, either to wisdom or goodness, are the greatest fools or deceivers. No wise man will trust them. God abhors them.

17. It ought effectually to cure high pretensions and vain boastings, that those, who have most abounded in them, have been left to commit the greatest folly, v. 23; even selecting the most hideous reptiles, yea, and vegetables, as fit representations of God.

18. Of all the inflictions of divine wrath none are more terrible than spiritual desertions, spiritual judgments and judicial blindness, vs. 24, 25, 28. It is a horrible thing to be *given up* or *given over* by God. From his throne never proceeds a more dismal sentence than this: "Let him alone." Calvin: "As Satan is the minister of God's wrath, and as it were the executioner, so he is armed against us, not through the connivance, but by the command of his judge. God, however, is not on this account cruel, nor are we innocent, inasmuch as Paul plainly shows, that we are not delivered up into his power, except when we deserve such a punishment." Olshausen: "Where God and His holy being is not, and therefore the vanity of the creature's self is the ruling power, there sin begets sin, and punishes itself by sin." Hodge: "God often punishes one sin by abandoning the sinner to the commission of others." Whatever confusion and error may have arisen in the minds of the self-sufficient on this and kindred subjects, these things are clear: God is not the author of sin, he is not the efficient cause of transgression, he works no iniquity, he is of purer eyes than to look upon unrighteousness; yet nothing happens in the world contrary to his sovereign and eternal purpose; if he had chosen, he could have prevented the existence of moral evil in the universe; he is Lord of all; he governs moral agents without interfering with their freedom, the wicked are his hand, his sword, the rod of his anger, Ps. 17 : 13, 14; Isa. 10 : 5; they can go no farther than he permits; God can and often does make a wicked man his own tempter and tormentor, he leaves him to himself, he throws the reins loose upon the neck of his lusts, putting comparatively little restraint upon his sinful propen-

sities. This desertion of the soul by the Lord is most righteous, it was desired by the wicked, it occurs only after stubborn resistance to the calls of mercy; in every instance wicked lives spring from wicked hearts, evil practices naturally follow human perversity. One of the sad things attending this judicial desertion is the fact that the sinner perceives it not, but flatters himself in his iniquity till it be found to be hateful. Not unfrequently the punishment is in kind; those who have been unfaithful to God are left to practise unfaithfulness to their wedding engagements; those who lie unto God become infamous by lying unto men; those who practise spiritual whoredom are left to commit all bodily lewdness and uncleanness till they are a loathing to others. and sometimes to themselves, Hos. 4 : 12–14.

19. The evils of idolatry have probably never been exaggerated, v. 23. It is full of grossness, absurdity and misery. 2 Ki. 17 : 15–18; Ps. 16 : 4; 115 : 4–8; Isa. 44 : 9–20; Acts 14 : 15; 17 : 29. If one would see the estimate of heathenism by those, who had been sunk in its pollutions, and then escaped its sorrows and abominations, let him read Lactantius' *de Ira Dei*, Eusebius' history, Augustin *de civitate Dei;* or let him for his own satisfaction read such works of modern authors as Leland on the advantage and necessity of the Christian Revelation, Jenkins' reasonableness of Christianity, Ward's India or some other books of that class. Cudworth has shown by ample quotations from ancient poets, philosophers, orators and historians, that the heathen held and knew that there was one supreme God; and yet in all Gentile literature is not found one hymn, as Estius says, in honor of the true God. Heathenism is as wicked as it is sottish. Chrysostom thus sums up the whole matter respecting the Gentile theology and worship: "The first charge is, that they did not find God; the second, that they failed to do so, although favored with the best and most manifest opportunities; the third, that they failed, though calling themselves wise; and the fourth, that they not merely did not find him, but degraded his worship to demons and stones." What but sin and misery, darkness and error could be introduced by sentiments and practices so corrupt and degrading?

20. Sin tends to the worst for both worlds, and in all respects, vs. 23, 26, 27. Its nature is to induce utter ruin.

21. People, who have the gospel, can never be sufficiently thankful for being saved from Paganism.

22. Lawgivers, moralists, pastors and parents cannot too wisely or carefully guard all, and especially the young against every sin of uncleanness, vs. 24, 26, 27. Any one form of it naturally

leads to its worst manifestations. Even the Israelites, when they forsook God, and were left to themselves, imitated the abominations of Sodom, 2 Ki. 23 : 7. Lewdness is the pit, into which the abhorred of the Lord falls, Pr. 22 : 14. Hodge: "Sins of uncleanness are peculiarly debasing and demoralizing." Nor is there any infallible preservative against them, if we forsake God and are forsaken of God.

23. It is a grave question whether private Christians in their speech and writings, and religious teachers in their public ministry abound, as they should, in doxology, v. 25. It is probable that the profaneness, with which some ungodly persons have bandied such phrases as "bless God," "thank the Lord," has brought into disesteem and desuetude the pious custom of reverently saying on all fit occasions, Bless the Lord, etc. The word of God contains a rich variety of these excellent forms of showing forth God's glory. Tholuck correctly says it is customary both for Jews and Mahometans to pronounce a doxology, whenever in their writings it becomes necessary to introduce even for refutation any notion or heresy unworthy of God. Haldane: "It denotes that we should never speak of God but with profound respect, and that this respect ought to be accompanied with praise and thanksgiving."

24. There is no reason to doubt the doctrine of human depravity, vs. 18–32. Every prison, and gibbet, and lock, and bolt, and bar, every good statute human and divine designed to restrain the outbreakings of lust and passion, every page of truthful history, every tear, and sigh, and wail, yea, the very lexicons and philology of the world prove how corrupt men are. Such a catalogue of sins as that given in vs. 29–31, if duly considered, would overwhelm any unconverted people with shame and self-condemnation. Like catalogues are given by Christ in Mark 7 : 21–23; and by Paul in Gal. 5 : 19–21.

25. However the vain expectations of men may be multiplied respecting impunity in transgression, yet God has published it (and he is of one mind and changeth not) that sin and sinners are *worthy of death*, v. 32. It cannot be safe to pursue a course which he who cannot lie, he who is love itself, he who cannot err, he who is to be our final Judge, has said is punished condignly only by the awful penalty—death. And if a course of iniquity among the heathen brought on them eternal ruin, what shall not God inflict on those who, living in the light of a pure gospel, shall commit the same or similar deeds! There is a dreadful hell. The heathen themselves spake of Tartarus as the prison house of the wicked.

26. Those who maintain the doctrine of total depravity find their views warranted by the word of God. The wicked are *filled with unrighteousness*, etc., and are *full of envy*, etc. vs. 29, 30. Other Scriptures say they have not the love of God in them, that they are in the bond of iniquity and in the gall of bitterness, that they are dead in trespasses and sins. John 5 : 42 ; Acts 8 : 23 ; Eph. 2 : 1.   Surely this language is as strong as any language ever used by sound theologians. By *total depravity* we do not understand that one man is as bad as another, or that any one sinner is as bad as he will be if he continues longer in sin ; but only that every unregenerate man is altogether destitute of holiness, is entirely without the image of God, and has no love to God.   Brown : " So mighty is the torrent of corruption in folks by nature, that if God would but give way, and give folks over unto their own perverse, reprobate minds, it would carry them headlong to all acts of iniquity, and run out to all, even to the most abominable wickedness whatsoever."

27. " Deceit lies in generals."   Let those who would deal faithfully with their own souls, or the souls of others, come to particulars as does our apostle in this part of his epistle.

28. To what fearful lengths many a sinner, even though dastardly as to all noble deeds, will go in sin, taking pleasure in the sins of his fellow men, even when they bring him no honor, wealth or advantage, but merely gratify his horrid enmity against God and man by letting him see Jehovah dishonored and souls madly rushing to ruin, v. 32.   The Scriptures everywhere speak of such in terms of alarm and abhorrence, Pr. 2 : 10–14 ; Ezek. 16 : 24–26. Chrysostom : " He that praiseth the sin is far worse than even he that trespasseth."   Calvin : " He, who is ashamed, is yet healable ; but when such an impudence is contracted through a sinful habit, that vices, and not virtues, please us, and are approved, there is no more hope of any reformation."   Pool : " Having pleasure in them that do evil is the highest kind of wickedness : such come nearest the devil, who take pleasure in evil because it is evil." Olshausen : " To take pleasure in the sins of others when one's own evil desires are more subdued, and therefore the voice of conscience is more easily heard, indicates a higher degree of sinful developement than the sinful action itself."   Slade : " To look with complacency on the vices of others is one of the last degrees of degeneracy."   Stuart : " The Apostle considers this as the very climax of all the charges which he had to bring against the heathen, that they not only plunged into acts of wickedness but had given their more deliberate approbation to such doings."

29. Hodge : " The most reprobate sinner carries about with

him a knowledge of his just exposure to the wrath of God. Conscience can never be entirely extirpated, v. 32." Of this truth we have proofs every day. Even where a man's avowed wicked principles are entirely opposed to a pure conscience, the case is not altered. Herod was a Sadducee, a gross infidel, denying angel and spirit, mocking the doctrine of the resurrection. With these principles he beheads John Baptist. This bloody crime goads him, makes him a coward, and his infidelity is no protection. When Jesus became a public person and his miracles were noised abroad, some of the people said he was Elias and some that he was one of the old prophets; but Herod in the teeth of his Sadduceeism said, I can tell you who he is—it is John whom I beheaded. If these things be so, it is in vain for the wicked to avoid a fearful looking for of judgment for doing those things which they know to be worthy of death.

30. The scope of the whole section under consideration is to show that salvation by the deeds of the law is impossible, and that if men are to be saved at all, there must be some method of justification altogether different from that, to which the human heart is so much wedded. Stuart: "It is clear that the Gentiles need a Saviour; it is equally clear that they need gratuitous justification, and that they must perish without such a provision for them." The necessity for a revelation of the gospel scheme for the Gentiles was urgent. They were living without God's image, without communion with him, without his favor, without holiness, without saving knowledge, with wrong beliefs, with wrong feelings, with wickedness in their hearts and breaking out in their lives. This matter should deeply affect the hearts of us sinners of the Gentiles, the descendants of those, whose characters are here depicted. We still carry about us some of the rags of heathenism, as in the names of the days of the week. This may remind us of the hole of the pit, whence we have been digged, and should make us greatly glory in the cross of Christ, in the glorious gospel of the blessed God.

Chapter 4

ROMANS 2
VERSES 1–11

AN ACKNOWLEDGMENT OF THE TRUTH DOES NOT
PROVE MEN TO BE WITHOUT SIN

THEREFORE thou art inexcusable, O man, whosoever thou art that judgest: for wherein thou judgest another, thou condemnest thyself; for thou that judgest doest the same things.

2 But we are sure that the judgment of God is according to truth against them which commit such things.

3 And thinkest thou this, O man, that judgest them which do such things, and doest the same, that thou shalt escape the judgment of God?

4 Or despisest thou the riches of his goodness and forbearance and longsuffering; not knowing that the goodness of God leadeth thee to repentance?

5 But, after thy hardness and impenitent heart, treasurest up unto thyself wrath against the day of wrath and revelation of the righteous judgment of God;

6 Who will render to every man according to his deeds:

7 To them who by patient continuance in well doing seek for glory and honour and immortality, eternal life:

8 But unto them that are contentious, and do not obey the truth, but obey unrighteousness, indignation and wrath,

9 Tribulation and anguish, upon every soul of man that doeth evil; of the Jew first, and also of the Gentile;

10 But glory, honour, and peace, to every man that worketh good; to the Jew first, and also to the Gentile:

11 For there is no respect of persons with God.

PAUL, having shown the atrocious guilt of the Gentiles, and the justice of their exposure to the Divine displeasure, now turns to the Jews, and by skilful approaches and logical arguments proves that they also were liable to wrath, and could not be justified by the works of the law. He begins by saying,

1. *Therefore thou art inexcusable, O man, whosoever thou art that judgest : for wherein thou judgest another, thou condemnest thyself ; for thou that judgest doest the same things.* The apostle does not here name the Jews, but leads on his readers to acknowledge that such immorality and impiety as he had de-

scribed were worthy of death, and then makes his appeal to *men*, as such; see also v. 3. It is not till he reaches v. 9 that he even names the Jews. The division of the sacred books into chapters, however advantageous in some respects, often breaks the connection. The first verse of this chapter and the last verse of chapter I. are closely connected. In that Paul first says that they which do such things are worthy of death. He then says that they which have pleasure in so vile wrong-doers are still more vile. In this verse he asserts the increased criminalty of those, who have the rule of right before them, and condemn those immoralities and impieties of which he had given a list, and yet practise the same sins. Other explanations of the connection indicated by *wherefore* have been given. But this seems most satisfactory. By saying such a man is *inexcusable*, he uses a figure of speech in which he says less than he intends to be understood. The meaning is he is wholly *indefensible* because he sins against clear light. *Inexcusable*, in chapter 1: 20 rendered *without excuse*. In pronouncing on the case of others, one passes sentence on himself as did David before Nathan. *Judge* and *condemn :* the first of these verbs is often rendered judge, condemn, sometimes sue at the law, go to law, determine, think, esteem. The second is always rendered condemn or damn. There is a striking resemblance between these two verbs. This is sufficiently preserved in the authorized version, also in the Syriac and Vulgate and often in more modern versions. On this verse Whitby has shown by ample quotations from Josephus that the very sins of the heathen were practised by the Jews. The Jewish historian says that his countrymen committed all kinds of wickedness, omitting none which ever came to the memory of man, esteeming the worst evils to be good.

2. *But we are sure that the judgment of God is according to truth against them which commit such things.* *But* here has the sense of and or further. *We are sure*, literally, we know, we understand, we are aware. The principles of God's moral government over the world were not concealed from mankind. *Judgment*, so rendered in many places, also damnation and condemnation. Here it means a condemning sentence, because it is *against* wrong-doers. This judgment is *according to truth*, i. e. it is righteous and proceeds from the exalted nature of God. It is not capricious. The Lord does not condemn in one man that which he commends in another. He does not look upon appearances, professions and plausibilities. What he loathes in a Greek he abhors in a Jew. We know thus much from the nature of God, from the course of his providence, from the convictions of our own consciences, and from the clear declarations of holy scripture. By *truth* Locke

understands not only that which is right and just; but truth
according to divine predictions and threats. But truth is often
synonymous with righteousness, and well nigh invariably supposes it.

3. *And thinkest thou this, O man, that judgest them which do such
things, and doest the same, that thou shalt escape the judgment of God?*
The doctrine of this verse is quite the same as that of the first.
The rendering of Wiclif is striking: But gessist thou man, that
demest hem that dose such thingis, and thou doist these thingis :
that thou shalt escape the dome of god? The word rendered
judgment here is the same as in v. 2, and is cognate to the word
judgest found thrice in v. 1. If men with all their blindness and
errors still see how righteous it is in God to punish iniquity, much
more does God see the enormity of sin and the righteousness of
retribution. And if God never errs, how can he fail to punish
those vices and sins which men justly and commonly condemn in
each other? It is not charged that every Jew practised all the
sins of the heathen, especially in the eyes of man, but that the
Jewish people, who rejected the gospel did these things at least in
their hearts, so as to be involved in a like condemnation. Tholuck :
" Knowledge without corresponding disposition is of no avail."
The ground of Paul's strong appeal in this verse is not history,
public rumor or any labored argument which he had submitted,
but the conscience of every man.

4. *Or despisest thou the riches of his goodness and forbearance and
long suffering; not knowing that the goodness of God leadeth thee to
repentance?* Peshito: Or wilt thou abuse the riches of his benevolence, and his long suffering, and the opportunity, which he giveth
thee? And dost thou not know that the benevolence of God
should bring thee to repentance? Wiclif: Where [whether] dis-
pisist thou the richessis of his goodnesse, and the paciens and the
long abidinge? knowist thou not that the benygnnyte of god
ledith thee to forthinkynge? *Despisest*, contemnest, thinkest
lightly of, a word rendered with absolute uniformity in the New
Testament. That the wicked contemn God is alike taught in the
Old Testament, Ps. 10 : 13; 107 : 11. *Goodness,* also rendered good,
Rom. 3 : 12; kindness, 2 Cor. 6 : 6 and elsewhere; gentleness,
Gal. 5 : 22. Haldane: Goodness is the best translation of the
word. *Forbearance,* found also in Rom. 3 : 25. It here means
God's delay to punish when he is highly provoked. Macknight :
"*Forbearance* is that disposition in God, by which he restrains
himself from instantly punishing sinners." *Long suffering,* com-
monly so rendered, also patience. It denotes the quiet and pro-
tracted endurance of God under insults and wrongs. In all these

perfections God has and manifests *riches*, a word rendered with entire uniformity. The amount of the first clause is that in order to continue in sin men must contemn an unspeakable amount of divine kindness. In the second clause the word rendered goodness is elsewhere uniformly an adjective, good, kind, gracious, but here used as a noun and well translated. Here we are taught that the appropriate effect of God's forbearance and kindness would be to work in us a thorough change of mind and behaviour. If God is good even to the unkind and the unthankful, surely the door of entrance to the divine favor is open to the penitent. The word repentance is that used to designate repentance unto life, and not mere regret without a change of heart. Wicked men pervert every thing. Until renewed by grace nothing moves men aright. They do not know, or acknowledge that a due consideration of the divine kindness ought to change their whole course.

5. *But, after thy hardness and impenitent heart treasurest up unto thyself wrath against the day of wrath and revelation of the righteous judgment of God:* Peshito: But, because of the hardness of thy unrepenting heart, thou art treasuring up a store of wrath against the day of wrath, and against the revelation of the righteous judgment of God. *Hardness,* Cranmer and Genevan have stubburnesse; Stuart, obstinacy; found here only, but the cognate adjective is rendered hard in Matt. 25 : 24; John 6 : 60; Jude 15, &c. *Impenitent,* that is without true repentance; Cranmer and Genevan: a heart that cannot repent. The other words of the verse are translated with a literal exactitude that cannot be surpassed. No more fearful thought has ever reached the human mind than is found in this verse. On wrath see above on Rom. 1 : 18. Proverbs 10 : 2 shews that the word treasure is not always used in a good sense. The day of wrath is a phrase found elsewhere, Rev. 6 : 17. Compare Zeph. 1 : 15. Clarke: "The *treasure of wrath* in this verse is opposed to the *riches of goodness* in the preceding." All this evil on the wicked is to be expected from the character of God,

6. *Who will render to every man according to his deeds.* A man's *works* are all those things, which evince his character. The doctrine here laid down is abundantly declared in Scripture. Job 34 : 11; Ps. 62 : 14; Pr. 24 : 12; Jer. 17 : 10; 32 : 19; Matt. 16 : 27; 1 Cor. 3 : 8; 2 Cor. 5 : 10; Rev. 2 : 23; 20 : 12; 22 : 12. These places teach the truth directly. Other passages as clearly declare it in other words. *Render,* elsewhere perform, yield, restore, pay, give, reward, recompense. It fully conveys the idea of retribution. The context shows that the *every* has special reference to Jew and Gentile, but those distinctions embrace the whole human

family. None are exempt from accountability—none. Therefore those able commentators Pareus and Haldane misapprehend the force of this passage when they suppose that Paul here speaks of salvation by the works of the law. We are compelled to believe that our destiny will be according as our works shall show that we are the friends or enemies of God, nor does this doctrine at all impair that of a gratuitous salvation by faith without works, for no man has faith, unless he shows it by his works. Calvin: " It is an absurd inference to deduce merit from reward." Rewards of grace will be among the most glorious of all recompenses. But even they will be proportioned to the faith and obedience of believers. Matt. 9 : 29; Gal. 6 : 7, 8; 2 Cor. 9 : 6. None will gain admission to heaven, whose lives prove that they are God's enemies ; and none will be banished into darkness, whose lives prove that they are God's friends. God's recompense shall be to all men according to their works, for he will render

7. *To them who by patient continuance in well doing seek for glory and honour and immortality, eternal life.* Peshito: To them who by perseverance in good works, seek for glory and honor and immortality, to them he will give eternal life. *By patient continuance in well doing* is good English, gives the sense, and is better than the literal would be—the *patience of good work.* *Glory,* as in 1 : 23 and often in this and in twelve other epistles of Paul. *Honor,* always so rendered in Romans and often elsewhere, though sometimes rendered price, precious. 1 Cor. 6 : 20; 7 : 33; 1 Pet. 2 : 7. It is often coupled with glory. Heb. 2 : 7; 1 Tim. 1 : 17; 1 Pet. 1 : 7. *Immortality,* see above on Rom. 1 : 23. Here it evidently means a blessed immortality. Tholuck thinks the three words are equivalent to *a glorious and honorable immortality.* *Eternal life* is perfectly literal, and points to enduring bliss beyond this world. Calvin: " The meaning is that the Lord will give eternal life to those who, by attention to good works, strive to attain immortality." Nor will God recompense the righteous alone ;

8. *But unto them that are contentious, and do not obey the truth, but obey unrighteousness,* [shall be] *indignation and wrath,*

9. *Tribulation and anguish, upon every soul of man that doeth evil; of the Jew first, and also of the Gentile.* *Contentious,* literally of contention, Peshito: obstinate ; Conybeare & Howson: men of selfish cunning; Diodati: resty ; Tyndale, rebellious. The Doway, Genevan and Rheims agree with the authorized version. *Not to obey the truth* is not to receive, love and practise it—to refuse submission to it—often rendered not to believe. *To obey unrighteousness* is to trust in it, to have confidence in it, and so to adopt it as a course of life, taking it as a principle of action. *Indignation,* com-

monly rendered wrath, sometimes fierceness. Rev. 16 : 19; 19 : 15. *Wrath*, as in v. 5. *Tribulation*, the only Greek word so rendered, often translated affliction ; the cognate verb signifies to press, press hard, oppress, distress. *Anguish*, so rendered here only, elsewhere distress. The four words, here used to describe the evils, which shall come on the incorrigibly wicked, are as strong as can be found in the Greek language. The evils here threatened shall come upon every sinful soul, without regard to nationality.

10. *But glory, honour, and peace* [shall be] *to every man that work-eth good; to the Jew first, and also to the Gentile. Glory and honor*, as in v. 7. *Peace*, as in Rom. 1 : 7 and often hereafter. These blessings shall come, not on him who sometimes does a thing in itself right, but who *worketh good*. It is his life work. He lives for it. Whatever his former history, his ancestry, his nationality, he shall not fail of eternal blessedness.

11. *For there is no respect of persons with God.* Tyndale : For ther is no parcialyte with God. *Respect of persons*, one word uniformly rendered. We have also the cognate parts of speech. In every instance where any form of the word occurs, the matter in hand shows that the inspired writer is speaking of those factitious distinctions so much gloried in by men, as nationality, Acts 10 : 34 and here; civil position as of master or servant, Eph. 6 : 9; Col. 3 : 25 ; social position as of rich and poor, Jas. 2 : 1–9. Of these and like things God makes no account whatever.

DOCTRINAL AND PRACTICAL REMARKS

1. However invincible ignorance of any one truth may *excuse* men respecting that, yet clearly no man is exempt from blame, who knows enough truth to pass righteous sentence on others, yet is himself guilty of the same offences, v. 1. The profane often justly reprehends professors of religion for things which he and they alike practise. The self-righteous moralist and formalist often justly condemn the irreligion of the openly wicked, when in heart they are all alike. All such will be judged out of their own mouths, Luke 19 : 22.

2. Nor can men complain if, applying just rules to the conduct of others, they find the same applied to their own lives, v. 1. Brown : " It is the most absurd, and most unreasonable thing in the world, for any to think to escape God's judgment for such sins, or the like, for which others cannot escape their sharp censure. How strict soever men be, God is more strict."

3. Therefore our just sagacity and discrimination in condemning others cannot save us. Indeed we ought thereby rather to be

alarmed than quieted. Scott: "The censures which men pass on their neighbors, who perhaps justly deserve them, may render themselves more inexcusable, while they do the same things, and yet trust in themselves that they are righteous and despise others."

4. So far is our own judgment of others from being a safeguard against our own ruin, that oftentimes the most severe are the vilest of men, v. 1. Compare Matt. 7 : 1. It was a mark of the special power of truth and of God's Spirit, when the accusers of that poor guilty woman slunk away, one by one, from the presence of Christ. So in the last day the truth will flash condemnation in the faces not only of the grossly censorious, but of all, who condemn in others what they tolerate in themselves.

5. Man's judgment may err; God's cannot, v 2. God's whole nature makes that *sure*. If God decides any matter, rule, right, character or destiny, he does it *according to truth*, and truth is eternal and unvarying.

6. Carnal security is one of the most dangerous foes. It lulls to sleep, it deludes into self-deception, it is a dangerous form of hypocrisy, it effectually prevents men from seeing their danger and from seeking salvation. Faithful preachers must give awful warnings against it, as Paul does here. Brown: "It is a great aggravation of folks guilt, when they know the hazard of their doings, and see what they do deserve, and yet notwithstanding malapertly go on, and hereby their mouths are stopped for ever."

7. Vain is the hope that God will interpose to save men, or for ever leave them unpunished, when they obstinately persist in doing such things as must be an offence to him, vs. 2, 3. God is too holy to look upon iniquity. Man is too weak to resist God. If God arise to judgment, man must fall. Any view of religious doctrine, which makes us careless about fleeing from sin and wrath and laying hold on Christ is false.

8. Every sin against God has in it more or less contempt of his glorious excellency; but when we clearly know the truth and yet persist in sin we do despite against his nature, and specially against his goodness, v. 4. Chrysostom: "As to them who rightly avail themselves of God's long suffering, it is a ground of safety; so to them that slight it, it is conducive to a greater vengeance." Haldane: "God's goodness is despised when it is not improved as a means to lead men to repentance, but, on the contrary, serves to harden them, from the supposition that God entirely overlooks their sin." Hodge: "The goodness of God has both the design and tendency to lead men to repentance. If it fails, the fault must be their own."

9. The reason, why such conduct brings wrath, is that it is so base and ignoble not to be melted and subdued by kindness, and especially by the goodness of God. When men harden themselves in pride and unbelief, turning the grace of God into lasciviousness, and being worse and worse, because God is good, all ingenuousness of nature is gone. When God is so good and forbearing as to remind us of his continual pity, the only way we can persist in sin is by a fearful obduracy, v. 5.

10. Let every man often ask himself, Does the goodness of God lead me to repentance? Am I humbled by mercies as well as by judgments? Is my sorrow for sin ingenuous? Do I hate every false way? Surely every man is bound to the most solemn and humbling duties of religion by the amazing kindnesses of Jehovah. In him we live and move and have our being. His patience and forbearance have no parallel, and these are shown to his foes, who deserve only ill at his hands.

11. All the work of the wicked is self-ruinous and self-destructive, v. 5. They are treasuring up wrath. They are digging into hell. They do in diligence and toil often excel the righteous in their endeavors. But they feed on wind. Sin is all a lie from beginning to end.

12. In the present state saints and sinners often have common mercies and miseries, and not in a few cases the righteous are greatly afflicted above others, but there is coming a time called the day, that day, the great day, the last day, the day of *wrath*, when things will assume a very different aspect. Even now Jehovah judges in the earth, but that will be the final as well as the *righteous judgment of God.* Then " the secrets of all hearts will be made manifest. Let us often reflect upon the awful result ; and consider, that indignation and wrath, tribulation and anguish will be our portion, if we are contentious and disobedient to the truth ; yea, if we do not by a patient continuance in well-doing, seek the promised glory, honor and immortality ; which if we do, we shall, through the grace of God, secure everlasting life. Vain will our knowledge and our profession be, and our testimony against the sins of others will only inflame the guilt of our own." We cannot entertain too frequent or too solemn thoughts of our great account. Cyprian said that he seemed all the time to hear the words, " Awake ye dead, and come to judgment." Though God may long keep silence and not seem to notice men's misdeeds, yet shall he in due time " reveal " himself as an avenger.

13. If God will render to every man according to his deeds, then where, say some, is there room for the insteppings of grace ? v. 6. The answer is that when God saves believers he saves them

on principles of everlasting righteousness. They enter not into glory trampling on the law of God. The object of the apostle here is to show that national, ecclesiastical, or hereditary relations will save no man; that the wicked will surely be lost, because they are wicked; and that the righteous will be saved, because they are righteous. And no man can prove that he is righteous but by holy living. The meritorious ground of a sinner's salvation is the righteousness of Christ. The instrument, by which he lays hold of the merits of the Redeemer is his faith. The only way in which he can prove his faith is by his good works. Gill: "God will render to evil men according to the true desert of their evil deeds: and of his own free grace will render to good men, whom he has made so by his grace, what is suitable and agreeable to those good works, which, by the assistance of his grace, they have been enabled to perform." The pure in heart shall see God. All others shall go into outer darkness.

14. Haldane: "There will not, as the Pharisees imagined, and as many nominal Christians suppose, be two accounts for each person, the one of his good works, the other of his sins, the judgment being favorable or unfavorable to him, according as the one or the other predominates; for there will be no balancing of this sort. . . The judgment of the great day will be to all men according to their works. The works of those who shall be condemned will be the evidence that they are wicked. The works of believers will not be appealed to as the *cause* of their acquittal, but as the *evidence* of their union with Christ, on account of which they will be pronounced *righteous*, for in them the law has been fulfilled in their Divine Surety."

15. If men shall receive according to their deeds, there will be no cause of just complaint in the final sentence of the unjust, v. 6. Indeed there will be no complaint on any score. "Every mouth will be stopped."

16. Nothing is more certain than final and righteous retribution, v. 6. The mouth of the Lord hath declared it.

17. The friends of virtue need not fear that their judgment will be passed over by their God, nor that he will be unmindful of their work of faith or their labor of love, vs. 7, 10.

18. True piety has, and is authorized to have regard to the recompense of reward, vs. 7, 10. A sordid bargaining for heaven is forbidden. But a believing expectation of glory is a virtue. Haldane: "Here we see a condemnation of that opinion which teaches, that a man should have no motive in what he does in the service of God but the love of God. The love of God, indeed, must be the predominant motive, and without it no action is morally good. But it is not the only motive. The Scriptures

everywhere address men's hopes and fears, and avail themselves of every motive that has a tendency to influence the human heart."

19. He, who would be saved, must resist temptation, hold on his way and persevere. It is only by patient continuance in well-doing that men can be saved, v. 7. Men go not to heaven by fits and starts, by spirts and paroxysms. " He that endureth to the end shall be saved." " Be thou faithful unto death, and I will give thee a crown of life."

20. It is impossible adequately to set forth heavenly things by any language known to mortals. The apostle here speaks of glory, honor, peace, immortality and eternal life, vs. 7, 10. These terms, though fit, are but feeble. Chrysostom : " He is unable to tell clearly the blessings, but speaketh of glory and honor. For in that they transcend all that man hath, he hath no image of them here to show, but by those things which have a semblance of brightness among us, even by them he sets them before us as far as may be, by glory, by honor, by life. For these be what men earnestly strive after." Our conceptions of heavenly things must always be poor, till we reach the blessed home of the redeemed. Compare John 3 : 12 ; 1 Cor. 13 : 12 ; 2 Cor. 12 : 4 ; Rev. 21 : 18. Of all the terms here employed none convey to many a weary pilgrim more pleasant conceptions than the word *peace*. Chrysostom : " For here whatever good things a man hath, he hath with many troubles, even if he be rich, if in power, if a king. For though he be not at variance with others, yet is he often so with himself, and has abundant war in his own thoughts."

21. It is a bad sign to be *contentious*, to oppose the truth, to be contrary, and especially to be found fighting against God and his truth, v. 8. There is no virtuous principle where men do not love and obey the truth. He, that loveth a lie, is a bad man. He, that, knowing the truth, obeys it not, is nigh unto cursing.

22. There is a wondrous, yes a heavenly elevation and nobleness in the character of the child of God ; for while others are seeking human applause, earthly riches, sordid pleasures, he is chiefly intent on the honor that comes from God, on the true riches and on the pleasures at God's right hand, vs. 7, 10. The world may now despise the servants of God as of a base spirit, but none aim so high ; and ere long all men will say so.

23. In character whether good or bad, positive and negative go together. If one does not obey the truth he is sure to obey unrighteousness, v. 8. He, who does no good, is sure to do harm. It is only he, who works righteousness and perfects holiness, that avoids the very appearance of evil. If men would cease to do evil, they must learn to do well.

24. No terms can adequately set forth the terribleness of the
final doom of the wicked.   Here we have indignation and wrath,
tribulation and anguish, vs. 8, 9.   But who knows the torment of
a future world, where remorse, despair, and all the evil passions
furnish ·elements on which the fierceness of the wrath of God
kindles for ever? Now the wicked sport themselves with their
own deceivings, are exceeding mad upon their idols, make light
of perdition, and call damnation a chimera; yet when they shall
be made sensible of the hot displeasure of God, and God shall
lay the weight of his hand upon them, and leave them to themselves, their undoing will be felt by them to be intolerable.
Eternal justice is so glorious that it must be terrible to all the
enemies of God.

25. Much that is highly esteemed among men is an abomination in the sight of God.   National, ecclesiastical and hereditary
advantages are of no avail with God.   A Jew in sin is and always
was as odious to God as a Gentile in sin.   A good work done by
an outcast is as pleasing to God as if done by one that has Abraham to his father.   The curse is on every soul of man that doeth
evil; the blessing on every man that worketh good, vs. 9, 10.   Let
none value themselves on those distinctions which will vanish
away.   Chrysostom: "It is not quality of persons, but difference
of actions, which God maketh inquisition for."   Hodge: "God
deals with men according to their real character."

26. Though our persons are not justified by our good works,
yet our profession of Christ's truth is thus approved.   So that he
who sets aside the law of holiness is an enemy of the truth.   It is
a great error not to distinguish between justification and sancti-
cation.   It is a greater error to separate them.   Brown; "However there be no intrinsical worth in men's seeking of immortal
life by well-doing, so as to merit at God's hand eternal life; yet it
hath pleased the Lord for the declaration of the incomprehensible-
ness of his goodness, out of free grace and love, to make such a
connection betwixt seeking of glory, in a constant course of well-
doing, and the enjoying of everlasting life, that now whosoever
shall do the one shall certainly enjoy the other."

27. Hodge: "The leading doctrine of this section is, that God
is just."   Let us never adopt any opinion, which could possibly
bring the divine rectitude into question.   Just and right ·is the
Most High in all he says and does.   Let us leave all the wicked in
the hands of God, and not assume the awful prerogative of vengeance.   The day of visitation will soon be here.   The highest
shall soon be brought down to hell, if he repent not.

28. If Jew or Gentile, Pagan or Christian be finally rejected,

it will be for their sins, and not because they were born in one age or country, and not in another. Doddridge: "The last day will be a most impartial as well as important day. Nor are we concerned to know how the heathen will fare in it: let it suffice us, that if they are condemned, they will be righteously condemned; not for remaining ignorant of the gospel they never had the opportunity of hearing, but for violating those precepts of the Divine law which were inscribed on their consciences."

29. Scott: "According to the whole tenor of Scripture, as well as the dictates of common sense, no *sinner* can do *well*, till he repents, submits to God, and seeks mercy from him." That truth should never, never be forgotten. All God's goodness and authority call us to break off our sins by righteousness. Otherwise iniquity will be our ruin. "Ungodliness is not a thing of tale and measure. It is a thing of weight and quality." It must be subdued, or we must perish.

30. Wicked men are very unlike each other in a thousand particulars. But this diversity will save no man from being a castaway. Chalmers: "Among the varieties both of taste and of habit which obtain with the different individuals of our species, there are modifications of disobedience agreeable to one class and disgustful to another class. The careful and calculating economist may never join in any of the excesses of dissipation; and the man of regardless expenditure may never send an unrelieved petitioner from his door; and the religious formalist may never omit either sermon or sacrament, that is held throughout the year in the place of his attendance; and the honorable merchant may never flinch or falsify, in any one of the transactions of business. Each has such points of conformity as suits him, and each has such other points of non-conformity as suits him; and thus the one may even despise or execrate the other for·that particular style of disobedience by which he indulges his own ·partialities; and the things which they respectively do, differ there can be no doubt as to the matter of them—but as to the mind of unconcern about God which all of them express, they are virtually and essentially the same."

31. Yet marvellous is the grace, which offers salvation to all, even to the vilest of our race, who will turn to God. Let us urge the gospel call on all around us. There is mercy for the chief of sinners. Let us despair of none whom the patience of God permits to live. Let us exhort and entreat men by all that is solemn and tender to lay hold on eternal life.

Chapter 5

ROMANS 2
VERSES 12–29

MEN HAVE VARIOUS DEGREES OF LIGHT. THE MORE LIGHT THE GREATER OUR RESPONSIBILITY, AND, IF WE ABUSE IT, THE GREATER OUR GUILT.

12 For as many as have sinned without law shall also perish without law; and as many as have sinned in the law shall be judged by the law;

13 (For not the hearers of the law *are* just before God, but the doers of the law shall be justified.

14 For when the Gentiles, which have not the law, do by nature the things contained in the law, these, having not the law, are a law unto themselves:

15 Which shew the work of the law written in their hearts, their conscience also bearing witness, and *their* thoughts the mean while accusing or else excusing one another;)

16 In the day when God shall judge the secrets of men by Jesus Christ according to my gospel.

17 Behold, thou art called a Jew, and restest in the law, and makest thy boast of God,

18 And knowest *his* will, and approvest the things that are more excellent, being instructed out of the law;

19 And art confident that thou thyself art a guide of the blind, a light of them which are in darkness,

20 An instructor of the foolish, a teacher of babes, which hast the form of knowledge and of the truth in the law.

21 Thou therefore which teachest another, teachest thou not thyself? thou that preachest a man should not steal, dost thou steal?

22 Thou that sayest a man should not commit adultery, dost thou commit adultery? thou that abhorrest idols, dost thou commit sacrilege?

23 Thou that makest thy boast of the law, through breaking the law dishonourest thou God?

24 For the name of God is blasphemed among the Gentiles through you, as it is written.

25 For circumcision verily profiteth, if thou keep the law: but if thou be a breaker of the law, thy circumcision is made uncircumcision.

26 Therefore, if the uncircumcision keep the righteousness of the law, shall not his uncircumcision be counted for circumcision?

27 And shall not uncircumcision which is by nature, if it fulfil the law, judge thee, who by the letter and circumcision dost trangress the law ?

28 For he is not a Jew, which is one outwardly; neither *is that* circumcision which is outward in the flesh :

29 But he *is* a Jew, which is one inwardly; and circumcision *is that* of the heart, in the spirit, *and* not in the letter; whose praise *is* not of men, but of God.

THE apostle, having established the foregoing truths proceeds to their application to the case of all, especially of the Jews. He begins by saying that the heathen and the Jew are in the eye of the law criminal.

12. *For as many as have sinned without law shall also perish without law ; and as many as have sinned in the law shall be judged by the law.* Peshito: For those without law, who sin, will also perish without law ; and those under the law, who sin, will be judged by the law. By the law we may here understand the entire revealed preceptive will of God ; Tholuck, the will of God ; Stuart, revelation ; Hodge, the rule of duty. This was not fully and in many cases not at all made known to the heathen, they having only the light of nature. And yet it is said they had sinned. This is true. Their consciences said so. The smoke of ten thousand altars declared the same. Their superstitious devices for quieting conscience and appeasing divine wrath confirmed the sad truth. Such, living contrary to the very light of nature and neither knowing nor accepting a Redeemer, shall *perish*. To sinners the light of nature is killing and condemning, not saving. And those, who had and knew the whole preceptive will of God, and heeded not that great light, but sinned still, shall be judged, yes, and condemned (for the word has that force; John 3 : 17, 18 and often) by the law. Hodge: " Men are to be judged by the light they have severally enjoyed. The ground of judgment is their works; the standard of judgment, their knowledge." Haldane: " In one word, the divine justice will only regard the sins of men; and wherever these are found it will condemn the sinner." The next three verses are parenthetical and explain the principle here laid down.

13. (*For not the hearers of the law* are *just before God, but the doers of the law shall be justified.* Here first in this epistle occur the words *just* and *justified.* This verse seems to be an answer to an objection that might be made by a Jew ; q. d. It is not fair or right to put us in the same condemnation with the heathen. We have Abraham to our father. We have Moses for our prophet. He is read in our synagogues every Sabbath. To us are committed the oracles of God. We hear the Scriptures, and we know

God's will. To this Paul replies that hearing is one thing and doing another thing; that knowledge of even the truth, if it be not loved and practised, so far from making our state safe, enhances our guilt. This is the doctrine of all the Scriptures. It commands the approval of the human conscience. *Before God*, in this verse means In the sight of God. In the sight of men acts of mere outward obedience are often highly esteemed, but with God they are worthless; he requires a holy heart and a holy life. Pool: " The scope of the apostle is not simply to show how sinners are now justified in the sight of God; but to show what is requisite to justification according to the tenor of the law, and that is to do all that is written therein, and to continue to do so." Diodati: " The law cannot bring any salvation to man, by the knowledge or profession thereof, as the Jews believe, but by the perfect observing of it, which being found no more in them than in other nations, they are also comprehended within the general curse, and bound to seek after their righteousness in Christ."

14. *For when the Gentiles, which have not the law, do by nature the things contained in the law, these, having not the law, are a law unto themselves.* The meaning is that the Gentiles, who are without a written revelation, and yet do what is taught them by the light of nature, are less criminal than the Jews who had the Scripture and broke it. One, who walks by the best light he has though it be small, is not so guilty as he who has ever so much light and rebels against it. In other words, it is not rules, or wit, or knowledge that can justify or save us. We must be conformed to the truth. Scott: " For even the Gentiles, who had not the written law, when from natural principles they performed any of those duties which the law required, were, in this respect, 'a law unto themselves;' and by obeying thus far *their own rule*, came nearer to righteousness, than the Jews who broke *their rule.*" All nations however benighted have some sense of right and wrong, some apprehension of moral law, and are not without conscience. They are a law to themselves.

15. *Which shew the work of the law written in their hearts, their conscience also bearing them witness, and* their *thoughts the meanwhile accusing or else excusing one another.* Peshito: And they show the work of the law, as it is inscribed on their heart; and their conscience beareth testimony to them, their own reflections rebuking or vindicating one another. The apostle in this verse shows that the heathen are under moral law, that their consciences are not extinguished by heathenism, and that their thoughts on questions of right and wrong are busy and active. They are not brutes. They have a moral sense. They are under law, though it is writ-

ten on their hearts only, and not in an inspired volume in their possession. The consciences and reasonings of the heathen do clearly condemn many sins and vices in *one another.* And if a man knows enough to judge others and rightly condemn them, he knows enough to condemn himself for doing the same or like things. This verse ends the parenthesis, and the next is to be read in close connection with v. 12.

16. *In the day when God shall judge the secrets of men by Jesus Christ according to my gospel.* That is, all men, Jews and Gentiles, shall be judged, and if they have no interest in Christ and are not partakers of his righteousness, they shall perish or be condemned; for then the secrets, the motives, the real principles that govern men shall be brought to light. This scrutiny and revelation of human character shall be conducted and effected by Jesus Christ in his own person. Many Scriptures so teach. John 5 : 22 ; Acts 10 : 42; 17 : 31; 2 Tim. 4 : 1, 8; 1 Pet. 4 : 5. And all this is according to the uniform teaching of the gospel, here called by Paul *my gospel,* because he was a preacher of it, had made it known to many, and prized it so highly that he rested the whole weight of his salvation upon the person of its author. And now for the direct application of these truths to those who bore the name of Jews.

17. *Behold, thou art called a Jew, and restest in the law, and makest thy boast of God.* The Jew had advantages, which he perverted, but which were no mean things. First, he was called a Jew, a name of great antiquity, highly honorable, pointing to a long list of renowned and pious ancestors, with a history unequalled, in the annals of all time, for stupendous miracles, with a lawgiver, whose eloquence was admired by the very heathen, with poets, who had sung the opera of all ages, with prophets, who had unfolded the history of·the world to its end. The best Jewish kings were types of Messiah himself. We first find the word Jew in Jer. 34 : 9. It is often found in the book of Esther. That evangelical prophet, Zechariah, speaks of the honor of being a Jew in high terms. It may have been used from a much earlier period, as Palestine is in Ps. 76 : 1 called Judah or Judea. Secondly, the Jew rested in the law. He unquestionably had the revealed will of God, abundantly supported by evidence as an authentic communication from heaven, so that he relied upon it as truth and for good cause, the best in the world—the divine attestation. His was no uncertain wisdom, like that of the philosophers. Thirdly, the Jew made his boast in God—not in dumb idols, not in lying vanities, not in dead men, whom superstition had deified; but in the living God, Jehovah, who had made his name terrible among the heathen and glorious among his saints. The God of the Jews

made and ruled heaven and earth, and they knew it.   Their government was a theocracy.   Jehovah was their king.   This God
was their Rock, Refuge, Governor and all.

18. *And knowest* his *will, and approvest the things that are more
excellent, being instructed out of the law.*   Fourthly, the Jew had
many means of knowing the will of God.   He had the lively oracles, educated teachers to expound it, with a splendid and divinely
appointed public service, full of instruction and solemnity, so that
it was nearly impossible to live even a short lifetime in Jewry
without acquiring a large amount of religious knowledge.   Compare Ps. 147 : 19.   *And approvest the things that are more excellent.*
Fifthly, the Jew had better laws, better songs, better philosophy,
better moral lessons, purer worship than any heathen nation, and
these commended themselves to his conscience and judgment, so
that he discerned, tried, allowed and approved more excellent
things, because he had inspired men for his guides, as Moses and
David and all the prophets.

19. *And art confident that thou thyself art a guide of the blind, a
light of them which are in darkness.*   Sixthly, he was conscious of
his superior light.   He knew how debased and ignorant were the
nations round about.   He was *confident* that he could tell them
many things of the greatest importance to all men.   He regarded,
and very justly too, the heathen as *blind*, and enveloped in darkness, and felt that he was able to be

20. *An instructor of the foolish, a teacher of babes, which hast the
form of knowledge and of the truth in the law.*   The rites, the philosophical dogmas, and even the mythology of the heathen abounded
in puerilities and absurdities.   They were besotted by their gods
and by their teachers.   But every tolerably intelligent Jew had
the *form*, pattern, or summary of divine knowledge and truth, as
made known in scripture.   But now for the reverse.   The Jew,
untaught by God's Spirit and without a new heart, relied on his
forms of knowledge and of worship for salvation, was proud and
scornful in his conscious superiority, superciliously contemned
others as babes, yea as dogs, and accursed, had a foolish self-confi-
dence in his attainments, vainly and sinfully boasted in God, relied
on ceremonies heartlessly observed, and on his national and ecclesiastical and ancestral connections for safety from wrath, and sadly
failed to practise with godly sincerity the plainest truths of his religion.   So the apostle challenges him :

21. *Thou therefore which teachest another teachest thou not thyself ?
thou that preachest a man should not steal, dost thou steal ?*   The
sense of this verse and of the next is not destroyed by dropping,
as do the Vulgate, Theophylact, Erasmus and Luther, the form of

interrogation, though it is perhaps best to follow the Syriac, Ethiopic, Arabic, Chrysostom etc. and retain it. The sum of the charge here made is that of gross inconsistency between profession and practice, with the aggravation of a wicked life following sufficient knowledge. Some think the apostle here charges stealing as a common sin upon the Jews of his time. If by stealing is understood what our law calls larceny, there is no evidence that this sin was peculiarly prevalent among the Jews at any period of their history. But if covetousness, overreaching, false weights and measures, extortion, usury, bribery, oppression, cheating, embezzling, unfaithfulness, holding back wages fairly earned, and like acts, which are clearly in violation of the whole spirit of the eighth commandment, are referred to, there is abundant evidence that these sins were often sadly prevalent, particularly in the latter days of the Jewish commonwealth. See the minor prophets. If our apostle was seeking an illustration of the principle he was discussing, he could find none more apt than that here selected, together with those of the following verse;

22. *Thou that sayest a man should not commit adultery, dost thou commit adultery? thou that abhorrest idols, dost thou commit sacrilege?*
There is not wanting evidence, that lewdness, in all the latter ages of the Jewish nation, was sadly prevalent. In our Saviour's day it had assumed one form, that if generally practised must have utterly subverted society. I refer to divorce for insufficient cause. In no way could our Saviour have attacked a more popular vice than that in Matt. 5 : 31, 32. Besides the law of chastity is spiritual, and a filthy thought is a clear violation of the seventh commandment. Matt. 5 : 27, 28. It is well known that after the Babylonish captivity the Jews never fell into open and gross idolatry, that many of them suffered greatly in consequence of their refusal to countenance this sin, and that the people generally expressed great abhorrence of every form of it. Yet they did other things no less clearly forbidden. The verb rendered to commit sacrilege signifies to *rob temples*. The law forbade the Jews to appropriate to their own use the spoils and treasures of even heathen temples, in countries conquered in lawful war : " The graven images of their gods shall ye burn with fire : thou shalt not desire the silver or gold that is on them, nor take it unto thee, lest thou be snared." Deut. 7 : 25. Whether any violation of this particular statute occurred near the beginning of the Christian era, we are not informed. It seems certain that in Paul's time it was not prevalent, for the Jews, living under a foreign government, had not for a long time made war on any people, so that if any of them robbed heathen temples, they must have acted

as common thieves, and not as invaders of a hostile country.   But
the word may designate such offences as were common among the
Jews, who robbed God in tithes and offerings, polluted the table
of the Lord, etc.   Mal. 1 : 8, 12–14 ; 3 : 8, 9.   See also Nehemiah
13 : 10–12.   The same occurs whenever men withhold from God
the worship, which is his, in particular when they refuse to give
him the love, honor, reverence and obedience, which are undoubtedly his due.   Hodge sums up the sin here charged, when he
speaks of " the wicked and profane abuse and perversion of sacred
things."   Stuart explains it " of every kind of act, which denies to
God his sovereign honors and claims."   This form of wickedness
always marks an irreligious people, and is involved in the very
nature of sin.   The apostle adds in general terms :

   23. *Thou that makest thy boast of the law, through breaking the law
dishonorest thou God ?*   The Jews never failed to speak of their law,
as something great and excellent.   They knew it had God for its
author, and was given and accompanied with the most awful sanctions.   It was therefore impossible for them lightly to esteem it,
or break its precepts, without grossly *dishonoring* God.   A sovereign can in no way be more insulted than by his subjects going
counter to his known will, and especially by violating his published laws.   Such conduct is against the peace and dignity of the
government, and tends to bring it into utter contempt.   So it is
added :

   24. *For the name of God is blasphemed among the Gentiles through
you, as it is written.*   *Blasphemed,* evil spoken of, reviled, railed at.
The meaning is ñot that the Jews spoke against God, but that the
Gentiles, taking occasion by the evil ways of the Jews, reviled
Jehovah, his word and his religion, q. d.   The Gentiles see how
you Jews are unfaithful, dishonest, profane, lewd and in many
ways immoral, and they say, The religion of Jehovah is no better
than that of Baal or Moloch.   Deliver us from a religion, whose
professors practise sins, which we abhor.   Various opinions are
expressed as to the Scripture referred to in the phrase, *It is written.*   Some cite Isa. 52 : 5.   But the context would hardly justify
such a use of that passage.   Others more safely refer to Ezek. 36 :
23, 24.   The context would fully justify this use of the passage.
But the same is virtually written in many places.   See Ezek. 16 :
51–59 and like places.

   25. *For circumcision verily profiteth, if thou keep the law : but if
thou be a breaker of the law, thy circumcision is made uncircumcision.*
Circumcision was an exceedingly ancient rite, instituted long
before the time of Moses, John 7 : 22.   It distinguished the Jews
from most surrounding nations.   To a Jew no epithet was more

odious than " uncircumcised." Gen. 34 : 14 ; Ex. 12 : 48 ; 1 Sam. 17 : 26 ; 2 Sam. 1 : 20 ; Isa. 52 : 1 ; Ezek. 28 : 10, etc. The Jews looked upon circumcision not only as initiatory but also as essential to fellowship with God's people, and to salvation. Now our apostle here argues that if this rite, which they so highly valued, was to be regarded as a mere rite and was not followed by conformity to the law, a Jew was no better than a heathen. The law not obeyed could save no one. In other aspects of circumcision, it was a solemn and useful rite, but when the circumcised lived in sin, and acted like the uncircumcised, they were no better, but circumcision became uncircumcision. Paul goes yet further :

26. *Therefore, if the uncircumcision keep the righteousness of the law, shall not his uncircumcision be counted for circumcision ?* Stuart: " Neither circumcision nor the want of it determines our deserts in the view of our Maker and Judge ; but a spirit of filial obedience." It is not supposed that Paul intended to say that any man, heathen or Jew, kept the whole law, for elsewhere he expressly teaches that there was no such case, Rom. 3 : 9. But he says, that if a heathen could be found with a blameless character, he would be accepted as readily as a Jew of like character. Haldane : " In reality, then, the Jews and Gentiles were on a level as to the impossibility of salvation by the law." This is really the drift of Paul's argument.

27. *And shall not uncircumcision, which is by nature, if it fulfil the law, judge thee, who by the letter and circumcision dost transgress the law ?* This verse teaches the same as that next preceding with the additional declaration that such a case, if found, would *condemn* the Jew, who fell short of the requirements of the law he professed to receive. It is true no such case was found. For both Jew and Gentile are guilty before God. But the great object of the apostle in these verses is to destroy the confidence of a Jew in his law, nationality and rites as means or even as pledges of salvation, if he were found, like other men, to be a sinner. He next announces that religion is internal and spiritual and that as a man thinketh in his heart, so is he :

28. *For he is not a Jew, which is one outwardly ; neither* is that *circumcision, which is outward in the flesh :*

29. *But he* is *a Jew, which is one inwardly : and circumcision* is *that of the heart, in the spirit,* and *not in the letter ; whose praise* is *not of men, but of God.* Haldane : " The essence and reality of things do not consist in names or external signs; and when nothing more is produced, God will not consider a man who possesses them as a true Jew, nor his circumcision as true circumcision. He is only a Jew in shadow and appearance, and his is only a figura-

tive circumcision void of its truth." In other words the holiness, which God approves, is in the heart. With him a name is nothing, profession nothing, but the reality is everything. For *outwardly* the Peshito reads *in that which is external*, and for *inwardly* it has *in what is hidden*. By the *spirit* in v. 29 we are not to understand the Holy Ghost, but the opposite of the letter. Haldane : " That which penetrates to the bottom of the soul; in one word, that which is real and effective." So also Locke, Slade, Macknight, Olshausen and others. But as the grace and renewal of the soul are by the Holy Spirit, there is no error taught by understanding the reference to be to the Holy Ghost. Hodge says : " This gives a better sense, Circumcision of the heart which is effected by the Spirit, and not made after the direction of the written law; compare Col. 2 : 11." Augustine, Oecumenius, Grotius, Dutch Annotations, Pool, Le Clerc, Tholuck, Doddridge and others favor this interpretation. Some unite the two and so cover the whole ground, as Evans, Clarke, etc. The result is the same in either case. *Whose praise is not of men, but of God.* " Man looketh on the outward appearance, but the Lord looketh on the heart." The heart, the spirit, the seat of the principles, affections and motives, is of chief importance. God cares nothing at all for mere show, mere profession, mere rites and appearances as deciding character. Such things are of no real worth in his sight.

DOCTRINAL AND PRACTICAL REMARKS

1. It is true that where there is no law, there is no transgression; but it is not true that where there is no written law, there is no wickedness. It is enough that the law be known by the light of nature. Paul admits that men " have sinned without law "—without a written revelation, v. 12. Yea, he admits that they have so sinned, that unless God shall show them mercy, their condemnation will be just, and they will *perish.*

2. God is a sovereign in all his acts and dispensations, v. 12. He dealt not with any ancient nation as with the Jews. Ps. 147 : 20; Amos 3 : 2. On the other hand for long centuries he suffered all other nations to walk in their own ways, Acts 14 : 16. No man can tell why this was so. " Even so, Father, for so it seemed good in thy sight," gives the only solution. Shall not the Lord do as he will with his own ? Behold here the goodness and severity of God.

3. But privileges are accompanied with corresponding obligations, and if these are unheeded, sin is aggravated. The greater

the light sinned against, the greater the guilt incurred.   So that it is less dreadful to perish without law than to be condemned by the law, v. 12.   To whom much is given, of him shall much be required.   Chrysostom : " The greater the attention he enjoyed, the greater the punishment he will suffer.   See how he urges on the Jews their greater need of a speedy recourse to grace." Doddridge : " We shall be judged by the dispensation we have enjoyed ; and, how devoutly so ever we may hear and speak of it, shall be condemned if we have not acted agreeably thereto." Hodge : " Superior knowledge enhances the guilt of sin, and in- creases the certainty, necessity and severity of punishment, with- out in itself increasing the power of resistance."

4. In every case the wages of sin is death.   Whether men sin without the law or in the law, they perish, they are condemned, if the merits of Christ are not counted to them for righteousness.

5. Legal justification to men is impossible, for they are all sin- ners, v. 13.   The law says, " Do and live."   " The soul that sin- neth, it shall die."   " Cursed is every one that continueth not in all things written in the book of the law to do them."   One failure infracts the covenant of works, and renders it impossible for us thereby to have good hope.   Brown : " Men are ready to imagine a more easy way whereby to stand justified at the bar of God, and expect absolution on easier terms than God ever carved out : and as men should look diligently that their imaginations .thus deceive them not, and that they stand on sure grounds ; so the faithful servants of God should be carefnl to undeceive people, and to discover the vanity of their imaginations, and show the true grounds on which a man must stand justified before God in the great day."   O sinner, on the score of personal merits there is no hope for thee.   Nor will it save any man to know that his own righteousnesses are all as filthy rags, and that Jesus Christ alone is the Lord our righteousness, unless he truly flees to him as his only hope and Redeemer.

6. Whatever dreams men have indulged, and however they may have imagined cases, in which, if one did right, it would go well with him, yet no such case is found.   There was never a mere man that did not at some time blush, or groan, or writhe under the consciousness of ill desert for some sin in the sight of God. Show us a man, whose nature is holy and who never in thought, word or deed broke the law, and we admit that the law has no charges against him.   But there is no such man.   It is only by refusing to look at the context, that men suppose our apostle ad- mits in any part of his argument that such cases are found. v. 14. All good men disclaim human merits and all bad men ought to

do the same. Chalmers: " What turns the virtues of earth into splendid sins, is that nothing of God is there. It is the want of this animating breath, which impresses upon them all the worthlessness of materialism. It is this which makes all the native loveliness of our moral world of as little account, in the pure and spiritual reckoning of the upper sanctuary, as is a mere efflorescence of beauty on the face of the vegetable creation."

7. So long as conscience gives forth her utterances in the solemn tones, which every man hears, it is in vain to deny the moral government of God over the world, v. 15.   Conscience *bears witness* in a way that none but scoffers will deny. Men cannot rid themselves of its power by adopting abominable principles. Athiests have confessed its power. Felons feel its frightful sting. If men have consciences, it must be because God has given them a moral nature and placed them under moral law.   If men are so constituted as to be a law to themselves, they are surely accountable to God. True, a long course of sinning will sadly sear the conscience, but even old and cruel monsters of depravity have confessed that they from conscience alone suffered death every day. Reader, have you a good conscience? Is it purified by atoning blood? Do you study to keep it void of offence towards God and man? If in any part of the world a man without a conscience could be found, we should justly pronounce him a monster.

8. There will be a day of Judgment, v. 16.   Why should there not be? There have been days of sinning, and days of acting, and days of suffering. Why should there not be a day of reckoning and of retribution? Scoffers may cry out against such an event as of old. 2 Pet. 3 : 3, 14. But scoffing will have no more effect to defer it, or avert its decisions than laughter will have in hindering the violence of a storm or the raging of the sea.

9. This great day will expose the *secrets* of men, v. 16. None will object to the public acknowledgment and rewarding of good deeds, performed from right motives, however secretly and modestly they may have been performed. This shall surely be done. Matt. 25 : 34–40. It is no less right that all, who have stubbornly and stoutly resisted God's love and authority, his mercy and his terrors should be condignly punished and their characters fully exposed. Some have asked, shall the sins of God's people be exposed on that day? If they shall be, it shall not be to their confusion, or condemnation, but only to the magnifying of the riches of the grace, which washed and saved them from their sins. And there the believer may let the matter rest, for he is willing that Christ should have all the glory of his salvation.

10. The last day will settle one controversy, that has long been conducted with heat and violence on one side, and with unflinching fidelity on the other—the doctrine of the divinity of Jesus Christ. Is he truly and supremely divine? If he does not know all things, all hearts, all motives, all rules of right, and how infallibly to apply them, how can he make the awards of the last day? To the devout and humble all this seems clear even now. But the human heart is terribly opposed to honoring the Son as most men admit they should honor the Father. Blessed be God, the man Christ Jesus, who poured out his life unto death, is to pass upon the case of all his people and of all their enemies.

11. Every generation witnesses a strong tendency to rely on names and forms, on rites and professions, on creeds and sacraments, and not on the Saviour and his Spirit for salvation, vs. 17–27. Ritualism is indigenous to the corrupt heart of man. It is as easy to trust in forms when simple as when splendid, when divinely ordered as when by man invented. The Pharisees were much more orthodox than the Sadducees or Essenes, yet they were vile hypocrites. The case is this. The human conscience oppresses one with some just sense of guilt. He says, I must do something to save my soul. Formalism says: Here is something you can do. Engage in it and you will feel better. The trial is made. The conscience becomes purblind and stupid. Some relief is felt. The devotee is encouraged to press on, till at length the sad delusion steals over him that this is piety. Then his blind self-love rivets that impression, and time only is required to make a full end of all good hopes and prospects for eternity, unless God in mercy opens his eyes to see the utter worthlessness of all he has done, and by his Spirit converts his poor carnal heart. This is sometimes done, and when it is, it is vastly to the praise of the glory of divine grace. For " when men grow secure because of privileges wherewith they are blessed of God, it is hard to get such roused up and awakened, and brought to some thorough conviction of their case and condition." There is nothing which the deceitfulness of the human heart may not pervert to its destruction. The law is of great use to give the knowledge of sin. Yet men go to it for justification. And if one thing seems to fail in these false foundations, men easily try another. Some plead that they are within the pale of the true church, are esteemed and trusted as pious, have the seals of the covenant and are exact in many decent forms of worship. Chalmers: " Were we asked to fix on a living counterpart in the present day to the Jew of the passage now under consideration—it would be on him, who, thoroughly versant in all the phrases and dexterous in all the arguments of orthodoxy, is, with-

out one affection of the old man circumcised, and without one
sanctified affection to mark him the new man in Christ Jesus our
Lord, withal, a zealous and stanch and sturdy controversialist.
He too rests in the form of sound words, and is confident that he
is a light of the blind, and founds a complacency on knowledge
without love and without regeneration."

12. It is therefore a solemn question for every man's consideration: " Is my evidence of acceptance with God under the gospel
at all better than that of this Jew under the law?" If the best
any man can say is : 'I am of my own choice and by public consent called a Christian, I rest in the Gospel, I make my boast of
God, I know his will, I approve the most excellent things, I am
instructed out of the gospel, I am capable of teaching others the
way of life and salvation, I instruct a Bible class, I am a communi-
cant or a minister in the church;' if this is all, it is nothing,
nothing to the purpose of salvation.   Hodge : " Membership in
the true church, considered as a visible society, is no security that
we shall obtain the favor of God."

13. The foregoing truth is manifest and of solemn weight in
your case, if your religious profession is, like that of this Jew, attended with dark signs, and especially with the bad mark of not
obeying the plainest and clearest truths known and professed, vs.
21–23. It is impossible, even if we could work miracles, to prove
that we are real Christians, unless we keep the commandments.
On this point God's word abounds in the clearest proofs. Hodge :
" Mere knowledge cannot commend us to God. It neither sanctifies the heart, nor of itself renders men more useful. When made
the ground of confidence, or the fuel of pride and arrogance, it is
perverted and destructive." Therefore the question, Are you a *consistent* Christian ? is as pertinent as this, Are you a Christian at all?
It is not reproving sin and error, but fleeing from them that proves
men right-minded. A wicked practice evinces a wicked heart.

14. So deceitful is the human heart and so cunning are self-deceivers that God's ministers must use great plainness and directness
of speech, as Paul does here, vs. 21–23. It will not save men's
souls from the snares of the devil to preach by hints, allusions and
indirect attacks on error and wickedness. Our Saviour and his
apostles as well as the prophets have left us admirable lessons and
examples on this matter.

15. The wicked may often greatly pervert things and may at
times tell many utter falsehoods respecting you. These things are
of course no test of character. But what do men truly say of you?
v. 24. If from the tenor of your life they fairly infer that you are
no better than men who profess no love to Christ, you are a bad

man. And you are the worse man for professing the true religion, and not acting accordingly.

16. But you have a name to live. Your profession is fair.
Your sincerity is unsuspected by just men. Yet what is all that
worth? It is not he, whom man commendeth, but whom the Lord
approveth, that shall be saved.

17. Are your virtues better than those of many heathen? v.
26. In justness of character would you compare with Aristides?
In despising the annoyances of life, as well as its vain show, are
you equal to Diogenes or Socrates? In honor are you equal to
Cicero? Well, we must have a higher standard of virtue than the
heathen, or be condemned by them.

18. It would therefore be a great matter if the world would
learn that " *he is not a Christian, who is one outwardly, nor is that
baptism, which is outward in the flesh ; but he is a Christian, that is
one inwardly, and baptism is that of the heart, in the spirit, and not in
the letter ; whose praise is not of men, but of God,*" vs. 28, 29.
Chalmers: " Faith is an inlet to holy affections. Its primary office
is to admit truth into the mind, but it is truth which impresses as
well as informs. The kingdom of God is not in word alone, nor
in argument alone—it is also in power, and while we bid you look
unto Jesus and be saved, it is such a look as will cause you to
mourn and be in heaviness—it is such a look as will liken you to
his image, and import into your own character the graces and the
affections which adorn his." If one be thus changed, it matters
not whether the world applauds or censures, peace is made with
God, and the soul is safe forever, through Jesus Christ.

19. Doddridge: " We pity the *Gentiles,* and we have reason to
do it; for they are lamentably blind and dissolute: but let us take
heed, lest those appearances of virtue, which are to be found
among some of them, *condemn us ;* who, with the *letter* of the *law,*
and the *gospel,* and with the solemn tokens of a *covenant relation to
God,* transgress his precepts, and violate our engagements to him ;
so turning the means of goodness and happiness into the occasion
of more aggravated guilt and misery."   .

20. There is no reason why we should not apply to the sacraments of the gospel the doctrine Paul here lays down respecting
circumcision. Sacraments have neither inherent nor invariable
efficacy, They are signs of great truths, and seals of great blessings; but unbelief hinders their good effect, and a wicked life is
proof of unbelief.

Chapter 6

ROMANS 3
VERSES 1–19

PAUL DOES NOT SLIGHT THE MOSAIC DISPENSATION. HE PROVES ALL MEN TO BE SINNERS.

What advantage then hath the Jew? or what profit *is there* of circumcision?

2 Much every way: chiefly, because that unto them were committed the oracles of God.

3 For what if some did not believe? shall their unbelief make the faith of God without effect?

4 God forbid: yea, let God be true, but every man a liar; as it is written, That thou mightest be justified in thy sayings, and mightest overcome when thou art judged.

5 But if our unrighteousness commend the righteousness of God, what shall we say? *Is* God unrighteous who taketh vengeance? (I speak as a man)

6 God forbid: for then how shall God judge the world?

7 For if the truth of God hath more abounded through my lie unto his glory; why yet am I also judged as a sinner?

8 And not *rather*, (as we be slanderously reported, and as some affirm that we say,) Let us do evil, that good may come? whose damnation is just.

9 What then? are we better *than they?* No, in no wise: for we have before proved both Jews and Gentiles, that they are all under sin;

10 As it is written, There is none righteous, no, not one:

11 There is none that understandeth, there is none that seeketh after God.

12 They are all gone out of the way, they are together become unprofitable; there is none that doeth good, no, not one.

13 Their throat *is* an open sepulchre; with their tongues they have used deceit; the poison of asps *is* under their lips:

14 Whose mouth *is* full of cursing and bitterness:

15 Their feet *are* swift to shed blood:

16 Destruction and misery *are* in their ways:

17 And the way of peace have they not known:

18 There is no fear of God before their eyes.

19 Now we know that what things soever the law saith, it saith to them who are under the law: that every mouth may be stopped, and all the world may become guilty before God.

1. *WHAT advantage then hath the Jew? or what profit is there of circumcision?* Peshito: What then is the superiority of the Jew? Or what is the advantage of circumcision? For *advantage* the Vulgate and Wiclif have *more;* Tyndale, Cranmer and Genevan have *preferment;* and Rheims has *pre-eminence.* Some of the ancient interpreters use excellence, meaning thereby pre-eminence. There is no need of making this dramatic by introducing a Jew as here making this objection. In his candor, Paul states it as one likely to occur to the mind of his countrymen. The force of the place is this: If the argument of the foregoing chapter, and particularly from the seventeenth verse to the close, is correct, may you not as well deny that the Jews had any privileges above others? If Jews could not secure salvation by their conformity to the letter of the law, how are they more privileged than others? If the Jews had generally regarded as valid this objection, it must have mightily hindered the Gospel among them. It was therefore important fairly to meet it, as Paul does thus:

2. *Much every way: chiefly, because that unto them were committed the oracles of God.* Wiclif renders the first clause, Myche bi alle wise; Tyndale, Cranmer and Genevan, Surely very much; Calvin, Very much. The objection of v. 1 was not to be entertained for a moment, for it was not true. God had greatly favored the Jews. Take a single particular and consider it in all its bearings. The Jews were the depository of the precious words of God. *Committed,* confided or intrusted. *Oracles,* found also in Acts 7 : 38; Heb. 5 : 12; 1 Pet. 4 : 11; and always rendered as here. Oracles were divine communications, or words uttered by God. Without slighting the words spoken for many generations by Urim and Thummim, the chief reference here is to the written word of God as we have it in the Old Testament. Think how much is here included—the history of creation, of the fall, of the deluge, of the dispersion, of the call and trials of Abraham, of the history of his descendants, of the exodus from Egypt; the law; the records of kings good and bad; the best proverbs; the sublimest songs; predictions respecting the course of events to the end of the world; and all these abounding in precepts, promises, warnings and encouragements of the most weighty character. Especially did these lively oracles animate the church with bright hopes respecting Messiah and the glory of his reign. These were the richest and most glorious matters, of which the Old Testament treats. And although the Gentiles had fragments of revelation among them, and so looked for some great Teacher and Deliverer, yet their ideas were confused, at least vague, and the Gentiles were never the custodians of the holy Scriptures, which are able to

make men wise unto salvation.   Chrysostom: "Do you see how he still counts up, not their good deeds, but the benefits they received from God?"

3. *For what if some did not believe? shall their unbelief make the faith of God without effect?*   Candor requires the admission that this is a difficult portion of the epistle.   The proof is found in the great diversity of explanations and conjectures offered.   Macknight varies the sense of the verse by a negative: Will not their unbelief destroy the faithfulness of God?   Calvin thinks the sense is this, "Is God's covenant so abrogated by the perfidiousness of the Jews, that it brings forth no fruit among them?"   Evans: "The infidelity and obstinacy of the Jews could not invalidate and over-throw those prophecies of the Messiah, which were contained in the *oracles committed to them.*"   Doddridge: "Shall their unbelief destroy God's fidelity to his promises, or prevent our receiving them, and owning their accomplishment?"   Olshausen supposes the point to be this: "Even if the blessing was lost to the nation collectively, it yet, according to God's faithfulness, remained even now confirmed to individual believers, and should hereafter also belong to the whole of Israel when God should have led them back by wondrous ways."   Conybeare & Howson: "Shall we imagine that God will break his covenant with the true Israel, because of the unfaithfulness of the false Israel?"   Clarke: "Shall the wickedness of some *annul* the PROMISE, which God made to Abraham, that he would, by an *everlasting* covenant, be a God to him and to his seed after him?"   Locke thinks the point is this, that the unbelief of some cannot render God's covenant of none effect to the nation so as not to bring them blessings in all coming generations.   Others suppose this to be the sense, If the Jews shall not believe, as many do not, this does not show that the covenant is not good, and its blessings great in themselves, and freely offered to the acceptance of men.   Hodge: "What if we have been unfaithful, or are as wicked and disobedient as you would make us appear, does that invalidate the promises of God?   Must he be unfaithful too?   Has he not promised to be our God, and that we should be his people?   These are promises not suspended on our good or evil conduct."   On these views it may be said: 1. that there is no authority for inserting, as Macknight does, a negative. 2. Whether we make the language of this verse to be that of a Jew or of Paul himself candidly stating an objection likely to be made does not necessarily change the sense.   It is admitted that the language is that of objection.   3. Several of the explanations offered though diverse are not adverse to each other.   4. It is probably safest to regard the apostle as closely confining himself

to the main matter in hand, viz. the impossibility of any one, even a Jew, being justified before God by the law. 5. Any sense put upon the question ought to make relevant the subsequent answer given by our apostle. Perhaps the judicious Thomas Scott has as nearly caught the spirit of the passage as any other: " What if some, if even the greater part of the nation of Israel, from worldly and ambitious motives, had obstinately and wickedly rejected the divine Saviour? Did their unbelief render the faithfulness of God ineffectual? He had fulfilled his promises to their fathers, and if they would not receive and submit to the ' Seed of Abraham,' and the Son of David, could they plead that God had failed of his word?" etc. In reply to the objection Paul says,

4. *God forbid: yea, let God be true, but every man a liar ; as it is written, that thou mightest be justified in thy sayings, and mightest overcome when thou art judged.* Peshito: Far be it ; For God is veracious, and every man false: as it is written: That thou mightest be upright in thy declarations, and be found pure when they judge thee. *God forbid.* The original of this phrase occurs ten times in this epistle. It is a very strong form of denial. It is rendered as here by Wiclif, Coverdale, Tyndale, Cranmer, Genevan and Rheims ; and yet in the Greek the name of God is not found. *Let it not be* is all the original warrants in any of the ten cases. We cannot defend this uncalled for appeal to God. We can account for it on the score of use, it having been for many centuries an idiomatic phrase among our ancestors, when they would give a strong denial. *Let God be true*, i. e. let him be accounted faithful to all his engagements, though by supposition every man be false, or faithless. It is safer to trust no man than it is to distrust God. It is better to discredit all men than not to believe God. Brought into comparison with God men are false, filthy, foolish. When Job had a clear discovery of the spotless purity of God, he abhorred himself and repented in dust and ashes. Paul refers to the case of David, who, though a great and good king, and held in high esteem in Israel, yet sinned, and in his confession admits that God was altogether and incomparably righteous. See Ps. 51 : 4. Paul quotes not the Hebrew, but gives literally the Septuagint version, with which his readers were familiar, and which for his purpose was as good as the Hebrew, or as a literal translation of it would have been. This verse is a rebuke to false reasonings and to daring charges against the Almighty. For an exposition of Ps. 51 : 4, see the author's " Studies in the Book of Psalms."

5. *But if our unrighteousness commend the righteousness of God, what shall we say ?* Is *God unrighteous who taketh vengeance ?* (*I speak as a man*). Peshito: But if our iniquity establish the recti-

tude of God, what shall we say? Is God unrighteous, when he uplifteth wrath? (I speak as a man.) This objection is of a like tone with those already stated; but it is perhaps more presumptuous. It is for substance this, that if the unbelief and wickedness of the Jews had served to show the faithfulness of God, and so to make his name glorious, shall we blame the Jews, or say that they shall be punished for that, which exalts God and sets forth his glorious and excellent nature? Shall we say that God is unrighteous when he taketh vengeance? Such an inference would be monstrous and blasphemous. Our apostle informs us that these reasonings do not meet his approval, and that he does not originate them : *I speak as a man ;* literally, I speak according to man; i. e. I am not the author of this objection; I do not even approve it; I am using the language of others. My own view I will now express :

6. *God forbid : for then how shall God judge the world ?* On the first clause, see above on v. 4. To *judge* the world, in this place, means to rule it and decide on its affairs. Calvin : "It is God's work to judge the world, that is, to rectify it by his own righteousness, and to reduce to the best order whatever there is in it out of order : he cannot then determine any thing unjustly." Three views are taken of this verse. One is that, if God punishes unjustly, he cannot be a fit judge and governor of the world, as we all now admit that he is. Another is that Paul is using the *argumentum ad hominem*, q. d. You Jews admit the doctrine of the divine judgment and authority over the world; but if you accuse God of unrighteousness in his dealings with men in this life, how can you expect righteousness in his awards to men? The third and perhaps the better view is that if sin ceases to be sin and cannot be punished because God overrules it, and makes it the occasion of glorifying him, and showing forth his excellent nature and providence ; then no sin can be punished, and so there is nothing to be condemned, and of course there is not and will not be any judgment of God on human conduct. Either of these views shews the necessity of vindicating the divine character against all aspersions. Not to do it is to give up all first principles in religion. But the bold assailants of divine truth are commonly very pertinacious, and have an amazing zeal in pressing their objections. So here :

7. *For if the truth of God hath more abounded through my lie unto his glory ; why yet am I also judged as a sinner.* Peshito : But if the truth of God has been furthered by my falsehood, to his glory ; why am I then condemned as a sinner? Cranmer : For if the trueth of God appeare more excellent thorow my lye, vnto his

prayse, why am I hence forth judged as a synner? Scott thus
paraphrases this verse: " Suppose the truth of God, in his predictions, promises, or denunciations, should be more abundantly
manifested to his glory, by any man's telling a wilful lie:
why should the liar be punished for giving occasion to the display of God's glory?" The answer is that our want of right
motives, our evil intentions and our violation of the law forbid-
ding all falsehood are the ground of condemnation. The good
brought out of moral evil by the overruling providence of God,
and the result have nothing to do in estimating the heinousness of
sin. So says the human conscience. So says God. The conduct
of Joseph's brethren was overruled to his and their great advantage, but they intended evil and they therefore had a just sense of
great criminality. The same may be said of the enemies and
murderers of Jesus Christ. The word here rendered *lie* is not
found elsewhere in the New Testament, but its cognates, rendered liar, lied, falsely, false witness, &c. are of frequent occurrence. *Lie* in this verse corresponds to *unrighteousness* in v. 5, just
as *truth* in this verse corresponds to *righteousness* in v. 5. Men are
rightly judged wicked when they do wickedly. " He that doeth
righteousness is righteous ; he that committeth sin is of the devil."
1 John 3 : 8.

8. *And not* rather, (*as we be slanderously reported, and as some
affirm that we say,*) *Let us do evil, that good may come ? whose damnation is just.* Peshito: Or shall we say—as some have slanderously
reported us to say :—We will do evil things that good [results]
may come? The condemnation of such is reserved for justice.
The reader will notice that the authorized version and the Peshito
differ, the former having a negative. The Peshito is probably
right. The particle rendered *not* often is a negative, but it is also
many times a mere sign of interrogation and has no negative
power whatever. It is perhaps so here. At least this is a satisfactory solution, is approved by Stuart, and supported by the
grammarians and Lexicons. The enmity against the grace of the
gospel is and always has been fearful. The enemies of the truth
have charged on those, who proclaim it, the worst principles; as
fair consequences of the most precious doctrine. Even the apostles were slanderously reported as favoring the loosest Antinomian
doctrines. The objector says that if Paul's doctrine, that God so
overrules all things as to exalt his glory, is true, shall we say, Let
us do evil, that good may come? Is this a fair inference? But if
we use the particle as a negative, then we should read thus, And
may we not say, Let us do evil, that good may come? So that we
reach the same result either way. The atrociously wicked nature

of the principle here stated is such that Paul does not hesitate to
declare that men, who favor it, are condemned, and that their condemnation is just.   The word " damnation " in this place clearly
means condemnation.

9. *What then ? are we better* than they? *No, in nowise : for we
have before proved both Jews and Gentiles, that they are all under sin.*
It is not an objector but Paul, who says, *What then ?* meaning
what is the fair result of this argument?   Does this course of
reasoning, or does the truth show that we [Jews] are better than
they [Gentiles]?   He answers, with an emphasis, No.   The word
rendered, *in nowise*, is elsewhere rendered *surely*, q. d.   No, not at
all, or No, in no respect. *Are we better*, one verb, have we the preference or pre-eminence over them?   Are we superior in the matter in hand—our legal standing in the sight of God?   *We have
before* proved [in Chap. I.] that the Gentiles, and [in Chap. II.]
that the Jews are all under sin, that is, are sinners, and so are
under condemnation, and need a gratuitous justification.   To
prove this incontestably in the minds of all, who reverence the
sacred Scriptures, he cites many passages of God's word.

10. *As it is written : There is none righteous, no, not one.   It is
written* is a phrase occurring about ninety times in the New Testament, eighteen times in this epistle.   It is the common notice of
quotation given by Christ and his apostles.   It was well understood as an appeal to the word of God.   The first citation is made
from the first and third verses of Psalms 14 and 53.   In verse 1
in each of those Psalms it is said *there is none that doeth good ;* in
verse third of each, it is added, *No, not one.*   Our apostle does not
literally quote either the Hebrew or the Septuagint, but he gives
the sense, *There is none righteous.*   All righteous men do good.
The chief question is, Does this verse apply to the Jews only, or
to all men?   The context both here and in the Psalms is conclusively
in favor of giving it a universal application.   Above in v. 9 Paul
expressly says that his doctrine and his argument embrace " both
Jews and Gentiles."   And in v. 2 of Psalms 14 and 53, it is said
that the inquisition of Jehovah was into the character, not of the
sons of Jacob, nor of the children of Israel, but of " the sons of
men " [Adam], a phrase embracing the human race.   There is,
however, no objection to giving the verse a pointed reference to
the Jews as their sacred writings are quoted, and as they held
that they were not in danger as the Gentiles were.

11. *There is none that understandeth, there is none that seeketh
after God.*   The words are chiefly taken from the 2d verse of
Psalms 14 and 53 ; only what is there an inquiry in a form implying negation is here a simple negative.   To *understand* God's will,

nature and loving kindness towards us, and our duty and obligations to him is so important a part of piety that it is often put
for the whole of religion.   He, who sees divine things in their
true nature, must love them; but alas! man without divine grace
is blind, 1 Cor. 2 : 14.   To such a one even Jesus Christ is without
form and comeliness.   Without God's Spirit man has no insight
into the real nature of heavenly things and no relish for them.
Accordingly he does *not seek after God.*   His heart goes not out
towards him in love and gratitude, in longings after him, in
prayers, or praises, or meditations concerning him.   And how
can such a man be otherwise than *under sin?*

     12. *They are all gone out of the way, they are together become
unprofitable; there is none that doeth good, no, not one.*   The Greek
is a literal quotation from the Septuagint rendering of Ps. 14 : 3,
and, with the exception of one word, of Ps. 53 : 3 also.   Peshito:
They have all turned aside, together; and become reprobates.
There is none that doeth good; no, not one.   On the last clause
of this verse see above on v. 10.   *Gone out of the way,* turned
aside, or gone away is a good rendering of the first verb.   The
second Greek verb is best rendered become unprofitable, though
the Hebrew has the idea of filthy.   The Hebrew also has the dis-
tributive form—every one, not all.   The whole verse teaches that
the corruption was total and universal.   See on this place the
author's "Studies in the Book of Psalms."   Such is the fruit of
ignorance of God, and of an aversion to his character and ways.
Ruin must follow in their train, even utter social debasement.

     13. *Their throat* is *an open sepulchre ; with their tongues they have
used deceit; the poison of asps* is *under their lips.*   The first and
second clauses in the Greek are literal quotations from the Septuagint version of Ps. 5 : 9.   The third is taken literally from the
Septuagint rendering of Ps. 140 : 3.   The figure of a sepulchre is
very striking and suggests two ideas.   One is that an open sepulchre sends forth offensive and pestilential vapors.   The other is
that an open sepulchre is insatiable and all devouring, being a
receptacle of all that is loathsome.   *Deceit,* flattery, lying, backbiting, cheating, how common and how detestable they are.   Men
are so guileful that they often deceive themselves.   The heart is
deceitful above all things.   The effects of evil speaking are sad
and terrible, like poison diffusing itself everywhere and producing
deadly effects.   The poison of serpents is used by Moses as an
emblem of the horrible nature of wickedness, Deut. 32 : 33.   See
also Ps. 58 : 4.   In the authorized version of Ps. 140 : 3 we have
adders, but the Septuagint has asps.   In the Hebrew the word
here rendered adders occurs nowhere else in the Bible.   There

are four Hebrew words rendered adder.   The bite of the asp was
fatal, and that almost instantly.

14. *Whose mouth* is *full of cursing and bitterness.*   The Greek
of Paul in this verse is the Septuagint version of Ps. 10 : 7.   *Cursing,* execration, imprecation.   *Bitterness,* the word includes the
idea of venom.   The two words embrace the most odious forms
of ill will and malignity, describing a character selfish and impious.

15. *Their feet* are *swift to shed blood.*   It is a quotation from
Isa. 59 : 7, chiefly in the rendering of the Septuagint.   On what
slender grounds most quarrels arise.   For how trivial a slight will
men murder.   Resentment, jealousy, covetousness and wantonness fill the world with constant fruits of violence and bloodshed.
How senseless and cruel wars devastate the globe.

16. *Destruction and misery* are *in their ways.*   This is a literal
quotation from the Septuagint version of Isa. 59 : 7.   *Destruction,*
describing ruin by violence, crushing, breaking in pieces by con-
cussion.   *Misery,* distress, affliction, wretchedness, as a fruit of the
violence before spoken of.   *In their ways,* in their paths, in their
courses.   Wherever they go they carry destruction and produce
misery.

17. *And the way of peace have they not known.*   Here the apostle
varies from the Septuagint version of Isa. 59 : 8, where the passage occurs, but the variation affects not the sense, being merely,
have not known, for have not seen.   By *the way of peace* we may
understand the method of securing their own quietude or that of
others.   They were the sons of strife.   They lived in contention
themselves and involved others in like quarrels and disquiet.

18. *There is no fear of God before their eyes.*   The Greek is a literal quotation from the Septuagint version of a part of Ps. 36 : 1.
The phrase has become famous, being in several countries adopted
into the forms of criminal indictment.   It is a description of a disposition generally depraved, utterly wanting in religious tone, for
when a man has *no fear* of God, he will regard nothing as sacred.

19. *Now we know that what things soever the law saith, it saith to
them who are under the law : that every mouth may be stopped, and all
the world may become guilty before God.*   The object of the first
clause is not, as some have thought, to assert that the quotations,
just considered, did not embrace the Gentiles, and cannot be
fairly cited to prove universal depravity, but only the depravity
of the Jews.   The statements are sweeping and universal.   They
as truly comprehend one nation as another.   But they have an
undeniable application to the Jews.   They are spoken by their
own prophets to themselves.   They contain language as strong

and decisive as any used by Paul. There is no way of escaping from their force but by denying the scriptures to be the word of God. That universal depravity, the Jews forming no exception, is by Paul himself intended to be taught is clear not only from verse 9, where he asserts what his object was in making the quotations, but also in this verse, where he declares the logical conclusion of his argument to be that every mouth [whether of Jew or Gentile] may be stopped, and all the world may become guilty before God. Could language be clearer?

DOCTRINAL AND PRACTICAL REMARKS

1. God is a sovereign. He does what he will with his own. He divides all his gifts severally as he will. He gives to some more, and to some less. He raised the Jews to heaven in point of privilege. He has a right to do these things, vs. 1, 2. He ought to do what seemeth good in his own eyes. He makes no mistakes.

2. It is a part of the perversity of man to turn outward blessings and privileges into the means of self-conceit and self-righteousness, instead of turning them to good account. The Jew had God's ordinances, and therefore he argued that he needed not forgiveness, conversion, or a Saviour. The merely nominal Christian has the Gospel and its sacraments, and in his folly and self-sufficiency he says he needs only baptism, the Lord's Supper and priestly absolution; but no change of heart, no regeneration by the Holy Ghost, and no gratuitous justification.

3. Those, who possess the Scriptures, have a treasure which exalts them above all others, who are without them, v. 2. No man, and no people have ever esteemed the word of God too highly. Doddridge: " Thankfully let us own the inestimable goodness of God in having favored us with his sacred *oracles*, and endeavor to improve in the knowledge of them." To take their liberties from a people is a great affliction to them ; but to take away God's word from them is one of the direst curses of heaven ever sent on a nation.

4. The holy Scriptures are God's word. They are his *oracles*, v. 2. Stephen called them the *lively oracles*. Holy men of God spoke as they were moved by the Holy Ghost. All scripture is given by inspiration of God. The oracles of God are *divine dictates*, as Hesychius defines the word. Brown: " God's word, and every truth that is held forth therein, of whatsoever nature, should have great weight with us, and be received with great reverence, fear and love, as having on it an impression of majesty, and should be believed as undoubted truth."

5. The great foe of piety, knowledge and virtue has been and still is unbelief, v. 3. Nero, speaking of his own vices to Seneca, said : " Do you suppose that I believe there is a God when I do such things ? " Men must deny God, his attributes and his word, if, in a land enlightened by revelation, they persist in sin. This they cannot do, but by indulging a wicked and criminal disregard of the divine testimony given in nature, or in Scripture, both in God's works and word. Unbelief has its seat in hatred of the truth.

6. Whatever men may allege to the contrary, every dispensation of God to man was instituted and has been administered in good faith, and in uprightness, v. 3. He has been sincere in all his offers, in all his engagements, in all his threatenings. Scott: " As the promises of God are made to believers alone ; the unbelief of some or of many professed Christians cannot make ' the faithfulness of God of none effect ; ' for he will fulfil his promises to his people, and execute his threatened vengeance on hypocrites and apostates." Covenant-breakers lose all that is promised and incur all that is threatened, but covenant-keepers shall never, do never complain of slackness in the Almighty.

7. Neither charity nor wisdom require us in the conduct of an argument for the truth to lay down our propositions in the most sweeping way that exact truth will admit. Paul talks of SOME not believing, v. 3. He might have said many, the great mass, and perhaps with truth too. But that was not essential to his argument, and might have given needless offence. Calvin: " There is here a sort of reticence, as he expresses less than he intended to be understood." Brown : " It is good sometimes, and Christian prudence requireth it, not to speak the worst of folks wickedness."

8. No matter what may happen, let us justify and glorify God. Such a course may cover us with shame, but it will be deserved shame. ' Let God be true,' Calvin well calls ' the primary maxim of all Christian philosophy'. It must never be given up. It is wicked to doubt it. One of the darkest signs in the character of some is their disposition to ward off all charges against themselves even at the cost of failing to justify the Most High. ' Let God be true, even if it involves the consequence that every man is a liar.'

9. God's threatenings will as surely be executed as his promises will be fulfilled, and for the same reason, because he is true. Hodge : " No promise or covenant of God can ever be rightfully urged in favor of exemption from the punishment of sin, or of impunity to those who live in it. God is faithful to his promises ; but he never promises to pardon the impenitently guilty."

10. The Scriptures make nothing clearer than that no mere man can stand, if God enter into judgment with him, vs. 4, 19. He cannot answer for one of a thousand of his offences. Omniscient purity sees enough in every man to justify any sentence of condemnation against him. In this fearful contest Jehovah must 'overcome.'

11. If we would not be found faithless to our solemn charge, we must bear bold and solemn witness against detestable and blasphemous opinions uttered in our hearing by profane men, unless their authors are mere scoffers. Compare vs. 4, 6; Pr. 9 : 8; Matt. 7 : 6. A wise man will regard time and judgment; but fidelity must not give way to timidity.

12. Of all the ways of opposing error and falsehood in religion, none is so safe or commonly so successful as a direct and solemn appeal to Scripture. This was Paul's plan, vs. 4, 10. Thus the Saviour taught us by his example. Matt. 4 : 4, 6, 10. I have known many a man to swear on when in human words reproved for profaneness; but I never have seen any man, not utterly abandoned, who was not silenced by the awful words of the third commandment, kindly and solemnly repeated.

13. Motives, not consequences, intentions, not results in human conduct, are the matter of praise or of blame, and will be the ground of reward or of doom, vs. 5, 7. God has brought glorious consequences out of the treachery of Iscariot. But the traitor thought only of his sordid gains and aims. Chrysostom: " God honored the Jews: they dishonored him. This gives him the victory, and shews the greatness of his love toward man, in that he honored them even such as they were." But no thanks to man for all this. Rather confusion of faces and penitence befit him.

14. God will punish none more than they deserve. He is ever righteous when he takes vengeance, v. 5. The slightest doubt on this point, if well founded, would subvert the moral government of the universe. The songs of heaven would cease, could it once be shewn that the King was not just and right in all his ways, Rev. 16 : 7.

15. The doctrine of God's providence and authority over the world is fundamental, and must never be given up, v. 6. It can be of no practical use to believe that there is what Voltaire calls " a supreme, eternal, incomprehensible intelligence," if we believe that he neither sees, nor knows, nor cares, nor helps, nor saves. A God without providence is unworthy of adoration. Atheism, whether speculative or practical, subverts all order and all religion. It would, if it could, annihilate moral government,

16. All wicked counsel shall come to naught. Yea, God will

make the wrath of man to praise him. Man's perfidy will exalt the divine faithfulness. Man's wickedness will shew forth the divine righteousness; and man's weakness, the divine power, vs. 5, 7. Let not the wicked boast himself. Utter confusion will cover all his impenitent and ungodly courses. And let not the righteous be afraid with any amazement. His enemies shall not triumph over him, but he shall surely triumph over them.

17. All sin is a lie, v. 7. It is guile and deceit. It fulfils none of its promises. Its least odious form is more to be dreaded than excruciating pains—than all temporal sufferings. The worst thing about it is that in any form it "is exceeding sinful." No man ever excessively hated, dreaded, or abhorred iniquity.

18. We may not cease to hold and teach true doctrines, because men abuse or misrepresent them, and us for inculcating them, v. 8. We may never yield the truth, whatever be the result. Paul taught that God could and would bring good out of evil. Then, said the wicked, the more we sin the more we honor God; and so the more wicked we are, the more deserving we are. This was all gross perversion. But shall we yield the doctrine of God's sovereign control over wicked men and their actions, because evil men thus pervert it? Never. Sin is wicked, and deserves punishment, not because it dethrones God, nor leaves him without rule, but because it is its aim to do these things. Chrysostom: "When Paul said *where sin abounded grace did much more abound*, in ridicule of him and by perverting what he said to another meaning, they said, We must cling to vice that we may get what is good. But Paul said not so." Against nothing has the wicked ingenuity of men been more exercised than against the doctrine of the divine sovereignty in all its parts. But we dare surrender none of it. Brown: "It is an old custom of Satan and his perverse followers, to be wronging the faithful servants of Christ, and fastening false doctrine upon them, as the maintainers thereof, which they never did approve of; and such an exercise as this should be taken in good part, seeing the apostles before us met with the like false imputations; yea, and Christ himself."

19. Let men remember that all their sophistry and merriment, all their perverseness and impudence cannot and will not shield them from the due reward of their evil deeds, vs. 5-7. Embracing a lie does not change it into truth. Denying damnation will not put out the flames of Tophet. Laughing at perdition will not keep us from perishing.

20. Let us ever oppose with abhorrence the baneful and baleful doctrines of Antinomianism, v. 8. They please the carnal nature of man, but they cannot be too much detested. Speaking

of such Calvin says: "Their perverseness was, on two accounts, to be condemned,—first, because this impiety had gained the assent of their minds; and secondly, because in traducing the gospel, they dared to draw from it their calumny." Hodge: "There is no better evidence against the truth of any doctrine, than that its tendency is immoral." Whatever makes men lax in their views of the precepts of God's law is dangerous.

21. The Lord is a great God, and a great King above all gods, and angels, and men. He so 'exerciseth his infinite wisdom, as a wise alchemist, extracting good and glory to himself out of the sinful carriages of wicked folks, as that he neither alloweth nor approveth of them in their sins, nor looseth the reins unto them to sin the more, nor shall they be any whit the less guilty, or less liable to judgment, because of that,' v. 7.

22. Let no man regard his personal, social or ecclesiastical advantages as constituting any refuge or palladium to him, v. 9. External privileges do but enhance responsibility, if they are abused. They cannot save men from either the guilt or the power of sin, v. 9. Yet such is the perverseness and self-righteousness of wicked men, that, like the Jews, they hug the delusion that sin cannot be fatal to them, because God has given them so many privileges above many of their fellow men. But the Saviour addressed a city of such when he plainly told them they should be thrust down to hell.

23. By nature every man is a sinner, and without divine grace no man is righteous in the sight of God, vs. 10–18. Tholuck well says that Paul here employs these verses "in order to describe the universal depravity of the whole human race." It makes the heart sick to see the glosses of Macknight, and the labored efforts of Taylor of Norwich and Stuart of Andover to make the impression that these verses do not prove what the apostle declares he quoted them to prove. If universal depravity in the human race is not proved by these verses, then are there no terms, by which that doctrine could be taught. President Edwards in reply to Taylor says: "What instance is there in the Scripture, or indeed any other writing, when the meaning is only the much greater part, where this meaning is signified by repeating such expressions—*They are all—they are all—they are all—together— every one—all the world;* joined to multiplied negative terms, to show the universality to be without exception; saying, *There is no flesh—there is none—there is none—there is none—there is none,* four times over; beside the addition of *no, not one—no, not one,* once and again! . . . Here the thing which I would prove, viz.: that mankind in their first state, before they are interested in the bene-

fits of Christ's redemption, are universally wicked, is declared with the utmost possible fulness and precision. So that, if here this matter be not set forth plainly, expressly, and fully, it must be because no words can do it; and it is not in the power of language, or any manner of terms or phrases, however contrived and heaped one upon another, determinately to signify any such thing." Words precisely to the same effect are used by Richard Watson: "Whoever reads that argument, in the third chapter of the epistle to the Romans, and considers the universality of the terms used, ALL, EVERY, ALL THE WORLD, BOTH JEWS AND GENTILES, must conclude, in all fairness of interpretation, that the whole human race, of every age, is intended." Scott: "It is proved beyond contradiction, that we are all, in ourselves, 'under sin.'"

23. If men are not *righteous* by nature, they must secure help from without, a righteousness not theirs by nature, or they must perish, v. 10. Can any thing be clearer than that they who are sick need a physician? The scope of all the apostle's reasoning hitherto has been to this very point. Hereafter he wonderfully shows how the Lord is our righteousness.

24. If men are so benighted as not to *understand* the plainest truths in religion, nor even to make any hearty efforts to become savingly acquainted with God (as is declared in v. 11); then surely there is the greatest necessity for the work and agency of God's Holy Spirit in the hearts of men. This necessity is imperative for there can be no genuine piety without saving knowledge, and a seeking after God.

25. It is amazing kindness in the good shepherd to go after the lost sheep. Poor things! they are all gone out of the way, v. 12. Nor would they ever find the path of safety, or the green pastures but for his sovereign mercy, that seeks them in their lost condition.

26. Men are not only lost, but in that state they are *unprofitable*, useless, v. 12. This aspect of the character of fallen men is often presented in God's word.

27. If a man does no good, it is impossible to prove that his piety is genuine, v. 12. All other distinctions between men vanish away before this, that some do good, and some do it not. Compare 1 John 3 : 7, 8.

28. The power of the tongue for evil is immense, incalculable, vs. 13, 14. It defiles the whole nature of man. It has the power of life and death, Pr. 18 : 10. Compare Pr. 30 : 14. It is a fire, a world of iniquity; it sets on fire the course of nature; and it is set on fire of hell. The tongue can no man tame; it is an unruly

evil, full of deadly poison, Jas. 3 : 6, 8.   No man has ever been too watchful over his tongue.   The evils of a tongue not restrained by grace are legion—blasphemy, profanity, perjury, cursing, murmuring, quarreling, foolish talking and jesting, vain reasoning, railing, reviling, flattering, silence when we ought to speak, speaking when we ought to be silent, perversion of facts, lying, detraction, talebearing, backbiting, whispering, rash and harsh judging, vain jangling, swelling words, idle words, boasting, false and foolish rumors, vows and promises of a sinful kind, etc.   If any offend not in word, the same is a perfect man.

29. Sin ruins and defiles everything.   All the faculties and parts of soul and body are corrupted, so that by nature we are utterly indisposed, disabled, and made opposite to all good, and wholly inclined to all evil, vs. 10–18.   The whole head is sick, the understanding darkened, the imagination evil, the memory polluted, the taste degraded, the heart faint, the hands full of wickedness, the feet running in forbidden paths, the lips poisoned, the eyes full of adultery, the breath murderous, the soul sunk down in irreligion, and the flesh triumphant.

30. How fearfully prevalent are bloody crimes, v. 15.   How often we read or hear of murders, manslaughters, rencontres, duels, shootings, stabbings, fightings, acts of revenge, malice, envy, hatred, woundings and provocations to violent deeds, together with a manifest delight in wars and scenes of horrid strife and slaughter.   Good men should everywhere testify their abhorrence of such things, and God's wrath against them.

31. It is of the very nature of sin to work ruin, to scatter abroad *destruction and misery*, v. 16.   Like fire sin destroys everything on which it kindles.   It has digged every grave.   It is the parent of every sigh from earth, or groan from hell.   God will surely not let sin or sinners have their way always.   He will surely, for his own glory, and the good of his saints, set bounds to lawlessness and to the lawless.   Blessed be his name for withholding man from compassing all the wickedness, to which his heart would incline him, and Satan seduce him.

32. Nor is it in the heart of man to make or to work peace, to impart or to enjoy it, v. 17.   As manifesting the temper of the ungodly see how they have martyred fifty millions of the saints in less than two thousand years, on an average more than a million and three-quarters for each century, or more than an average of seventeen hundred every year during the Christian era.

33. The fear of God is an essential element in rightly swaying the hearts of men, v. 18.   There is no piety without it.   Where there is none of it, there is no safety for life, liberty, or property.

Doddridge: "Let us bless God that we have been preserved from falling *into such enormities*, as those described in this chapter, and from falling *by them*."

34. If you would induce men to be virtuous, persuade them to be pious. He, who fears not God, will not regard man. Hodge: "Piety and morality cannot be separated." He, who is bold enough to break with God, cannot be relied upon to keep friendship with man.

35. Jesus Christ and his apostles freely quoted the Septuagint version of the holy Scriptures, as Paul does here, vs. 10–18. This shews the lawfulness of making and using translations of God's word, and circulating them, even if they are not inspired or perfect.

36. We, who have both the law and the gospel, are under manifold obligations to hear, love and keep the words of God. What they say they say to us who are under them, v. 19. Our responsibility is awfully solemn. To whomsoever much is given, of him shall much be required.

37. And now have we not fairly reached by the apostle's argument the unavoidable conclusion that for men of every race and of every age there is no justification by the law? vs. 9–19. Stuart: "Plainly the apostle's design is, to shew that there is but *one* method of acceptance with God now possible; and this is in the way of gratuitous pardon or justification." Chalmers: "Be assured that there is a delusion in all the complacency that you associate with your own righteousness. It is the want of a godly principle that vitiates the whole." Hodge: "The office of the law is neither to justify nor sanctify. It convinces and condemns." If salvation is not a gratuity, all men are in a state of hopeless misery; for all are sinners, and before God every mouth must be stopped and all the world stand condemned.

Chapter 7

ROMANS 3

VERSES 20–31

PAUL AFFIRMS THE SUM OF HIS ARGUMENT. HE ANNOUNCES THE GOSPEL SCHEME OF JUSTIFICATION, WHICH IS FOR JEW AND GENTILE INDISCRIMINATELY.

20 Therefore by the deeds of the law there shall no flesh be justified in his sight : for by the law *is* the knowledge of sin.

21 But now the righteousness of God without the law is manifested, being witnessed by the law and the prophets ;

22 Even the righteousness of God *which is* by faith of Jesus Christ unto all and upon all them that believe; for there is no difference :

23 For all have sinned, and come short of the glory of God;

24 Being justified freely by his grace through the redemption that is in Christ Jesus :

25 Whom God hath set forth *to be* a propitiation through faith in his blood, to declare his righteousness for the remission of sins that are past, through the forbearance of God;

26 To declare, *I say,* at this time his righteousness : that he might be just, and the justifier of him which believeth in Jesus.

27 Where *is* boasting then? It is excluded. By what law? of works? Nay; but by the law of faith.

28 Therefore we conclude that a man is justified by faith without the deeds of the law.

29 *Is he* the God of the Jews only? *is he* not also of the Gentiles? Yes, of the Gentiles also :

30 Seeing *it is* one God, which shall justify the circumcision by faith, and uncircumcision through faith.

31 Do we then make void the law through faith? God forbid; yea, we establish the law.

20. *THEREFORE by the deeds of the law there shall no flesh be justified in his sight, for by the law* is *the knowledge of sin.* Peshito : Wherefore by the deeds of the law, no flesh is justified before him; for, by the law, sin is known. The Doway

exactly agrees with the English, except that the first word is
because instead of therefore. The parallel passages are many.
See Rom 1 : 17; Acts 13 : 39; Gal. 2 : 16; 3 : 11; Eph. 2 : 8, 9;
Tit. 3 : 4–7. *Therefore* marks the connection with the whole foregoing argument. This is the conclusion from those impregnable
positions taken and maintained from the 17th verse of the first
chapter to the 19th verse of this. It is refreshing to find even
Macknight thus paraphrasing this verse: " *Wherefore, by works of
law,* whether natural or revealed, moral or ceremonial, *there shall
no man be justified meritoriously, in God's sight; because law makes
men sensible that they are sinners,* without giving them any hope of
pardon, consequently instead of entitling them to life, it subjects
them to punishment." With this Locke substantially agrees.
Ferme is more brief and very clear: " The righteousness of man
in the sight of God is not from the law, nor its deeds. For
through the law is the knowledge of sin." Beza: " The apostle's
purpose is to teach that no man can be justified in any other way
than by faith in Christ."

By *the deeds of the law* Paul means acts of obedience required
by law, by any law, known to man. It is a miserable drivelling
of Pelagian writers and of some not Pelagian in other points,
when they assert that Paul here merely denies that men can be
justified by acts done in conformity to the Mosaic ritual. For, as
Whitby says, " This knowledge of sin being chiefly by the moral
law (Rom. 7 : 7) shows that the Apostle excludes as well that, as
the ceremonial, from Justification, and evident it is, that the
antithesis runs all along, not between *Moral* and *Ceremonial* Works,
but between Works in general, and Faith, vs. 20, 22." Stuart:
" Surely the object of Paul in the present case is to show that
both Gentiles and Jews need that gratuitous justification which
the gospel proclaims, and which Christ has procured." Tholuck:
" His object, throughout the whole of the foregoing inquiry, had
been to show that the Jew is guilty, because he does not keep the
divine law, outwardly imposing obligations upon him ; and that,
for the same reason, the heathen is guilty, even as transgressing
that law implanted by nature within him and which is also outwardly obligatory." The reason why the law would not justify
was no imperfection or fault in it. The law has ever justified unsinning angels. In Eden before his fall it justified Adam. To the
innocent it utters no threat; against the unoffending, no curse.
Perfect conformity to all God's will is a faultless righteousness,
and never was by God rejected. Paul admits that the doers of the
law shall be justified, Rom. 2 : 13. The difficulty is that no mere
man, since the fall of Adam, has kept the law and without any

failure done the commandments. So that if men are saved it must be by gratuity, not by human merits. Rom. 3 : 27; 4 : 2-5, 13–16; 11 : 6; Eph. 2 : 8–10; 2 Tim. 1 : 9; Tit. 3 : 5.

No flesh as explained by David is *no man living*, Ps. 143 : 2, and by Paul as *no man*, Gal. 3 : 11. In Scripture the word flesh is used very variously; sometimes for all animal bodies, whether of man or any other living thing, Lev. 13 : 10; Num. 11 : 33; 1 Cor. 15 : 39; sometimes for animals, whether human or brute, living on the dry land, Gen. 6 : 13; sometimes for a kinsman, or one of the same stock, Gen. 37 : 27; 2 Sam. 19 : 12, 13; sometimes for every one having the same nature with ourselves, Isa. 58 : 7; sometimes for the state of the present life, Phil. 1 : 24; sometimes for the human body as now constituted, 1 Cor. 15 : 50; sometimes for the best qualities and powers of man, Matt. 16 : 17; sometimes for our corporeal nature, Matt. 26 : 41; sometimes for carnal ordinances, Phil. 3 : 3–6; once for the works of the law, Gal. 3 : 2, 3; and sometimes for the natural, corrupt state of man, Rom. 8 : 8. In our verse it is used for the human race, for men, embracing Jews and Gentiles. The whole course of the apostle's argument requires us so to understand it. The term flesh is never applied to angels, and our verse does not say that those unfallen spirits are not justified by law. But Paul's argument refers solely to the human race, and it embraces the whole of it.

Justified, the term points to the legal standing of men before God. Barrow: "God's justifying us doth solely or chiefly, import his acquitting us from guilt, condemnation, and punishment, by free pardon and remission of our sins, accounting us and dealing with us as just persons, as upright and innocent in his sight and esteem." Hodge: "*To justify* is to declare just, to pronounce righteous according to the standard of the law." The term is judicial, or pertains to courts. The apostle's whole argument goes on these suppositions: 1. that the moral law is holy, just and good in its precept, and its penalty; 2. that the obedience it requires is personal, perfect and perpetual; 3. that God will not clear the guilty, but will surely condemn the wicked; 4. what he has already and at length proven in chapters I., II. and III. viz. that all men, of every nation, have broken the law, and so cannot be accounted otherwise than as rebels and as under the curse.

In his sight, in his view, judgment or estimation; before him. In one's own sight many a man is justified. Pr. 21 : 2; Luke 16 : 15. Compare 2 Cor. 10 : 18. In the sight of their neighbors sinners often stand well. Frequently men justify those, whom God condemns, for that which is highly esteemed among men is abomination in the sight of God.

21. *But now the righteousness of God without the law is mani-fested, being witnessed by the law and the prophet*s. Peshito : But now, the righteousness of God without the law is manifested ; and the law and the prophets testify of it. On the phrase righteous-ness of God, see above on Rom. 1 : 17. This righteousness is here said to be without the law, literally *without law*, that is without deeds done by man in obedience to the precepts of the law, or as Tyndale expresses it, " without the fulfillinge of the lawe." The righteousness by which sinners are saved is not a legal righteous-ness. It is a great righteousness—even the righteousness of God. It is pleasing to God. In the case of sinners God will accept it and none other. This righteousness *is manifested*, is shewed, is declared, is made known, has appeared, or has come abroad. In Rom. 1 : 17 this righteousness is said to be *revealed*. Yet it had been known by the church of God for long ages. The doctrine of it was no novelty ; for it was *witnessed* (Doddridge attested, Schleusner pre-dicted and promised) *by the law and the prophets*. Moses in the Pen-tateuch and later prophets had testified or borne record of this very way of securing a good standing before God, so that as Chrysostom says this way was " old, but concealed." The Old Testament was sometimes spoken of as *the law*, Matt. 11 : 13 ; John 10 : 34 ; some-times as *the prophets*, Acts 10 : 43 ; 13 : 27 ; Rom. 16 : 26 ; some-times as *Moses and the prophets*, Luke 16 : 29 ; 24 : 27 ; sometimes as *the law and the prophets*, Matt. 5 : 17 ; 7 : 12 ; 22 : 40 ; Luke 16 : 16 ; Acts 13 : 15 ; and sometimes as the law of Moses, the Psalms and the prophets, Luke 24 : 44. In each of these cases all the holy Scriptures then written were designated. How Moses pointed out the true and only way of justification for sinners may be seen in the sacrifices and other rites prescribed in the law, as well as in the case of Abraham mentioned in Rom. 4 : 1–3. David, who was a prophet, Acts 2 : 30, also taught this way of life, Rom. 4 : 6–8. Habakkuk did the same, Rom. 1 : 17. See also John 5 : 46, 47 ; Gen. 3 : 15 ; 15 : 6 ; 22 : 18 ; Isa. 53 : 11 ; Dan. 9 : 24. Nor did other prophets fail to teach this doctrine of righteousness,

22. *Even the righteousness of God which is by faith of Jesus Christ unto all and upon all them that believe ; for there is no differ-ence*. It is clear that *righteousness* in this connection cannot mean the attribute of justice in God, for in no sense is that by *faith ;* and it is as much unto and upon infidels as upon believers. But it is a righteousness received by faith, not in God merely, nor in the general truths of religion, but in *Jesus Christ*. Stuart : " Most clearly it is not faith which belongs to Christ himself, but the faith of sinners towards him." In Acts 3 : 16 Through faith in his name is literally through faith of his name. See also Gal. 2 : 20.

On the nature of faith see above on Rom. 1 : 8, 12, 17. The righteousness of faith is the merit of Christ received by faith, and is *unto all and upon all them that believe*. Some think that *unto all* is to be connected with *is manifested* in the preceding verse, and that the rest of the clause stands by itself. Stuart: "The offer is made to all men without exception; *believers* only, however, are entitled to the actual reception of it." There is no error of doctrine thus taught, but the difficulty is in the grammatical construction. It is better to regard the prepositions *unto* and *upon*, as covering the whole case, and excluding all other justification. We are not without examples of the accumulation of prepositions intended to be intensive and to exclude all counter conceptions, as in Rom. 11 : 36. "Of him, and through him, and to him are all things." Indeed this very chapter, v. 30, gives an instance of the same kind, where *by* and *through* are used to explain and intensify the same idea. We might even add other prepositions without teaching any error, and say this righteousness is unto all, and upon all, and for all, and over all, and with all that believe. Peshito has for every one, and on every one. This righteousness is suited to all. It is offered to all, who hear the gospel. It is upon all, who are willing to receive it. Neither in its own nature, nor in its gracious offer is it confined to bond or free, to rich or poor, to learned or ignorant, to rude or civilized, to Jew or Gentile. All, all need it, *for there is no difference*. Peshito & Rhiems: For there is no distinction. The word occurs in two other places, Rom. 10 : 12 ; 1 Cor. 14 : 7, and is once rendered difference and once distinction. The sense is, that in the matter in hand—the sinfulness of our nature, and the need of a gratuitous justification, all mere men stand on the same ground, the Jew as truly requiring grace and mercy as the Gentile.

23. *For all have sinned and come short of the glory of God.* Peshito : For they have all sinned, and failed of the glory of God. *All*, that is, all men, Jews and Gentiles, have *sinned*, missed the mark, erred, done wrong, neglected duty, and so are exposed to the curse of the law. And all have *come short*, failed, are lacking, are behind, are sadly deficient. They have failed *of the glory of God*. This term may be taken in either of four ways. 1. They have failed to honor God as they were bound to do. They were made for his glory, but they have been a shame unto him, 1 Cor. 10 : 31. 2. They have failed to secure his approval or praise, John 5 : 41, 44. 3. They have failed to secure the glory, which God bestows on the innocent, or on the penitent. John 9 : 24 ; Eph. 1 : 14; 1 Pet. 5 : 4. God has not honored them as his friends. 4. Chrysostom, Beausobre, Slade and others explain it of the

glory of heaven—or the glorified state.   Beza expressly says that
Paul speaks of eternal life, which consists in a participation of the
glory of God.   All these interpretations are coincident and they
may be all true.   Either one of them implies the others.   The first
is the righteous ground of the rest.

24. *Being justified freely by his grace through the redemption that
is in Christ Jesus.*   Peshito: And they are justified gratuitously,
by grace, and by the redemption which is in Jesus Messiah.
Being justified, a passive participle in the masculine plural.   It refers
to Jews and Gentiles, to *all* who are justified.   They are justified
freely, gratuitously, or as Doway and Rheims express it, *gratis ;*
Coverdale, without deservynge ; in 2 Thess. 3 : 8 the same word is
rendered *for naught ;* and in John 15 : 25 *without a cause,* that is,
all, who are justified, are justified without any desert of theirs,
without any meritorious cause in themselves, but wholly *by God's
grace,* or favor.   Yet God's saving grace flows only in one channel.
So it is all *through the redemption that is in Christ Jesus. Redemption,* the word so rendered is found ten times in the New Testament, and is with one exception translated as here.   Chrysostom
renders it here entire redemption.   Sometimes the word means
simply deliverance and is once so rendered, Heb. 11 : 35.   But it
commonly refers to deliverance from sin and wrath by Jesus
Christ, who gave his life a ransom for us. Eph. 1 : 7 ; Col. 1 : 14.
The idea of redemption may be either Hebrew or Roman.   In
Israel when a man was so heavily in debt that he could not pay
what he owed, the creditor might lawfully sell him or any of his
family as servants until the year of jubilee. 2 Kings 4 : 1 ; Matt.
18 : 25.   Sometimes a poor man sold himself even to a foreigner,
Lev. 25 : 47–49.   In either of these cases any one that was nigh of
kin to the poor servant might, and by the law of brotherhood was
bound in certain cases to redeem him, by paying all for which he
was in bondage.   Again, in the early ages of the world prisoners
of war were generally put to death.   In the course of time cupid-
ity, or in some cases humanity dictated that they should, by their
conquerors, be sold as servants.   Sometimes during the war, and
often after it was over, a man's country or his kin sent money, and
bought him out of bondage, thus 'redeeming him with corruptible
things as silver and gold.'   Suidas defines ransom as "the price
given to be redeemed from the slavery of the barbarians."   For
many ages redemption was thus effected, and so the idea of
redemption was familiar to mankind.   In the Old Testament
the same word is rendered kinsman, avenger and redeemer.
Avenging of blood and redeeming from bondage both devolved
on the nearest male relative.   In the New Testament are three

words rendered *redeem.* One means simply to *buy.* It is found more than thirty times. Our Lord uses it when he speaks of *buying* a field, *buying* oxen, *buying* victuals. Paul uses it twice : " Ye are *bought* with a price," 1 Cor. 6 : 20 ; 7 : 23. John uses it in Rev. 5 : 9 ; 14 : 3, 4. " Thou hast *redeemed* us to God by thy blood." Sometimes another word, a compound of the foregoing, is used. It occurs four times. Christ hath *redeemed* us from the curse of the law. See Gal. 3 : 13 ; 4 : 4, 5. There is still another verb rendered redeem, Luke 24 : 21 ; Tit. 2 : 14 ; 1 Pet. 1 : 18. This is cognate to the noun in our text rendered *redemption.* Then we have two words corresponding to this noun. They are both rendered ransom. For the first see Matt. 20 : 28 ; Mark 10 : 45 ; for the second 1 Tim. 2 : 6. The ransom was the price of release.

This redemption is *in Christ Jesus.* It was effected by him. The price was paid by him. The redemption is applied to us when we believe in him. We are not redeemed by Christ's example, precepts, doctrines, or power ; but by his laying down his life a ransom for us, by his blood, by his death, by his stripes, Matt. 20 : 28 ; Eph. 1 : 7 ; Col. 1 : 14 ; Heb. 9 : 15 ; Isa. 53 : 5. Jesus was every way fit to be our Redeemer by becoming our *kinsman,* by taking upon him human nature entire ; but in such a way that he was holy, harmless and undefiled. To believers the effect of redemption is full, complete, gratuitous, eternal salvation. It brings great glory to Christ,

25. *Whom God hath set forth* to be *a propitiation through faith in his blood, to declare his righteousness for the remission of sins that are past, through the forbearance of God.* Instead of *set forth* Peshito has preconstituted ; Wiclif, ordeyned ; Rheims, Pool and Doddridge, proposed ; Chrysostom and Margin, fore-ordained : Chalmers, exhibited. Every where else the word is rendered purposed, and the cognate noun is more commonly than otherwise rendered purpose. But manifestation also belongs to the word for it is the word used to express *shew* bread, or bread of setting forth. God has set him forth in his purpose, in sending him into the world, and in sending forth preachers, 2 Tim. 1 : 9–11 ; 1 Pet. 1 : 20–22. The words *to be* are not in the original, and might as well be dropped. If any thing be supplied, *as* would be better. *Propitiation,* the original word occurs but once elsewhere in the New Testament, Heb. 8 : 12, where it is rendered mercy-seat. It is doubtless borrowed from the Septuagint version of the Old Testament. See Ex. 25 : 18–20 ; Lev. 16 : 13–16. It is explained in these four ways : 1. Some render it propitiatory, or mercy-seat ; so Whitby, Locke, Macknight, Assembly's Annotations, Tyndale, Olshausen, and others. The advantages of this exposition are first

that it takes the word in its common signification, once in the Greek Testament and often in the Septuagint; secondly, that by using the term comprehensively we get a good sense, that as the Israelites obtained pardon and acceptance as public worshippers by the sprinkling of blood on the mercy-seat, so eternal life is dispensed from Christ. The objection to this explanation is that it presents to us an unusual figure, that of Christ himself as a mercy-seat. 2. Some render the word propitiator. This is the explanation preferred by Cranmer and Rosenmuller. It makes the word rendered propitiation, which is an adjective, to agree with *whom*. This teaches no error, nor does it necessarily weaken the true doctrine. 3. Others think the word is in the neuter and that we are to supply the word victim or sacrifice after it. This explanation is preferred by Calvin, Schlichting, Le Clerc, Bucer, Turrettin, Kypke, Magee, Tholuck, Stuart, Chalmers, Conybeare & Howson, Haldane and Hodge. 4. Others unite the first and third of these. Hawker: " CHRIST indeed is both the propitiation and the propitiatory. He is the propitiation, or sacrifice; the propitiatory or mercy-seat and altar, on which that sacrifice was offered." See also Olshausen, p. 153. Whichsoever of these we prefer we may still lay fast hold on the great doctrine of the atonement, by which God is reconciled to man. We have also the cognate word *propitiation* twice in the Scriptures. 1 John 2 : 2; 4 : 10. Of the correctness of this rendering there is no room for doubt. Then we have the cognate verb *make reconciliation for* the sins of the people, Heb. 2 : 17.

All these words no doubt have allusion to the mercy-seat, which was the lid of the ark of the testimony. In the Hebrew this is called the cover. It occurs frequently in Exodus and Leviticus, once in Numbers and once in 1 Chronicles. Its cognate noun is always rendered atonement as in Ex. 29 : 36; Lev. 23 : 27, 28. Over this lid stood the two cherubim with their wings extended. On this lid of the ark the blood of the sacrifice was sprinkled; over it rested the visible glory, and from it as from a throne God shewed himself propitious. Elsewhere Christ is called our passover, an offering and a sacrifice, and a lamb, a lamb slain, yea, a lamb slain from the foundation of the world, 1 Cor. 5 : 7; Eph. 5 : 2; John 1 : 36; Rev. 5 : 6, 9, 12; 13 : 8. All these forms of expression clearly point to atonement or reconciliation by Jesus Christ. Olshausen: " Every sacrifice is intended to *expiate* the guilt of men, and *propitiate* the anger of God, consequently the sacrifice of all sacrifices, in which alone all the rest have their truth, must *effect* that which the others only foreshadow." In what sense is Christ our pass-

over, if his death does not avert from us death and destruction? In what sense is he an offering and a sacrifice for others,
if he expiated no guilt, endured no curse, bore no wrath, and
exhausted no penalty for them? In what sense was he a lamb
slain, if he was not a victim offered for the sins of many?
How can a lamb take away sin except as a sacrifice? Christ is
set forth a propitiation *through faith in his blood,* and not otherwise. On *faith* see above on Rom. 1 : 8, 12, 17. *In his blood:*
the Scriptures often speak of the blood of Christ in a way that
ought not to be forgotten. In instituting the Lord's supper
our Saviour says, This is my blood of the new testament; or,
This is the new testament in my blood, Matt. 26 : 28; Mark
14 : 24; Luke 22 : 20. In John 6 : 53–56 the Lord informs us that
we must by faith drink his blood. In Acts 20 : 28 we are informed that the flock of God was purchased with his own blood.
In Rom. 5 : 9 saints are said to be justified by his blood. In
1 Cor. 10 : 16 the Lord's supper is called the communion of the
blood of Christ. In Eph. 1 : 7 we are said to have redemption
through his blood. In Eph. 2 : 13 it is said we are made nigh
by the blood of Christ. In Col. 1 : 14 we are said to have redemption through his blood. In Col. 1 : 20 we are said to have
peace through his blood. In Heb. 9 : 14 the blood of Christ is
said to purge the conscience from dead works to serve the living God, and it is said to do this *much more* than the blood
of bulls and goats fitted men of old to be public worshippers.
In Heb. 10 : 14 saints are said to enter into the holiest by the
blood of Jesus. In Heb. 10 : 29 Christ's blood is called the blood
of the covenant. In Heb. 12 : 24 it is called the blood of sprinkling. In Heb. 13 : 12 Christ is said to sanctify the people with
his own blood. In Heb. 13 : 20 his blood is called the blood
of the everlasting covenant. In 1 John 1 : 7 it is said the blood
of Jesus Christ God's Son cleanseth us from all sin. In Rev.
1 : 5 it is said he hath washed us from our sins in his own blood.
In Rev. 5 : 9 the saints in glory say to him, Thou hast redeemed
us unto God by thy blood. In Rev. 7 : 14 the saved are said
to have washed their robes and made them white in the blood
of the Lamb. In Rev. 12 : 11 it is said the conquerors overcame
by the blood of the Lamb. Indeed this aspect of truth is both
prominent and permanent. Two remarks may here be fairly
made. One is that the Jewish church lived under a dispensation, wherein almost all things were purged with blood, the altar,
the mercy-seat, the tabernacle and the worshippers, Heb. 9 : 21,
22; 10 : 19. So that the significance of blood as a sacrifice, expiat-
ing guilt, was well understood by all Israel. The other remark is

that if the Scriptures teach any thing clearly and by a great variety of terms and phrases, they do teach that Jesus Christ shed his blood, not for his own sins, for he had none; but for the sins of his people. He suffered the just for the unjust. And faith in his blood, reliance on his sacrifice, is the only way of salvation to men ordained by God. If this truth be not received, we hear the Gospel in vain; for God has set forth his Son *to declare*, shew, point out, or manifest *his righteousness for the remission of sins that are past*. The *righteousness* here spoken of cannot be God's attribute of justice; for in the case of sinners, for whom no full and complete atonement is made, justice calls for condemnation, which would be giving every sinner his due; but this righteousness is for a very different end, even for remission of sins. Nor can the term righteousness here mean God's method of justification for the remission of sins, for that is tautology. Locke explains it of God's righteousness in keeping his word, but how can God's veracity procure the remission of sins till they are atoned for? *The righteousness of God* undoubtedly points to Christ's complete fulfilment of the precepts of the law, and his endurance of its whole penalty in our room and stead. Thus believers in Christ are so perfectly righteous in the eye of the law that they are said to be made the righteousness of God, 2 Cor. 5 : 21. But see above on Rom. 1 : 17. This righteousness, imputed by God and received by faith, secures the *remission of sins that are past*. The word here rendered *remission* is not found elsewhere, but no better rendering has been proposed. The word literally means *passing by*. But it is one of the glories of God that he *passeth by the transgression* of his people, Mic. 7 : 18. When the apostle speaks of the remission of *sins*, he means all sorts of sins, sins against God and against man, sins of omission and of commission, open sins and secret sins. The blood of Christ cleanseth us from all sin. The phrase, *sins that are past*, is capable of two constructions. One is that the apostle declares remission for sins already committed by any one. God actually forgives no sin till it is committed, but in accepting a sinner who believes, God gloriously purposes and promises no more to impute sin to him, and he never does judicially condemn him, but puts away his sin as soon as committed, 2 Sam. 12 ; 13. Howbeit a believer by sin incurs God's fatherly displeasure and chastisements. But there is to such no forensic condemnation. *For the remission*, some would read *through the remission*. But there is a grammatical difficulty in the way. Nor could we then retain the accepted meaning of the word righteousness. God has declared a righteousness of such an excellent nature that he can grant the remission of sins in a way honorable to himself and safe for man. Brown: "Though God decreed from all eternity to pardon the sins of his own chosen, and so their sins may be said, in so far, to be pardoned *intentionally* before they are committed, and laid our sins on Christ, who in due time satisfied for them and so *meritoriously* they may be said to be pardoned, yet they are not *actually* pardoned, until the sinner, convinced of a necessity, flee in to that price, and lean to it. . . In justification they have their iniquities pardoned, all their by-past transgressions are covered and remitted." Another and more common construction of the phrase, *sins that are past*, refers it to sins committed under the former dispensation. Some give it no other construction. This seems to derive strength from the phrase, *at this time*, in the next verse. If we supply *and* between the verses this will be grammatical and right. Thus Ferme: "To be *past* here signifies that the world had lived in them, and that they had reigned in the world before Christ was known." Doddridge: "This remission extends not only to the present, but former age, and to all the offences *which are* long since *past, according to the forbearance of God*, who has forborne to execute judgment upon sinners, in reference to that atonement which he knew should in due time be made." There is no doubt of either of the following truths; 1. God had a people justified, redeemed and saved, before the coming of Christ. 2. All, who have ever been saved had redemption in the blood of Christ. 3. There is no more difficulty in giving prospective than there is in giving retrospective efficacy to the work of Christ. One is startled at Olshausen: "In the O. T. there was no *real* but only a symbolical forgiveness of sins." But of old believers looked to Messias to come as we look to Messias already come. They were saved as we are by reliance on a Redeemer, John 8 : 56. Compare 1 Kings 8 : 30; Ps. 32 : 1 ; 103 : 3 ; 130 : 4, and many other places.

All this propitiation, righteousness and remission are secured to men *through the forbearance of God*, i. e. through his long-suffering whereby he delays to punish those who richly deserve his wrath, and holds back the merited stroke of vengeance from those who have insulted him. See above on Rom. 2 : 4. How patient and merciful is God in giving time and opportunity to repent and believe the Gospel. How great is his mercy in setting forth Christ

26. *To declare*, I say, *at this time his righteousness: that he might be just and the justifier of him which believeth.* The words rendered *declare* and *righteousness* are quite the same and teach the same as they do in v. 25. *At this time* no doubt refers to the Gospel dispensation. Some, as has been stated above, think it is set over

against *sins that are past*, as pertaining solely to the old dispensa-tion.　And it is certainly true that believers in all ages have obtained remission of sins and acceptance solely by one and the same glorious righteousness.　It is added that this righteousness is manifested that God *might be just and the justifier of him that believeth.*　It is God that justifieth.　None else can do it.　None else has jurisdiction in the moral government of the world.　It is God's law that is broken.　Even when men sin against each other, their great offence is against God, Ps. 51 : 4.　Jehovah is judge of all the earth.　None else is fit to dispense pardons and salvation. To give up this prerogative to others would be to deny himself. God often condemns men and deeds, which mortals justify; and he as often justifies men and deeds, which mortals condemn.　He is right in all cases.　He is not governed by appearances.　He judges by the ken of omniscience.　Consequently there are no errors committed in his awards.　Whom he will he justifies and whom he will he condemns; but whether he saves or destroys he acts righteously.　If men are cast off for their sins, if condign punishment banishes them from God, none can complain of any want of equity, for they receive the reward of their evil deeds.　In like manner when God for Christ's sake forgives and accepts the sinner, when he imputes to him the infinite merits of Christ, and clothes him in the righteousness wrought out by the obedience and sufferings of his great substitute, justice is satisfied, the law is satisfied; for Christ *finished* the work of reconciliation; yea, both in its precept and in its penalty he magnified the law and made it honorable, so that now when we confess our sins, he is faithful and just to forgive our sins and to cleanse us from all unrighteousness, 1 John 1 : 9.　This justification is to *him that believeth*, and to none else.　Unbelief rejects a free gratuitous salvation.　It stubbornly refuses submission to God's method of justification.　It is impos-sible that one, who rejects the only remedy provided, should escape death.　The unbeliever will not come to Christ, John 5 : 40.　On *faith* see above on Rom. 1 : 8, 12, 17.　Here the literal rendering is *him who is of the faith of Jesus*, but the English version gives the exact meaning and in idiomatic phrase.

27. *Where* is *boasting then ?　It is excluded.　By what law ? of works ?　Nay ; but by the law of faith.　Boasting*, often rendered rejoicing or glorying; everywhere else used in a good sense.　Here the apostle declares that by the Gospel plan of salvation, self-esteem, self-righteousness, self-complacency, self-approbation are cut up by the roots.　The accepted worshipper never makes mention of his own merits, or of his own works as a ground of acceptance with God.　He abases himself and exalts God.　He is nothing;

Christ is all in all. His righteousnesses are, not only in God's esteem but in his own also, as filthy rags. Were he to rejoice in his own doings, he would boast in a thing of naught. Self-glorying is excluded, or shut out, not by the rule, plan or scheme of works, but by the rule, which now should govern the world, the doctrine of the Gospel, by which we shall be judged ; the scheme of faith in, by and through Jesus Christ. For the meaning of the word *law* compare Isa. 2 : 3 ; 42 : 4.

28. *Therefore we conclude that a man is justified by faith without the deeds of the law.* We *conclude,* literally we reckon, reason, count, or judge ; Tyndale has suppose ; Cranmer, holde ; Genevan, gather ; Rheims, account ; or we reason out. We reach this conclusion by a fair and logical process, viz. : that a man is justified *by faith,* i. e. by faith alone, without anything on man's part but a simple reception of Christ's righteousness. *Without the deeds of the law,* literally without deeds of law, i. e. deeds performed in obedience to any law, the law of nature, the moral law, the law of ceremonies, or any other law. On *deeds of law* see above on Rom. 3 : 20. Simple faith in Christ, a hearty reception of him secures salvation. So clear and direct is this testimony that the Doway Bible has a note flatly denying that the apostle here excludes such works " as follow faith, and proceed from it." But the apostle, both by his terms and by his train of reasoning, excludes all works of man from any and from all share in his own justification. That is precisely the point of his whole argument, and what he has asserted over and over again.

29. Is he *the God of the Jews only ?* is he *not also of the Gentiles ? Yes, of the Gentiles also.* The Jews themselves could not with any show of truth deny that Jehovah created, fed and governed all nations ; that he did much good to them, filling their hearts with food and gladness, making many of them the objects of his special care. Jehovah was much more than a national God. He was God over all. We should not therefore be surprised to find him offering mercy and grace to all nations on the same terms without money and without price.

30. *Seeing* it is *one* God, *which shall justify the circumcision by faith, and uncircumcision through faith.* God is one, and has no divided counsels. He does not save one sinner in one way and another sinner in another way. The Jews themselves hold that the Lord our God is one Lord, and that the nations have no real God but the same, who is the God of Israel. Why then should any cavil against God for justifying Jew and Gentile in the same way, viz. : *by* faith, or *through* faith ? Some attempt to make a distinction between these forms of expression, but they quite fail to make

it obvious. Both words mean the same thing. Locke thinks that in this verse the apostle has special reference to Zechariah 14 : 9, " The Lord shall be King over all the earth : in that day shall there be one Lord, and his name one."

31. *Do we then make void the law through faith ? God forbid : yea, we establish the law.* For *make void* we have various meanings and paraphrases, all however confirming the true doctrine, as Peshito, nullify ; Tyndale, Cranmer, Rheims, Vulgate and Doway, destroy ; Genevan, make unprofitable ; Locke and Macknight, make useless ; Conybeare and Howson, bring to naught. The meaning is, Do we, by teaching that life to man is solely by grace through faith, put dishonor upon any other revelations God has made to man ? By no means. Verily not at all. On the unhappy rendering *God forbid* see above on Rom. 3 : 4. For *establish* Coverdale, Tyndale and Cranmer have mayntayne ; Dutch Annotations and Stuart, confirm. We contend that so far from making useless the law—all the law God has ever given—we assign to it its true use as giving the knowledge of sin, shewing the necessity of a better righteousness than men ever attain to by their own works, furnishing a perfect rule of life, and bringing great glory to God, its author, because as a transcript of his character it is holy, just and good.

DOCTRINAL AND PRACTICAL REMARKS

1. All attempts at justification by our own works are vain and presumptuous, v. 20. They all go on the supposition that God is not holy and omniscient, or that man is not sinful and guilty. Every thoughtful man knows that in countless ways he has offended in thought, word and deed. Both by original and actual sin every man is wholly broken and bankrupt, without strength, merit, holiness or righteousness. Left to themselves men are in as hopeless and helpless a state as are the fallen angels, John 8 : 41, 44. Man cannot be justified by a law, which wholly condemns him. Scott : " There is no law of God, which any man has kept : therefore no law by the deeds of which any man can be justified." It is worse than common folly to seek life by a door that is for ever shut against us.

2. Though the law cannot save but must condemn us, yet in other respects it is of excellent use. By it we learn our sinfulness and ruin, v. 20. It shows what sin is, how much sin is chargeable to us, and what sin deserves. It shews us the pure and exalted character of God. It teaches us what our duty is. But it cannot both justify and condemn. It cannot give the knowledge of sin

and of salvation too. Brown : " Much of our ignorance of our sinful condition, of the sinful nature of many of our actions, of the vileness and abominableness of sin, and of the just and dreadful desert thereof floweth from our being strangers to the law : and much humble and diligent study of the law would help us to discover many latent corruptions, and to be better acquainted with the stratagems of sin, and the dangerous snares we are drawn into thereby." Any teaching, therefore which represents the law as useless or of none effect, is false and mischievous.

3. But though the law condemns us there is a way of salvation. Nor can we ever sufficiently praise and bless God for making it known to us. It is a matter of pure revelation, v. 21, as well as a matter of pure and sovereign mercy. Scott : " Proud men will be offended at this, and strive to establish some distinction between themselves and more *scandalous* and *vulgar* sinners : but they labor in vain. . . The meanest and most guilty of the human species, who comes in God's appointed and manifested way, shall be justified freely by his grace through the redemption of his Son : while all, who persist in the attempt of justifying themselves, will assuredly perish under the wrath of God."

4. It would surely free us from many foolish notions and from much self flattery and self delusion, if we would but remember that all our judgments and actions must undergo the scrutiny of God. It is only as acts, words or thoughts are good or bad *in his sight* that they shall affect us hereafter. Our hearts are so deceitful and our minds are so corrupt that not only will most private opinions, but many public judgments also be set aside, in part or in whole, at the last day. Men search not the heart, men are vile, men love darkness and falsehood, men are slow to find any fault with themselves. But to God, who is our judge, all things are naked and open ; he never clears the guilty, he never condemns the innocent. He is holy. The stars are not pure in his eyes. Oh that men would cease to flatter either their neighbors or themselves.

5. Sad as is our case by nature, it is not beyond remedy. Though we are prisoners of ignorance, of guilt, of corruption and of misery, yet we are prisoners of *hope*. Even we can have a righteousness commensurate to the demands of God's law and every way suited to our case, vs. 21, 22, 25, 26. Nothing in the whole book of God more concerns us than this. Nothing more sets forth the divine wisdom or glory. Nothing else reconciles justice in God with good *hope* in man. True it is not originally *our righteousness*, Dan. 9 : 18 ; Rom. 10 : 3 ; Phil. 3 : 9 ; nor *righteousness by the law*, Gal. 3 : 21 ; nor *righteousness of the law*, Rom. 2 :

26; 10 : 5 ; nor *righteousness by works*, Tit. 3: 5 ; nor *righteousness in the law*, Phil. 3 : 6.   But it is and is called the *righteousness of God*, Rom. 1 : 17; 3 : 21, 22, 25, 26; 10 : 3 ; the *righteousness which is of God*; Phil. 3 : 9; *righteousuess by faith of
Jesus Christ*, Rom. 3 : 22; *righteousness through the faith of
Christ*, Phil. 3 : 9; Rev. 5 : 9; *righteousness not our own*, Phil. 3 : 9;
righteousness imputed, Rom. 4 : 6, 10, 11.   This righteousness is the
fine linen, clean and white, in which the redeemed in glory are
arrayed.   Rev. 19 : 8.   It is celebrated in all ages of the church.
The true doctrine on this matter has not been at any time a novelty ; but has been in some form declared from the beginning,
though often obscured and sometimes denied by wicked teachers.
See Ps. 24 : 5 ; 85 : 10, 13; 89 : 16; 145 : 7 ; Isa. 42 : 21 ; 45 : 8, 24,
25; 46 : 13; 53 : 11; 54:17; 56 : 1 ; 61 : 11 ; 62 : 1, 2; Jer. 23 : 5 ;
Dan. 9 : 24; Hos. 10: 12.   Haldane: " To Balaam, who beheld the
Saviour at a distance he appeared as a *star ; There shall come a star
out of Jacob*, Num. 24 : 17 ; while to Malachi, the last of the prophets,
on his nearer approach, he appeared as the *sun of righteousness*,"
Mal. 4 : 2.   This righteousness is manifested, declared.   The way
of salvation by it is clearly pointed out in both Testaments.   Were
men not perverse and filled with hatred to the truth, they would
all at once receive it.   It suits their case exactly.   It is without
law, i. e. without deeds done in obedience to law.   It is by faith,
faith in Jesus Christ.   Simply believe.   It is perfect and needs no
addition, no amendment, no work of man or angel to complete it.
It is just what all men need.   It is unto all and upon all that receive it.   Prince and peasant, Jew and Gentile, bond and free, old
and young alike need it and, on accepting it, are alike adorned
with it.   This is the righteousness of God.   1. He devised it,
wrought it out, and applies it.   2. He freely gives it, Rom. 5 : 17.
3. He graciously accepts it.   He will from man accept none else.
4. He is well pleased with it, delights in it, and bestows all blessings on those, who lay hold of it, Isa. 42 : 21 ; Rom. 8 : 32.   5. This
is the great righteousness.   It is the most glorious robe worn by
any creature in heaven.   The robe of innocence is not so radiant.

This righteousness is exclusive of all other righteousness.   We
must take this alone, or not at all.   Chalmers: " The foundation
of your trust before God must be either your own righteousness
out and out, or the righteousness of Christ out and out. . . If you
are to lean upon your own merit, lean upon it wholly.   If you are
to lean upon Christ, lean upon Him wholly.   The two will not
amalgamate together ; and it is the attempt to do so, which keeps
many a weary and heavy-laden inquirer at a distance from rest,
and at a distance from the truth of the Gospel.   Maintain a clear

and consistent posture.   Stand not before God with one foot upon
a rock, and the other upon a treacherous quicksand . . . Make no
reservations . . . We call upon you, not to lean so much as the
weight of one grain or scruple of your confidence upon your own
doings—to leave this ground entirely, and to come over entirely on
the ground of a Redeemer's blood and a Redeemer's righteousness.   Then you may stand firm and erect on a foundation strong
enough and broad enough to bear you.   You will feel that your
feet are on a sure place."

Nothing is of more importance than our views and treatment
of this righteousness of God.   Yet no doctrine of the Gospel is
more maligned or slandered.   Many will hear you with apparent
candor on the evidences of Christianity, on the morality or benevolence of the Gospel; but the moment you summon their attention
to the righteousness of Christ as the ground of a sinner's acceptance, they are offended, or begin to stumble.   Hence error on
this subject is rife.   One contends that the righteousness of God
in this chapter and generally in Paul's writings means a system of
morals approved by God; another, God's mercy; another, God's
attribute of justice; another, God's method of justifying sinners;
another, God's method of saving sinners.   These teachings are
not all alike wide of the truth.   One may so explain either of the
last two, as to embrace enough of the Gospel to be saved thereby.
But how can man be saved by God's attribute of justice, when it
pours curses on the head of every transgressor?   Or how can
God's mercy save a sinner, if he is to enter heaven trampling on
the divine government, and eternally standing naked before God,
with not one precept of the law fulfilled and with all his sins unatoned?   Or how can any code of morals be any purer or better
than that of Sinai, which is holy, just and good, and which only
failed to secure life because the flesh has proved itself wholly
unable to keep its precepts and so meet its demands? Rom. 8 : 3.
Why will not men allow God, in executing his glorious plans to
provide for believing sinners a righteousness equal in all respects
to the demands of the precept and the penalty of God's law, a
righteousness resulting from the perfect fulfilment of all the law
requires in the way of obedience or suffering?   Why will men
write treatises on justification and never mention the word righteousness, and never say that by it the believer is righteous?   Did
Paul so write?   Why will men cavil, and higgle, and boggle, and
make a thousand pleas and excuses, and state a thousand difficulties, respecting a doctrine and a scheme so honorable to God,
so safe for man, so suited to advance the divine glory, and so fully
meeting the demands of an enlightened conscience?   Nor should

men be offended at this doctrine, nor at the frank and earnest assertion of it.   It alone gives ground of good hope to sinners. It alone harmonizes many of the statements of Scripture.   It alone shews how God can be just when he justifies the ungodly.   It has been the joy of believers in long ages gone by.   Nothing in Scripture has been more clearly stated or firmly held.   See the author's "Grace of Christ," Chapter XXI.   Guyse: "By the righteousness of God I mean the mediatorial Suretyship Right eousness of Jesus Christ God-man, which consists in his active and passive obedience to the law, in the room and stead of sin- ners, which for its transcendent excellence and glory, as well as on other accounts, may be styled the righteousness of God."

It is true this doctrine is very humbling to the sinner.   He had no part in devising this righteousness, nor in providing it, nor in manifesting it; nor can he add anything to it.   Nor can he, without humbling his heart, avail himself of it.   All he can do is to put on this blessed robe, wear it, and adore the grace that pro- vided it.   This he ought to do; for it is in several respects a wonderful righteousness: 1. None but God could have devised a plan, in which all the demands of the law should be fully met, precept and penalty magnified, and justice and mercy, truth and grace reconciled.   2. None but he, who was both God and man, could render an obedience and suffer a curse so as to bring in such a righteousness.   Our Surety must be man to sympathize, and suffer, and obey.   He must be divine to supererogate, or to give infinite value to what he did and suffered.   Jesus Christ was called and anointed to the very end that he might be every way prepared for this work and this suffering, which have no parallel in the universe.   3. Such is the mystery of love and wisdom dis- played in this whole scheme that without the aid of the Holy Ghost no man would ever receive it, or in anywise credit the truth of it, 1 Cor. 2 : 14.   To each believer it becomes known by what Christ and Paul did not hesitate (and why should we hesi- tate?) to call a revelation, Luke 10 : 22; Gal. 1 : 16.   4. This righteousness is entire—wanting nothing; perfect—without spot or defect; complete—full in every particular.   If justice or con- science demands a sinless Surety, a spotless, bleeding victim, a holy faultless substitute both in keeping the law and in bearing its curse, behold the Lamb of God.   It was by his being made a curse for us, and in no other way that we are redeemed from the curse of the law, Gal. 3 : 13.   It was by his obedience to all the divine requirements that many are made righteous, Rom. 5 : 19. 5. This righteousness has no end.   It is infinite in duration.   It is an everlasting righteousness, Dan. 9 : 24.   And it is infinite in value. It cannot be exhausted. The righteousness, which superabounds at all, can have no limit. It is the peculiar glory of him who wrought it out and brought it in, that there is none like him, none with him, none beside him. His undertaking was unique. His glory is unparallelled. He deservedly has a name above every name.

This righteousness is *unto and upon* men, not within nor from them. It is not inherent, nor infused, nor imparted. But it is imputed, counted, reckoned to believers; for it is *of faith, through faith and by faith*, Rom. 4 : 11, 13 ; 9 : 30 ; Phil. 3 : 9. It is unto and upon them that believe, vs. 22, 25. Men are the children of God by faith in Christ Jesus, Gal. 3 : 26. This faith has Christ for its chief object. Nor has there ever been but this one way of salvation for sinners, vs. 21, 22. The Gospel was preached to Abraham, and by it all the saints have been justified. The Jew and the Gentile, the babe in Christ and the man of hoary head, the antediluvian and the last man that shall be saved all come to God, and obtain life in one and the same way. Hawker: "The Lord, whose righteousness it is, gives it to all with an equal hand, and loves all with an equal love, and justifies all with an equal freeness of grace. For it is not what they are in themselves, but what they are in CHRIST, which makes them the objects of the divine favor. . . He that hath little faith, and is in CHRIST, is as completely justified by CHRIST, as he that hath the largest portions of faith to apprehend with greater delight his mercies."

6. The portion of this epistle now under consideration casts much light on the right manner of preaching. It instructs us to shew men their sinful and ruined estate by nature, the impossibility of having any good standing before God by their own works of morality or of reformation, and then to proclaim a free and full salvation by grace alone, for rich and poor, rude and learned, polite and vulgar. Hodge: "All modes of preaching must be erroneous, which do not lead sinners to feel that the great thing to be done, and done first, is to receive the Lord Jesus Christ, and to turn to God through him. And all religious experience must be defective, which does not embrace distinctly a sense of the justice of our condemnation, and a conviction of the sufficiency of the work of Christ, and an exclusive reliance upon it as such." Ministers are not sent to amuse men with novelties, nor to show their own learning, ingenuity or oratory, nor to correct the philosophical, political or financial errors of mankind, but to proclaim the Gospel. "Preach the preaching that I bid thee." "What is the chaff to the wheat?"

7. Nor need there be any great diversity in the manner of an-

nouncing God's truth in different places. Climate, government, manners, rites, customs in a nation may produce some considerable outward effects. But in the matter of guilt, the necessity of the new birth and of a gratuitous justification, "there is no difference," v. 22. Never was a people found, to whom all the blessings of the Gospel were not suited and seasonable. Every one needs all that is promised.

8. Paul would have us never forget that depravity is universal, v. 23. He had before proven this at length, vs. 9–18.

9. Sad is the state of man, that in every sense of the phrase he has *come short of the glory of God*, v. 23. Should there be no remedy for this, utter ruin must follow.

10. Let us loudly and earnestly proclaim the doctrine of *free grace*, unbought mercy, undeserved favor, v. 24. The humble will hear it and be glad. The proud may be offended at it, but if anything can bring down their high looks, this will. At all events this doctrine is true, is taught by God, is found in all the Scriptures, is necessary to be believed, and, if rejected by men, they are left without excuse.

11. And with it let us bring forth the glories of *redemption*, v. 24. How can we ever bless God enough for such an expression of his love and kindness, his wisdom and condescension? Redemption will enter into the songs of the ransomed, while eternity endures. It was provided, when wrath might justly have been sent; when the whole plan must be devised, executed and applied by him, against whom man had sinned; when it cost more than could have been paid by any but a divine sufferer, and when the state of man was such that unless the Father should give him faith he would utterly reject all the mercy and grace offered in the gospel.

12. There is no mistake in the scriptural method of salvation. It is *set forth* by God himself, v. 25. Yes, he, who is the way, the truth and the life, has *declared* it.

13. Nor let us ever be offended but rather admire and adore, when we read and hear that all the salvation wrought for us is by *blood*, v. 25. "Without the shedding of blood there is no remission," Heb. 9 : 22. Olshausen: "As the vial of balsam, if it is to refresh all those who are in the house by the odor of its contents, must be opened and poured forth, so also did the Redeemer breathe forth into the dead world that fulness of life which was contained in him, by pouring forth his holy blood, the supporter of his life, and this voluntarily, since none could take his life from him, John 10 : 18." Brown: "Christ was a testator, and a testament is of no force until the testator die, Heb. 9 : 16, 17." The

best men know not which most to admire, the love of the Father in giving his Son, John 3 : 16; and in not sparing him, but delivering him up to death, Rom. 8 : 32; or the love of the Son in coming in the flesh, in suffering all his enemies could do to him, and in laying down his own life a ransom. Nor need such a point be settled, nor can it be determined. In either case we are lost among the infinites. None can gauge the compassion of God.

14. If men were duly sensible of their sad case by nature, sunk down as they are in guilt, pollution and misery, they surely would not stand carping and asking foolish questions, and sometimes venting blasphemies against the Father, Son and Holy Ghost, when we speak to them of the *remission of sins*, v. 25. Let us magnify the grace of God in the forgiveness of sins. 1. To how many sinners does he extend pardon. 2. How many sins in each case does he pardon. 3. How terribly aggravated are many of the sins remitted. They have been long persisted in. They have been committed against light, against vows, against warnings, against mercies, against convictions. 4. Jehovah remits our sins so freely, without money and without price. 5. Then God forgives for ever. His gifts are without repentance. 6. He so pardons as not to weaken government. His forgiveness is not connivance at sin; it is not hushing up a bad case; it is remission wholly consistent with righteousness. 7. It is not bare pardon. It is accompanied with acceptance, adoption, the indwelling of the Spirit and great grace. 8. It is followed by eternal glory.

15. Every thing is traced to God at last, v. 25. If Jesus Christ comes, he is sent of God. If a propitiation is made, it is made by divine arrangement and by a divine person. If righteousness is provided, it is the righteousness of God. " Of him, and through him, ánd to him, are all things; to whom be glory for ever. Amen," Rom. 11 : 36.

16. As God has very graciously set forth and declared his plan for man's salvation, so let us concur in this amazing benevolence and beneficence, and spread the good news and make known the joyful tidings in all their fulness. Let us be imitators of God, vs. 25, 26. In particular let us hold forth the truth that the salvation of the Gospel is all the richer because it is not in derogation of justice. Clarke: " Because Jesus was an *atonement*, a *ransom price* for the sin of the world, therefore God can consistently with his *justice*, pardon every soul that believeth in Jesus." This is the only way of salvation that duly honors the spotless purity, and inflexible justice of God. All others represent the saving of the sinner as in some way a conniving at sin. Some are so opposed to the idea of punishing sin in the person of Christ, and so averse

to the doctrine of divine justice in all things that for *just* in v. 26 they propose to read clement or merciful. This is sufficiently answered by Whitby, who says that the word, rendered *just*, "is used about eighty times in the New Testament, and not once in the sense of clemency." Hodge: "In the Gospel all is harmonious; justice and mercy, as it regards God; freedom from the law and the strongest obligations to obedience, as it regards men." And herein is a marvellous thing revealed to us, not merely that "God should be faithful to his promises, and merciful, when justifying believers. But that he should be *just* in such an act, might have seemed incredible, had we not received such an account of the atonement."

17. And here comes up fairly and prominently the doctrine of justification, v. 27. No subject is more important; for Luther truly says: "The article of justification being lost, all Christian doctrine perishes with it." This witness is true. Let us then look a little into this matter. Remarks offered on v. 23 need not be here repeated. See on that place. One rarely meets with a better definition than this: "Justification is an act of God's free grace wherein he pardoneth all our sins, and accepteth us as righteous in his sight, only for the righteousness of Christ imputed to us, and received by faith alone." 1. Justification is an act, not a work or series of acts. It is a sentence passed by God, an acquittal of one, who has been under condemnation. It is perfect in itself. It is not progressive. Every man is wholly justified or wholly condemned—either in favor with God, or out of favor with God. There is no middle ground. 2. Justification is an act of *God*. He is the *justifier*, v. 26. See also v. 30. "It is God that justifieth," Rom. 8 : 33. The reasons are obvious. (*A*) It is God's law that is violated and God's government that is insulted by sinners, and he only has jurisdiction. (*B*) He alone is competent to decide when, how and upon what grounds transgressors may be restored to the divine favor. (*C*) From all the awards of men, all judgments of mortals there lies an appeal to the tribunal of God and there human judgments may be reversed. But the sentence of justification cannot be set aside, because it is pronounced by a tribunal from which lies no appeal. The Homily of the Church of England on this subject justly says: "Justification is the office of God only, and is not a thing which we render unto him, but which we receive of him." (*D*) God is one and will not deny himself. He is of one mind, and who can turn him? Job 23 : 13. "I am God, and there is none else; I am God, and there is none like me, declaring the end from the beginning, and from ancient times the things that are not yet done, saying, my counsel shall

stand, and I will do all my pleasure," Isa. 46 : 9, 10. The sentence of justification is therefore irreversible. What if Satan and the whole world shall hate, and curse, and accuse the believer, his judgment is with his God. It is a small matter to such a one to have his name cast out as evil. 3. Justification is an act of God's *free grace*. So says Paul : " Justified freely by his grace," v. 24. Eternal life is the *gift* of God, Rom. 6 : 23. Compare Rom. 5 : 16–19 ; 1 Cor. 6 : 11 ; Eph. 2 : 7–10; Tit. 3 : 5–7. If man's justification were not wholly gratuitous, it would not be possible, for he has broken the law. He is a sinner. He is by nature justly condemned by a law that is holy, just and good. By human merits, by works of law, by the deeds of the law shall no flesh, no man living he justified in the sight of God, Rom. 3 : 20; Gal. 2 : 16. From first to last a sinner's justification is of grace. Nor is this grace less free or less glorious because it is bestowed entirely through the channel of Christ's priesthood ; for it was God that gave Christ as a surety, that accepted his work, that for his sake remits sins and that bestows the very faith, with which men believe. So that it is all of God's grace. The Lord justifies the ungodly, Rom. 4 : 5 ; because Christ died for the ungodly, Rom. 5 : 6. Even Macknight admits that Paul's " plain meaning is, that men are justified by faith, and not meritoriously, by perfect obedience to any law whatever." Nor should we ever forget that all men are guilty. " For," says Haldane, " if there had been any excepted, there would have been two different methods of justification, and consequently two true religions, and two true churches, and believers would not have had that oneness of communion, which grace produces." 4. In justification there is granted a full pardon of all sins. (A) If one sin remained unforgiven, it would blast all hope. It is expressly said of him that he " forgiveth all thine iniquities," Ps. 103 : 3. This forgiveness therefore is total. (B) It is effectual, " In those days, and in that time, saith the Lord, the iniquity of Israel shall be sought for, and there shall be none ; and the sins of Judah, and they shall not be found : for I will pardon them whom I reserve," Jer. 50 : 20. (C) This justification is not granted on account of any thing in man. God is self-moved to the whole thing : " I, even I, am he that blotteth out thy transgressions *for my own sake*, and will not remember thy sins," Isa. 43 : 25. (D) This pardon is expressed in a great variety of ways, such as not imputing, not remembering, taking away, removing, scattering like a thick cloud, washing, cleansing, burying, blotting out, remitting, hiding the face from beholding, etc. All this pardon is by the blood of the covenant, the blood of Christ. On this point the Scripture is full and clear. See above on v. 26.

So important is the Scriptural doctrine of the forgiveness of sins, and so much is said of it, that there have not been wanting a set of divines, who have maintained that pardon was the whole of justification. But the Scriptures so clearly teach the contrary and the friends of sound theology have been so earnest in maining the true doctrine that even Mr. Barnes, whom none will suspect of seeking too much after old ideas, in a tract on Justification says: " Justification in the gospel does not mean mere pardon. It has been supposed by many that this is all that is denoted by it. But there are insuperable objections to this opinion. One is that it is a departure from the common use of language. When a man who has been sentenced to the penitentiary is pardoned before the term of his sentence is expired, we never think of saying that he is justified. The offence is forgiven and the penalty is remitted; but the use of the word *justify* in his case would convey a very different idea from the word pardon. Another objection is that the sacred writers have so carefully and so constantly used the word *justify*. If mere pardon or forgiveness were all that is intended, it is difficult to see why another word has been constantly employed, and a word so different in its signification. And another objection is, that mere forgiveness is *not* all that the case seems to demand. There was required a reinstating in the favor of God ; a restoration to forfeited immunities and privileges, and a purpose in regard to future treatment which is not necessarily involved in the word pardon."

Indeed mere pardon leaves a sinner for ever to stand naked before God. It grants him no robe of righteousness. Nor would it ever meet all the demands of an enlightened conscience.

It is therefore a doctrine full of comfort that,

5. The believer is not only forgiven. He is also taken into favor —"accepted in the Beloved." His standing is good before God. " God is not ashamed to be called his God," Heb. 11 : 16; and though he suffer, he is not ashamed, 2 Tim. 1 : 12. He is a friend, a child, an heir, an heir of God, and a joint heir with Christ. Perfect pardon would save one from hell. It would give him no title to heaven. It would take off our chains, but it would put ho rings on our fingers. It would turn the rebel loose, but it would give him no ticket to the king's table. It would lift the curse, but it would of itself give us no *authority to become the sons of God,* no *right to the tree of life,* John 1 : 12 ; Rev. 22 : 14. The redeemed are not held for ever in the state of mere abjects, no, nor of abjects at all. By grace through righteousness they have a title to heaven. That righteousness is the righteousness of Christ, 2 Pet. 1 : 1, and is their own by a gracious gift, and to all the ends of a complete

justification. See above on verses 22, 25, 26, and the extended statement of this righteousness in *Doctrinal and Practical Remarks* No. 4 of this section. 6. This righteousness is made ours by the *imputation* of God. In the next section this subject will be distinctly brought up by the apostle himself, Rom. 4 : 3, 5, 6, 8. It is wholly idle for men to endeavor to cover this doctrine with odium and to overthrow it by saying that we claim to be saved by a *putative* or supposed, and not by a real righteousness; or to assert that the term *imputed* is not a fit term because unintelligible; or that we can better express the Scripture doctrine in some other way. There is no more mystery in imputing righteousness than in imputing sin. But see the next section. 7. The righteousness of Christ is received by faith alone. On the nature and office of faith see above on Rom. 1 : 8, 12, 17. When we say by faith *alone*, we mean to say that our reception of it is by faith, not by love, not by patience, not by repentance, nor by any other grace; nor by works, which we have done or can do. Faith is a receiving grace, John 1 : 12. Its office is to take Christ as he is freely offered, in all the fulness of his merits, in all the blessedness of his mediation. Calvin : " You now see how the righteousness of faith is the righteousness of Christ. When therefore we are justified, the efficient cause is the mercy of God, the meritorious cause is Christ, the instrumental cause is the word in connection with faith. Hence faith is said to justify, because it is the instrument by which we receive Christ, in whom righteousness is conveyed to us." How sadly therefore does a modern writer pervert the true doctrine of justification when he says that " we are justified by faith and holiness ; " for what is holiness but conformity to law, the very law which we have broken, and which denounces curses on him who has sinned even once? James 2 : 10. Such teaching presents altogether another scheme and has no countenance from God's word. From such error how pleasant it is to turn away to such a sentence as this from Tholuck : " By the believing appropriation of that, which Jesus Christ, during the whole course of his blessed life, until it terminated in his bloody death, was, and did, for the human race, men are made partakers of justification before God." O yes! This is our life. Brown : " There is such a privilege vouchsafed upon sinners who have fled in to Christ by faith, as justification, whereby they get their iniquities and transgressions pardoned, only because of the propitiation which Christ made by his bloody sacrifice ; so as they are accepted of as righteous, not for any thing in themselves, or done by them, but allenarly by the righteousness of Christ, imputed to us, and accepted by faith."

18. The whole aim of the gospel plan is to exalt God and abase man, v. 27. What say you, Dear Reader, to such a result? Do you approve it? Your temper here is decisive. Scott: "The apostle decides that all boasting by any of the human race is excluded, and can have no admission, in consistency with truth and justice." Does such a view offend you? or do you glory in it that while you justly lose all self-gratulation, Christ rises higher and higher? Are you satisfied, if Christ is glorified?

19. When first principles or leading truths in religion are settled, hold on to them, v. 28. Never let them go. Let the state of your mind be a rational, fixed, unalterable *conclusion*. This is not obstinacy, nor prejudice. It is practical wisdom.

20. Any scheme of religious belief, which represents Jehovah as a partial God is false, and is dishonorable to him, v. 29. He is kind to all. His tender mercies are over all. He sends rain and sun and zephyrs and food to all. He is Lord of all. Chrysostom: "The same is the Master of both these and those." Hodge: "God is a universal Father, and all men are brethren." No people need pique themselves on their privileges, as though oracles and ordinances had made or would make them better, without saving faith in Christ Jesus.

21. The unity of God is a great truth and of great use, v. 30. It should never be doubted. It is necessary to be believed on many accounts. If God is not one, divine counsels cannot be harmonious, moral government cannot be every where the same, and the mode of worship by one mediator cannot be suited to all. In short error on this point is fundamental, for "there is one God and one Mediator between God and man, the man Christ Jesus," 1 Tim. 2 : 5.

22. We need not fear to publish the doctrines of free grace and abounding mercy in the most earnest manner, lest we should weaken the respect of men for the law of God, v. 31. The Almighty can vindicate his own honor and maintain the dignity of his own government, without our assistance. Our wisdom and our business is to obey his will and proclaim his readiness to save and bless all penitent sinners. Olshausen: "The gospel establishes the law, because it is the most sublime manifestation of the holiness and strictness of God. Sin never appears more fearful than at Golgotha; where, on account of it, God spared not his own Son." Calvin: "Let us bear in mind so to dispense the Gospel that by our mode of teaching, the law may be confirmed; but let it be sustained by no other strength than that of faith in Christ." Chrysostom: "Three things Paul has demonstrated, first, that without the law it is possible to be justified, next, that this the

law could not effect, and that faith is not opposed to the law."
Bengel : "This is the great evangelical paradox, for in the law God
is seen to be just while he condemns, in the gospel just while he
justifies sinners." Brown : "Licentious spirits, who love not to
be bound by the law of God, liking rather to walk according to
the lusts of their own heart, are ready to turn the grace of God
into lasciviousness, and to suck rank poison from the most comfortable points of truth. . . It is no new thing to see men of corrupt minds, loving to follow pernicious principles, smoothing over
their corrupt opinions with fair and specious colors, and pretend-
ing a gospel privilege warranting them thereto, and so with fair
shews of reason and plausible pretexts, hide their damnable and
soul-destroying designs and practices." Scott : "Whatever
Pharisees, Sadducees, or infidels may object ; whatever Antino-
mians, or Enthusiasts may plead, or profess ; the doctrine of faith
establishes the law in its real honor, and lays the true foundation
for all holy obedience ; and this doctrine alone 'establishes the
law.' "

23. How wondrously the undertaking of Christ exalts him
and endears him to his saints. Even here they admire the everlasting bulwarks of strength, with which he has surrounded Zion.
Hawker : "PRECIOUS LORD JESUS, be thou my propitiation, my
high priest, my altar, the Lord my righteousness now ; and sure
I am thou wilt be my everlasting glory."

NOTE. I cannot forbear to call the reader's attention to the
last ten or twelve pages of Chrysostom's Seventh Homily on this
epistle. It is searching ; it is eloquent, it is eminently practical ; it
breathes that exalted spirit of a noble nature, refined by grace, for
which he was so remarkable. Portions of it would have been
here quoted, but it was found to be best as a whole.

Chapter 8

ROMANS 4
VERSES 1–15

PAUL CONTINUES HIS ARGUMENT, GIVES THE EXAMPLES OF ABRAHAM AND THE TESTIMONY OF DAVID, AND SHEWS THAT RITES NEVER JUSTIFIED.

W HAT shall we say then that Abraham our father, as pertaining to the flesh, hath found ?

2 For if Abraham were justified by works, he hath *whereof* to glory ; but not before God.

3 For what saith the Scripture ? Abraham believed God, and it was counted unto him for righteousness.

4 Now to him that worketh is the reward not reckoned of grace, but of debt.

5 But to him that worketh not, but believeth on him that justifieth the ungodly, his faith is counted for righteousness.

6 Even as David also describeth the blessedness of the man, unto whom God imputeth righteousness without works,

7 *Saying*, Blessed *are* they whose iniquities are forgiven, and whose sins are covered.

8 Blessed *is* the man to whom the Lord will not impute sin.

9 *Cometh* this blessedness then upon the circumcision *only*, or upon the uncircumcision also ? for we say that faith was reckoned to Abraham for righteousness.

10 How was it then reckoned ? when he was in circumcision or in uncircumcision ? Not in circumcision, but in uncircumcision.

11 And he received the sign of circumcision, a seal of the righteousness of the faith which *he had yet* being uncircumcised : that he might be the father of all them that believe, though they be not circumcised ; that righteousness might be imputed unto them also :

12 And the father of circumcision to them who are not of the circumcision only, but who also walk in the steps of that faith of our father Abraham, which *he had* being *yet* uncircumcised.

13 For the promise, that he should be the heir of the world, *was* not to Abraham, or to his seed, through the law, but through the righteousness of faith.

14 For if they which are of the law *be* heirs, faith is made void, and the promise made of none effect :

15 Because the law worketh wrath : for where no law is, *there is* no transgression.

1. *WHAT shall we say then, that Abraham our father as pertaining to the flesh, hath found?* The connection with the preceding argument is marked by the particle rendered *then;* q. d. if we maintain such doctrine respecting the necessity of a gratuitous justification, without any human merits, what shall we say of the case of Abraham? The general tone of the verse is not very different from that of Rom. 3 : 1, 3, 5. It is virtually, perhaps not formally, the language of an objector. *As pertaining to the flesh* is the most difficult clause in the verse. Our version connects it with *father*. This is supported by Chrysostom, Theophylact, Vulgate, Erasmus, Limborch, Wiclif, Coverdale, Tyndale, Cranmer, Genevan, Rheims, Doway, Calvin, Doddridge, Locke and others. Not a few put it, as in some of the best MSS., after *hath found*. This reading is sustained by the original, Peshito, Arabic, Beza, Ferme, Piscator, Brown, Evans, Hammond, Whitby, Macknight, Olshausen, Haldane, Conybeare and Howson, Hodge and others. If the collocation of words in the authorized version is correct, the phrase merely teaches that the Jews, of whom Paul was one, were of the lineage of Abraham. If the latter view is right (and probably it is) then the word *flesh* must have another meaning. Dutch Annotations : " Some take this word *flesh* for the state of an unregenerate man : but that cannot be here, because Abraham was regenerated long before, and had served God, before this testimony in Gen. 15 : 6 was given." Nor is the explanation of Diodati that *flesh* means " considered in himself, in his own natural state," free from objection. Wetstein, Michaelis and Clarke think *flesh* here refers to the sign of circumcision in Abraham's flesh. Circumcision was probably included in the apostle's idea. But may we not give a more extended meaning to the term *flesh?* In more than one place in Scripture *flesh* seems to designate carnal ordinances—all those in which a Jew was apt to value himself, Gal. 6 : 12; Phil. 3 : 3–6. Compare Heb. 7 : 16; 9 : 10. But at least once Paul by *flesh* seems to understand *works of the law*, Gal. 3 : 2, 3. Hammond thinks that in our verse *as pertaining to the flesh* means the same as *by works* in v. 2. For the various significations of the term *flesh* see above on Rom. 3 : 20. If we are right thus far, then we may read the verse as Peshito : " What then shall we say concerning Abraham the patriarch, that by the flesh he obtained?" or with Hammond, " What shall we say then? shall we say that Abraham our father found according to the flesh?" *Found*, in Heb. 9 : 12 *obtained;* in Luke 9 : 12 *got*, i. e. secured, or obtained. We have the same verb in Luke 1 : 30; Heb. 4 : 16 *find* grace; in 2 Tim. 1 : 18 *find* mercy; in Acts 17 : 27 *find* God; in Matt. 10 : 39 *find* life. In the

verse something is to be supplied.   Hath Abraham found life, or acceptance, or justification by the flesh, or by works?   Beza fairly states the course of argument: " In whatever way Abraham, the father of believers was justified, in the same must all his children (that is, all believers) be justified ; but Abraham was not justified, and made the father of the faithful, by any of his own works, either preceding or following his faith in Christ."   The verse is in the form of interrogatory or perhaps challenge.   If a question is asked, the answer is supposed to be in the negative.   If a challenge is given, silence is the proper sequent.

2. *For if Abraham were justified by works, he hath* whereof *to glory : but not before God.*   This verse also is elliptical.   The sense is that if Abraham were justified by works, he had cause for boasting ; but it can be shown that, however distinguished among believers, he had no such cause of boasting *before God.*   Calvin : " He calls that glorying when we pretend to have any thing of our own to which a reward is supposed to be due at God's tribunal."   Macknight gives the sense of the verse in his paraphrase : " *For if Abraham were justified* meritoriously *by works* of any kind, *he might boast* that his justification is no favor, but a debt due to him : *But* such a ground of boasting he hath not *before God.*"   And this the apostle at once proceeds to prove.

3. *For what saith the Scripture ?   Abraham believed God, and it was counted unto him for righteousness.*   The sacred writer here relied on is Moses himself, whom all the Jews professed to receive as an infallible witness.   This testimony is found in Gen. 15 : 6, and is given without any change (except in the connecting particle) from the Septuagint version, which differs slightly in form, though not in import, from the Hebrew, and not more than the English version here differs from that in Gen. 15 : 6.   *Scripture,* see above on Rom. 1 : 2.   *Believed,* see above on Rom. 1 : 8, 12, 17.   *Righteousness,* see above Doctrinal and Practical Remark No. 4 on Rom. 3 : 21, 22, 25, 26.   Here we meet with the verb *was counted,* in the sense of reckoned or imputed.   It occurs in ten other places in this chapter in the same sense, see vs. 4, 5, 6, 8, 9, 10, 11, 22, 23, 24.   It cannot be denied that the whole argument of this chapter turns very much on a right understanding of this term.   On the meaning of it see the author's " *Studies in the Book of Psalms,*" on Ps. 32 : 2, p. 398.   The Greek word rendered *impute* sometimes means to number, count, esteem, think, reason, conclude and then to reckon, impute,. set to the account or lay to the charge of one.   The corresponding Hebrew word has a yet wider range of rendering, according to its connections, but in two conjugations is fitly rendered impute, in the sense of reckon, count, account.

The word occurs often.   There is seldom cause of reasonable
doubt as to the fit rendering in any given case.   We get our word
impute from the Latin.   Its classical use assigns to it these significations, to impute, ascribe, charge, lay blame, account, reckon.
Its theological use as fully authorizes us to employ it in the sense
of imputing merit as blame.   The English word *impute* has the
same significations, to reckon, ascribe, attribute, set to the account
of one, to reckon to one what does not belong to him.   So that in
Hebrew, Greek, Latin and English you will seldom find a word
better understood.   A few things are very noticeable here.   1.
Although we certainly know that there were pious men before
Abraham, as Abel, Enoch and Noah, yet the man whose justification is first distinctly and formally stated in scripture is Abraham.
2. His justification is not simply announced as a fact, but the
means and ground of it are given.   3. In verses 23, 24 of this same
chapter we are told that this is a model case, a real pattern for the
instruction of men in all coming ages: " Now it was not written
for his sake alone, that it was imputed to him ; but for us also, to
whom it shall be imputed, if we believe" etc.   Abraham was the
father of all believers, Rom. 3 : 11, 16.   4. This justification is expressly said to be by *counting* him as righteous, or by imputing
righteousness to him.   5. In this same epistle Paul twice informs
us that the fatal mistake of the Jews was their rejection of the very
righteousness here said to have been imputed to their great ancestor, Rom. 9 : 31 ; 10 : 3, 4.   6. As a historic fact it is true that
for three hundred years past the great enemies of the doctrine of
imputed righteousness have been Romanists, who hold to the
merit of penance, and to justification by grace infused, and Socinians and other enemies of the divinity and vicarious atonement of
Jesus Christ.   There is no risk in asserting that for three centuries there has not been a respectable body of Protestant Christians, who have hesitated to receive and adopt the doctrine of
human salvation by the righteousness of Christ imputed to believers.   See the Creeds and Confessions.

What then is imputation?   1. There is an imputation by mistake.   Thus Judah *thought* Tamar to be a harlot, and Eli *thought*
Hannah was drunk.   In each of these cases we have the same
word rendered *impute* in many places.   2. Then we have imputation from malice, or passion or contempt.   Thus those that dwelt
in Job's house and his maids *counted* him for a stranger, Job 19 :
15.   That is they regarded and treated him as if he were a stranger.   The word is the same we render *impute*.   But God never
thus imputes either sin or righteousness.   He makes no mistakes ;
he is never moved by passion or caprice.   When he imputes, he

does no wrong.   3. There is a just imputation of that which
fairly belongs to one. " Behold, the nations are as a drop of a
bucket, and are *counted* as the small dust of a balance ... All nations
before him are as nothing, and they are *counted* to him less than
nothing, and vanity," Isa. 40 : 15, 17.   That is, God reckons or imputes to them the insignificance that really belongs to them.   So
Shimei said to David : " Let not my Lord *impute* iniquity unto me,
neither do thou remember that which thy servant did perversely,"
&c. 2 Sam. 19 : 19.   He admits such imputation would be just.
He deserved ill treatment.   He had acted perversely.   Such imputation is but counting to a man that which is already his own,
and so is a simple judgment according to truth and a corresponding course of conduct.   Jacob said : " My righteousness shall answer for me," Gen. 30 : 33.   4. Then on account of one's relations
sometimes that, which is not properly his own, may be imputed to
him.   Thus a man is held and treated as a debtor when his foolish
or wicked partner wastes the property of the firm, or makes ruinous adventures in trade, even when he violates the terms of co-
partnership.   Or one is held and treated as a wise man and a
great merchant when all his success is due to the foresight of another, who had control.   Thus the Israelites bore the sins of their
fathers, Num. 14 : 33.   Thus the first sin of the first Adam is imputed to his posterity because in the covenant he stood for them
and they sinned in him and fell with him.   5. One may become the
willing surety of another, and so be fairly held responsible for his
debts, his fines, or his misconduct.   Thus Paul writes to Philemon
that if Onesimus " hath wronged thee, or oweth thee aught, put
that on mine account," v. 18 ; literally *impute* it to me.   From this
time forth Paul was by his own willing act and promise bound to
make good all damages previously done to Philemon by Onesimus.
Thus also Christ became the surety of his people, and God " laid
on him the iniquity of us all."   So that Isaiah is very bold and
says : " Surely he hath borne our griefs, and carried our sorrows ;
he was wounded for our transgressions, he was bruised for our iniquities ; the chastisement of our peace was upon him ; and with
his stripes we are healed."   And because he was our surety and
substitute, " it pleased the Lord to bruise him," to " put him to
grief," and to " make his soul an offering for sin," Isa. 53 : 4, 6, 10.
Nor is Paul less bold.   He says that God " hath made him to be
sin for us," 2 Cor. 5 : 21.   And yet he is careful to tell us that even
then Christ was personally innocent.   He " knew no sin."   6.
Then there is the imputation of Christ's righteousness to his people.   They are " made the righteousness of God in him," 2 Cor. 5 :
21.   In the eye of God's law they share his righteousness, are joint-

heirs with him, are in him the children of God by faith.   7. Imputation does not of itself change the character, but only the relations
of men.   Christ was as holy and personally as pleasing to God,
after our sins were laid upon him, as he had ever been or ever shall
be ; but by that imputation he became the great sin-bearer, and so
was obnoxious to the sword of justice, the wrath of God.   And
when one receives Christ by faith, he does it as a believing *sinner*,
as one in himself *ungodly*, Rom. 4 : 5.   Jesus Christ did in no sense
commit the sins that were laid upon him ; nor do believers in any
sense work out the righteousness which justifies them, for it is the
righteousness of God ; yea, it is "the righteousness of God and
our Saviour Jesus Christ," 2 Pet. 1 : 1.   He imputes it to them,
regards and treats them as kindly and lovingly and gloriously as
if they had wrought out their own righteousness.   Yet neither have
they on that account any just cause of increased self-esteem, any
just sense of personal worthiness, any ground for *boasting;* as
Christ their surety had no remorse, no sense of personal ill-desert
before God, when the iniquity of us all was laid upon him.   He
knew that his whole course was pleasing to his Father, for he said,
"I know that thou hearest me always," and twice did a voice from
heaven proclaim, "This is my beloved Son, in whom I am well
pleased."   The imputation of our sins to Christ was no mistake,
no erroneous judgment, but a gracious act of God in accordance
with the voluntary undertaking of Christ; nor is the imputation
of Christ's righteousness to his people, whereby they are justified,
a false estimate, an erroneous judgment passed on them, but a gracious reckoning of the Redeemer's merits to their account.   8. It
is impossible that any righteousness imperfect in God's esteem
should justify any creature in his sight.   If it could, it would be
an acknowledgment either that the precept of the law was too
strict or that the penalty was too rigorous, and so God had consented to some abatement or relaxation of his requirements.   And
this would be denying and contradicting himself.   This consideration alone shows that God cannot accept the act of faith itself as
a meritorious ground of justification, for in every case that faith is
imperfect.   Besides it is the gift of God.   Nor is it so great a
grace as love, 1 Cor. 13 : 13, and therefore it cannot by reason of
its own nature be entitled to such pre-eminence as to justify.
Abraham himself was justified by faith in the merits of the Redeemer.   Jesus says : "Abraham saw my day and was glad,"
John 8 : 56.   9. The only way, in which faith can justify a sinner
before God, is by laying hold of the righteousness of Christ, receiving it, and appropriating it according to the free and gracious
offer of God to reckon it to all, who heartily accept it.   Thus every

demand of the law is met in the righteousness of Christ. This is the sense in which the Christian world has long held this doctrine, so precious to the people of God, and to none less than the glorious martyrs. 10. By this imputation the righteousness of Christ is so reckoned to the believer that it becomes his, not by infusion nor by any transfer of moral character, which is absurd and impossible, but his to all the ends of a complete justification. Owen: "This imputation is an act of God, of his mere love and grace, whereby on the consideration of the mediation of Christ, he makes an effectual grant and donation of a true, real, perfect righteousness, even that of Christ himself unto all that do believe, and accounting it as theirs, on his own gracious act, both absolves them from sin, and granteth them right and title unto eternal life." Well does he add: "To say that the righteousness of Christ, that is, his obedience and sufferings are imputed unto us only as unto their effects, is to say that we have the benefit of them, and no more; but imputation itself is denied. So say the Socinians, but they know well enough, and ingenuously grant that they overthrow all real imputation thereby." Again: "To say the righteousness of Christ is not imputed unto us, only its effects are so, is really to overthrow all imputation," It is like saying that all the warmth and ornament of a robe shall be ours, but the robe itself we must not wear. 11. This righteousness is indeed imputed to us by a most gracious act on the part of God. It is wholly a gift, but it is a gift which God will not revoke, Rom. 11 : 29, or, as Owen says, it is "an effectual grant and donation." All, that men justly put a high value upon, is enjoyed by the gift of God. Life, reason, understanding, parents, children, friends, health, food, raiment belong to us by his donation. We have no better right to any of them than this, that God freely bestowed them on us. These are gifts in the order of nature, granted to men out of God's sovereign bounty, as governor of the world, and bestowed alike on saints and sinners; but the gift of righteousness imputed to us is an act of special grace, the fruit of redeeming love. We can have and we need no better title to any thing than that it is freely given us of God through Jesus Christ. 12. By this imputed righteousness we have *power*, authority, right to become the sons of God ; by it we have *right*, title, authority to the tree of life, John 1 : 12; Rev. 22 : 14. 13. We may now see why the Scriptures everywhere speak of God's people as the just, the righteous, and not merely as those that are treated as if they were righteous. Yea more, they allow saints to speak of *our* Lord Jesus Christ, and not merely of the Lord Jesus Christ. Even the Old Testament gives to the Redeemer this title—" The Lord *our* righteousness." How then dare

any one say that Christ's righteousness is in no proper sense
ours? The opposite of *proper* is *figurative*. Have believers naught
but a figurative or typical interest in Christ? Let us beware of a
doctrine so contrary to Scripture, so destructive of solid grounds
of comfort in the hearts of the pious, and so contrary to the faith
of God's elect.

We can now fully understand our apostle when he says that
Abraham's faith was counted to him for righteousness, or unto
righteousness, as we have it in Rom. 10 : 10; or in order to righteousness, as Doddridge renders it. Abraham was not justified by
the flesh, by works, by anything that could allow him to boast
before God. And yet he was fully justified. His guilt was
removed. Pardoned sin is no ground of condemnation; else pardon is no more pardon. The only legal obstruction to the salvation of sinners is found in the penalty of God's law, but Christ has
borne that, as the scriptures expressly state, Gal. 3 : 13; and so,
on accepting Christ, that obstruction no longer remains. All
guilt is removed by the accepted sacrifice of Calvary. Jesus
exhausted the penalty on the cross. The believer is also accepted,
regarded and treated as righteous. His righteousness, received
by faith and imputed by God, is perfect, is all the law demands;
it is the spotless righteousness of our substitute. Thus Christ is
the end of the law for righteousness to every one that believeth,
Rom. 10 : 4.

If, as some contend, faith itself is taken as the ground of acceptance, then what is the meaning of all those passages that say we
are saved by Christ's blood, by his propitiation, by his sacrifice, by
his intercession? And that we are not justified by works of any
kind, legal or evangelical, moral or ceremonial, has been abundantly declared. See above on Rom. 3 : 20. Nor is it true that
we are ever said to be saved on account of our faith, but by it or
through it as the instrument. If we are justified by faith itself as
a righteousness, it is absurd to speak of the righteousness of God,
or righteousness by faith. It is monstrous, therefore, to find men
exalting faith to the rank of a meritorious righteousness, a work to
be rewarded with eternal life. In the succeeding context Paul
argues to the contrary.

4. *Now to him that worketh is the reward not reckoned of grace,
but of debt.* By *him that worketh* some understand him whose
works are perfect before God. Such a one no doubt would be
accepted as in himself righteous. He would not be saved by
grace. But there is no such mere man. Others think that by him
that worketh is meant him, who doeth any work. This is more in
the line of Paul's argument. He has shown that debt and grace

are distinct and different, yea that they are irreconcilable, as schemes of good standing before God. He, who does anything and relies on it for righteousness, renounces all hope of gratuitous justification. All he asks is to have his dues paid him. Abraham *found* or obtained righteousness not by his sweet submissive virtues, nor by his superior confidence in God, nor by anything that he could claim as ground of self-exaltation. He did not hold that God was in his "*debt.*"

5. *But to him that worketh not, but believeth on him that justifieth the ungodly, his faith is counted for righteousness. To him that worketh not*, i. e. worketh not in the hope of being thereby justified, but simply *believeth on him that justifieth the ungodly*, one who admits that all his own righteousnesses are as filthy rags, and that he has nothing in himself, whereof to glory before God, and yet looks to Christ alone, his faith is counted unto righteousness. That, which he presents before God as a ground of acceptance, that on which he relies for justification, is so perfect that it meets all the demands of God's infinite law. God looks upon him as in himself lost, ruined, *ungodly*, as he certainly is; yet on this ungodly man accepting the Saviour he is justified. To all the ends and purposes of justification no sinner does anything meritorious. The believer looks away from himself. In the matter of justification his best doings are in fact and in his own esteem, utterly worthless. Even if his obedience now and henceforth were sinless, it is all due to God, and can in no way make amends for past deficiencies, Luke 17 : 10. To pardon and accept a sinner as righteous is a favor wholly undeserved—is purely a gratuity. The word rendered *ungodly* is found nine times in the New Testament, is everywhere rendered as here, and beyond a doubt designates a wicked man. Such is every sinful child of Adam until he believes. Then and not till then does he cease to be ungodly; then and not till then is he invested with the robe of the Redeemer's righteousness, and his heart changed, and he turned unto God. Not only has he no merits, but he has in himself great demerits. Christ is all our salvation. All this is illustrated in the case of Abraham. The same truth is taught in other scriptures;

6. *Even as David also describeth the blessedness of the man, unto whom God imputeth righteousness without works.* David was a great warrior, a good king, the sweet singer of Israel, the man after God's heart, chosen by Jehovah to be Saul's successor, because God saw in him something well fitting him to be the ruler of Israel, 1 Sam. 16 : 6–13. He was a prophet, and a type and lineal ancestor of Christ. Next to Abraham and Moses he was probably the most prominent in the habitual thoughts of the Jews. What

is David's testimony respecting justification and the ground of it? It is all in the same direction—a gratuitous justification by imputed righteousness, righteousness without works.

David's sad fall is commemorated by two penitential psalms, the 32d and the 51st. Paul's reference here is to the 32d. On turning to it, we do not find in any part of the psalm the word righteousness. Perhaps it is well we do not. Paul was inspired not only to write new scriptures but to interpret Old Testament books. Peter's interpretations of scripture on the day of Pentecost have by the church of God ever been regarded as of infallible authority. And so Paul's exposition of the true meaning of the prophet David is infallible. Accepting this as correct, these things certainly follow: 1. The doctrine of salvation by grace alone, or, which is the same thing, the doctrine of gratuitous justification by imputed righteousness was understood and devoutly celebrated by the great poet and prophet David. 2. He taught that justification was *without works*. So says Paul. He means not only works of one kind, but of every kind, legal, evangelical, moral, ceremonial, done before justification or after justification. Calvin thus begins his commentary on this verse: " We hence see the sheer sophistry of those who limit the works of the law to ceremonies; for he now simply calls those works, without anything added, which he had before called the works of the law. Since no one can deny that a simple and unrestricted mode of speaking, such as we find here, ought to be understood of every work without any difference, the same view must be held throughout the argument. There is indeed nothing less reasonable than to remove from ceremonies only the power of justifying, since Paul excludes all works indefinitely." 3. Justification does not consist wholly and solely in the pardon of sin, or in the non-imputation of sin. Paul infallibly informs us that when David wrote that ode he taught more than the great doctrine of the forgiveness of sins. 4. Paul declares that David taught the doctrine of *imputed righteousness*. He uses the very phrase. Yea more, he says this has always in the church of God been to pious souls a precious doctrine. " David describeth the blessedness of the man, unto whom God imputeth righteousness." And that we may certainly know that Paul is not citing some other part of scripture he proceeds to quote the 1st and 2d verses of the 32d Psalm. *Imputeth*, the same verb found in vs. 3, 4, 5, 9, 10 and rendered *counted* or *reckoned ;* and in vs. 8, 11, 22, 23, 24, and rendered *impute*. The *righteousness* thus imputed is the righteousness so long celebrated in the church on earth and the church in heaven. It is the righteousness of God. Peter calls it "the righteousness of God and our Saviour Jesus Christ." Humble men, good men have long made mention of that and of that only. If the reader would put the right value on this verse he must remember that although in parts of Ps. 32 David speaks of his personal experience, yet in the verses here cited by Paul, he speaks of all believers.   Nor did he utter these truths of himself, but God was speaking *by the mouth of his servant David*, Acts 4 : 26.   Let all flesh listen, cease cavilling and be wise.

7. *Saying, Blessed* are *they whose iniquities are forgiven, and whose sins are covered.*   There is no significancy in having here the plural instead of the singular as in the original, or *they* instead of *he*. The apostle closely follows the Septuagint.   *Blessed*, the Hebrew is a plural noun, "O the blessednesses."   The Septuagint, which Paul here quotes, is literally "Happy."   It is the same word rendered blessed in Matt. 5 : 3–11.   *Iniquities*, the word has not before occurred in this epistle.   It is found fifteen times in the Greek Testament, is commonly rendered iniquity, once unrighteousness, 2 Cor. 6: 14, once transgression, 1 John 3 : 4.   It literally means *want of conformity to law*.   The Hebrew word in the place here cited is always rendered *trespass* or *transgression*.   It occurs frequently, and, when applied to political affairs, signifies revolt, or rebellion.   *Forgiven*, the word used in the Lord's Prayer, and often so rendered; also put away.   It means to send away, dismiss from one's thoughts, or attention.   Men sometimes say they will forgive, but not forget; but Jehovah says, your sins and your iniquities will I remember no more.   The Hebrew word rendered *forgiven* in Ps. 32 : 1 means *lifted up*, as when a cloud is raised, or *borne away*, as when the scape-goat bore away the sins of the people into a land uninhabited.   *Sins*, a word of frequent occurrence, rendered with absolute uniformity in the New Testament; the same word used by the Septuagint in Ps. 32 : 1. *Covered*, there is no better rendering ; as Pharaoh and his hosts were covered in the Red sea, Ex. 15 : 10; buried out of sight, cast into a deep sea, Mic. 7 : 19.   The compound verb here rendered *covered* is not found elsewhere in the New Testament, but the simple word occurs several times, and is applied to *hiding* or *covering* sins, Jas. 5 : 20; 1 Pet. 4 : 8.   Neither the Psalmist nor the apostle stops here ; it is added :

8. *Blessed* is *the man to whom the Lord will not impute sin.   Sin*, in the Greek the same word in the singular as is in v. 7 in the plural rendered sins, but in the Hebrew we have a different word, commonly rendered iniquity ; sometimes fault or mischief, in a few cases punishment, or punishment of iniquity.   The Hebrew expresses perverseness.   *Impute*, see above on v. 3.   The scope and bearing of vs. 7, 8 is the same.   Three forms of expression

are used to teach the doctrine of the pardon of sin, which is an essential part of justification, though not the whole of it. But where God grants forgiveness, he never withholds acceptance, but surely imputes righteousness, as Paul teaches in v. 6. Hodge: " To *impute sin* is to lay sin to the charge of any one, and to treat him accordingly, as is universally admitted; so to *impute righteousness* is to set righteousness to one's account, and to treat him accordingly." Owen of Thrussington: " It is a striking proof of what the apostle had in view here, that he stops short and does not quote the whole of Ps. 32: 2. He leaves out, 'and in whose spirit there is no guile:' and why? Evidently because his subject is justification, and not sanctification. He has thus most clearly marked the difference between the two." Paul quotes all that is pertinent to his argument and to the matter in hand. Not that sanctification is unimportant; nor that it is ever separated from justification, though both Testaments distinguish between them; but the apostle is now absorbed with one point only— justification.

9. Cometh *this blessedness then upon the circumcision* only, *or upon the uncircumcision also? for we say that faith was reckoned to Abraham for righteousness.* Paul had not dropped the case of Abraham, but had confirmed it by the testimony of David to the same truths. He asks whether such blessings as David speaks of were enjoyed by none but the circumcision. Did justification by imputed righteousness depend on circumcision? Did not God always, and in gospel times does he not abundantly grant salvation and good hope to believers of every nation? See Acts 10: 34, 35. Does righteousness come to men through carnal ordinances? *We say*, probably meaning we Jews commonly admit; though Stuart regards them as uttered by an objector. We must admit (for Moses our great prophet records it of our great ancestor) that faith was reckoned to Abraham for [unto] righteousness.

10. *How was it then reckoned? when he was in circumcision or in uncircumcision? Not in circumcision, but in uncircumcision.* In Gen. 15 : 6, we are told that Abraham was justified by faith. But the command of circumcision was not given for several (some say fifteen and all agree that it was as much as thirteen or fourteen) years afterwards; and neither Abraham, nor any of his family were circumcised till the patriarch was ninety-nine years old, Gen. 17 : 24. Clearly then to Abraham God imputed righteousness, and so justified him, when he was uncircumcised, and his justification therefore could not be by an ordinance not as yet given, and of course not obeyed. So far from circumcision being the ground of Abraham's justification, it was not in

any sense even a condition of his acceptance with God. If he was justified before he was circumcised, he could not be justified by being circumcised. But such a view of circumcision was very contrary to the views of many Jews. Some of their learned men said, and many believed that no circumcised descendant of Abraham could perish. Paul's doctrine was therefore likely to awaken the most violent opposition, and Jews might say, that he virtually denied that circumcision was a divine institution, or held that it was of no avail, or had no meaning. He therefore proceeds to tell what circumcision was and what were its uses:

11. *And he received the sign of circumcision, a seal of the righteousness of the faith which* he had yet *being uncircumcised : that he might be the father of all them that believed though they be not circumcised ; that righteousness might be imputed to them also. The sign of circumcision* means the sign circumcision and no more. Such forms of speech are not uncommon in the Scriptures. In English we speak of the ordinance of baptism, meaning the ordinance baptism, and of the sacrament of the supper, meaning that sacrament, which we call the Lord's supper. The meaning is not that something signified circumcision, but that circumcision signified something. Of what was it a sign? It signified that the heart must undergo a great change, that the natural corruption of men's natures must be removed by the blood and spirit of Christ, his redemption being applied to them. Moses himself so explained it, when he said: "Circumcise therefore the foreskin of your heart, and be no more stiff-necked," Deut. 10 : 16. Again : "The Lord thy God will circumcise thine heart, and the heart of thy seed, to love the Lord thy God with all thine heart, and with all thy soul, that thou mayest live," Deut. 30 : 6. A later prophet says : "Circumcise yourselves to the Lord, and take away the foreskins of your heart," &c. Jer. 4 : 4. In this epistle Paul says : "He is not a Jew, which is one outwardly ; neither is that circumcision, which is outward in the flesh : but he is a Jew, which is one inwardly ; and circumcision is that of the heart, in the spirit, and not in the letter ; whose praise is not of men but of God," Rom. 2 : 28, 29. Elsewhere he says, "We are the circumcision, which worship God in the Spirit, and rejoice in Christ Jesus, and have no confidence in the flesh," Phil. 3 : 3. "In whom [Christ] also ye are circumcised with the circumcision made without hands in putting off the body of the sins of the flesh by the circumcision of Christ." Col. 2 : 11. Circumcision was a sign of the cleansing of our natures by divine grace. In Gen. 17 : 11 God calls it a "token of the covenant." But this rite was more than a sign or token. It was also a pledge, a seal or confirmation of the righteousness of faith ; not the means

of begetting faith, much less the efficient cause of it; nor a seal of faith itself; no: but a seal or assurance of the righteousness, which had been imputed to him long before his circumcision, even when he believed God—*the righteousness of the faith which he had yet being uncircumcised.* Circumcision was to be kept up in the church till Christ should come. In Abraham's *seed*, which was Christ, all the families of the earth were to be blessed. The promise was of a great salvation by a Redeemer, who should spring out of Abraham's loins, and who should bring in everlasting righteousness. Abraham believed the promise·long before his circumcision, and so became the father, the leader, the pattern, the first teacher, the first recorded instance of any man being justified by or through faith. As Jabal was the father of such as dwell in tents and have cattle; as Jubal was the father of all such as handle the harp and organ; and as Tubal-cain was an instructor of every artificer in brass and iron, Gen. 4: 20–22; so Abraham was the model, the instructor, the pattern *of all them that believe though they be not circumcised; that righteousness* [the righteousness of God our Saviour Jesus Christ] *might be imputed to them also.* It is very true that Abel, Enoch and Noah, and all the pious, who lived before Abraham were justified and saved by faith, but we learn this from reasonings and revelations found in the New Testament, especially in the epistles to the Romans, Galatians and Hebrews, but not from any record in the Old Testament that they believed God, and that their faith was counted for or unto righteousness. It is then true that if men have like precious faith with Abraham, they shall have like glorious righteousness with him also, whether they be circumcised or not. For in Christ Jesus neither circumcision availeth any thing, nor uncircumcision, but faith, which worked by love, Gal. 5 : 6. Calvin : " Mark how the circumcision of Abraham confirms our faith with regard to gratuitous righteousness; for it was the sealing of the righteousness of faith, that righteousness might be imputed to us also." So that circumcision was not only confirmatory of imputed righteousness to ancient believers, but through them to us also, even us, who are sinners of the Gentiles. Abraham's faith made him the father of Gentile believers,

12. *And the father of circumcision to them who are not of the circumcision only, but who also walk in the steps of that faith of our father Abraham, which* he had *being* yet *uncircumcised.* That is, Abraham was a model, the first recorded instance of faith, a spiritual father, not only to believing Gentiles, but also to Jews, who rely not on circumcision itself, but have a faith like that of Abraham, believing all God speaks to them, and in particular re-

joicing in a Redeemer, whose righteousness is imputed to believers without regard to nationality. One emphatic word in
this verse is *only*. All are not Israel, who are of Israel. Haldane : " While all Abraham's children were circumcised, he
was not equally the father of them all. It was only to such of
them as had his faith that he was a father in what is spiritually represented by circumcision." Christ denied that the unbelieving
Jews were the children of Abraham, or the children of God, but
asserted that they were of their father the devil, John 8 : 39–44.

13. *For the promise, that he should be the heir of the world, was
not to Abraham, or to his seed, through the law, but through the righteousness of faith.* The argument grows stronger and stronger.
It now assumes the form it takes in Gal. 3 : 16–18. He had before
proven that justification was not by circumcision, for Abraham
was justified before he was circumcised. He now proves that
Abraham's acceptance with God and his high distinction as the
father of the faithful could not have been by the law, for the law
was not given for hundreds of years after he became pre-eminently
the friend of God. I say *the* law, for although the article is wanting in the Greek, yet it is supplied by every English version now
at hand, Wiclif, Coverdale, Tyndale, Cranmer, Genevan, Rheims
and Doway ; also by Peshito and Conybeare and Howson, though
Stuart omits it. That it is properly supplied is manifest from the
fact that to a Jew the very mention of law suggested the great
law given by Moses, and Paul is here arguing with a Jew. That
was to him *the* law, so as nothing else was. But if any prefer to
read simply *law*, there is no objection to his doing so, for that includes the law of Moses and all law of every kind, and the argument still relates to justification by gratuity and not by human
merit. But what are we to understand by Abraham's being *heir
of the world ?* With diffidence the author ventures to suggest a
train of thought that he finds in no commentary that he has consulted. First, what is meant by the *world ?* In the Greek Testament are four words sometimes rendered world. One of these
(aion) signifies duration, past, present or future, but often with a
limit. In the plural it often means eternity. Our Lord uses it
when he speaks of "this world," of "that world," of "the end of
the world," and of "the world to come." In Rom. 12 : 3 we have
this word: "Be not conformed to this *world*." In Acts 17 : 31 we
have another word [oikoumene) rendered world : "He hath appointed a day in the which he will judge the *world*." It is so
rendered everywhere else except in Luke 21 : 26 where we read
earth. In Luke 2 : 1 it is put for the Roman empire, because that
embraced most of the world then known. That is the word in

Matt. 24 : 14 : " This gospel of the kingdom shall be preached in all the world, for a witness unto all nations." Commonly this word means the *habitable earth,* once at least *the inhabitants of the earth.* It occurs in Rom. 10 : 18 : " Their words unto the ends of the *world.*" Then in Rev. 13 : 3 we have a third word (ge) rendered world, but its ordinary signification is ground, land or earth, once country : " Blessed are the meek ; for they shall inherit the earth," Matt. 5 : 5. In the Greek Testament is still another word (kosmos) rendered world. It is found in Acts 17 : 24 : " God that made the world." Often it means the earth, and then its inhabitants. It is often used in connection with the last judgment. " God shall judge the world," Rom. 3 : 6. This is the word used in our verse. Abraham was heir of the world (kosmos). It is found in such passages as these : " Ye are the light of the world ;" " The field is the world ;" " Go ye into all the world ;" " The Lamb of God that taketh away the sins of the world ;" " God so loved the world ;" " I am the light of the world ;" " He will reprove the world of sin ;" " The saints shall judge the world ;" " Came into the world to save sinners ;" " The world passeth away ;" " The Saviour of the world," etc. It would therefore seem improbable that by the world in this verse can be meant anything so narrow as any one country, such as Palestine. It must embrace something as extensive as the habitable part of our globe. What then is it to be the *heir* of the world ? In Gal. 3 : 18 we read : " If the inheritance be of the law, it is no more of promise : but God gave it to Abraham by promise." Here the same idea of heirship is preserved. Representing the blessings of the gospel in this way is very common : " If children, then heirs, heirs of God, and joint heirs with Jesus Christ," Rom. 8 : 17 ; " That the Gentiles should be fellow heirs," Eph. 3 : 6 ; " Heirs according to the hope of eternal life," Tit. 3 : 7 ; " Heirs of salvation," Heb. 1 : 14 ; " Heirs of the righteousness by faith," Heb. 11 : 7 ; " Heirs together of the grace of life," 1 Pet. 3 : 7. In like manner we have the phrases : " Inherit everlasting life ;" " Inherit the kingdom of God ;" " Inherit a blessing," etc. Sometimes the language is very strong : " He that overcometh shall inherit all things ; and I will be his God, and he shall be my son," Rev. 21 : 7. Heavenly benefits are often spoken of as an inheritance : " An inheritance among all them that are sanctified ;" " We have obtained an inheritance ;" " The earnest of our inheritance ;" " The inheritance of the saints ;" " An inheritance incorruptible, and undefiled, and that fadeth not away, reserved in heaven for you," 1 Pet. 1 : 4. Several of these places—in particular 1 Pet. 1 : 4 ; Rev. 21 : 7—distinctly teach that all believers have as great and glorious benefits, and *by inheritance too*, as are said to have been conferred on Abraham when he is called "the heir of the world." And that we may not suppose that. by his being heir of the world any peculiar spiritual good was conferred on him, Paul says to Christians generally : " If ye be Christ's, then are ye Abraham's seed, and heirs according to the promise," Gal. 3 : 29. This is in the very connection in which he discusses the heirship of Abraham. The phrase *the heir of the world* therefore does not necessarily mean anything greater than the phrase " the blessing of Abraham," Gal. 3 : 14, that is the bless- ing which Abraham received, viz., full and irrevocable justification by imputed righteousness; nothing greater than the phrase *the father of all them that believe*, the pattern, exemplar, illustrious leader, forerunner, the first recorded instance of a man being justi- fied by faith, and intended to teach men everywhere, Jew and Gentile, that they must be saved as Abraham was. The same *blessedness*, that Abraham secured comes on believers in all *the world*. The *blessing*, intended by the phrase *the heir of the world*, whatever it may be, was obtained precisely as justification was, not *through law but through the righteousness of faith*. And to sin- ners no greater blessing comes than a gratuitous justification. Is Abraham the heir of the world? believers are the light of the world. So the faith of the Romans was spoken of throughout the whole world, Rom. 1 : 8 ; and if that church had been the first known instance of a people believing unto righteousness, it would have had the pre-eminence here given to Abraham ; it would have been the mother of all that believe and the heir of the world. Beyond complete justification and the honor of shewing to all men by his example how we are to be saved, what did Abraham possess beyond what is in many places promised to all believers? Thus Jesus: " Verily I say unto you, There is no man that hath left house, or brethren, or sisters, or father, or mother, or wife, or children, or lands, for my sake and the gospel's, but he shall receive an hundredfold now in this time, houses, and brethren, and sisters, and mothers, and children, and lands, and persecutions ; and in the world to come eternal life," Mark 10 : 29, 30. So Paul : " All things are yours; whether Paul, or Apollos, or Cephas, or the world, or life, or death, or things present, or things to come ; all are yours; and ye are Christ's; and Christ is God's," 1 Cor. 3 : 21–23. The words of Rev. 21 : 7 have been already cited. These passages engage to all believers infinite blessings, blessings as great as they can enjoy ; therefore as great as were probably intended to be intimated by the phrase *the heir of the world*, even if we take it in the sense of Abraham inheriting the world. The views differing from this are commonly embraced under one of

these heads: 1. That to be the heir of the world is to inherit
Canaan. But Canaan is not the world, and is never called the
world, but the land, or the earth. The Greek uses different words.
Besides the blessing, which Abraham received, was to be shared
by the Gentiles, Gal. 3 : 14. Moreover when Abraham actually
lived in Canaan, it was hardly as proprietor, for when Sarah died
he had to buy a place of burial. Like the other patriarchs he confessed he was a stranger and a pilgrim. "By faith he sojourned
in the land of promise, as in a strange country." "He looked
[was looking] for a city which hath foundations." 2. Another explanation is that he became the heir of the heavenly Canaan, of
which the earthly was but a type. But all believers shall possess
that good land and enter that heavenly country. Nor is heaven
ever called *the world*, although in Luke 20 : 35 we have the terms
that world applied to the blissful period of duration following this
life, but the word there rendered world is *age*, elsewhere rendered
world to come. 3. Some think as God promised a numerous posterity to Abraham, Gen. 15 : 6; 17 : 5; and as these have been
widely scattered in the world that in this sense the patriarch may
be said to be heir of the world. But the Jews do not constitute
the hundredth part of the human family, generally own very little
land, and never possessed much political power in the world. Nor
is our apostle conducting any argument on such a subject as national power, but an argument on justification by faith.

4. Some regard the phrase *heir of the world* as indicating great
happiness, and point to the promises in Ps. 37 and in Matt. 5 : 5 in
proof. No doubt Abraham was happy, greatly blessed, but so is
every child of God, and our verse closely points to some pre-eminent distinction. Besides, the word rendered earth or land in
those places both in Hebrew and Greek has a very different signification from that rendered world in our verse.

5. Some think that by heir of the world we are to understand
that Abraham in some way became inheritor of the world through
his seed Jesus Christ, in whom all nations were to be blessed,
Gen. 12 : 3. Yet the *first* promise of Messiah was made to our
first parents in Eden and not to Abraham. And as to his being
the lineal ancestor of Christ, so were Isaac, Jacob, Judah, David,
Solomon, and others. Still it is undeniable that Messiah is Lord
of all and that he shall have dominion from sea to sea and from the
river to the ends of the earth, and that in him shall all the families of the earth be blessed. And although the promise of a seed
did certainly have a special reference to Christ, as Paul asserts,
Gal. 3 : 16, yet that promise was no more precious and no more
sure than that made to David hundreds of years after, 2 Sam. 7 :

16. So that this can hardly be the mind of the Spirit in this place. Our verse admits that the promise that he should be the heir of the world was not only to Abraham, but to his seed, and that through the righteousness of faith. His seed therefore here cannot mean Christ, for he did not enter heaven through the righteousness of faith, but by his own merits. Therefore it must mean his spiritual seed, believers. 6. The phrase *heir of the world*, therefore, probably, means an heir of God known to all the world of believers, a very prominent child of God, just as Paul says that the apostles were made "a spectacle unto the world, kosmos, and to angels, and to men," i. e. were very prominent before the world [perhaps of believers]. Just so Abraham's prominence is indicated by his being "the heir of the world" and "the father of all that believe," and by the phrase "the blessing of Abraham coming on the Gentiles." This gives a good sense and agrees with the preceding and succeeding context. In the next verse all the saved are called heirs. This view also coincides with the whole scope of the argument which Paul is conducting—an argument respecting gratuitous justification by the merits of the Redeemer.

14. *For if they which are of the law* be *heirs, faith is made void, and the promise made of none effect.* Respecting the persons here spoken of opinions are divided. Mr. Locke thinks that by *them which are of the law* we are to understand "them only who had the law of Moses given them." Clarke agrees with him and says the phrase points to "the Jews only." But a large class give an interpretation more coincident with the line of the apostle's argument. Doddridge says the terms used designate "those who depend upon the law;" Tholuck: "those who trust to their works;" "*they which are of the law* is the exact parallel of *as many as are of the works of the law,* Gal. 3 : 10;" Hodge: "*legalists,* those who seek justification by the works of the law." This is doubtless the right view. Calvin : "He takes his argument from what is impossible and absurd." Haldane: "The case is supposed, though not admitted, which would be contrary to the whole train of the apostle's argument." If it were possible for men to become *heirs* of salvation by the law, the whole gospel would be subverted, and its provisions rendered nugatory. Calvin: "If the condition had been interposed—that God would favor those only with adoption who deserved it, or who fulfilled the law, no one could have dared to feel confident that it belonged to him." Diodati : "If it were so that by works man might obtain that inheritance, all faith, covenant of grace, and promises would be void, which is wicked and most absurd to think." Whitby : "If they which are of the law be heirs faith is made void to them which are not of the

law [because then they cannot by it be made heirs] and it is also
made void to them that are of the law [because they were heirs
before] and may still be so without it; v. 15." Hawker: "It is
of no use for God to promise, if the accomplishment depends upon
man's performance of the law. And as man cannot come up to
the law, so man can never attain the promise if it depends on his
obedience. It is of no use to hold forth any blessings, if those
blessings depend upon man's taking them when they are out of
his reach." The apostle proceeds to give the reason:

15. *Because the law worketh wrath: for where no law is*, there is
no transgression. The law wherever known among men works
wrath or brings a curse, not because the law is not holy, just and
good, nor because it was not ordained to life, and suited to the
very case of all that are free from all sin, but because men are
wicked, break the law and transgress its holy precepts, and so
incur its righteous penalty. If men were not subjects of moral
government, if neither by the light of nature, nor by the light of
revelation they had any knowledge of the law of their being and
the right rule of living, then they would have had no sin. Tholuck: "The idea of *law*, and the idea of penal justice are correla-
tive, because it is impossible to conceive of man, except as a transgressor." Chalmers: "There have been infractions of the law by
all, and all therefore are the children of wrath." Scott: "The
clearer, the more copious and the more express the law is, the
more numerous, evident, and aggravated must man's transgressions appear.'

DOCTRINAL AND PRACTICAL REMARKS

1. The doctrine of justification by faith is true, for God's word
teaches it; it is important, for God's word urges it; it is vastly
weighty, for God's word greatly insists upon it. It is the great
theme of two of Paul's epistles, this, and that to the Galatians.
Elsewhere it is brought up again and again. If God says a thing
once, we know it is true. If he says it often, we should think of
it habitually, vs. 1–14. Brown: "Justification, and the right way
thereof, being a matter of great necessity to be known, and a truth
which Satan hath early and late bent his strength against, a great
necessity lieth upon all to be thoroughly clear in this matter; and
ministers should labor to explain it fully unto people, and use all
means to make plain the way, and to confirm them in the truth
thereof."

2. All claim of personal merit or desert of good before God on
the part of us sinners is monstrous—monstrous error, monstrous

arrogance, monstrous folly, monstrous wickedness, v. 2. Olshausen: "Works give merit, merit justifies a person in making demands or in boasting ; no grace therefore can consist with works, but only a relation of debt." Hodge: "The renunciation of a legal self-righteous spirit is the first requisition of the gospel." If God's word teaches any thing, it certainly teaches that any and every form of self-glorification in the sight of heaven is vain, is vile, is wicked, is dangerous.

3. There has never been but one method of a sinner's acceptance before God. God's word speaks of but one. It condemns all others, vs. 1–13. Saving faith rests on Christ, not on self; on the Son of God, not on the son of man ; on atoning blood, not on tears of penitence. No two things are more opposite than faith or grace on the one hand, and works or debt on the other. All scripture shuts up men to a wholly gratuitous salvation. This suits our case exactly.

4. But this is a very humbling method. It abases man. It cuts up pride by the roots. It leaves no room for boasting. It forbids glorying, v. 2. Hence the offensiveness of this doctrine. Pool: "Abraham was a man that had faith and works both, yet he was justified by faith, and not by works." He humbled himself to receive the gratuity, and so must we, if we would inherit eternal life. If we expect to pursue any course which shall in strict justice to us bring God under any obligation to save us, we shall perish in our folly. Even Abraham had nothing whereof to glory *before God.*

5. It is one thing to be judged of men. It is another, and a very different thing to be judged of the Lord, v. 2. Compared with many other men how bright was the character of Abraham ! Compared with the perfect law of God, he needed absolutely pardoning grace and justifying righteousness, just like every other sinful man. If there was any sense in which he might glory before men, there was no sense in which he could boast before God. And if he, "a patriarch whose virtues had canonized him in the hearts of all his descendants ; and who, from the heights of a very remote antiquity, still stands forth to the people of this distant age, as the most venerably attired in the worth and piety and all the primitive and sterling virtues of the older dispensation," had nothing whereof to glory before God, how dare any of us trust our souls to any but a plan of unmingled grace ?

6. The simple fact is, merits we have none. Demerits cluster on us all. We are born in sin. Our best deeds are full of imperfection. "In many things we all offend." "There is not a just man upon earth that liveth and sinneth not." "All our righteous-

nesses are as filthy rags." Eternal confusion must cover us if there is not some gracious method of making us righteous before God. We must be found naked, if we are not " found in Christ, not having our own righteousness."

7. We may always, with safety and profit, refer our sentiments and reasonings, our belief and practice to the unerring rule of *scripture*, v. 3. " To the law and to the testimony : if they speak not according to this word, it is because there is no light in them," Isa. 8 : 20. Haldane : " Paul's proof is drawn from the historical records of the Old Testament, and thus he sets his seal to its complete verbal inspiration, quoting what is there recorded as the decision of God." Brown : " Old Testament scriptures are yet in force to us under the gospel, and may safely be made use of to confirm and illustrate truths." Scripture binds the conscience of all good men, yea, it often speaks with awful authority even to bad men. Let no man—in particular let no minister—handle the word of God deceitfully, nor imagine that any merely human logic can control the heart of man as holy scripture can. It is " the sword of the Spirit."

8. Although faith has in it nothing to merit God's favor and is itself never by him regarded as righteousness, or in any wise commensurate to the requirements of the law, yet it is necessary to salvation—so necessary that without it there is no man saved. Even Abraham had not been justified, if he had not *believed*, vs. 3, 5. Chalmers : " They who have the faith of Abraham are his children, though they have not the circumcision. They who have the circumcision are not his children, if they have not the faith. The sign without the thing signified will avail them nothing." Chrysostom : " To him that worketh a reward is given : to him that believeth righteousness. Now righteousness is much greater than a reward." Great and numerous have been the just commendations of faith ; but our apostle commends it here, because it lays hold on Christ's righteousness. This is what man can do in no other way than by believing. Yet let us eschew the dangerous error that faith is itself a justifying righteousness. O no ! if we are ever righteous before God, it must be by receiving the righteousness of God, which is by or through faith. On the other hand " without faith it is impossible to please God ; " for unbelief is a refusal to set our seal to the covenant of grace. Nor can believers too often renew their hold of Christ and his righteousness. The great cure of uncertainty respecting our interest in Christ is found in frequently renewed acts of faith in him.

9. Let men, especially those, who bear the Christian name, cease to oppose and oppugn the blessed doctrine of the *imputation*

of Christ's righteousness, seeing it is so clearly taught in many scriptures, vs. 3, 4, 5, 6, 8, 9, 10, 11.   The violence and ingenuity manifested against the doctrine of imputation have often been amazing, sometimes blasphemous, and sometimes scornful, sometimes claiming great love for the truth, sometimes promising to remove difficulties, but always involving us in uncertainty.   The latest form of opposition claims to be very mild and gentle.   But there is no yielding of the disputed point.   A living writer says, " It is not uncommon to say, that Christ's righteousness is imputed to us, or that it becomes ours."   He then adds that " this language to many minds does not convey a very definite conception," and that " on other minds it conveys erroneous impressions, and seems to be irreconcilable with the common notions of men about moral character."   These terms are mild compared with those used by Socinus on the same subject, but they are not a whit less insidious or dangerous.   Here is an absolute refusal to employ terms used by David and Paul, by the greatest reformers, by the most glorious martyrs, and by the church of God for long ages; and all under the plea that they are not definite, that they may mislead, and that they do not tally with men's notions.   One may search the Christian world through and through, and he will find no terms touching the mystery of salvation better understood for centuries past by the learned and by the common people, or better defined in massive treatises or in concise formulas of doctrine than *imputed righteousness.* Yet we read some modern treatises, avowedly on justification, and never meet these terms except to find some slighting remark, some cavil respecting them.   When men shall succeed in excluding imputation from the terms of theology, it will not be long till they will be found disusing or even opposing the word righteousness.   The two must stand or fall together.   And what will the preaching of the gospel be, when no righteousness remains to be offered to the penitent?   No mortal has ever suggested any possible way, in which the believing sinner may avail himself of the righteousness of Christ, if the Lord shall not freely impute it to him.   The great objection, flippantly urged, is that imputation involves a transfer of moral character.   But who has ever taught that absurdity?   What respectable man has ever held such an opinion?   Surely the Christian world never taught it. Christ in his own character was truly, wholly, personally innocent ; but when our sins were laid on him he was in the eye of the law, and as our substitute, by imputation guilty, under the curse ; yet our moral character was not transferred to him.   It would be blasphemy to say that his holy soul was defiled.   And yet God so laid on him the iniquities of us all, that he was made sin for us.

So we are truly, whol y, personally vile, and when Christ's righteousness is imputed to us, it does not make us personally pure or
worthy, but it gives us a title good in the eyes of the law to all the
blessings of the covenant of grace. Hodge truly says : " It never
was the doctrine of the Reformation, or of the Lutheran or Cal-
vinistic divines, that the imputation of righteousness affected the
moral character of those concerned. It is true, whom God justifies he also sanctifies, but justification is not sanctification, and the
imputation of righteousness is not the infusion of righteousness."
Nor has the church of God ever taught otherwise. Justin Martyr :
" God gave his Son a ransom for us ; the holy for transgressors ;
the innocent for the evil ; the just for the unjust ; the incorruptible for the corrupt ; the immortal for mortals. For what else
could hide or cover our sins but his righteousness ? In whom else
could we wicked and ungodly ones be justified, but in the Son of
God alone ? O precious permutation. O unsearchable operation.
O beneficence surpassing all expectation ! that the sin of many
should be hid in one just person, and the righteousness of one
should justify many transgressors."

There is a class of writers, not very numerous, nor respectable,
but confident and pushing, who to avoid the doctrine of the imputation of the righteousness of God our Saviour, declare that our
faith itself is accepted by God as righteousness ; that faith itself
is reckoned as righteousness. If our faith were perfect, this would
be accepting one perfect act instead of the perfect obedience due
all our lives. But every man's faith, especially as he first lays hold
of the gospel, is imperfect, and the best men are the most conscious of such imperfection, Mark 9 : 24. One of the best prayers
ever offered by the disciples was, Lord, increase our faith. If God
should accept any one act of faith, or all acts of faith as the meritorious ground of our acceptance, it would be admitting that his
law had been too strict, that an imperfect obedience was all he
now required, and that Jesus Christ had lived and died in vain ;
at least, that he satisfied not the demands of the law or justice,
that he brought in no righteousness, and that believing sinners
were saved in derogation of perfect righteousness. The same
class of writers often urge that God merely treats the sinner as
just, and that this is the mercy of God in Christ. But if any one
is not righteous, how can God treat him, as if he were righteous?
The Bible never speaks of men as *quasi* just, but it often speaks
of the just, the righteous. If God acquits as just those who in
every sense in the eye of justice are guilty and have no righteousness, what hinders him from saving unbelievers as well as believers ? Such a view utterly confounds the distinction made by the

apostle between faith and works, the righteousness of God and the deeds of the law. Guyse: " The act of faith itself is as much a *work*, as any other commanded duty, and were that to be reckoned to us for righteousness, the reward in justifying us would be a debt, due to us, on account of our having performed that work." Pool: " Remission of sins presupposeth imputation of righteousness; and he, that hath his sins remitted, hath Christ's righteousness first imputed, that so they may be remitted and forgiven to sinners." It is therefore but a miserable mockery of the sad state of men to represent justification in any case, as Macknight has done: " In judging Abraham, God will place on the one side of the account his *duties*, and on the other his *performances*. And on the side of his performances he will place his faith, and by mere favor will value it as equal to a complete performance of his duties, and reward him as if he were a righteous man." Can it be wondered at that when such sentiments are presented to men, every pious and intelligent Christian is shocked, and every penitent sinner asks, Am I after all left without hope except that God will save me by my own merits, or at least without any righteousness commensurate to his law ? It is impossible ever to quiet an enlightened and tender conscience in man, until you can show him such a righteousness, meeting all the demands of God's law, and let him see how he may make it his own to all the ends of a complete justification, vs. 3, 5, 6, 7, 8. The great importance of this matter to Christian comfort is well stated by Chrysostom : " Paul is now intent upon shewing that this salvation, so far from being matter of shame, was even the cause of a bright glory, and a greater than that through works. For since the being saved, yet with shame, had somewhat of dejection in it, he next takes away this suspicion too. And indeed he has hinted at the same already, by calling it not barely salvation but *righteousness. Therein* (he says) *is the righteousness of God revealed.* For he that is saved as a righteous man has a confidence accompanying his salvation. And he calls it not *righteousness* only, but also the setting forth of the righteousness of God. But God is set forth in things which are glorious, and shining, and great." No ·right minded man wishes to go to heaven in derogation of the divine honor or the glory of the divine government. Nor is it possible for us in any wise to please God, until we ourselves are graciously accepted, for as Calvin says: " The righteousness of works is the effect of the righteousness of God, and the blessedness arising from works is the effect of the blessedness which proceeds from the remission of sins." Nor can we otherwise have any good hope, for the Dutch Annotations truly says: " The ground of our salvation consists in remission of sins and imputation of the righteousness of Christ." And Hawker well says: "That which was and is counted for righteousness, is not our faith in that righteousness, but the righteousness itself imputed to the persons of the faithful, from their union and oneness in Christ." We cannot give up the distinction between faith and works, grace and debt, Christ's righteousness and human merits. It must be made and maintained at all costs and at all hazards, vs. 4, 5. Nor need we fear that we shall dishonor God by exalting his grace. In no way can we so shew forth his glory as by believing in his Son and accepting his righteousness. Chrysostom: "He indeed honors God, who fulfils the commandments, but he doth so in a much higher degree who thus followeth wisdom by his faith. The former obeys him, but the latter has that estimate of him, which is fitting, and glorifies him, and is full of wonder at him more than can be evinced by works." Brown: "This imputation of Christ is no chimera, or groundless imagination, however it seemeth absurd to carnal reason, but a real thing, founded upon the obedience of Christ, which is no fiction."

10. The truth puts man in a low place and gives him a low estimate of himself. By the gospel scheme boasting is excluded. God justifies the *ungodly*, v. 5. Olshausen: "*All* men in respect of God are in a state of *ungodliness*, and unable by their own powers to raise themselves into any other condition. . . . Every one, who desires to come to Christ, must altogether, and in every thing, recognize himself as a sinner." Blessed be God! his mercies are for the needy; his salvation for the lost. We are sick and "ungodliness is the radical and pervading ingredient of the disease of our nature, and it is here said of God that he justifies the ungodly. The discharge is as ample as the debt." Hodge: "As God justifies the ungodly, it cannot be on the ground of their own merit." No mere man deserves at God's hand any benefit whatever.

11. How perfect is the remission of sins, and how rich is the variety of terms and phrases employed to assure believers of the completeness of their deliverance from the condemning power of the law, vs. 7, 8. Forgiveness or remission, covering or hiding, not imputing, or not setting to one's account are the terms used. What more could we ask? 'Evans: "Justification does not make the sin not to have been, or not to have been sin;" and yet odious, abominable, offensive as is every form of iniquity the Lord casts it behind his back; he averts his face and refuses to look at it. Blessed be his name for his mercy. Blessed is the man, who shares it.

12. The grace of God in the pardon of sin is the more illustrious when we consider the nature of it, vs. 7, 8. It is iniquity, it is transgression, it is evil, it is an offence, it is a horrible thing, an unnatural crime, it is contempt of God, it is robbery, it is rebellion, it is perversity, it is lawlessness, it is enmity against God. It is odious, vile, loathsome, ruinous. It digs every grave. It makes the torments of hell what they are.

13. The justification of the believer is entire, wanting nothing, complete, full, finished, perfect, vs. 6–8. Every man needs all that is promised, but no man needs more. Chrysostom: "Punishment is removed, and righteousness through faith succeeds; there is then no obstacle to our becoming heirs of the promise." Who does not call Abraham blessed? yet all 'they that are of faith are blessed with faithful Abraham.'

14. Nor does the Scripture leave us in any doubt as to the character of those, who receive so great a blessing. They are believers and none else, v. 9. By nationality they may be Jews, or Gentiles; in manners they may be rude or refined; in education they may be learned or uncultivated; in man's esteem they may be base or honorable; but if they accept from the heart the mercy offered in Christ, they shall be saved. Michaelis: "To him who does works, the reward is not said to be *reckoned*, an expression which makes it appear as if it were given from grace, but he obtains it because it is his due."

15. Let not the pious reader fear that our apostle in dwelling so long on justification will overlook sanctification. There is no conflict between these things. The truth respecting forgiveness and acceptance is not unfriendly to purity. Ere we close our study of this epistle we shall see that Paul is as stanch a friend of holiness as ever wrote a book of scripture.

16. Let every man beware lest he become enamored of rites and ceremonies, of forms and ordinances rather than in love with Christ, v. 10. It is quite as easy to put gospel ordinances in the place the Saviour should occupy, as it was to put the Jewish ritual in the place of justifying righteousness.

17. Let us seek to understand and hold fast the true doctrine of the sacraments of God's house, v. 11. "A sacrament is a holy ordinance instituted by Christ; wherein, by sensible signs, Christ and the benefits of the new covenant are represented, sealed, and applied to believers." A sacrament is a sign, a sign of some truth. It sets forth something which it concerns us to know and receive. And it is a seal, confirming some engagement on the part of God. If there were no covenant of grace, there could be no fitness in any sacrament. In its very nature, a sacrament has no inherent

virtue, no invariable efficacy.   Nor does its usefulness depend on
the sanctity of him, who administers it.   Unbelief is a rejection of
its usefulness and makes it a curse rather than a blessing.   Conybeare & Howson: " Abraham received circumcision as an outward sign of inward things, a seal to attest the righteousness which
belonged to his faith while he was yet uncircumcised."   The
sacraments are not righteousness, nor the cause of righteousness,
nor a substitute for faith, nor even a seal of faith, but a seal of
righteousness received by faith.   To those, who reject Christ himself, they are powerless for good.   Not that our unbelief changes
their nature, any more than it changes the nature of God's word ;
but to us it deprives them of all good effect.   Nor is there the
least authority for the opinion that the sacraments of this dispensation, more than those of the former, have any justifying power.
Men are justified by faith, not by ordinances.   Yet sacraments are
ordained by God, are full of meaning, and to the humble and penitent great comforts, making sure, by our senses, what we receive
by faith.   Chalmers: " The term sign may be generally defined a
mark of indication, as when we speak of the signs of the times, or
of the signs of the weather.   A sign becomes a seal, when it is the
mark of any deed or any declaration, having actually come forth
from him who professes to be the author of it.   It authenticates it
to be his—so that should it be a promise, it binds him to performance."   We therefore fitly speak of sacraments as sealing ordinances.   To contemn them is to despise the ordinance of God.   Yet
Abraham was justified long before he was circumcised.   The penitent thief was never baptized, and never partook of the Lord's
Supper, yet he was saved.   Simon Magus was duly baptized, yet
continued in the bond of iniquity and in the gall of bitterness.
Some of the Corinthians in partaking of the Lord's Supper ate
judgment to themselves.   Sacraments rightly used are great blessings; but sacraments put in the place of the grace and Spirit of
God are the means of confirming men in fatal delusions.   To
assert that baptism is regeneration is as great error in our day, as
it was of old to teach that circumcision was complete righteousness before God.

18. It is a great honor to be a pattern and an encouragement
to even a few souls in teaching them by example the way of salvation.   How great then was the honor conferred on Abraham that
he should be the father of the faithful, the heir of the world, vs.
11–13.

19. So rich are the promises of God, that one of the chief
difficulties we have is in comprehending their glorious fulness,
v. 13.

20. We can never yield the doctrine of salvation by grace through faith. To do so makes the promises of God of none effect, v. 14. To do so puts us into tormenting uncertainty concerning salvation. Proof of this is found in the churches of Galatia, Gal. 4 : 15; and in the Romish church, which utterly denies the doctrine of assurance of faith and of hope.

21. There must be something very malignant in the nature of sin to cause the law to work wrath, and to cause God to execute wrath, v. 15. The law was ordained to life, but, when sin entered, it was found to be unto death. Chalmers: "Admit the arbitrations of the law, and wrath will be wrought out of them. Condemnation will be the sure result of this process. It must and will pronounce the guilt of transgression upon all, and, to get quit of this, there must be some way or other of so disposing of the law, as that it shall not be brought to bear in judgment on the sinner. It has been so disposed of." Jesus Christ was made a curse for us. Jesus Christ obeyed in our room and stead. He brought in everlasting righteousness. Calvin: "The law can indeed show to the good and the perfect the way of life: but as it prescribes to the sinful and corrupt what they ought to do, and supplies them with no power for doing, it exhibits them as guilty before God."

22. Let no man who fails to lay hold of the righteousness of Christ, indulge the hope of escaping the curse of the law, the punishment of his sins, the wrath of God, v. 15. Every wise man cries: "Enter not into judgment with thy servant: for in thy sight shall no man living be justified," Ps. 143 : 2. All men know better than they do. All have come short of the glory of God.

23. Unspeakable are the blessings of salvation. Those who embrace it are the *faithful*, *heirs*, heirs of God, joint heirs with Christ. The only people, who are truly blessed, or to whom existence is on the whole desirable, are the justified. They have everlasting riches, treasure inexhaustible. No blessing can be imagined that is not vouchsafed to the true child of God. All things are his. Pardon, peace, acceptance, authority to become a son of God, purification, victory final and complete, eternal life in a glorified state—all are secured to him, who believes in Jesus and takes him as his wisdom, righteousness, sanctification and redemption.

Chapter 9

ROMANS 4

VERSES 16–25

JUSTIFICATION BY FAITH AND BY GRACE THE
SAME. ABRAHAM'S FAITH STRONG. HIS EX-
AMPLE COMMENDED. WHY CHRIST DIED AND
ROSE AGAIN.

16 Therefore *it is* of faith, that *it might be* by grace; to the end the promise
might be sure to all the seed; not to that only which is of the law, but to that
also which is of the faith of Abraham; who is the father of us all,

17 (As it is written, I have made thee a father of many nations,) before him
whom he believed, *even* God, who quickeneth the dead, and calleth those things
which be not as though they were:

18 Who against hope believed in hope, that he might become the father of
many nations, according to that which was spoken, So shall thy seed be.

19 And being not weak in faith, he considered not his own body now dead,
when he was about a hundred years old, neither yet the deadness of Sarah's
womb:

20 HE staggered not at the promise of God through unbelief; but was strong
in faith, giving glory to God;

21 And being fully persuaded, that what he had promised, he was able also to
perform.

22 And therefore it was imputed to him for righteousness.

23 Now it was not written for his sake alone, that it was imputed to him;

24 But for us also, to whom it shall be imputed, if we believe on him that
raised up Jesus our Lord from the dead;

25 Who was delivered for our offences, and was raised again for our justification.

16. *THEREFORE*, it is *of faith, that* it might be *by grace; to
the end the promise might be sure to all the seed; not to that
only, which is of the law, but to that also which is of the faith of Abraham; who is the father of us all. Therefore* connects this verse not
so much with the preceding verse, as with the whole of the preceding argument. The first part is very elliptical. Our translators leave it vague, supplying *it*. The Assembly's Annotations
understand the way of obtaining life; Hammond, the promise

182

of reward ; Scott, a title to the promised blessings ; Dutch Annotations, the promise of this inheritance ; Stuart, justification.
Wiclif supplies rightfulness ; Chrysostom, Coverdale, Evans,
Doddridge, Clarke, Olshausen and others, promise ; Calvin, Tyndale, Cranmer, Genevan, Locke, Ferme, Brown, Pool, Macknight,
Slade, Conybeare and Howson, inheritance.   Either promise, inheritance, righteousness or blessedness gives the general idea of
the apostle.   Perhaps inheritance is the best, Gal. 3 : 18.   Some of
the old versions give a rendering slightly varied ; Peshito : Wherefore, it is by the faith which is by grace, that we are justified ;
Arabic : Therefore they are heirs through faith, that it might be
according to his grace ; Ethiopic : And moreover God has appointed justification by faith, that justification might be by his
grace ; Vulgate : Therefore it is of faith, that through grace the
promise might be firm to all the seed.   The objection to each of
these is that the Greek hardly allows it.   The apostle's object is
to prove that the whole work of our salvation is of grace, not of
our merit ; by favor, not by debt.   It is well for us sinners that it
is so.   If our heirship at all depended on our personal conformity
to the law, it would certainly fail ; for in many things we all offend.
But if it depends on faith graciously given us by God, it clearly
depends on God's unmerited and boundless kindness, given us in
God's eternal purpose, promised in the covenant of peace, expressed to us in the cross of Christ, and applied to us in the work
of the Spirit.   Thus the *promise* is indeed *sure, firm, steadfast, of
force,* (so the word is elsewhere rendered, Heb. 3 : 6, 14 ; 9 : 17) to
all *the seed,* to all Abraham's spiritual children ; *not to that only
which is of the law,* or Jews by birth, *but to that also, which is of the
faith of Abraham,* i. e. to those who sustain none but a spiritual relation to Abraham, and are his seed only because they have like
precious faith with him.   This is the most important for he *is the
father of us all,* Jews and Gentiles, who believe as he believed.
" If ye be Christ's, then are ye Abraham's seed, and heirs according to the promise," Gal. 3 : 29.   Stuart : " If the promise were to
be fulfilled only on condition of entire obedience to the law, then
would it never have any fulfilment, inasmuch as no mere man
ever did or will exhibit perfect obedience."   Calvin : " The promise then only stands firm, when it recumbs on grace."   Paul now
confirms this doctrine by a quotation from Gen. 17 : 5 :

17 (*As it is written, I have made thee a father of many nations,*) *before
him whom he believed,* even *God, who quickeneth the dead, and calleth
those things which be not as though they were.*   This promise to Abraham was made when he was an old man, and some time before the
birth of Isaac.   Yet God says I *have* already done it.   So unfail-

ing is God's counsel that what he purposes is as good as accomplished, and is often so spoken of in the prophetic writings; therefore it may be well said that he *calleth those things which be not* [but which he has determined on] *as though they were.* Some have found difficulty with the word *calleth*, as though it contained some mysterious meaning. It may be taken in either of two senses, both obvious and both agreeing with the use of the word elsewhere. 1. *Calling things that are not*, according to some is authoritatively commanding them into existence. Bp. Hall: "By his mighty word he is able to make those things to be which are not." Olshausen: "It is the creative call of the Almighty." 2. *Calling* often means giving names to persons or things, or speaking of them under certain designations. See many instances in all the gospels, as Matt. 1: 21, 23, 25; also Acts 1: 12, 19, 23; Jas. 2: 23; 1 Pet. 3: 6; 1 John 3: 1; Rev. 1: 9 and often. Macknight: "He *speaketh* of things in the remotest futurity, *which exist not*, with as much certainty, *as if they existed.*" This is the simpler, and perhaps the better meaning here. The pertinency of saying in this place that God *quickeneth the dead* is not merely that the power which effects resurrection, can accomplish any thing; but it has special reference to the age and infirmities of Abraham and Sarah when the promise of a great posterity was made. See v. 19. Cranmer, Genevan, Rheims and Doway agree with the authorized version in putting the quotation in parenthesis. This is doubtless correct. If so, we must join some words in this with the preceding verse: He *is the father of us all before him whom he believed, even God,* i. e. in the sight, view, or estimation of Jehovah Abraham was the spiritual father of great multitudes, who should believe, both Jews and Gentiles; even as he was according to the flesh the ancestor of all that lineally descended from him. Other explanations are offered, but they are forced, or aside from the drift of Paul's argument. This is pertinent and agrees with what follows. He makes a great deal of the faith of Abraham:

18. *Who against hope believed in hope, that he might become the father of many nations, according to that which was spoken, So shall thy seed be.* To believe in hope is confidently to believe; and to believe in hope *against hope* is confidently to believe when appearances would lead to a very different conclusion. Doddridge: "*Against* all human and probable *hope*, he *believed* with an assured and joyful hope;" Locke: "Without any hope, which the natural course of things could afford, he did in hope believe." He believed that according to God's promise he should become, or he believed the promise that he might thus become the father of many nations. Other constructions have been put on these words,

but either of these is better, coinciding entirely with the scope of the argument. Some have contended that Abraham understood not the spiritual nature of the blessings promised to him by the Lord. But Christ says: "Abraham rejoiced to see my day, and he saw it and was glad," John 8 : 56. Compare Gal. 3 : 14, 16. If any say that the promise was so glorious that even Abraham with all his faith did not fully comprehend it; the same may be said of all the promises and of all believers. *So shall thy seed be* is a quotation from Gen. 15 : 5, where it is promised that his seed shall be in number like the stars. This is more illustriously fulfilled in the spiritual children than in the descendants according to the flesh.

19. *And being not weak in faith, he considered not his own body now dead, when he was about a hundred years old, neither yet the deadness of Sarah's womb.* Every record of Abraham's faith shews that it was strong and unfaltering. Yet its strength arose entirely from his confidence in the truth and power of God, and not at all from anything he saw. Indeed as to any likelihood of his becoming a father or Sarah becoming a mother of the promised seed, nothing seemed more improbable, for both of them were old, and as to this matter, *dead.* Both Tyndale and Cranmer for *dead* in the case of Sarah have *past chylde beringe.* In Heb. 11 : 11 Paul says she was *past age ;* and in Heb. 11 : 12 he says of Abraham that at the time named *he was as good as dead.* That was so ; for he was *about a hundred years old,* and Sarah was ninety years old, Gen. 17 : 17.

20. *He staggered not at the promise of God through unbelief ; but was strong in faith, giving glory to God.* In the preceding verse he was said to have been *not weak in faith ;* in this he is said to have been *strong in faith.* And we are here told that faith is strong when it has no such admixture of unbelief as produces uncertainty. *Staggering,* nowhere else so rendered, but commonly doubting, wavering, disputing, judging. God had spoken and Abraham took him at his word, did not sit in judgment on his engagement, did not dispute nor waver respecting it. Thus he was found *giving glory to God,* i. e. so confiding in the faithfulness and power of God, that then and ever since Abraham's faith has honored God, and also caused others to trust and glorify him.

21. *And being fully persuaded, that what he had promised, he was able also to perform.* Here Abraham's faith is spoken of in terms still stronger. It now amounts to a *full persuasion.* It lacks nothing. It puts the highest honor on God. It can do no more. Such faith can walk in darkness and have no light, and yet trust in the Lord to make good all he has engaged. *Able* here and often implies both power and willingness.

22. *And therefore it was imputed to him for righteousness.*   Its strength evinced its perfect genuineness. It could not be doubted. He became righteous not by any works, but wholly by his faith, laying hold of the covenant of grace and thus receiving the right-eousness therein set forth.

23. *Now it was not written for his sake alone, that it was imputed to him.* He might have believed, been justified, had righteousness imputed to him, and gone to glory, and no man living after him have known anything about him. God did not make his a case of record to please Abraham's vanity, or to exalt his self-esteem. The great thing for the patriarch was that a perfect, glorious, righteousness was graciously imputed to him. It was written not for his sake alone ;

24. *But for us also, to whom it shall be imputed, if we believe on him that raised up Jesus our Lord from the dead.* Abraham was a pattern, a leader, an heir, a father of all such as believe ; and all, who have faith, leading them to embrace the truths of the gos-pel now clearly revealed, shall have the same glorious right-eousness, the righteousness of our God and Saviour Jesus Christ imputed to them also. One of the great truths necessary to be believed, a fundamental truth of Christianity, was the resurrec-tion of Christ. If this were doubted, preaching and faith were both vain. We must look to Jesus ;

25. *Who was delivered for our offences, and was raised again for our justification.* He *was delivered,* given up, or given over, Rom. 1 : 24, 26, 28 ; betrayed, Matt. 17 : 22 ; 1 Cor. 11 : 23 ; delivered in a good sense, Acts 16 : 14 ; 1 Cor. 15 : 24. The same word is used to express the treacherous act of Judas, the malignant conduct of the chief priests in bringing him before Pilate, the cowardly act of Pilate in giving him over to crucifixion, the act of God in sub-jecting him to the curse for us and his own act in giving up the ghost, Matt. 20 : 18, 19 ; John 19 : 16 ; Rom. 8 : 32 ; John 21 : 20. In this place it chiefly refers to the act of his Father in laying on him the iniquity of us all, in bruising him, in putting him to grief, in making his soul an offering for sin, Isa. 53 : 6, 10. But this was not done without his voluntary act of giving himself up to suffering, Gal. 2 : 20 ; where the same word is used. *For our offences* ; Peshito and Ethiopic, on account of our sins ; Arabic and Vulgate, for our faults. The word is rendered faults, sins, trespasses, offences ; but he was delivered up not for his own sins, for he had none ; but for *our* sins, and for ours only. He was de-livered to the curse, to death, to the grave. " He was wounded [margin tormented] for our transgressions, he was bruised for our iniquities, and the chastisement of our peace [that procured our

peace] was upon him," Isa. 53 : 5. The word rendered *for* is one
of the prepositions, which as Hornbeck and others have shewed,
is used to teach Christ's substitution. In no way could he suffer
for our sins except that they were imputed to him. He "was
made sin for us." "He hath loved us, and hath given himself
for us an offering and a sacrifice to God for a sweet smelling
savour," 2 Cor. 5 : 21 ; Eph. 5 : 2. *And was raised again for our
justification.* On Christ's resurrection see above, the exposition
of Rom. 1 : 4, and Doctrinal and Practical Remarks thereon.
Here Christ's resurrection is said to be *for our justification*, for the
purpose of effecting our justification, or on that account. He
was our Surety. Had he remained a prisoner in the grave it
would have proven that the work of atonement was incomplete,
that his sacrifice had not been accepted, and that we were still
under condemnation, 1 Cor. 15 : 17. Nor could Christ without
rising from the dead have entered into heaven there to present
his most precious blood, and intercede for his people. In this
epistle we have already frequently met with the adjective just
or righteous, with the verb to justify or to be justified, and
with the noun uniformly rendered righteousness. In this verse
we first meet with the noun justification. The same word occurs
in Rom. 5 : 19 and no where else in the New Testament, though
in Rom. 5 : 16 we have a cognate noun rendered justification.
These two words are sometimes used in the same sense both in
the Septuagint and by Paul, though the latter is also rendered
ordinance, judgment and righteousness.

DOCTRINAL AND PRACTICAL REMARKS

1. All God's plans and works are perfect. None of them can
be amended. When we diligently and successfully study them
we are continually finding out new and important relations in
them. The apostle closed the preceding chapter by saying that
through faith we establish the law. Here he shews that by the
same doctrine of gratuitous salvation by faith we establish the
promises of God, v. 16. Were the promises of God suspended
in the least on human merits, or human strength, all men would
perish. Now every man's case is met and every man's necessities
are provided for in the gospel scheme.

2. As the doctrine of salvation by grace through faith in the
Redeemer is vital, it is well that we have line upon line, and are
taught the same thing over and over again, in all fitting forms of
speech, that there may be left open no door for reasonable doubt,
v. 16. This plan is " grounded upon God and his immutable pleas-

ure, and upon Christ's perfect and everlasting righteousness, and not upon men's variable will, and inconstant obedience." As Jehovah found cause not in us but in himself to provide salvation for us, so he finds cause in himself alone for accomplishing all he has undertaken. Olshausen: " Every thing, which depends upon the decision, faithfulness and constancy of such an irresolute and wavering being as man, is, in St. Paul's view, extremely uncertain; but that which depends upon God, 'with whom is no variableness neither shadow of turning,' is firmly established." It is a sad mistake in not a few that they make faith itself a work, and put it in the place both of perfect obedience to the law, and of Christ's righteousness, and thus look upon God's favor " as a premium, not a premium for doing, it is true, but a premium for believing." To make a new law out of the gospel is to destroy all the solid foundations of Christian joy and peace.

3. Things are great and good, or small and evil, as they are *before God*, v. 17. His estimate of all things and of all beings is alone infallible. It is a small matter to be judged of man's judgment. Man is a worm. Man is a fool. Man is a sinner. Man is horribly perverted in his affections, warped in his judgments, erratic in his conduct. But God knows the end from the beginning. That, which shall be a thousand ages hence, is as well known to God as that which occurred yesterday. Let us never forget that he, which judgeth us, is the Lord.

4. He, who can raise the dead, can do any thing, v. 17. Well may the challenge be given, Is any thing too hard for the Lord? Gen. 18 : 14. He, who is able of the stones to raise up children unto Abraham, can never be straitened in his resources, Matt. 3 : 9. When the prophet was asked if the dry bones in the valley of vision could live, he replied to the Lord, Thou knowest. Whether a thing is to be or not to be, to be vile or honorable, useful or hurtful, turns altogether on the relations of God to it.

5. God's being, wisdom, power, holiness, justice, goodness and truth are a sufficient offset to any appearances whatever, v. 18. "One almighty is more mighty than all the mighties in the universe." The Amen cannot but be faithful. He is the best and the wisest man, who with the most childlike simplicity believes every word God utters. Implicit faith in man is great folly. Implicit faith in God is the height of wisdom. Chalmers: " Such is the way in which the message of the gospel is constructed—such are the terms of that embassy with which its ministers are charged, that the promise of God as a shield, and of God as an exceeding great reward, is as good as laid down at the door of every individual who hears it. It is true the promise thus laid down will not be

fulfilled upon him, unless he take it up, or, in other words, unless he believe it. Now there is a difficulty in the way of nature believing any such thing. There is a struggle that it must make with its own fears and its own suspicions, ere it can admit the credibility of a holy God thus taking sinners into acceptance." The shorter that struggle is the better for us. Unbelief is folly, is perversity, is ruin. Faith believes best when it reasons least. It relies most, and has most comfort, and shews most wisdom, when it simply says, " Good is the word of the Lord ;" " For ever, O Lord, thy word is settled in heaven ;" " Thy faithfulness is unto all generations."

6. The scripture cannot be broken. God said that Abraham's seed should be in number like the stars, and like the stars they became, v. 18. It could not be otherwise. Calvin : " The past tense of the verb, according to the common usage of Scripture, denotes the certainty of the divine counsel." If God speaks, it is done. If he commands, it stands fast. If it could be shewn that according to its true intent any word of God had failed, all confidence and comfort in him would vanish. A justly suspected God could be no solace to a sinking soul. Faithfulness that is not unimpeachable is not divine.

7. Let us not therefore dwell so much on our circumstances as on our covenant relations, not so much on the means of support and deliverance as on God the promiser.

8. The wisest thing any mortal can do is without questioning or hesitancy to believe everything God has spoken, v. 20. Chrysostom : " From the case of Abraham we learn, that if God promises even countless impossibilities, and he that heareth doth not receive them, it is not the nature of the things that is to blame, but the unreasonableness of him who receiveth them not." Even Balaam's theology carried him so far as to say : " God is not a man that he should lie ; neither the son of man, that he should repent ; hath he said, and shall he not do it? or hath he spoken and shall he not make it good?" Num. 23 : 19. If any should think that the days are past when a strong faith is necessary, he is wholly mistaken. Here is one, who has always led a life of ungodliness. At last his soul is awaked from its sleep of death. He sees that there is a God, who governs the world by a law that is holy, just and good ; that against that law he himself has transgressed in times and ways innumerable. His iniquities take hold of him like armed men and are dragging him to the prison of despair. Go to him, and attempt to persuade him to exercise faith in the promises of God to those, who have sinned as he has done, and what a task you have on hand! Tell him of God's spotless rectitude, and he says

I know it; I have sinned against it; I am sadly contrary to it. Point him to the divine veracity, the great pillar of hope, and he rejoins, That is even so, but the same unfailing truth has said, " The soul that sinneth, it shall die." Exhort him to fix his stead-fast eye on the divine compassion expressed in the cross of Christ, and he says, God is merciful, but I have long slighted and abused his grace and been cold to his loving kindness. Tell him of the penitent thief, converted on the cross, and he reminds you that his case was extraordinary, and that inspiration alike tells us of his companion in crime dying in his sins. Hold up before him that great pattern of mercy, Paul; and he says, Yea, but his great sins were committed ignorantly in unbelief, but I have sinned against light, vows and convictions. To him it looks as if everything in God were against him; for the saving view of divine truth has not yet been revealed to him. All within him is dark. His history is black with offences. His prospects are dismal. He is sinking into sadness bordering on despair. To him it looks as if everything was against him. Everything in God is to his mind tremendous. He cannot persuade himself that Jehovah looks or ever can look on him but as an enemy, an outcast from the hopes of the right-eous. He sees not how he, who is accustomed to do evil, shall ever learn to do well. He is fearfully holden with the cords of his sins. Of the renewal of his fallen nature he has no experience and no hope. So far is he gone in the downward road of rebellion and remorse, that it is clear as day that if he shall ever have peace in believing, it must be by a faith, which shall be the gift of God. No human persuasion can ever fetch him up from the depths, to which he has fallen. It must be given him from above to believe in the great sacrifice of Calvary, and there in the cross of Christ see all the divine attributes harmonizing in his salvation. Even then his faith may be weak, compared with that of others, com-pared with what it shall be, but it is yet precious faith and a mighty principle that can change his entire relations to God and all things.

9. Such faith glorifies God, v. 20. It puts all honor on his word, his grace, his power, his wisdom, his faithfulness. Chrysostom: " The very privilege of glorifying God were itself a glory." This is the highest aim of unfallen angels and redeemed men. It is the high-est destiny of any creature to glorify God and enjoy him for ever.

10. But let us not confound the astonishment of true faith with the perplexity of unbelief. The latter is a vice; the former a vir-tue. The pious Jews released from Babylon were "like them that dream." Peter released from prison "wist not that it was true which was done by the angel; but thought he saw a vision."

Calvin: "Abraham asked indeed, how it could come to pass, but that was the asking of one astonished; as the case was with the Virgin Mary, when she inquired of the angel how could that be which he had announced." Pious wonder will never cease. Calvin: "No greater honor can be given to God than by faith to seal his truth; as, on the other hand, no greater dishonor can be done to him, than to refuse his offered favor or to discredit his word." We may wonder; we must not disbelieve.

11. True faith obeys as well as trusts. We must walk in the steps of believers. We must act as if all God had spoken was true. It is in vain to say in words, We trust, and to say by deeds, We have no confidence. Concerning all the promises made him and commandments given him Abraham behaved as if he believed every word. Our weakness cannot check God's operations. Let not our lives prove that our faith is heartless.

12. Genuine and strong faith begets undoubting persuasion of all that God promises, however new and difficult may be our circumstances, v. 21. Abraham could look back to no example, where God had done such wonders as were promised to him. He looked at himself and he was as good as dead. He looked at Sarah and she seemed far too old to be a mother, and besides had always been barren; and yet he was fully persuaded, that what God had promised, he would perform. God knows and governs all causes and all hindrances, and so is never defeated, never nonplused.

13. Faith is at the greatest possible remove from fancy, from dreams, from vagaries. It lives and exults when it reads or hears the promise of Jehovah. It believes God, not the creature, v. 22. It is such faith that is imputed for righteousness, for such faith will accept the grace of the gospel. Calvin: "It becomes now more clear, how and in what manner faith brought righteousness to Abraham; and that was, because he, leaning on God's word, rejected not the promised favor." If we are now believers in Christ, we have assurance of the final triumph, an assurance confirmed to us more and more as we advance in knowledge of God's word, and in experience.

14. Abraham was in many things a model of piety, yet his works could not save him. But for his faith in the Redeemer he would have perished, v. 22. The same is true of us, Gal. 3 : 9.

15. No Scripture is of any private interpretation, but whatsoever things were written of old, were written for our learning, that we through patience and comfort of the scriptures might have hope, vs. 23, 24. There is one and but one way of obtaining righteousness, of gaining the victory over the world, the flesh and the devil, and that is the way of faith in a Redeemer.

16. As Abraham came off victorious, so shall all his spiritual children. Hawker: " Beyond all doubt, notwithstanding all that is said of this venerable patriarch in commendation of his faith; the humblest and poorest believer is equally interested in all the blessings of CHRIST in right of redemption. And for this plain reason all is God's gift, not man's worth. The patriarch had no more faith than was given him. Hence all he had he owed to the LORD." The same is true of all the faithful.

17. We cannot too often revert to the great fact and doctrine of the atonement of Christ, v. 25. Christ was *delivered* by the determinate counsel and foreknowledge of God, Acts 2 : 23. But he was delivered for our offences. Then, if we accept him, we need not die for our own sins. And if his blood, not being yet shed, saved Abraham, surely his blood sprinkled on the mercy-seat above can save us. Abraham believed in a Saviour yet to come. We believe in a Saviour already come. Abraham and his spiritual seed have all had the same kind of faith and the same object of faith. Bp. Hall: " Christ was delivered to death for the full satisfaction for all our sins, in that he paid for us that debt which we were never able to have discharged." He who rejects this truth refuses salvation on God's terms, and God accepts sinners on no other terms. This is a fundamental doctrine. So is also the next truth stated:

18. The resurrection of Christ cannot be given up on any account, vs. 24, 25. If Christ, who is our life, is still under the power of death, we are under the power of condemnation. But he has surely risen for our justification. He lives to intercede for us. Calvin: " When we possess the benefit of Christ's death and resurrection, there is nothing wanting to the completion of perfect righteousness." Stuart: " As justification, in its *full* sense, comprehends not only forgiveness, but the accepting and treating of any one as righteous, it implies of course the being advanced to a state of glory. The resurrection of Christ was connected with this." Doddridge: " By faith shall the righteousness of our Redeemer be reckoned as ours, to all the purposes of our justification and acceptance with God." Hodge: " As surely as Christ has risen, so surely shall believers be saved." We have an ever-living Saviour ; and because he lives we shall live also.

19. The gospel consists not of a number of detached truths but of a system of doctrines, facts and principles, making one harmonious whole, gloriously exalting God, reconciling things apparently antagonistic, and giving faithful men the strongest assurauce of eternal life.

Chapter 10

ROMANS 5
VERSES 1–11

HAVING SHEWN MAN'S NEED OF GRATUITOUS
SALVATION, AND HOW IT IS OBTAINED, THE
APOSTLE PROCEEDS TO STATE THE BLESSED
EFFECTS OF JUSTIFICATION.

THEREFORE being justified by faith, we have peace with God through our Lord
Jesus Christ :

2. By whom also we have access by faith into this grace wherein we stand, and
rejoice in hope of the glory of God.

3 And not only *so*, but we glory in tribulations also ; knowing that tribulation
worketh patience ;

4 And patience, experience ; and experience, hope :

5 And hope maketh not ashamed ; because the love of God is shed abroad in
our hearts by the Holy Ghost which is given unto us.

6 For when we were yet without strength, in due time Christ died for the ungodly.

7 For scarcely for a righteous man will one die : yet peradventure for a good
man some would even dare to die.

8 But God commendeth his love toward us, in that, while we were yet sinners, Christ died for us.

9 Much more then, being now justified by his blood, we shall be saved from
wrath through him.

10 For if, when we were enemies, we were reconciled to God by the death of
his Son, much more, being reconciled, we shall be saved by his life.

11 And not only *so*, but we also joy in God through our Lord Jesus Christ,
by whom we have now received the atonement.

1. *THEREFORE being justified by faith, we have peace with God
through our Lord Jesus Christ*. For *we have peace*, Peshito
has, we shall have peace ; Doway and Rheims, let us have peace.
But the authorized version follows the original, and is sustained
by most interpreters, versions and manuscripts. This verse is an
inference from the whole preceding argument, marked by the

word *Therefore*, which some render Then.   But either word
shews the connection.   On *justified*, see above on Rom. 2 : 13; 3 :
20, 26.   *By faith*, see above on Rom. 1 : 8, 12, 17.   On the ground
of what righteousness a sinner is justified, see Doctrinal and Practical Remark No. 5 on Rom. 3 : 20–31.   On the whole nature of
justification, see Doctrinal and Practical Remark No. 17 on Rom.
3 : 20–31.   Macknight contends that in this verse *justified* either
means "delivered from wickedness and ignorance through the influence of faith;" or that it signifies that "believers have *the
promise of justification* given them."   But neither of these explanations can for a moment be received without subverting the entire
argument of the apostle, and destroying all ground of solid comfort.   O this is not the gospel.   If Paul makes any thing plain, he
certainly teaches that believers are, on accepting Christ, actually,
fully and irrevocably justified by the Lord through faith in the
Redeemer, whose righteousness is imputed to them by himself.
Such receive incalculable benefits from their justification.   The
first is mentioned in this verse—*peace with God*.   There is much
said in scripture concerning peace, which is the opposite of war,
persecution, temptation, condemnation, alarm, tumult, strife, controversy.   Several times does Paul speak of "the God of peace."
Jesus Christ is called "our peace" and the "Prince of peace."
The reason is that "the chastisement of our peace was upon him."
He was sent to "guide our feet into the way of peace," Luke
1 : 79.   He says: "Peace I leave with you ; my peace I give unto
you."   Peace is often included in the apostolic salutations and
benedictions.   In our verse it is used in one or both of these two
senses: 1. Actual peace with God, whereby we are no longer
condemned by him, are no longer counted as enemies, and are no
longer engaged in a controversy with him.   By faith in Jesus
Christ we receive reconciliation with God.   The Almighty then
no more regards us as outcasts.   Christ is our Surety, our Sacrifice, our Peace.   The objection to this explanation is that it makes
our verse tautological; for justification clearly includes all this.
2. The other explanation is that the peace here spoken of is peace
of conscience towards God, or, as some express it, conscious
peace towards God.   This is an inestimble blessing.   For it there
is no substitute.   Without it there can be no abiding rest to the
soul.   In the angels, peace of conscience is the fruit of innocence.
In believers it is the fruit of the Saviour's obedience and sufferings..   We cannot be made perfect, as pertaining to the conscience, "without blood," Heb. 9 : 7–12.   The want of this peace
dooms the wicked to misery.   To them there is no peace, Isa. 48 :
22; 57 : 21.   This is the view taken of this passage by many

Calvin: " Peace means tranquillity of conscience, which arises from this—that it feels itself to be reconciled to God." Diodati: " God is made propitious unto us in Christ, who by the faith which he creates in us, causeth us to enjoy this reconciliation, by virtue whereof our conscience is firmly grounded," etc. Hodge: " We have conscious peace with God, that is, we have neither any longer the present upbraidings of an unappeased conscience, nor the dread of divine vengeance." Some unite both senses. Dutch Annotations: " Peace with God is the friendship of God, and the assurance thereof in our mind, whereby we are set at rest in God." The peace, which believers have, is, like justification, wholly gracious. It is " through our Lord Jesus Christ." Like all other graces it is the fruit of the Spirit. It is essential to the symmetry of Christian character. It is abiding. This is the first benefit of a free justification by the merits of the Redeemer.

2. *By whom also we have access by faith into this grace wherein we stand, and rejoice in hope of the glory of God. By whom,* i. e. by Jesus Christ, through whom alone all the benefits of the covenant of grace are conveyed to men. There is but one Mediator, one Prophet, one Priest, one King in Zion. Himself says: " I am the way, the truth, and the life ; no man cometh unto the Father but by me." This verse mentions two other benefits flowing from justification. One is admission into a state of grace, where we permanently enjoy the favor of God, so that our relation to him becomes to all the ends of salvation the same as that of Abraham. We are in covenant with God, who has graciously and in the most solemn manner bound himself not to forsake us, nor leave us to our own strength, wisdom or righteousness. *Access,* found also in Eph. 2 : 18 ; 3 : 12, and uniformly rendered. Peshito: By whom we are brought by faith into this grace. Yet Evans and others for *access* read introduction. This does not materially vary the sense. Access or admission doubtless gives the main idea, which is more than once presented in the scripture. The cognate verb is found in 1 Pet. 3 : 18, " Christ also hath once suffered for us, the just for the unjust, that he *might bring* us [give us access] to God." The same idea in other words is found in Eph. 2 : 13, " Now in Christ Jesus, ye who sometimes were far off, *are made nigh* by the blood of Christ." Some make the clause under consideration substantially a repetition of the latter clause of v. 1. It is true that all the benefits of justification here enumerated are inseparably connected ; but in his account of them the apostle mentions several benefits. In his enumeration he makes delightful progress. If *peace with God* tells us of friendship with God, *access into this grace* points to a covenant relation in which all needed

grace is pledged and supplied.   Haldane: "Peace denotes a particular blessing; access into grace, or a state of favor, general
blessings."   *We stand*, we stand fast, we stand firm, we stand
still, we continue, we are established.   The verb often expresses
stability.   The other benefit of justification noticed in this verse
is solid joy arising from good hopes and bright prospects: *We
rejoice in hope of the glory of God.*   The Jews had seen the visible
glory resting over the tabernacle or over the ark.   And that was
a great sight.   But the glory yet to be revealed is ineffably greater.
It is the glory that excelleth.   It is the far more exceeding and
eternal weight of glory; that which is connected with being forever with the Lord, and enjoying the ineffable bliss of a never-
ending residence in the glorious presence of God and the Lamb.
Into that state of perfection and enjoyment God's people, still in
this world, have not yet entered.   But they have a well grounded
hope, a hope begotten in them by God's Spirit, a hope that cannot
deceive or make ashamed, that in due time, and at no distant day,
all the glories and blessings of heaven shall be theirs.   All Christians are "looking for that blessed hope, and the glorious appearing of our God and Saviour Jesus Christ."   *We rejoice*, in Rom.
2 : 17, 23, make boast; in Rom. 5 : 3, glory; in Rom. 5 : 11, joy.   It
is used in both a good and bad sense, the context determines
which.   In Gal. 6 : 14 it is rendered glory: "God forbid that I
should *glory* save in the cross of our Lord Jesus Christ."

3. *And not only* so, *but we glory in tribulations also, knowing that
tribulation worketh patience.*   In this verse two other benefits flowing to believers from justification are stated.   The first is this.   So
far from being overwhelmed by afflictions they *joy* and rejoice,
they boast and glory in the worst of them.   It is the same verb as
in v. 2, on which see above.   *Tribulation*, we have in this verse the
same noun in both the singular and the plural.   It is often so rendered, also affliction, trouble, anguish, persecution.   It is sometimes connected with persecution, as in Matt. 13 : 21; Mark 4 : 17.
In not a few cases it at least implies persecution for Christ's sake.
See above on Rom. 2 : 9.   The sermon on the mount and many
parts of God's word authorized this glorying in tribulation, especially when it comes for Christ's sake, Matt. 5 : 11, 12; Acts 5 : 41;
Jas. 1 : 2; 1 Pet. 4 : 13.   How common and wonderful this exultation in sore trials was is told in the history of every persecution.
No greater joy have the saints ever had than in the midst of trials
the most appalling.   All this is referable to the power of that grace
wherein we stand.   Hodge: "Since our relation to God is changed,
the relation of all things to us is changed."   "Whom the Lord
loveth he chasteneth, and scourgeth every son whom he receiveth,"

Heb. 12 : 6. A reason for this exultation in suffering is found in its tendency, through grace, to produce the peaceable fruit of righteousness. *Tribulation worketh patience.* In the Greek Testament are two words, rendered patience. One of them is more frequently rendered long-suffering. It means patient endurance. Compare Rom. 2 : 4; Heb. 6 : 12, 15. The other word rendered patience is found in our verse. It is once rendered patient continuance, and signifies endurance, constancy. It is an element of all truly great souls. Towards God it is resigned, saying, " Not as I will, but as thou wilt." Towards Christians, who are faithful in reproof, it meekly says, "Let the righteous smite me." Towards the wicked who afflict and mock us, it says, " Rejoice not against me, O mine enemy." To the ills, which afflict us, it gives a kind entertainment. Without malice it bears insults and injuries. Under delays it is still constant. When others blanch and quail, it plays the hero. The world often counts it obstinacy. But in God's esteem it is a sublime virtue. It is worth all it costs to acquire it. It is a fruit of the Spirit much commended. It is a great grace.

4. *And patience, experience ; and experience, hope.* Patience effects in us *experience.* Everywhere else the word is rendered proof, trial, or experiment. Here it seems to mean that proof, which, by patient endurance of evil, we obtain of the value of our principles and the power of divine grace in its effectual working in us. So, if by experience we understand knowledge gained by being exercised in any matter, experience is a good rendering here. If any prefer proof to experience, there is no objection to that rendering. Such, however, will doubtless admit with Haldane that "proof implies that the trial has proved the genuineness of the tried person and also of the faithfulness and support of God, which will enable us to overcome every difficulty." This is religious experience. And experience worketh *hope.* The apostle spoke of hope in v. 2. See on that place. It is brought up again to shew that as we prove God and ourselves, our hope, instead of diminishing, grows stronger and stronger. Before David met Goliath, he had had experience of great dangers. He did encourage himself by his past experience in encountering terrible enemies and assailants, 1 Sam. 17 : 37. So does the hope of the child of God become more and more an anchor to the soul, as the power of God's grace and his faithfulness are illustrated in its history.

5. *And hope maketh not ashamed; because the love of God is shed abroad in our hearts by the Holy Ghost which is given unto us. Ashamed,* often so rendered; also confounded; sometimes dishonored. Either rendering suits here. The hope here spoken of is that good

hope through grace, which God grants to his chosen. *Such* hope will never bring dishonor, confusion, shame. The apostle here and often uses a figure, common to most, if not all languages. He expresses less than he intends us to understand. His real meaning is that this hope gives a holy and joyful confidence, which nothing can abash. It is of the nature of hope to embolden. It is of the nature of the Christian's hope to make him fearless and faithful in professing the true religion, in adhering to Christ's cause, and in doing one's duty in the face of the most unreasonable and wicked opposition. This hope derives its great strength and animation from the love of God—*because the love of God is shed abroad in our hearts by the Holy Ghost which is given unto us.* Interpreters give three explanations of the phrase *love of God* in this verse. In other places it is clearly used in two different senses; God's love to us, as in Rom. 5 : 6 ; 8 : 39 ; our love to God, as in Luke 11 : 42 ; John 5 : 42 ; Jude 21. The mere words therefore determine nothing in this matter. Others so interpret the phrase as to include both God's love to us and ours to him. 1. Chrysostom thinks it means God's love to us, whereby he has " shed abroad the full fountain of his blessings." The same view is substantially taken by Theophylact, Ambrose, Luther, Melancthon, Calvin, Ferme, Piscator, Cajetan, Toletus, Assembly's Annotations, Dutch Annotations, Schlichting, Pareus, Grotius, Beza, Bp. Hall, Whitby, Brown, Hammond, Evans, Locke, Guyse, Burkitt, Schleusner, Gill, Macknight, Olshausen, Hodge, Haldane and Chalmers. Beza says the apostle is speaking of " the love whereby we are beloved of God, as not only the train of argument shews, but as Paul himself explains in v. 8." All that Rosenmuller makes of the whole clause is that " the divine love is abundantly testified to us." 2. Others seem no less clear that our love to God is here spoken of. So Theodoret, Augustine, Bernard, Anselm, Mede, Doddridge, Hawker, Clarke, Scott and Stuart. The Council of Trent concurs in this view. The arguments for this interpretation are strong. How can God's love to us evince that our hope will not make us ashamed, unless it shall cause him to put his Spirit within us, to work in us all graces and in particular love to God, without which all other supposed evidences of an interest in Christ are vain ? Then our apostle is now in several verses speaking of Christian graces as hope, patience, constancy, etc. This context is nearer than that of v. 8; to which many refer. The apostle is speaking, be it remembered, of a good hope, not of a delusion, and of something enjoyed or experienced by us, which nourishes and supports a good hope. Then our love to God is by Paul elsewhere expressly put down as a fruit of the

Spirit, Gal. 5 : 22. And God's love to us is not the fruit of the
Spirit, but it flows from the glorious nature of each person of the
Godhead. The verb *is shed abroad* is the word so often used, in
some of its forms, to express the effusion of the Holy Spirit in his
gifts or graces, Acts 2 : 17, 18, 33 ; 10 : 45 ; Tit. 3 : 6. That the indwelling of the Holy Spirit, working his graces in our hearts, and
making us his temples, and so evincing our sonship with God, is
an idea familiar to the inspired writers none can doubt, 1 Cor. 3 :
16 ; 6 : 19 ; 2 Cor. 1 : 22 ; 6 : 16 ; Eph. 1 : 13, 14. This view derives
force from the fact that those, who adopt the first view, are not
satisfied with it, but make explanations, which, if they have any
force, virtually admit this second interpretation. Thus Locke :
" Because the sense of the love of God is poured out into our
hearts, &c. But the apostle says nothing about a *sense* of the love
of God. He speaks of the love of God itself. And what is a just
sense of the love of God to us, if it be not our love towards God ?
So Gill explains himself by speaking of the " full and comfortable
sensation which believers have of the love of God to them." But
Paul says not a word about any *sensation ;* and, if he did, to what
could he refer but to our love to God ? Bp. Hall also says :
" Hope disappointeth us not ; because the sense and comfortable
assurance of that love, wherewith he embraceth us, is shed abroad,"
&c. Diodati also says that here " the love of God means the assurance we have of God's love to us." Yet how can any one have
a " comfortable assurance," or any " assurance " of God's love to
him but by the love, which he has towards God ? 1 John 3 : 19. So
Guyse : " This sort of hope will not turn to our confusion ; because it rests, not upon any merit in ourselves, but upon the free
favor of God towards us, which in its gracious and effectual operation is poured forth into, and abundantly fills our souls with its
lovely manifestations and distinguishing fruits ; and so inflames
them with love to him again," &c. This is almost all that could
be asked by those, who think that in our verse *love to God* means
our love to him. So also Hodge : " This manifestation of divine
love is not any external revelation of it in the works of Providence, or even in redemption, but it is *in our hearts.*" It will
probably be denied by none that if the apostle had designed to
teach that the gracious affection of love in the soul was enkindled
by the Holy Ghost he could have selected no better language
than we have in this verse. Tholuck : " We must naturally view
it as implying a *consciousness in the heart*, such as is spoken of in
Rom. 8 : 16 ; 2 Cor. 1 : 22. On Rom. 5 : 1 Chalmers says : " The
whole passage, for several verses, looks to be a narrative of the
personal experience of believers—of their rejoicing, and of their

hoping, and of their glorying;" and why may we not add—of their loving? A third view of this verse has been presented and seems to be favored by Origen, Oecumenius and Aquinas. It unites the two senses above given. It supposes discoveries of God's love to us to be made by the Spirit in such a way as to enkindle our love to him. It explains it of love *created* in us by the love of God *uncreated* towards us. This is substantially the view of not a few others, some of whom have been already cited. Thus Olshausen: " The love of God in the apostle's meaning is the love of God to man, which however awakens in him reciprocal love, (1 John 4 : 19,) not indeed proceeding from his own mere natural powers, but from the higher powers of the divine Spirit." The objection to this third view is that it makes the same word in the same sentence denote two things so different as God's love to us and ours to him. For the reasons given the second view is to be preferred. It is pleasant to the believer to find that all commentators agree that God's Spirit reveals to his people, so as to enable them to view aright God's love to them, and at the same time implants and nourishes in them a sincere and supreme love to him. On those points all good men are agreed. Nor do they differ in their judgment respecting the gratuitous bestowment of the Holy Spirit. He is "given unto us." He cannot be purchased.

6. *For when we were yet without strength, in due time Christ died for the ungodly.* In this and the next three verses the apostle uses four words to describe, not the state of the Gentiles only, as Locke contends, but of all men before the grace of God. These words we render " without strength," " ungodly," " sinners," and " enemies;" all applied to the same persons, and either of them making a sad yet just representation of the natural state of man. The first is rendered, " without strength." In Matt. 25 : 39, 43, 44; Luke 10 : 9; Acts 5 : 15, 16, it is rendered *sick;* in Acts 4 : 9 *impotent;* in 1 Cor. 12 : 22 *feeble;* often *weak;* the rendering in our verse is literal. Coverdale, Tyndale, Cranmer, Rheims and Doway have *weak;* Conybeare and Howson, *helpless.* Our case is by nature sad indeed. We have no might to do good, Isa. 40 : 29. We cannot keep the law. Clarke: " Neither able to resist *sin* nor *do* any *good;* utterly devoid of *power* to extricate themselves from the misery of their situation." We cannot atone for our sins. We cannot regenerate our hearts. We cannot keep ourselves in the way of life. We are sick, impotent, broken, yea dead in trespasses and sins. In a state of nature the soul performs none of the functions of spiritual life. This our inability is universal, perpetual, sinful, and by all human powers incurable. Spiritually we are

sick unto death. We are also "ungodly." On this word see above on Rom. 4 : 5. The word is uniformly rendered. It is the same used by the Septuagint in Ps. 1. and elsewhere, rendered ungodly, more frequently wicked. Clarke : " Satan lived in, ruled and enslaved their hearts." God justifies the ungodly, Rom. 4 : 5. Christ died for the ungodly. He died *for* the ungodly, i. e. he died in their place, in their stead, as their substitute. Often has the Greek preposition this sense : " Will he *for* a fish give him a serpent?" Luke 11 : 11. See also 1 Cor. 11 : 15. In Matt. 2 : 22 it is rendered *in the room*. Twice it is said of Christ that he gave " his life a ransom *for* many," Matt. 20 : 28 ; Mark 10 : 45. So he died *for* the ungodly, *in due time*. Coverdale, Tyndale, Cranmer, Rheims and Doway, according to the time ; Rosenmuller and others, at the appointed time. The word means a time, a season, a set time, a fit time, and often occurs. Other terms of like import are employed, Gal. 4 : 4 ; 1 Pet. 1 : 20. In this verse the most difficult word is the particle *for* at the beginning. It may connect this verse with the last clause of v. 5, or with the first clause of v. 5, or with the first clause of v. 1, or with the whole train of the apostle's argument. In the first case we have proof of God's grace in giving us the Holy Spirit through Christ Jesus ; in the second the ground of our good hope is brought out ; in the third we see why we are justified and have peace with God ; in the last we have a recurrence to the ground of the kindness shewn to believing sinners, securing to them all the blessings of the covenant by the work and sufferings of Christ. The fact is that truths of this class are often so inwoven into the texture of inspired discourses that they relate to the train of thoughts, and to many particular parts thereof. Many both ancient and modern writers are disposed specially to connect this verse with the *hoping* of vs. 2, 5. Some regard vs. 6–10 as containing a parenthesis. Perhaps they do ; but the thoughts presented are as weighty and as rich as any in the chapter, and well accord with the rest.

  7. *For scarcely for a righteous man will one die : yet peradventure for a good man some would even dare to die. For*, the first word, is simply affirmative. Peshito : " For rarely doth one die for the ungodly : though for the good, some one perhaps might venture to die." Beza says he could approve this rendering but for the want of authority in the MSS. This is wholly wanting. The Syriac doubtless took the word *ungodly* from the preceding verse. But the contrast in this verse is not between a *wicked* man and a *good* man ; but between a *just*, righteous, equitable, or upright man and the *good*, kind, useful man, who obliges many. Rarely indeed will men die for one another, even when most benevolent and beneficent, or

most highly esteemed. But for a man who is merely upright, and has done no great public service, nor conferred marked benefits on any one, who has ever offered to die? Sacred history tells us of the love Jonathan had to David. He did *risk* his life for him. We have too the affecting story of Damon and Pythias. " Lilloe stepped between the murderer and King Edward his master. Nicholas Ribische lost his life to preserve Prince Maurice at the siege of Pista." Still these are rare cases. When they occur, men unite in saying that they are *daring.* Our verse says the same. There is no act of more boldness. Perhaps in most cases like those cited the hero expects to survive and has no settled design of dying. Indeed there is but a slight *peradventure* that any man would deliberately die for his best friend. Compare John 15 : 13 ; 1 John 3 : 16.

8. *But God commendeth his love towards us, in that, while we were yet sinners, Christ died for us.* In v. 6 it is said Christ died for the ungodly, and here that he died for us *sinners.* This word is rendered with great uniformity. It denotes those who have missed the mark, at which they should aim—the honor of God, and the mark at which they did aim—their own happiness. They have plunged themselves into guilt and pollution and wretchedness. And such were we all, Jews and Gentiles, old and young, for whom, in whose stead Christ died. This was wonderful love, indeed. It has no parallel. God *commendeth* it, i. e. sets it forth, manifests it in a wonderful manner. See above on Rom. 3 : 5 where we have the same word.

9. *Much more then, being now justified by his blood, we shall be saved from wrath through him.* No part of the Bible is a treatise on logic, nor was designed to teach logic ; but no book contains finer specimens of the art of reasoning than can be found in many of the sacred pages. In particular Paul gives us many specimens of irrefragable argument. Our verse contains a sample of the *argument a fortiori.* If God loved us and gave his Son for us while sinners, he will beyond all doubt save us when we are justified. Justification includes the forgiveness of sins and the acceptance of the sinner as righteous before God. Often is a part, an important part, put for the whole. The shedding of Christ's blood was an important matter, as essential as his holy life, his resurrection or his intercession. It seems to be put here for his whole undertaking. The active and passive obedience of Christ are never separated, though they are distinguished. Christ's righteousness consists of his conformity to the precept and his endurance of the penalty of the law, and we are justified by his righteousness. But as men are constantly liable to pervert the

truth, and especially the true doctrine of justification, God teaches us the right way by a great variety of phrases and terms. Take the matter here adduced. One scripture says that men are justified by faith. Another says they are justified through faith. Another declares that they are justified by Christ. Another declares that we are justified freely by his grace. Another teaches that we are justified in the name of the Lord Jesus Christ. In our verse we are said to be justified by the blood of Christ. Compare Rom. 3 : 24, 30; 1 Cor. 6 : 11; Gal. 2 : 17. These statements are not contradictory, but mightly serve to guard us against mistake. When men are said to be justified by faith, some say it means that faith is the procuring cause of our pardon and acceptance; or that our faith is accepted in lieu of a perfect righteousness. No! says our verse, we are justified by the blood of the Redeemer, as the procuring cause. And so none but the wilful and perverse can mistake the truth. And so being justified, it is certain we shall be delivered from the penal consequences of transgression or from wrath—the wrath to come, and all through Christ.

10. *For if, when we were enemies. we were reconciled to God by the death of his Son ; much more, being reconciled, we shall be saved by his life.* The preceding verse contained a sample of the argument *a fortiori*. This contains that form of argument duplicated. The first antithesis is between *enemies* and persons *reconciled*. The second is between Christ's *death* and his *life*. If a *dying* Saviour can effect the reconciliation of *enemies ;* much more can a *living* Redeemer do all that is required to the complete deliverance of his *friends*. Where in all the range of knowledge can more powerful argument be found? *Enemies !* What a fearful thought. Clarke: "Sin, indulged, increases in strength; evil *acts* engender fixed and rooted *habits;* the mind, everywhere poisoned with sin, increases in averseness from good, and mere *aversion* produces enmity; and *enmity, acts of hostility*." No word can more clearly denote real adversaries. Against such God must have a holy and inflexible displeasure, or *wrath. Reconciled,* a word not before found in this epistle. The cognate noun is found in the next verse, and is rendered *atonement*. Everywhere else these words are rendered reconciled and reconciliation, Rom. 11 : 15; 2 Cor. 5 : 18, 19, 20. An at-one-ment is a reconciliation, a bringing together those, who have been at variance. We have forsaken, insulted and rebelled against God. He has been good to us, following us with mercies, reproofs and invitations. God is holy, and hates sin. Out of mere pity he provided a mode of reconciliation by the life and death of his Son. Jesus Christ is the great,

the only Reconciler. God is the offended and we are the offenders. To be reconciled to God is to be brought into relations of friendship with him, and this can be done only by an atonement. Grotius correctly says that in heathen authors men's *being reconciled to their gods* is always understood to signify appeasing the anger of their gods. Jesus Christ satisfied the demands of justice against us. By his death he averted from his people the righteous indignation of God. As is said in the preceding verse he *saved* them *from wrath*, meaning deserved punishment. He propitiated the Most High towards us offenders. He met all the claims of law against us. This reconciliation took place *intentionally*, in God's eternal purpose; *meritoriously*, in the completion of Christ's humiliation; *actually*, when in true faith we embraced the offer of the Gospel. The apostle is here speaking of those who were *actually* reconciled. We are reconciled by the *blood of Christ*, as it is expressed in v. 9; for to be actually reconciled is virtually the same as to be justified. Our reconciliation with God is by *the death of his Son*, who made the propitiation for us, who suffered the just for the unjust. That this is the true view of *reconciled* is proven from the scriptural use of that term, 1 Sam. 29 : 4; Matt. 5 : 23, 24. The same is taught by a variety of phrases of like import in the Scriptures, in which God says his anger is turned away, he is pacified, he has taken away his wrath, etc.

11. *And not only so, but we also joy in God through our Lord Jesus Christ, by whom we have now received the atonement.* *Joy*, in v. 2 rendered rejoice; in v. 3, glory; elsewhere boast. The meaning is we now exult in God. *Received*, a literal rendering. Paul has been enumerating the benefits of justification. In doing so he more than once reverts to the same idea. In vs. 2, 5 he dwells on *hope;* in vs. 3, 11 he speaks of joy, exultant joy; and in vs. 1, 10, 11 he speaks of peace and reconciliation with God. The whole is designed to be a triumphant and exultant deduction of his argument as to the blessedness of the man, who enjoys a gratuitous justification. This conclusion is honorable to Jehovah. *We joy in God*, not in ourselves, not in our ancestry, not in ,rites, not in works of righteousness which we have done, but in God alone, *through our Lord Jesus Christ.* We pray in his name, we give thanks in his name, we trust in his name, we do all in his name. Our names are worthless, because we are sinners. The names of angels are worthless because they are fellow creatures and fellow servants, Rev. 22 : 9. But the name of Jesus is far above every name that is named, not only in this world, but in that which is to come, Eph 1 : 21. *By him* we have received the atonement; by him we shall gain the final victory, by him we shall be raised from

the dead, by him we shall rise to eternal glory.   And all this is
through the great *atonement* he has made.   Had he been only a
Prophet and a King to his chosen he would not have saved them.
They were indeed ignorant and needed a teacher. They were feeble
and needed a ruler and defender.   But they were guilty, and so
must have a sacrifice, an atoning and an interceding High Priest.

DOCTRINAL AND PRACTICAL REMARKS

1. Let us not weary of sound scriptural instruction on the
great doctrine of justification, v. 1, It is a glorious theme, and we
should not cease to give thanks that we have line upon line respecting it.   Nor can we possibly too deeply impress on our
minds vital truths on this subject.   When we are said to be justified by faith, the meaning is that we are justified by a faith that
lays hold of the righteousness of our God and Saviour Jesus
Christ.   Faith is the instrument.   The righteousness of Christ
is the ground.   This righteousness of God is by faith of Jesus
Christ, unto all, and upon all them that believe.   Men are saved
not by their works, merits or efforts, but by God's grace and
mercy in and through Jesus Christ.   This great gift of righteousness is an unspeakable benefit, having in its train innumerable
blessings.   By it is the life of our souls.

2. Let us imitate Paul in frequently and formally acknowledging our indebtedness to the blessed Saviour.   Here in vs. 1, 9, 11
he says we have these great blessings *through* Jesus Christ; and in
v. 2 our access is said to be *by* him; in v. 9 our justification is said
to be *by* his blood; in v. 10 our reconciliation is said to be *by* his
death; and in v. 11 it is said that *by* him we have received the
atonement; while in vs. 6, 8 it is said he died for us.   Let us dwell
on his name with hearty and grateful joy.   Let us make him the
first and the last.   There is no danger that we shall love him too
much, commend him too highly, or serve him too devotedly.
Blessed Lamb of God, we owe thee all, we would give thee all.
Oh that men would look to him, and to him alone.   Chalmers:
"The children of Israel might have as soon been healed by looking downwardly upon their wounds, rather than upwardly to the
brazen serpent, as the conscience-stricken sinner will find relief
from any one object that can meet his eye, in that abyss of darkness and distemper to which he has turned his own laboring
bosom."

3. Though justification and sanctification are as distinct as any
two gifts of God to men, and ought ever to be so spoken of, and
never confounded; yet they are never separated.   Where one is,

the other is not wanting Whoever is justified in the name of the Lord Jesus is sure to be sanctified by the Spirit of our God, 1 Cor. 1 : 30; 6 : 11. And yet in justification God imputes the righteousness of Christ; in sanctification he by his Spirit works in us both to will and to do of his good pleasure; in the former, sin is pardoned; in the latter, sin is subdued; in the one, all are equally freed from condemnation and fully accepted; in the other, very unequal attainments are made; one is from the first perfect; the other is progressive; the former being an act, the latter a work. Yet God never justifies a man that he does not also make him holy, and infuse into him all Christian graces, as we see here, vs. 1-5.

4. Inestimable is the blessing of *peace* with God, in whatever scriptural sense we use that term. If by it here we understand peace of conscience towards God, what do men in all ages and countries need more than this? To the Roman Senate Caligula said, "I suffer death every day." Plato: "When a man is near the time when he must expect to die, there come into his mind a fear and anxiety about things that were never so thought of before." Herod was a Sadducee. He believed in neither angel, nor spirit, nor resurrection. Yet when Jesus began to do his wonders, all Herod's principles forsook him, and he said, "It is John, whom I beheaded; he is risen from the dead," Mark 6 : 16. No other scheme or system but that of the Gospel is at once "righteousness, and peace, and joy in the Holy Ghost." God's plan meets all the demands of law, and justice, and conscience.

5. Let us seek to have sound and clear views of faith, of its nature and of its offices, vs. 1, 2. True faith is no conceit, no dream, no wild and irrational apprehension. It is real, sober, regardful of evidence. It believes on the authority and testimony of Jehovah. Even when it lays hold on Christ, it believes the testimony of God concerning his Son. It is wise to credit every word of God, on the simple ground that he cannot lie. Faith relies on Christ as he is freely offered. It embraces the promises graciously made. It is a great grace, Heb. 11 : 1-38. Well did John Bunyan call it by the name of Mr. Greatheart.

6. There is such a thing as a state of grace, and believers are admitted into it, v. 2. Chrysostom: "This is the nature of God's grace. It hath no end, it knows no bound, but evermore is on the advance to greater things, which in human affairs is not so. Take an instance of what I mean. One has acquired rule and glory and authority, yet he does not stand therein continuously, but is speedily cast out of it. Or if man take it not from him, death comes, and is sure to take it from him. But God's gifts are not of

this kind ; for neither man, nor occasion, nor crisis ot affairs, nor even the devil, nor death can come and cast us out of them. But when we are dead, we then more strictly speaking have possession of them, and keep going on enjoying more and more." This state of grace enjoyed by believers secures to them communion with God, so that all of them may say, " Truly our fellowship is with the Father, and with his Son Jesus Christ," 1 John 1 : 3. " The secret of the Lord is with them that fear him ; and he will shew them his covenant," Ps. 25 : 14. This access to grace is not a vanity, such as self-deceivers often boast of, but it is a great advantage possessed by those and those only, who are justified by faith. Scott : " The believer has free access to the mercy-seat ; he is established in the grace and favor of God ; and he may now rejoice and triumphantly exult in the hope of everlasting glory ; though perhaps he just before trembled from well-grounded apprehensions of deserved vengeance."

7. The state of believers is not changeable but has great stability. In it they stand firm. Their moods and frames of feeling change. Their views on many things undergo modifications. Their characters are constantly changing for the better. But their state is fixed by the purpose and grace of God. In it they *stand*, stand firm, v. 2. And why should it not be so? Their hope is in the Lord, who changes not, Mal. 3 : 6. And are not these his promises unfailing? " They shall be my people, and I will be their God . . . And I will make an everlasting covenant with them, that I will not turn away from them, to do them good : but I will put my fear in their hearts, that they shall not depart from me," Jer. 32 : 38, 40. God's people are not only admitted to his favor ; but they are confirmed in it. Evans : " It is not in the court of heaven as in earthly courts, where high places are slippery places ; but we stand in an humble confidence of this very thing, *that he who has begun the good work, will perform it*," Phil. 1 : 6. The grace manifested in bringing men to embrace the gospel is quite sufficient to hold them up in any trial. The seed of God remains in the regenerate. The sentence of justification is irrevocable. And the intercession of Christ is full security that our faith shall not fail, Luke 22 : 31, 32.

8. So that we may and should labor with earnest and confident expectation of success for a full assurance of understanding in all the truths of religion, for a full assurance of faith, that we may stagger at no promise of God, and for a full assurance of hope of final salvation, Col. 2 : 2 ; Heb. 6 : 11 ; 10 : 22. In the covenant of grace provision is made and encouragement is given to us to make our calling and election sure. Calvin correctly designates

these dogmas as "pestilent," first "bidding Christians to be satisfied with moral conjecture as to the perception of God's favor
towards them, and secondly, teaching that all are uncertain as to
their final perseverance." Nor is any thing further from pride
and overweening conceit of ourselves than strong genuine confidence in our final salvation. Hodge : "Assurance of the love of
God never produces self-complacency or pride ; but always
humility, self-abasement, wonder, gratitude and praise." That such
assurance is attainable many scriptures declare, Job 19 : 25 ; Ps.
116 : 16 ; 119 : 125 ; 143 : 12 ; 2 Tim. 4 : 6–8 ; 1 John 3 : 19.

9. Let us cultivate a joyful state of heart and mind, vs. 2, 3, 11.
Ample provision is made for great joy in the Lord, in the power
of his might, in the abundance of his grace, in the wisdom of his
plans, and in the riches of the inheritance he has provided for his
saints. It is sometimes forgotten that holy joy is enjoined as a
duty ; but no command is more clear : "Rejoice in the Lord, O ye
righteous," Ps. 33 : 1 ; 97 : 12, "Rejoice in the Lord always : and
again I say, Rejoice," Phil. 4 : 4. If our joy is *in the Lord,* in his
being, his perfections, his providence, his word, his ordinances
and his grace, it cannot rise too high. It is a tormenting vanity
to rejoice in a thing of naught, to be very glad in a gourd, but it
is a blessedness to glory in Jehovah. Let us rejoice in what God
is, in what he has done and in what he has promised.

10. And let not our hope be faint or trembling. Only let it
rest on God's word and it cannot be too confident, or expect too
much, even including enduring riches, unending pleasures and
everlasting honors, yea the joy and glory of God. Chrysostom :
"What then ? do our goods lie in hopes ? Yes, in hopes—but
not mere human hopes, which often slip away, and put to shame
him that hoped ; when some one, who was expected to patronize
him, dies, or is changed, though he lives. No such lot is ours,
our hope is sure, and unmoveable. For he, who hath made the
promise, ever liveth." Chalmers distinguishes between the kinds
of hope enjoyed by the Christian, calling them ' the hope of faith
and the hope of experience.' By the former he means the hope
awakened by the simple promise of God ; by the latter, the expectation arising from an actual experience of God's faithfulness
in trials through which we have passed. But these are not different kinds of hope. When we rightly hear and believe God's
promise, we hope in his mercy ; when we experience the fulfilment of his gracious engagements to strengthen and help us, our
hope is confirmed. That seems to be all that can be made of the
distinction. Haldane : "At first hope springs solely from a view
of the mediation and work of our Lord Jesus Christ. Here it ac-

quires a new force from the proof the believer has of the reality of
his union with the Saviour, by his being filled with the fruits of
righteousness which are by Jesus Christ. Thus the ' good hope
through grace' must be produced solely by faith, and confirmed,
not produced, by the fruits of faith."

11. Wondrous is the grace, which God grants to his people,
when he enables them not only to bear meekly divers trials, but
many times even to glory in the sharpest of them, v. 3. What but
love to Christ and his sustaining grace ever caused a truthful
record to be made like this?   " They departed from the presence,
of the council, rejoicing that they were counted worthy to suffer
shame for the name of Jesus," Acts 5 : 41. It is true that no affliction is in itself joyous but on the contrary grievous. The *tribulations* of God's people are *great*. Flesh and blood must sink under
them. But divine grace can bear them aloft. They who have it
sing with their backs all cut with scourging, and their feet fast in
the stocks, Acts 16 : 25. The worst case, into which a disciple of
strong faith may be put, will not hinder him from singing the
old song of Christendom : " If we be dead with him, we shall
also live with him : if we suffer, we shall also reign with him : if we
deny him, he also will deny us : if we believe not, yet he abideth
faithful."   God's people may be troubled on every side, yet not
distressed; perplexed, but not in despair; persecuted, but not forsaken ; cast down, but not destroyed, 2 Cor. 4 : 8, 9. Thousands
of years ago one of the most afflicted servants of God sang:
" Thou hast dealt well with thy servant, O Lord, according unto
thy word. . . Before I was afflicted I went astray : but now have
I kept thy word. . . It is good for me that I have been afflicted;
that I might learn thy statutes," Ps. 119 : 65, 67, 71.   This was
under a dispensation not near so luminous as that under which we
live. Brown: " Though natural people, who are strangers to God
and to his way of dealing, may judge them best beloved who are
least troubled with outward crosses and tribulations; yet, as no
man knoweth either love or hatred by all such external dispensations, so God's love towards his people will not exeem them from
external crosses, nor will external tribulations and crossing dispensations give any just ground of questioning God's love."   So far
from it, himself has said: " As many as I love, I rebuke and
chasten." " Whom the Lord loveth he chasteneth, and scourgeth
every son whom he receiveth," Rev. 3 : 19; Heb. 12 : 6.

12. Another excellent grace, which all should cultivate is
patience, or constancy, unflinching endurance and resolution, vs.
3, 4. No gracious quality is more essential. " Behold, we count
them happy who endure," Jas. 5 : 11. " He that endureth to the

end shall be saved," Matt. 10 : 22. In both these cases the verb rendered *endure* is cognate to our noun *patience*. This grace is indispensable. " Be thou faithful unto death, and I will give thee a crown of life." " He that overcometh shall inherit all things ; and I will be his God, and he shall be my son," Rev. 2 : 10 : 21 : 7. Evans : "*Patience* does us more good than *tribulations* can do us hurt." Let us therefore doubly guard our spirits against all that is contrary to true constancy of soul. Brown : " Impatience and fretting under God's dispensations do so blind souls that they cannot see nor observe how God is proving himself even then gracious, merciful, powerful and faithful." " The patient in spirit is better than the proud in spirit." Ecc. 7 : 8.

13. Nor is there any substitute for that practical and *experimental* knowledge of divine things, which we obtain by being *proved* and tested, and by *proving* the faithfulness of God in divers trials and tribulations, v. 4. Very little does the young believer, genuine though his faith may be, know of the rich and blessed import of the promises. He is a novice. Once Paul speaks of *carnal* and *babes in Christ* as very much the same, 1 Cor. 3 : 1. But the aged believer, who has long been taking lessons in the school of Christ and in the school of adversity, has a blessed apprehension of such covenant engagements as these : " When thou passest through the waters, I will be with thee ; and through the rivers, they shall not overflow thee : when thou walkest through the fire, thou shalt not be burned ; neither shall the flame kindle upon thee." " When the poor and needy seek water, and there is none, and their tongue faileth for thirst, I the Lord will hear them, I the God of Israel will not forsake them. I will open rivers in high places, and fountains in the midst of the valleys : I will make the wilderness a pool of water, and the dry land springs of water," Isa. 41 : 17, 18 ; 43 : 2. Wondrously does ' the God of all comfort comfort us in all our tribulation, that we may be able to comfort them which are in any trouble by the comfort wherewith we ourselves are comforted of God,' 2 Cor. 1 : 3, 4. Any thing is good for us if it leads us to know more of God and of his grace in us and toward us. What a wonderful teacher experience is, especially experience in adversity. It instructs us so fully respecting our own ignorance and weakness, the world's vanity and fickleness, Satan's malice and power, the tenderness and sympathy of real Christians and the wisdom, power, love and faithfulness of God.

14. Nor is there a nobler attainment made by the pious than love to God, which was insisted on as fully by Moses as by John, Deut. 6 : 5 ; 7 : 9 ; 10 : 12 ; 11 : 1, 13, 22 ; 19 : 9 ; 30 : 6. This grace is shed abroad in our hearts by the Holy Ghost, v. 5. The first

necessary quality of this love is that it be genuine not spurious; sincere not in pretence; efficient, not in word only; supreme, admitting no rivals; stable, not fitful; universal, not partial, extending to all God's character, laws and decisions, ways and works. Scott: " This seal of God cannot be broken, and Satan evidently and peculiarly fails in his attempts to counterfeit it: for all false affections, and enthusiastic confidences are liable to be consumed in the furnace of long-continued afflictions; and they never can communicate that reciprocal, steady, pre-eminent and abiding love of God in Christ, which no fire can burn, no waters can quench, and which in ten thousands of instances has proved stronger than the fear of death in its most tremendous forms, and has enabled a feeble believer to disregard the cruelty of a savage executioner, in comparison of the anguish of wilfully denying or disobeying his beloved Lord." If we love not God, we are yet in our sins. Love is greater than faith, greater than hope. It bears all things, endures all things, 1 Cor. 13 : 7, 13.

15. There is an amazing work going on for God's people, for the whole church. Many a time has God rebuked kings for the sake of an humble believer. He has made the sun to stand still, and the stars in their courses to fight the battles of his people. To them the Valley of Achor is for a door of hope. Jehovah has made a covenant for his people with the beasts of the field, and with the fowls of heaven, and with the creeping things of the ground. Yea, his saints are in league with the stones of the field; and the wild beasts of the field are at peace with them. God himself is their God, and guide, and portion. And by the work he is doing in them, he is evincing his readiness to do all these things and much more for his people. This is specially manifested by the blessed sisterhood of graces, begotten and nourished in them by the Holy Ghost, which is given unto them, vs. 1–5.

16. There is such a thing as symmetry of Christian character, a proportion in the graces of a renewed soul. Its excellences are not all faith, or peace, or joy, or hope, or exultation, or patience, or experience, or boldness, or love; but all of these combined in harmony, vs. 1–5. And these are united with the other graces of the Spirit, named in Matt. 5 : 1–10; Gal. 5 : 22, 23; James 3 : 17 : 2 Pet. 1 : 5–9. Let us undervalue no kind of moral excellence. Every grace is necessary to the completeness of a good character. It is God's plan to take his people home to glory without spot, or wrinkle, or blemish, or any such thing, especially without such a blemish as would exist, if they had faith without penitence, courage without humility, zeal without meekness, hope without reverence, or fear without love. There are no monsters in the

kingdom of heaven. To this very end God has instituted a ministry to labor in the church on earth, " till we all come in the unity
of the faith, and of the knowledge of the Son of God, unto a perfect man, unto the measure of the stature of the fulness of Christ:
that we henceforth be no more children, tossed to and fro, and
carried about with every wind of doctrine by the sleight of
men, and cunning craftiness, whereby they lie in wait to deceive,
but speaking the truth in love, may grow up into him in all things,
which is the head even Christ."

17. It is much to be regretted that the true doctrine respecting the Holy Ghost is not better understood and his offices in the
church more thought of. On this subject the scriptures are very
clear. In particular Paul never fails to embrace a fit opportunity
for reminding us of this great author of all holiness in the human
heart. See v. 5. In scripture he is called the Spirit, the Spirit of
the Lord, the Spirit of God, the Spirit of Christ, the Holy Spirit,
and the Holy Ghost. Ghost is a Saxon word and means Spirit.
Spirit is a Latin word and means Ghost. Ghost and Spirit are
used interchangeably as the rendering of the same word. He is
the Spirit of truth, of holiness, of wisdom, of counsel, of knowledge, of might, of revelation, of adoption, of grace and of supplication, because by him we receive these blessings. He is said
to be free, because he cannot be bought or commanded. His
work is all of grace. He is said to be good, because such is his
nature, and he is the fountain of goodness. He is loving, pitiful
and condescending. He is the Sanctifier, the author of regeneration and of all holiness in man. He is the Comforter in the souls
of believers, taking of the things of Christ, and shewing them to
his people. He indites the prayers of the righteous. On him we
depend for spiritual life, and for all Christian graces. He calls
men to repentance. He is a divine person. It is as true of him
as of the Father or the Son : " Them that honor me will I honor."
No improvements in theology, in preaching, in religious instruction or in religious effort can render unnecessary his influences.
He must illuminate, impress, renew, guide and purify us, or we
shall perish. His indwelling is the earnest of our inheritance.
Chrysostom : " Had not God been willing to present us after our
labors with great crowns, he would never have given us such
mighty gifts before our labors. But now the warmth of his love
is hence made apparent, that it is not gradually and little by little
that he honors us, but he hath shed abroad the full fountain of his
blessings, and this too before our struggles." Our dependence on
the Spirit is absolute. We are not sufficient as of ourselves to
think anything. Men may read and hear the gospel faithfully

preached all their days, without any saving effect, if the Spirit open not their hearts to attend unto the things of salvation.   Nor can converted souls make any advancement in saving knowledge or holy affections, except as the Holy Ghost is granted unto them.   He is that unction, which teacheth all things.   " Not by might, nor by power, but by my Spirit, saith the Lord."

18. Let us do all in our power to stir up ourselves to take hold on God, and in particular to ' keep ourselves in the love of God,' v. 5.   Let us cultivate all those habits of devotion, especially in our closets, which will conduce to the fervor of our love.   Dodd-ridge : " To excite our love to God, let us be daily meditating upon the wonders of redeeming love and grace ; adoring that *seasonable* interposition of divine mercy, that when we were *weak* and guilty creatures, when we lay for ever helpless under a sentence of everlasting condemnation, Christ died for us."

19. In v. 6 we are taught that our Lord died in the time that was due, or set, or appointed.   This is proven by many scriptures. He was to come during the time of the second temple, before all political power was taken from Judah, and at the end of Daniel's weeks.   Christ himself knew the very hour when he was to die. Now though no prophecy has revealed the time of the death of any man living, yet in the counsels of God the time and manner of every man's departure out of this world are fixed.   So teaches the oldest book of Scripture : " His days are determined, the number of his months are with thee, thou hast appointed his bounds that he cannot pass," Job. 14 : 5.   It is a comfort to a good man to know that he cannot die till his time comes—the time set by infinite wisdom and immeasurable love.

20. It seems strange that any one, who regards the authority of the sacred oracles, should find any difficulty or be at any loss about the scriptural doctrine of the fallen state of man by nature. We have met this subject in previous pages of this work ; but in the verses under consideration, is not the language as decisive? Men are said to be " without strength " " ungodly " or impious, " sinners " and " enemies."   What more can be said?   What more need be said to depict our ruined condition ?   God is of purer eyes than to behold evil, and cannot look on iniquity, Hab. 1 : 13. If God's word regards and represents us as helpless, impious, sinners, enemies, we may rest assured that in that representation there is no exaggeration, no extravagance, but the simple verity.

21. How could God love men as he did ?   Only because he was God and had in his own bosom an ocean of unspeakable benevolence, vs. 6, 8.   It is common and it is just to say that God's love is unparalleled.   But an old writer, who lived a few centuries

ago, uses a word that is no longer found in English classics. He says God's love to man is *unparallelable*. And this is true. It cannot be matched. This love of God to sinners is no novelty. It dates from the remotest antiquity, Jer. 31 : 3. It has been very costly. It did not cost God even an effort to make the universe. But it cost the agony of Gethsemane and the awful scenes of Calvary to redeem men. God's love to sinners brings to all who accept his grace blessings more precious than are enjoyed by any creatures God has made. God's love to sinners is infinite. As it spared no cost or pains, it withholds no good thing. This love was the love of Father, Son and Holy Ghost. The Father gave the Son to die for us. The Son offered himself a victim, as a sacrifice for us. The Spirit sets forth the love of the Father in just terms, and applies the redemption that is in Christ Jesus, new creating the souls of all the chosen. A government has sometimes paid large sums of money to redeem one of its citizens from captivity. But who, besides the Prince of life, ever gave himself a ransom for his enemies?

22. While the reigning motive in the pious heart is not fear but love, not mere dread of torment but a joyful trust in God's grace, yet it is well for us often to think of the hole of the pit whence we were digged, and of the miry clay whence our feet were taken. We should never forget that salvation is not only to something great and glorious, but that it is from something exceedingly dreadful, even from *wrath*, v. 9. It is said that one man was awakened and converted just by hearing Mr. Whitefield pronounce the words—*The wrath of the Lamb.* Such words ought to move any heart.

23. The scriptures make much of the *blood* of Christ, and well they may, v. 9. But it was not enough that he shed a little blood for us. It is sometimes foolishly said that one drop of his blood was enough to atone for the sins of the world. But there is no truth in such a statement. Had it been so, the work of propitiation would have been finished in Gethsemane, for there " his sweat was as it were great drops of blood falling down to the ground," Luke 22 : 44. Accordingly that, which in v. 9 is said to have been effected by the blood of Christ, is in v. 10 ascribed to his death. If Christ himself would save us, it must be by his tasting *death* for every man. Every time we celebrate the Lord's Supper, we do shew the Lord's *death* till he come.

24. In our thoughts, speeches and writings concerning scriptural truths, in particular respecting the great doctrines of salvation let us beware of the bad art of dwarfing or dwindling the glorious things of salvation. On v. 9 Macknight says: " Here *justified by*

his blood, means that, in view of Christ's shedding his blood, Adam and Eve were respited from death, and being allowed to live, he and they were placed under a new covenant, by which they might regain immortality.   This is what is called *justification of life*, v. 18." Again he says: "Here persons are said to be justified by Christ's blood, who are not saved from wrath through him." Was there ever more wild or foolish speech than this? It is not a whit the less to be regretted because it is the language of a scholar, who in some other things has done good service to the church. How refreshing now to read such words as these from Hodge: "The primary object of the death of Christ was to render God propitious, to satisfy his justice; and not to influence human conduct, or display the divine character for the sake of the moral effect of that exhibition.   Among its infinitely diversified results, all of which were designed, some of the most important, no doubt, are the sanctification of men, the display of the divine perfections, the prevention of sin, the happiness of the universe, etc., etc.   But the object of a sacrifice, as such, is to propitiate, vs. 9, 10; Heb. 2 : 17."   Compare 1 Pet. 1 ; 18; Rev. 5 : 9.   Chrysostom: "There were two difficulties in the way of our being saved; our being sinners, and our salvation requiring the Lord's Death, a thing which was quite incredible before it took place, and required exceeding love for it to take place.   But now, since this has come about, other requisites are easier.   For we have become friends, and there is no further need of Deaths.   Shall then he who hath so spared his enemies as not to spare his Son, fail to defend them now they are become friends, when he hath no longer any need to give up his Son?"

25. We cannot too highly prize the *atonement*, v. 11.   Some wish us to give up the name; but the name is a very good one. It is in the Bible.   Some wish us to give up what is meant by the atonement, but we cannot.   It is our life.   Give up that, and what have we left?   Whitby quotes Crellius as excepting to the phrase *we have now received the atonement*.   He would read, *obtained this conversion to God*.   But for such a rendering there is not the slightest reason or authority.   To receive an atonement, or obtain reconciliation by blood-shedding was an idea perfectly familiar both to Jews and Gentiles.   We cannot too much guard our thoughts and words on the whole subject of our reconciliation to God.   It is never by ourselves but by Christ Jesus, never by our sufferings or merits, but always by the sacrifice and death of Jesus Christ that we are represented as obtaining reconciliation.

26. There is a difference between saints and sinners.   They are not alike.   They do not fare alike.   What sinner has such a char-

acter as is described in vs. 1–5? Who that is living without
Christ has such privileges as are described in vs. 1–11? Stuart:
"To rejoice in God as our God, expresses the consummation of
all the Christian's happiness." Well does Luther say: "Although
I am a sinner by the law, and under condemnation of the law, yet
I despair not, I die not, because Christ liveth, who is both my
righteousness and my everlasting life. In that righteousness and
life I have no sin, no fear, no sting of conscience, no care of death.
I am, indeed a sinner, as touching this present life, and the righteousness thereof, as the child of Adam; where the law accuses
me, death reigns over me, and at length would devour me. But
I have another righteousness and life above this life, which is
Christ, the Son of God, who knoweth no sin, nor death, but righteousness and life eternal; by whom this, my body, being dead,
and brought into dust, shall be raised up again, and delivered
from the bondage of the law, and sin, and shall be sanctified together with the spirit." Who may *joy* in God, if such a man
may not?

27. The instruction given in these verses 1–11, is rich and full.
In them we have our attention turned to the three persons of the
Godhead, the Father, Son and Holy Ghost, as united in the accomplishment of human salvation. We have a catalogue, not
perfect, indeed, yet quite comprehensive, of the benefits enjoyed
by believers, through the great scheme of redemption. Whatever else is wanted is found in the covenant. Sometimes particulars are stated, going down to bread and water, yea even to the
hairs of our heads. Nothing is omitted, which faith and love and
hope need to sustain and encourage them. Tribulations are indeed
the lot of God's people: but "the pain of them will soon be over;
the happy consequences of them will be as lasting as our immortal
souls." Justification is neither sanctification, nor glorification,
yet "in it there is a real relative change of the man's state before
God, so that in a moral and law sense he goeth for another man
than he was formerly, and that even in God's account."

28. Christianity is true, and one proof of its divine origin is
the fact that it comes to men loaded with unspeakable blessings,
blessings such as no system of error has ever conveyed to mortals. See the list in vs. 1–11. The true and infinitely wise and
good God, and he alone could devise a scheme at once so perfect,
so honorable to its author, and at the same time conveying such
blessings to poor, lost, ignorant, guilty and depraved man.

Chapter 11

ROMANS 5
VERSES 12–21

OUR JUSTIFICATION IN CHRIST ILLUSTRATED BY
OUR FALL IN ADAM. THE DIFFERENCE BE-
TWEEN THESE OUR REPRESENTATIVES. THE
RICHES OF GOD'S GRACE.

12 Wherefore, as by one man sin entered into the world, and death by sin;
and so death passed upon all men, for that all have sinned :

13 (For until the law sin was in the world : but sin is not imputed when there
is no law·

14 Nevertheless death reigned from Adam to Moses, even over them that had
not sinned after the similitude of Adam's transgression, who is the figure of him
that was to come.

15 But not as the offence, so also *is* the free gift : for if through the offence
of one many be dead, much more the grace of God, and the gift by grace, *which
is* by one man, Jesus Christ, hath abounded unto many.

16 And not as *it was* by one that sinned, *so is* the gift : for the judgment *was*
by one to condemnation, but the free gift *is* of many offences unto justification.

17 For if by one man's offence death reigned by one ; much more they which
receive abundance of grace and of the gift of righteousness shall reign in life by one,
Jesus Christ.)

18 Therefore, as by the offence of one *judgment came* upon all men to condemnation ; even so by the righteousness of one *the free gift came* upon all men
unto justification of life.

19 For as by one man's disobedience many were made sinners, so by the
obedience of one shall many be made righteous.

20 Moreover the law entered, that the offence might abound. But where sin
abounded, grace did much more abound :

21 That as sin hath reigned unto death, even so might grace reign through
righteousness unto eternal life by Jesus Christ our Lord.

RESPECTING this portion of God's word a few preliminary
remarks are submitted.

1. It is instructive to see different classes of commentators approach this passage. Those, who entertain Pelagian or Semi-
Pelagian views, or are unsound or doubtful on the great doctrines

of Original Sin, the Nature of Sin, the Work of Christ, or Justification, seem to look upon verses 12–19 with alarm, if not dread.
John Taylor of Norwich among moderns took the lead in this
course. He has been followed, more or less closely, by a multitude, whose preliminary remarks on the passage commonly notify
you of what is coming. Frequently they early announce that
they have had great labor on the passage, and have found it full
of difficulty. Stuart says: " That this is one of the most difficult
passages in all the New Testament, will be conceded, I believe,
by all sober and reflecting critics. As I have before remarked,
I have bestowed repeated and long-continued efforts upon the
study of it. I do not say this, however, as affording in itself even
a presumptive proof that I have at last attained to a right understanding of it; but only to shew that I have felt, and in some
measure rightly estimated, the difficulties attendant upon the
nature of an undertaking to explain it, and have not neglected
any efforts within my power to overcome them." Similar remarks
might easily be cited from other writers of the same class.

That there are unsearchable riches and unfathomable depths
of love and wisdom and knowledge in this and in many other
portions of God's word is readily conceded by all good men.
Paul himself in this epistle and elsewhere frankly and adoringly
admits all this, Rom. 11 : 33–36; Eph. 3 : 17–21.

That those, who oppose the sound view, have often shown
great ingenuity, if not perversity, in making objections of various
kinds, philological, philosophical, and rationalistic, and thus succeeded in perplexing some of the unlearned is also admitted. In
some cases these views have been carried so far as to subvert the
gospel. It is of the nature of all religious error to eat as doth a
canker.

Sound expositors, to defend the truths here taught, have often
laid out much strength in showing the mistakes of errorists, and
in vindicating the old orthodox interpretation. They admit the
passage has been so perverted as to require a lucid exposition of
its leading ideas, and an exposure of the glosses of errorists, who,
while complaining of the theories of others, present their own
conceits, and would have us follow them. But it is not true that
the great body of sound divines have found this portion of God's
word perplexing and hard to be understood. That this is a correct statement it would be easy to show in many ways. They
come to it as to any other part of scripture. They take the terms
and phrases in their connection and in their obvious sense, and
they rest on the divine word as conclusive. One opens the
volumes written by the fathers in the church for the last fifteen or

sixteen hundred years, and he finds them from the days of Chrysostom down handling this scripture with great love and reverence,
but never seeming to think the apostle was obscure, or that this
passage was very difficult, or calculated to perplex rather than
edify plain godly people.

The elder President Edwards has borne a noble testimony on
these matters : " Now I think this care and exactness of the
Apostle no where appears more than in the place we are upon.
[Rom. 5 : 12–19.]   Nay I scarcely know another instance equal to
this, of the apostle's care to be well understood, by being very
particular, explicit, and precise, setting the matter forth in every
light, going over and over again with his doctrine, clearly to
exhibit, and fully to settle and determine the thing at which he
aims."

Again : " No wonder, when the apostle is treating so fully and
largely of our restoration, righteousness, and life by Christ, that
he is led by it to consider our fall, sin, death, and ruin by Adam ;
and to observe wherein these two opposite heads of mankind
agree, and wherein they differ, in the manner of conveyance of
opposite influences and communications from each.

" Thus, if the place be understood, as it used to be understood
by orthodox divines, the whole stands in a natural, easy, and clear
connection with the preceding part of the chapter, and all the
former part of the epistle ; and in a plain agreement with all the
apostle had been saying ; and also in connection with the words
last before spoken, as introduced by the two immediately preceding verses, where he is speaking of our justification, reconciliation, and salvation by Christ ; which leads the apostle directly to
observe, how, on the contrary, we have sin and death by Adam.
Taking this discourse of the apostle in its true and plain sense,
there is no need of great extent of learning, or depth of criticism
to find out the connection ; but if it be understood in Dr. Taylor's
sense, the plain scope and connection are wholly lost, and there
was truly need of a skill in criticism, and the art of discerning,
beyond or at least different from that of former divines, and a
faculty of seeing what other men's sight could not reach, in order
to find out the connection."   Works, Vol. 2, pp. 499–502.   Similar
remarks are made by Guyse and others.

2. On the object and interpretation of this portion of scripture
sound divines have been remarkably agreed.   It would be easy to
fill pages with extracts from the best writers of the last fifteen
hundred years in proof of this assertion.   There is a general agreement that this part of the epistle is written in confirmation and
elucidation of what the apostle had already taught respecting

man's justification by the imputed righteousness of Christ.   There is no notice of any change of topic.   All that is said admits of a satisfactory explanation on this view of the case.   Perhaps not a single writer, who denies this to be the design and bearing of these verses, escapes either mistake or confusion, while not a few are led into strange contradictions, or dangerous errors.

3. Although this is the design of the passage, the method of carrying it out is quite different from anything yet presented in this epistle.   The illustration of our recovery in Christ is borrowed from the fact and manner of our ruin in Adam.   Paul's object is not to discuss and explain original sin, but by original sin to explain the method of justification.   In doing this he does in a most instructive and satisfactory manner explain to us the entrance of sin, and our relations to the father of the human race.   Indeed no equal portion of scripture casts such light on the introduction of evil, as it involves the human race.   All this is the more satisfactory because the apostle does not attempt to prove anything respecting original sin.   He either takes it for granted that his positions on that subject will be admitted by all, or he intends by the authority of God's Spirit to make known to us the leading truths respecting original sin, and that for the purpose of letting us see more clearly the manner and the glory of our recovery in Christ.   And all this comes in most naturally.   He had delivered a great argument evincing these truths, that mankind, Jews and Gentiles, were sinners; that their justification by the deeds of the law was out of the question; that the gospel scheme had in it a righteousness commensurate to the demands of the law; that this righteousness was wrought out and brought in by Jesus Christ; that we become interested in that righteousness when God imputes it to us, and we receive it by faith; that there is no other method of justification for any mere man; that Abraham himself was justified by faith; and that the writings of Moses settled that fact beyond all doubt.   He then in the early part of this chapter dwells briefly on the benefits of this justification, and on the greatness of the love and humiliation by which our justification and reconciliation were effected.   Having in chapter IV. disposed of the truth respecting Abraham, the father of believers, he now goes back to Adam, the father of the human race, and borrows an illustration of his argument and principles from him.   As he had said Abraham was a pattern of all believers, so he now says Adam was a *figure*, literally a *type*, of our Saviour.

4. If these things are so, then there is a clear and definite object before the mind of the apostle, and all that is said is harmonious with what has gone before, and is as easily understood as any other

part of the epistle, the terms being simple, and the connection obvious.   But Stuart says, " The *main design* of this passage is . . . to exalt our views respecting the blessings which Christ has procured for us by a comparison of them with the evil consequences, which ensued upon the fall of our first ancestor, and by shewing that the blessings in question not only extend to the removal of these evils, but even far beyond this; so that the grace of the gospel has not only abounded, but *superabounded*."   But what is said of *superabounding* grace is a remark very just indeed but wholly by the way, is no part of the main argument, yet grows out of the illustration used.   No wonder this writer should find himself sadly perplexed and embarrassed at every step of his exposition when he misapprehends the scope of the passage.   The same may be said of others, who have alike mistaken the design of the apostle. All these things show the justice of what is said by the elder President Edwards: " It is really no less than *abusing* the scripture and its readers to represent this paragraph as the most *obscure* of all the places of scripture, that speak of the consequences of Adam's sin; and to treat it as if there was need first to consider other places as more *plain*.   Whereas it is most manifestly a place in which these things are declared, the most plainly, particularly, precisely, and of set purpose, by that great apostle, who has most fully explained to us those doctrines in general, which relate to the redemption by Christ, and the sin and misery we are redeemed from."   Works, Vol. 2, p. 511.   These things being so, let us consider these verses in detail.

12. *Wherefore, as by one man sin entered into the world, and death by sin; and so death passed upon all men, for that all have sinned.* Peshito: As by means of one man, sin entered into the world, and, by means of sin, death; and so death passed upon all the sons of men, inasmuch as they all have sinned.   The old English versions are very much the same as the authorized translation.   The verse may be fairly thus paraphrased: Having largely explained to you the lost and guilty state of mankind, and shewn that they are involved in universal ruin; and having stated the method of recovery by the righteousness of Jesus Christ, in which we become interested by the imputation of God when we believe, I *am led* to notice a *resemblance* between the method of our ruin and of our recovery.   Our justification is not by many, but by *one man*, the man Christ Jesus, even as our condemnation was not by many but by *one man*.   Condemnation was followed by *death*, and among rational and accountable creatures, *death is by sin*.   That is a first principle in this matter so plain that I shall not argue it, but take it for granted.   This dreadful curse and condemnation came, not

only on the first transgressor of the covenant of works, but on all his posterity; for he was their representative, and his first sin, his *one offence* had such an effect that *death passed upon all men;* for by the fall of Adam *all* became *sinners,* and so were liable to the curse of God, expressed in the word *death,* and manifested in the miseries of men here and hereafter, especially in this life in the dissolution of the body, then in separation of the soul from God, and finally in the liability of both soul and body to the pains of hell forever.

The first word *wherefore* marks the connection with the whole of the foregoing argument, more especially as summarily stated in vs. 9, 10, 11.   In Rom. 4 : 13 we have precisely the same words rendered Therefore.   If they are illative there, why are they not illative here?   This is by far the more common rendering, and there are many instances of this use in the New Testament beginning with the sermon on the mount, running through all the Gospels, Acts, etc. down to Revelation.   It shows the great straits, into which some are brought that this *wherefore* should be so troublesome to them, and they set about with much zeal to show that it means something else.   Stuart makes a great effort to prove that it does not mean here what it *usually* means.   He shows very clearly that he is *perplexed,* and says others have been, yet he has the candor to state that Tholuck and Flatt give their suffrage in favor of the common view, which makes it illative.   But Stuart labors to show that it neither notes a deduction nor is it a formula of transition.   But these *perplexities* would never have arisen, if the plain obvious teaching of these few verses had not been contrary to favorite theories.   We are at no loss to know who is the *one man* mentioned in this verse.   The history of the race points to the father of all mankind.   A single person is spoken of here and in verses 14–19.   This language excludes Eve, not from the sin of eating the forbidden fruit, nor from being a tempter to her husband, nor from suffering the displeasure of God, but from being the federal head of the human family.   Eve was not a public person. Had she alone sinned, she alone would have suffered.   Scott: " Adam was the federal head, surety and representative of all his posterity ; nor did sin enter, save to the personal condemnation of Eve, till he also ate the forbidden fruit."   Adam and Eve were indeed " *one flesh;* " yet no more so than are every lawfully married man and woman.   But they were not one person.   They had not the same consciousness.   There was a time when Adam existed and Eve did not exist.   There was a time when Eve was a sinner and Adam was holy.   Nor is there in scripture the least hint that Eve was a public person, a federal head, a representative of any.

In these eight verses our ruin is twice distinctly said to have come
on us by *Adam;* three times by *one man*, and four times by *one*,
meaning either one person or one act.

By this one man sin entered.   *Sin*, the word usually so rendered.   All unrighteousness is sin.   All want of righteousness is
sin.   All transgression of law is sin.   All want of conformity to
law is sin.   Men may sin by defect or by excess, by not coming
up to the law or by overleaping its prohibitions, by omission of
duty, or by commission of deeds of iniquity.   We sin when we
fail to love, serve and obey God, or when we love, serve and obey
any thing in the place of God.   Sometimes the word sin denotes
a state of sinfulness; sometimes, a principle of wickedness; sometimes, a wicked influence having the mastery over us: but in all
cases it involves the idea of guiltiness, or righteous liability to
God's displeasure.   Sometimes this is the prominent thought.   So
far do the scriptures carry this idea that they have the same word
for sin and sin-offering.   Sometimes sin is personified, but that
does not dismiss either the idea of wickedness or of exposure to
wrath.   Even when one of these ideas is prominent, the other still
inheres, either as a basis or an accompaniment.   Often the prominent idea suggested by the word is the guilt of sin, its power to
subject us to wrath, liability to punishment.   So when we read of
the remission of sins, or the forgiveness of sins, it is the guilt of
sin that is meant.   The pollution or stain of sin is removed by
sanctification, not by remission.   Pardon excludes punishment.
It does not render unnecessary the purification of the heart.   That
must still go on.   When it is said "Christ was once offered to
bear the sins of many," Heb. 9 : 28, it is blasphemy to say that he
bore the pollution, the stain of sin, while it is glorious doctrine to
say that he bore the guilt of our sins, the punishment due to us for
sin, our legal liability to righteous indignation.   So when it is
said "he hath made him to be sin for us," it cannot mean that
Christ was stained or polluted with sin, for it is immediately
added that he "knew no sin."   The meaning is that he bore the
guilt of sin, the curse of the broken law, in our room and stead,
though personally innocent and holy.   Sin *entered into*.   No word
in Scripture has a meaning less variant.   It is always rendered as
here, or came into, or went into, but always retains the idea of
entrance.   "Enter into thy closet," "enter ye in at the strait
gate," "enter into life," "entered into the swine," "entered into
rest" are samples of its use.   Sin entered into *the world*, the
same word as in Rom. 4 : 13, on which see comment.   It includes
all the inhabitants of the earth, Jews and Gentiles.

What then is the meaning of the whole clause: "*By one*

man sin entered into the world?" Some say it simply teaches that
Adam was the first sinner in this world. But this is not true.
"Adam was first formed, then Eve." But Eve first sinned, then
Adam. So all the accounts agree in teaching. Adam was not
the first sinner. He did not commit the first sin. He did not
set the first example of disobedience. The woman did that.
The clause says: "By one *man* sin entered into the world."
Some teach that simply as progenitor of the race, under that
law of nature, that *like begets like*, Adam becoming a sinner introduced depravity into the world. No doubt like begets like.
No doubt our depravity is native, and that all Adam's descendants have naturally sinful affections, corrupt natures derived
from him as their root. But in the same sense men derive
their sinful nature from Eve, as she was the mother of all living. And "who can bring a clean thing out of an unclean?"
When David speaks of his hereditary depravity, he does not
even mention his father, though doubtless he was included in
his thoughts: "Behold I was shapen in iniquity; and in sin did
my *mother* conceive me," Ps. 51 : 5. *By one man sin entered* certainly means more than that Adam set us a bad example. Every
man, who has ever done a known wrong, has set a bad example.
And the phrase certainly means more than that Adam's descendants inherit from him a fallen nature; for they inherit it no less
from their immediate ancestry, as David confesses. This whole
clause is explained in this very chapter by such phrases as these:
"Through the offence of one many be dead;" "The judgment
was by one to condemnation;" "By one man's offence death
reigned by one;" "By the offence of one judgment came upon
all men to condemnation;" "By one man's disobedience many
were made sinners." The true interpretation of these phrases is
clearly indicated by the language respecting the second Adam
who produced effects directly opposite: "The gift by grace, which
is by one man, Jesus Christ;" "They which receive abundance of
grace, and of the gift of righteousness, shall reign in life by one,
Jesus Christ;" "By the righteousness of one the free gift came
upon all men unto justification of life;" "By the obedience of one
shall many be made righteous." None but the loosest thinkers
will say that all, which these latter passages teach, is that by his
example Jesus Christ taught us the way of righteousness; or how
to secure the gift of righteousness; or that his example and doctrine and sufferings are suited to win us to righteousness. Yet
these phrases respecting Christ are in complete antithesis to those
respecting Adam. Whatever is meant by one class is just the
opposite of what is meant by the other. Jesus Christ saves us as

Adam ruined us. Jesus Christ brings us into a state of justification, as Adam brought us into a state of condemnation. By the
latter we have eternal life as a free gift, yea, and abundance of
grace, as by the former we received judgment unto condemnation.
If ever any eight verses of scripture clearly interpreted themselves,
these verses do that very thing. *And death* [entered] *by sin.* The
Scriptures are entirely uniform and harmonious in accounting for
the entrance of *death* into the world: "In the day thou eatest
thereof thou shalt surely die;" "The soul that sinneth, it shall
die;" "The wages of sin is death;" "Sin, when it is finished,
bringeth forth death," Gen. 2:17; Ezek. 18:4; Rom. 6:23;
James 1:15. But what is the meaning of *death* in this passage?
Below we have these phrases "death reigned," "many be dead,"
"judgment was by one to condemnation," "judgment came upon
all men to condemnation," vs. 14–18. Death is the opposite of
life. There is a natural life, and there is a natural death. In Scripture the word death often means simply that change effected by
the separation of soul and body, John 11:13; Rom. 8:38; Phil.
1:20; Heb. 7:23. All, who treat the word of God with reverence, admit that death in this passage includes natural death, or,
as it is often called, temporal death. Some indeed contend that
no other evil under the name of death is here meant. But this
cannot be so. Even if the word never had in itself another distinct meaning, yet we ask what is this awful event? As to the
body, it is corruption and dissolution. It is the extinction of animal life. It is the destruction of our material organism. This is
its effect on the body. But what is the effect of death on the
soul? There is an impression very common among thinking people, and particularly among devout students of God's word, that
when the dust returns to the earth as it was, the spirit returns
unto God who gave it; and that the immediate consequences of
temporal death are of the most solemn and momentous character, either for bliss or for woe. Besides, if the death of the body,
or the loss of natural life exhausts the penalty of transgression,
from what did Christ redeem us? It is admitted that but two
men of former generations ever escaped natural death; and that
since Christ left the world not one of his followers has been exempt
from temporal death. What then has Christ done for his people?
Their bodies go into the grave as do also those of other men.
From what then did Christ save them? Nor can we reconcile
this view of the term death with the language of other verses in
this connection. To *reign in life by one, Jesus Christ* (v. 17) surely
is not escaping temporal death, and yet it is the opposite of
death reigning. The *justification of life* (v. 18) is certainly not ex-

emption from temporal death, and yet it is the opposite of *judgment coming unto condemnation*. *Many being made righteous* (v. 19)
is the opposite of *many being made sinners*, and yet we must believe that all Christ did for his people was nothing worth naming,
if he merely lived and died to save them from a temporal death,
from which after all he did not save them, for like other men they
die. This has led some to take the ground that all Christ did was
to secure a suspension of the execution of the sentence of death
until men should have time to repent and turn to God—a respite
of a few months or years, But this is manifestly trifling with the
clearest teachings of Scripture. " God so loved the world that
he gave his only begotten Son that whosoever believeth on him
might not perish, but have everlasting life," John 3 : 16. In scripture death is used as a term to denote all the penal consequences
of sin whatever they .may be. The death of the body under the
displeasure of God is still a part of that penalty. All the pains
and woes that lead to such a death are a part of that penalty.
The life Adam led before his fall was joyous, exultant, bright and
brightening. The life men lead in a state of alienation from God
is sad, dark and full of evil forebodings. Before his fall Adam
had delightful fellowship with God. By his disobedience he lost
communion with God. The Holy Ghost no longer made a temple
of his person. All the miseries, the unblest sorrows, of life are
the fruit of transgressing the law, whose penalty is death. A
soul forsaken by God is a poor, withered, shrivelled thing, " dead
in trespasses and sins," however vigorous natural life may be, and
however great may be one's apparent success in schemes of earthly
enjoyment or aggrandizement. Then there is a life beyond this
world. It is often mentioned by Christ and Paul, also by Peter,
John and Jude. It is often spoken of simply as *life*, Matt, 7 : 14 ;
18 : 8, 9 ; Rom. 8 : 6 ; 1 John 5 : 12 ; as *eternal life*, Matt. 25 : 46 ;
Mark 10 : 17 ; Acts 13 : 48 ; 1 Tim. 6 : 19 ; 1 John 5 : 20 ; also as
everlasting life, Matt. 19 : 29 ; John 3 : 16 ; Acts 13 : 46 ; Rom. 6 : 22.
This same life was often promised in the Old Testament, Deut.
30 : 15, 19 ; Pr. 12 : 28. The opposite of this life is *death*, several
times called the *second death*, John 8 : 51, 52 ; Rom. 1 : 32 ; 6 : 21 ;
7 : 5 ; 2 Tim. 1 : 10 ; Heb. 2 : 14 ; Jas. 5 : 20 ; Rev. 2 : 11 ; 20 : 6 ;
21 : 8. This death is as enduring as the life to which it is opposed.
It is everlasting, Dan. 12 : 2 ; Matt. 25 : 46. It is by Christ himself
called *everlasting punishment*. This is the death, which the Lord
Christ says the righteous shall never die, John 6 : 50 ; 8 : 51 ; 11 : 26.
This everlasting punishment, this second death, that has no end,
results from the sin of man in opposing the wise and holy will of
God. It is the chief penalty for sinning against God. It is indeed

dreadful, but not too dreadful. The law of God, of which it is the sanction, is holy, just, good, grand and awful. Dreadful as is the penalty, it is not found sufficient to deter many from very bold sinning. When man endures the penalty of the broken law in his own person, it is eternal, because God has made man immortal; because it inheres in man that once lost he cannot by his own strength or merit recover himself; because, when in a Christian land he dies in his sins, he has proven himself incorrigible, having persistently rejected the strength and righteousness offered him; and because going into the eternal world will not terminate his accountability for his moral conduct there. Well may we therefore understand why death should be so uniformly, at least so frequently spoken of in God's word as a very great, an exceedingly terrible evil, and be associated as it several times is in Revelation even with hell itself.

In Scripture death is a name often given to capital punishment inflicted as a penalty. Of this many instances are found, see Matt. 26: 66; Mark 14; 64; Luke 23: 15; Acts 23: 29 and many other places. That is, the extreme penalty of human law is expressed by the term death, which includes the pain and the ignominy of such a punishment, as well as the extinction of natural life. So in the word of God death is a name for penal suffering, whatever may be its form, or however lasting may be its duration. Therefore, when it is said *death entered by sin* the meaning is that penal suffering came into the world by sin. God's law denounces no one kind of suffering, as exclusively penal. It places our race under *the curse of the law*, as Paul calls it in Gal. 3; 13; but in what precise way and to what precise extent that *curse* shall come on any one man is reserved for his own decision by the Judge of all the earth, who is too wise to make mistakes, too holy to be unjust, too good to practise any cruelty, too pure to look on evil, too upright to clear the guilty, and too mighty to be resisted. Paul has proven that before grace comes men are universally given up to work wickedness and to be tormented with wretchedness. See the former part of this epistle. If sin defiles all his works, destruction and misery are necessarily in his ways: for he has done things worthy of death. The curse has come upon our entire race, or as our verse has it, *And so death passed upon all men*. A good deal has been said about the connecting words *and so*. Nor are they without significance. The Greek for *so* is also rendered *thus, even so, likewise, on this wise, after this manner*. All these renderings in this connection would direct attention to the entrance of sin and death on all men by the act of one man. It looks like levity in men to say that all Paul teaches is that as Adam sinned and died, so all men sin and die. Surely our apostle is not uttering in this place that proposition. The use of the word in this connection naturally points to the manner of death passing on all men by the sin of one man. Even those most opposed to this interpretation admit that the *and so* is capable of this interpretation. *Passed upon*, some prefer reading passed over to all men, or passed through to all men. Both of these renderings of the verb are common. Either of them gives a good sense. Neither of them need mislead any one. Death has passed over the human race so as a wave or a tide passes over objects. It also has passed through the world, laying claim to all men as its victims. *For that all have sinned.* *For that*, literally *in whom*. This is the rendering of the Vulgate, Chrysostom, Beza, Piscator, Doway, Dutch Annotations, Assembly's Annotations, Evans, Gill, Guyse, Pool and Scott. Wiclif has *in whiche man*. This is a fair rendering, as every scholar must see on examining the original. Following it makes the sense rather more obvious to the common mind. But the sound interpretation is fairly reached, if we follow the common version. The meaning is well expressed by Guyse: " In Adam they all sinned, as in their public head and representative, in whose loins they likewise were ; in so much that they, on this account, are by legal estimation deemed sinners in him, his offence being imputed, and punished in them." Hawker uses like language : " By the sin of the first *Adam* the whole race were equally involved in the guilt and punishment due to original corruption, although they had no hand in actual transgression." Haldane: " The meaning is that death passed upon all men because all are sinners . . . All have really sinned, though not in their own persons . . . In the guilt of Adam's sin, as well as in its consequences, they became partakers." Hodge: " By one man all men became sinners, and hence death passed upon all men, *through that one man*, in whom all sinned . . . By one man all men became sinners, and were exposed to death, and thus death passed on all men, since all were regarded as sinners on his account." The above statements fairly represent the true doctrine so long held in the Christian world.

That there is nothing forced in explaining the terms and clauses of this verse so as to draw out the meaning given above might be shown by many considerations. 1. The whole verse is to be explained in consistency with the fact, established by the context and by the terms employed, that Paul is expounding and illustrating justification and not sanctification. If this is so, then the point of all he says relates to condemnation, not to corruption of nature by Adam, as some maintain. Such an interpretation would quite destroy the apostle's reasoning, and make him speak thus : As

Adam introduced corruption, so Christ introduces purity. And this is directly opposed to his own language: " Judgment was by one to condemnation;" "Judgment came upon all men to condemnation." It is certainly true that we derive our sinful nature from Adam, and it is no less true that Christ is made unto us sanctification; but clearly those are not the truths here presented. 2. Edwards, Knapp and others have abundantly shown that the doctrine of the apostle in these verses respecting our condemnation in Adam was for ages the received doctrine of the Jews. So that the apostle was teaching no startling truth, was broaching no new doctrine when he said that our ruin came by one act of one man. This very fact may account for the manner in which he manages the argument. He finds in the accepted theology of his day a sound principle, a great fact relied on and not disputed. Under the guidance of God's Spirit he knows it is true. It well suits his purpose. He reproduces it to enable him the better to explain his great theme, justification by Christ's righteousness. Thus explained the whole is pointed and pertinent. Every clause tells. The whole is lucid and irrefragable. But on any other method of interpretation we have nothing but perplexity. This is so whether we consider the eight verses as a whole, or the various clauses by themselves. Yea, even the connecting particles, though of frequent occurrence, give much trouble, and require pages to explain them away, and at last some impotent conclusion is reached, such as this: As Adam sinned and died, so all men sin and die—a conclusion, which Pelagius himself not only did not deny, but fully accepted. He admitted that death was by sin, but maintained that sin was by "imitation." He said, " The sin of Adam has not injured those not sinning."

3. Beyond dispute, if the apostle would have us regard him as teaching the doctrine as stated above, he has used the appropriate terms and phrases; so that his language *seems* to teach it. Thus the great body of the Christian world have long understood him as teaching. Can it be that the people of God have so generally misapprehended the mind of the Spirit? Is it possible that none but Pelagians and their followers have rightly understood the apostle, although he has stated his points so clearly and so variously?

In this verse the word *as* remains to be noticed. Its consideration has been intentionally deferred to the last, that we may more easily understand some remarks concerning it. It is generally agreed that *as* introduces a comparison, the first member, or proposition of which is in these words, *as by one man sin entered into the world, and death by sin.* Where is the second part of the comparison—the application? Some insist that it is found in this verse itself; but where is it? If Paul is not comparing Adam and his posterity, the second member of the comparison is not in this verse, unless we adopt opinions now generally discarded. One is that we should read the verse thus: As by one man sin entered into the world, so death entered by sin. The other mode of reading suggested by some is this: Wherefore as by one man we have received the atonement, so by one man sin entered the world. The objection to each of these is that it takes too great liberties with the text. Neither of them has now any respectable defender. Even Macknight says that neither the apostle's argument nor the original will admit of the first. This remark is as true of the second. We need not therefore spend time upon them. Doubtless the correct way of explaining the comparison is reached by making verses 13–17 parenthetical, and finding the comparison renewed and finished in verses 18, 19. The sense requires this. We have it so in the authorized version. Calvin, Ferme, Grotius, Wetstein, Flatt, Hodge and others admit that there is a parenthesis. Stuart: "With the majority of interpreters, therefore, I hesitate not to regard verses 13–17 as substantially a parenthesis. . . In this manner, and only in this can I find the real antithesis or comparison to be fully made out, which the apostle designs to make." The note of Conybeare & Howson, in which there is an attempt to shew that Matt. 25 : 14 is like this, and that in neither case is any answering *so* found, is very inconclusive and unsatisfactory.

If the reader will revert to the paraphrase given early in the comment on this verse and read it again, it will give him a summary of the results reached. Having in elucidation of our justification in Christ stated the fact of our condemnation by the sin of Adam, the apostle proceeds in parenthesis to explain and confirm some matters, which naturally suggest themselves:

13. (*For until the law sin was in the world: but sin is not imputed when there is no law.* The rendering of Peshito quite destroys the sense: For until the law, sin, although it was in the world, was not accounted sin, because there was no law. One can hardly conceive of a rendering more utterly subversive of the words and the sense of the passage. The same may be said of the Arabic version, which is very much the same. *For* clearly connects this with v. 12. That contained a statement of a truth. This and v. 14 contain the proofs. *Until the law.* The chief difficulty in the mind of the English reader arises from the word *until*, elsewhere rendered unto, even to. The meaning is that from the fall of Adam *even to* the giving of the law we find just such proofs of the existence of sin as we find in later periods of the world. *Until*

the law, therefore, points to the whole of that long period from the fall of Adam to the giving of the law on Mount Sinai. In the next verse the same idea is expressed by the words "from Adam to Moses," designating a period of over twenty-five hundred years. Sin was in the world all that time. Men were regarded and treated as sinners. It was during that period that two of the most terrific judgments, of which we have any record, befell mankind. One was the Noachic deluge, proofs of which are still abundant on our earth. The other was the overthrow of the cities of the plain, and forming on the plain that monument of God's wrath the Dead Sea. These awful instances of the anger of heaven against the human race as well as the miseries and death that reigned all that time evince that beyond a doubt God even then regarded and treated men as sinners. And he did this justly and truly, for they were sinners. A constitution older than that of Sinai had been broken. God's will had been disregarded in the covenant of works. God had made man upright, but he sought out many inventions. Some propose to read our clause thus: From the fall even to the giving of the law on Sinai sin was imputed or counted in the world. Macknight favors this paraphrase. This is not authorized; nor does it relieve any difficulty. *But sin is not imputed where there is no law.* The fact that men were regarded and treated as sinners is proof enough that some law had been broken. What law could that be? The true answer is, the law of Eden, "Of the tree of the knowledge of good and evil, thou shalt not eat of it: for in the day that thou eatest thereof thou shalt surely die." The violation of this law brought down the curse, and from that day, even the law of nature written on the heart of man was constantly violated, and to a fearful extent men committed such things as are worthy of death, although they knew the judgment of God against them. During all this time sin was imputed, not only the first sin of the first man against the law of probation, but also the personal sins of all men against the will of God made known by such faithful men as Abel, Enoch and Noah, and especially as made known in the law of God written on the heart. Never was there closer reasoning than that of Paul. In v. 12 he says death in the human family proves the existence of sin. Here he says sin proves the existence of law. One wonders when he finds Stuart following Bretschneider seriously and after long argument maintaining that the clause, *sin is not imputed when there is no law*, means simply that *men* did not regard sin as sin, did not esteem themselves sinners, during that period. Tholuck well designates this as "another expedient of rather a violent kind, which many have adopted for removing the difficulties of this text." And it is a relief to find Stuart himself full of misgivings about his own exposition. He says: "I admit that a *modified* sense of the expression is to be regarded as the true one, viz. it is not to be considered so absolute as to convey the idea that *no* sense of sin existed among the heathen in any measure, for this would contradict fact, and contradict what Paul says in chap. 2 : 14, 15." See Stuart on that place. Nor has this exposition any pertinency to the matter in hand. Paul is shewing how men are justified in Christ. In doing this he refers to the manner of their condemnation in Adam. That condemnation was manifested by death reigning. Whether men during those twenty-five hundred years in their own consciences excused or condemned themselves we well know, but the fact in that matter has nothing to do with Paul's argument. By God's judgment death reigned over mankind and that proves beyond a doubt that some law had existed before Moses, that its penalty death had been incurred, and that thus sin had been imputed by God, for it was punished by his judgment. It is pleasant to find Stuart successfully combatting the idea of some Germans "that although the *guilt* of men, who sinned against the law of nature, was not taken away absolutely, yet their accountability for it was in a good measure *superseded*." The texts relied on to prove this dangerous position were Acts 17 : 30; Rom. 3 : 26. But Stuart well says: "Both of these instances, however, relate to *deferring punishment*, not to a remission of accountability; compare 2 Pet. 3 : 8, 9. Such a remission of punishment would directly contradict what Paul has fully and strongly asserted, in Rom. 2 : 6–16."

This verse may well be paraphrased thus: I have stated that by the sin of Adam men were no longer in covenant with God but were under the penalty of a broken law, as is proven by the reign of death, by the horrors of men's consciences, by their just apprehension of wrath to come, by all the miseries they endure and by death itself, all which things are not accidental, but penal, not misfortunes but punishments for sin, and thus all men are proven to be sinners. In elucidation and confirmation of this position I further observe, that the penalty of death, whose existence was proven by conscience, by human wretchedness and by temporal death, establishes the fact that sin was in the world from the fall of Adam, that the origin of sin therefore cannot be traced to the giving or the breach of the law of Moses; for the Lord is holy and just. He sends not suffering on those who are rightly regarded as innocent. Under his government men cannot suffer unless they are charged with the guilt of sin. Nor does God charge men with guilt by a mere arbitrary act of his own. Where the penalty is inflicted, sin is charged; and where sin is charged, some law (and all God's laws are holy, just and good) must have been broken. But all the generations of men *before* the giving of the law on Sinai both suffered and died. This proves that they were guilty in God's account ; and that some law must have been broken. What that law and its penalty were we learn in Gen. 2 : 17—a law given and a curse pronounced very early in the history of the human race. It was Adam's breach of the covenant, his violation of the law of his probation, that made all men sinners. Of this we may rest assured for God never imputes sin where no law is violated. After Adam no one ate of the forbidden fruit.

14. *Nevertheless death reigned from Adam to Moses, even over them that had not sinned after the similitude of Adam's transgression, who is the figure of him that was to come.* *Nevertheless*, the same word is commonly rendered but, or yet, or howbeit. Here we shall best get the sense by reading Yet or And yet, for it is clearly the continuation of his argument. He had said, " Sin is not imputed where there is no law." He now adds, And yet death reigned from Adam to Moses, i. e. death held sway in the history of the world from Adam to Moses, and in God's treatment of man death is by sin, and so it is a penalty, and where penal suffering is there must be sin, and where sin is, there must be a law broken. Thus far the verse reiterates in other words what was said in v. 13— " Until the law sin was in the world." The apostle now goes further, and says that death reigned, *even over them that had not sinned after the similitude of Adam's transgression.* What was the *likeness* of Adam's transgression ? His transgression was personal and actual disobedience to God's will. Now who ever lived between the fall of Adam and the time of Moses, that did not in any case or in any degree personally or actually disobey God's will ? There is but one class of the human family who in that age or any other suit this description, namely infants. Calvin gives it a more extended application but adds : " Infants are at the same time included in this number." Diodati : " *Over them,* namely, over little children, who were not come to the age of judgment, and consequently could not be guilty of an actual, deliberate and voluntary sin, such a one as Adam's was." Cornelius a Lapide : " You will object that where there is no law, there can be no sin. As the men, however, in the interval between Adam and Moses died, it is evident that they must necessarily have been sinners. And in case you may perchance insinuate that this is merely a proof of their actual sins, and not of original guilt, I appeal to children, who though they had not offended against any divine law, were also, during that period, subject to death." Ferme : " Death reigned not only over those who sinned actually,

as did Adam, but even over those who could not sin in like manner, on account of their age, as infants unconscious of the law." Guyse: " Death with all its dreadful and unknown attendants, exercised a terrible and universal dominion, not only over grown persons, that sinned actually, as *Adam* did, but even over infants themselves; witness those of the old world, that perished in the deluge; and those that were cut off in the tremendous destruction of *Sodom* and *Gomorrah*, as well as all the little children that were sick, convulsed, tortured, and then died, in every generation, though none of them could have committed any actual sin to deserve such punishment, as *Adam* had done."   Evans: " Death reigned over those that had not sinned any actual sin, never sinned in their own persons as Adam did ; which is to be understood of infants, that were never guilty of actual sin, and yet died, because Adam's sin was imputed to them."   The remarks of the judicious Thomas Scott on these verses are guarded and must commend themselves to serious Christians: " In proof of this our union with Adam [he had said Adam was our federal head, surety and representative], and our concern in his first transgression, which the proud heart of man is prone to deny, or object to, even with blasphemous enmity, it should be observed, that for two thousand five hundred years before the giving of the law, sin prevailed in the world, and was punished with death ; but sin cannot he imputed, where no law is, of which it is a transgression.   None of the immense multitudes, who died between the fall of. Adam and the promulgation of the law, could personally violate the prohibition, to which the penalty of death had been originally annexed ; yet they were included in the sentence denounced against Adam, and after much toil and suffering, 'returned to the dust whence they were taken.'   And, though adults might be thought to die for their personal violation of the law of tradition, or of their own reason and conscience; yet, during this long interval, an innumerable multitude had been subjected to death, who had never broken any law 'after the similitude of Adam's transgression ;' that is wilfully and deliberately.   For the number of infants, who had been cut off with great pain and agony, previously to their commission of actual sin, had been immensely great."   Edwards: " I can see no reason, why that explanation of this clause, which has been more commonly given, viz. That by *them who have not sinned after the similitude of Adam's transgression*, are meant infants ; who though they have indeed sinned in Adam, yet never sinned as Adam did, by actually transgressing in their own persons; unlesss it be that this interpretation is *too old, and too common* . . . We read of two ways of men being like Adam, or in which a similitude is ascribed to men ; one is, being

begotten or born in his *image* or likeness, Gen. 5 : 3.   Another is
transgressing God's covenant or law, like him, Hos. 6 : 7.   *They
like Adam,* (so in the Hebrew and Latin Vulgate) have *transgressed
the covenant.*   Infants have the former similitude but not the latter."
pp. 506, 507.   The same writer has a whole chapter (P. 1. Ch. 2) to
prove that " Universal Mortality proves Original Sin, particularly
the Death of Infants, with its various Circumstances."   And when
Taylor stated that death was sent as a *benefit* to make us moderate, to
mortify pride, &c., and not as a curse or penalty, Edwards asked : " Is
it not strange that it should fall so heavily on infants, who are not
capable of making any such improvement of it ; so that many more
of mankind suffer death in infancy than in any other equal part
of the age of man ?" p. 398.   " The apostle's main point evidently
is that *sin and guilt, and just exposedness to death and ruin,* come into
the world by Adam's sin ; as *righteousness, justification* and a *title to
eternal life* come by Christ.   Which point he confirms by this consideration, that from the very time when Adam sinned, sin, guilt,
and desert of ruin became *universal* in the world, long before the
law given by Moses to the Jewish nation had any being." p. 503.
Are not these things clear ?   Is not all this fair, logical, scriptural
reasoning ?   Could it be more indubitably stated that it is not
men's relation to parents, to Moses, to Abraham or to any other
person but to Adam only, that determines "our native moral
state ?"

   In elucidation and establishment of his main position that
life, justification and righteousness come to us by Jesus Christ in a
manner resembling that whereby death, ruin and condemnation
came to us by Adam, the apostle in this same verse says of Adam
that he " *was the figure of him that was to come,*" i. e. Christ.   This
is another step in the same direction with what is found in several
preceding clauses.   The word rendered *figure* is the Greek, from
which we get our word *type.*   It is elsewhere rendered pattern,
example, ensample.   Our theological term *type* suits well here.
Now it may be asked, in the way of challenge, in what conceivable
sense was Adam a type, a pattern, an ensample, a figure of Christ,
unless he was so in this that he was a public person acting for others, the federal or covenant head, the representative of his seed as
Christ was of his?   Calvin : " In saying that Adam bore a resemblance to Christ, there is nothing incongruous ; for some likeness
often appears in things wholly contrary.   As then we are all lost
through Adam's sin, so we are restored through Christ's righteousness : hence he calls Adam not inaptly the type of Christ.
But observe, that Adam is not said to be the type of sin, nor
Christ the type of righteousness, as though they led the way only

by their example, but that the one is contrasted with the other."
It makes one's heart sink into sadness to read in Stuart: "The
actual and principal point of similitude is that each individual respectively, viz. Adam and Christ, was the cause or occasion, in
consequence of what he did, of greatly affecting the whole human
race; although in an opposite way." His subsequent remarks
chime in with this. And has it come to this? Are we all to continue in doubt whether Christ was the *cause*, or the *occasion* of salvation? From God's word many have been led to believe that
Jesus Christ was the "author of life," "the author of salvation,"
Acts 3 : 15; Heb. 5 : 9; that he had "made an end of sins, and
made reconciliation for iniquity, and brought in everlasting righteousness," Dan. 9 : 24; that he himself was "the way, the truth and
the life;" John 14 : 6; that if there was such a thing known as an
efficient and a sufficient *cause*, Jesus Christ was such. But this
writer thinks he may have been only the *occasion* of good to men,
as Adam was the *occasion* of evil to his descendants. But no man
ever *wrought* mischief on a great scale like Adam. His sin combined in it many things calculated to make it blameworthy and
destructive—unbelief, belief of the devil, ingratitude, ambition,
wilfulness, deliberation, pride, discontent, luxuriousness, desperation and the involving of all his posterity. For extent of influence
and vastness of results no man has ever wielded a millionth part of
the power for evil, wielded by Adam, or has ever wrought a
millionth part of the ruin and destruction effected by him. The
fruit, the legitimate fruit of his doings will be felt through all the
cycles of eternity. For sweep of influence he never had but one
equal, and that was his antitype. It was in his federal headship,
his representative character that Adam was a type of Christ.
Take this away, and he is no more a type of Christ than any
other man among the patriarchs. Indeed this is the point, the
only point where the globe touches the plane.

   Some object to this whole matter, that Adam in his simplicity
did not know that he was acting for his posterity. To this several
things should be said in reply. 1. Men cannot prove that Adam
did not know that his acts would involve others. It is on their
part a mere conjecture, and may be sufficiently answered by a
counter conjecture. 2. Adam was not a child in understanding.
He had a mind full of vigor, fresh from the breath of God. He
conversed with God as a man with his friend. The inspiration of
the Almighty gave him understanding. He had already such intelligence that the Lord appointed him to name every beast of the
field, every fowl of the air and all cattle. Adam's *simplicity*, when
appointed by God our representative, consisted not in ignorance,

or puerility, or imbecility, but in virtue and purity.   3. It is
doubtless true that Adam did not know *all* the bearings or any
considerable part of the effects of his actions on his posterity.   It
is seldom if ever given to mortals to see the end from the beginning of any matter.   That is the prerogative of omniscience
alone.   Nor is it necessary to the fairness of any probation that
he, who undergoes it, should be as God, knowing all things.
Indeed there often would be no test at all, if men knew what God
afterwards reveals.   This was strikingly illustrated in Abraham's
offering of Isaac.   Had that patriarch known what the precise
issue would be, there would have been no trial at all.   4. It is
enough for the guidance of any one rightly disposed under trial to
understand the preceptive will of God, whether he knows or does
not know all of the reasons for it, or all of the remote or immediate bearings of obedience or of transgression.   Thus Abraham
saw not how the promises were to be fulfilled, if Isaac were
sacrificed.   But God's command was clear, and God's power was
unlimited, and he believed God could raise him from the dead;
and he did his duty.   In the case of Adam the prohibitory precept was perfectly clear : " Of the tree of the knowledge of good
and evil thou shalt not eat of it."   Nothing could be clearer.   5.
The penalty was clearly annexed : " In the day thou eatest thereof
thou shalt surely die."   The Hebrew is if possible still stronger.
Beyond a doubt Adam knew that a curse, the curse of God,
would follow disobedience.   If he did not know *all* that was
included in death, neither does any living man know all that is
now meant by death, temporal or eternal.   Yet who will say the
sinner has not fair warning, when Jehovah says, " The soul that
sinneth it shall die?"   6. The first three chapters of Genesis
make it highly probable that Adam well understood that the
welfare or misery of his posterity was involved in the course he
should pursue.   When Taylor said, " Observe here is not one
word relating to Adam's posterity;" Edwards replied : " But it
may be observed in opposition to this, that there is scarcely *one
word* that we have an account of, which God ever said to Adam
or Eve, but what does manifestly include their posterity in the
meaning and design of it.   There is as much of *a word* said about
Adam's posterity in that threatening [*Thou shalt surely die*], as
there is in those words of God to Adam and Eve, Gen. 1 : 28, *Be
fruitful, and multiply, and replenish the earth and subdue it ;* and as
much in events, to lead us to suppose Adam's posterity to be included.   There is as much of *a word* of his posterity in that
threatening as in those words, Gen. 1 : 29, *Behold I have given you
every herb bearing seed, which is upon the face of all the earth, and*

every tree, in the which is the fruit of a tree yielding seed: to you it shall be for meat. Even when God was about to make man, what he said on that occasion had not respect to Adam only, but to his posterity, Gen. 1 : 26: *Let us make man in our image, and let them have dominion over the fish of the sea, &c.* And, what is more remarkable, there is as much of *a word* said about Adam's posterity in the threatening of death, as there is in that sentence, (Gen. 3 : 19,) *Unto dust thou shalt return,*" pp. 424, 425. Is there a serious student of scripture, who doubts that this *sentence* exactly corresponds to the *threatening,* or that Adam knew that his descendants were included in the sentence? I know not of any. Why then should we doubt that he knew his posterity were included in the threatening?

When it has been stated that Adam was the representative of his posterity, some wits, with a glibness bordering on profanity, have given currency to the remark: "Adam was not my representative—I never voted for him." No doubt those, who speak thus, think they give some proof of cleverness. But such a remark has no manner of pertinency to the business in hand, for this reason: God's government over the world is not a democracy, nor a representative republic, nor an oligarchy, nor a limited monarchy. It is a government of one infinitely holy, just, good and omnipotent Sovereign, who has not a cabinet council, nor any advisers, nor any checks upon his plans outside of his own ineffable and glorious nature, Isa. 40 : 13, 14; 46: 10; Jer. 32 : 19; Acts 5 : 38, 39; Rom. 11 : 34; Eph. 1 : 11; Heb. 6 : 17. Jehovah kills, and he makes alive; he wounds, and he heals; he sets up on high those that be low; he raiseth up the poor out of the dust, and lifteth up the beggar from the dunghill, to set them among princes; promotion cometh neither from the east, nor from the west, nor from the south. But God is the judge: He putteth down one, and setteth up another. Deut. 32 : 39; 1 Sam. 2 : 8; Job 5 : 11; Ps. 75 ; 6, 7. In laying his plans and putting man under a constitution God asked the advice of neither man nor angel. If men, who use such language as that given above, mean anything more than to make a laugh, if they are in solemn earnest, they might as well object to their own lineal ancestry, even to a natural descent from Adam, because they did not vote for him as their first parent. No man ever votes on his own lineage. Yet lineage carries with it honor or dishonor, good health or a feeble constitution, riches or poverty, and affects our destiny in a thousand things. Not a British subject, living or dead, ever voted that Victoria should be his monarch. When the laws of the realm are promulged, they may greatly and injuriously affect the welfare of

a given man or class, but can they evade their force, or their binding obligation by saying, I never voted for Victoria to be my
sovereign? Even in our own land, America, the great majority
of the people, women and minors, never vote for their rulers.
Does this fact in the slightest degree relax their obligations to
submit, in the Lord, to the powers that be? No good man so
affirms. By the holy, sovereign, uncontrollable will of God Adam
was made the covenant head of his seed, and there the matter
must rest. In this he was a *figure* or type of Christ.

Very few men, who profess the least reverence for God's word,
deny that pain and temporal death came on mankind *by one man*,
by the one offence of Adam. Even Locke says that Paul here
" teaches that by Adam's lapse all men were brought into a state
of death." Macknight also: " Death, the punishment of sin,
reigned from Adam to Moses, even over infants," etc. During the
XVIII. century some taught that Adam's first sin, though truly
imputed to *infants*, so that they are thereby exposed to a proper
punishment, is not imputed to them in so high a *degree* as to Adam
himself. To all such remarks it is sufficient to say as Edwards
does: " To suppose God imputes not *all* the guilt of Adam's sin,
but only some *little* part of it, relieves nothing but one's *imagination. . .* But it does not at all relieve one's *reason. . .* All the
reasons (if there be any) lie against the *imputation;* not the *quantity* or *degree of what is imputed*," p. 561. If Adam had successfully
stood his probation, would his obedience have profited his posterity but a little? or would they have been for ever confirmed in
holiness and God's favor just as he would have been? Probably
but one answer will be given to that interrogatory. The fact is
that if Adam was at all a public person, if he at all acted as a
representative, he did so to this extent, that he and his posterity
should fare alike in the results of his probation. If he stood, he
and they would be regarded and treated as righteous; if he fell, he
and they would be regarded and treated as sinners. This communion in guilt might be confirmed by a detailed examination of
the sentence passed on our first parents, as we see it executed in
our own time. Did Adam die a temporal death? So do his
posterity. Can any one shew that there was anything appalling
in the manner of his death? It could hardly have been more so
than what may be witnessed every day in this world among old
and young. Was the ground cursed for his sake, so that in sorrow
he ate bread all the days of his life, the earth bringing forth thorns
and thistles to him, and he in the sweat of his face eating bread
till he returned to the ground? Gen. 3 : 17, 18. The very same
thing occurs all over the earth all the time. The rich are no ex-

ception, for often their abundance will not suffer them even to sleep, Ecc. 5 : 12. Did the Lord multiply the sorrows and conception of the first woman, so that in sorrow she brought forth children? Gen. 3 : 16. Is not the same as true of Adam's daughters to this day? We have then the great fact beyond dispute among serious students of the Bible. God visits on all our race the very evils that he sent on the first pair — toil, sorrow, pangs and death. All this does not argue that all incorrigible sinners, who spend their lifetime on earth in impenitence, are equally ill deserving and will suffer equally in the next world for their own ungodly deeds and speeches. Far from it. He, that knew his Lord's will, and did it not, shall be beaten with many stripes; but he that knew it not, and did commit things worthy of stripes, shall be beaten with few stripes, Luke 12 : 47, 48. Human accountability was in no sense exhausted in the garden of Eden; nor will it be exhausted in this life, no, nor in eternity.

It may here be observed that from the history of theological doctrine it appears that ordinarily when men have denied our representation in Adam they have also hesitated in receiving the orthodox doctrine on the subject of native depravity. Laxity in the former almost uniformly results in looseness respecting the latter. It was so in the days of Pelagius. He and Julian and Coelestius attacked both branches of the doctrine of Original Sin. It was so in the XVII. and XVIII. centuries both in Great Britain and on the Continent. It has been so in this century and in this country. Another historic fact is no less admonitory. It is that when men deny or explain away the federal headship of Adam, or the imputation of the guilt of his first sin to his seed, we almost invariably find them in doubt respecting the imputation of the sins of the elect to Christ, and of Christ's righteousness to his believing people. In other words, men, who are unsound on the manner of our condemnation, are seldom clear and scriptural on the subject of our justification. Now and then we meet with cases, where, by a happy inconsistency, men are sound on one of these points, and yet erroneous on the rest. Such cases, are, however, rare. Commonly errors are grouped together. And it is the tendency of error to make continual aggressions. On the other hand there is a consanguinity between religious truths. Truth is one. Error is multiform.

In summing up the argument we may thus paraphrase our verse : It has been admitted that where there is no law there is no sin, *and yet* there meet us as strong proofs of the reign of death during the first twenty-five hundred years of the world as we find even in our own time. In this whole argument it is a first princi-

ple that wherever death is found among men, it is proof of the existence of sin, and where sin is, some law must have been broken.
Now none of these people had the law of Sinai, and their sin
could not have been against that. Nor did any of them but the
first pair actually eat the forbidden fruit, yet we find men subject
to death then as at other times. We find too a law given in Eden
with the sanction of a death penalty. That law was violated by
Adam, who was not only the father but the covenant head of the
race and acted for them. This is the law, whose violation constituted in God's esteem all men sinners, and subjected all to death.
So that even infants, of whom no man can prove and very few if
any will assert that they have committed any actual sin, have from
the earliest ages to the present time not only died, but died in
great numbers and often in great agony. The explanation of these
amazing scenes of woe is to be found in the fact that Jehovah constituted Adam a public person, and in his infinite wisdom ordained
that he should act for others as well as for himself. In this way,
as a federal head, Adam became a type of Christ; as Christ acted
for his seed so did Adam act for his seed. The mode and results
of action in these two cases were very different; but the principle
of representation in both was the same. Else in what possible
sense was Adam a figure of him that was to come?

15. *But not as the offence, so also* is *the free gift: for if through
the offence of one many be dead, much more the grace of God, and the
gift by grace*, which is *by one man, Jesus Christ, hath abounded unto
many.* Here the apostle guards us against mistaking his teaching,
by commencing to shew that Adam was not in all or even in many
respects a figure or type of Christ. The similitude on which he
has insisted is exhausted in the one point of the federal headship,
the representative character of each. Wardlaw: "The parallel
lies chiefly in one point; namely, that the first and second Adam
acted each a public part, standing for others and not for themselves merely; a part from which important results were to arise
to those whom they are considered respectively as representing."
This is enough. This aids and elucidates the argument on justification by the righteousness of Christ. But the effects of this
headship respectively are as diverse as any things, of which we
can conceive. On one side are sin, misery and death; on the
other obedience, reconciliation, life. *The offence*, so rendered nowhere else but in four verses here closely connected, and in Rom.
4:25; elsewhere fall, fault, sin, trespass. The offence, here alluded
to, was the breach of covenant with God in eating the forbidden
fruit. *Free gift*, so rendered here only and in v. 16; everywhere
else, *gift*. But a gift, properly so called, is of course unbought.

It is *free*, without money and without price.   It is the same word
used in Rom. 6 : 23, "The *gift* of God is eternal life," and in
Rom. 11 : 29, "The *gifts* and calling of God are without repentance."   It is elsewhere used to denote spiritual *gifts*, miraculously
bestowed, for the edification of the church.   Now, says Paul, the
effect of our fall in Adam was wholly diverse from the effect of
our recovery by Christ.   One brought death; the other brings
life.   The former was in the course of righteous judgment on the
race; the latter is the most amazing expression of divine compassion. *For if through the offence of one many be dead*, many be
fallen under the penalty of a broken covenant, and so are dead, as
we have already shewn to be the case, *much more the grace of God,
and the gift by grace, which is by one man Jesus Christ, hath abounded
unto many. Offence*, as in the preceding clause.   *Grace of God*, explained on Rom. 1 : 5.   It here points out God's undeserved kindness. *Gift*, not the same word as *free gift* in this verse, but another
not cognate but nearly synonymous, always rendered gift.   The
cognate adverb occurs in Rom. 3 : 24, and is rendered *freely*, on
which see above.   What is here called the gift by grace is in the
next verse called the *free gift*, which brings the pardon of *many
offences* and goes on *unto justification;* in v. 17 it is called the *gift
of righteousness;* and in v. 18, *justification of life.*   Even if we had
not these explanations in the immediate context, the whole train
of argument in several preceding chapters shews that the great
benefits derived from Christ, and here made the subject of discourse, are justifying righteousness and its inseparable concomi-
tants. *Many*, the numerous seed of each respectively; Locke:
"the multitude;" Hodge: "the mass;" Conybeare and Howson:
"the many."   No doubt the term in each clause includes all that
the first and second Adam respectively represented.   In v. 18 the
word *all* is used as an equivalent.   What is precisely meant by
these words, *all* and *many*, will be considered when we reach v. 18.
In v. 15 now under consideration the most difficult phrase to explain is *much more*.   The rendering is literal and undisputed.
There are various views taken of the significancy of these words.
All agree that they indicate the argument *a fortiori*.   But in what
particular does the *grace* of the work of the second Adam so *much
more abound*, than did the death brought on men by the first Adam?
Some have said the meaning is that the pre-eminence consists in
the fact that a greater number are saved by Christ than were lost
in Adam.   To make this appear they have alleged that great
numbers of men were not made subject to death by Adam's fall,
but only by their own sins.   But any argument, by which the
people of any particular age or country can be shewn not to

have been involved in penal suffering by the lapse of Adam, will as fully prove that he acted for no one except himself, and then how is he the type of Christ? Those, who hold this view, maintain that those, who perished in the deluge, died for their own sins. No doubt their death by so awful a judgment and in so dreadful manner, was, and was intended to be understood as an expression of God's abhorrence of their great personal wickedness. The same may be said of those, who perished in Sodom and Gomorrah, Admah and Zeboim, yea, and of vast multitudes, who have been cut off by terrific judgments. But does any one believe, and if he so believes, can he prove that these people would never have died at all but for their actual atrocious sins? Their superadding the guilt of many and aggravated sins did not before God obscure the guilt of original sin, and did not set aside but caused to be executed, before the time indicated by the course of nature, the sentence of death brought on the race by Adam. Locke: "By their own sins they were not made mortal: they were so before, by their father Adam's eating the forbidden fruit: so that what they paid for their own sins, was not immortality, which they had not." It is believed that none maintain that Christ has saved or will save a greater number than were lost in Adam except those, who contend that mere temporal death and the pains which lead to it exhausted the penalty of breaking the covenant of Eden, and that even that penalty made not all men mortal, but many died solely because of their enormous actual sins. In the comment on v. 12 it has been shewn that the penalty did indeed include temporal death, but extended much farther also.

Locke suggests another way in which the grace of God and the gift by grace excel the offence: "It seems to lie in this, that Adam's lapse came barely for the satisfaction of his own appetite, and desire of good to himself; but the restoration was from the exuberant bounty and good-will of Christ towards men, who, at the cost of his own painful death, purchased life for them." No doubt sin in all its stages and in all its workings is very inferior to holiness. No doubt the sin of Adam had in it the element of low personal gratification; and we know the love of Christ for men was transcendant, vs. 6–8. But does Paul take no higher view in this verse than merely to state the superiority of benevolence over selfishness? The apostle does not seem to be speaking of human estimates of things, so much as of the exceedingly excellent nature of the benefits received by Christ, especially as contrasted with the ruin wrought by Adam. In other words he is laboring to make our views conform to the facts in the case as they are known and estimated by God. It is a fact that the undertaking of

Christ does *abound* in a way that the fall of Adam does not, whatever men's views of these matters may be. Wardlaw has probably given a better statement of the whole case: "There is one more general, and there are three more particular points of contrast here. The general point is, that whereas the condemnation and death which came by the first Adam were the due wages of sin; the righteousness and life which came by the second Adam are the bestowment of pure grace, of entirely unmerited favor. This, indeed, runs through the whole passage, and it forms the characteristic distinction between the law and the gospel. The sentence of death pronounced on Adam, and in him on his posterity, is the sentence of justice incurred by transgression, deserved by guilt. The Supreme Ruler, therefore, by whom it had been pronounced, was under no obligation of righteousness to deliver from it. He was rather under the obligation of truth and justice to see it executed. A condemned malefactor, if pardoned, must be pardoned by grace; if his condemnation be in justice, the remission of his sentence must be in clemency. Where death is due, life must be a gift. Where a curse is merited, the blessing must flow from purely spontaneous favor," Vol. 2; pp. 283–4. He then mentions three more particular points of contrast between our representation in the first and second Adam. "The first appears to me to relate to the superior dignity of the second Adam, in whom sinners have life, above the first, in whom they died. The second relates to the superabundance of pardoning grace, as extending beyond the guilt of the one offence, by which sin entered, even to all the multiplied acts and words, and thoughts of personal transgression—'many offences.' The third has respect to the superiority of the life to which sinners are brought by grace, to that life which they lost by Adam's sin," p. 284. These points of contrast duly carried out seem to cover very much the whole ground, not only given us in this verse but also in vs. 16–19. In this verse very much of the sense depends on the right place being given to the *one man, Jesus Christ.* The same is true of v. 17.

16. *And not as* it was *by one that sinned,* so is *the gift: for the judgment* was *by one to condemnation, but the free gift* is *of many offences unto justification. One that sinned* beyond a doubt points to Adam. *Gift,* the word is found nowhere else in the New Testament, except in Jas. 1:17. It is a noun cognate to that rendered gift in v. 15. *Judgment,* often so rendered; also damnation, condemnation. See above on Rom. 2:2, 3; 3:8. *Condemnation,* the word so rendered is found in the New Testament here only, in v. 18, and in Rom. 8:1. The cognate verb occurs often and is commonly rendered condemned, also damned. We met it in Rom. 2:1.

Free gift as in v. 15. The one, that sinned, by one act brought a condemning sentence, ready to be executed at any moment, and now continually in a course of rapid execution on all his posterity. But the Son of God shows his great power to save by blotting out innumerable transgressions committed by innumerable sinners, as well as washing away the guilt of original sin from their souls, and not leaving them merely pardoned. He accepts them as righteous and so secures to them full justification. Whenever called to appear before God, their raiment will be shining, exceeding white as snow ; so as no fuller on earth can white them. That the above gives the true sense of the passage is made plain by the very terms employed, and by the context.

17. *For if by one man's offence death reigned by one ; much more they which receive abundance of grace and of the gift of righteousness shall reign in life by one, Jesus Christ.* This verse terminates the parenthesis begun in v. 13. This verse is remarkably clear. It changes the form but not the purport of the antithesis, which is found in several preceding verses. Here we have death reigning by one and the redeemed reigning in life by one. The first Adam brought ruin by one offence. The second, abundance of grace and of the gift of righteousness. *Abundance*, not elsewhere in this epistle, but well rendered. We have the same word in 2 Cor. 8 : 2 ; in Jas. 1 : 21 it is rendered superfluity. It expresses superabundance, overflowing riches. *Gift* as in v. 15. *Righteousness*, as already explained at large. The general course of the argument here is very clear and pointed. If one man and he a mere man, by one act, in which we partook in no other way than that by divine appointment he acted for us, as well as for himself, installed death as a tyrant over us, much more shall one, who is at once man and man's maker, when we cordially embrace him as our Saviour, and accept his offers, cause us to be kings and sharers of the vast treasures of his grace, one of whose richest fruits is the gift of righteousness, so as to make sure to us the blessings of eternal life, of which we have the pledge in the newness of life granted us in this world.

18. *Therefore, as by the offence of one* judgment came *upon all men to condemnation ; even so by the righteousness of one* the free gift came *upon all men unto justificaton of life. Therefore* the two words so rendered are not the same as those rendered wherefore in v. 12. But they are of like import, and clearly mark the connection of this with v. 12. The comparison there begun, and interrupted by the parenthesis, is here fully carried out, only the leading terms *judgment* and *free gift*, being properly borrowed by our translators from preceding sentences. Some prefer to read *one offence*

and *one righteousness*, instead of *the offence of one* and the *righteousness of one*. No doubt Adam brought ruin on us by *one* act. Nor does the grammar forbid this rendering. Yet the objections to it are perhaps sufficient to cause its rejection. They are such as these: 1. The term *one* in the context uniformly applies to one person. Both in vs. 17, 19, *one man* is named. The sense in v. 18 is best reached by understanding one person in each case. At all events there is no improvement in the force of the argument by the proposed change. 2. Throughout the passage the apostle all along carefully marks the distinction between the *one* and the *all*, the *one* and the *many*. 3. If the phrase *one righteousness* is found elsewhere in scripture, the author does not remember it. 4. Those, who contend for the change do ask us to believe that Christ saves us by one act of righteousness, viz. his obedience unto death, understanding that phrase to mean his obedience in dying. This is not safe doctrine. Speaking of the proposed change and the reason of it Wardlaw says: " It seems to be not merely a superfluous refinement, but moreover to proceed from a false principle with regard to what is necessary as the ground of acceptance and of life. And without entering largely into the discussion about the active and passive obedience of Christ, I would say it seems to give us a more complete and satisfactory view of the finished work of Jesus, when we consider him as not only bearing the curse which forms the sanction of the law, but also as rendering to its requirements that sinless obedience, which, according to the original engagement of God, entitles to life. That the Lord our righteousness did render such a sinless obedience to all the great spiritual principles and requirements of the law cannot be doubted," p. 281. All Christ did and all he bore was for our salvation. He suffered in obeying. He obeyed in suffering. No fair criticism can ever shew that *righteousness* in this verse or *obedience* in v. 19 means simply his sufferings, much less his obedience in the mere act of dying. His circumcision and baptism were as much in fulfilment of all righteousness as his death. His perfect love to God and his equal love to man, evinced in every way, were essential to his righteousness. There is a sense in which Christ's righteousness is one. It is a seamless robe. There is no rent in it. It is undivided. It cannot be divided. But this is a very different thing from saying that Christ wrought out his righteousness the last few hours of his life. The parallel between Adam and Christ is not intended to be preserved in the shortness of the time in which, or the ease with which ruin and recovery were wrought. No? Destruction is easy. Recovery is difficult. It is so in every thing. A rash act of one may destroy a thousand lives, but all the power of men and angels cannot restore one life. A child may in a few hours burn down a city, which ten thousand men could not build in a year. In a moment Adam brought down ruin. It required the *righteousness* and *obedience* of the life of Christ and his agony in the garden and on the cross to bring us to God. Yea, to the same end he ever liveth to make intercession for us. " The truth is, the work of Christ is just the whole of his humiliation, with all that he did and all he suffered in the nature which he humbled himself to assume. That on account of which God exalted and glorified Christ, is that on account of which he justifies and glorifies sinners."

In considering a previous verse a promise was made to consider the meaning of the terms *many* and *all*, when we should reach this verse. In this verse we twice have *all men ;* in vs. 15, 16, 19, we have *many*, or *the many*. Evidently these terms are used interchangeably. The *all* of this verse corresponds to the *many* of the other verses. On this there is no dispute. As to the extent of meaning of these terms, there are five distinct views. 1. The old Universalists held that in both cases all mere men were embraced ; that is, Adam on the one hand brought down the curse of the law on his posterity, descending from him by ordinary generation ; and Christ, being truly divine, and having lived and died with the purpose of saving all men, his atonement being strictly vicarious and designed to save all men, all men shall surely be saved by Christ and raised to the everlasting enjoyment of God in heaven. These persons were consistent in their interpretation of the terms *all* and *many*. But they flatly contradicted many clear, positive declarations of God's word when they asserted that every man would be saved, Dan. 12 : 2 ; Matt. 25 : 46 ; John 5 : 28, 29 ; and many other places.

2. Another class of writers maintain that the whole extent of the curse brought on us by the fall of Adam was temporal death, and that all Christ is here said to have done for us was to secure to us natural life ; that Adam brought temporal death on all his posterity, and that Christ secured to all men a temporal life. If Locke is not misunderstood, this is his view. His language is : " The apostle teaches them that by Adam's lapse all men were brought into a state of death, and by Christ's death all were restored to life." In his paraphrase he seems to express himself to the same effect. And in a note he pleads for his rendering of the phrase *all have sinned*, as meaning no more than this *all became mortal*. If Adam brought only temporal death, the parallel would suggest that Christ merely secured temporal life. In commenting on v. 12 it has been shewn that temporal death was not all nor even the

chief evil brought on us by Adam. And surely Christ has done much more for men than to secure a short and miserable temporal existence. Some human beings are never even born. The womb is their grave. Others live a minute, others an hour, others a day, others a week, others a year, and the general limit is three score and ten. This whole existence is sometimes spent in pain. Surely Jesus Christ did more for those he represented than to secure a temporal life to man. But see above on v. 12. This mode of explanation would make the _all_ and the _many_ in every case include every human being that ever lived or ever shall live.

3. Another explanation given by some is that Adam involved his posterity in penal evils, including temporal death and that Jesus Christ, by his undertaking, removed not the curse of temporal death which remains, but brought literally all the race of man into a state, where it was possible they might be saved. These agree, as we do, that the curse fell on all who descended from Adam by ordinary generation. They contend that the effect of Christ's work in removing the curse extends to as many of Adam's descendants as were under the penalty of death, so that to all men capable of understanding anything a sincere offer of salvation is made. But in the first place there are millions on millions, to whom no such offer was ever made. It is only within the last three or four hundred years that Jesus Christ's name was ever pronounced on the continent of America. Did all, who lived here before that time reap any such benefit from the work of Christ as to have even an offer of eternal life by his blood made to them? No one will contend for that. Nor will any, who hold this view, contend that all these people were saved. If they were all, old and young, eternally saved, then there would be consistency in interpreting the words _many_ and _all_ as they do, but other Scriptures would be strangely opposed and contradicted. And in our chapter there is not a word about men being merely brought into a state of salvability by Christ. On the contrary they are said to be justified, to have peace with God, access into grace, joy, hope, triumph in afflictions, patience, love, all Christian graces. And in the immediate context we read of their sharing in _the grace of God_ and _the gift by grace_, of _the free gift_ [of remission] _of many offences unto jnstification_, of _the abundance of grace_ and _of the gift of righteousness_, and that _by the righteousness of one the free gift came unto the justification of life_. Surely these terms and phrases express a great deal more than that those here spoken of are brought into a state, in which it is possible they may be saved. They are saved, else to what use is the grace of God, the gift by grace, the free gift, the abundance of grace, the gift of righteousness, justification unto

life? Such language denotes actual salvation, not mere salvability.

4. Another explanation of the terms is that *all men*, which of course includes the *many*, here, as in some other places, means, not all men without exception, but all men without discrimination. Diodati: "All manner of persons indifferently, though not all universally." Wardlaw argues for this at length. He says the phrase is frequently used in this sense; and so it is. He might have cited Tit. 2 : 11 and many other verses in proof. He also says that the argument in the epistle shews that men without regard to nationality are included. This is also true. Conceding these points, the explanation will still probably be generally regarded as unsatisfactory. Indeed it has been generally so esteemed. Very few adopt it.

5. The method of explaining these terms adopted by sound writers generally is that the *many* and *all men* are to be understood of all who are represented by Adam and Christ respectively. In other words these and like terms here as in other places are to be construed according to the subject and connection, in which they are found. This explanation is thought to be fair and conclusive for the following reasons: 1. We are compelled to limit the term *all* even in regard to Adam; for the man Christ Jesus, though according to the flesh descended from Adam, was not represented in Adam and was not chargeable with original sin. Here is one exception. Eve was another, who was not brought under the penalty for Adam's but for her own sin. She was a sinner, and under the penalty of death, while Adam was yet an unfallen creature. How long she was so we know not, but if she was a sinner and under wrath the smallest portion of time, it is sufficient for our purpose. Here then we have two human beings not included in the all represented in Adam. 2. The language of the apostle clearly confines the *all* men represented by the second Adam to such as derive saving benefits from him. They are such as have *the grace of God, and the gift by grace, the free gift, abundance of grace,* and *of the gift of righteousness, justification, righteousness, justification of life.* Yea, it is expressly said, they *shall reign in life by one, Jesus Christ.* No language could more clearly mark a class of persons distinguished from the rest of mankind by having the redemption of Christ actually applied to them. We freely admit that all, who sinned in Adam and fell with him, are embraced in the *many* and *all men* where they first occur in these verses. We as freely concede that all men, who *shall reign in life,* who have or shall ever have *abundance of grace,* and *justification unto life,* are embraced in the terms *many* and *all men,* where they occur in the

latter clauses of these verses. 3. The construction contended for is clearly supported by the fact that Adam was a type of Christ. And Edwards justly says: " The agreement between Adam as the type or figure of him that was to come, and Christ as the antitype, appears full and clear, if we suppose that ALL who are IN CHRIST (to use the common scripture phrase) have the benefit of his obedience even as ALL who are IN ADAM have the sorrowful fruit of his disobedience." 4. Other scriptures use the term *many* in the very sense contended for in this place. In Rom. 12 : 5 Paul says: " We being many are one body in Christ; " and in 1 Cor. 10 : 17 " We being many are one bread, and one body." The Greek is exactly the same as in Rom. 5, *the many*, the mass, the multitude. Indeed in Rom. 4 : 18 the spiritual seed of Abraham is spoken of as ' *many nations*,' words indicating as vast and comprehensive a multitude as any phrase employed here. So also we read in Rom. 8 : 29 of Christ being " the firstborn among *many* brethren," where we have the same word. 5. The same line of remark may be applied to the words *all men*. We hardly have begun to read the New Testament until we find such language incapable of any other than a limited meaning: " Then went out to him Jerusalem, and all Judea, and all the region round about Jordan, and were baptized of him in Jordan, confessing their sins," Matt. 3 : 5, 6. That this language may not be so understood as to embrace *all* the people there is declared by Christ himself, Matt. 21 : 32. So in Luke 2 : 1 it is said " there went out a decree from Cesar Augustus, that all the world should be taxed." It is probable that only Syria is here intended. But it is certain that it cannot mean more than the Roman empire, which though a very important part of the world did not embrace the half of it, as every one knows. In John 12 : 32 Jesus says: " And I, if I be lifted up from the earth, will draw all men unto me." All men have not embraced Christ, although a great multitude of all sorts and ranks of men have believed on him. Great numbers of texts might be adduced to the same effect. 6. That passage in 1 Cor. 15 : 21, 22 uses the same language and yet on the one side none but Christ's own people are meant. " For since by man came death, by man came also the resurrection of the dead. For as in Adam all die, even so in Christ shall all be made alive." Now the whole context, preceding and subsequent, for many verses together, shews that the apostle is speaking not at all of the resurrection of the wicked, but of those that are *fallen asleep in Jesus*, of *those who have hope in Christ*, of those, *who shall be raised in glory, in incorruption*, in immortality, of those, who shall at last sing, O death, where is thy sting? O grave, where is thy victory? Even many, who oppose the precise

views given in this commentary admit that it is the resurrection
of the just, not of the unjust, that is spoken of throughout the 15th
chapter of 1 Corinthians. Even Stuart admits this. 7. Hodge :
" In a multitude of cases, the words *all, all things*, mean the all
spoken of in the context, and not all without exception ; see Eph.
1 : 10; Col. 1 : 20; 1 Cor. 15 : 51; 2 Cor. 5 : 14, 15." This list of
texts might be greatly extended. 8. This explanation covers the
whole case, and makes all plain and consistent. In this view all,
who are in Christ, who are his seed, his redeemed, have the *grace
of God*, and *the gift by grace*, the *free gift* of forgiveness of *many
offences unto justification, abundance of grace and of the gift of righteousness*, the *justification of life*, and *shall reign in life by one, Jesus
Christ*. These things cannot be said of the wicked, the ungodly,
but only of believers in the Lord Jesus Christ. So that we are
compelled at last to admit that those, who are never saved, are
not partakers of the benefits of Christ's undertaking as here described. Some would evade the force of this reasoning by saying
that these blessings are indeed not bestowed on all men, but that
they are sincerely offered to them. It is admitted that all God's
offers and proposals to men are sincere. He never mocks his
creatures. But to the greater part of mankind the Gospel has
never been preached, nor its offers made known. So this view
does not relieve the difficulty. Nor is this the only difficulty.
There is not a word said in this whole passage respecting the *offer*
of *grace*, or of *justification*, or of any blessing. All that is spoken
relates to the possession and enjoyment of these benefits.

19. *For as by one man's disobedience many were made sinners, so
by the obedience of one shall many be made righteous.* Perhaps there
never was a better, or more conclusive summing up of an argument than we have in this verse. Peshito: For as, on account of
the disobedience of one man, many became sinners ; so also, on
account of the obedience of one, many become righteous. Wiclif:
For as bi inobedience of o man many ben made synners : so bi
the obedience of oon many shuln be just. Stuart: For as by the
disobedience of one man the many were constituted sinners, so
by the obedience of one the many will be constituted righteous.
In the creed of Andover Seminary the language used on this
point is borrowed from Beza and we have it in the translation
above cited from the Andover Professor—many were constituted
sinners. No one holding the common view objects to such a
rendering. The word rendered were made, became, or were constituted is a strong word and is rendered *ordained*, Heb. 5 : 1; 8 : 3;
and in the active voice *make*, or *made*, Matt. 24 : 45, 47 ; 25 : 21, 23 ;
appoint, Acts 6 : 3. They were *made*, or *constituted* sinners, so as

to be regarded and treated as sinners. They are *made* just, or *con-stituted* righteous in the eye of the law, so that they are by the Judge of all the earth regarded and treated as just persons. The condemnation is here spoken of in the past tense, because Adam's work of ruin was actually finished and in operation on every liv-ing man. On the other hand the benefit of justification had not yet reached every man, who should share in that blessing, and so it is spoken of in the future.

20. *Moreover the law entered, that the offence might abound. But where sin abounded, grace did much more abound.* Having in v. 19 completed his illustration of the manner of our justification in Christ furnished by the manner of our condemnation in Adam, the apostle proceeds to state that the effect of the entrance of the law, so far from making a gratuitous justification by the righteous-ness of Christ unnecessary either in appearance or in reality, had just the contrary effect in two respects. First it revealed in many ways the true nature of sin, and shewed how greatly men had already departed from the rule of rectitude. Thus by the law was the knowledge of sin. Secondly, the very enjoining of many things and the prohibition of others in the law, so far from re-pressing sinful inclinations, did in many cases inflame them, and awaken unholy desires in a fearful manner. So Augustine and many others. That this latter effect in an unregenerate heart is often produced by the existence of law is matter of common ex-perience, and is clearly stated in this epistle. Indeed both these ideas are by Paul explicitly declared in Rom. 7 : 7, 8. The effect of the law in awakening opposition is no fault of the law itself, for it is holy, just and good, honorable to God and in all respects worthy of him. But because men are wicked and their hearts perverse, they abuse this great revelation of his will to the race of men, and thus that which was ordained unto life is found to be unto death. The divine procedure in this matter may be illus-trated by the conduct of a wise and faithful pastor, who often and ably expounds and enforces the law of God with the express design of awakening attention, creating alarm, convincing of sin and making men feel the need of deliverance, by the grace of God in Christ, from their guilt and depravity. So that there should be no hesitancy in admitting that it was entirely consistent with the divine benevolence to give the law, knowing that it would be the innocent occasion of stirring up the enmity of the human heart, while at the same time it revealed the number, ag-gravations, guilt and odiousness of sins already committed. This view is correct whether we interpret the word *law* as meaning only the moral law, or whether we make it to embrace the whole

of the Mosaic institute, of which the decalogue was the heart and centre.   The latter is probably the better explanation, and what is thus taught is certainly true.   *Entered,* very well rendered, though some prefer the word supervened, to which there is no serious objection.   But the apostle would not have us forget that if the ministration of death was glorious, much more doth the ministration of righteousness exceed in glory, 2 Cor. 3 : 7–9 ; that if the Mosaic dispensation, so honorable to God, had brought home to men so deep convictions of their sin and ruin, much more was the gospel honorable to God in displaying boundless stores of mercy and truth ; and that whereas sin did much abound and fill men with great and just alarm, so now grace, justifying and saving grace, did *much more abound.*   This is in full accordance with the teachings of the Old Testament, Isa. 40 : 2 ; 55 : 7 ; Zech. 9 : 12.   God does not barely save the soul that hopes in his mercy. He *abundantly pardons.*   He *renders double* for all our sins.   He ministers an *entrance abundantly* into his everlasting kingdom.   If sin and death reigned as tyrants, truth and righteousness shall much more reign in glory by Jesus Christ.   So illustrious is God's plan of bringing men to a saving knowledge of himself, and so wondrous the salvation he thus bestows, that there is no mistake in saying, that where sin abounded, grace did much more abound.

21. *That as sin hath reigned unto death, even so might grace reign through righteousness unto eternal life by Jesus Christ our Lord.* How sin has *reigned* over men is written in the history of the world.   How it has reigned *unto death* is written in every grave-yard, in every hospital, in every disease, in every groan, in every tormenting apprehension awakened by a guilty conscience, and in Tophet ordained of old—the prison-house of despair.   The world has been made a vast charnel-house, and all by sin.   But Jesus Christ is stronger than the strong man armed.   Grace is more mighty than sin.   Nor is the power of grace displayed in derogation of the claims of law and justice, truth and purity, but reigns entirely *through righteousness,* a righteousness every way commensurate to the demands of omniscient and infinite purity ; a righteousness that satisfies every demand of God's eternal law, both precept and penalty.   Nor does grace merely mitigate the horrors of our guilty state, nor does it merely save us from all the evils of the fall.   It reigns *unto eternal life.*   In this verse death and life are in antithesis.   If one is eternal, as life is said to be, so is the other.   There is no good reason for varying from the usual meaning of the word righteousness here and rendering it justification. It is, indeed, a righteousness, which secures justification to all

who in their hearts accept it, and it is the ground of their pardon and acceptance, but it is not the pardon and acceptance themselves. It is righteousness, strictly so called, as explained already at length. As to the manner in which grace so superabounds see above on v. 15.

DOCTRINAL AND PRACTICAL REMARKS

1. It is in the plan of God to subject all his rational creatures to a probation. And surely he has a right to do what he will with his own. What the probation of angels was we know not. In it some stood and some fell. What man's probation was the scriptures clearly state. One difference between the probation of angels and that of men was that in the former case each one seems to have stood for himself, in the latter one man stood for the race. For it was by one man that sin entered into the world, v. 12.

2. The probation of man in Adam was not only divinely appointed, but was very fair. Adam was in the full vigor of his powers. The will of God was very clearly made known to him. The test was as slight as we can well conceive a test to be. He doubtless knew that his conduct would affect his posterity. Great liberty was granted him, the fruit of one tree only being denied him. His communion with God had been intimate and delightful. He was endowed with knowledge, righteousness and true holiness. In short the probabilities all seemed to indicate a most favorable result of the probation, yet the fact was that sin entered by one man, and death by sin. There is no comparison between a probation thus conducted, and that, for which some have pleaded, that each member of the human family in his infancy should have stood for himself. Nor is it conceivable that in any stage of man's existence on earth so strong inducements to right conduct could have been brought to bear on each one as seem to have pressed on Adam in his probation. Cavil as men may, it is a great fact that we had our trial in Adam, and that by a divine constitution ordered in all respects in wisdom, holiness, justice, goodness and truth, and yet ruin came upon us like a desolation.

3. Great debates have been held, and are still going on respecting the origin of evil in the world; but they have not been fruitful of good results. The fact is that the history of the apostasy of man as given in the Bible is clear enough for all practical purposes. There wisdom would dictate that we pause. But folly never had any modesty, and pushes on till it is involved in inextricable difficulties or lost in wild confusion. Sin entered by

one man on trial as described in Genesis. We know no more. We can know no more in this world, perhaps never.

4. Let us not despise the day of small things either in good or evil. "Man knows the beginning of sin," said Francis Spira, "but who can tell the bounds thereof?" Every groan and sigh from men on earth or in hell may be traced back to the first sin in Eden, as in some way its cause. In this life we seldom have any adequate apprehension of the fruit of our doings, good or bad. Human conduct reaches much farther, and has consequences much more remote and much more potential for good or ill than we ever conceive. The beginning of sin is as when one letteth out water. Behold what a great matter a little fire kindleth. Whatsoever a man soweth that shall he also reap. Nor is it evil only that has a long course to run. The same is true of good also, "Good deeds never die." A class of men make light of the trial and fall of Adam. They say he sinned but once and then he merely ate an apple. What was the particular fruit that he ate, we know not. Nor is it of any importance that we should. It was forbidden by God. Nor is it a mark of either piety or wisdom to speak with levity respecting any act or word which has moral bearings. *One* sin may ruin a family. Nor is the length of time employed in doing an act the gauge by which to learn its dimensions for good or for evil. The work of a moment may bring forth fruit to all eternity.

5. It is plain to all serious students of God's word that the *death*, threatened against disobedience and incurred by transgression, was something very momentous, v. 12. Even temporal death is styled by Aristotle "the terrible of terribles," and by Bildad "the king of terrors." If the death of the body were all that were brought on us by sin, it would be something dreadful. But much more is included, as has been shewn. Guyse: "The Death, which, the apostle says, *passed upon all men, by one man's sin*, is manifestly the same with that, which the *one man* himself was exposed to by his sin, according to God's threatening, that *in the day he should eat* of the forbidden fruit, *he should surely die*, Gen. 2 : 17. And what was the death therein threatened, but a deprivation of the holy and happy life of soul and body, in the image and favor of God, and in communion with him, which he enjoyed, and should otherwise have been confirmed in with rich advantages for ever? Accordingly upon *Adam's* sin he was liable, not only to diseases and death of the body, but also to inward dread and horror of the soul, under a sense of divine wrath, as appeared in his being afraid, and seeking to hide himself from the presence of the Lord ... And as the death of the body by no means infers

an extinction of the soul, and divine revelation assures us, that the soul survives the body; it seems necessarily to follow from hence that this death extends, not merely to a separation of soul and body, but likewise to all the uneasiness and distress, that flow from the disorderly, ungovernable, and unsatisfied principles, inclinations and appetites, that were introduced by sin; from the loss of the image and favor of God, and communion with him; and from a sense of guilt, and of divine displeasure on that account, with dismal despair of being ever recovered to a state of happiness again: nor could such recovery have been expected, to prevent this death's being eternal, unless God himself, in the abundance of his own mercy, were to find out a way of relief; which, blessed be his name, he has done by our Lord Jesus Christ." By *death* no doubt all penal evil is pointed out. In the case of men living and dying without salvation these penal evils include death temporal, spiritual and eternal. The fact that to such this death is spiritual results from the nature of the soul, and its dependence on God; and the fact that it is eternal results from the fact that a lost soul cannot recover itself; can never pay the debt it owes, and will be eternally responsible for all its emotions and acts. Diodati: "Death is not an accident natural to man, as to plants and beasts, but is the reward of sin," Rom. 6: 23.

.6. Any solution of the questions arising respecting the pains and death of men, that does not include the case of every human being, is of course unsatisfactory, because it is unsound. The true solution will embrace all, who have sinned after the similitude of Adam's transgression, and all who have not sinned after the similitude of Adam's transgression, those who sinned and died before Moses as well as those who sinned and died after Moses, vs. 13, 14. If in reasoning any thing is clear, the principle here asserted is so. And it cuts off at once many shallow interpretations of Rom. 5: 12–19.

7. The most wonderful personage in all history, sacred and profane, is Jesus Christ. Not only is his very name called wonderful, Isa. 9: 6; not only were his sermons and his works full of amazing wonders; but there is hardly a great character mentioned in the Old Testament, who was not in some respects a *type* of Christ, beginning with Adam and coming down to Joshua the high-priest, v. 14. Sometimes there is a single point of similitude, and sometimes there are several. Chrysostom: "How was Adam a type of Christ? Why in that, as the former became to those who were sprung from him, although they had not eaten of the tree, the cause of that death which by his eating was introduced; so

also did Christ become to those sprung from him, even though they had not wrought righteousness, the provider of that righteousness which through his cross he graciously bestowed on us all." Then the sacrifices, the brazen serpent, the manna and in fact almost every thing had a typical reference to Messiah. " The law had a shadow of good things to come." And in and by Jesus Christ the good things came, and we now have them. Glorious is our Redeemer.

8. If men are ever saved it must be by grace, rich unmerited grace, unbought favor, vs. 15–21. How can he, who deserves death, have life but by a free gift? Chrysostom : " The case is as if any one were to cast into prison a person, who owed ten mites, and not cast in the man only, but his wife and children and servants for his sake ; and another were to come and not pay down the ten mites only, but give also ten thousand talents of gold, and to lead the prisoner into the king's courts, and to the throne of the highest power, and were to make him partaker of the highest honor and every kind of magnificence, the creditor would not be able to remember the ten mites ; so has our case been. For Christ has paid down far more than we owe, yea, as much more as the illimitable ocean is much more than a little drop." Brown : " Whatever blessing or privilege we enjoy in and through Christ, all is of free and undeserved grace ; and however Christ paid dear for any thing we get, yet to us it is a free gift." Nor is this doctrine to a pious mind offensive, but delightful. The truly humble soul would rather ascribe its salvation to the grace of God than to its own powers or merits, not merely because it delights in the truth, but because it delights to honor him whom the virgins love.

9. This section (particularly verses 12–19) brings before us fairly the doctrine of original sin, which " consists in the guilt of Adam's first sin, the want of original righteousness, and the corruption of our whole nature." This is the statement of this doctrine by the Westminster Assembly, and it is correct. On the universal spread of original sin, its desert of God's sore displeasure, its depriving us of all native holiness, and corrupting our whole nature, there has long been a very general agreement in the church of God. She has spoken more clearly and harmoniously on very few points. The Belgic Confession says : " Original sin is so base and execrable, that it suffices to the condemnation of the whole human race. . . God saw that man had so cast himself into the condemnation of death, both corporeal and spiritual, and was made altogether miserable and accursed." *Arts. XV* and *XVII.* The church of England says : " Original sin standeth not in the following of Adam (*in imita-*

tione Adami) as the Pelagians do vainly talk (*fabulantur*); but it is the fault and corruption of the nature of every man, that naturally is engendered, of the offspring of Adam, whereby man is very far gone (*quam longissime distet*) from original righteousness, and is, of his own nature, inclined to evil; so that the flesh lusteth always, contrary to the Spirit; and therefore, in every person born into this world, it deserveth God's wrath and damnation." *Art. IX.* The Moravian Confession says: "Since Adam's fall all mankind naturally engendered of him, are conceived and born in sin; that is, that they from the very womb are full of evil lusts and inclinations: and have by nature no true fear of God, no true faith in God, nor can have. Also that this innate disease and original sin, is truly sin; and condemns, under God's eternal wrath, all those who are not born again through water and the Holy Ghost." *Art. II.* The Synod of Dort "rejects the errors of those, who teach that 'It cannot properly be said, that original sin (*peccatum originis*) suffices of itself for the condemnation of the whole human race, or the desert of temporal and eternal punishments.'" We might quote from many other formularies to the same effect. Eminent teachers in the church of Christ have long borne a like testimony. Thus Calvin: "The natural depravity which we bring from our mother's womb, though it brings not forth immediately its own fruits, is yet sin before God, and deserves his vengeance: and this is that sin which they call original." Diodati: "Sin hath reigned unto death, shewing its pestilent power in the present and everlasting death, which it causeth of its own natural property to all men." John Owen of Oxford: "That the doctrine of original sin is one of the fundamental truths of our Christian profession, hath been always owned in the church of God." In like manner we might quote many pages of testimony from others, shewing how the church of God has maintained the truth on this great doctrine. The passages of scripture supporting the whole doctrine are many, such as Ps. 51:5; John 1:13, 29; Rom. 5:12-19; Eph. 2:3. Some falsely assert that the old doctrine of original sin involves the idea of physical depravity, or a corruption of the substance of the soul. A flat denial ought to be a sufficient answer to so groundless a charge. What sound divines have long maintained is that by his fall Adam brought on us penal suffering, the loss of original righteousness, and consequently the corruption of our moral nature. But where is the respectable defender of these doctrines, who at any time has favored the doctrine of physical depravity? Adam did indeed bring on all he represented the curse as just stated. But Christ has redeemed us from the curse of the law, being made a curse for us, and by his Spirit he renews our moral (not our physical) natures, and so fits us for heaven.

10. This passage of scripture (Rom. 5 : 12–19) certainly illustrates and so very clearly teaches the doctrine of imputation—imputation as a principle of the divine government. See above comment on Rom. 5 : 3, and Doctrinal and Practical Remark No. 9 on Rom. 4 : 1–15. Remarks there made need not be here repeated. The doctrine of imputation is applied to three matters in theology,—1. the imputation of Adam's first sin to his posterity; 2. the imputation of the sins of his people to Christ; 3. the imputation of Christ's righteousness to his people. It is the first and third of these that are presented in Rom. 5 : 12–19; the first for the sake of illustrating the third. For we should not forget (what was stated at the beginning of the exposition of these verses) that Paul's object in referring to Adam is to explain the work of Christ. We have on the one hand considered the various phrases that "by one man sin entered into the world," "that through the offence of one many be dead," " that the judgment was by one to condemnation," "that by one man's offence death reigned by one," and "that by one man's disobedience many were made sinners;" and, on the other the phrases, "the grace of God, and the gift by grace, which is by one man, hath abounded unto many," " that the free gift is of many offences unto justification," "they which receive abundance of grace and of the gift of righteousness shall reign in life by one, Jesus Christ," " by the righteousness of one the free gift came upon all men to justification of life," and that "by the obedience of one shall many be made righteous." I do not remember ever to have met with any writing that denied that these clauses respectively were antithetical, and that a parallel (with a contrast in several verses) was run between Adam and Christ. If any man should so deny, it could not possibly do any good to argue with him on these matters. Admitting these things to be so, we have the following conceivable methods of explaining these verses. One is the Pelagian theory, that Adam brought damage to us only by setting us a bad example which we imitated. It is probably not necessary at length to refute an error, which is not avowed by any existing church, however corrupt in other respects it may have become. If all Adam did for our ruin was to set us a *bad* example, then we must in fairness say that all Christ did for us was to set us a *good* example. No one, who is likely to be profited by this work, will avow an opinion so flatly contradictory of many clear statements of God's word, and of this portion of scripture in particular. Like remarks are applicable to the statement that Adam injured us and Christ benefited us only by instruction. It

is true that the lessons we learn from Jesus of Nazareth are of the most weighty character, but we have no account whatever of any bad instruction communicated by Adam to his posterity beyond that taught by his example. And it is confounding all language and denying to it any fixed meaning to say that *one offence* and *one man's disobedience* mean some bad lessons taught us; or that *the free gift, righteousness,* and *the obedience of one* mean the sermons and teachings of our Lord. Nor will it be seriously contended that our *death, condemnation* or *judgment* was by Adam infusing sin into us by *one offence,* or that Christ's *obedience* is imparted to us, or infused into us. The passage is not speaking of purification or sanctification, but of *judgment, condemnation,* the penal evil, *death,* and of *justification, justification of life,* being *made righteous.* Nor is there left to us any other way of conceiving how the guilt of Adam's sin or the righteousness of Christ can be made ours but by imputation alone. A class of modern writers refuse this and all definite terms, and insist that all we can say is that we are subject to death *in consequence* of Adam's sin and are saved *in consequence* of Christ's undertaking. But this language is never used in the word of God. In his Works Vol. 2, p. 351, Dr. Leonard Woods of Andover says: " As to those, who deny the doctrine of native depravity, and the doctrine of imputation, and the doctrine of John Taylor and the Unitarians, and yet profess to believe that we are depraved and ruined *in consequence of Adam's sin,* I am at a loss to know what their belief amounts to. They say, Adam's sin had an influence; but they deny all the conceivable ways in which it could have an influence, and particularly the ways which are most clearly brought to view in Rom. 5, and in other parts of scripture." And when such are asked whether they mean to speak of a *legal* consequence, they either say no, and thus deny the substance of scriptural teaching, or they say yes, and then we ask what is a legal consequence to us, but imputation? There is no conceivable way in which Adam's one act could ruin us, or Christ's obedience save us but by imputation. The Bible uses this term often, as we have seen in Rom. 4 : 3, 4, 5, 6, 8, 9, 10. It is well defined in systems of theology, and has been accepted by nearly all the Christian world for centuries.

Some indeed say that this view of things involves us in mystery and is unintelligible. But there is no more mystery in the simple fact of Adam representing us and the fruit of his doings being counted to us, than there is in a general representing his army, or an ambassador his nation. It is the fact of representation, and not the greatness of the results, that involves the difficulty, if there is difficulty. All, by whom this book is likely to

be read, admit that the fall of Adam ruined our race. Let them
tell us how that was done, if they can. We say it was done by
his being by divine appointment our federal head. We say the
guilt of his sin was imputed to his posterity, and so they became
guilty. Our explanation is according to the severest rules of interpreting terms, phrases and statements. We deny that there is
anything unintelligible in the simple doctrine of imputed sin, or
imputed righteousness, which doctrines must stand or fall together.
For as Turrettin well expresses it : " We are constituted sinners
in Adam in the same way in which we are constituted righteous
in Christ."

Others seem to think that in some way they can reject the old
orthodox view without being in any danger of serious error. But
is this so? Olshausen (p. 186) correctly says: "Antiquity knew
only two different stations from which to consider this passage,
and, although under altered names and forms with shades of distinction and modifications, the same have continued to the present
essentially like what they were, since the time they were first
keenly expressed ; the *Augustinian* and the *Pelagian*. The difference between these two carefully considered is not in *some*, but in
all points, and they deviate specifically upon all the great prob-
lems; any reconciliation, therefore, between them is out of the
question." He afterwards says that Semi-Pelagianism is involved
in as many difficulties as Pelagianism. And this is true also. If
the fall of Adam made us in the eye of the law sinners, we ought not
to say, and we relieve no difficulty by saying that we become sinners without any probation at all, or by a probation in the dawn
of our infancy, when we have so little understanding, that it is
mocking us to say that each one undergoes a probation for himself.
From the days of Chrysostom down to our time the best writers,
those, who have stood foremost as advocates of the truth have
contended that to be *made sinners* "means to be made liable to
death and condemned to death." Chrys. p. 154.

If men say that the ruin of the race by one act of one man
and the salvation of believers by the obedience of another are
quite contrary to the natural conceptions of most men, it is freely
admitted by all candid writers. Hodge: "The idea of men being
regarded and treated, not according to their own merits, but the
merit of another is contrary to the common mode of thinking
among men." But shall not the Judge of all the earth do right?
Is man, the worm, the fool, the sinner, capable of revising the
ways of Providence? Is it not wiser with Paul to say, "O the
depth of the riches both of the wisdom and knowledge of God !
how unsearchable are his judgments, and his ways past finding

out!" than to sit in judgment on the ways of the Almighty? If God says a thing, we know it is true; if God does a thing we know it is right. Wisdom would dictate that modesty should stop just there. Haldane: "Our duty is to understand the import of what is testified, and to receive it on that authority—not to inquire into the justice of the constitution from which our guilt results. . . . It is highly dishonorable to God to refuse to submit to his decisions till we can demonstrate their justice." Moses: "The secret things belong unto the Lord our God: but those things which are revealed belong unto us, and to our children for ever." Elihu: "God is greater than man. Why dost thou strive against him? for he giveth not account of any of his matters." Deut. 29 : 29; Job 33 : 12, 13.

Of no more force is the objection of Macknight, repeated by several of his American imitators, that "to argue with Beza, that to entitle believers to eternal life, Christ's righteousness must be imputed to them, is to contradict the scripture, which constantly represents eternal life, not as a debt due to believers, but as a free gift from God." But what lover of sound doctrine ever held that eternal life was to the believer anything but a *free gift, a gift by grace*, unmerited kindness? And does it not magnify the grace of God to sinners to know that it is bestowed at a great cost, even the humiliation and sufferings of the Son of God? To man salvation from first to last is all gratuity, but not a whit less so, because it is bestowed in a manner consistent with all the requirements of the eternal law of God. To Christ, who obeyed and suffered, the salvation of his people is due, because he has paid the ransom for them. Those, who are saved, are pardoned and accepted through Christ, in a way perfectly consistent with the demands of justice, for Christ has fully satisfied all the claims of God's infinite and unspotted rectitude for his people. But to the sinner saved, all is grace, all is mercy, all is a free gift through Jesus Christ.

Perhaps the most popular and wide-spread objection to the doctrine of the imputation of Adam's sin to his posterity is one that is stated with various degrees of coarseness and harshness, holding up the friends of truth as maintaining the doctrine that infants dying in infancy are eternally lost. On this objection the changes are rung with great dexterity, and often with deep malignity. I may say with boldness that in the reading of my lifetime I have found nothing to justify such a charge, but a great deal to the contrary. Hear the Synod of Dort: "Seeing that we are to judge of the will of God by his word, which testifies that the children of believers are holy, not indeed by nature, but by the benefit of the gracious covenant, in which they are comprehended along with their parents; pious parents ought not to doubt of the election and salvation of their children, whom God hath called in infancy out of this life." On this article the judicious Thomas Scott of the church of England, in a note to his translation of the Acts of the Synod of Dort, says: "The salvation of the offspring of believers, dying in infancy, is here scripturally stated, and not limited to such as are baptized. Nothing is said of the children of unbelievers dying in infancy; and the scripture says nothing. But why might not these Calvinists have as favorable a hope of all infants dying before actual sin, as anti-calvinists can have?" Surely this is sound speech that cannot be condemned. Guyse: "How far the righteousness of the second Adam may extend to them that die in infancy, to prevent an execution of the curse in the future miseries of another world, is not for us to determine; we may quietly leave them in the hands of a merciful God, who we are sure can do them no wrong. And believing parents may with great satisfaction hope well concerning the eternal happiness of their dying infants; since they never lived to cast off God's gracious covenant, into which he has taken believers and their seed, under that better Head, *in whom all nations are blessed.* But then it should be remembered, that infants needing Christ's redemption supposes them to have been under a charge of guilt; otherwise there would have been no occasion for any redemption of them; and if they have not the benefit of redemption in the other world, they have none at all, since they are afflicted and die in this." Chalmers: "For anything we know, the mediation of Christ may have affected, in a most essential way, the general state of humanity; and, by some mode unexplained and inexplicable, may it have bettered the condition of those who die in infancy." Hodge: "If without personal participation in the sin of Adam, all men are subject to death, may we not hope that, without personal acceptance of the righteousness of Christ, all who die in infancy are saved?" In his beautiful poem "The Work and Contention of Heaven," the pious Ralph Erskine, to the joy of saints, thus opens the scene:

> "Babes thither caught from womb and breast
> Claim right to sing above the rest;
> Because they found the happy shore,
> They never knew nor sought before."

Wardlaw: "This I believe and delight in believing, that to whatever extent the curse may reach them, they are all included in the efficacy of the redemption, amongst the objects of saving mercy.

Their salvation is entirely on the ground of Christ's mediation." Vol. 2, p. 269. Dr. Archibald Alexander uses language very strong on this subject. See his Life, p. 455 : " It can do harm to hope as much as we can respecting the dead. Let us be as rigid as we please in regard to the living; but it is no dishonor to God, nor disparagement of his truth, to entertain enlarged views of his mercy." A reason, why God may in mercy have said no more on this subject, is that wicked parents may be restrained from infanticide. As it is, many a child is murdered by the parent, to put it out of misery. Wardlaw goes too far—goes beyond what is revealed—when he says : " I believe that even in heathen lands, Christ makes his great adversary outwit himself. The amount of infanticides, produced by ruthless and unnatural superstition, has been fearfully great. But the Redeemer, without its in the least mitigating the atrocious guilt of the perpetrators, has thus, by means of idolatry itself, been multiplying the number of his subjects and peopling heaven." We must not be wise above what is written. We must not lay before ungodly men an inducement to murder their own offspring that they may put them for ever beyond the reach of misery. The Lord will do right. Let us leave all in his hands. Let us trust him for ever. He has revealed all that faith requires. Thus we see it is not true that the friends of sound doctrine are chargeable with holding any gloomy, or unscriptural views on the subject of infant salvation. They hold not a principle, which forbids them to entertain as cheerful and enlarged views on the subject as any other persons who believe the Bible. But they do contend, and justly too, that whoever of our race is saved at all, is saved entirely by Christ, and not by native innocence. The pious parent, whose infant offspring has preceded him, exults in the thought that he and they shall sing the same song unto him that loved them, and washed them in his blood.

It might well be remembered that all, who live long enough to reject the gospel, do by that act justify Adam in his trangressing the covenant of works, just as Jerusalem justified Sodom and Samaria by sinning worse than they, Ezek. 16 : 51, 52. Great as was Adam's first sin, it was a sin against goodness, law and authority ; but he, who rejects the gospel, sins against the greatest love and mercy and wisdom, and against the most awful authority too. " This is the condemnation [the worst and most dreadful condemnation] that light is come into the word, and men have loved darkness rather than light," John 3 : 19.

Some have objected to the doctrine of the imputation of Adam's sin to his posterity that it teaches that everlasting misery is or may be sent on those whose souls and lives are wholly pure

and innocent.   But who has at any time taught such a doctrine?
Surely no approved divine of this or any other age.   Thus Calvin :
" By Adam's sin we are not condemned through imputation alone,
as though we were punished only for the sin of another; but we
suffer his punishment, because we also ourselves are guilty ; for as
our nature is vitiated in him, it is regarded by God as having committed sin."   Hodge : " As the term *death* is used for any and
every evil judicially inflicted as the punishment of sin, the amount
and nature of the evil not being expressed by the word, it is no
part of the apostle's doctrine that eternal misery is inflicted on any
man for the sin of Adam, irrespective of inherent depravity or
actual transgression.   It is enough for all the purposes of his argument that that sin was the ground of the loss of the divine favor,
the withholding of divine influence, and the consequent corruption of our nature."   Haldane is no less clear and decided on the
same point.   The same view was maintained by David Pareus and
other eminent divines of the XVI. century, as well as by the best
divines of the XVII. and XVIII. centuries.   So far did the old
Hopkinsians carry this matter that they were understood to insist
that newborn infants committed actual sin.   See Dr. Leonard
Woods' Works, Vol. 2, p. 352.   But that is an extreme opinion,
generally rejected on both sides of the Atlantic.

It would not be difficult to shew by the writings of many serious men, who oppose the doctrine of the imputation of Adam's sin,
that they do often concede all that any calm and enlightened friend
of the old and sound doctrine of the imputation of Adam's sin contends for.   Hodge has collected a number of such.   The number
of proofs might be almost indefinitely extended.   Locke : " Paul
proves that all men became mortal, by Adam's eating the forbidden fruit, and by that alone. . .   Men's dying before the law of
Moses, was purely in consequence of Adam's sin, in eating the forbidden fruit. . .   By one offence, Adam's eating the forbidden
fruit, all men fell under the condemnation of death."   So also
Macknight : " Death hath come on all men for Adam's sin. . .
Through the disobedience of one man, all were made liable to
sin and punishment, notwithstanding many of them never heard
of Adam, or of his disobedience."   Any of these concedes all the
principle contended for in imputation, viz. that one may act for
another, and in such a way as the fruit of his doings, the legal consequences of his acts may, by the just providence of God, come to
that other, as if they were his own.

It is a pleasing thought that in the actual administration of
human affairs by the headship of Adam and of Christ, there is so
great a superiority and glory in the headship of Christ.   Paul

mentions this several times in Rom. 5 : 12–19. Chrysostom takes up the same note: "Sin and grace are not equivalents, death and life are not equivalents, the Devil and God are not equivalents, but there is a boundless space between them. . . If sin had so extensive effects, and the sin of one man too; how can grace, and that the grace of God, not the Father only, but also the Son, do otherwise than be the more abundant of the two? For the latter is far the more reasonable supposition. For that one man should be punished on account of another does not seem to be much in accordance with reason. But for one to be saved on account of another is at once more suitable and reasonable. If then the former took place, much more the latter." Hodge: "The benefits of the one dispensation far exceed the evils of the other. For the condemnation was for one offence; the justification is of many. Christ saves us from much more than the guilt of Adam's sin. . . It is far more consistent with our views of the character of God, that many should be benefitted by the merit of one man, than that they should suffer for the sin of one. If the latter has happened, MUCH MORE may we expect the former to occur." The point of the thought from the *much more* of the apostle is this: The principle of representation in the government of God has by the fall of Adam brought great evil, but by the obedience of Christ it has wrought out results the most glorious to God, and the most beneficial to man—results as far excelling those of the fall as Christ is superior to Adam. How much that is the scriptures clearly state: "The first man Adam was made a living soul, the last Adam was made a quickening Spirit. . . The first man is of the earth, earthy: the second man is the Lord from heaven. As is the earthy, such are they also that are earthy: and as is the heavenly, such are they also that are heavenly. And as we have borne the image of the earthy, we shall also bear the image of the heavenly," 1 Cor. 15 : 45, 47–49. It evinces amazing wisdom, power and goodness to bring any good out of any evil; but to bring infinite and everlasting, yea the greatest good out of the apostasy of man manifests such infinite perfections as must for ever fill the soul of the devout and humble with unceasing wonder, admiration and thanksgiving.

11. Sin is as bad, as mischievous, as ruinous to man, as dishonoring to God, as it has ever been represented to be. "Death entered by sin;" "through the offence of one many are dead;" by it "death reigned by one;" by it "judgment came upon all men to condemnation;" "by one man's disobedience many were made sinners." Sin is carnal, sensual, devilish. It is the sting of death; it is the venom of perdition. It digs every grave; it builds every

prison; it forges every chain; it erects every gibbet; it made strong the bars of hell; it is horrible. Not a sigh, or groan, or wail is heard on earth or in hell, but that sin is the cause of it. In the wretchedness of man on earth, in the screams of the damned in hell, above all in the cross of Christ, let men learn the evil of sin. Look at that mysterious sufferer in Gethsemane! Why is he in such agony? He is bearing sin for others. What must sin not be, when it required so amazing humiliation and suffering in the holy Jesus to redeem us from it?

12. The law of God is of excellent use in many ways. Nor is its value in shewing us how wicked and guilty we are one of the lest important of its uses, v. 20. Calvin: "Without the law reproving us, we in a manner sleep in our sins; and though we are not ignorant that we do evil, we yet suppress as much as we can the knowledge of evil offered to us, at least we obliterate it by quickly forgetting it." T. Adam: "Keep your thoughts close to this idea of the divine law; establish it with the apostle, as the sacred, invariable rule by which you are to be tried; and then ask yourself, what part of your life has been answerable to it." The law is still a schoolmaster to lead men to Christ. Those converts to Christ, who have but a slight law-work on their hearts, are apt to take but a feeble hold on the Redeemer; while those, who are soundly troubled in their consciences, at least see the need of just such a salvation as is provided in the gospel.

13. If poor sinners, saved by grace, can, after long study and prayer, get a comparatively good insight into the doctrines of gratuitous justification, such as is revealed in this epistle, and in this chapter, what a glorious doctrine must it be in the eyes of angels, who never sinned, and especially in the esteem of the spirits of just men made perfect in heaven, vs. 18, 19, 21. See Doctrinal and Practical Remarks on Rom. 5 : 1–11. Diodati: "Christ's righteousness consisteth in his full and perfect obedience unto God his Father in fulfilling the law. Now Saint Paul saith here, that all this righteousness is imputed unto us, and we thereby are perfectly righteous before God, as if we ourselves had wholly fulfilled the law." T. Adam: "Paul takes occasion to plead for such a remedy as is suited to the urgency of our case; declares the nature of it as plainly as words can do, and tells us precisely both what it is, and what it is not; that it is only and altogether the grace of God, and the gift by grace, the abundance of grace and of the gift of righteousness, by Jesus Christ, to the glory of God, from the bowels of his mercy, and to the utter exclusion of all other pretensions, human merit or qualification." If a perfectly gratuitous justification is not taught in this epistle, there are

no words left whereby such a doctrine may be taught. There is
but one sense, in which the righteousness, by which we are justified before God, is our own; and that is, it is imputed to us, or set
down to our account, to all the ends and purposes of perfect pardon and complete acceptance with God. Otherwise it is wholly
and entirely the righteousness of God, the righteousness of Christ,
Rom. 3 : 21, 22; 10 : 3; 2 Cor. 5 : 21; 2 Pet. 1 : 11. Chalmers:
" God now is not only merciful to forgive—he is faithful and just
to forgive. He will not draw upon the surety, and upon the debtor
both. He will have a full reckoning with guilt; but he will not have
more than a full reckoning by exacting both a penalty and a propitiation : and the man who trusts to the propitiation, may be very
sure that the penalty will never reach him. The destroying angel,
on finding him marked with the blood of Christ, will pass him by."
Glory be to God for such heavenly doctrine. As the scarlet thread
made Rahab safe in the midst of the convulsions of Jericho, so the
precious blood of Christ and his infinite righteousness will give
boldness to the redeemed when all nature shall be dissolving.

14. Every right view of scripture doctrine, of God's glory, or
man's feebleness, of human wickedness or of man's recovery by
Christ Jesus, teaches us a lesson of humility. Nor is it possible for
us to be too lowly before God. If we ever rise, it must be by
sinking. If we are ever exalted, it must be by humbling ourselves. Our place is in the dust. Our great error is in our lofti-
ness. Oh for self-emptiness. The best man on earth is the humblest man on earth. The most exalted creature before the
blazing throne above is the one that makes the most profound
obeisance of all his nature in the presence of his Maker. Come
down, ye mountains of pride. Be abased all ye lofty thoughts
that exalt yourselves against God. Scott: " Let us learn habitually to look upon ourselves and the whole human race as lying in
the ruins of the fall; sinners by nature and practice, exposed to
condemnation, and no more able to save our own souls from hell,
than to rescue our bodies from the grave. Instead of perplexing
ourselves about the awfully deep and incomprehensible, but most
righteous dispensation of God, in permitting the entrance of sin
and death; let us learn to adore his grace for providing so adequate a remedy for that awful catastrophe, which we are sure was
consistent with all his glorious perfections." Such a course as
this would prove that we were already taught of God, and had
found the way of life. God's judgments are indeed terrible;
but his mercies endure for ever. . True, clouds and darkness
are round about him, but righteousness and judgment are the
habitation of his throne. If we were but as humble as our state

and character require, we should avoid all the serious mistakes of men, and make delightful progress in the knowledge of God and in conformity to the will of God.   If any man would be wise, let him become a fool that he may be wise.

15. If such is the sad and fallen condition of our whole race, as we have seen it to be, vs. 12–19, how zealous should be our endeavors, how faithful our instructions, and how fervent our prayers in behalf of our sinful offspring.   Monica said she travailed in birth more for the soul than for the body of her son, Augustine.   It is sad to see our loved ones in the snare of the devil.   But it is glorious to see Christ rescuing the captives, and opening the prison to them that are bound.   He is able to bind the strong man and spoil his goods.   Scott: " As our children have evidently, through us, received a sinful, suffering and dying nature from the first Adam ; we should be stirred up, even by their pains and sorrows in helpless infancy, to seek for them the blessings of the second Adam's righteousness and salvation."   And our prayers should be full of ardor.   " Elijah's prayer brought down fire from heaven, because being fervent it carried fire up to heaven."   In nothing is there a greater deficiency in our day than in the matter of prayer.

16. The way of salvation is by the Redeemer's blood and righteousness, and by them alone, Out of Christ God is a consuming fire.   We cannot be saved by any finite power or merit.   Brown : " There is no inheriting eternal life until first we be covered with a righteousness, seeing we are altogether unclean and unholy of ourselves ; and as grace certainly carries us to heaven, so grace certainly provides the means, and the way how to win it, and finds out a way how poor sinners shall become righteous saints."   That is just what we need, just what we should accept.   It is offered to us by the Lord—offered without money and without price.   The air we breathe is not more free than the grace of the gospel.   O sinful man ! does not that quite suit your case ?   And will you not at once close in with the overtures of mercy ?   Chalmers : " Jesus Christ our Lord by his death bore the punishment that you should have borne.   He by his obedience won a righteousness, the reckoning and the reward of which are transferred unto you ; and you, by giving credit to the good news, are deemed by God as having accepted all these benefits, and will be dealt with accordingly. You cannot trust too simply to the Saviour.   You cannot place too strong a reliance on his death as your discharge."   Oh come to Jesus Christ and be saved.

17. There is great danger that many will lose their souls by idle questions, and false reasonings, and deceitful hopes respecting their case.   In our day men have learned fearfully to sin by cavil-

ling at almost every thing declared even in the gospel. Some say, How can these things be? And while men are disputing, life passes away, and they find themselves in the fixedness of an eternal state, but without the needful preparation. Wardlaw: " Whatever may be the amount of curse arising directly from your relation to the first sinner, O do not allow any speculations on a subject so full of mystery, to draw away your thoughts from the consideration of your actual guilt. Do not think hardly of God on account of his dealings towards you, and towards the race. Be assured he is the Judge of all the earth ; and has done and can do only that which is right. While he visits transgressions with punitive vengeance, think how he has visited sinners in tender mercy. 'He delighteth in mercy.' If his dealings by the first Adam manifest his righteousness, his dealings by the second Adam reveal the everlasting riches of his love. I must do as my Bible does. There I find all men spoken of, and spoken to, as children of wrath till they turn unto God by Jesus Christ. Even those who have experienced the renewing power of grace are spoken of as having been so previously. The way of escape is set before men. Ample and immediate encouragement is held out to them to come to God for pardon and full salvation, through the overflowing abundance of his grace in Christ Jesus. The righteousness of Christ is infinitely more than a counterbalance to Adam's sin and to their own. Grace reigns through this righteousness." Will you, O will you be saved? When shall it once be?

Chapter 12

ROMANS 6

VERSES 1–11

THE SCRIPTURAL DOCTRINE OF GRATUITOUS JUS-
TIFICATION DOES NOT LEAD TO LICENTIOUS-
NESS, BUT TO HOLINESS.

WHAT shall we say then? Shall we continue in sin, that grace may abound?

2 God forbid. How shall we, that are dead to sin, live any longer therein?

3 Know ye not, that so many of us as were baptized into Jesus Christ were baptized into his death?

4 Therefore we are buried with him by baptism into death: that like as Christ was raised up from the dead by the glory of the Father, even so we also should walk in newness of life.

5 For if we have been planted together in the likeness of his death, we shall be also *in the likeness* of *his* resurrection:

6 Knowing this, that our old man is crucified with *him*, that the body of sin might be destroyed, that henceforth we should not serve sin.

7 For he that is dead is freed from sin.

8 Now if we be dead with Christ, we believe that we shall also live with him:

9 Knowing that Christ being raised from the dead dieth no more; death hath no more dominion over him.

10 For in that he died, he died unto sin once; but in that he liveth, he liveth unto God.

11 Likewise reckon ye also yourselves to be dead indeed unto sin, but alive unto God through Jesus Christ our Lord.

1. *WHAT shall we say then? Shall we continue in sin that grace may abound?* The apostle, having established the necessity of a gratuitous salvation, having shown how we obtain it by the righteousness of Christ, having evinced that Abraham himself was thus saved, having illustrated the method of our recovery by the method of our ruin, and having declared how grace is glorious in proportion to the dreadfulness of the apostasy, from which Jesus Christ saves us, he informally, not dramatically, refers to a specious objection, likely to be made by the opposers, or by the ill-informed, who might say, What shall we say then? as if one should say: Your doctrine is new to me. I am startled by it.

It is very different from my long cherished opinions. I had looked to the law of Moses for salvation. But your doctrine is that by the deeds of the law no flesh shall be justified, and that where sin abounds, grace does much more abound. Does it not follow from your doctrine that we may continue in the love and practice of sin that grace may abound yet more ?

2. *God forbid. How shall we, that are dead to sin, live any longer therein? God forbid*, literally, *Let it not be*, let it never be so, q. d. to argue that way would be perverseness indeed.• See above on Rom. 3 : 4. He expresses abhorrence of the thought. *How shall we, who are dead to sin, live any longer therein?* Peshito·: For if we are persons, who have died to sin, how can we again live in it? Hodge : " It is no fair inference from the fact that God has brought so much good out of the fall and sinfulness of men, that they may continue in sin." Calvin : " He who sins certainly lives to sin ; we have died to sin through the grace of Christ ; then it is false, that what abolishes sin gives vigor to it." In the preceding chapter he had shewed how death had justly come on the whole race for one sin of one man. It could not then be that under the government of a God, who so hates sin, provision should be made whereby God's chosen people in their march to glory should allowedly indulge in conduct offensive to the Most High. The chief difficulty in explaining this scripture satisfactorily is found in the question, What is it to be *dead to sin ?* If light can be had from the use of the same or like phrases, we may find it in Rom. 6 : 6, 7, 8 ; 7 : 4 ; 8 : 13 ; Gal. 2 : 19 ; 5 : 24 ; 6 : 14 ; Col. 2 : 20 ; 3 : 3, 5 ; 1 Pet. 2 : 24. One, who looks at these passages is very apt to think that he understands precisely what is intended to be taught. But when he comes to express himself definitely, he is often at a loss. The fact is that *death* used figuratively has so many and wide reaching applications, all resulting from the nature of death itself, that we are apt to become confused. Where the scriptures speak of *mortifying* [putting to death] *the deeds of the body* and *our members which are upon the earth*, the meaning is clear. We are called to spare no sin, to kill it, knowing that our contest with it must prove fatal to it or to us. If we put not it to death, it will put us to death. So when the scripture speaks of our *crucifying the flesh, with the affections and lusts*, it is clear that the work done is that of warring against our carnal nature with a determination to destroy all its power over us ; even though it lingers and struggles for the ascendancy. So when Paul says, The world is crucified unto me, and I unto the world, clearly the meaning is that to the world Paul was an object as little regarded as the crucified malefactor ; and that the world was to him as one cruci-

fied. He sought not its smiles, its favors, its portion, its wealth,
honors or pleasures. So when Paul says he is *dead to the law*, the
meaning is that he looked no longer to the law for life and justification. He had no desire to be saved by his own works. Then
we have the phrase *dead with Christ*, which in its connection shows
that by and through Christ his people have wholly ceased to trust
to rites and ceremonies, Jewish or Pagan ; they rely not on them
at all. Then again Paul says, Ye are dead, and your life is hid with
Christ in God, where he teaches that they were dead to their old
hopes, plans and objects of desire, and that their present reliance
was on Christ Jesus, by the secret communications of his grace,
unseen by the world. In 1 Pet. 2 : 24 we have the phrase *we being
dead to sins*, sins of all sorts. The question still recurs what is it to
be *dead to sin ?* Is it not explained by such phrases as *not serve sin,
dead with Christ, living with Christ*, etc. found in vs. 6, 8, etc?
Still is it the guilt or the power of sin that is spoken of in this
place? Venema, Haldane and Chalmers think that it means we
are dead to the guilt of sin. It looks as if 1 Pet. 2 : 24 referred also
to be being freed from the guilt of sin. And it cannot be denied
that such a sense agrees with the argument of former chapters.
Nor are these writers without support from the subsequent
context. For instance in v. 10 Christ is said to have *died unto sin
once*, where we must understand that he died for sin, or on
account of sin ; that is, he bore and so put away the guilt of sin.
Others, and there are not a few of them, regard the apostle as
speaking only of the power of sin, as a reigning principle. They
rely much on the context to sustain this view. Paul's language in
this chapter is very bold and highly figurative. Yet I believe no
commentator has attempted to unite these two interpretations, and
present sin as a tyrant and task master, tormenting his servants
with the horrors of guilt, and wielding his vile power to seduce
them into deeper pollution. Certainly *some* of the phrases seem
inapplicable to an interpretation that would include both these
ideas, but others do not. Owen of Thrussington says, " The question, ' Shall we continue in sin ? ' surely does not mean shall we
continue in or under the guilt of sin ? but in its service, and in the
practice of it." It was the charge of practical licentiousness that
the apostle rebuts ; and he employs an argument suitable to the
purpose, " If we are dead to sin, freed from it as our master, how
absurd it is to suppose that we can live any longer therein."
Then being dead to sin, it is contended, is just the opposite of
living in sin. Evans : " We must not be as we have been, nor do
as we have done. The time past of our life must suffice to have
wrought the will of the flesh. Though there are none that live

without sin, yet, blessed be God, there are those that do not live *in sin ;* do not live in it as their element, do not make a trade of it." This is the substance of what is contended for by the great body of expositors.

3. *Know ye not, that so many of us as were baptized into Jesus Christ, were baptized into his death ? Baptized into Jesus Christ ;* in 1 Cor. 1 : 13 we have baptized in the name of Paul; in 1 Cor. 10 : 2, baptized unto Moses ; in Matt. 3 : 11 we have baptize you with water unto repentance ; in Mark 1 : 4, the baptism of repentance unto the remission of sins ; in 1 Cor. 12 : 13, baptized into one body. In each of these cases we have the same Greek word rendered, in, into, or unto. To be baptized unto or into Moses expresses the relation of the baptized to that great prophet. So when Paul denies that the Corinthians were baptized in or into his name, he denies that by their baptism he became their leader, denies that in their baptism they professed any subjection to him. To be baptized unto repentance, or unto the remission of sins expresses the relations of the baptized to the doctrines and dispensations of repentance and of remission of sins. By baptism then our union with Christ is professed and declared. But those, who cordially receive Christ and with true faith profess their subjection to him, are *baptized into his death,* that is, have a union with him in his death, not only partaking of the benefits thereof, but as his death separated him from the world and terminated his work as a sin-bearer, so our baptism declares that we have done with the world as a portion, and with sin as a practice. We have died unto sin, and in baptism we so profess. Thus the first formal argument against the loose living, to which some allege the doctrines of free grace lead, is that a sinful life is contrary to our sacramental engagements. If baptism teaches anything, it teaches our cleansing from sin. He, who is baptized and lives in sin, is a hypocrite, a mere pretender. He has not put on Christ. He is not like Christ. He is not subject to Christ. If Christ does not save us from sin, he does not save us from wrath. His name was " JESUS, for he shall save his people from their sins," Matt. 1 : 21. Compare Tit. 2 : 14.

4. *Therefore we are buried with him by baptism into death : that like as Christ was raised up from the dead by the glory of the Father, even so we also should walk in newness of life.* Death is followed by burial. Death cuts us off from the world. Burial quite secludes us from it, puts us entirely out of it. So we are dead to sin; we are by baptism, if rightly received, separated from wickedness, and devoted unto Christ. But this death and burial must not be misunderstood. They are not without a resurrec-

tion. No! They are followed by a new life. Calvin: " He rightly makes a transition from a fellowship in death to a fellow-ship in life; for these things are connected together by an in-dissoluble knot—that the old man is destroyed by the death of Christ, and that his resurrection brings righteousness, and renders us new creatures. And surely, since Christ has been given to us for life, to what purpose is it that we die with him except that we may rise to a better life?" By the death of Christ on the cross, the power of sin was broken. By our death unto sin, its domin-ion over us is destroyed, and this is signified in baptism. That it is not the mere rite of baptism, but the thing signified thereby, that he speaks of, is clear. Saving effects are said to follow. Many from the days of Simon Magus have been baptized but the power of their sins has continued unbroken. So in Col. 2 : 11, 12, where Paul teaches that circumcision and baptism have the same signifi-cancy, viz. putting off the body of the sins of the flesh, and rising with Christ through faith, we learn the same lesson, the necessity of holiness, as inculcated by every ordinance of God, especially the sacraments. *By the glory of the Father;* Peshito: Into the glory of his Father; Arabic: In the glory of the Father; Gene-van: Unto the glory of the Father; Beza: To the glory of the Father. Were the word glory in the accusative, there would be no difficulty in adopting the rendering of the Genevan translation. But the preposition here used when it governs the genitive never signifies unto, or for the sake of. We know nothing to justify the rendering of the Peshito or Arabic, though each gives a good sense. *By the glory of the Father* must be taken as the fair render-ing of the clause; and the meaning may be by the power of the Father, or by the divine nature, all of which is glorious. Bucer regards *glory* as denoting " the extraordinary presence of the God-head." Tholuck: " Glory denotes the sum of the divine perfec-tions." Power and glory are often united in the New Testament, as in Matt. 24 : 30; Mark 13 : 26; Luke 21 : 27; Rev. 5 : 12, 13. Compare Col. 1 : 11. Scholars point us to Ps. 68 : 34; Isa. 12 : 2; 45 : 25 as instances, in which the Septuagint employs the term here rendered *glory* to express the power or strength of Jehovah. In fact the word may be so understood in John 2 : 11; 11 : 40. We cannot conceive of a resurrection but by God's power, 1 Cor. 6 : 14; 2 Cor. 13 : 4; Eph. 1 : 19, 20. By *newness of life* we understand the *new life*, which we lead after becoming *new* creatures and re-ceiving a *new* heart and a *new* spirit, as the scriptures speak, Gal. 6 : 15; Ezek. 18 : 31.

Some are fond of making this passage designate the mode of baptism by immersion. But evidently it has no bearing on that

matter. Christ's burial consisted in laying his body in a new tomb,
hewn out of a rock, and in rolling a great stone to the door of
the sepulchre, Matt. 27 : 60; Mark 15 : 46; Luke 23 : 53. His body
was not covered up in the ground. Whatever is meant by the
language here used is in v. 5 expressed by being *planted*. Scott :
" Great stress has been laid upon the expression, ' buried with him
by baptism into death,' as proving that baptism ought to be performed by *immersion*, to which the apostle is supposed to allude.
But we are said also to be ' crucified with Christ,' and ' circumcised with him,' without any allusion to the outward manner in
which crucifixion and circumcision were performed : and, as baptism is far more frequently mentioned, with reference to the '*pouring out*' of the Holy Ghost (Notes Acts 1 : 4-8; 2 : 14-21; Tit.
3 : 4-7), and as the apostle is evidently treating on the inward
meaning, not the outward form, of that ordinance; no conclusive
argument is deducible from the expression, shewing that immersion is *necessary* to baptism, or even, apart from other proof, that
baptism was generally thus administered."

   5. *For if we have been planted together in the likeness of his death,
we shall be also* in the likeness of his *resurrection*. For *planted*,
Coverdale, Tyndale, Cranmer and Genevan, Calvin, Pareus, Bp.
Hall, Locke, Hammond, Conybeare and Howson, and others have
graft, grafted, or *ingrafted*. This would involve a figure of which
Paul elsewhere makes use, Rom. 11 : 17-24, though for a different
purpose. But later writers altogether reject the idea of grafting.
Stuart renders the verse thus : For if we have become kindred
with him by a death like his, then we shall be also by a resurrection. Doddridge leads the way in an explanation followed by
many : " If we are thus made to grow together in the likeness of
his death." Robinson renders it, " If we are grown together with
the likeness of his death." Without dwelling on the mere word
used, it will probably be agreed that the planting together, grafting together, or growing together implies what Hodge calls " an
intimate and vital union with Christ, such as exists between a vine
and its branches." But it may be observed that in nature this
vital union between different trees can be effected in no way but
by some kind of ingrafting or inarching. If sap and nourishment
are to be derived such a union must be formed. Owen of
Thrussington : " Evidently the truth intended to be conveyed
is, that as the Christian's death to sin bears likeness to Christ's
death, so his rising to a spiritual life is certain to bear a similar
likeness to Christ's resurrection." Chrysostom explains the latter
clause of the verse without supplying any words as our translators do, as declaring we shall be of the resurrection, or " we

shall belong to the resurrection," making it of like import with
that phrase in Luke 20 : 36, ye shall be "the children of the
resurrection." The meaning usually drawn from the passage is
thus obtained without supplying anything. But the blessed resurrection of the last day pre-supposes, in ordinary cases, a spiritual
resurrection, a renewal of our moral nature followed by newness
of life.

6. *Knowing this, that our old man is crucified with* him, *that the
body of sin might be destroyed, that henceforth we should not serve sin.*
Knowing agrees with *we. Old man*, we find quite the same in Eph.
4 : 22; Col. 3 : 9: "That ye put off concerning the former conversation the old man, which is corrupt according to the deceitful
lusts." "Lie not one to another, seeing that ye have put off the
old man with his deeds." These passages taken together clearly
point to the sinful nature within us, which we bring into this
world, and which we act out, until divine grace makes us new
creatures in Christ Jesus. *Crucified;* some think it refers to the
painful, lingering and ignominious death to which the believer
subjects his old carnal nature, and in this respect the similitude is
indeed striking. But two other ideas were probably foremost in
the apostle's mind. The first is that it was by the cross of Christ
that the old man was subdued, that from the death of Christ for
sin it was made manifest that sin must die, and that by Christ's
death sin was slain. The other is that to the new man, or regenerate nature, the old man is an object of aversion and abhorrence,
as the crucified were to men generally. *The body of sin* may mean
the mass of corruption in us, substantially the same as *the old man.*
This form of expression is probably taken from the fact that nothing was crucified but living men, who of course had bodies. The
body of sin is therefore but a continuance of the figure introduced
by *crucifying* the old man. In Col. 2 : 11 we have the body of the
sins of the flesh. Chrysostom : "He does not give that name to
this body of ours, but to all iniquity." Oecumenius : "The body
of sin is a circumlocution for sin itself." This body of sin must be
destroyed, made of none effect, brought to naught, done away, put
down, abolished, as the same word is elsewhere rendered. It is
destroyed at and by the cross of Christ. It can be put to death in
no other way. But in this way it can be so destroyed, Peshito :
abolished, *that henceforth we should not serve sin,* or be the slaves of
sin, as the verb means; Doddridge : "That we might no longer be
in bondage to sin." The Canaanites did indeed tempt, annoy and
seduce the Israelites after Joshua took possession of the promised
land, but they were its masters and rulers no longer.

7. *For he that is dead is freed from sin.* There is considerable

diversity in rendering and interpreting this verse, and this diversity is rather increased by the fact that most of these interpretations give a good sense.   Peshito: He that is dead [to it] is emancipated from sin.   The Arabic, Vulgate, Wiclif, Tyndale, Cranmer,
Rheims, Doway, Calvin and Conybeare and Howson render it:
He that is dead is justified from sin; Coverdale: "He that is dead
is righteous from sin."   The word rendered *freed* is everywhere
else rendered justified, except in Rev. 22: 11 where it is righteous.
Nor is there more than one other place where it is claimed that
the word means freed (Acts 13 : 39), and there the rendering of
the authorized version is justified, and the sense thus obtained is
good.   The rendering of the common version is sustained by
Chrysostom, Ferme, Bp. Hall, Rosenmuller, Macknight, Scott,
Stuart and others,   As to the meaning of being *dead to sin*, see
above on v. 2.   The various views taken of the passage may be
thus classified: 1. Conybeare and Howson say the meaning is
"that if a criminal charge is brought against a man who died before the perpetration of the crime, he must be acquitted, since he
could not have committed the act charged against him."   The
objection to this explanation is that it is recondite, not obvious,
and not very pertinent to Paul's argument.   2. The second explanation is suggested by Ferme, viz. that Christ who died for sin
did by his passion effect the complete liberation, both of himself
as our surety and of his believing people, from sin and guilt. This
is true, and it is pertinent to the leading doctrine of the epistle;
but seems hardly to belong to this portion of it.   Yet Ferme
regards the very next verse as probably a logical inference
from it.   If it *is* so, he is right.   Some regard 1 Pet 4 : 1 as lend-
ing support to this exposition.   No doubt Christ and his people
are one in law, so that his death for sin secured their death to sin,
and his life in heaven secures their justification, sanctification, adoption and glorification.   But is this what Paul would here teach
us?   3. Another explanation is that he, who is dead to sin, is
freed from its dominion.   Some, who thus expound the place, find
support, as they think, from the idea of servitude to sin spoken of
in v. 6 and in subsequent parts of the epistle.   Locke's paraphrase
is: "He that is dead is set free from the vassalage of sin, as a slave
is from the vassalage of his master."   Macknight: "Sin has no
title to rule you; for as the slave, who is dead, is freed from his
master, he, who hath been put to death by sin, is freed from sin."
In illustration of this thought Diodati and Evans refer to that
beautiful description given by the man of Uz of the effect of death,
in which he says, "the servant is free from his master," Job 3 : 19.
4. The other opinion is that the mind of the Spirit in this verse is

this: " He that is dead to sin, and has renounced it, and abhors it, is a justified man, being absolved from the guilt of all his sins. His hatred of sin proves his justification before God." Doddridge says that the sense indicated by the English version is so uncommon, that he is in much doubt whether it ought not to be rendered *justified* here. And it cannot be denied that the term has a very decided forensic import. Indeed it is not certain that it can ever be taken in a sense different. This view is strengthened if we understand after *dead*, the words *with Christ*, as seems very reasonable we should. In v. 3 it is said we are *baptized into his death;* in v. 4 that we are *buried with him;* in v. 5 that we are *planted in the likeness of his death;* in v. 6 that we are *crucified with him,* and in v. 8 that we are *dead with him,* and shall *live with him.*

8. *Now if we be dead with Christ, we believe that we shall also live with him.* *Now* indicates a connection, in the way of argument, between this and the preceding verse. The first clause clearly expresses communion with Christ in his death and sufferings; the latter, in his endless and glorious *life* and joy. The scripture often speaks of our communion with Christ in his sufferings and glory: " For as the sufferings of Christ abound in us, so our consolation also aboundeth by Christ:" " That I may know him, and the power of his resurrection, and the fellowship of his sufferings, being made conformable unto his death; if by any means I might attain unto the resurrection of the dead;" " Rejoice, inasmuch as ye are partakers of Christ's sufferings; that, when his glory shall be revealed, ye may be glad also with exceeding joy," 2 Cor. 1:5; Phil. 3:10; 1 Pet. 4:13. Paul does not hesitate to call his sufferings " the afflictions of Christ," Col. 1:24. In the last day Christ will say to each of his saints: " Enter thou into the joy of thy lord," Matt. 25:21, not merely the joy which he has prepared and will bestow, but the joy of which he is a partaker. The same is taught by our Lord in his intercessory prayer: " I in them, and thou in me, that they may be made perfect in one," John 17:23. Indeed the church is a mystical body, of which Christ is the Head, and believers are the members. If one member suffers, all suffer. When Saul waged war on Christians, Jesus did not say, Why persecutest thou these good people? but, " Why persecutest thou me?" Now as Christ's resurrection and glory inevitably followed his humiliation and death, so the believer's death to sin by the cross of Christ shall certainly be followed by a *life* and glory which will, in its measure, be like the life and glory won by Christ. Only he possesses his by his own merits. His people hold entirely under him and by his righteousness. The pledge of this future glory is given in three ways, one

of which is mentioned in the context, viz., death to sin. Another is the sure promise of God variously given, and the third is the new life which is in all believers, which they live by the faith of the Son of God, and which is in God's word sometimes called eternal life, because it shall never become extinct, John 6 : 54 ; 10 : 28 ; 17 ; 3 ; 1 John 5 : 13.

9. *Knowing that Christ being raised from the dead dieth no more; death hath no more dominion over him.* The scripture informs us that Christ suffered and died, and it as carefully informs us that he suffered and died but *once*, Rom. 6 : 10 ; Heb. 7 : 27 : 9 : 25–28 ; 10 : 2, 11–14 ; 1 Pet. 3 : 18. This point is made so clear that there is no doubt left on the mind of any of God's people respecting it. Not one believes that Christ died twice or oftener, or that he ever will die again. This is for a perpetual joy to the saints in many ways. A second humiliation and death would argue the insufficiency of the first. Besides, how could believers have any confidence in their own salvation and the permanency of their spiritual or heavenly state, if their Lord must leave his throne and again become a man of sorrows? It is essential to the stability of Christian hopes, that Christ being raised from the dead *dieth no more ;* yea, that he can die no more ; for *death hath no more dominion ;* Wiclif: lordship ; Tyndale, Cranmer, Genevan : power *over him.* It has no commission against him, no claim upon him. He has satisfied the law ; he has made an end of transgression ; he has borne the whole curse ; he has exhausted the penalty. His resurrection was the public and glorious acknowledgment before all worlds that the ransom price was all paid. Death once had a just claim on Christ, because he stood in the place of sinners and bore their guilt. But the shedding of his blood fully satisfied all the claims of the law, and now there is no cause for his suffering more.

10. *For in that he died, he died unto sin once : but in that he liveth, he liveth unto God. Once,* in Heb. 10 : 10 the same word is rendered once *for all.* There can be but one sense in which Christ literally died to sin, and that is, he died on account of sin. See above on v. 2. But if we look on him as the Head of the mystical body and as having his people in union with him, in him they died unto sin, for he died " to redeem them from all iniquity and purify unto himself a peculiar people, zealous of good works," Tit. 2 : 14. Christ's work and sufferings were unto all the ends of a full and perfect deliverance of all his people from the guilt and power of sin, and from death as the curse, the penal consequence of sin. His release from suffering and humiliation is the token that his work was all done, and in that he liveth, *he liveth unto God,* that is

he lives to the perpetual honor, the highest and everlasting glory of God, he has an eternal life in the most blessed enjoyment of God. And in this his people are and ever shall be, in their measure, conformed to him. Because he lives, they shall live also, John 14: 19. Their life is hid with Christ in God, Col. 3: 3. As he lives and shall ever live unto God, so shall they.

11. *Likewise reckon ye also yourselves to be dead indeed unto sin, but alive unto God through Jesus Christ our Lord.* The meaning is, Understand aright the true nature of your relations to Christ. Look upon yourselves as having died and been crucified with Christ, that both the guilt and power of sin might be for ever taken away, and that you may always live or be alive unto God. You are dead and buried with Christ, you are planted and crucified with him, that as he arose and became the most famous and the most exalted of all creation, and ever lives in glory and renown, so you also may arise in newness of life, glorifying God here, and in due season, in your order, ascend and dwell with him in glory, partaking of his endless life and entering for ever into his joy. The life of a Christian on earth ought to be, and in some degree, is like the life of Christ in glory. It is unto God. Even here the life we live is so entirely by the faith of the Son of God, that Paul is very bold and says: "I live, yet not I, but Christ liveth in me," Gal. 2 : 19; yea, he says that Christ is formed in believers the hope of glory, Gal. 4 : 19; Col. 1 : 27. Nor is such an attainment in holiness or happiness impossible. Nothing is more confidently to be looked for, because it is all *through Jesus Christ our Lord.* If God gave us his Son, why should we be surprised at his giving us all things through him, or *in him,* as some prefer to read it, and as the Greek allows us to read it? Men do rightly construe the doctrine of the union of believers with Christ when they "love, serve, and glorify God, in thought, word and deed, as being quickened with a new principle of supernatural life, which is communicated from Jesus Christ our Lord, who lives, as well as died for us."

DOCTRINAL AND PRACTICAL REMARKS

1. If we would be able and faithful ministers, we must state the doctrines of scripture clearly, and guard them well against abuse and perversion, vs. 1–11. Then if any wrest them, it will be their fault and not ours. It is no sign of fidelity or of Christian intrepidity to state any doctrine either harshly or unguardedly, and leave it exposed to all manner of cavil and objection. For such a course we cannot plead inspired example.

2. Every doctrine in religion, whether true or false, has logical consequences, v. 1. This is delightfully true of great evangelical doctrines. We cannot state one of them, that may not fairly be followed by the interrogatory, What shall we say then? What is the fair consequence of such teaching? Truth is one, is harmonious. God is of one mind. He never contradicts himself. If we teach any principle or embrace any aspect of doctrine, which fairly contradicts any settled principle of truth or morals, we may know it is false.

3. All scripture doctrine may be abused, has been abused, even when stated in the most fitting manner. Let not the friends of sound doctrine think that any strange thing has happened to them, because from age to age they find their words wrested, and their meaning perverted. It has always been so. Brown: "Men of corrupt minds, who are filled with prejudice against any truth, cannot be soon satisfied with any answer that is made to any of the grounds of their stumbling, and gained to the truth; but the more that is said to satisfy them, they will have the more still to reply." Hawker: "Dear *Paul!* hadst thou lived in the present day of the church, and seen, as we see, thy sweet truths taught thee by the HOLY GHOST, wire-drawn by many of the various professors; divinely inspired as thou wert when writing this epistle, thou wouldest hardly have escaped the odium which is thrown upon those who subscribe with full consent of soul, and from the same teaching, to the doctrine of free grace!"

4. The fact that the truth is opposed and its friends maligned is no reason why we should waver in our profession and preaching of the doctrines of God's word, vs. 1-11. It is rather a reason why we should be steadfast and intrepid in making known with all meekness the truth as it is, in Jesus. T. Adam: "Observe, that the strength of the objection consists altogether in the supposition, that he really did teach and establish salvation by grace, or the imputed righteousness of Christ, through faith, in the plain, simple meaning of the words, and to the exclusion of all human righteousness, works, or merit, from any share in our justification. For if he had intended solely, or chiefly, to exclude works done before faith, or works of the ceremonial law, and not all works whatever, from the office of justification, there could have been no room for the objection; and now, if ever, was the time for him to have had recourse to such distinctions, and strike at the root of this prejudice, by denying the ground of it." That would not have been faithfulness but faithlessness to Christ and his truth. Guyse: "The objection that carnal minds are naturally apt to make against justification by God's grace through the

righteousness of Christ, is not to be answered by allowing that our own righteousness is to be joined in part with his to justify us, for, on that supposition, there would be no room for the objection : but it is to be answered by shewing, as the apostle doth, the indispensable necessity of personal holiness, on other accounts, in them that are justified, and the inseparable connection that is fixed, by the ordination of God in the gospel, between these things, without blending them together, or confounding one with the other." If sanctification were our sole object, we cannot attain to it but by cordially receiving the truth respecting justification. The world contains no record of any sinner being persuaded to righteousness and piety but by the hearty embracing of Jesus Christ as the Lord our righteousness. All scripture, the gospel in particular, says: "This is the will of God, even your sanctification," 1 Thess. 4 : 3. Brown : "Such as imagine that justification by the imputed righteousness of another is a doctrine tending to open a door for licentiousness, do grossly bewray their ignorance of the state and condition of such as are justified by faith, and know not how they have changed masters, when once they have fled in to Christ, and have now a new nature, and a new principle of life in them." There is nothing more absurd than for one, who loves iniquity, to claim to be pardoned and accepted through Christ.

5. Of all the forms of error none is more loathsome to a pure mind than Antinomianism. To a renewed heart it is most sickening to see the friend of the world and the slave of sin going up to the cross of Christ, and saying, There in the death of my Lord, is my full license for drinking in iniquity. Hodge : "Antinomianism is not only an error ; but it is a falsehood and a slander. It pronounces valid the very objection against the gospel which Paul pronounces a contradiction and absurdity, and which he evidently regards as a fatal objection, were it well founded, vs. 2–4." The man, who so sins as to bring on him the curse of the law, is in a sad state indeed ; but he, who so perverts the gospel as to make its best promises and richest provisions the means of sinking him lower in corruption, has a marked foulness and a deep damnation as his portion.

6. All objections to truth are capable of a fair answer, and should be fairly answered. We are not bound to give heed to mere cavils or frivolous objections. Much less may we waste time in foolish wranglings, or in a war of words. But when men show difficulties resulting from our scriptural teachings, we should with meekness, candor and ability show that they are of no force, or that they are fully met by a statement of the whole truth involved.

This is not surrendering the truth. It is following the example of Christ and his apostles in establishing the faith. Calvin: " Since every thing that is announced concerning Christ seems very paradoxical to human judgment, it ought not to be deemed a new thing, that the flesh, hearing of justification by faith, should so often strike, as it were, against so many stumbling stones. Let us, however, go on in our course ; nor let Christ be suppressed. . . We ought at the same time, ever to obviate unreasonable questions, lest the Christian faith should appear to contain any thing absurd."

7. While we make the freest possible proclamation of the gospel, let us never forget or fail to state that pardon and renewal, acceptance and holiness alike flow from the grace of God, and though always distinguishable, are yet never separable, vs. 1–11. Sanctification and justification always go together. The necessity of both is clearly taught in scripture.   Calvin : " It would be a most strange inversion of the work of God were sin to gather strength on account of the grace which is offered to us in Christ ; for medicine is not a feeder of the disease which it destroys." So surely as we are accepted for the sake of the blood and righteousness of the Redeemer, so surely are we made partakers of the Holy Spirit, the author of the restored image of God on the heart of man.   Paul does indeed preach the death of legal hope, but he no less clearly proclaims the death of the body of sin. Justification of the sinner by grace is with him a welcome theme ; but the condemnation of the sin, which made such gratuity necessary, is no less welcome. He never takes part with the sinner against God or his law. But he never takes sides with the Pharisee in favor of salvation by our own deservings.   In all this he is consistent.

8. Wickedness in any is vile, in one acquainted with the gospel is very ungrateful, but in one professing subjection to Christ is monstrous, v. 2.   If it were possible for any to receive Christ's righteousness and yet really to cherish sin, the long mooted question, Whether there are any moral monsters? would be answered. Calvin : " Throughout this chapter the apostle proves, that they who imagine that gratuitous righteousness is given us by him, apart from newness of life, shamefully rend Christ asunder." Chrysostom : " When the fornicator becomes chaste, the covetous man merciful, the harsh mild, a resurrection takes place ; an earnest of the resurrection of life."   Diodati : " Christ is dead not only to expiate the guilt of sin, but also to take away all its strength and power over us ; and to gain us wholly to God, and frame and consecrate us to his service."   A hearty embracing of the gospel is of necessity fatal to corruption.

9. It is cruel to teach men that they can find the way of life and savingly embrace it without the aid and teaching of the Holy Ghost. The road to heaven is like the way that Jonathan and his armor-bearer went; there is a sharp rock on one side and a sharp rock on the other side. If unaided nature comes to the cross, it stumbles at every thing. Were it possible to impart to the unenlightened soul a confidence of full acceptance, it would sin the more. Call on the carnal to be holy, and, if they make any serious effort at purity, they at once present their good deeds as some ground of acceptance before God. Thus "self-righteous pride and antinomian licentiousness are two fatal rocks, on which immense multitudes are continually wrecked, and between which none but the Holy Spirit can pilot us." Compare 1 Cor. 2 : 14. The true gospel plan is understood aright by none but those, to whom it is revealed.

10. Yet the love of Christ in bestowing his grace and righteousness is a powerful constraining motive to hearty and entire obedience to the known will of God. No man ever works righteousness with all his heart, until with all his heart he accepts the righteousness wrought out by the Son of God. Hodge : " Instead of holiness being in order to pardon, pardon is in order to holiness. This is the mystery of evangelical morals, v. 4." This has been evinced by a thousand practical demonstrations. Chalmers proved it in his early ministry, as he informs us. Brainerd proved it among the savages, to whom his ministry was blessed as he tells us at length. When the love of Christ enters the soul, we see marvellously illustrated " the expulsive power of a new affection."

11. Baptism is a most solemn and significant rite, as much so as circumcision that preceded it, as much so as the Lord's Supper that accompanies it, vs. 3, 4. We have no prescribed worship more binding in its nature than baptism, and none that teaches more important lessons. It is both a sign and a seal of our union with Christ. To those, who rightly receive it, it confirms all the blessings of Christ's mediatorial work. It seals to them all the blessings promised in the covenant of grace. Some, indeed, who boast of their baptism, live as if ' the use and purpose of baptism had been altered, so as to allow a covenant with sin, and an agreement with hell.' But their perversion of this sacred rite can take nothing from its excellence to those, who receive it aright. True, it has been sadly perverted. Some have maintained and some still maintain that it is by *opus operatum* and by the inherent efficacy of the rite itself, that we are profited. Others contend that its efficacy is confined to the time of administration, and that sins after baptism are irremissible. But let us not despise the

ordinance because it has been abused. Baptism does certainly teach our death to sin, our separation from it, our mortification to it, and all by our blessed union with Christ. Voluntarily to live in sin after baptism is to follow the sow that was washed to her wallowing in the mire. If, after we have by baptism given in our adhesion to Christ, we turn away from the holy commandment, we do declare, as Simon Magus did, that we have no part nor lot in this matter, but are in the bond of iniquity and in the gall of bitterness. How can he who is baptized into the death of Christ, and claims the benefits of that death, by allowed sin renounce all good and give sentence against his own soul? How can he thus act, unless by unbelief his baptism was a mockery of sacred things?

12. It is and shall be for a lamentation that so many wrong notions have been attached to baptism and that great stress has been laid on things of no importance whatever in regard to this ordinance. Some contend that the whole body must be immersed at once, else there is no baptism. Others have practiced trine immersion, and contended that is was obligatory. Others insist on making the sign of the cross at the time to make the rite complete. But all these and many other things are mere human inventions. The less stress we lay upon them, the better.

13. God's people are conformable to Christ, vs. 3–8. All the terms and images used to express their relations to Christ either imply or declare it. Is the church a glorious temple unto the Lord? Christ is the chief corner stone, and believers are lively stones built up a spiritual house. Is Christ a husband? His church is his spouse, and is subject to him as her Beloved. Is he a vine? Believers are the branches. Is he a Shepherd? Saints are his flock, and feeble saints his lambs, carried in his bosom. Did Christ die? They are baptized into his death. Was he crucified? They are crucified with him. Is he risen from the dead? They are already risen from their death in sin, and shall, in their order, rise from their graves, and ascend up where the Son of man is, and sit down with him in his throne. True, any of these figures of speech, or methods of conveying precious truth, may be overstrained, and so perverted. Men may try to find resemblances where there are none. Calvin notices one of the many of these overstrained figures: "Between the grafting of trees, and this which is spiritual, a disparity soon meets us. In the former the graft draws its aliment from the root, but retains its own nature in the fruit; but in the latter not only do we derive the vigor and nourishment of life from Christ, but we also pass from our own to his nature." This illustration is itself sufficient to show us the

folly of carrying any metaphorical language beyond the bounds of sobriety—beyond the simple point or points intended to be thereby illustrated.

14. All true piety begins with right views of the person, work and death of Christ, v. 5.

15. As the death of believers to sin is not a sinking down into abiding inertness and sloth, but is early followed by a resurrection from death in sin to a life of holiness; so the temporal death of believers is not an eternal sleep but shall, at the right time, be followed by a blessed resurrection of the body, it being made like unto the glorious body of our Lord Jesus Christ, v. 5. Seeing that these things are so, ' let us set ourselves as in the presence of the God of our renewed lives, and account that time lost in which we are not acting for him,' living unto him, drawing our motives from him, and hasting to his coming. Brown: " This life, which believers in Christ have gotten through quickening influence from him, is not an idle, fruitless life, without fruits of holiness, but an active stirring principle, setting folk on work constantly, and in this life believers can never win to perfection, but are still advancing and growing in grace."

16. If the gospel fails to destroy the *body of sin* it fails wholly of accomplishing its great work, vs. 5, 6. Luther: " The old man is not to be gradually sanctified, but must die as a sinner. . . We must scourge the old man, and strike him on the face, pain him with thorns, and pierce him through with nails, until he bow his head and give up the ghost." Tholuck: " Crucifixion first painfully robs a man of all power of action. He still lives, but lives under constraint and torture. By slow degrees does he sink away, until the breaking of his limbs puts an end to him at last. In like manner might it be said, is the love of sin pierced through by the impressions which the Holy Spirit makes upon the heart. It can no more do what it would, but still it does not expire. As the opposite thirst for holiness, however, which flows from and keeps pace with the believer's growing passion for his soul's invisible friend, augments in fervor, the love of sin feels itself miserable and tormented, and declines apace until death inflicts upon it the finishing stroke, and conducts the Christian, purified by the contest, into the peaceful bosom of his Saviour." Glory be to God.

17. We must not so construe, as some have done, the phrases *old man* and *body of sin*, as to teach that our animal nature is the cause of our sinfulness, or that sin is a substance, so that if we were disembodied, we should be sinless, or that our corruption controls us in some·way rather than as moral agents, justly accountable to

God for all our sinful emotions, thoughts, words and deeds, vs. 6, 7. It is a spiritual disease that infects our nature. It is a spiritual death to sin that we must undergo, in order to salvation. It is not our bodies, nor our mental constitutions, but our fall in Adam, the want of rectitude in our moral nature and the consequent corruption, which have made us what we are. Here is the source of all those evils, which sink and debase us, and make it necessary that we should die, yea, that we should be crucified with Christ.

18. If death unto sin proves men to be justified, the perfection of holiness finally secured by that death will be a great element in their glorification, vs. 8, 9. As Christ dieth no more, his people cannot perish. Himself thus reasons and teaches us to reason, John 14 : 19. Glorious truth! Let us hold it fast for ever. What will not be the joy of the redeemed when they awake in the likeness of God, without spot, or wrinkle, or any such thing.

19. Even in this world sin has lost its dominion over the justified, vs. 6–8. It has not power to condemn them. It has not power to control them. They are not the servants of sin. They are tempted, they are sometimes ensnared, they sometimes lose a battle, but in the war they always come off conquerors.

20. Let not the godly complain that they are not made at once partakers of all the benefits of Christ's redemption. If now they are justified and regenerated, in due time they shall be perfected and glorified. If they are dead with Christ, they shall live with him, v. 8. Christ is never to any one a Prophet that he is not to him also a Priest and a King. He never begins a good work that he does not carry on to the day of Jesus Christ. In no sense is Christ divided. To each believer he is as complete and glorious a Saviour as if he had but one soul to save.

21. The prospects of the Christian are very bright, vs. 8–11. A noble life has he here in and by Christ. That noble life shall itself be ennobled in the perfection and glory of heaven.

22. Saints on earth should learn to put a more just estimate upon their state and prospects. They greatly need more faith, and hope, and courage, not fewer trials, crosses and difficulties.

23. All that the righteous possess, or enjoy, or have in reversion, or hope for is in, by and through Jesus Christ. Oh that all Christ's friends made more of him in their plans, their prayers, their conflicts with the adversary. Clarke: " Die as truly *unto* sin, as Jesus Christ died *for* sin. Live as truly *unto* God as he lives *with* God." Let us fervently pray that such may be our aim and endeavor. Hawker: " Do thou, dearest Lord, cause me to have my redemption by thee always in remembrance. May my soul be

more and more humbled to the dust before thee that my GOD and SAVIOUR may be more and more exalted.   Through life, in death, and for ever more, be it my joy to acknowledge that there can be no wages mine, but the wages of sin, which is death; and all the Lord bestows, even eternal life, with all its preliminaries, can only be the free, the sovereign, the unmerited gift of God through JESUS CHRIST OUR LORD."

Chapter 13

ROMANS 6
VERSES 12–23

AN EXHORTATION TO HOLINESS. THE TRUE DOCTRINE OF GRACE LEADS TO SANCTIFICATION. ALL ENDS WELL.

12 Let not sin therefore reign in your mortal body, that ye should obey it in the lusts thereof.

13 Neither yield ye your members *as* instruments of unrighteousness unto sin: but yield yourselves unto God, as those that are alive from the dead, and your members *as* instruments of righteousness unto God.

14 For sin shall not have dominion over you: for ye are not under the law, but under grace.

15 What then? shall we sin, because we are not under the law, but under grace? God forbid.

16 Know ye not, that to whom ye yield yourselves servants to obey, his servants ye are to whom ye obey; whether of sin unto death, or of obedience unto righteousness?

17 But God be thanked, that ye were the servants of sin, but ye have obeyed from the heart that form of doctrine which was delivered you.

18 Being then made free from sin, ye became the servants of righteousness.

19 I speak after the manner of men because of the infirmity of your flesh: for as ye have yielded your members servants to uncleanness and to iniquity unto iniquity; even so now yield your members servants to righteousness unto holiness.

20 For when ye were the servants of sin, ye were free from righteousness.

21 What fruit had ye then in those things whereof ye are now ashamed? for the end of those things *is* death.

22 But now being made free from sin, and become servants to God, ye have your fruit unto holiness, and the end everlasting life.

23 For the wages of sin *is* death; but the gift of God *is* eternal life through Jesus Christ our Lord.

12. *LET not sin therefore reign in your mortal body, that ye should obey it in the lusts thereof.* There is not an agreement respecting the latter part of the text. Griesbach has nothing after *obey;* the Hexapla, nothing after obey *it;* Flatt and Goschen omit *it,* and read *obey the lusts thereof.* Knapp and many others

admit the whole as we have it in the common Greek text and in the authorized version, in the old English versions, Peshito, Arabic and Vulgate. Several of these, however, drop *it* out of the verse. The apostle is still using bold figures of speech. In this verse sin is presented as a tyrant, lording it over men, *reigning,* wielding a sceptre of dominion, subjecting them to his vile wishes. *Mortal body,* variously understood. Locke: "Permit not, therefore, sin to reign over you by your mortal bodies, which you will do if you obey your carnal lusts." In a note he defends this paraphrase, contending that the apostle 'places the root of sin in the body.' But we have seen this is not so. By your *mortal body* Rosenmuller and others understand yourselves. Diodati paraphrases it, "Whilst you live this corporeal life, which being also subject to death, it appears thereby that there are still some relics of sin against which we must fight, to mortify and suppress them." Olshausen thinks the words here used signify that sin "commonly makes itself known in the body by the excited sensuality." Chalmers thinks it "denotes all that may be designated by the single word *carnality*." Others think it means the physical body which is mortal. So Chrysostom, Doddridge, Macknight, Tholuck, Stuart, Conybeare and Howson. Bengel: "The lusts of the body are the fuel; sin is the fire." Some have referred the *mortal body* to the body of sin in v. 6. Several of these views give a good sense. By the *body* in Rom. 1 : 24 ; 12 : 1 we may understand the whole person ; and why not here? It is said to be mortal, for we are dying creatures, and the sentence of death is upon us. The apostle designed to exhort us not to let sin reign in our persons, mind, will, affections, or corporeal nature. Calvin : "The word *body* is not to be taken for flesh, and skin, and bones, but, so to speak, for the whole of what man is." Speaking of our mortality was not intended to give us gloomy thoughts, but to remind us that the conflict would be short. *It* refers to *sin,* and *thereof* to the body. *Obey,* it occurs again in vs. 16, 17. It is always rendered as here except once, where it is *hearken,* Acts 12 : 13. The sense is obvious. To obey sin in the lusts of the body is to suffer sin to sway us in our whole nature.

13. *Neither yield ye your members* as *instruments of unrighteousness unto sin : but yield yourselves unto God, as those that are alive from the dead, and your members* as *instruments of righteousness unto God. Members,* the same word twice in this verse and twice in v. 19. As the body is composed of members, so the whole person consists of various powers or faculties, some mental and some corporeal, any and all of which may become aids to vice or virtue, to sin or holiness according as they are directed. To yield our

powers to sin is to decline the great spiritual warfare, is to let sin reign in us. To yield ourselves to God is to subject our whole nature to God, so that our powers and faculties of every kind shall be used for his honor. It seems impossible by *body* and *members* to understand less than our whole nature. Indeed in this verse the apostle has *yourselves* and in the next verse *you* as expressive of the same idea. If this is so, this verse is a repetition in other words of the exhortation of v. 12—this being more minute and particular than that. *Yield*, in Rom. 12 : 1 and elsewhere *present;* it occurs again twice in v. 19. Stuart renders it proffer; several old versions, give, or give up.

14. *For sin shall not have dominion over you : for ye are not under the law, but under grace.* Instead of *for* at the beginning of the verse Peshito has *and;* Tyndale, Cranmer and Genevan, *let not, &c.* But the authorized version follows the original. *For* points to a reason. That reason is found in the foregoing argument. It is this: God has made provision for the death of sin—for destroying its power over his people; so that they are inexcusable for living in its service. By the whole work of Christ they are delivered from its condemning power and from its sovereign sway, and therefore it is reasonable that they should yield themselves, soul and body, unto God, to work righteousness. *For ye are not under the law.* In the Greek is no article : ye are not under law. God is not exacting of you in your own persons an impossible satisfaction to law, which you have broken, nor has he placed you under a covenant, where you must work out your own righteousness, and in your own strength perfect holiness. Christ has redeemed them that were under the law, Gal. 4 : 5. The strength of sin is the law, but sin has no power over any except those under law. It is a shallow attempt to fritter away the meaning of scripture to say that by *law* here Paul means only the *ceremonial* law. Stuart well says that such an explanation would " give the passage a sense frigid and inept." Hodge : "Freedom from the Mosaic institutions is no security that sin shall not have dominion over us." Being thus free from the curse of broken law, from law as a covenant of works, from law to which without help from God you must be morally conformed or perish, the dominant power, Wiclif the *lordship* of sin is broken, can be, and ought to be cast off. *Ye are under grace,* under a plan of unmerited favor, where the condemnation of sin is removed, where a glorious righteousness is provided and freely bestowed, where the feeble are by God's Spirit made strong, and the timid courageous, and the vile cleansed and sanctified. On *grace* see above on Rom. 1 : 5 ; 3 : 24. Such being the system, under which believers are placed, their spirit

corresponds thereto. They are not slaves but children. They
feel that they are under grace. They are under restraint, but it
is the restraint of filial fear. They are under constraint, but it is
the love of Christ that constrains them.

15. *What then? shall we sin, because we are not under the law,
but under grace? God forbid.* This is the third time that Paul has
virtually presented this objection, first in Rom. 3: 19; then in
Rom. 6: 1 ; and now again. He blinked no fair or important point
in his argument. He had established in the early part of the
epistle that justification by law, by any law, was impossible, that
God's plan of justifying sinners was by righteousness wrought
out by Jesus Christ, and gratuitously bestowed, the sinner simply·
receiving it by faith. He now proves at length, his argument beginning in this chapter and running into the VIII., that our sanctification is effected, not by the precepts and penalties of the law,
restraining and terrifying us, but by the same blessed scheme of
gratuitous salvation — a scheme that brings in all-conquering
love and infinite kindness as motives and methods of recovery.
Stuart : " The legalist would ask, ' Is not the law holy? Does it
not forbid all sins? And does not grace *forgive* sin? How
then can grace *restrain* sin?' That is, Why may we not sin, if we
are under grace merely, and not under law?" In his usual
indignant style expressive of his abhorrence he says, Let it never
be. On *God forbid* see above on Rom. 3: 4. ' Freedom from
the law is not freedom from moral obligation.' Who ever so
charges slanders the gospel and perverts the grace of God.

16. ·*Know ye not, that to whom ye yield yourselves servants to obey,
his servants ye are to whom ye obey ; whether of sin unto death, or of
obedience unto righteousness.* In his sermon on the mount our
Lord gave us the principle, which settles this matter: " No man
can serve two masters : for either he will hate the one and love the
other; or else he will hold to the one and despise the other,"
Matt. 6: 24. It is both a natural and a moral impossibility for
one man to serve two masters. Sin and holiness, obedience and
disobedience, righteousness and unrighteousness are utterly opposite. A state of grace and a state of nature are wholly irre-
concileable. A man cannot go North and South at the same
time and in the same sense. Scott: " The apostle demanded
whether it might not be proved what master any one served,
by observing the constant tenor of any one's conduct. A person may do an occasional service for one, to whom he is not
servant : but no doubt he is the servant of that man, to whom
he habitually yields and addicts himself, and in whose work he
spends his time and strength, and skill, and abilities, day after

day, and year after year." The principle is of easy application
to any case. If one obeys sin, allowedly and habitually yielding
his faculties or any of them to wickedness, he is not the servant
of obedience or of righteousness. The forms of speech, *sin unto
death* and *obedience unto righteousness*, are not only intensive, but
show the results reached in each case by the natural tendency
of both good and evil to growth. The apostle often employs
this or like manner of speech. See Rom. 1 : 17; 2 : 5–10; 6 : 19.
Paul is still using highly figurative but very appropriate language
to express his conceptions.

17. *But God be thanked, that ye were the servants of sin, but ye
have obeyed from the heart that form of doctrine which was delivered
you.* No pious reader of the scripture supposes that the apostle
intends to express gratitude that his Roman brethren had at any
time lived in sin. His thanks to God are that their vile servitude
to sin was *past*, and that *now* there was a great change. Owen of
Thrussington renders it : "Thanks be to God; for ye have been
the servants of sin, but have obeyed the form of doctrine, in which
ye have been taught." Paul had previously used the words *obey*
and *obedience*. In carrying out his personification he retains the
same conception. But here the idea is all pleasant. They have
obeyed, that is, they have given good heed, considered and yielded
to the truth. The *form*, literally the *type* of doctrine, meaning the
pattern or rule of doctrine. It is a just and beautiful figure to
represent the soul as receiving the exact impress of the system of
revealed truth, as the wax receives that of the stamp, or the melted
metal, that of the mould into which it is cast. Only this is no
mechanical or material process, for it is effected through God's
Spirit, by the soul yielding a *hearty obedience* to the truth. This
obedience was not the result of a hasty or inconsiderate purpose,
nor of a reluctant or irksome action of the mind. It was a cheer-
full, sincere, universal acceptance of the truth and submission to
it as far as known. It excepted to no commandment—cavilled at
no precept as being too strict—rejected no scripture doctrine as
being too humbling. What the form of doctrine delivered to the
Romans was, may be learned from all the New Testament. It
was the truth as it is in Jesus, *delivered* by Christ and his apostles.
From the heart indicates the cordiality with which the message
of mercy and of obedience had been received. The attempt of
some to prove thereby the ability of the soul without divine grace
to turn to God has of course been a failure. Whenever the gospel is received so as to secure salvation, it is received with the
whole heart. But grace to do this is from God. "Thy people
shall be willing [willingnesses, free-will offerings] in the day of thy

power," Ps. 110 : 3, is the secret of any hearty consent to being saved on gospel terms. How then can one, who has had his mind, will and affections cast into the mould of gospel doctrine, live like a heathen or a sinner?

18. *Being then made free from sin, ye became the servants of righteousness.* There is no better rendering of the verse. The thought is the same already presented. No man can serve two masters. Ye were once the slaves of wickedness. The Son of God has made you free from that hard bondage, and then and thus were ye made the servants of righteousness, leading a life conformed to law. Chrysostom: "God has done the same as if one were to take an orphan, who had been carried away by savages into their own country, and were not only to free him from captivity, but were to set himself as a kind father over him, and bring him to very great dignity. This has been done in our case."

19. *I speak after the manner of men because of the infirmity of your flesh: for as ye have yielded your members servants to uncleanness and to iniquity unto iniquity; even so now yield your members servants to righteousness unto holiness.* The first clause is nó doubt parenthetical. *I speak after the manner of men.* i. e. I borrow an illustration from common life, which you will all understand, as in Rome you are specially familiar with servitude, with the fact of servants changing masters, and with their being freed. Other explanations have been given but this is the best. He says he used this homely metaphor because of the *infirmity of their flesh.* Locke: "because you are weak in these matters, being more accustomed to fleshly than spiritual things;" Macknight: "on account of the weakness of your understanding in spiritual matters;" Bp. Hall: "I use this familiar similitude of service and freedom, because I would descend to your weak capacity; that, by these secular and civil things, ye might understand the spiritual." He repeats in words somewhat varied what he had said before, but retains the leading idea: *for as ye have yielded your members servants to uncleanness and to iniquity unto iniquity.* That is, Formerly ye were the willing slaves of low vices and degrading practices; ye waxed worse and worse; your course was only downward, from bad to worse, from worse to worst; Locke: "wholly employed in all manner of iniquity;" Conybeare and Howson: "slaves of uncleanness and licentiousness, to work the deeds of license;" Theophylact: "when you committed a sin, you did not stop at that; it but proved an incentive to further transgression." This is a better explanation than that which makes the clause merely mean that their course of uncleanness and iniquity terminated in iniquity. How could it terminate in anything

else ? It *began* in iniquity. It was all iniquity. See above on v.
16. This mode of explanation is applicable to the next clause :
even so now yield your members servants to righteousness unto holiness.
Personal righteousness is holiness. But *righteousness unto holiness*
is growing conformity to God, embracing all acts of sobriety,
equity and piety. As they had sinned with a will, so now he ex-
horts them to yield their whole natures to the service of God.
The idea suggested by *service* is not unsuitable to the matter in
hand, for God is the absolute proprietor and owner of the soul
and body, and has a sovereign and exclusive right to the highest
worship and best services we can possibly render. The queen of
Sheba thought it a great honor and privilege for one to be a servant of Solomon. Angels regard it as their glory to be the servants of God and implicitly to obey his will. All the redeemed
are of the same mind. David never thought himself more
honored than when for cause he esteemed himself the servant
of the Lord.

20. *For when ye were the servants of sin, ye were free from righteousness.* Ye never did serve both God and Satan, both sin and righteousness. In the days of your unregeneracy, righteousness had
not the mastery over you. It is as if he had said, When ye
did serve sin, you served it without hesitancy or double mindedness. You were wholly free from the restraints of righteousness; you had but one purpose. Let it be so now. Serve the
Lord with all your might. Indeed if it were possible you ought
to serve righteousness far more zealously than ye did sin, for in
God's service ye shall have a rich blessing ; whereas in evil courses
you found no advantage whatever. I challenge you to tell me a
single thing in which you were real gainers.

21. *What fruit had ye then in those things whereof ye are now
ashamed? for the end of those things* is *death.* *Fruit* means good
fruit, real profit, solid advantage. They had reaped a great harvest of disappointment, remorse, sorrow and often disease from
their wicked courses. Destruction and misery had been in their
ways of wickedness. They had indeed now repented of them, the
proof of which was found in the fact that they were heartily
ashamed of them, Ezek. 16: 63; 36: 32. But they ought not to
forget the unprofitableness of their former courses, lest they be
tempted to return to any of them ; and especially lest they should
slight the distinguished privileges they enjoyed under the gospel.
Calvin : " The godly, as soon as they begin to be illuminated by
the Spirit of Christ and the preaching of the Gospel, do freely acknowledge their past life, which they have lived without Christ,
to have been worthy of condemnation; and so far are they from

endeavoring to excuse it, that, on the contrary, they feel ashamed of themselves." *The end of those things* [which ye once unblushingly practised] is *death*.   They are all followed by dire penal consequences—consequences, many of which are natural but not a whit the less penal because by the constitution of things God has made them natural.   On *death* see above on Rom. 1 : 32 ; 5 : 12.

22. *But now being made free from sin, and become servants to God, ye have your fruit unto holiness, and the end everlasting life.*   Among the Romans were the *liberi* or free men, the *liberati* or freedmen, and the *servi* or slaves.   Paul here takes his forms of speech from the latter two.   A freed man was no longer under the control of his former master.   He was the friend of him, who redeemed him with silver or gold from his bondage, and he clung to him for life.   Sometimes the service he rendered was more important as well as every way more agreeable than that which he had rendered in servitude.   Cicero had such a freed man, who was his friend and correspondent.   God's servants were once the slaves of corruption.   Jesus freed them from the penalty and power of sin.   Then with joyful and hearty willingness they became the servants of God, who had by his Son redeemed them.   To him they held themselves firmly and for ever bound by ties which death could not dissolve, to devote all their powers of mind and body, their time, their property, their all.   *Fruit*, the same word as in v. 21, but used in a different though legitimate sense.   Before it meant the retribution of conduct.   Here it means conduct consequent upon a reception of the gospel—holy living.   Conybeare and Howson have another view : " The fruit which you gain tends to produce holiness."   It is *unto holiness*.   The same form of sentence is found in several parts of this section.   See above on vs. 16, 19.   " Herein is my Father glorified, that ye bear much fruit ; so shall ye be my disciples," John 15 : 8.   Holiness in his creatures greatly honors God.   Nor is the *end* any thing but good to the creature.   The end is not yet.   It will come in due season, accompanied with great results—here expressed by *everlasting life.*   On this phrase see above on Rom. 2: 7 ; 5 : 12.

23. *For the wages of sin* is *death ; but the gift of God* is *eternal life through Jesus Christ our Lord.*   *Wages*, a word found four times in the New Testament ; Luke 3: 14 John says to the soldiers, " Be content with your *wages ;*" 1 Cor. 9 : 7 " No man goeth a warfare at his own *charges ;*" 2 Cor. 11 : 8 " Taking *wages* of them to do you service."   It denotes primarily the rations, raiment and hire of soldiers.   The Greek word is transferred into the Latin without any change of sound.   Yet the Latin word more commonly used was stipendium.   See Augustine.   Its meaning was well under-

stood in Rome. The idea of desert and perhaps that of stipulated reward is involved in the word here. Nothing is more justly deserved than the rewards of unrighteousness. On no matter has God more faithfully forewarned men. Tholuck: " At the time a man surrenders himself to the sway of sin, it promises, indeed, something very different, but while he seeks what is durable, sin deceives him with apparent blessings, which prove afterwards to be destruction, his true nature being altogether overlooked in the enjoyment they impart." *Death*, see above on v. 21, and places there referred to. *The gift of God*, Chrysostom: " He does not say, the wages of your good deeds, *but the gift of God ;* to shew, that it was not of themselves that they were freed, nor was it a due they received, neither a return, nor a recompense of labors, but by grace all these things came about." The same substantially is said by every respectable commentator. *Gift*, the same as in Rom. 5 : 15, 16 rendered *free gift*. It is a gift wholly gratuitous. And it is all in, by and *through Jesus Christ our Lord*. In him are hid all the treasures of wisdom, and knowledge, and love, and mercy, and grace.

DOCTRINAL AND PRACTICAL REMARKS

1. Let good doctrine be followed by good exhortation, vs. 12–23. We have had much sound instruction in all the former part of this epistle. It is fitting we should now have a lively application of it to our own hearts and consciences. Many a modern discussion is powerless for good because it is not pointed. No practical use is made of it.

2. Let us never be found with the formalist and the enemies of righteousness, objecting to the doctrines of free grace, or abusing them to vile purposes. If sinners cannot be *freely* justified, they cannot be saved. Hawker: " No child of God, with grace in his heart, can act but from that grace in all his deliberate purposes. The Lord hath put his fear in his heart that he shall not depart from him, Jer. 32 : 40. And this childlike fear becomes the most persuasive of all motives to love and obedience." It is a fact in the history of theological doctrine that no class of men have held so high a standard of pious living, as those who have been stanch advocates of the doctrine of gratuitous justification.

3. Let us dread sin, and teach others to dread it. It is easy to have an excessive fear of pain, of reproach, or of poverty ; but it is not possible for any one excessively to abhor iniquity, v. 12. The reasons are many and obvious to any devout student of God's word. The motives to purity are drawn from heaven, earth and

hell, from ourselves, our neighbor and our God, from Mount Sinai, from Gethsemane and from Calvary. Of all these the most potent are those drawn from the goodness and love of God. Where there is the least ingenuousness of moral character, it will and must argue from the cross of Christ to the death of sin; from the love of God towards us to our infinite and pleasing obligations to seek his glory, and delight in his service.

4. And if we would avoid sin, we should avoid all needless trial of our principles. Indeed, if we would avoid sin, we must avoid occasions naturally leading thereto. We all ought daily to pray: "Lead us not into temptation." And when we sincerely thus pray, we shall be in the fear of the Lord all the day long. And the fear of the Lord is a fountain of life to depart from the snares of death.

5. We must also from love to Christ and with gratitude for mercies already received guard all our powers and faculties, that we sin not against God, vs. 12, 13. We must make a covenant with our eyes, not to look upon evil; for the eye affects the heart. Job 31 : 1; Lam. 3 : 51. When Eve gave her ear to the tempter, she began to fall. When the memory is stored with vanity and folly, the greater its retentiveness, the more it is a snare. When the imagination is under the control of the wicked one, the more vigorous it is, the more it runs riot. A mild disposition sometimes leads to sinful compliances. A rough temper sometimes causes men to say bitter things to those whom the Lord greatly loves. A hasty spirit leads to many a false step, which is followed by tears. A sad soul is in danger of yielding to the lessons of unbelief. A gay spirit is specially in danger of falling into sinful levity. Thus every power and faculty of soul and body may become an instrument of wickedness. Chrysostom : "If the eye be curious after the beauty of another, it becomes an instrument of iniquity, through the fault of the thought which commands it. But if you bridle it, it becomes an instrument of righteousness. Thus with the tongue, thus with the hands, thus with all the other members." Calvin : " As the soldier has ever his arms ready, that he may use them whenever he is ordered by his commander, and as he never uses them but at his command; so Christians ought to regard all their faculties to be weapons of the spiritual warfare : if then they employ any of their members in the indulgence of depravity, they are in the service of sin. But they have made the oath of soldiers to God and to Christ, and by this they are held bound: it hence behoves them to be far away from any intercourse with the camps of sin."

6. Sin has dominion over the wicked. They are under law,

not under grace, v. 14. The condemning power of sin over them
is perfect. Fallen angels are not under a more righteous sentence.
He that believeth not is condemned already. Then sin itself has
the mastery over them. They are the willing slaves of corruption
not all in the same way or to the same extent. Some commit
beastly sins; others, the sins of devils. Some glory in their shame;
some cover up their iniquity. Some cast off all restraint; others
hug one darling vice. But every one, who has not fled to Jesus,
is the bond-slave of depravity. "His own iniquities shall take the
wicked himself, and he shall be holden with the cords of his sins.
He shall die without instruction; and in the greatness of his folly
he shall go astray," Pr. 5 ; 22, 23.

7. Sin has not dominion over the righteous; they are not under
law, but under grace, v. 14. The law condemns not one of them.
They are free from its curse. They are free from it as a covenant
of works. They are free to do the will of God. The highest class
of motive actuates them to serve God, and that joyfully. They are
redeemed and set at liberty. Their eternal life depends not on
their own works or deservings. They believe in Christ as though
they had no works; and yet they work far more than if they believed
not, and all from love. Chrysostom: "The law promised them
crown after toils, but grace crowned them first, and then led them
to the contest." Evans: "God's promises to us are more powerful and effectual for the mortifying of sin than our promises to
God. Sin may struggle in a believer, and may create him a great
deal of trouble; but it shall not have dominion; may vex him, but
it shall not rule over him. Hagar troubled Sarah not a little,
but Sarah was Hagar's mistress all the time."

8. God's children are not lawless, nor without law to God, but
under law to Christ. Compare 1 Cor. 9 : 21. Their freedom from
a legal spirit and from legal hopes mightily inclines them to walk
in the way of holiness—to keep the commandments. This is
effected by grace alone. Such is its power over the believer that
he is dead unto sin, is risen with Christ, is one with Christ, is a
new creature, is alive unto God by Jesus Christ. No man more
heartily approves the preceptive will of God than he, who owns
that he is saved by grace alone. Nay, no other man has any principle that works by love, that makes him desire holiness as in itself
a good thing. If Paul has made anything clear, it is that all believers are dead to the law as a covenant, are dead to sin as a master, are alive unto God in a way pleasing to God, and are pleased
to do and to suffer his entire known will. Such people cannot but
loathe and detest sin.

9. It is therefore right, safe and scriptural to proclaim, as Paul

teaches, that saints are under grace, v. 14. The effect of grace is amazing. It wholly changes our relations to God, as we have seen in the former part of the epistle. It no less entirely changes our dispositions towards God, towards duty, and everything of a moral nature. It mortifies sin. It restores the soul to a heavenly life. It makes one long to be like Christ and to be with Christ. It admires and imitates the blessed Saviour. Sin made devils out of angels. Grace makes saints out of sinners, heirs of glory out of the heirs of perdition. If ever the world is to be made better, it will be by mankind embracing the true doctrines of grace. The history of the world furnishes no instance of a sinner being brought to love holiness, but by a just apprehension of the mild and winning truths of religion. Take an enemy of God to Mount Sinai; let its thunders roll, and he will exceedingly fear and quake, but he will sin on, secretly, if not openly. But let any man have a true apprehension of the mercy of God as displayed in the cross of Cavalry, and he says of his sins, They shall die. " Behold what manner of love the Father hath bestowed on us that we should be called the sons of God!" Does John speak thus to encourage loose living? Far from it: " Every man that hath this hope in him purifieth himself as he is pure," 1 John 3 : 1, 3.

10. But the adversary is very subtle and very untiring. Wickedness perverts every thing. It turns even the grace of God into lasciviousness. It specially delights in a show of reasoning. It pleads over and over again, that this humbling method of saving men after all leads to free sinning: at least, it asks, If there is not danger that free forgiveness will have such an effect? Paul answers with an indignant negative for the third time, v. 15. The renewed heart is the best preservative against such filthy fallacies. It abhors them. It cannot consent to the systematic dishonoring of God, who has lavished his kindness upon the undeserving, and shows mercy to the chief of sinners.

11. Nothing is clearer than that one's life evinces his real character, v. 16. A good tree brings forth good fruit; and a corrupt tree, evil fruit. Even a child is known by his doings. There is no more shallow pretence than that the heart is right when the life is sinful and irregular. " His servants ye are to whom ye obey," is the infallible rule. Fairly applied it always brings out the truth. Christ himself will apply it in the last day, Matt. 25 : 31–46. If this rule were not correct in all cases, moral distinctions would be obliterated, and wild confusion would reign; the humble man would have all the insolence of manner pertaining to the proud; the meek would display malignancy; the generous would act like the churl; the hypocrite would be as consis-

tent as the good man, and none could tell whether he himself were
on the road to heaven or to hell.

12. Every change from sin to holiness, from Satan unto God, is
to all right minded men matter of thankfulness to God, v. 17. So
great is such an event, and so far-reaching its influence that it is
made known to the happy inhabitants of the heavenly country,
and among them awakens new joys, Luke 15 : 7, 10. Nor is this
strange. A soul is saved from death. Immortal honor to God
and immortal happiness to a soul that shall never die are thus secured. On this matter all converted men are agreed. Brown :
" A gracious soul that has ever tasted of the sweetness of the work
of God in his own soul will be unfeignedly glad at the work of
God in others." How could it be otherwise ? True religion makes
men glad when God is glorified and when men are made truly
happy. Both these things are done when a soul is soundly converted.

13. It is one of the glories of the gospel that it seeks and suits
great sinners, and makes them, as well as others less foul and
guilty, the monuments of its justifying and sanctifying power,
v. 17. Nor do any on earth or in heaven more magnify the grace
of God than those, who once were the vile servants of sin, sinning
with greediness, and wantoning in wickedness. O how such will
shine as illustrious patterns of what sovereign love can do. Never
will all its wonders be told. Never will the song of redemption
pall on the tongues of the redeemed.

14. The great change from the service of sin to the service of
God has so many, and so pleasing aspects, that to the pious it is
ever a welcome theme. Sometimes we are instructed in its necessity. Sometimes we are told of its divine author, God's Spirit.
Sometimes we hear of its effects. Sometimes we have many
points all brought out in few words in one terse sentence : " Ye
have purified your souls in obeying the truth through the Spirit
unto unfeigned love of the brethren," 1 Pet. 1 : 22. Here we have
the means and process of renovation described. " Ye have obeyed
from the heart the form of doctrine," v. 17. The soul is renewed
when it is moulded into conformity to the model of truth, and
when it heartily loves that truth. All professed conversions,
which are not by the truth but by falsehood, which are not to the
truth, but to a sect or to a new set of human opinions, are utterly
worthless.

15. Nor is it difficult to know when we have obeyed the truth
from the heart. The rule of safe judgment is that in practice we
follow it, wherever it leads, and are conformed to it in all things,
so that we love the whole law as a rule to live by, and the whole
gospel as a method of salvation.

16. True **Christians** would enjoy their spiritual privileges and advantages more, if they would oftener look back to the wretched bondage, far worse than that of Egypt, in which they so foolishly served divers lusts, and treasured up wrath.   Israelites were wisely taught to say, " A Syrian ready to perish was my father." Good men are specially called upon to " look unto the rock whence they are hewn, and to the hole of the pit whence they are digged," Deut. 26 : 5 ; Isa. 51 : 1.   Brown : " It is profitable now and then to be calling to mind the black and doleful state of nature which we were sometimes in, and out of which we are now delivered through free grace, that the unspeakable riches of his grace may never grow little bulked in our estimation."   Surely if good men had a constant and more adequate estimate of what Christ has done for them, they would do more for Christ.

17. There is a *form of doctrine* delivered us.   To it we ought to be conformed.   To it we must be conformed.   We are not left at liberty to choose out of the mass of human opinions and systems what pleases our fancy, our taste, or our practice ; but we must receive and hold fast the form of sound words taught us in the Scriptures.   " Thy word is truth."   We must receive it as the very word of Jehovah, who cannot lie.   We are to read and hear God's word, not as critics but as criminals, not as judges but as perishing sinners.   Brown : " Wherever the gospel of Jesus Christ is kindly, heartily and sincerely welcomed and embraced, it will not be halved, or any way divided, but wholly accepted of, as all necessary, useful, and desirable."

18. Salvation is not merely a negation of evil, it is something positive.   It sets those who receive it free from sin ; it also makes them the servants of righteousness, v. 18.   They not only cease to do evil ; they learn to do well.   Nor is a good man afraid of being too much broken off from corruption and unrighteousness ; nor is he cautious lest he should serve God too devotedly.   Nothing so works on the renewed nature of man as just thoughts of the grace manifested in the scheme of mercy.   T. Adam : " There is great force of argument, great advantage for pure obedience, and a powerful inducement to it, in the belief and acknowledgment of complete deliverance from the guilt of sin, and restoration to eternal life, by the grace of God in Christ Jesus."   The holy angels have had long experience of the excellence of God's service, and of his faithfulness to his obedient creatures.   But it has sometimes seemed to me that one just born into the kingdom of grace has ties to bind him to God, which ought to be unspeakably more potent than any resting on those, who never sinned, and, consequently, never felt the power of redeeming love.

19. Every man will serve something, v. 18. There is no such thing as a state of moral indifference. Each one is God's friend, or God's foe; serves sin, or serves righteousness; willingly obeys God or the great adversary. The world over an affected neutrality is a declaration of hostility to God; because he not only has a right to our secret but also to our open and avowed friendship.

20. On this 18th verse Chrysostom has a long and eloquent appeal and exhortation, warning men against various sins. He is specially earnest and eloquent on the sin of covetousness: " *The love of money is the root of all evils.* Hence come fightings, and enmities, and wars; hence emulations, and railings, and suspicions, and insults; hence murders, and thefts, and violations of sepulchres. Through this, not cities and villages only, but roads, and habitable and inhabitable parts, and mountains, and groves, and hills, and, in a word, all places are filled with blood and murder. And not even from the sea has this evil withdrawn, but even there also with great fury hath it revelled, since pirates beset on all sides, thus devising a new mode of robbery. Through this have the laws of nature been subverted, and the claims of relationship set aside, and the laws of our very being broken through." Such are some of the fruits of being under the mastery of one sin. But there are many other whelps in the same horrid den. Chrysostom dwells at length and with great eloquence on the superfluities and vain ostentation of his times. If our religion does not conquer our strongest evil inclinations, it is worthless. The Philippian jailor was a wretch, accustomed to acts of cruelty; but as soon as converted he was as tender as a woman. Saul of Tarsus was exceeding mad against Christ and his people; but when his heart was changed, he preached Christ, and was as tender to the disciples as a nurse to her children. A sound conversion conquers the strongest sinful inclinations, and gives scope to the noblest principles and motions.

21. Let us cheerfully condescend to men's weakness of understanding, if by any means we may do them good, v. 19. Compare 1 Cor. 9 : 18–23. A slovenly dress ill befits the truths of the gospel. But a plain, homely attire is by no means unbecoming the great things of salvation. If men insist on using the words, which man's wisdom teaches, they must not be surprised if they labor very much in vain. When the sword of the Spirit is all wrapped up in wreaths of flowers, its keen edge is often hardly felt. Mankind are very dull, and slow to believe, or even to apprehend the truth. Let us show no mercy to a guilty conscience. Let us use great plainness, and even familiarity of speech.

22. Everything, good and bad, is growing. Wickedness proceeds from iniquity unto iniquity. Evil men and seducers are waxing worse and worse. Saints are growing in grace and in the knowledge of Christ. Babes in Christ are becoming strong young men. The redeemed are servants of righteousness unto holiness. Their past constancy and greediness in sinning ought to make the children of God the more diligent and zealous in his service. They have lost much time in sin; they have but little time left; therefore they should greatly bestir themselves with all their might.

23. Some think it a great thing to be free from the restraints and self-denial required by the laws of righteousness; but at that very time they are in a slavery, which will yet fill them with utter dismay, v. 20. No Algerine bondage was ever so cruel as that of sin. No prison, with its dungeons and victims, ever exhibited to a benevolent mind so appalling a spectacle as that of a soul, delivered over to iniquity, its noble faculties and affections subjected to the cruel tyranny of the devil. The burden of men's guilt is itself sufficient to sink them into the deepest sadness. Sometimes it does this very thing, even in the midst of their prosperity; and if they die unpardoned, it is a millstone around their necks for ever, and sinks them into the lowest hell.

24. Let us not attempt to serve two masters, v. 20. It cannot be done. The friend of the world is the enemy of God. The friend of God is the enemy of sin.

25. How sad is the history of every child of God up to the time of his new birth! v. 21. His works were the works of the devil; his principles and habits were all corrupt; he was tossed from vanity to vanity; his life was full of vexation and disappointment; his hopes were illusory; his fears were tormenting; his virtues were but polished vices. Good fruit there is none remaining. Clarke: " Among the Greeks and Romans, under a *bad* master, the lot of the slave was most oppressive and dreadful; his ease and comfort were never consulted; he was treated worse than a beast; and in many cases his life hung on the mere caprice of the master. This state is the state of every poor miserable sinner; he is the slave of Satan, and his own evil lusts and appetites are his most cruel task-masters." It would be a great thing if it were possible for us to induce the wicked to make an inventory of all they have gained in the service of sin. But commonly they will not think. Satan rushes them madly on from one thing to another till their doom is sealed. A rich man dying said: " What have I now of all my estates, except that they fearfully swell my account at the tribunal of God?" Byron said that in his life he could

remember but eleven days that he would care to live over. Voltaire exclaimed : " I wish I had never been born ! " Solomon tried everything that could please the carnal nature, and his solemn judgment was that it was all vanity of vanities.

26. Well may all men blush and be ashamed of a course of sin, v. 21. The righteous are so indeed. The wonder is that all are not so. The brazen face exhibited by many shows how desperate their case is. God himself so speaks of them, Jer. 6 : 15 ; 8 : 12. Chrysostom : " Ye were injured in two ways, in doing things calling for shame, and in not even knowing what it was to be ashamed." If sin is of so foul and dreadful a nature as to make all good men ashamed, even when they know it is pardoned, it must be most malignant and dreadful. Nor is it possible for any man to be too much afraid of it or excessively to detest it. In temporal affairs the wicked often regret what they have done. But it is only in moral matters that men pursue a course, which they know they will be sorry for, and which they hope they will be deeply sorry for and heartily ashamed of before they leave this world, knowing that if they shall not weep for it here, they will howl for vexation of spirit for ever.

27. The penal consequence of sinful courses is *death*, v. 21. In many cases penal consequences seem to be natural and inevitable. We may finally discover that they are so in all cases. None but the omniscient eye can trace all the connections of things ; but sin certainly leads to hell, and it certainly leads nowhere else. It leads to the gulf of wo as naturally as the Mississippi leads to the Gulf of Mexico. It is in vain for men to delude themselves with the hope that shame and everlasting contempt will not follow transgression, or, if they do, that it will be only by some arbitrary arrangement. When the poor drunkard began his career, little did he dream that it would end in rags, and poverty, and beggary, and crime, and hell.

28. Great is the grace and rich are its provisions for effecting and completing the work of salvation, even here breaking the bondage of corruption, freeing believers from its dominion, and from all its roots and effects before they stand before the Lord in judgment, v. 22. And how great is this work of purification. The converted man could have no greater work, or one that called for greater help from heaven than to *perfect holiness*. Oh that all, who name the name of Christ, would depart from iniquity.

29. It is impossible to overstate the necessity of a godly life, in which we bear fruit unto holiness, bear much fruit to the glory of God, v. 22. To such a course not only all that is awful and authoritative in the character of God, but all that is mild and winning in

the dispensation of the gospel urges us.   T. Adam : " Gratitude
runs low in the nature of man ; but if there is one spark of it in the
heart, the belief of deliverance from death, and eternal life merited
for us by the Son of God, will kindle it into a flame." Chalmers :
" Let me urge that you proceed on the inseparable alliance, which
the gospel has established, between your deliverance from the
penalty of sin and your deliverance from its power—that you evidence the interest you have in the first of these privileges, by a
life graced and exalted by the second of them." Without holiness
no man shall see the Lord.

30. To those, who rely on the righteousness of Christ alone for
justification, and heartily forsake their sins and serve God with a
willing mind, *everlasting life* is certain. It is the *end* to which their
present conduct tends ; the *end* God has in view in all his dealings
with them ; the *end* they have before their minds in their best
frames, v. 22. They are as sure of that as God's word can make
such poor doubting souls.

31. All the penal sufferings of the wicked are deserved. They
receive only the fruit of their doings. Death is their wages, v. 23.
They are earning all the wo that will yet come upon them. The
law of retribution returns into their own bosom all their evil deeds.
They cannot justly complain of a righteous recompense.

32. But heaven is a gift—a free gift, without money and without price. Eternal life is deserved by no mere men. It is wholly
free, v. 23. Nor is this a painful but an animating thought to the
renewed soul. He is willing that God should have all the glory
of salvation. The crown of glory cannot be purchased with such
tin and dross as mingle with our best services. Clarke : " A man
may MERIT *hell*, but he cannot MERIT *heaven.* The apostle does
not say that the *wages of righteousness is eternal life :* no, but that
this eternal life, even to the righteous, is *the gracious* GIFT *of* God ;
and even this gracious gift comes *through Jesus Christ our Lord.*
He alone has procured it ; and it is given to all those who find redemption in his blood. A sinner goes to hell because he *deserves
it ;* a righteous man goes to heaven, because Christ has *died for
him :* and communicated that grace by which his sin is pardoned,
and his soul made holy."

33. What a wonderful person is *Jesus Christ our Lord.* By him
the worlds were made. By him all things consist. All the angels
worship him. All the virgins love him. If our sins are washed
away, it is by his blood. If we are accepted, it is in the Beloved.
If we have sore conflicts here, and yet come off conquerors, it is
because his grace is sufficient for us. He is all and in all, the first
and the last, the author and the finisher of faith. Who would not

join with Hawker and say? " Through life, in death, and for evermore, be it my joy to acknowledge that there can be no wages mine, but the wages of sin, which is death; and all the Lord bestows, even eternal life, with all its preliminaries, can only be the free, the sovereign, the unmerited gift of GOD through JESUS CHRIST our LORD."

Chapter 14

ROMANS 7
VERSES 1–6

BELIEVERS ARE IN NO SENSE UNDER LAW AS A MOTIVE TO HOLINESS. THEY ARE MOVED BY A MORE EFFECTIVE PRINCIPLE.

1 Know ye not, brethren, (for I speak to them that know the law,) how that the law hath dominion over a man as long as he liveth?

2 For the woman which hath a husband is bound by the law to *her* husband so long as he liveth; but if the husband be dead, she is loosed from the law of *her* husband.

3 So then if, while *her* husband liveth, she be married to another man, she shall be called an adulteress: but if her husband be dead, she is free from that law; so that she is no adulteress, though she be married to another man.

4 Wherefore, my brethren, ye also are become dead to the law by the body of Christ; that ye should be married to another, *even* to him who is raised from the dead, that we should bring forth fruit unto God.

5 For when we were in the flesh, the motions of sins, which were by the law, did work in our members to bring forth fruit unto death.

6 But now we are delivered from the law, that being dead wherein we were held; that we should serve in newness of spirit, and not *in* the oldness of the letter.

1. *KNOW ye not, brethren, (for I speak to them that know the law,) how that the law hath dominion over a man as long as he liveth?* Most will agree that the apostle, having answered the objection stated in Rom. 6:15, and having completed the exhortation fitly growing out of that answer, here resumes the matter announced in Rom. 5:14: *Sin shall not have dominion over you: for ye are not under the law, but under grace.* He proceeds to show how we are not under law. Many for *he* read *it.* So Wiclif, Tyndale, Cranmer, Grotius, Bp. Hall and others. The Doway in the text has *it liveth;* but in a note admits that we may read, *he liveth.* The Vulgate does not decide the matter, omitting the pronoun, as does also the Greek. The doctrine is the same which way soever one decides. The death of either party in a marriage contract releases the survivor. And whatever the apostle intends to teach

in v. 1, it is something consistent with this idea, for he expressly introduces it in v. 2.   The word rendered *man* in this verse is the generic word, corresponding to the Latin *homo*, meaning one of the human family, a man or woman, a human being.   It is not the word corresponding to the Latin *vir*, meaning one of the male sex.   Schleusner even thinks that the word here denotes a *woman*. Wolf and Pool interpret it indifferently of *male* or *female*, supposing, as Olshausen and some others do, that the *law* even in this verse means the law of marriage.   Thus the passage would teach that the death of either party releases the other in marriage. Clarke thinks it all the same whether we read *he liveth* or *it liveth*. Speaking of these two renderings Chalmers says, "that either supposition, of the law being dead or of the subject being dead, stands linked with very important and unquestionable truth so that by admitting both, you may exhibit this passage as the envelope of two meanings or lessons, both of which are incontrovertibly sound and practically of very great consequence."   But it is better to confine the attention to one rather than to both of these conceptions.   Each seems to have some claims to consideration. The great objection to reading *it liveth* is that stated by Wolf— " It is very unusual and surely unknown to scripture to say that the *law liveth*, or the *law is dead*."   The only place cited to prove such language admissible is v. 6 of this section, and there a different reading is accepted by many.   The great argument in favor of the sense gathered from the authorized version is that it coincides well with Paul's language in v. 4, where he says Christians themselves are *dead to the law*, not the law dead to them.   But what does Paul here mean by the *law* ?   Some say he points to the ceremonial law.   But why should we thus hold?   Men were sanctified while obeying the ceremonial law, and observing (not abusing) its precepts.   It was indeed burdensome, and those, who put it in the place of the grace of God, sadly perverted it.   But men might be dead to it as a way of salvation, and yet not be in a state of salvation, relying on the moral law to save them.   With the necessary qualifications the same things may be said of the Mosaic institute as a whole.   But why may we not apply the term to law generally—to all law as a method of justification or of sanctification?   This covers the whole ground, well agrees with what Paul has said elsewhere, and leaves no room for evasion.   Some, indeed, think that in this verse the apostle by *law* means the law of marriage only.   But that is not necessary to a right understanding of the verse.   The law of marriage is an illustration of the principle here avowed, and a very good one too, brought forward in vs. 2, 3.   Some have suggested that this argument is specially addressed to Jewish converts to Christianity; but all the early Christians were, according to their several grades of intelligence, acquainted with the moral law, even as contained in the decalogue, yes, and even with the general character of the old dispensation, And nothing could hinder even the Gentiles from knowing the general character of the moral law, for it was written on their hearts. And Jew and Gentile are alike wedded to law as a scheme of commending themselves to God and of assimilating their characters to his. Now God's people have no more to do with moral law as a method of salvation, nothing more to do with the covenant of works as a means of pardon, acceptance or sanctification, than a dead man has to do with laws of any kind enacted for the government of the living. One's death releases him from any and every law, by which man ever held him in subjection or had dominion over him. We might thus express the sense: " My brethren, whether Jews or Gentiles in origin, I have fully showed you that justification is by no means to be obtained by any conformity sinful men can acquire to the precepts of law. I have in the last chapter shown that neither can holiness be acquired by a legal spirit, nor by motives drawn from the rigors of law. If you would obtain sanctification, you must seek it by the *grace* of the gospel. I wish this matter to be understood by you, and well settled in your minds. So I ask your intelligent attention to an illustrated argument on the subject. Will you not admit thus much that one's death releases him from the binding force of any law, under which he may have lived? Will you not concede that neither good nor bad governments have power to pursue a man beyond the grave? Even the prisoner and the slave are free among the dead. Now, my argument is that you are dead to the law; you are dead with Christ, who is the head and surety of the covenant of grace, and so no law, as a means of salvation, can bind you. I have proved that no man can be justified by any law. I am now proving that his heart cannot be purified by any law, as a master or as a means, supplying adequate motives or helps thereto."

2. *For the woman which hath a husband is bound by the law to* her *husband so long as he liveth; but if the husband be dead, she is loosed from the law of* her *husband.* The single word rendered, *which hath a husband,* is found nowhere else in the New Testament; but we have it in the Septuagint in Num. ,5 : 29. There is no doubt that it is correctly rendered. The *law of her husband* is the law of marriage which binds her to her husband. *He liveth,* in this verse corresponds to the same words in v. 1, and shows that the rendering there is probably correct.

3. *So then if, while* her *husband liveth, she be married to another man, she shall be called an adulteress : but if her husband be dead, she is free from that law ; so that she is no adulteress, though she be married to another man.* The terms and phrases are simple and easily understood. The principle avowed is that even the law of marriage, sacred as it is, binds not after either party has departed this life. For *adulteress* Tyndale and Cranmer read *wedlocke breaker ;* but the sense is the same. This verse and the preceding contain the illustration plainly stated. Some indeed find difficulty from trying to make the illustration *in all things* parallel to the matter illustrated. But this can seldom be done. It certainly cannot be done here. The application of the illustration is found in verse

4. *Wherefore, my brethren, ye also are become dead to the law by the body of Christ ; that ye should be married to another,* even *to him who is raised from the dead, that we should bring forth fruit unto God.* Believers are dead in two senses. 1. They are said to have died with Christ, to have been crucified with him. See above on Rom. 6 : 2–13. In his death they are so much interested and their union with him is so close, that his death is spoken of as if it were theirs. This is probably the sense here. 2. Believers are as to their hopes dead to the law. They have no expectation whatever of salvation from that quarter. If they had nothing better to look to, they know they are all dead men. The death of believers to the law is *by the body of Christ.* This phrase in its connection receives various explanations. 1. By far the most common is that which refers it to the death of Christ on Calvary. Chrysostom explains it as "through the Lord's death ;" Calvin : "through his body, as fixed to the cross ;" Bp. Hall : "By that all-sufficient sacrifice which Christ offered up in his flesh for us ;" Pool : "by the sacrifice of Christ's body upon the cross ;" Doddridge : "Christ's death and sufferings having now accomplished the design of the law, and abrogated its authority ;" Scott : "by his incarnation, obedience and sacrifice on the cross for their transgressions ;" Stuart : "He must of course mean, the body of Christ as crucified, as having suffered in order to redeem us from the curse of the law ;" Hodge : "by the sacrifice of that body, or by his death." The texts relied on as sustaining this interpretation are Rom. 8 : 2 ; Gal. 2 : 19 ; 3 : 13 ; Eph. 2 : 13, 15, 16 ; Col. 1 : 22 ; 2 : 14 ; Tit. 2 : 14 ; Heb. 10 : 5–10 ; 1 Pet. 2 : 24 ; 3 : 18. This is by far the most common and it is the best method of explanation. 2. Others think that the prominent idea is that of our union with Christ in his mystical body. Locke : "By the body of Christ, in which you as members died with him ;" Macknight : "Believers being considered as members of Christ's body

on account of the intimate union which subsists between them and him, every thing happening to him is in scripture said to have happened to them." The texts relied on to justify such an explanation are such as Col. 2 : 11, 20. 3. Evans unites these views : " *By the body of Christ,* that is, by the sufferings of Christ in his body, by his crucified body, which abrogated the law, answered the demands of it, made satisfaction for our violation of it, purchased for us a covenant of grace, in which righteousness and strength are laid up for us, such as were not, nor could be, by the law. We are dead to the law by our union with the mystical *body of Christ;* by being incorporated into Christ in our baptism professedly, in our believing powerfully and effectually, we are dead to the law, have no more to do with it than the dead servant, that is free from his master, hath to do with the master's yoke." 4. Ferme says : " ' We are dead to the law in the body of Christ '—first, because we die to the law with Christ ; secondly, because Christ died in the body only ; and thirdly, because we are in a manner crucified with the crucified body of Christ, inasmuch as his crucified body was a ransom for all: so that by his one death we are all set free from and dead to the law and sin." 5. Not a few Roman Catholic expositors by *the body of Christ* understand the church, into which we are introduced by baptism, and refer to 1 Cor. 12 : 12–27; Eph. 4 : 12 etc., in proof. The first of these views covers the ground and is to be preferred. Being thus dead to the law, believers are lawfully married to Christ, who is raised from the dead to the very end that we might be effectually placed under a system of grace, where both justification (see Rom. 4 : 25) and sanctification might be secured to us ; *that we should bring forth fruit unto God;* at the command and to the glory of God, and so be like him. This fruit-bearing is the only infallible sign of renewal and of sanctification. That this fruitfulness is most reasonably to be expected might be argued from the new state of those, who had accepted Christ, and were *under grace.* To this the brethren at Rome were urged (and the same might have been said to the brethren of any of the churches) by the fact that in their unregenerate state they had been diligent in doing wickedness, and had done much dishonor to God :

5. *For when we were in the flesh, the motions of sins, which were by the law, did work in our members to bring forth fruit unto death.* On the term *flesh* see above on Rom. 3 : 20. Here it evidently means the natural corrupt state of man previous to a work of grace on the heart. *The motions of sins,* an expression not elsewhere found in scripture. In the Greek Testament the word rendered motions occurs sixteen times, is eleven times rendered *sufferings* or in

the singular *suffering;* three times, *afflictions;* once, *affections;* here, only, *motions.*   In Gal. 5 : 24 where it is rendered *affections* it has very much the same signification as here.   Peshito has emotions of sin; Wiclif, Rheims, Arabic and Doway, passions of sin; Tyndale and Cranmer, lustes of synne; Coverdale, synful lustes; Stuart, Conybeare and Howson, sinful passions; Macknight, sinful inclinations, Diodati, the perverse affections; Grotius, lusts; Scott, those desires and affections which the law forbade; Clarke, the evil propensities to sins; Hodge, the emotions or feelings of sin.   The word *passions* as it was understood two or three centuries ago would be the best rendering.   Perhaps *sinful affections* more nearly expresses the exact idea than any other words.   These sinful affections were *by the law;* Chrysostom: were produced by the law; Calvin: the law excited in us evil emotions, which exerted their influence through all our faculties; Diodati: the perverse affections, which are the roots of sins, being pricked forward, rather than corrected or repressed by the law, did produce their effects in all the parts of our souls; Guyse: the violent passions of indwelling corruption, which were irritated by the opposition, that the purity of the precepts and the severity of the curse of the law made against them, powerfully worked and exerted themselves in the whole man, unto the employing and commanding of all the members of our bodies, and all the faculties of our souls, as instruments of unrighteousness unto sin.   *Members,* as in Rom. 6: 13, 19, on which see above.   *We should bring forth fruit,* in the Greek one word, a verb well rendered, found several times in the New Testament.   We had it in v. 4.   Here the fruit is *unto death,* to the promotion of death in ourselves and others, to the service and honor of death, personified as a tyrant, and opposed *to God,* in v. 4.

6. *But now we are delivered from the law, that being dead wherein we were held; that we should serve in newness of spirit, and not* in *the oldness of the letter.*   If this is the correct reading of this verse, then in v. 1 we may read *it liveth.*   But it is probable it should read, *we being dead to that wherein we were held.*   The weight of authority is quite that way.   This reading is supported by Peshito, Arabic, Ethiopic, Wiclif, Coverdale, Tyndale, Cranmer, Genevan, Rheims, Erasmus, Calvin, Knapp, Ferme, Bengel, Mill, Wetstein, Stephens, Griesbach, Rosenmuller, Conybeare and Howson, Stuart and others.   Very seldom is there so strong ground for giving up a received English reading.   Not a single manuscript supports our authorized version.   The Doway, following the Vulgate reads: But now we are loosed from the law of death wherein we were detained.   It is true indeed that the same doctrine is taught whether we read we

are dead to the law, or the law is dead to us ; but it is best to follow the true Greek text, and to preserve, as far as we can, the harmony of the figures of scripture.   All agree that we are delivered
from the law, but to what intent ?   *That we should serve in newness
of spirit*. It is perhaps best to supply *God* after *serve*. For it is to
him all religious service is due.   In the latter part of the preceding chapter he had spoken of our being the *servants of God*.
This is better than any other construction proposed.   Some think
the meaning is, we serve the Holy Spirit.   All God's people do
indeed serve him, but that is hardly the truth taught here.   *Newness of spirit* here corresponds to *newness of life* in Rom. 6 : 4 ;
only here we have the source of strength pointed out—even the
Holy Spirit.   God's regenerated servants have new apprehensions of truth and of duty, of privilege and of obligation ; new dispositions towards God and man, towards God's word and people,
his laws and his promises ; new qualities of heart, loving what
they once hated, hating what they once loved, fearing and hoping
as they never did before ; faith displacing unbelief, love super-
seding enmity and penitence taking the place of hardness of heart.
And all this is done with a freshness of spirit, a vigor and an
earnestness, which wholly distinguish it from the *oldness of the
letter*, in which they had once lived ; formalism, servility, the spirit
of bondage, and dead works marking the whole of that old life,
even where there was some form of godliness, sin virtually gaining an advantage all the time.   For an account of the great effects
of conversion to and by the Gospel read Acts 2 : 41–47.

DOCTRINAL AND PRACTICAL REMARKS

1. If we would profit others, we must speak to them as kindly
as truth will allow, following the example of Paul, who here addresses the Romans as brethren, vs. 1, 4.   However we may be
grieved by the dulness and apparent perverseness of men, we must
have that charity which beareth all things, and remember that the
wrath of man worketh not the righteousness of God.   We may
not indulge suspicious and harsh tempers.   Our Saviour carried
his gentleness so far that he even called Judas *friend*, in the very
moment of betrayal.   The law of kindness never reigns more
gracefully than in the speech of God's ministers.   Brown : "If
people were thoroughly convinced that they had a room in the
affections of pastors, it would much help them to profit by them,
and to receive the truth at their hands."   It is a saying not less than
fourteen or fifteen hundred years old, "Love and say what you
please."

2. If truths are manifestly scriptural and important, let us thoroughly explain them, and earnestly insist upon them; so that if men reject or misapprehend them, the fault shall be wholly their own.   In Rom. 6: 14 Paul had laid down the great truth that we are not under law, but under grace; that as justification had been shown to be impossible by the deeds of the law, so sanctification was no less unattainable by legal means or in a legal spirit,   In chapter VI. he had stated and proven that we were free from sin as a master, that it had not dominion over us.   Here he shows that we are free from the law, and this was necessary, for the strength of sin is the law.   If we are still under the reign of law, we are still under the reign of sin.   The power of sin is in the power of the law, as a covenant of works, vs. 1–6.   If one even religiously believes any thing, and yet the church of God does not receive it, the best and ablest men looking upon it as doubtful, or of slight importance, he may well keep silence respecting it, Rom. 14: 22. But where we surely have the mind of the Spirit, and a doctrine or practice is weighty, and of present importance, let us spare no pains truly to set it forth.

3. It is a great advantage to the cause of Christ when in vindicating and establishing the truth we have intelligent hearers or readers, v. 1.   It is well indeed that in malice men should be children, but in understanding they should be men, 1 Cor. 14: 20. We should therefore labor to come, and to bring others to a full assurance of understanding in all the great things of God, Col. 2 : 2.

4. As we are bound not to exaggerate the errors or infirmities of our brethren, so we ought candidly to admit their attainments and excellencies as Paul does here, saying, *I speak to them that know the law*, v. 1.   Augustin freely admitted the good moral character of Pelagius.   When one of the Reformers used harsh language to Calvin, the Genevan replied : " If thou shouldest call me a devil, I would still esteem thee an eminent servant of Christ." We strengthen no good cause (and we ought not by any means to strengthen a bad cause) by suspicious or slanderous allegations against any.

5. Scriptural holiness, no less than Christian comfort, requires of us that we insist upon the truth (and never fail, on a fit occasion, to vindicate it), that believers are dead to the law, or that it is dead to them, as a means, or as a motive to holy living, no less than as a means of justification before God, vs. 1–6.   Chrysostom : " The marvel is that it is the law itself acquits us who are divorced from it of any charge, and so the mind of it was that we should become Christ's."   We must be dead to the law before we can be

joined to Christ; and until we are joined to Christ we can do nothing, John 15: 5. It is greatly to be regretted that so many, who seem to begin in the right way, aim to be made perfect in the wrong way. T. Adam: "O! what pains are taken to conjure up the ghost of the law, and how many mistaken souls frighten themselves all their days with the ghastly apparition of it, instead of seeing it slain by Christ, and rejoicing over it as a dead enemy. Reader, do not charge me with Antinomianism: I abhor the imputation: it is the desire of my soul to say with the Psalmist, ' Lord, how love I thy law!' I believe it to be the rule of our duty, and that it will be the measure of our reward or condemnation. I believe, from my heart, that we are only miserable by transgressing it, and can never be happy but in conforming to it. But then I must learn·from St. Paul the Spirit's order of coming to the love of it. And I understand from him, that I can never look upon it with a friendly eye till I see the sting of death taken out of it, never be in a fruit-bearing state according to it, nor delight in it as a rule, till I am freed from it as a covenant."

6. In its nature marriage is of perpetual obligation, and can be dissolved in no way during the life of the parties but by some crime, which wholly subverts its design. The scriptures mention two such, adultery, and wilful permanent desertion, Matt. 5: 32; 19: 9; Mark 16: 18; 1 Cor. 7: 15.

Irritability of temper, want of congeniality, ungodliness, scolding, penuriousness, insanity, incurable disease, helplessness, or consent of parties can give no right to dissolve the marriage bond. The law of God is decisive. The laws of man should be no less so. Nor is it possible that either piety or good morals should pervade a community, where the marriage relation is not maintained in its purity. "Marriage is honorable in all and the bed undefiled." Only let neither men, nor churches attempt to make marriage more holy than it is, nor surround it with hindrances that are not sanctioned by God himself. Scott: "It would be foreign to the apostle's design to interpret his words, as meaning that a woman, who had been equitably divorced for consanguinity, which rendered her former marriage a nullity, or for any other cause, would be guilty of adultery, if she married again during her former husband's life; for neither the law of Moses, nor the precepts of Christ inculcate any such thing." Nor should churches or christians discourage second marriages, where death has loosed the bond, vs. 2, 3. There may be as good reason for a second or third as for a first marriage; and it is every way as lawful, 1 Cor. 7: 39.

7. Good men, enlightened from above, have given up all ex-

pectation of being saved by a righteousness founded on their personal obedience to law, or by motives drawn from the covenant of
works, v. 4. The legal spirit is a great enemy of the gospel.
Legal repentance is wholly diverse from evangelical sorrow for
sin. Mount Sinai is far from Mount Calvary. It was Joshua, not
Moses, that led Israel into Canaan.

8. The state of unbelievers is sad indeed. They are wedded
to a law, which they never kept, which presents no incentives
strong enough to secure obedience, and which pours its curses on
the heads of all, who continue not in all things which it requires.
The law demands perfect obedience, but gives no strength ; unspotted holiness, but provides no means or motives, that can control the heart even for a day, The thought of foolishness is sin,
Pr. 24 : 9 ; but vain thoughts lodge within ·the unrenewed all the
time. Their ploughing is sin, Pr. 21 : 4 ; for they plough like
atheists. Their sacrifice is an abomination, Pr. 21 : 27 ; because
they bring it with a wicked mind. Without faith it is impossible
to please God, Heb. 11 : 6 ; but they utterly discredit in their
hearts the testimony of God concerning his Son. Without holiness no man shall see the Lord, Heb. 12 : 14 ; but they wear the
image and do the works of the wicked one. Redemption by
blood, without money and without price, is offered to them ; but
in their self-righteousness they reject it. The yoke of Christ is
tendered to them ; but in their self-will they say, We will not
have this man to reign over us. The gates of the kingdom of
heaven are thrown open to them ; but they madly press on till
they drop into hell. Nothing can be so dismal as the future of an
incorrigible sinner, who has heard the gospel, and died without
repentance. So many of them say before they leave the world.
So God's word says.

9. The incarnation and death of Christ are truly wonderful in
their nature and in their effects. They reach so far, delivering
poor lost souls from sin, and wrath, and guilty fears. Indeed it is
by his body sacrificed for us that we become dead to the law, cease
to strive for heaven by a self-righteous course, and become zealous
of good works, and perfect holiness in the fear of God. We must
thus be dead to the law before we can lay hold on Christ. The
gospel plan in its very nature requires an utter renunciation of all
other plans. Christ will divide the glories of redemption with
none other. He alone will save us entirely or not at all. And
there is no other name under heaven, given among men, whereby
we must be saved.

10. Great is the mystery of godliness, whereby poor lost souls
are *married to Christ*, v. 4. Of all the forms of speech used to

express the relations of saints to the Saviour and of the Saviour to saints none is more appropriate, more refreshing or perhaps oftener adopted in scripture than that of marriage.   In Ps. 45 : 8–15 is a beautiful illustration of this remark.   Then we have the whole of the Song of Songs, which is Solomon's, entirely on the same subject.   No equal portion of scripture has probably been more admired by the experienced child of God.   Then by the evangelical prophet God brings forth the same idea : " Thy Maker is thy husband, the Lord of hosts is his name," Isa. 54 : 5.   Then by the husband of Gomer the daughter of Diblaim God says : " I will betroth thee unto me for ever ; yea, I will betroth thee unto me in righteousness, and in judgment, and in loving kindness, and in mercies.   I will even betroth thee unto me in faithfulness ; and thou shalt know the Lord," Hos. 2 : 19, 20.   Paul takes up the same glorious truth and says : " I have espoused you to one husband, that I may present you as a chaste virgin to Christ," 2 Cor. 11 : 2.   And in another epistle he has an allegory on the same blessed theme, Eph. 5 : 22–32.   In the Apocalypse John has much to say about the bride, the Lamb's wife.   With a splendor that shall amaze men and angels her nuptials shall be publicly celebrated on the evening of the day of judgment.

11. It is by forgetting her marriage covenant and turning to folly that the church brings on herself such disgrace and such misery.   So that God often charges her with harlotry and whoredom, a form of wickedness detestable in all ages ; and yet in comparison of unfaithfulness to God small is the sin against man of unfaithfulness in the marriage bond.   Oh that every backsliding soul and church would say : " I will go and return to my first husband ; for then was it better with me than now," Hos. 2 : 7.   Such a return would but be in response to the Lord's glorious invitation : " Thou hast played the harlot with many lovers ; yet return again to me, saith the Lord," Jer. 3 : 1.

12. All religious profession and service without holy living— *fruit unto God*—are vain and worthless, v. 4.   Evans : " The great end of our marriage to Christ is our fruitfulness in love, and grace, and every good work.   That is *fruit unto God*, pleasing to God, according to his will, aiming at his glory."   But let us never forget that it is only in Christ Jesus that we are created unto good works, Eph. 2 : 10.   The way in which the church avoids the sin and shame of not honoring her head is by holiness in life.   Otherwise the foul blot of at least practical antinomianism would attach to her.   Chalmers : " While the law is abolished as a covenant, it is not abolished as a rule of life.   Though not under the economy of do and live, still you are under the economy of live and do.

Your obedience to the law is no longer the purchase-money, by which heaven is bought; but still your obedience to the law is the preparation by which you are beautified and arrayed for heaven. It is no longer the righteousness by which the rewards of eternity are earned; but still it is the righteousness, which fits us to enjoy the sacred rest, and the hallowed recreations of eternity." Blessed be God, the King's highway is the way of holiness.

13. Let Christians hold fast the fact and the doctrine of Christ's resurrection from the dead, v. 4. It can never be yielded without surrendering the gospel. No truth is fundamental, if this is not. It is connected with all good hopes, with all right practice, with salvation itself. He had power to lay down his life; but he had power to take it again, John 10 : 18. Compare 1 Cor. 15 : 14–20; were he not the first begotten of the dead, he would not be the prince of the kings of the earth.

14. A good deal may be learned concerning our spiritual state by observing our thoughts and words respecting our conduct in that state, which we confess to have been one of unregeneracy, v. 5. If our former sinfulness is dwelt upon with pleasure, it is a dark sign. But if it is used as an incentive to greater humility, diligence and love, it is a good sign. Those, who have been strong sinners, should not be feeble saints. Let the zeal of God's house consume us.

15. What a horrible thing sin is. Its very *motions* so *work* as to *bring forth fruit unto death*, v. 5. Since the world began sin has produced evil, only evil and that continually. Though in his infinite wisdom, power and goodness God has brought great good out of evil, making the wrath of men to praise him, yet sin works no good to man, nor glory to God. It brings no good out of itself. It is *evil;* it is *rebellion;* it is *iniquity;* it is *transgression;* it is *unrighteousness;* it is want of *conformity to law;* it is the *folly of fools;* it is a *lie.* God hates it with the whole of his nature. It is the only thing he does hate. The worst thing that can be said of sin is not that it carries death and hell in its train; but that it is *exceeding sinful.* It is so stubborn that if divine grace were not armed with omnipotence, even it would not be able to bend the will.

16. The natural state of man is, therefore, very alarming. It is a state of unregeneracy, of impenitence, of unbelief, of war with God. The heart is naturally dead to good, but keenly alive to evil. It is deceitful above all things and desperately wicked. The affections are all disordered and far from God. The whole tends directly to death and ruin. No awakened sinner ever had

too strong a sense of his lost condition, too dark a view of the heinousness of his sins.

17. The *deliverance from the law* as a covenant was a great deliverance, v. 6.   None but God could devise, execute or apply any fit scheme of redeeming mercy.   The power that *held* men, though not almighty, was too mighty for any arm of flesh.   They were in the hands of the *strong man.*   Great is the salvation of our Lord Jesus Christ.

18. Why should not God's people lead a new life? v. 6.   They have new views, new hopes, new fears, new joys, new principles, new objects of attraction, new motives.   Our righteousness must exceed the righteousness of the scribes and pharisees.   We must not only not murder; we must not strike ; we must not slander ; we must not bear ill-will.   We must love purity for its own sake.   And if we do, we will surely shew it in our walk.   If we become not like Christ, we may not hope to be with him.

19. No wonder the *oldness of the letter* amounts to nothing in the service of God.   The letter killeth.   It is stern, inexorable. It is clothed with terrors.   It goads the conscience to madness. It works wrath.   Those, who cling to it, make no progress in overcoming the world.   They live and die the slaves of corruption.

Chapter 15

ROMANS 7
VERSES 7-13

THOUGH THE LAW NEITHER JUSTIFIES NOR SANC-
TIFIES, YET IT IS EXCELLENT, AND USEFUL IN
OTHER WAYS.   BUT MAN IS QUITE WRONG;
AND HIS FALLEN NATURE PERVERTS THE LAW.

7 What shall we say then?   *Is* the law sin?   God forbid.   Nay, I had not known sin, but by the law: for I had not known lust, except the law had said, Thou shalt not covet.

8 But sin, taking occasion by the commandment, wrought in me all manner of concupiscence.   For without the law sin *was* dead.

9 For I was alive without the law once: but when the commandment came, sin revived, and I died.

10 And the commandment, which *was ordained* to life, I found *to be* unto death.

11 For sin, taking occasion by the commandment, deceived me, and by it slew *me.*

12 Wherefore the law *is* holy, and the commandment holy, and just, and good.

13 Was then that which is good made death unto me?   God forbid.   But sin, that it might appear sin, working death in me by that which is good; that sin by the commandment might become exceeding sinful.

7. *WHAT shall we say then?*   Is *the law sin?   God forbid.   Nay I had not known sin, but by the law: for I had not known lust, except the law had said, Thou shalt not covet.   What shall we say then?*   This form of interrogation, after the main argument on a point is finished, is quite common with Paul, Rom. 3: 27; 4: 1; 6: 1, 15.   It clearly marks the close logical connection.   *Is the law sin?*   Those, who would make Paul a fautor of sin, can do so only by imputing to him sentiments of which he expresses abhorrence, yes, indignant abhorrence, as here.   Compare Rom. 6: 1, 2, 11-15.   Paul was no friend of loose living.   Nor was he an enemy of the law.   He never said the law was sin, or favored sin, or produced sin.   It was not itself evil, nor did it countenance evil.   Ambrose: "The law discovers sin, it does not beget sin."   *God forbid,* let it not be.   See above on Rom. 3: 4.   *Nay, I had not known sin, but by the law.*   So far

322

from the law favoring sin, it was the great reprover of sin. It made known its true nature, odiousness and guilt. The word rendered *nay* is in Rom. 3 : 31 rendered *yea ;* in Rom. 8 : 31 *nay ;* in Rom. 5 : 14 *nevertheless.* It is a following up of the *Let it not be* with notice of further statement or argument. *I had not known sin ;* Tyndale and Genevan: I knewe not what synne meant; Conybeare and Howson: I should not have known what sin was. The meaning seems to be this : I should never have understood the real nature of sin, the enormity of my guilt, nor the multitude of my offences but for the law. One way of discovering the uncleanness of an apartment in a house is to bring in a light. One way of discovering the crookedness of a wall is to apply the plumbline to it, Ps. 119 : 105 ; Amos 7 : 7, 8. God's law is such a light and such a line. Paul gives a particular illustration : *I had not known lust, except the law had said, Thou shalt not covet.* This tenth commandment was the key that unlocked the mystery of iniquity in the heart of the great apostle. It showed him the great storehouse of iniquity in his bosom. *I had not known lust ;* Tyndale, Cranmer and Genevan: I had not knowne what lust had meant; Conybeare and Howson: I should not have known the sin of coveting ; Locke: I had not known concupiscence to be sin ; Bp. Hall : I had not known or observed lust to be a sin ; Stuart: I had not known even inordinate desire. Calvin: " Municipal laws do indeed declare that intentions, and not results are to be punished. Philosophers also, with more refinement, place vices as well as virtues in the soul. But by this precept God goes deeper, and notices coveting, which is more hidden than the will ; and this is not deemed a vice. It was pardoned not only by philosophers, but at this day the Papists fiercely contend that it is no sin in the regenerate. But Paul says he had found out his guilt from this hidden disease : it hence follows, that all those, who labor under it, are by no means free from guilt, except God pardons their sin. We ought, at the same time, to remember the difference between evil lustings or covetings which gain consent, and the lusting which tempts and moves our hearts, but stops in the midst of its course." Evil desires are evil things. It is sinful to indulge or even have them.

8. *But sin, taking occasion by the commandment, wrought in me all manner of concupiscence. For without the law sin was dead.* The word rendered *occasion* is found six times in the New Testament, twice in this chapter, and always rendered *occasion*, except in Gal. 5 : 13, where we read *liberty.* It never means *impunity*, as Grotius thinks it does here. There is no better rendering than occasion. So thought Wiclif, Coverdale, Tyndale, Cranmer, Genevan,

Rheims, Doway, and many others. Peshito: Sin found occasion. How sin flamed out so terribly is here declared. The precept and penalty of the law both offended the carnal heart by bringing to light and by stirring up its evil inclinations. Pride, self-will and enmity refused to be restrained by the law or by the curse. In previous chapters Paul had dropped a hint to the same effect, Rom. 4 : 15 ; 5 : 20. Here he declares it in plain and strong terms. Chrysostom : " When we desire a thing, and then are hindered of it, the flame of the desire is but increased. Now this came not of the law ; for it hindered us in a way to keep us off from it : but sin, that is, thy own listlessness and bad disposition used what was good for the reverse." Calvin : " The law is only the occasion. And though he may seem to speak only of that excitement, by which our lusting is instigated through the law, so that it boils out with greater fury ; yet I refer this chiefly to the knowledge the law conveys ; as though he had said, ' It has discovered to me every lust or coveting, which, being hid, seemed somehow to have no existence.' " Stuart : " Opposition to the desires and passions of unsanctified men inflames them, and renders them more intense and unyielding." Hodge : " The effect of the law operating upon our corrupt hearts is to arouse their evil passions, and to lead to the desire of the very objects which the law forbids." *Concupiscence,* the same word rendered *lust* in v. 7, on which see above. It is sometimes used in a good sense for strong *desire,* Luke 22 : 15 ; 1 Thess. 2 : 17 ; but commonly in a bad sense ; as *lust* of the eyes, wordly *lusts,* fleshly *lusts,* hurtful *lusts,* deceitful *lusts,* ungodly *lusts.* *For without the law sin* was *dead.* By *dead* Chrysostom understands " not so ascertainable ;" Calvin : " Without the law sin is buried ;" Locke : " Not able to hurt me ;" Diodati : " As it were asleep and deaded, if it were not kindled again by the law working lively on the conscience ;" Pool : " Comparatively dead ;" Doddridge : " I was no more aware of any danger from it, or any power it had to hurt me, than if it had been a dead enemy ;" Guyse : " Sin was a trivial harmless thing in my account : it did not terrify my con- science ; but seemed, like a dead man, to have no strength in me, and to carry no danger in it ; " Stuart : " Comparatively sluggish and inoperative ; " Hodge : " Inactive, unproductive and unobserved." The principles involved in the exposition are these : 1. Where there is absolutely no law, there is absolutely no sin, Rom. 4 : 15. 2. But all men have some knowledge of right and wrong, and therefore some conscience of sin, Rom. 2 : 15. 3. Ignorance of law naturally begets low conceptions of sin. 4. In the absence of law, sin is not felt even where it does actually exist. 5. The clear shining of the law discovers sins where none were

supposed to exist. 6. The restraints of law are irksome to the carnal
nature of man, and actually provoke his evil desires. 7. But this
provoking of lusts is wholly chargeable to the evil nature of sin,
and not at all to the law itself; the law merely showing us the
nature, prevalence and power of sin. The question, most mooted
respecting verses 7, 8, is whether Paul is here speaking of himself,
or merely stating a general truth in the first person singular. Calvin: " I wonder what could have come into the minds of interpreters
to render the passage in the preterimperfect tense, as though Paul
was speaking of himself; for it is easy to see that his purpose was
to begin with a general proposition, and then to explain the subject by his own example." Doddridge thinks the apostle is " personating another character." But is this so ? 1. Paul uses the
only form of speech he could use, if he were speaking of himself.
He has *I* and *me*. 2. It must be admitted that in subsequent
verses the apostle does speak of himself, and why not here ? The
general structure of these and of subsequent verses is the same.
3. One clause of v. 7 absolutely requires us to understand the
apostle as revealing his personal experience. He says that the
tenth commandment was the means in the hand of the Spirit of
showing him the true nature of sin or of evil desires. The experience of every converted man is not that the tenth commandment
first opened his eyes to a just view of his lost condition. God
often uses other portions of Scripture to bring about the same
thing. 4. At some time Paul certainly had the experience here
recorded, for it is substantially the experience of all God's people
in the early stages of their religious impressions. That is, in some
way, by some truth their eyes have been opened to see the number, heinousness and sinfulness of their sins. Paul was no exception.

9. *For I was alive without the law once : but when the commandment came, sin revived, and I died.* The same experience in its
consummation is related in Gal. 2 : 19, and more fully in Phil.
3 : 4-10. *I was alive without the law once;* Wiclif: I lyued with
outen the lawe sumtyme ; Tyndale and Cranmer : I once lived
with out lawe ; Peshito : I, without the law, was alive formerly.;
Doway : I lived some time without the law ; Stuart : I was alive,
once, without the law. In the Greek the article is wanting before
law. The chief difficulty arises from the word rendered *was alive.*
Some think it means, I lived, that is, I had my earthly existence.
Mr. Locke so understands it, and applies the whole verse to one,
who lived before and after the giving of the law of Moses. But
this does not at all agree with the context, nor with the facts in
the case. The contrast is twofold. First, we have the antithesis

between *was alive* and *died;* and secondly, between *without law* and *the commandment came.* To be *alive* cannot mean natural life unless to have *died* means to have died a temporal death. In what sense then may we understand these terms? By being *alive* Chrysostom understands, " I was not so much condemned;" and by *died,* he understands that Paul was distinctly made acquainted with the fact that he had been sinning. Calvin: " When I sinned, having not the knowledge of the law, the sin, which I did not observe, was so laid to sleep, that it seemed to be dead; on the other hand, as I seemed not to myself to be a sinner, I was satisfied with myself, thinking that I had a life of my own. But the death of sin is the life of man, and again the life of sin is the death of man." Paul was bred a Pharisee, and was early made acquainted with the letter of the law. But the letter convinces none of sin. None were more self-righteous than the Pharisees. But when God's Spirit opens the eyes to see the extent and spirituality of the law, a very different state of things is produced in the mind of even a Pharisee. His self-esteem *dies;* his hope of heaven by his own worthiness *dies;* his peace of mind leaves him; his false ideas of safety all forsake him. No man is absolutely *without law.* Paul certainly never was so. That phrase therefore here must point to the time, when spiritual blindness excluded from his mind just apprehensions of the holiness, strictness, extent and spirituality of the law. So when *the commandment came* points to the time when by the tenth precept of the law his eyes were opened to see how his thoughts, words and deeds were at war with the true intent and just demands of the law. Then *sin revived,* came to life, i. e. I became sensible of the number and power of my sins and then *died,* as a legalist. When this great change in Paul's views occurred, he does not here inform us. But it doubtless began about the time that Jesus arrested him on his way to Damascus. Something of this sort occurs in the case of all truly converted men, nor does the change thus indicated cease till sanctification is complete.

10. *And the commandment, which* was ordained *to life, I found* to be *unto death. The commandment,* either the last precept of the decalogue, or the whole law. *Was ordained* is added also by Tyndale, Cranmer, Genevan, Doway, Bp. Hall and others. The moral law is unto life among unsinning angels. It was unto life to our first parents till they ate the forbidden fruit. Had they and their posterity perfectly obeyed it, it would have been unto life to them all for ever. It is the law of heaven, and its observance there conduces to the highest good of that blessed society. But every man, who has had true conviction of sin, has, like Paul,

found the law to be *unto death,* that is to condemnation, to the death of legal hope, and to the arousing of wicked principles in the soul into lively action. The law, rightly used, conduces to holiness and happiness; broken or misused, it conduces only to sin and misery.

11. *For sin, taking occasion by the commandment, deceived me, and by it slew* me. Notice it was *sin* that did this. Holiness would have done just the opposite. As in v. 8 so here *sin* doubtless means the sinful principle in our fallen nature. *Occasion,* opportunity or advantage, as in v. 8, on which see above. The strength of sin is the law. It gives sin its damning power, and its power to make men vile and miserable; but it does all this by mans' abuse and perversion. In this way sin deceives by the commandment. The law shows a good way, a very good way, an angelical way, for the holy. Sin puts a veil over the heart, and persuades the poor sinner that he can win God's favor by deeds of law, by the law restrain and remove his corruptions, by degrees become tolerably good, and so secure heaven. All this was through the great treachery and desperate wickedness of the carnal heart. But the deceitfulness of sin knows no bounds. It does its work perfectly. None but God can countervail it. Acute as was Saul of Tarsus it *deceived* him; yea more it *slew* him. Sin sunk him in guilt and misery, fastening upon him the fetters of iniquity and the chains of a fiery condemnation. It then showed him his sad condition, and let him see that by law he was a dead man—dead in the sight of God's purity, justice and omniscience—dead in trespasses and sins. *Deceived,* in 2 Cor. 11 : 3 *beguiled.* But the law itself is not seductive ; it is sin alone that does the mischief.

12. *Wherefore the law* is *holy, and the commandment holy, and just, and good.* T. Adam's paraphrase is: "Wherefore the law is (not sin, as might be objected, nor the cause of sin, but) holy (in its nature, end, and purpose); and the commandment holy (in itself), just (as coming from God), and good (for men)." Three explanations may be given of the terms *law* and *commandment* in this verse in their relation to each other. One is that these terms are used synonymously for the decalogue. Another is that by *law* Paul means the decalogue, and by *commandment* the tenth precept of the decalogue, which he had specially named in v. 7. The third is that by *law* he means the decalogue, and by *commandment* he means each precept separately. The whole law and the precepts thereof severally are *holy,* pure, manifesting the rectitude of the divine Lawgiver ; *just,* equitable, capable of being shown to be *righteous* before any competent tribunal; and *good,* worthy of him, who alone has original and infinite goodness in his nature,

and displays his benevolence in all his works and ways.   There are perhaps no three words in the New Testament of so frequent occurrence, that vary less in their meaning than these three adjectives, which we render *holy, just and good*.   The apostle, having proven what he asserted in v. 7, that the precepts of the law are not sin, but that they are holy, just and good, that they are of excellent use in showing us the true nature of sin and our lost condition by nature, proceeds to show that the penalty of the law cannot be fairly objected to, that death is the fruit and fault of *sin*, that the law curses no one who keeps it, and that we cannot blame the law but only sin for all our miseries.

13. *Was then that which is good made death unto me ?   God forbid. But sin, that it might appear sin, working death in me by that which is good ; that sin by the commandment might become exceeding sinful.* By *that which is good* he of course means the law.   Was it the law that brought death ?   By no means.   On *God forbid* see above on Rom. 3 : 4.   It was not the law, but the transgression of the law that brought death.   Sin did this that its true, its deadly nature might be seen, *that it might appear sin*.   The worst thing that can be said of any thing, even of sin, is that it is sin ; for it *works death by that which is good*, it perverts the very best things, even the excellent law of God, to the condemnation and ruin of the soul.   Sin reveres no authority, however high and glorious.   It bows to no will, even though it be that of God.   It goes further still.   It perverts the very gospel to its own ends, and thus to death.   The effect of all this is that to the discerning sin *becomes*, that is appears to be exceeding *sinful*, literally sinful to a *hyperbole*, overleaping all bounds, knowing nothing but lawlessness, doing nothing but working wrath, ruin and death, and thus exposing to our view its mischievous and malignant nature.

DOCTRINAL AND PRACTICAL REMARKS

1. Let us not blame what is good for what is evil, v. 7.   Nathan was in no way a partaker of David's sin, because he brought it to his remembrance, and brought him to repentance for it.   If David's zeal and indignation had been turned against the prophet, and not against his sin, it would have shown that he was yet unhumbled.   And if we find fault with the law, and not with ourselves for breaking the law, we may know that all is still wrong in us.   The law is not sin.   If the law were not perfect, it would not be worthy of God ; and how can a bad man be saved by a good law ?

2. Whoever undertakes to expound any part of the truth of God should guard it against any liability to reasonable misappre-

hension, and defend it against plausible objections, v. 7.   Much
damage has been done to the law of God and to the gospel also
by the loose statements of professed friends.   God's word is exact, precise.   Let us not fall into habits of careless or confused
thinking or speaking on divine things.   If men pervert what we
say, let the fault be wholly theirs, and not partly ours.   This care
on our part is the more necessary in proportion as our readers or
hearers are ignorant, prejudiced or sinful.   Let us never consent,
or seem to consent that any part of God's word is not very pure.

5. Against one form of error—antinominanism—it is hardly
possible too carefully to guard our statements or mankind, v. 7.
Every man in love with sin is at heart an enemy of the law in its
true intent and spirit.   Some express their opposition to the law
by shamelessly breaking it, others by secretly sinning against it,
others by arguing against it, and others by turning the grace of
God into licentiousness.   Let us have no fellowship with either
class of these opposers of righteousness.   For the very reason
that the law is too strict to justify us, and of a nature utterly at
war with the carnal nature of man, we ought to commend it, and
blame ourselves.   It is its purity that gives it its power to reveal
our sinfulness.

4. It is a pleasing truth that God puts honor on all the truths
of scripture in awakening the careless, in convincing the self-
righteous, in leading men to hope in his mercy, and in carrying
on the work of sanctification, v. 7.   Some writers of the XVIIth
century tell of a man whose attention was called to religion by the
words " and he died," which occur so often in Gen. 5.   The late
Dr. Hamilton of London in one of his fine tracts has brought together the cases of several, whose religious experience began or
was very much moulded by different portions of God's word, as
that of Paul by the tenth commandment, the elder Jonathan Edwards by 1 Tim. 1 : 17, etc.   It is perhaps he who suggests that if
we knew the minute religious history of all the pious, and should
mark with red the text blessed to the conversion of each, nearly
the whole Bible would thus be *rubric*.

5. There is such a thing as religious experience, vs. 7–13.   That
is, God's Spirit does lead men to feel and be exercised by the truths
of the divine word.   This experience begins when men's attention
is truly awakened to the word of God, nor is it ended till they
pass over Jordan.   But a peculiar interest always attaches to the
early stages of such personal religious history.   A scriptural discourse on conviction and conversion is sure to be eagerly listened
to by real Christians.   That, which has awakened so strong prejudice against public narrations of God's dealings with one's soul,

is the ignorance, the self-conceit and the imprudence, with which men have often spoken of themselves. But does not Paul often tell his religious experience? Did not David often do the same? And where is the good man that is prepared to condemn or even censure Bunyan's "Grace Abounding," or the memoirs of Halyburton, Brainerd, John Newton, Henry Martyn, Scott's "Force of Truth," or a multitude of such books? Truth is chiefly valuable as it can be wrought into our experience and thus mould our characters. Who ever received the Lord Jesus as all his salvation till he saw and felt that in himself he was poor, and blind, and naked, and guilty, and vile, and wretched, and helpless? Hodge: "If our religious experience does not correspond with that of the people of God, as detailed in the scriptures, we cannot be true Christians. Unless we have felt as Paul felt, we have not the religion of Paul, and cannot expect to share his rewards."

6. The law of God and God himself look chiefly at the heart, v. 7. As a man thinketh in his heart, so is he, Pr. 23 : 7. In God's esteem covetousness is as truly idolatry as bowing down to images of wood and stone, Col. 3 : 5 ; hatred is murder, Matt. 5 : 22; and lust is adultery, Matt. 5 : 28. That was a fearful charge Christ brought against some, "I know you that ye have not the love of God in you," John 5 : 42. And it is as fearful to be without the love of God now as it ever was. To be in that state proves that one is every day breaking, in their true spirit, all the commandments. For long years Saul of Tarsus had been a Pharisee, proud, self-righteous, and confident of his being in favor with God, but when his eyes were opened to see the spiritual nature of one precept, he soon saw himself guilty of violating all. All inordinate and irregular desires and affections are as truly sin as overt acts against the letter of the commandments. The very first impulses to evil are evil. How very low poor human nature is fallen! Aims, motives, dispositions and inclinations may be as truly offensive to God as words and overt acts. This should never be forgotten. Otherwise we shall continually make fatal mistakes, calling bitter sweet, and evil good. Let men everywhere study the law as expounded in all the scriptures, especially in the sermon on the mount. It is not our enemy, even when it condemns us, although it cannot justify or sanctify us. But by God's blessing it can show us that we are sick and need a Physician, weak and need a Helper, guilty and need a Redeemer.

7. We must make just distinctions, and we must heed those made in the word of God. A sound discrimination in things temporal is a mark of earthly wisdom ; in things spiritual it is a

mark of heavenly wisdom. If the law were the *cause* of sin it would be sin. But its being the occasion of sin argues nothing against it, v. 8. Abel's acceptance before God was the occasion of Cain's violence ; but the cause of his murderous conduct was his own wicked envy. Naboth's inheritance of a vineyard gave occasion to Ahab and Jezebel to shed innocent blood. But the cause of that crime was their accursed cruelty and covetousness. We must regard moral distinctions. To do this aright we must rightly use our powers of discrimination. Some distinctions are wide and obvious; but others are nice and minute. Some of this latter class are as important as any we make. Refinements of thought, which are merely for scholastic or dialectic purposes, may easily be perverted to bad ends; but anything which enables us the more clearly to apprehend truth, in particular moral and religious truth, is of importance to us.

8. Spiritual Christians will study and faithful ministers will preach the law of God. Salvation is not by the law, but by it is the knowledge of sin. The law is itself no means of sanctification, but it presents the true standard of holiness. The corruption, which the law stirs up, exists before the law comes, and is not created by the law, v. 8. Brown: " It is not unsuitable unto the days of the gospel, for ministers to be treating of the law, and explaining it unto people, nor ought they for so doing, to be reproachfully styled legal preachers." On this point Paul has instructed us by his example, and Paul's Master did the same. A considerable part of the sermon on the mount was directed to the rescuing of the law from false glosses and popular errors. Hodge: " Though the law cannot save us, it must prepare us for salvation."

9. There must be something very dreadful in the nature of sin, for it not only flies in the face of law, contemns law and refuses subjection to law, but is by it actually aroused into greater activity and desperateness, so that by the law it excites many unholy desires, and ' so works in men all manner of concupiscence,' v. 8. Fraser: " The more the law, with its authority, light, and terror, reached the heart and sin in it, sin exerted itself the more vehemently." A running stream may be dammed up for a while but it is gaining head and force all the while, and must in the end rise above the obstruction or sweep it away. Brown: " So prone are these naturally corrupted hearts of ours to break out into all manner of actual transgressions, till grace make a change, and diminish the strength and vigor of original corruption, that what should prove a curb, proves a spur." Sin perverts everything, law, authority, love and mercy.

10. It is no marvel that, without any right rule of moral judgment before their minds, men should have high though false hopes of even heavenly felicity, v. 9. How could it be otherwise? When men believe that God is either the patron of vice, or indifferent to moral character, that wicked desires and affections, which are not acted out, are not sinful, or that God will accept a moral reformation or some tears of sorrow for atonement, why should they not be confident of future happiness, at least some measure of it? Blindness of mind, stupidity of conscience, popular errors among worldly men, false religious doctrines, the seductions of Satan and self-flattery may well account for all the delusive dreams entertained by men concerning their spiritual state. Such self-deception is not uncommon. Many a man might save his soul, if he would give up his false hope; but if he hugs his hope to the last, his damnation is sure.

11. Yet the slumber of the soul under such delusion may be broken at any time; for no man can tell when the *commandment may come* with such light and power as shall at once plunge him into the deepest distress, v. 9. Scott: "The proudest Pharisee on earth would, from his towering height of vain confidence, sink into despair, if the commandments of God were once discovered to his soul, in all their spirituality and excellency, without a correspondent view of the salvation of Christ." Great activity in corruption is not at all inconsistent with excessive spiritual pride. High conceits and high looks entirely consist with a depravity, which will frighten any one, whose eyes are by divine grace opened to see his true character in the glass of God's word.

12. Sin may sleep without dying, v. 9. Sometimes for a season Satan seems to leave a man, corruption seems to be very much gone, but if the change is not owing to a thorough work of grace, these specious appearances will all vanish. Our Saviour told us how all this was, Matt. 12 : 43–45.

13. Knowing God's will and not doing it will save no man. Non-compliance with truth revealed will turn all divine revelations into means of sorer destruction. Through sin Paul found even the law to be *unto death*, v. 10. Thousands have done the same. Yea more, by unbelief, which is the great master sin, the glorious gospel of the blessed God, becomes a savor of death unto death. "Sin overturneth all things." In our fallen state we never rightly regard the law, till we see how to us by reason of sin it works death.

14. Sin is a terrible delusion. It deceives and seduces in many ways, v. 11. There is danger that even converted men will be

hardened through the deceitfulness of sin, for the old man is very corrupt according to the deceitful lusts, Heb. 3 : 13 ; Eph. 4 : 22. The heart is deceitful above all things and desperately wicked, Jer. 17 : 9.   Men cannot be too much on their guard, lest there should be among them a root that beareth gall and wormwood ; and it come to pass that when they hear the very words of the curse, that they bless themselves in their hearts saying, We shall have peace, though we walk in the imagination of our hearts, Deut. 29 : 18, 19.

15. It is a sad error into which some fall that even a bias to sin is not sinful, that sinful inclinations are not themselves wicked, or that there may be a proper cause of sin, which is not sinful. This whole section condemns such doctrine.   Lust, covetousness, evil concupiscence are as truly worthy of God's displeasure as overt acts of profaneness or violence.

16. The wrath of God, foreshadowed by men's alarms of conscience and by conviction for sin, slaying all false hopes, does not come on men capriciously but by the measure of a holy, just and good law, v. 11.   Death is by sin and the strength of sin, in working man's ruin, is the law.   The great trouble with a very sick man is that his disease turns both food and medicine to his further injury. Cathartics weaken him. Stimulants produce febrile action. Sedatives nauseate him.   Every thing works against him.   Just so sin makes law and gospel, precepts and promises, warnings and threatenings all conducive to the death of the sinner.

17. Let us, therefore, at all times defend the law against all charges brought against it, and study it with care.   Luther said that if for a day he ceased to meditate on the law, he was sensible of a decline in his pious feelings.   True the law has curses, but they are all deserved.   It has precepts too strict for a sinner to keep perfectly, but they are all holy, just and good.   It forbids nothing that omniscience regards as good for us.   The only perfectly happy society in the universe is one where the law is perfectly and universally obeyed. Chalmers : " God loves what is wise and holy and just and good in the world of mind ; and with a far higher affection too, than he loves what is fair and graceful and comely in the world of matter."   Let our taste coincide with his.

18. We cannot be too guarded against a temper that shall lead us to pervert the right ways of God, find fault with his orderings, or oppose his known will. Reasonable difficulties we may properly state that they may be solved ; but the spirit of cavilling is as wicked as it is foolish.   We may never find fault with God.   To do so is impiety.   To accuse his law of *working death* is wicked, v. 13.

19. It is bad to oe justly charged with want of civility. Even awkwardness may do harm. But the worst thing that can be truly said of any thing is that it is sinful. Yea, the worst thing that can be said of sin itself is that it *is exceeding sinful*, v. 13. Pool: "Sin is so evil, that he cannot call it by a worse name than its own."

Chapter 16

ROMANS 7
VERSES 14-25

THE GREAT SPIRITUAL WARFARE OF THE CHRIS-
TIAN

14 For we know that the law is spiritual: but I am carnal, sold under sin.

15 For that which I do, I allow not: for what I would, that do I not; but what I hate, that do I.

16 If then I do that which I would not, I consent unto the law that *it is* good.

17 Now then it is no more I that do it, but sin that dwelleth in me.

18 For I know that in me (that is, in my flesh,) dwelleth no good thing: for to will is present with me; but *how* to perform that which is good I find not.

19 For the good that I would, I do not: but the evil which I would not, that I do.

20 Now if I do that I would not, it is no more I that do it, but sin that dwelleth in me.

21 I find then a law, that, when I would do good, evil is present with me.

22 For I delight in the law of God after the inward man:

23 But I see another law in my members, warring against the law of my mind, and bringing me into captivity to the law of sin which is in my members.

24 O wretched man that I am! who shall deliver me from the body of this death?

25 I thank God through Jesus Christ our Lord. So then with the mind I myself serve the law of God; but with the flesh the law of sin.

FROM this to the end of the chapter we have twelve verses, giving us a full account of the spiritual warfare, carried on in the heart of believers. That this is the real subject of these verses has long been held by many in the church of God. But this view has been by some much opposed. In particular Whitby and Stuart have shown great zeal in attempting to prove that these verses do not describe the exercises of a converted man. Instead of arguing this matter in each verse, it will be more satis-factory to make the discussion of it preliminary to the exposition of these verses. Whitby: " I think, nothing can be more evident, and unquestionably true than this, that the apostle doth not here speak of himself in his own person, or in the state he was then in."

335

Stuart: "I suppose the apostle to be here speaking of himself when in a *legal state*, or under the law, and before he was united to Christ." These writers are agreed in their interpretation only negatively, viz. that Paul is not speaking of himself in a regenerate state. Stuart admits that Paul is speaking of himself, but Whitby thinks he is speaking "only in the person of a Jew, conflicting with the motions of his lusts, only by the assistance of the letter of the law, without the aids and powerful assistance of the Holy Spirit." These general remarks are offered.

1. The controversy respecting this portion of scripture is not to be settled by scorn or vituperation. Stuart seems greatly moved on this subject and exclaims: "When will it be believed, that scorn is not critical acumen, and that calling men heretics, is not an argument that will convince such as take the liberty to think and examine for themselves? When will such appeals cease? And when shall we have reasons instead of assertions, criticism in the place of denunciation, and a full practical exhibition of the truth, that the simple testimony of the divine word stands immeasurably higher than all human authority?" If this quotation has any pertinency to the matter in hand, it is a pretty distinct intimation from the Andover Professor, that those, who hold views directly opposite to his are deficient in " critical acumen," do not " think and examine for themselves," offer " assertions" instead of reasons, and denunciation in the place of " criticism," put " human authority" above the " divine word," or along side of it; and that they resort to scorn and vituperation instead of argument. If this is the intent and meaning of the words quoted, they contain more that is harsh and scornful towards opponents than I have yet found in all the writers on the other side. The same author says a good deal that is quite as harsh. Whitby says that those who hold the view commonly approved by sound divines present " as great an instance of the force of prejudice, and the heat of opposition, to pervert the plainest truths as can be haply produced." Whitby was of course not ignorant of the instance of prejudice and heated opposition furnished by the history of the enemies of Christ, and recorded in the gospels, for he had written much about it, and yet he thinks that no greater than that of the many good and learned men, who think Paul is here speaking of himself while in a state of grace! Is not *scorn* or something very much like it apparent here? Many instances of a like strain of remark from writers on the same side could easily be pointed out. Take one more. Clarke: " This opinion has most pitifully and most shamefully lowered the standard of Christianity, and even destroyed its influence and disgraced its character." Again: " Of Paul the apostle

all here said would be monstrous, and absurd, if not blasphemous."
Is this critical acumen?   Is this reasoning?   Is it any thing better
than railing?   Socinus himself warning men against understanding
this passage of persons regenerate and under grace exclaims : " Beware as of the pestilence."   Of course he means a deadly pestilence.

2. It has been shown, (see above on v. 8) that Paul is there for
several verses preceding the 14th, speaking of himself, and if now
he begins to speak of another man, or of himself merely as personating a Jew, let it be manifested.   It has not yet been made to appear.   The place so much relied on to prove that Paul is in the habit
of personating others or of using himself merely as a figure to
teach important truth can have no pertinency to this matter :
" These things, brethren, I have in a figure transferred to myself
and to Apollos, for your sakes; that ye might learn in us not to
think of men above that which is written," 1 Cor. 4 : 6.   Whatever
may be the precise idea here suggested, it cannot be regarded as
proving that in Rom. 7 : 14–25 Paul is speaking of some one else
than himself for two reasons : 1. In 1 Cor. 4 : 6 he gives fair notice
that he had in a figure transferred certain things to himself and
Apollos; but he gives no such notice in Rom. 7 : 14–25.   2. In 1
Cor. he says nothing of himself or of Apollos, that is not true
of himself or of Apollos, as is apparent on the face of the
text.   See the place.   Now if it is admitted that all Paul says
here is literally true of himself as well as of other good men,
we have made some progress towards ending the controversy.
For those, who take the view of the best divines, admit that Paul
is here giving his own experience, not as peculiar to himself, but
in common with the body of believers.   And Stuart says : " Does
the apostle mean to designate himself specially and peculiarly, or
does he include others with himself?   Others certainly are included, understand him as you please.   If he speaks of himself
while under the law, he means by a parity of reasoning to include
all others who are in the same condition.   If he speaks of himself
as a Christian, he means in the same manner to include all other
Christians, who of course must have similar experience. . . Whatever ground of exegesis one takes, as to chap VII. in general, the
principle that Paul speaks of himself only as an example of what
others are in like circumstances, must of course be admitted."

3. Stuart admits, and very correctly too, that what is said in vs.
14–25 is substantially Christian experience.   His language is clear :
" The question is not whether it be true that there is a contest in
the breast of Christians, which might (at least for the most part)
be well described by the words there found; but whether such a
view of the subject is congruous with the present design and ar-

gument of the apostle." Again: " I concede, in the first place, that Christians have a contest with sin; and that this is as plain and certain, as that they are not wholly sanctified in this life. It is developed by almost every page of scripture, and by every day's experience. That this contest is often a vehement one; that the passions rage, yea, that they do sometimes gain the victory; is equally plain and certain. It follows now, of course, that as the language of Rom. 7 : 14–25 is intended to describe a contest between the good principle and the bad one in men, and also a contest in which the evil principle comes off victorious; so this language can hardly fail of being appropriate to describe all those cases in a Christian's experience, in which sin triumphs. Every Christian at once recognizes and feels, that such cases may be described in language like that which the apostle employs." This is a concession called for by the very nature of the case. Rightly used it may aid us in coming at the truth. Here then it is conceded that the language of Rom. 7 : 14–25 is appropriate to the case of Christians; that all Christians have a contest like that here described; and that the matter is of a very weighty character—a matter of universal Christian experience, than which nothing is to us more important to be rightly understood.

4. This controversy cannot be settled by human authority, although the friends of truth need not blush to let it be known what company they are in. It is freely admitted that among the early fathers of the church Origen, Tertullian, Chrysostom and Theodoret interpreted the passage of an unregenerate man. Grotius is so delighted with this fact that he exclaims: " Praise be to God, that the best Christians, those of the first three centuries, understood this place, as they ought," etc. But Stuart goes too far when he says, " that Augustine was the first, who suggested the idea that it (Rom. 7 : 14–25) must be applied to Christian experience." Augustine himself in his Retractions B. I. Chap. 23, expressly denies this: " Hence it came to pass, that I came to understand these things, as HILARY, GREGORY, AMBROSE and other holy and famous [noti] doctors of the church understood them, who thought that the apostle himself strenuously struggled against carnal lusts, which he was unwilling to have, and yet had, and that he bore witness to this conflict in these words." Stuart is altogether wrong also in saying that Augustine was led to his views " in the heat of dispute with Pelagius," and that he " felt himself pressed" by the arguments of Pelagius, and " *made his escape* by protesting against the exegesis of his antagonist." That Augustine did at one time regard Rom. 7 : 14–25 as inapplicable

to one in a state of grace is denied by no one, not even by himself. " But as a deeper insight into his own heart" [says Hodge] "and a more thorough investigation of the scriptures, led to the modifi- cation of his opinions on so many other points, they produced a change on this also. This general alteration of his views cannot be attributed to his controversy with Pelagius, because it took place long before that controversy commenced. It is to be ascribed to his religious experience, and his study of the word of God." Beyond controversy this is the fair historic verity. On the same side with the earlier fathers we find Photius in the IX. and Oecumenius in the X. century. After them came Erasmus, Alfonso Turrettin, Le Clerc, Bengel, Arminius, Epis- copius, Limborch, Locke, Bull, Hammond, Whitby, Doddridge, Kettlewell, Macknight, Tholuck, Storr, Flatt, Stier, Conybeare and Howson, and others, whose names have already been men- tioned.

On the other side we have Augustine (with his matured views), Anselm, Thomas Aquinas, Cornelius a Lapide, Luther, Melanc- thon, Calvin, Beza, Diodati, Buddaeus, T. Adam, Bp. Hall, Ferme, John Owen of Oxford, John Brown of Wamphray, Guyse, Burkitt, Dutch Annotations, Assembly's Annotations, Gill, Pool, Koppe, Dickinson, Hawker, Scott, Fraser, Wardlaw, Andrew, Fuller, Haldane, Chalmers, and others. The great treatise of Owen on "Indwelling Sin" is founded on this portion of scripture. Hawker says, " Nothing can be more plain, than that it is *Paul's* own history he writes, and his own experience in the very moment of writing ; and which the Holy Ghost taught him to instruct the church concerning. And sure I am, that every child of God, savingly called of God, and long taught of God as *Paul* was when he thus committed to writing what daily passed in his heart, will not only bear testimony to the same, but bless God the Holy Ghost for the history, for it is most precious." Those, who em- brace the views defended in this work, are generally very decided in their utterances. Their convictions seem to be very clear. Commonly they appeal to the universal experience of God's peo- ple in confirmation of their views ; nor do they appeal in vain, if we take as a proof the exercises of the most experienced servants of God.

5. If the apostle had designed to speak of himself in a state of grace, he has certainly used the appropriate terms and forms of speech to that end. We have in the passage itself the personal pronoun, *I, my, me*, repeated fifteen or sixteen times ; and that there may be no room left for doubt as to the designation Paul once says *I myself*. Then we thrice have the participle or adjec-

tive agreeing with this pronoun, and in more than twenty cases we have the verb in the first person singular. It very seldom happens that in the space of twelve verses there is so remarkable a combination of verbs, participles, adjectives and pronouns determining the person spoken of, and this appears in every translation now at hand. And after the apostle begins to speak of himself in v. 14 he does never change the person or the number. It is *I, my, me* to the end of the chapter. This is the more remarkable as Paul does sometimes make a transition from the singular to the plural and back again to the singular, as in 1 Cor. 13 : 11, 12. If the language of Psalms 32, 51 points out David as speaking of himself, these twelve verses do as clearly make Paul to speak of himself.

6. This view is strengthened by the fact that in vs. 7–13 Paul invariably uses the past tense ; but in vs. 14–25 he uses the present tense, when speaking of himself, never varying from it. Here are verbs found more than twenty times in the present tense, without one exception, while just before Paul had for seven verses as carefully used the past tense. In no writer adopting the views of Whitby, Stuart, etc. have I found the least, respectful notice of this change in tenses. Yet many, who favor their views, could not be ignorant of the fact that in construing an author such a change ought to affect the sense, and should therefore be carefully noticed. The Dutch Annotations on v. 14 says : "Hitherto the apostle hath spoken of the power of the law and of sin, in the corrupt and unregenerate man ; as he himself also had formerly experienced, when he was yet in such a state, v. 9, but now he cometh and speaketh of himself as he then was, and declares what power the remainder of sinful flesh had still in him, now after that he was delivered from the dominion of sin, like as all his reasons, which follow, speak of the present time, and not of the time past." Fraser : " He had been speaking of himself in the past tense. . . He now from v. 14. speaks of himself in the present tense." Olshausen notes the same thing : " The passage (Rom. 7 : 7–13), indeed, according to the opinion of *all* expositors, applies to the state *before* regeneration, as the apostle also sufficiently indicates by the *aorist* that the state described is gone by ; but whether the passage (Rom. 7 : 14–24) is likewise to be considered as before regeneration, seems very uncertain, since in this section Paul makes use of the *present* only, while in Rom. 8 : 2 the *aorist* again appears." Wardlaw : " Of this change this transition from past to present time, neither Tholuck nor Stuart takes any notice. Yet surely it is no unimportant item in the case. . . When a man has once been speaking of the views which he once entertained, and which

he had continued for a length of time to hold, respecting his own
character and state, and in doing so uses the past tense, and then
makes a transition from the past to the present, it cannot but appear unnatural in a high degree to consider him as still meaning
the past, and still continuing to speak of what he had been.
When the same man, in speaking of his own views and principles
and character, says first I was, and then changes to I am, is it not
reasonable to conceive that he is speaking of his former and his
present self?" See also Guyse and others to the same effect. If
there is no significance in this change of tense, it seems useless to
pay any attention to the grammar of a language. If this matter
is not important here, it is important no where. Nor can anything
like this construction of verbs in an extended passage be found
elsewhere in Paul's writings or in the New Testament, unless this
is significant.

7. In these twelve verses there are things said, which can by no
fair interpretation be applied to an unregenerate man, and therefore they must refer to Paul or some one in a state of grace. If
any thing in religious character is decisive, it is one's state of mind
towards the law of God. On this matter the scriptures are decisive and harmonious. One of David's marks of a good man is
that " his delight is in the law of the Lord : and in his law doth he
meditate day and night," Ps. 1 : 2 ; " The law of thy mouth is better
unto me than thousands of gold and silver," Ps. 119 : 72. " I will
meditate in thy precepts," Ps. 119 : 78. " Blessed is the man that
feareth the Lord, that delighteth greatly in his commandments,"
Ps. 112 : 1. " Then shall I not be ashamed when I have respect
unto all thy commandments," Ps. 119 : 6. So in many other places
human character is said to be good or bad, as it stands well or ill
affected to the law of God. In the portion of scripture under consideration the apostle makes three statements respecting the law,
either of which ought to be regarded as decisive of his real state
of mind and of heart in the sight of God. One is in v. 16, " I consent unto the law that it is good." One is in v. 22, " For I delight
in the law of God after the inward man." The other is in v. 25,
" So then with the mind I myself serve the law of God." Some
very strange things have been said to do away with these declarations, which upon the face of them seem to be decisive of the
whole matter. Clarke says : " So far is it from being true that
none but a REGENERATE *man can delight in the law of God*, we find
even a *proud, unhumbled* Pharisee can do it." And that this is no
careless assertion is evident from much more that he says like it :
" If it be said, that it is not possible for an unregenerate man to
delight in the law of God, the experience of millions contradicts the

assertion. Every true *penitent* admires the moral law : longs most earnestly for a conformity to it : and feels that he never can be happy till he awakes up after this divine likeness ; and he hates himself, because he feels that he has *broken* it, and that his evil passions are still in a state of hostility to it." One hardly knows how to cease to wonder at such language. An *unregenerate* man is stated to be a *true penitent !* No man can be saved without the new birth. Yet here is a *true penitent* still unregenerate ; and an unregenerate true penitent, who still gives the very best scriptural evidence of being a new creature. Can any but a renewed heart love holiness ? Yet the law of God is holy, and is the standard of holiness. How can one, who is not in a state of grace, love holiness, or the perfect law that enjoins it ? The language of each of the three clauses is, and upon their face was evidently intended to be unmistakeable : " I consent unto the law that it is good." He does not say " I assent to the law ;" that would be merely an act of the understanding, and might be cold and heartless. But he says " I consent " to it. He here uses a word found no where else in the New Testament. Wiclif, Cranmer, Rheims, Doway and Stuart render it *consent*. He consents to the law that it is *good*. An unregenerate man may see and say that the law is strict and rigorous, but when did an unrenewed man ever say that the law, the whole law, was *good*, good for himself, good for every man ? He adds : " I delight in the law of God after the inward man." Here each important word may in succession be emphasised and the sense will be evolved and not obscured. Paul expresses *delight* in the law of God. Here too we have a word found no where else in the New Testament. It is very strong—I *delight myself* in the law. What is it but saying—" I delight in real, hearty, entire, universal obedience and holiness, just such as the law demands ? " What more did David mean when he said ? " Thy law is my delight," Ps. 119 : 77, 174 ; " Thy testimonies are my delight," Ps. 119 : 24 ; " I will delight myself in thy statutes," Ps. 119 : 16, 35 ; " Make me to go in the path of thy commandments; for therein do I delight," Ps. 119 : 35 ; " I will delight myself in thy commandments, which I have loved," Ps. 119 : 47 ; " For I delight in thy law," Ps. 119 : 70. For ages the church of God has regarded delight in the law of God, as a conclusive evidence of a renewed heart. Nor was this a wild notion as we have seen. " The carnal mind is enmity against God : for it is not subject to the law of God, neither indeed can be," Rom. 8 : 7. And that there may be no mistake in his meaning he says : " I delight in the law of God *after the inward man.*" The word rendered inward or *inner* is an adverb and means *within*. He delights in the law of

God after the *man within*. It is not some outward or carnal delight. We have precisely the same words rendered the *inner man* in Eph. 3:16. What do they mean there? What can they mean but the *renewed heart of man?* They are very explicit: " That he would grant you according to the riches of his glory, to be strengthened with might by his Spirit in the *inner man*." Does not this mean the new nature, the new creature, the new man? Is not that what needs *strengthening?* Is it not that which is strengthened *with might by the Spirit?* Paul was not praying that their natural faculties might be invigorated, but that their gracious habits and principles might be increased in power. Then we have a cognate adverb, just the same as this except in termination and rendered as in Rom. 7:22. "For which cause we faint not; but though our outward man perish, yet the *inward* man is renewed day by day." Does this mean that the natural faculties were growing while the body was decaying? Surely not. Often the mental powers of aged Christians are daily losing their vigor, while they are rapidly ripening for heaven, and their gracious characters are becoming exceedingly refined, elevated and invigorated. The third of these remarkable expressions concerning the law is this: "So then with the mind I myself serve the law." Here *mind* evidently means the same as the *inward man* in v. 22; for although the word does often mean the *understanding*, yet it also means the controlling moral character of the man; and so we read of a "reprobate mind," "the renewing of your mind," "the vanity of their mind," "fleshly mind," "men of corrupt minds," Rom. 1:28; 12:2; Eph. 4:17; Col. 2:18; 2 Tim. 3:8. In Eph. 4:23, Paul says, "And be renewed in the spirit of your *mind*." Here the very same word is used as in Rom. 7:25. Evidently the meaning is, my heart goes out after the law and truly engages me to serve it. That he means as much as this is evident from the use of the two pronouns, *I myself*. There is no dispute concerning the Greek text. There ought to be none about the rendering. We have quite the same in these places: "It is *I myself*," Luke 24:39; "I could wish that *myself* were accursed," Rom. 9:3; "*I myself* am persuaded," Rom. 15:14; "Now *I* Paul *myself* beseech you," 2 Cor. 10:1; "*I myself* was not burdensome to you," 2 Cor. 12:13. If anything can settle entire identity these words must be allowed that power. *Serve*, the same verb so rendered in Rom. 6:6; 7:6. Its cognate noun is rendered *servant* in Rom. 1:1; 6:16, 17, 20. It expresses subjection and obedience. "His servants ye are to whom ye obey." Here it expresses the willing service rendered to the precepts of God's law. I am *minded* to keep God's law. My soul by divine grace is set on this thing. My new nature inclines me that way. I do it. I myself do it.

In these verses are many other things, which can by no fair interpretation be applied to an unregenerate man, as the reader will see in the exposition. But it has been shown that there are three such. One ought to be sufficient for the purpose of satisfying a fair mind.

8. In these twelve verses there is nothing said, which may not enter into the experience of a regenerate man; nothing said stronger than is said of good men by themselves or by others in various parts of scripture. This will of course be more and more manifest as we consider in detail the several verses. At this time attention is called to several direct declarations of God's word on the matter of human imperfection. " There is no man that sinneth not," 1 Kings 8 : 46. If possible the following language is still stronger: "There is not a just man upon earth that doeth good, and sinneth not," Ecc. 7 : 20. " Who can understand his errors? cleanse thou me from secret faults," Ps. 19 : 12. " Who can say, I have made my heart clean, I am pure from my sins? " Pr. 20 : 9. " In many things we offend all," Jas. 3 : 2. " If we say that we have no sin, we deceive ourselves and the truth is not in us," 1 John 1 : 8. In like manner the best of mere men in telling us their thoughts of themselves use language as strong as any Paul employs in Rom. 7 : 14–25. After unusual discoveries of the glory, majesty and holiness of God, Job says: " I abhor myself and repent in dust and ashes," Job 42 : 6. David in several penitential Psalms bewails his depravity, and pleads for mercy. " Peter fell down at Jesus' knees, saying, Depart from me; for I am a sinful man, O Lord," Luke 5 : 8. Elsewhere Paul thus speaks of himself, " Not as though I had already attained, either were already perfect," Phil. 3 : 12. There is as much strength in these expressions as in any found in Rom. 7 : 14–25. If Paul says, " The evil that I would not, that I do ;" David says, " Iniquities prevail against me." If Paul says, " O wretched man that I am ;" Isaiah says, " Wo is me ! for I am undone; because I am a man of unclean lips." If Paul says, " I know that in me (that is in my flesh,) dwelleth no good thing ;" Isaiah says, " We are all as an unclean thing, and all our righteousnesses are as filthy rags; and we all do fade as a leaf; and our inquities, like the wind, have taken us away," Isa. 64 : 6. If Paul here says of himself, " The good that I would, I do not ;" he elsewhere says the same of the churches in a whole province : " The flesh lusteth against the spirt, and the spirit against the flesh ; and these are contrary the one to the other; so that ye cannot do the things that ye would," Gal. 5 : 17. Instead, therefore,

of regarding a man as a bad man because he has a deep sense of
his own vileness and weakness, the scriptures teach us to form an
estimate just the reverse. Perhaps no one has ever dared to say
that Job was an unregenerate man because he said, " Behold, I
am vile; what shall I answer thee? I will lay my hand upon my
mouth," Job 40 : 4. The very book that says of Job that he was
" perfect and upright, and one that feared God, and eschewed
evil," yea, God himself said, " There is none like him," Job 1 : 1, 8,
brings that good man before us saying : " If I wash myself in snow
water, and make my hands never so clean ; yet shalt thou plunge
me in the ditch, and mine own clothes shall abhor me," Job 9 : 30,
31. The fact is that no man's piety goes beyond his humility.
Saul of Tarsus, though a murderer of holy men and women, was
full of self-complacency ; but Paul the apostle says, " I am not
worthy to be called an apostle," " I am less than the least of all
saints ;" and, just before he leaves the world, " I am the chief of
sinners." The worse a man is the better he thinks himself to be.
The better a man is, the lower is his estimate of his own righteousness. The more the light shines into an apartment, the easier it
is to see millions of particles of dust before unperceived. To interpret Rom. 7 : 14-25 aright, it must be remembered that it is a
complaint, that the apostle is bitterly bemoaning his state, and
that his language is that of a heart-broken penitent, every word of
which is felt to be true, as he stands in the presence of omniscient
purity. Such notes are never heard from the Pharisee, from the
careless, nor from the unregenerate. Wardlaw : " We never expect to hear an unrenewed man bewailing his carnality and opposition to the divine law, as through the whole of the passage before
us, this writer does. But on the other hand, the more truly holy
a person becomes—the more spiritual in mind and affections, the
stronger will be his impressions of the evil of sin, and of his own
sin, and of the extent of his disconformity to the character and
law of God. . . As a man advances in holiness, corruption at the
same time remaining in him, he will be disposed to express his
abhorrence of himself in exceedingly strong and vehement terms,
in proportion as the loathing of the spiritual nature is experienced
as regards everything that is evil." Fraser : " The expressions
here are not used by another concerning a person historically ; but
by himself in the way of bitter regret and complaint. A man may
in this way, and in the bitterness of his heart, say very strong
things concerning himself and his condition, which it were unjust
and absurd for another to say of him, in giving his character historically." The renewed and experienced Christian knows the
plague of his own heart, and speaks of himself in much lowliness

as of sincerity, as of God, in the sight of God. It is no mock
humility. Every word he utters respecting his own sinfulness is
sincere and is true. By the Holy Spirit he is taught how exceedingly broad is the commandment. And yet in the main his walk
before men is upright, and it would be mere uncharitableness for
other men, not inspired, to charge him with what his own heart
and the Most High know he is chargeable with before God.

9. Stuart insists that it is "a fundamental point in the interpretation of the whole" that Rom. 7 : 7–25 is plainly a comment on
Rom. 7 : 5 ; and that Rom. 8 : 1–17 is plainly a comment on Rom.
7 : 6; and that there is plainly and certainly an antithesis between
Rom. 7 : 7–25 and Rom. 8 : 1–25. This is a favorite postulate of
writers of the same school. It takes for granted that Rom. 7 : 5 is
in antithesis with Rom. 7 : 6, and then that Rom. 7 : 7–25 is a comment on Rom. 7 : 5, in antithesis with the comment on Rom. 7 : 6
found in Rom. 8 : 1–17. To maintain this mode of explanation
they take for granted that there are such comments and antitheses,
and give their exposition accordingly, and then from their exposition prove that there are such comments and antitheses. The first
objection to this mode of explanation is that it is a mere assumption,
the text and context hinting no such thing. A second objection
is that it is a very awkward kind of assumption, making the apostle lay down a truth, then drop it, and lay down another, then drop
it, and then argue the first at the length of 18 verses, and then
drop it, and without any hint to that effect take up the second and
argue it. A third objection is that this assumption takes no notice
of the change of tense at v. 14. It is a fatal objection that antithesis is assumed for exposition and the exposition is cited to prove
antithesis. Wardlaw well says : "This is not fair," and quotes some
one as saying : "A particular interpretation cannot first be assumed to make out the antithesis, and then the antithesis be assumed to justify the interpretation." In other words, we cannot
argue in a circle. So the "fundamental point in the interpretation" of this passage wholly vanishes out of sight. It will not
bear its own weight.

10. Another demand often made by writers of the same class
is that we shall look upon Paul as endeavoring to allay prejudice
by using soft words, and by insinuating offensive truth into the
minds of the prejudiced. Thus Whitby : "He saith not, you that
are under the law are carnal, but representing what belonged to
them in his own person, and so taking off the harshness, and molli-
fying the invidiousness of the sentence, by speaking of it in his
own person, he saith, I am carnal, sold under sin." He cites
Photius and Oecumenius as endorsing this sentiment. Others fol-

low Whitby. Now what is the truth respecting Paul's course as
to candor and the avoiding of prejudice? 1. None will deny that
he displayed consummate ministerial address. He availed himself
of all lawful and fair means to allay prejudices, and to commend
his Master's cause. 2. We have no proof that Paul ever resorted
to the arts of the sophists or orators of ancient times to win favor
to himself, or to avoid odium on account of the character of the
doctrines he was called to preach. Himself says, we "have renounced the hidden things of dishonesty, not walking in craftiness,
nor handling the word of God deceitfully; but by manifestation
of the truth, commending ourselves to every man's conscience in
the sight of God," 2 Cor. 4 : 2. Much more does he say to the
same effect. 3. In this epistle Paul has everywhere else displayed
great candor, and entire fearlessness in directly stating the doctrines of the gospel most offensive to Pharisaic pride and Jewish
prejudice. Why should he now begin to mince matters, or to
speak by indirection, and that on a point surely not more calculated to give offence than others, which he had stated in the plainest
manner and the most direct terms? If, as some contend, Paul was
addressing Jews already converted to Christianity, he had already
informed them that they were dead to the law, and were delivered
from the law, vs. 4, 6. There is nothing here to offend them, if
Paul is speaking of a man under law, and not under grace. None
will contend that Paul is here addressing unbelieving Jews. If he
had been, his language would have been of a very different sort,
as we know from samples left us of his addresses to such. Had this
epistle been sent to such, they would doubtless have consented
that Paul was even a worse man than any fair exposition of this
chapter could make him appear. 4. "If it be allowed, that, on
some occasions, Paul doth in very few words express arguments,
objections and reproaches used by others against himself, his doctrine or conduct; yet in every such case the thing evidently appears by the obvious import of the expressions, and by the
answers immediately subjoined; so that there is no room left for
mistaking." All such cases are very different from a discourse
running through twelve verses, and peculiarly marked as pertaining to himself.

   11. It is remarkable that while in these twelve verses Paul constantly speaks of his *will* (as much as six or seven times) and of his
delight (one of the highest pleasurable affections), yet of all those
who hold that he is here speaking of an unregenerate man, few,
perhaps none, pay any serious attention to the true state of case,
and generally hold that when he says anything good of himself
he is merely telling what his reason and conscience urge and de-

mand. So Stuart: " Nothing can be more unfounded, than the supposition that moral good is put to the account of the sinner, merely because one assigns to him reason to discern its nature, and conscience to approve it." The context shows that all he admits this man to have is what is here expressed, some intellect and some conscience. To admit that the man here spoken of had a *will* to that, which is good, would be fatal to his interpretation. And yet it is the *will* Paul chiefly speaks of, and never here once in any form mentions his conscience. Nor is this the course of one scholar merely. It seems to have been so generally.   Grotius took the same course. And Fraser, who died in 1769, says the same course was pursued in his day: " They, who hold this interpretation, do most commonly seem to understand by what good is here ascribed to the unregenerate, no more than the light of reason in the mind or understanding; with the urgent testimony for duty, and against sin, that is in the conscience of the unregenerate, with different degrees of light and force."   Should we apply this mode of explanation to other parts of scripture what sad havoc we should make of the truth. In Rom. 1 : 13 Paul says: " I *would* not have you ignorant," etc. In Rom. 16 : 19 he says : " I *would* have you wise." Does he mean no more than that his reason and conscience are in favor of their being wise and intelligent? or does he not declare that his heart was set upon their making these attainments? Many other cases where the same verb is used might be cited with as much pertinency as those just given. Of a like character is the attempt to ignore all the significancy of the word *delight*. Whitby thus paraphrases the words, " I delight in the law of God," " my mind approving for some time, and being pleased with its good and holy precepts."   In like manner expositions of this scripture by writers of the same school do much tend to show that the apostle meant very little by anything he said unless it is something that can be used to show that he is speaking of one unregenerate.

12. A number of writers, who in the main expound these twelve verses of an unregenerate man, do yet admit that in them are many things that a true Christian might say and think of himself. This has been done to such an extent that Olshausen actually proposes an interpretation which shall show " what is right and what erroneous" in these two classes. He has probably satisfied very few that his middle way is feasible. But that is not the matter now before us. His testimony to the concessions of others is striking: " After Spener, Franke, Bengel, Gottfreid Arnold, Zinzendorf, the words of the apostle were again begun to be explained of the state before regeneration, and Stier, Tholuck, Ruckert, De

Wette, Meyer follow them in their interpretation. These learned men nevertheless quite rightly acknowledge, that the Augustinian representation has also something true in it, since that in the life of the regenerate moments occur, in which they must speak entirely as Paul expresses himself here; and, moreover, as it is only by degrees that the transforming power of the gospel penetrates the different tendencies of the inner life, congenial phenomena extend through the whole life of the believer; and this leads to the thought, that the two views might admit of being united in a higher one. For it is little probable that men like Augustine and the reformers should have entirely erred in the conception of so important a passage." This quotation is weighty and important. It concedes as much as most sound interpreters would desire as the basis of an exposition.

13. If the exposition, to which we object, is correct, what need is there of divine grace to accomplish the salvation of unregenerate men? If a man, not under grace, can "consent to the law that it is good," can "delight in the law of God after the inward man," can himself "with his mind serve the law of God," can "hate" sin, can "will" all that God's word demands and enjoins, and can in the midst of his greatest conflicts with temptation and sin still sing out in triumph, "I thank God through Jesus Christ our Lord," there seems to be nothing left to be accomplished in setting one in the strait and narrow way that leads to life and peace. If "the moral powers of nature" can do all these things, why cannot these same moral powers without special grace go on and complete the work so happily begun? Encouragement would no doubt be acceptable to any one, moral suasion would certainly not be amiss, but surely they would not be essential. And if an unregenerate man himself without God's grace can do all these wonderful things, what could not a man do who was regenerate even if he were left to work his way without God's Spirit? Yet how differently do the scriptures speak. In one place Paul confesses the total inability of himself and his brethren even to think a good thought: "Not that we are sufficient of ourselves to think any thing as of ourselves; but our sufficiency is of God," 2 Cor. 3: 5. In another place he declares the inability of even Christians to approach God acceptably in prayer unless God teaches and helps 'them: "Likewise the Spirit also helpeth our infirmities: for we know not what we should pray for as we ought: but the Spirit itself maketh intercession for us with groanings which cannot be uttered," Rom. 8: 26. If even Christians and apostles converted and experienced, can neither think nor pray aright without special help from God, how shall an unregen-

erate man, " with his mind serve the law," which is holy, just and good, and which forbids all sin and enjoins all obedience pleasing to God: yes, and also "hate" all that is opposed to it, and "delight" (Stuart translates it *take pleasure*) "in the law of God after the inward man?" Fraser: "If a natural man, destitute of the Holy Spirit, can sincerely will, love, delight, and hate, as is here said; I would wish to know, what is left for divine grace to do in regeneration, according to the sentiments of these writers? What but external revelation, and moral suasion well inculcated, to give the proper excitement to the more languid will, inclination and affection towards holiness, which a man in nature hath, from rational nature itself, that these may exert themselves with due activity and force? This is divine grace, and the human will consenting to this suasion, and so exerting itself in practice, is, according to them, regeneration.

" Moral suasion must indeed have its own place, in dealing with rational creatures. They are not dealt with as stocks or stones under the hand of the mechanic. Conversion to God through Jesus Christ, and to holiness, is the consequence of proper evidence, and of proper motives. Conversion is the effect of suasion; but not of that merely: suasion is not of itself a cause adequate to such an effect in sinful men. In using that suasion, and that the proper evidence and motives should have effect on the hearts of men, there is needful the immediate operation and influence of divine power and grace on the hearts of men." How necessary God's almighty power and grace, and the effectual working of his Spirit are in regeneration the scriptures very fully declare, John 1 : 13 ; 3 : 5 ; Eph. 1 : 18–20 ; 3 : 7 ; Jas, 1 : 18. That the same power and grace are necessary to keep believers in the right way after regeneration is no less clear, John 10 : 28, 29 ; 1 Pet. 1 : 5 ; Jude 1. But how is this, if one not under grace can do all that is in Rom. 7 : 14–25 said to be done?

14. If the passage (Rom. 7 : 14–25) does not teach what is claimed for it by Whitby, Stuart, and that class of writers, it may be asked what does it teach? This is a fair question. The object in connection with the great argument of the apostle is very important indeed. He had demonstrated that justification was not and could not be by deeds of law; that it was by faith laying hold of the righteousness of Jesus Christ; that the fruits of gratuitous justification were exceedingly rich; that man's recovery by the second Adam, like his ruin by the first Adam, was by representation and covenant headship; that as a consequence believers are dead to sin and alive to God by Jesus Christ; that believers are dead to the law as a covenant; that when those,

who are now God's children, were unregenerate, they had a thorough experience of the impossibility of gaining by the law the mastery over their sins, but were by it only made acquainted with their number, guilt and power. This brings him to the end of the thirteenth verse of the seventh chapter of this epistle. Then in vs. 14–25 he shows the utter powerlessness of law to carry on the work of sanctification even in the hearts of renewed men, thus warning them against the legal spirit. Even in converted men mere precepts do not day by day renew the soul. That is peculiarly the effect of evangelical doctrine and truth. So that to believers Jesus Christ is of God made wisdom, and righteousness, and *sanctification*, and redemption. The capital error of the Galatian churches was that having begun in the gospel, they sought to be made perfect by the law, Gal. 3 : 3. They so changed their base of proceeding as to bring on themselves many and sore calamities, confusion, perplexity and loss of comfort. It must be so in every case. Hodge: " The law excites in the unrenewed mind opposition and hatred ; in the pious mind complacency and delight ; but in neither case can it break the power of sin, or introduce the soul into the true liberty of the children of God."

Let us now proceed to a consideration of the several verses.

14. *For we know that the law is spiritual : but I am carnal, sold under sin. We know*, we, Christians generally, have no doubt on the point. All admit it. It is one of the truths learned in the early stages of a saving acquaintance with the gospel. Some prefer to read *I know indeed* and the Greek admits either. The change does not affect the sense of the context. *The law is spiritual*, the context shows that it is the moral law of which he speaks. *Spiritual*, a word found in the New Testament as much as twenty-five times. It is sometimes the opposite of natural. Thus speaking of the human body in death and the resurrection Paul says: " It is sown a natural body ; it is raised a spiritual body," 1 Cor. 15 : 44. Compare 1 Cor. 2 : 14, 15. Sometimes it is the opposite of secular or temporal. " If we have sown unto you spiritual things, is it a great thing if we shall reap your carnal things?" 1 Cor. 9 : 11. The context shows that he is speaking of the temporal support of ministers of the gospel. Compare Rom. 15 : 27. In both these verses we may read secular or temporal as the opposite of spiritual, and we shall get the sense. So when Paul speaks of *spiritual songs* he designates not only such as were the opposite of lascivious, profane, or idolatrous, but such as were the opposite of secular, witty, amusing, though they might be free from any thing wicked. Then it is used to designate things the opposite of material, which material things set forth blessings

or privileges provided by Christ. So we read of spiritual meat, spiritual drink and spiritual Rock, 1 Cor. 10 : 3, 4, a spiritual house and spiritual sacrifices, 1 Pet. 2 : 5. Spiritual is also an epithet applied to consistent Christians, who by the Spirit of God have attained a good degree of holiness and stability. Thus Paul says : " I brethren could not speak unto you as unto spiritual, but as unto carnal, even as unto babes in Christ," 1 Cor. 3 : 1. Here spiritual designates a strong or matured believer in opposition to a feeble one. The word spiritual evidently has the same meaning in Gal. 6 : 1. Sometimes the word simply means pertaining to spirits as where we read of spiritual wickedness, Eph. 6 : 12. But what is the precise meaning of the word here? Wardlaw : " Spiritual, as contrasted with carnal, evidently signifies not only the law's reaching to the inward thoughts, affections and desires ; but its perfection of accordance in all that it requires, both inwardly and outwardly, with the character and mind of God's Spirit, as opposite to the moral corruption of man's fallen nature, called the flesh." Stuart : " The law enjoins those things which are agreeable to the mind of the Spirit." Owen of Thrussington : " As *carnal* means what is sinful and corrupt, so spiritual imports what is holy, just and good." Hodge : " The word spiritual is here expressive· of general excellence, and includes all that is meant by holy, just and good." The ideas of excellence, holiness, justness and goodness are in scripture always connected with the law of God, but we must on no account drop the idea that the law is spiritual in the sense of being a discerner of the thoughts and intents of the heart. It was by this means that Paul formerly received conviction of the true nature and terrible extent of sin as stated, vs. 8–12. *I am carnal.* In considering the word spiritual, we have seen that the opposite in some cases is carnal. See also above on Rom. 3 : 20 where the cognate noun *flesh* is explained. So here Paul admits the excellence of the law and his own vileness. If the law is holy, he is sadly deficient in holiness. If it is just, he sees he is far from being personally righteous as the law requires. If it is good, he is so evil as to be a loathing to himself. In considering 1 Cor. 3 : 1 it has been shown that the word carnal does sometimes mean comparatively carnal. Paul might say, *I am carnal*, compared with the perfect and holy law of God, compared with my own imperfect perceptions of what the law demands, compared with what I sincerely desire to be. See also 1 Cor. 3 : 3, 4. To be *carnal* is not in scripture the same as to be in the flesh ; for Paul addresses the Corinthians as *brethren*, which he would not have done, if he had regarded them as unregenerate. Surely this place demonstrates that saints, brethren, may in some respects be sadly carnal, even in the eyes of other good and charitable men.   Much more may a man in his own eyes have many remains of sin in him.   So that he may truly utter the complaint of this verse *Sold under sin.*   There were two classes of slaves.   One was so by voluntary act.   Provision was made for men becoming so in the Jewish commonwealth, Ex. 21 : 6.   Such were willing slaves. They preferred that state to freedom.   If they had any good principles they served their masters with a will.   Ahab was like one of these, in this that it was his own perverse and continued choice to work wickedness.   He sold himself to work evil in the sight of the Lord, 1 Kings 21 : 20, 25.   God tells us of others who willingly and greedily wrought evil and so sold themselves to do evil, 2 Kings 17 : 17.   The other way of being a slave was without the consent of the slave.   He was sold for debt, or as a prisoner of war.   In no sense did he sell himself; yet he had a master whom he was forced to serve.   He did so reluctantly, wishing all the time that he should be free from his master.   This was the servitude of Paul.   He *hated* his tyrant, indwelling sin, and hoped to be wholly free in God's good time ; but now he was a captive.

15. *For that which I do I allow not ; for what I would, that do I not ; but what I hate that I do.* For *allow* Stuart reads *approve.* The original is literally *know*, but must here be taken, as the word often is, in the sense of allowing, approving, or owning as friends, Matt. 7 : 23 ; 2 Cor. 5 : 21 ; 2 Tim. 2 : 19 ; 1 John 3 : 1.   When he says *that which I do I allow not*, he does not mean all that he does, but whatever he does in his spiritual captivity.   He did not mean to say that he did not approve of praying, preaching, and serving Christ ; but he says that in the service he renders to God there is such deficiency as fills him with shame and self-reproach.   The same limitation must be applied to the next clause : *for what I would, that do I not*, q. d. the will of my renewed nature is to serve God perfectly ; I wish to be entirely holy, and do God's will as the angels and spirits of just men made perfect in heaven do.   But I continually come short of even my own standard, and certainly I come short of the law of God.   *But what I hate, that do I.*   Every translation at hand has *hate*.   The Greek admits of no other rendering.   No unregenerate man hates sin, abhors himself for it, repenting in dust and ashes.   It is sometimes said that the three verbs in this verse rendered *do* must exclusively refer to external acts.   But the context clearly uses them of acts of the mind and heart.   Every experienced Christian knows that when he has made the greatest attainments in holiness, he has the deepest sense of his own vileness.   Hodge : " The language of this verse may not be metaphysical, though it is perfectly correct language.   It is the

language of common life, which as it proceeds from the common consciousness of men, is often a better indication of what that consciousness teaches than the language of the schools."

16. *If then I do that which I would not, I consent unto the law that it is good.* He does not say, nor mean to intimate that he is not responsible for his failures, much less does he deny that his failures are sinful. But he does declare that all the time his conflict is going on, his better, his new nature resisted temptation. In proof he gave his hearty *consent to the law*, which is the standard of moral exccllence. On *consenting to the law* see above preliminary remarks No. 7. Hodge: " To disapprove and condemn what the law forbids, is to assent to the excellence of the law."

17. *Now then it is no more I that do it, but sin that dwelleth in me.* The apostle could not more decidedly adhere to the profession of his confidence in the reality of his great change from a state of nature to a state of grace. It was not he, not his new nature, not his better part, that did wrong or failed to do right. No! it was the old man, the fallen nature, the flesh that thus involved him in trouble. Fraser: " It is reasonable to consider it as a fixed point, that to consent to the goodness of the law, as it is spiritual, giving rule to men's spirits, which is the apostle's special view in this place, is far from the disposition of any unregenerated soul." Could words more clearly state that the Christian man Paul, whom he calls *I* was truly sincere, and his heart in the main right with God? It was sin that gave all the trouble, not Paul's new nature.

18. *For I know that in me (that is, in my flesh,) dwelleth no good thing: for to will is present with me; but* how *to perform that which is good I find not.* Divine grace makes a wonderful change, long before it brings its subjects to spotless purity and angelic perfection. The unrenewed sinner's heart is fully set in him to do evil, he will not accept the gospel offer. His will and affections are bent to evil. The remains of this sinful nature, called the flesh, had in it no good thing. It did not see, or think, or feel, or purpose, or act aright. But Paul's will, in his new nature, was right. If he could have had his way he never would have sinned any more. Grace wrought this change, and it was a great one. But he had such temptations, and sin was so urgent and instant that he often found himself unable to carry out his best volitions and purposes, at least to the degree which the law justly demanded. That *willing* what is holy is a fruit of God's spirit and is proof of the presence of divine grace is evident from Phil. 2 : 13, " It is God that worketh in you both to *will* and to do of his good pleasure." Here is a direct and unmistakeable assertion that we are as dependent on divine grace for a right will as for anything else.

19. *For the good that I would, I do not : but the evil which I would not, that I do.* He still maintains that his *will* is for the good, for *would* is the same verb and in precisely the same form as in v. 18 is rendered *will*. Stuart does not alter the force of the argument by substituting *desire* for *would* in this verse. For real hearty desires after holiness prove a man to have been born again. On this verse some, who plead for the application of the passage to an unregenerate man, bring many quotations from heathen authors to show that what Paul says of himself here might be said of a man not under grace. And it is freely admitted that conscience has often mightily moved men in favor of the right, and that at times they are full of grief for misconduct, which has brought on them much disappointment and vexation. But when was the will of the unrenewed man ever set on the good? when did he earnestly desire holiness?

20. *Now if I do that I would not, it is no more I that do it, but sin that dwelleth in me.* This is nearly a repetition of v. 17. The object of saying the matter again probably is to remove all doubt on the point that Paul speaks as a Christian, having the will of his new nature right before God, and yet unwillingly led into sad imperfections. Arminius has labored to show that the word *dwelleth* found here signifies the possession of dominion. If he had succeeded in his argument, it would have been fatal to the interpretation maintained in this work. It is true that the indwelling of the Holy Spirit does always *imply* dominion over the soul, Rom. 8 : 9, 11 ; 1 Cor. 3 : 16. This results from the sovereign authority and glorious nature of the third person of the Trinity. But that there is no such idea as sovereign sway involved in the word dwell is perfectly manifest. In 1 Cor. 7 : 12 Paul says: " If any brother hath a wife that believeth not, and she be pleased to *dwell* with him, let him not put her away." Surely he does not mean that the wife should rule her husband. Here we have the same word rendered dwell as in our verse. The only idea essentially connected with the word dwelling is habitation, as every scholar must see on examining the word and its cognates.

21. *I find then a law, that, when I would do good, evil is present with me. I find,* I have experience of the fact. With me it is no matter of conjecture, nor of vague theory. I have the sad reality to deal with. I find a *law;* in v. 20 he told us what this law was— " sin that dwelleth in me." The term *law* here denotes a powerful principle. Owen of Oxford: " It is not an outward, written, commanding, directing law, but an inbred, working, impelling, urging law. A law proposed to us is not to be compared for efficacy to a law inbred in us." By the power of divine grace we are set free

from the dominion but not from the annoyance of sin. The tribes of Canaanites were not the Lords of Palestine after the days of Joshua, but they still dwelt in the land and greatly tempted, vexed and harassed the people of God. In the unregenerate this law is unbroken in its power. They obey it habitually and promptly. Their wills yield to its demands. In the regenerate its dominion is cast off, but it still has great force to mar their good works, and hinder their conformity to God. It does not lord it over the saints, but it seduces them. It is terribly deceitful and terribly wicked. That we may thus understand the word law, as synonymous with inward, urging principle is clear. See v. 23 and compare Rom. 8 : 2. This law has power in a renewed man, one that *would do good*, one the prevailing inclinations of whose will are right. As Owen says this indwelling sin 'is a law or power in believers, but it is not a law unto them.' It meets not their approval; it commends not itself to their consciences, nor to their spiritual tastes. They were once fully under its dominion; but that is now broken. Yet old habits of sinning, the weakness of grace and the urgency of temptation do still give it much power, to annoy, vex and betray the soul. The apostle specially mentions the urgency of sin. *Evil is present with me.* The tow is always in our hearts, so long as our sanctification is incomplete, and we know not at what moment the enemy may hurl his fiery darts.

22. *For I delight in the law of God after the inward man.* For an explanation of the terms and phrases of this verse, see above preliminary remarks No. 7. *The law of God* certainly includes the ten commandments as explained in scripture. Sometimes law is a name given to the whole word of God, of which his preceptive will forms an important part. For *delight* Taylor of Norwich has *esteem*. But this is trifling. That this verse describes the exercises of a renewed man is as clear as any mark of regeneration laid down in scripture. If an unregenerate man can delight in the law of God, why cannot he love God supremely and his neighbor equally ? why cannot he love the brethren and do every thing else required of men ? The fact is the carnal mind is enmity against God : it is not subject to his law. How then can it delight in anything holy ? for the law is to us the standard of holiness.

23. *But I see another law in my members, warring against the law of my mind, and bringing me into captivity to the law of sin which is in my members.* Here again we have the word *law* in the same sense as in v. 21 ; and in contrast with the *law of God* in v. 22. *Members*, the same word so rendered in Rom. 6 : 13, 19 ; 7 : 5, on which see above. *Warring against*, the word is literally rendered. Indwelling sin never reasons or remonstrates but seduces, de-

ceives, wages war, and commits acts of violence. It arrays its whole forces against the inner man, or new creature, *the law of the mind*, established in regeneration. God had so far fulfilled the provisions of the covenant as to write the law on Paul's heart, Jer. 31 : 33 ; Heb. 8 : 10. Yet the remains of his fallen nature brought him into the condition of an unwilling captive, who felt the force though he hated the power of that which kept him in bondage. The law of his mind was utterly contrary to the law of sin. Though the latter had long had possession, yet it had no longer in any sense a right there. All it claimed and controlled was by usurpation. Wardlaw : " *Bringing me into captivity* has been interpreted as if it signified that he was uniformly overcome, actually brought into full captivity. But it expresses no such thing, as that the power of corruption was either uniformly, or even prevailingly successful. Similar expressions are used to denote a tendency that has not effect. It was the case with the apostle, and it is the case with every saint of God, that he feels this law in his members bringing him, i. e. he feels it to be its constant tendency to bring him into captivity ; so that were it not resisted by ' the law of his mind,' by the energy of the new man under the influence of the Spirit of God, such would infallibly be its effect." This is all that can fairly be educed from these words. Thus much they do certainly teach. The same truth is expressly set forth in Gal. 5 : 17. Some have cited Ezek. 24 : 13 as conveying the same truth. Possibly it does, but it fairly admits of another exposition.

24. *O wretched man that I am ! who shall deliver me from the body of this death ? Wretched*, the word occurs but once more in the New Testament, Rev. 3 : 17, and is rendered as here. The cognate noun occurs twice and is rendered *misery*, Rom. 3 : 16 ; as. 5 : 1. The cognate verb occurs once and is rendered, *Be afflicted*, Jas. 4 : 9. It expresses extreme unhappiness. Rheims has *unhappie*. The language is so strong that some have said it cannot possibly apply to the Christian for he is happy not wretched. Wardlaw well says: " It is truly marvellous that such an argument should ever have been used. One is strongly tempted to suspect that he by whom such an argument could be used, can never himself have felt the burden of corruption, the plagues of his own heart. Is it not the very man whose heart is most under the influence of holiness and the love of God that feels most acutely the anguish of a sense of remaining corruption?" The fact is these words express the same idea made familiar to us by patriarchs and prophets, as has been already shown. In this whole section the apostle has not been expressing an apprehension of

wrath for unpardoned sin, but a sense of self-loathing on account of indwelling corruption. The word rendered *deliver* has not before occured in this epistle. It is very strong. Owen of Thrussington says it means to pluck out, rescue, take away by force, and is applied to a forcible act, effected by power. By *the body of this death* some understand this mortal body, and think the speaker here was expressing a wish to die. But such an exposition certainly does not suit Paul. He himself tells us that on the subject of dying he was in a strait, Phil. 1 : 23, 24. Nor does it suit the case of an awakened unregenerate man ; for he, who rightly sees his sins and does not behold the Lamb of God, is for very good cause, the best cause in the world, both afraid and unwilling to die and meet God in judgment. His cry " is not the utterance of despair, but of longing and vehement desire." The next verse clearly shows this. By the body of this death others understand the body of sin consisting of the members; Hall: " the mass of inward corruption ;" Stuart : " the seat of carnal and sinful principles ;" Hodge: " it may be taken metaphorically for sin considered as a body." Some give an illustration of the conception in the apostle's mind by referring us to an ancient mode of punishment resorted to in some cases, where the culprit—perhaps a murderer—was punished by having a dead human body fastened firmly to his own, limb to limb, and then the criminal turned loose. Soon the stench was horrible ; soon the virus of the corrupting body communicated its deadly poison, and a horrible though not a very speedy death ensued. No doubt Paul was aware of this practice. Nor is it improbable that he here alludes to it. So think Scott, Clarke and others.

25. *I thank God through Jesus Christ our Lord. So then with my mind I myself serve the law of God; but with the flesh the law of sin.* Fraser : " I thank God, who hath provided comfort for me with respect to this my present wretchedness, through Jesus Christ our Lord : by virtue of whose cross the old man in me is crucified : which gives me the sure and delightful prospect, that this body of sin and death shall, in due time, be absolutely destroyed, and I completely and for ever delivered from it." This paraphrase seems to cover very much the ground of thankfulness here expressed. This language puts the grace of Christ in strong contrast with the rigors of law and its powerlessness to aid a sinner in his conflict with inbred sin. For many verses the apostle had been describing the great conflict of his renewed nature with indwelling sin, the law yielding him no help in the fight, until at last he utters that bitter cry, *O wretched man !* But he lets us see that he is not in despair. He yields not to the enemy, but direct-

ing the eye of his faith to the great *Deliverer*, he says the first cheerful word we have had for many verses: I thank God through
Jesus Christ our Lord.   Instead of *I thank God*, the Vulgate,
Wiclif, Rheims, Doway, Locke and others, following the Cler-
mont, and other Greek manuscripts read, *the grace of God*.   This
requires but a slight change in the Greek and gives a good sense.
Paul says, Who shall deliver me?   The answer is, The grace of
God through or by Jesus Christ our Lord shall deliver me.   But
we do virtually get the same idea from the authorized version.
Sanctification, no more than justification, is by the law, but both
of them are by grace, which is in Christ Jesus our Lord.   But for
the gospel men might well despair of pardon, acceptance, any fitness for communion with God, or any victory over sin.   Pleasant
as this theme is he dwells no longer on it, but reverts to the burden of the paragraph.   *So then with the mind*, with the will, with
the person so often called *I*, with the inward man, with the *law of
my mind*, with the affection of *delight*, which so influences cheerful
obedience, *I myself*, I Paul, who *hate* sin, and *will* what is good,
serve the law of God.   In this I am not deceived, nor am I a
deceiver—I am no hypocrite—my heart is truly engaged—I love
the law—my most animating hope is that I shall be as holy as the
law requires; *but with the flesh*, with *sin*, with *another law* in my
members, I serve the law of sin.   This warfare I have, and expect
to have, till I close my earthly career.   But I will fight on.   I
shall never be satisfied till I awake in the likeness of the Redeemer.
Some have objected to the general view taken of these verses that
no man can serve two masters.   And it is true that no man can in
the same sense and to the same extent serve two masters.   But
neither of these things occurred with Paul.   Sin had not dominion
over him, though it had power against him.   He did highly and
prevailingly please Christ, and did not willingly or habitually
serve sin.   He was imperfect, but not a hypocrite, a true penitent,
not a self-deceiver.

DOCTRINAL AND PRACTICAL REMARKS

1. There is such a thing as religious experience, and it is
dangerous to treat it with contempt or despite, vs. 14–25.   No
man has any more piety which will stand the tests of the last day,
than has made itself felt in the depths of his nature.   One may be
a real child of God without having yet experienced all Paul felt;
but as he advances in the divine life, he will know more and more
of what is here described.   Scott: "Every believer knows a little
of the things spoken of by the apostle in these verses, when he

first flees for refuge to the hope of the gospel: but his subsequent experience gives him still further insight into them." Owen of Thrussington: "The apostle says nothing here of himself, but what every real Christian finds to be true. It was the saying of a good man, lately gone to his rest, whose extended pilgrimage was ninety-three years, that he must often have been swallowed up by despair, had it not been for the seventh chapter of the epistle to the Romans. The best interpreter of many things in scripture is spiritual experience." Hawker: "Blessed and eternal SPIRIT! I praise thee for the account, which thou hast caused thy servant the apostle to give of himself in this sweet chapter." True, indeed, much odium has been cast on the subject of Christian experience by the ignorance, folly, and self-conceit of some, who have spoken much on the matter. But it is not wise to give up any thing vital in religion because it has sometimes been abused.

2. There is a vast difference between sin indulged and sin resisted, between corruption nourished and corruption lamented. This marks one of the prominent distinctions between good and bad men in this world. No two things are more contrary to each other than sin and grace, the flesh and the spirit. Chalmers: "In the case of an unconverted man, the flesh is weak and the spirit is *not* willing; and so there is no conflict—nothing that can force those outcries of shame and remorse and bitter lamentation, that we have in the passage before us. With a Christian the flesh is weak too but the spirit is willing; and under its influence there must from the necessary connection that there is between the human faculties, there must from the desires of his heart be such an efflux of doings upon his history, as shall make his life distinguishable in the world, and most distinguishable on the day of judgment from the life of an unbeliever." The difference between the weakest of converted men and the most amiable of the unregenerate is the difference between friendship and hostility to God. Wardlaw: "Indulged corruption, indeed, may and ought to lead to doubt and despair. But corruption itself should not. It should only lead us to have more constant and simple-hearted recourse to the blood of sprinkling, and to more earnest supplications for the restraining and sanctifying influences of the promised Spirit."

3. Christ's people may fall into melancholy and write more bitter things against themselves than the truth demands or allows; but even real, exemplary Christians, contemplated in the light of God's holy word and of Christ's perfect example, are poor creatures. So Paul judged of himself, vs. 14–25. So others judge of themselves. Fraser: "All professed Christians will acknowledge, that it is very consistent with a state of grace, to have much im-

perfection in holiness, and much remaining sinfulness.   Upon this view it is most reasonable to suppose, that the farther one is advanced in holiness, and the more his heart is truly sanctified, he will have the greater sensibility with regard to sin, and it must give him the more pain and bitterness."   Increase of sanctification is not increase of sanctimoniousness, nor is it marked by grimace, or pomp, or high self-estimation, but by humility, gentleness and modesty.

4. Let no man think his spiritual state good, who does not in his heart consent to the excellence of the law of God, vs. 14, 16, 22, 25.   If one objects to the perfection of that standard, the evidence against him is very strong.   Guyse: " How excellent is the moral law, as the rule of obedience!   In this view of it, it is unchangeably and everlastingly binding, and is fit and worthy to be so ; for it is all holy, just and good, and reaches to the thoughts of the heart, as well as to the actions of the life: it discovers and strictly forbids every sin, and stands clear of all charges of defect ;" aye, and of excess also.   Wardlaw: " The whole system of salvation by grace has its foundation in the absolute and immutable perfection of the law.   It is in this that the necessity of a scheme of grace originates."   The right estimate of the excellence of the law is necessary to a believer in many ways.   One is suggested by this section, viz. it keeps a good man from despair when he can look at that perfect rule of right, and say I esteem it right, I consent to it, I serve it, I delight in it.   No man in such a state of mind can ever be depressed beyond recovery.   He who looks on the law as all right and sin as hateful need not seriously doubt his own regeneration.

5. On the other hand, as Hodge says, " it is an evidence of an unrenewed heart to express or feel opposition to the law of God as though it were too strict ; or to be disposed to throw off the blame of our want of conformity to the divine will from ourselves upon the law as unreasonable."   When the boy, that would learn to write, finds fault with the perfection of the copy set him, and not with himself for his want of skill, there is but little hope that he will soon hold the pen of a ready writer, or ever become a proficient in the art of penmanship.   The illustration is easily applied.

6. Where the carnal nature has the mastery, and one is led captive by the devil at his will, and no hearty resistance is made to sin, there is no scriptural piety.   So teach the scriptures.   So, when rightly interpreted, teach these verses.   The reason, why the wicked lament not their state is not that it is good, but because it is very bad.   Owen of Oxford: " Many there are in the world who, whatever they may have been taught in the word, have

not a spiritual sense and experience of the power of indwelling sin, and that because they are wholly under the dominion of it. They find not that there is darkness and folly in their minds, because they are darkness itself, and darkness will discover nothing. They find not deadness and an indisposition in their hearts and wills to God, because they are dead wholly in trespasses and sins. They are at peace with their lusts, by being in bondage unto them." In human limbs and bodies insensibility attends mortification. One of the saddest signs in many is the entire absence of alarm respecting their spiritual affairs.

7. Let us watch carefully all our sentiments and opinions respecting the moral law. Low views of it are always injurious to piety. Let us always consent to it that it is good, and delight in it in our inmost souls, vs. 16, 22, Durham: "There was never so much matter and marrow, with so much admirably holy cunning, compended, couched and conveyed in so few words by the most laconic, concise, sententious and singularly significant spokesman in the world as we find in the moral law." Colquhoun: "If a man have not just and spiritual apprehensions of the holy law, he cannot have spiritual and transforming discoveries of the glorious gospel." T. Watson: "Though the moral law is not a Christ to justify us, yet it is a rule to instruct us." John Newton: "Ignorance of the nature and design of the law is at the bottom of most religious mistakes." It is not possible for man to tell whether Pharisaic self-righteousness in the letter of the law or Sadducean laxity concerning its obligation most effectually defeats God's benevolent design in giving us his perfect law.

8. It is a great thing to have a good will, rightly set, in the things of God, vs. 15, 16, 19–21. The state of the will decides the character. He, who wills what is evil, is evil. He, who wills what is good, is a renewed man. But a will is more than a wish. It is settled and controls the man, if not wholly, yet in the main. And a will to that, which is good, is the gift of grace.

9. Where inability results from a sinful nature or from sinful habits, it is itself sinful, and so is no excuse for a failure to do our whole duty. It is not by way of excuse, but in humiliation and self-abhorrence that Paul cries: "What I hate, that do I;" "how to perform that which is good I find not," etc. Let us beware how we spare, excuse or justify sin or imperfection. To us it is more dangerous in our own hearts than in the hearts of others. We have destroyed and cannot save ourselves. But we have done all this by sin; and sin is not a misfortune; it is a crime. Any course of reasoning that makes us think lightly of indwelling sin is false and detestable.

10. It is a popular, yet a gross error that to have strong inclinations to evil, if they gain not the mastery over us, evinces higher virtue than to live virtuously without such inclinations. Such a doctrine makes the virtuous principle in a renewed man more amiable than in an angel who never sinned, more amiable in an imperfect Christian than in the spirits of just men made perfect. Surely the virtue of him, who is my companion on a long journey and never meditates anything but kindness is far better than that of him who frequently harbors thoughts of robbing and murdering me, though he carries not out his plans.

11. Yet if we overcome evil principles, and have a deadly aversion to sin, and are not brought into willing captivity to evil, let us not be discouraged. He, who lives and dies fighting against sin, shall not lose his soul, but shall yet wear a conqueror's crown.

12. We cannot be too much on our guard against the lust of the eye, the lust of the flesh, the pride of life, and all the brood of unholy affections. T. Adam: " We are so accustomed to overlook the depravation of nature in coveting, or evil lusting, and so confident that it will not be laid to our charge, if it is in some measure resisted, and does not generally break out into gross acts of transgression, that for this reason we do not understand the apostle when he is imputing it to himself for sin, lamenting his bondage under it, exulting in the grace that is by Jesus Christ, and holding it forth to all as the necessary means of deliverance from the guilt that is upon us; and therefore fly to some other method of interpretation, as supposing neither him nor ourselves to be culpable on this account before God, and obnoxious to the sentence of his law on this account." He, who would avoid the worst evils must make war on the evils of his heart. Owen of Oxford: " Would you not dishonor God and his gospel, would you not scandalize the saints and ways of God, would you not wound your consciences and endanger your souls, would you not grieve the good and Holy Spirit of God, the author of all your comforts, would you keep your garments undefiled, and escape the woful temptations and pollutions of the days wherein we live, would you be preserved from the number of the apostates in these latter days; awake to the consideration of this cursed enemy [indwelling sin], which is the spring of all these and innumerable other evils, as also of the ruin of all the souls that perish in the world." " Dearly beloved, I beseech you as strangers and pilgrims, abstain from fleshly lusts, which war against the soul," 1 Pet. 2 : 11. Who ever lamented that he had watched and prayed too much?

13. Nor can we have too much jealousy over our own hearts,

nor too earnestly inquire into their state. "Grace is as sharp-sighted and searching, as it is humble and heart-humbling." It is but self-deception to think or hope that we shall be finally tested by any rules less rigorous than God has laid down in his word. Self-examination, not candidly conducted, can avail for no good thing.

14. In every stage and shape sin is horrible. It may be pardoned, and pardon is a great mercy, but forgiveness makes not sin the less detestable. We may confidently hope for final victory over it, but that abates nothing of its odiousness, vs. 23, 24. How could it be otherwise? If there were no hell, sin would be abominable. It is to be abhorred not because it is to be punished; but it is to be punished, because it is to be abhorred. How can one, who finds his best purposes crossed, his best desires frustrated, his best prayers followed by lapses into sin, but look with detestation on the *cause* of his wretchedness? In some things there is great danger of excess; but no man need fear that he loves God or hates sin excessively.

15. The doctrines of the power of indwelling sin and of the spiritual warfare, though true and of great importance, may be, and have been perverted and abused. How many, whose minds perceived their own errors, and whose consciences remonstrated against their evil courses, have pleaded that it was not they that did the evil, but sin that dwelt in them, while all the time they loved these hateful courses with an undivided heart. Their wills were not at all averse to the evil they practised. If a man laments not from the heart any evil still adhering to him; if he *allows* the evil he does; if he *hates* not sin in every shape; if he excuses wrong because it is in himself; if he serves the law in his members with a cheerful heart; if he longs not to be delivered from all sin, there is no solid ground of comfort for him in the experience of Paul here recorded.

16. Nor is it ever idle to inquire whether we have clear, just and growing views of the beauty of holiness. If we have not, we stand in great need of a change of heart. He, who sees nothing lovely in holiness, does not love it or practise it. An easy test on this point is furnished us in our feelings towards the law of God. Do we delight in it, in the whole of it, in all its precepts? v. 22. It is the standard of holiness.

17. There is one blessed truth relating to indwelling sin in believers, stated by Owen in his treatise: "The more they find its power, the less they will feel its effects." This sounds almost like a contradiction, but the children of wisdom know what it means. To them it is a cheering truth. "Proportionally to their discovery

of it, will be their earnestness for grace ; nor will it rise higher. All watchfulness and diligence in obedience will be answerable also thereunto."

18. The Christian is a wonder! He is a wonder unto many. He is a wonder to himself. He has glorious hopes, yet mortifying failures ; he has intense longings after holiness, yet is strangely led away from the right path in many things. 'The wrongs he does he knows not, he approves not, he excuses not, he palliates not.' The good he does, he does not of himself, but by the grace of God. Of course he boasts not of it as coming from his own sufficiency. With one breath he cries, O wretched man that I am ; with the next, Thanks be unto God. How amazing is that grace, which shall take away his divided heart, and give him one heart, one mind, one will, as he has now one God, one Redeemer, one Comforter.

19. It is vain to hope that an unrenewed man will understand aright the bitterness of a soul grieved for its own sins with a godly sorrow. Paul was no chicken-hearted man. He bore stripes, bonds, imprisonments, stonings, shipwrecks, perils by land and by sea, by robbers and by his countrymen ; he was hungry and thirsty and weary ; but none of these things moved him. Yea, when the sword hung over him, and he knew it was about to close his earthly existence for ever, he said 'I am ready ;' but when corruption displayed its deformities within him, his cry was piteous : O wretched man that I am, who shall deliver me from the body of this death? And there is so much corruption remaining in the best men on earth that a sight of it would extort a cry no less bitter. Brown : " Corruption seems no contemptible enemy unto believers." Nor is it to be despised. It has slain many mighty men. It has wounded many others, and they have gone lame all their days.

20. Most admit it is foolish and dangerous to seek justification by the law ; it is no less unwise or perilous to seek sanctification by the law. This Section proves this, if it proves anything. Brown : " As in and through Christ, we got the pardon of our sin ; so it is in and through him, who died, that he might sanctify and cleanse his church, and present her glorious without spot or wrinkle, holy and without blemish, that believers are kept up in the battle against corruption, so that they are not quite overthrown thereby, and that grace is always growing, and corruption decaying." Christ is all our salvation. Let him be all our desire.

21. Let every man, who would save his soul, make up his mind to warfare. There is no possibility of evading it. Compare Rom.

8 : 24 ; 2 Cor. 5 : 2–4. It has always been so. It is so now. It will be so to the end of time. Whoever would go to heaven must go against the tide of wordliness without and of indwelling sin within. Owen : " Never let us reckon that our work in contend- ing against sin, in crucifying, mortifying and subduing it, is at an end. . . Many conquerors have been ruined by their carelessness after a victory ; and many have been spiritually wounded after great success against this enemy. . . The heart hath a thousand wiles and deceits, and if we are in the least off from our watch, we may be sure to be surprised.'' It is always wise to cry, Search me, O God, and know me. Fight on, my soul, till death.

22. Sad as is the case of the believer, all will yet be well, he himself being judge. He is borne down but he is not borne away by trials ; he is encumbered, but not drowned in wordly lusts, he is grieved, but not in despair respecting his state. He knows God shall yet lift up his head above all his enemies round about. The final victory is sure and shall be glorious.

23. How sweet the rest of heaven will be—rest not merely from toil, and pain, and bereavement but above all from sins and temp- tations. " How reviving are the hopes of relief in Christ against these evils." Glory be to God, the battle may last all day, but it shall not last for ever. It may be fierce and terrific, but the issue is not doubtful.

24. All solid advantages and real profit in the spiritual conflict, yea, in the divine life, are only by and through Jesus Christ. This is right. It is just that he should have all the glory of all the vic- tories won by his elect. He is the Captain of their salvation. By him they conquer. To him they bow and give glory. He is worthy to receive power, and riches, and honor, and glory, and blessing, for ever and ever. Amen.

Chapter 17

ROMANS 8
VERSES 1–11

THE SAFETY OF BELIEVERS. THEY ARE JUSTI-FIED. THEY ARE SANCTIFIED. THE SPIRIT DWELLS IN THEM. THEY DIFFER FROM THE WICKED.

THERE is therefore now no condemnation to them which are in Christ Jesus, who walk not after the flesh, but after the Spirit.

2 For the law of the Spirit of life in Christ Jesus hath made me free from the law of sin and death.

3 For what the law could not do, in that it was weak through the flesh, God sending his own Son in the likeness of sinful flesh, and for sin, condemned sin in the flesh :

4 That the righteousness of the law might be fulfilled in us, who walk not after the flesh but after the Spirit.

5 For they that are after the flesh do mind the things of the flesh ; but they that are after the Spirit, the things of the Spirit.

6 For to be carnally minded *is* death ;· but to be spiritually minded *is* life and peace.

7 Because the carnal mind *is* enmity against God : for it is not subject to the law of God, neither indeed can be.

8 So then they that are in the flesh cannot please God.

9 But ye are not in the flesh, but in the Spirit, if so be that the Spirit of God dwell in you.   Now if any man have not the Spirit of Christ, he is none of his.

10 And if Christ *be* in you, the body *is* dead because of sin ; but the Spirit *is* life because of righteousness.

11 But if the Spirit of him that raised up Jesus from the dead dwell in you, he that raised up Christ from the dead shall also quicken your mortal bodies by his Spirit that dwelleth in you.

WE now proceed to consider a chapter long regarded with peculiar delight by the pious. Some have spoken of it as the crowning gem of this epistle. Hitherto we have commonly had logical argument, with digressions to answer important objections, and to make some application of the truths taught. Now for thirty-nine verses we have as strong language of triumph as is commonly found even in the most exultant parts of scripture. Nothing in the song of Miriam, or in the song of Deborah can compare with portions of this chapter for sublimity. A noble young hero of the cross, Rev. William Hoge, D.D., whose sun not long since went down in a blaze of glory, such as never surrounds any but the dying Christian, in a manuscript kindly lent me by surviving friends, says: "For fervor and strength of expression, for rapidity and vigor of argument, for richness in doctrine, for revelation of high and precious mysteries, and for a noble elevation of sentiments, which pervades the whole, and bursts out at the end with irrepressible ardor, there are few passages equal to it, even in the sacred oracles, and certainly none out of them." This witness is true.

This chapter brings to a happy and practical conclusion all that had been stated in the former part of the epistle respecting justification by union with Christ, sanctification by the gospel, and victory over corruption by believers, even if their spiritual warfare is long and distressing. It shows many of the excellent uses of these doctrines. Very few sound commentators deny that the first verse contains the pregnant truths, on which depends the just exultation, which follows.

1. There is *therefore now no condemnation to them which are in Christ Jesus, who walk not after the flesh, but after the Spirit.* *Therefore* connects this chapter with the whole preceding argument. The meaning is, that the truths of the gospel being thus clear and settled, it is not possible there should be condemnation resting on believers. *Condemnation,* in many old English versions damnation; the same word occurs in the Greek in Rom. 5 : 16, 18, and nowhere else in the New Testament. The reason why believers are free from a condemning sentence is that they are *in Christ Jesus.* These words point to a vital union with Christ, such as the branch has with the vine, the limb with the body. Locke says it means "the professing the religion and owning a subjection to the law of Christ." But Whitby justly observes that it must mean much more than being members of the Christian church by profession. And Paul in more than one place teaches the same thing: "If any man be in Christ, he is a new creature," 2 Cor. 5 : 17. Compare 1 Thess. 4 : 16 and many other places. It has been an old device of the adversary to corrupt the truth, that justification is not perfect without some rite or addition, and that it may become imperfect, even when real. This verse is fatal to both these errors. If justification exists at all, it is complete. There is to him that is

a partaker of this benefit *no* condemnation; none for old sins, none
for sins committed after admission to the church; none for original sin, none for actual sin.   There was special propriety in here
presenting the truth contained in v. 1, for the apostle had dwelt
considerably on the infirmity, temptation and trouble of a child
of God.   It was very fitting that he should announce that the
spiritual warfare did in no way impair the completeness of justification.   He adds that those who are in Christ Jesus prove it in a
very decisive way: they walk *not after the flesh, but after the spirit.*
This part of the verse is entirely omitted in the Greek text of the
English Hexapla, and also by Griesbach, Mill and others.   But
the Greek manuscripts generally retain it, as we do on their
authority.   It is all found in v. 4.   In Eph. 3 : 1 the words *hath he
quickened* in the English translation are very properly brought
forward from v. 5, where they are found in the original.   So here,
there is no *error* taught by inserting these words, though we may
not vary the text without authority.   They are all admitted by
Wiclif, Coverdale, Tyndale, Cranmer, Genevan, Rheims and Bp.
Hall; and the first clause is admitted by the Vulgate, Doway,
Bengel, Morus and Peshito.   To *walk* in both Testaments indicates
the course of the life.   Compare Ps. 1 : 1; 2 Cor. 10 : 2; 12 : 18;
Gal. 2 : 14; Eph. 2 : 2.   To walk *after the flesh* therefore is to be
habitually or prevailingly governed by carnal inclinations.   So
to walk *after the Spirit* is to be governed by his word, and actuated
by his motions.   In Ps. 32 : 2 David in like manner unites justification and sanctification: "Blessed is the man unto whom the
Lord imputeth not iniquity, and in whose spirit there is no guile."
Compare Rom. 4 : 6–8.

  2. *For the law of the Spirit of life in Christ Jesus hath made
me free from the law of sin and death.*   For the Spirit of life Tyndale has the Spirit that bringeth life.   For set free Peshito has
emancipated.   We had the same word in Rom. 6 : 18, 22.   It occurs again in v. 21.   Our Lord used it when he said, The truth
shall make you free; the Son shall make you free, John 8 : 32, 36.
In the exposition of Rom. 7 : 21 the word law was explained as
having the same import as here, that of a powerful impelling
principle in the soul.   If the former, the law of sin, was potential
for evil, much more is this, the law of the Spirit of life, mighty
for good; for it liberates believers from the law of sin and death.
That exposition is supported by Owen of Oxford and many others.
It makes the work of grace by the Spirit efficacious in destroying
the work of sin and death in the soul.   It has destroyed the
dominion of sin.   It is destroying its power, and it shall finally
destroy the whole force of sin and death in the soul, not leaving

spot, or wrinkle or any such thing.   The whole efficacy of this law
in Christ Jesus is by the Spirit.   This is substantially the view
taken by Chrysostom, Calvin, Diodati, Beza, Vitringa, Doddridge,
Scott, Stuart and Chalmers.   But Ambrose, Pareus, Witsius,
Hodge, Haldane and others prefer another explanation, which
may be thus stated.   Believers are not under the moral law as a
covenant of works, or as a means of sanctification.   They are not
under law but under grace.   They are thus freed from the moral
law by the law of the Spirit of life in Christ Jesus, that is by the
gospel, of which the Spirit is the author—the gospel revealing a
scheme of gratuitous justification.   The obvious objections to this
exposition are such as these.   1. It is unusual to call the gospel a
law.   It is sometimes done, Rom. 3 : 27, but it is in such a
connection and with such explanations as leave no room for mistake.   2. It is still more unusual to denominate the moral law by
such terms as are here employed.   Calvin: " I dare not, with
some, take *the law of sin and death* for the law of God, because it
seems a harsh expression."   This consideration is the more
weighty inasmuch as Paul has been in the preceding context carefully guarding against views derogatory to the excellence of the
law.   3. Believers are so far made free from the law of sin and
death within them, that sin no longer lords it over them, nor has
dominion over them, nor controls their *wills*, nor shall it prove to
them a law of death, for it shall itself be utterly destroyed.   It
does indeed vex and harass the good man, but like the house
of Saul it waxes weaker and weaker, while the gracious principle, like the house of David, waxes stronger and stronger.
4.   The plea for connection with v. 1 quite overlooks all of
that verse but the first clause of it.   5. The subsequent context
may without any violation of the laws of language as well be connected with v. 1, if we follow the former as the latter exposition.
But if any still prefer the latter, we have no contention with
them.

   3. *For what the law could not do, in that it was weak through the
flesh, God sending his own Son in the likeness of sinful flesh, and for
sin, condemned sin in the flesh.*   Here *the law* no doubt means the
moral law.   It was impotent for justification and for sanctification
also.   It condemned ; it could not justify.   It gave the knowledge
but not the cure of sin.   It is said to have been *weak*, wanting
strength, lacking power.   This was no inherent fault of the law ;
in fact its working wrath arose from its very perfection, which
brought a knowledge of the heinous nature of sin, revealed its
power, and unmistakeably threatened righteous and awful retribution on the transgressor.   Nor could it give any strength to

believer or unbeliever to resist the seductions of fallen human
nature. To each and all of these ends it was impotent. In this
our sad state the Lord undertook for us, sent his own Son in the
likeness of sinful flesh. God's own Son was he, who counted it
not robbery to be equal with God. He was with God and he was
God. The likeness of sinful flesh is not sinful flesh, but " the likeness of that flesh which was sinful," elsewhere expressed by the
phrase in the likeness of men, Phil. 2 : 7. He was in all things
made like unto his brethren, having a true body and a reasonable
soul, Heb. 2 : 16–18. But he was not born in sin, nor did he ever
offend against God, but was holy, harmless, undefiled and separate
from sinners. His Father, his friends, his judge, his betrayer all
pronounced him faultless. It is said God sent his Son *for sin*,
Peshito, on account of sin ; Theophylact, in respect of sin. But
from Augustine down many have explained the words *for sin* as
meaning for a sin-offering. So Melancthon, Calvin and many
others. Whitby cites more than thirty cases in the Septuagint
where the same words mean for a sin-offering. In Heb. 10 : 6
undoubtedly this is the meaning. The margin in this place has a
sacrifice for sin. The foregoing, among good writers, is the more
common method of exposition. But some contend that Paul is
still speaking of sanctification, not of justification. Nor can it be
denied that in many parts of scripture the sanctification of believers
is stated in close connection with the sacrifice and sufferings of the
Lord Jesus Christ, John 17 : 19 ; Eph. 5 : 25, 26 ; Tit. 2 : 14 ; 1 Pet.
1 : 18, 19. Nor is it safe to deny that by a figure of speech often
only one thing in salvation is named, when the whole is intended
to be included. And Fraser is quite confident that in this verse
Paul is still showing how men must be sanctified. He says : " The
general point is clear, that the scripture connects making men
free from the dominion of sin with Christ's sufferings and sacrifice." He also cites Gal. 3 : 13, 14 in confirmation of the truth
that the Spirit is received through the faith which lays hold of the
redemption of Christ. We may and we must distinguish, but we
may never separate between justification and sacntification, and
either of these words, or their synonymes may be chosen to represent to us all the benefits obtained by believers in Christ Jesus.
Condemned, always so rendered except a few times where it is
rendered damned. It is found again in v. 34 of this chapter.
Peshito has condemned ; Schleusner, Hodge and Haldane :
punished ; Locke : put to death, extinguished or suppressed ;
Conybeare and Howson : overcome or conquered. The prominent idea in the verb is that of sentencing to death, or of putting
to death in execution of a sentence. The doubt among interpret-

ers is whether Paul is speaking of justification or sanctification, of
the removal of the guilt of sin or of the destruction of its power.
On this point they are much divided. Venema, Pareus, Pool,
Bp. Hall, Whitby, Hodge and Haldane refer it to justification.
But Chrysostom, Fraser, Locke, Doddridge, Scott, Macknight,
Owen of Thrussington and Stuart refer it to sanctification. Many
admit that in this verse sin is personified. If it is, we know how
it fared in the sacrifice of Calvary. It was punished, condemned
and overcome. By that one offering it was made certain that sin
should be put down, or as Calvin says: " cast down from its
power, so that it does not now hold us subject to itself." The
chains of its guilt are knocked off; the sceptre of its power is
broken; it is no longer lord over any one who is in Christ Jesus.
The more these verses are considered, the more it looks as if Paul
was not nicely discriminating between the guilt and the power of
sin, but was speaking of its utter destruction in every sense, so
that it shall neither condemn us nor hold us in bondage. The
word condemned is cognate to the word condemnation in v. 1.
Those who are in Christ are not in any sense condemned, but sin
is in every sense condemned. The sentence has gone forth, the
death on Calvary was decisive, and the application of redemption
by the Spirit is giving the victory more and more, till in all who
are in Christ there shall be left neither spot nor wrinkle. In other
words complete deliverance from sin itself and from all its effects
seems to be spoken of in these verses, by a figure of speech, a part
being often put for the whole. This mode of explanation seems
to have been in the mind of Evans: " By the appearance of Christ
sin was *condemned*, that is, God did therein more than ever manifest his hatred of sin ; and not only so, but for all that are Christ's
both the damning and the domineering power of sin is broken
and taken out of the way. He that is *condemned* can neither *accuse*
nor *rule ;* his testimony is null, and his authority null. Thus by
Christ is sin condemned, though it live and remain, its life in the
saints is still but that of a condemned malefactor. It was by the
condemning of sin that death was disarmed, and the devil, who
had the power of death, destroyed. The condemning of sin saved
the sinner from condemnation." This mode of explanation, taking a part for the whole, and personifying sin, covers the whole
ground, and allows us to see how by the union of the legal and
moral effects of Christ's death believers have full salvation. It is
said that God condemned sin *in the flesh.* Two explanations are
offered. One is that God condemned sin in the flesh of Christ.
So Peshito. The other is that he condemned it in human nature.
But it is better to unite the two and say that God condemned sin

in human nature, of which Christ is a partaker. All this was done,

4. *That the righteousness of the law might be fulfilled in us, who walk not after the flesh, but after the Spirit.* Perhaps the best method of expounding this verse is the same as that adopted in v. 3. The righteousness of the law is the righteousness which the law demands. By living union with Jesus Christ we receive his perfect active and passive obedience to the law in our room and stead as our justifying righteousness. The law demands no more. This robe is without a rent; and so the righteousness of the law is perfectly fulfilled in our justification. Some contend that this is all. But if the view given of v. 3 is correct, we may in the same way add that this verse also embraces the sanctification of believers; and that the righteousness of the law through Jesus Christ and by his Spirit is fulfilled in them just so far and so fast as their sanctification progresses. The great objection urged to this view is that the law calls for perfect conformity to its demands, and that the best of mere men freely confess they come far short of perfection. In answer it may be said 1. that whatever may be the imperfection of good men in this life, it shall not be so always. They shall at last have in their hearts and characters all that holiness which the law requires. If the gospel should fail in producing this effect, it would fail utterly in bringing glory to God or good to men. 2. Although the holiness of a believer is not in degree what the law requires, yet to a pleasing extent it is in kind much what the commandments call for. 1. This obedience is personal. 2. It is to the law as coming from God, having his authority and expressing his will. 3. It is from the heart. 4. It flows from love to God. 5. It flows from godly fear. 6. It springs from true and lively faith. 7. It is humble and accompanied by a just and deep sense of imperfection. 8. It is universal, extending without partiality to all the commands of God. 9. It is habitual and not by fits and starts. 10. It is evangelical, drawing its strongest motives from the love of God manifested in the cross of Christ. Colquhoun: " True holiness is spiritual and sincere obedience to the law as a *rule of life*, in the hand of the blessed Mediator, and is commonly styled evangelical holiness or true godliness." Were this obedience perfect, as it is sincere ; spotless, as it is accepted and rewarded of God; without defect, as soon it shall be ; it would in every respect be the very righteousness of the law, that is, the very holiness of the spirits of just men made perfect. Even now regenerate men walk not *after the flesh.* They are often carnal to an extent very mortifying to themselves, but the tenor of their lives and the aim of their hearts even now are towards holiness, not sin, after the Spirit,

not after the flesh. Without holiness no man shall see the Lord. A professed reliance on the merits of Christ, not followed by conformity to the preceptive will of God, is utterly vain and unprofitable.

5. *For they that are after the flesh do mind the things of the flesh; but they that are after the Spirit, the things of the Spirit.* The same doctrine is taught by our Lord : " That which is born of the flesh, is flesh ; and that which is born of the Spirit, is spirit ;" " It is the Spirit that quickeneth; the flesh profiteth nothing," John 3 : 6 ; 6 : 63. It is much the same as that announcement by the great prophet of the captivity : " The wicked shall do wickedly ; but the wise shall understand," Dan. 12 : 10; or by Christ in the sermon on the mount : " Every good tree bringeth forth good fruit ; but a corrupt tree bringeth forth evil fruit," Matt. 7 : 17. In other words, sin and holiness have very different fruits, appropriate to their respective natures. The special object of introducing these thoughts here is to show that we in vain plead that we are in Christ, if we have not the Spirit of Christ, and walk not in his footsteps; and that we are certainly corrupt and unregenerate if our lives are wicked. The word *mind* is to be taken in the sense of fixing the attention and setting the heart on any thing. In Matt. 16 : 32 and elsewhere it is rendered *savorest*. In Rom. 14 : 6 it is four times rendered *regard*. In Col. 3 : 2 it is rendered, *set* your *affection on* things above. Elsewhere we read, " Let us *mind* the same thing ;" " who *mind* earthly things," etc. Here it clearly designates two very opposite characters, as evinced by their diverse preferences; one hotly pursuing carnal things ; the other eagerly turning to spiritual things.

6. *For to be carnally minded* is *death*; *but to be spiritually minded* is *life and peace.* The word rendered *minded*, which occurs twice in this verse is a noun, the same rendered mind in vs. 7, 27. It is cognate to the verb rendered mind in v. 5. It embraces the whole moral man, mind, will and affections. To have these under the control of our sinful nature is *death*, is spiritual death, which, unless removed, will be followed by eternal death. In all cases the wages of sin is death, Rom. 6 : 23. But to have the mind, will and affections set on spiritual things is eternal life and the peace of God begun in the soul, giving an infallible pledge of eternal life and undying peace in the heavenly world. Calvin thinks this *minding* corresponds to the word imagination as used by Moses, Gen. 6 : 5 ; 8 : 21 ; and that peace is equivalent to every kind of happiness. It does not materially alter the sense whether we make *for* refer to v. 4 or to v. 5, as they both are very much on the same subject; though the more natural connection is with v.

5. The *aim* of v. 6 is to show the fatal end of sin and the happy issue of true piety.

7. *Because the carnal mind* is *enmity against God: for it is not subject to the law of God, neither indeed can he.* Sin is no trifle, no unconscious aberration, no unfortunate mistake. O no. It is wholly contrary to all that is lovely and righteous in the character of God. Even if it breaks not forth in crimes to be punished by the judges, yet the *minding of the flesh,* the going out of the heart after the things that perish, is wicked and wholly opposed to the divine will, law and nature. It is *enmity against God.* In Gal. 5 : 20 the same word is rendered hatred; every where else, enmity, as in Jas. 4 : 4 "the friendship of the world is enmity with God." The cognate noun, which occurs often, is always rendered enemy or foe. We met it in Rom. 5 : 10, and shall meet it again in chapters XI. and XII. The language of the apostle is very strong. He does not say that the natural mind of man has some shyness, prejudice, or aversion to some things pertaining to God ; but it is *enmity, hostility, against God,* against his attributes, against his will, his government. Nothing is more contrary to any other thing, than is the carnal mind, to God. Stuart : " It is inimical to God, or (in plain terms) hates him, dislikes his precepts, his character, and his ways." Compare John 15 : 18, 19, 24, 25 ; 1 Cor. 2 : 14 ; Gal. 5 : 17. *It is not subject to the law of God.* It does not consent to the law that it is good, it does not serve the law, it does not delight in the law of God, it does not submit to the law. The will of the carnal mind is hostile to the will of God. Where is the man, who, without the Spirit, ever makes it his business to know, study and practice the precepts of the decalogue, because they are ordained by God. What wicked man feels his conscience fully bound by that code ? Where he is outwardly conformed to the letter of it, it is not because he loves God, or has reverently submitted to his authority. This is proven by the fact that such in their hearts break the very commandments whose letter they seem to observe. *Neither indeed can he.* On opening a whole class of commentators one cannot avoid the impression that they find this clause inconvenient. They at once begin to complain of metaphysics. They propose to take broader views than the apostle. They do fairly wriggle. But Paul had used no metaphysics ; and the interpreters, who follow him most literally, are those whose opinions are most offensive to this school. The great and plain fact is that Paul says the carnal or unrenewed mind *cannot be subject* to that law which is holy, just and good. There is no dispute about the Greek text. There is no doubt concerning the translation. There ought to be no doubt concerning the doc-

trine taught. It is never said that men ought not to obey the law, but that unrenewed men cannot submit to it. The next verse asserts the same thing in another form.

8. *So then they that are in the flesh cannot please God.* How can they please him when they cast off his whole law; when they are so much opposed to him that they *cannot be subject* to his authority; when his revealed will is in every shape offensive to them? They cast off the yoke of the decalogue; they refuse submission to the will of God made known in his providence; they will not wear the yoke of Jesus Christ. No unregenerate man with the heart believes in Jesus Christ, nor loves the precious Saviour. How then can he please God? If he ploughs, or sows, or reaps, he does all irrespective of God's will or authority. God's will, precepts, authority, nature, justice, love, mercy and holiness are most opposite to the heart and will of him, who is and who walks after the flesh. All this is the fruit of that sad fall of our first parent, by which we come into the world, children of wrath, Eph. 2 : 3. The want of original righteousness is the infallible sign of the image of the wicked one. Such a one neither loves, nor fears, nor regards, nor trusts, nor obeys God so as is his due. And this is true of every man, who is not renewed by the Holy Ghost; he does not please God. If the matter of the act is right, the manner or the motive is wrong.

9. *But ye are not in the flesh, but in the Spirit, if so be that the Spirit of God dwell in you. Now if any man have not the Spirit of Christ, he is none of his.* Paul had in vs. 1, 4, 5 stated a contrast between the children of God and the children of the wicked one. The latter were after the flesh. The former were after the Spirit. In vs. 7, 8 he had shown why and how a carnal mind was death. He now proceeds to show the blessedness of a spiritual mind. First, he asserts that all men are not in the flesh. Some are changed. In particular he admits that the body of the church, to which he was writing, were, in the judgment of charity, converted people. Ye are in the Spirit. Secondly, he asserts that permanent effects will follow a saving change wrought in the soul. The " Spirit of God dwells " in such. Thirdly, the lack of the indwelling of the Spirit is fatal to any pretensions to a saving change of heart, or to a safe spiritual state. " If any man have not the Spirit of Christ, he is none of his." Fourthly, the Spirit of God is the Spirit of Christ. The terms are convertible. Perhaps no equally brief portion of scripture presents more weighty, practical truths, clearly stated and well guarded.

10. *And if Christ* be *in you, the body* is *dead because of sin; but the Spirit* is *life because of righteousness.* In v. 9 he spoke of the

Spirit of Christ being in you ; here he speaks of Christ being in you. Verse 9 explains verse 10, so far that it tells us how Christ dwells in his people, viz. by his Spirit. This solves what would otherwise be to us a painful mystery concerning the presence of Christ in and with his people. Christ dwells in us by his Spirit. But this does not save us from temporal death. Notwithstanding this great spiritual renovation, "the body is dead because of sin." Death is by sin. The sins of believers are all pardoned, yet believers still die. How is this?   The answers are many and solid. 1. If we had no light on the subject any more than Abraham had in the matter of offering Isaac, yet it would be no great thing in us to trust the living and the loving Lord that it was all right, and wise and every way best for us to die.   2. Our Saviour died.   Is it not right that we should be made conformable to his death? Phil. 3 : 10.   How could we otherwise so well know the fellowship of his sufferings?   How otherwise could we so fully know by personal experience the power of his resurrection?   3. In the death of believers there is no curse.   The sting of death is sin ; and the strength of sin is the law ; but thanks be to God who giveth us the victory through our Lord Jesus Christ, 1 Cor. 15 : 56, 57.   4. In no sense essentially, but only in appearance, does the righteous die as the wicked dieth.   The wicked is driven away in his wickedness.   The righteous is taken away from the evil to come.   He shall enter into peace : they shall rest in their beds, Pr. 14 : 32 ; Isa. 57 ; 1, 2.   5. The body of the believer is not fit for the heavenly state, and cannot be fit for it, without dying and being raised, or without undergoing a change equivalent to death and the resurrection.   It is now in *corruption ;* it must be brought into a state of *incorruption.*   It is now in *dishonor ;* it must be put into a state to fit it for *glory.*   It is now full of *weakness ;* it must be filled with *power.*   It is now a *natural* body ; to be fit for heaven, it must be fashioned anew by the Holy Ghost, and so become a *spiritual* body, 1 Cor. 15 : 42–44.   6. The death of Christ was followed by the most glorious results to him—results dependent on his death.   No doubt the same is true in their measure of his people, John 12 : 24 ; 1 Cor. 15 : 36–38.   7. When a believer dies there is a real and rich blessing resting upon him.   " Blessed are the dead which die in the Lord from henceforth," Rev. 14 : 13.   8. Believers shall finally and fully be in every sense delivered from death.   " The last enemy that shall be destroyed is death," 1 Cor. 15 : 26.   9. We know that when Christ shall appear, we shall be like him, for we shall see him as he is, 1 John 3 : 8.   Compare 2 Cor. 5 : 6, 8. *The Spirit is life,* that is the new nature wrought in men by the Spirit, the opposite of the flesh.   Our Lord uses the word Spirit in application to the new nature imparted by him, John 3 : 6. This new nature is not dead nor dying, it is living, yea it is *life*, eternal life begun in the soul, having in it the elements of an imperishable vitality, John 6 : 54. All the saints are born of incorruptible seed, 1 Pet. 1 : 23. Then what secures beyond all doubt the perpetuity of this life is that the Holy Spirit, who gave it, nourishes it. And all this is so *because of righteousness*. Righteousness may mean either, 1. the rectitude of God, by which he is faithful to all his covenant engagements; 2. the righteousness of Christ, wrought out for believers and imputed to them when they believe, thus securing to them the blessings of the covenant ordered in all things and sure ; or 3. the righteousness wrought in the souls of believers, thus quite changing their natures, and conforming them to God. Though the rectitude of God is always to be regarded as lying at the foundation of his engagements, and though the righteousness of Christ is essential to the covering of the nakedness of his people, yet it is probable that the prominent idea in the word *righteousness* in this verse is newness of nature, holiness inwrought in believers by the Holy Ghost, producing a blessed conformity to the whole revealed will of God in their views, tempers, aims, thoughts, words and deeds. Thus is the Spirit life because of righteousness. Other expositions of this verse are given even by sound and scholarly commentators. But this best coincides with the context, is the most simple, taking the terms in a sense acknowledged by all to be scriptural and common.

11. *But if the Spirit that raised up Jesus from the dead dwell in you, he that raised up Christ from the dead shall also quicken your mortal bodies.* The resurrection of Christ is ascribed first to his own power, John 2 : 19; 10 : 18; then to the power of the Father, Acts 2 : 24, 32 ; 3 : 15, 26; 4 : 12; 5 : 30; 10 : 40 and often; then in our verse he is said to have been raised by the Spirit. Creation was the joint work of Father, Son and Holy Ghost; so is the providential care of the world; so is salvation; so is that crowning work of salvation, the resurrection of the body and glorification of the entire person of the believer. Chrysostom : " Wheresoever one person of the Trinity is, there the whole Trinity is present." Such language need produce no confusion. Jesus says, " my Father worketh hitherto and I work," John 5 : 17. Compare John 10 : 37, 38. The indwelling of the Spirit makes certain the resurrection of believers in two ways. 1. His presence is the pledge and proof of their sonship with God. He has begun in them a great and good work, and it would be unworthy of him to drop it in the midst and leave it unfinished. We read of the earnest of the Spirit. God could give us nothing else so suita-

ble and so satisfying as an earnest.   2. The Spirit has the energy to raise up believers and is already in them as a power.   By that power the body of Christ was raised up.   By the same power the souls of believers have been regenerated.   They are born of the Spirit, John 3 : 5.   In Eph. 1 : 19, 20 these two great works, the implanting of grace and the raising of Christ from the dead are compared, and both are said to have been effected by the exceeding greatness of God's power, etc.   Thus the resurrection and eternal life of believers is made, not merely probable, but infallibly certain.   One can but regret that some respectable commentators explain this verse as though " mortal bodies " meant the remains of sin, or the fallen natures of men.

DOCTRINAL AND PRACTICAL REMARKS

1. It is both pleasing and edifying to the pious to notice the connections of divine truth.   Paul closed chapter VII. with a declaration of the sad power of indwelling sin.   He begins this by stating that notwithstanding inbred corruption the justification of the believer is complete, and that with it is connected a sanctification that even now prevails to the government of the life or *walk* of the justified.   The scheme of salvation is a golden chain of many links.   Let us hold fast the truth in its connections.   All scripture is profitable for doctrine.

2. We may rest assured that we are on the domain of error, if we in any way divorce justification and sanctification, v. 1.   What God hath joined together let not man put asunder.   It is as dangerous to rest on a justification unattended with holiness, as it is to rest on a justification that has our works for its basis.

3. Nor can we easily present with too much frequency or with too great simplicity each of these doctrines in its scriptural connections, v. 1.   We need not, we must not deny the reality of our need of a free pardon and a gratuitous acceptance, nor of the absolute necessity of a thorough cleansing of our nature in renewal begun in regeneration and completed in the work of the Spirit.   And let us declare how these inestimable benefits may be secured.   They are to be had in Christ Jesus.   His mediation has made all needed provision.   It has fully satisfied justice and truth.   It has secured to us the gift of the Spirit.   It shall finally effect a complete deliverance from all sin and from all the effects of sin.

4. There is in scripture no ground for the doctrine of a partial forgiveness of sins.   God forgives all sin or none at all, v. 1.   There is *no* condemnation to them who are in Christ Jesus.   David loudly calls on his soul to bless the Lord, ' who forgiveth all thine ini-

quities,' Ps. 103 : 3. To forgive all but one in a thousand would save no man's soul.

5. It is in vain for us to hope for any saving blessings without a vital union with Christ. We must be in him, v. 1. Out of Christ all is wrath and ruin to a sinner; God is a consuming fire to such ; their sins are their tyrants, and will surely deliver them over to the tormentors. Our union with Christ is not personal but mystical. He and believers are not one as his human and divine natures are one person. But he and believers are one as the stock and the branches are one vine, as the head and the members are one body. From him his people derive sap and nourishment, guidance and wisdom, supplies of all needed spiritual things.

6. There is such a thing as the tenor of one's life, his course, his way, his conversation, his *walk*, vs. 1, 4, 5. The course of Enoch's life was heavenly and divine. He *walked* with God. A good man *walketh* not in the counsel of the ungodly, Ps. 1 : 1. This tenor decides the character. It was the habit of Judas to steal. It was not the habit of Peter to deny his master.

7. A life of sin and a life of holiness are alike in one thing— they are active, always advancing. Every man is *walking* after the flesh or after the Spirit, vs. 1, 4. Every man is making daily attainments in good or evil. The longer he lives, the better or the worse man he is. As in a life of sin those, who are now Christians, were once very diligent and untiring, now that they have turned to the Lord they ought to be mightily stirred up to take hold on God and to run with patience the race that is set before them. Nor does it in fact repress any genuine feeling of zeal to know that our justification is wholly gratuitous, or that our sanctification is by the gospel, not by the law ; for of all the principles of obedience in the heart of sinful man, none is so mighty as the love of gratitude for undeserved kindness.

8. In preaching great pains should be taken to state the doctrines of the gospel with clearness and discrimination, as well as in their connection, v. 1. If glorious privileges are preached, let it be done in such a way as not to lead to antinomian laxity. This will require a statement of the awful responsibilities, under which men live and act. Indiscriminate comfort to all classes of men is as unscriptural as indiscriminate denunciation. Say ye to the righteous, that it shall be *well* with *him*. Wo to the wicked, it shall be *ill* with *him*, Isa. 3 : 10, 11. A loose mode of stating truth does it great injustice, and sometimes, because the truth is misunderstood, has the same effect as error.

9. No two things are more opposed than flesh and Spirit, vs. 1,

4, 5. One is darkness; the other is light. One is earthly, sensual, devilish; the other is holy, godly, heavenly. One is folly; the other is wisdom. One is death; the other is life and peace. How could it be otherwise? One is sin, which wars on God and goodness, on all that is lovely and of good report, on all that is sacred· and divine, on all that honors God. The other is gospel holiness, which, abasing itself in the dust, and declaring itself deserving of no good thing, out of admiration of the glorious character of God and out of gratitude for his saving mercies in Christ, gladly works and suffers for him, to whom all is due.

10. The true doctrine of the divinity, personality, and agency of the Holy Spirit in man's salvation is of vital importance, vs. 1, 4, 5, 6, 9–11. Without the mediation of Christ we should not be in a more hopeless case than we should be without the effectual working and mighty energy of the Holy Ghost. Poor deluded souls, still sunk in gross ignorance and under the power of the wicked one, have sometimes brought great reproach upon this precious doctrine by their hypocritical cant and ungodly lives; but what doctrine have such men or others not abused? Let us not for a moment yield the truth because some pervert it and others scoff at it. It is freely conceded that the miraculous gifts of the Holy Ghost, so abundantly granted at the first planting of churches, have ceased; but his ordinary and special influences in the church are as much needed as ever. The promise of the Holy Spirit to all God's people is one of the vital promises of the covenant of grace, Isa. 44 : 3–5; Ezek. 36 : 25–27. Nor have we higher authority or more encouragement to seek for anything than we have to pray for large measures of the Holy Spirit, Matt. 7 : 11; Luke 11 : 13; John 4 : 10. The gift of the Holy Spirit is a chief fruit of Christ's undertaking, Acts 2 : 33. It is alike a fruit of his intercession, John 14 : 16, 17. The fact is, we are powerless for any good, unless we have the presence and aid of the Spirit. If there have been fanatics and filthy dreamers in the world, let us not turn formalists, and renounce the unspeakable blessing of the gift of the Spirit. Without him we be all dead men.

11. There is a power in true piety, a mighty power. It is a *law*, v. 2. It is the law of the Spirit of life. If anything is efficient, that is. No greater wonders have ever been manifested in this world than in the case of martyrs and confessors, who have leaped for joy at the prospect of a death intended to be made horrible by the cruel arts of persecutors. The best men now in this world, were once darkness, but now are they light in the Lord; once aliens and strangers, but now brought nigh by the blood and Spirit of Christ. The law of the Spirit must be prodigious when it has

already weakened and shall finally abolish the law of sin and death. Chalmers: " It is like the awakening of man to a new moral existence, when he is awakened to the love of that God whom before he was glad to forget, and of whom he never thought but as a being shrouded in unapproachable majesty, and compassed about with the jealousies of a law that had been violated. It is like a resurrection from the grave, when, quickened and aroused from the deep oblivion of nature, man enters into living fellowship with his God ; and he, who ere now had been regarded with terror or utterly disregarded, hath at length reclaimed to himself all our trust and all our tenderness." If there is power anywhere displayed in this world, it is in the glorious gospel of the happy God.

12. But let us never forget that all the vitality and power of even true religion is from the Holy Ghost, v. 2. If he shall not take of the things of Christ and show them unto us, we shall never see them aright. Chalmers: " The doctrine of the Holy Ghost is too much neglected in practice. It is not adverted to that all acceptable virtue in man is the product of a creating energy, that is actually put forth upon him ; and that it is his business to wrestle in supplication with Heaven, that it may be put forth upon him." Jesus Christ taught that the gift of the Holy Ghost was the sum of all good things. Oh that all his people acted on that truth. It is only by the Holy Ghost that any man can say that Jesus Christ is Lord ; or that he can see in Christ anything but a root out of a dry ground.

13. Until the gospel is carried to the heart with power by the Holy Ghost, it is amazing in what undisturbed possession the strong man keeps his goods. Tyrannical despotisms, when fully set up, are the most quiet governments in the world. They open not the house of their prisoners. They silence outcries and clamor by measures the most effectual. Pass through a country thus ruled and you shall hardly hear a complaint. So it is with the wicked. They are under the cruel tyranny of the devil. Their noblest faculties are loaded with the chains of iniquity. The dungeons of the Bastile exhibited no sights so mournful as those revealed to a man, when he first fairly sees himself a prisoner of sin and Satan, a man wholly after the flesh.

14. It is proof of amazing madness and folly that, after all man has done and God has taught, men will still fly to the law for justification and sanctification. The law is *weak*, impotent to either of these ends, v. 3. Read the decalogue through and you shall find not one word of mercy for the guilty. Do and live, sin and die, is all it says. Calvin: " It is absurd to measure human

strength by the precepts of the law; as though God in requiring
what is justly due had regarded what and how much we are able
to do." The law never demanded more than was holy, just and
good. It can demand no less. The gospel is not an apology to
man for having given him the law. God never acts more righteously than in demanding perfect obedience to the moral law on
pain of his sore displeasure—even death itself. But the gospel
does suit our case. It is not weak. It is mighty through God to
the pulling down of strongholds. It is the power of God unto salvation. How could it be otherwise?

15. Its author is God's *own Son*, v. 3. He is not the son of God
as Adam was and as the angels were, by creation; nor as Christians are, by the renewing of the Holy Ghost. But he is God's
own Son by an eternal generation. He is the brightness of the
Father's glory and the express image of his person. He is the
only begotten Son of God, John 1 : 18 ; 3 : 16. He often called
himself the Son of God, and the whole controversy concerning
his sonship and divinity ought to have been settled, and to all well
taught from heaven was settled by his resurrection from the dead.
See above comment and remarks on Rom. 1 : 4.

16. Paul never utters a doubt respecting the fact or the necessity of the incarnation of Jesus Christ, v. 3. It was human nature
that had fallen, and was to be redeemed. It was right that the
nature which sinned should bear the punishment of sin, be exalted
to honor and glory, and should appear for us in heaven. We
needed a High Priest, who should not only be equal with God,
and be able to lay his hand on the eternal throne, because he was
the Fellow of the Father, but who should also be bone of our
bone, and not be ashamed to call us brethren, that he might be a
merciful High Priest. This incarnation, involving so profound
humiliation on the part of Christ, is, when duly considered, very
humbling to us. It was designed to " remind us that righteousness by no means dwells in us, for it is to be sought from him, and
that men in vain confide in their own merits, who become not just
but at the pleasure of another, or who obtain righteousness from
that expiation which Christ accomplished in his own flesh."
Christ took our nature, its innocent infirmities, our place under
the law, our load of guilt, the curse due to us ; and in his love and
mercy he gives us his blessing, his righteousness, his Spirit, his
glory, his joy, his kingdom, a seat with him on his throne. It
would be worse than swollen bombast to say these things, but God
has taught them all to us.

17. Sin is condemned, was condemned on Calvary, v. 3. It
was condemned and punished as outlawry, as usurpation, as de-

serving God's wrath and curse, and man's abhorrence and detestation for ever.   Diodati : " God has as it were by his sovereign
decree taken away all command over believers from sin, has crucified and mortified it in them, whilst they live in this animal and
corporeal life.   He has done this *in the flesh,* to the end that we
may not doubt of the forgiveness of our sins, which are destroyed
in our proper nature, which the Son of God has taken upon him."
Whatever sin is or does, it is and does without any rightful claim.
Once those, who are now believers, were held as lawful captives;
but all who accept of Christ, are no longer under the dominion of
its guilt or of its power.   The guilt is all removed, and in the
matter of sanctification they have made by the grace of Christ a
blessed beginning, which is a sure pledge of final and complete
victory.

18. How clearly in all the scriptures the doctrine of a sacrifice
for sin is so taught as to imply its absolute necessity, v. 3.   Indeed
who can believe that God would have sent his own Son to endure
any pain or shame, if our case had not been such as to require it ?
If remission without the shedding of blood could have been had,
there would have been no blood shed.   Under the law almost all
things were purged with blood ; not that God regarded as of any
saving efficacy the sacrifice of an innocent lamb, but he thus taught
the pious to look away from all human merits and offerings to the
one great sacrifice on Calvary.   Here is a vital matter.   Men
may be saved without science, without literature, without wealth,
without civilization ; but without faith in the atonement of Christ
there is no hope of future blessedness.   " If ye believe not that I
am he, ye shall die in your sins."

19. Men are not saved in derogation of the honor of God's
government.   They enter not paradise trampling on the holy
sovereignty of the Most High.   The righteousness of the law is
fulfilled in them.   First their justifying righteousness, being the
spotless obedience of the Lord Jesus, is without any defect.   No
sinner, however guilty and terribly awakened to a sense of his lost
condition on account of the number and aggravation of his sins,
when brought to rest on Christ alone for salvation, ever found any
rent in his seamless robe, any spot in his glorious righteousness.
How could he ?   Omniscient purity itself pronounced it faultless,
and so released Christ from all further humiliation and raised him
to glory and honor at God's right hand.   The Lord Jesus was
made under the law, under its precept for obedience and under
its penalty for the suffering of death, that he might redeem them
that were under the law and should believe on him.   Then the
righteousness, which the law demands, is finally and perfectly

wrought in the souls of believers by the power of the Holy Ghost. This work is begun in regeneration. It is carried on by the same divine power until in glory the redeemed soul finds itself without spot, or wrinkle, or any such thing. Believers do in no sense enter heaven in derogation of law. Men are not saved without righteousness, both justifying and sanctifying.

20. As God has condemned sin, let us condemn it also, v. 3. As he abhors it, so let us abhor it. As he has punished it, so let us mortify it and crucify it. There is no danger of excess in our hatred of sin. It is horrible. It is a horrible dishonor to God, a horrible defilement of the soul, a horrible torment to him, in whom it reigns, and followed by torments so horrible, that if the gayest sinner had a just view of his sad state and dismal prospects he would never smile again unless he could be brought to believe in Jesus. Chalmers: "However zealously the righteousness of Christ must be contended for as the alone plea of a sinner's acceptance, yet the benefit thereof rests upon none save those who walk not after the flesh but after the Spirit. Light where it may, it must carry a sanctifying power with it; and you have no part nor lot in the matter, if you are not pressing onward in grace and in all godliness. It is not enough that upon Christ all its honors have been amply vindicated—upon you who believe in Christ all its virtues must be engraven." All ye that love the Lord hate iniquity. If you do not kill sin, it will kill you. If you do not crucify it, it will torment you for ever.

21. If a man can discover the bent of his mind, will and affections, he can know whether he is a child of God, or of the wicked one. If he *minds* the things of the flesh, he is a wicked man; if he *minds* the things of the Spirit, he is a new man, v. 5. Old things have passed away. As a man thinketh in his heart so is he. He, whose heart goes out after his covetousness, is an idolater. He, whose soul followeth hard after God, is regenerate. He, who *studies* to gratify his unholy desires, is not born from above. Evans: "The man is as the mind is. The mind is the forge of thoughts. Which way do the thoughts move with most pleasure? On what do they dwell with most satisfaction? Which way go the projects and contrivances?" What kind of news is most refreshing, that which relates to the kingdom of Christ, or that which is secular? Are you eager after those things which the Gentiles seek? Matt. 6 : 32. Your heart is where your treasure is,

22. Death must attend and follow a carnal mind, v. 6. It cannot be otherwise. A carnal mind is always at war with the very laws of our being. It outrages all the principles conducive to our

well-being. It never rests till it drags the soul down from all that
is ennobling. Even here it is a death, an extinction of all that
should lift the soul above low and sordid things. Chalmers:
" Such a death is not merely a thing of negation, but a thing of
positive wretchedness. For with the want of all that is sacred or
spiritual about him, there is still a remainder of feeling which
makes him sensible of his want—a general restlessness of the soul,
on whose capacities there has been inflicted a sore mutilation."
Wars sometimes close, leaving poor mutilated men in hospitals—
men who have neither leg nor arm left. The sight of them often
brings tears in the eyes of spectators. Yet such may walk with
God, may have the noblest aspirations, thoughts and hopes. But
a poor soul under the sway of carnality is a body without a spirit,
a mass of death, still, however, responsible, still waxing worse and
worse, still preparing for the second death. " Woful and sad is the
change that has turned a friend into a foe, a favorite into an enemy,
displaced the spiritual, enthroned the sensual, máde the very
imaginations of the heart only evil, and that continually, and clad
with carnality sense, affection, desire, and all the powers of the
soul."

23. Nor can it be but that life and peace accompany and follow a spiritual mind, v. 6. It is impossible that the good Spirit
of the Lord should work in us anything contrary to our well-
being. A spiritual mind is *life*, it is all activity. Its energies
are drawn forth by thoughts of time misspent, mercies abused,
kindness insulted, the divine glory obscured and souls perishing. This *life* was bought by blood, was infused by the Spirit,
and consists of the noblest thoughts, emotions and principles.
It is the life of God in the soul of man. It is indeed even now
eternal life, John 6 : 47. Its best hopes will in the future be far
more than realized. This life is hid with Christ in God. But
he who has this life has *peace* also. Carking care reigns not in
him. The discords of the people agitate him not. His spirit is
calm and hushed on the bosom of his God. His conscience approves of all that is right in his aims, principles and hopes. He
has peace with God, and peace within, and peace (at least in his
heart) with all men. Chalmers in his lecture on this place em-
bodies a fine story respecting a clerk in Calcutta, who gave up a
fine situation that he might devote his time to spreading the gospel among the heathen. His employer, amazed at his conduct,
applied to Dr. Carey of Serampore for an explanation of so remarkable a procedure, and when he found that no emoluments, no
honors, no pleasures (that suit the taste of the carnal) were to be
secured, his amazement was surpassing. The secret of holy,

heavenly peace was unknown to him. Hodge: "God has made the connection between sin and misery, holiness and happiness, necessary and immutable. . . The divine Spirit is a well-spring within of joy and peace to all who are sanctified. In itself considered, therefore, moral purity is essentially connected with happiness, as cause and effect." It must be so. God has ordained it.

24. No wonder men must be born again; the carnal mind is enmity against God. No wonder men are distressed for their sins of heart, so soon as they see the real state of case; for the carnal mind is enmity against God. No wonder God has set the whole of his nature and the whole course of his providence against sin; for the carnal mind is enmity against God. No wonder finally impenitent sinners are finally lost; for the carnal mind is enmity against God. On this point we have the very words of inspiration, expressed in terms both clear and various. We have also great facts in sacred and secular history, and presented to our personal observation, such as these: 1. Men prove their hatred to God by the dislike which they manifest to a sound knowledge of him. In two periods of the history of the world, once in the family of Adam and once in the family of Noah, every human being on earth possessed the true knowledge of the true God. But because men held the truth in unrighteousness and did not like to retain God in their knowledge; ignorance, superstition, idolatry and cruelty soon obtained a fearful prevalence and hold it still. For thousands of years God has raised up great companies of faithful and able witnesses for the true knowledge of himself, and they have proclaimed it with zeal. And yet how many even in Christian lands have not the saving knowledge of God. This great fact cannot be accounted for, if the carnal mind is not enmity against God. 2. Men evince their hostility to God by the manner in which they treat his name. They take it in vain with mournful frequency. They mingle it up with profane oaths and horrid curses. The ungodly often use his names and titles in connection with their senseless and malignant ribaldry, or with their wicked prejudices or religious errors. Millions profane his name, and when reproved, declare that they do it without being aware of the fact. The name of no pest of society, no scourge of mortals, is so often used in scorn or contempt as is the name of the loving and glorious God. Does not this prove that the carnal mind is enmity against God? 3. Men prove their enmity to God by their unwillingness to see his honor advanced. When Joseph's brethren saw that their father tenderly loved him, they hated him, and could not speak peaceably to him, Gen. 37:4. And when his prophetic dreams told of his coming honors, they hated him yet the

more for his dreams and for his words ; and they envied him, Gen. 37 : 8, 11. They were hostile to him. The higher he rose, the stronger was their dislike of him. So sinners are pained when God is honored. ".When the chief priests and scribes saw the wonderful things that Jesus did, and the children crying in the temple, and saying, Hosanna to the Son of David, they were sore displeased," Matt. 21 : 15. Why? Because their minds were enmity against him. 4. Men evidence their hostility to God by their opposition to his law and government. Every unrenewed man on earth does daily, willingly, allowedly break the spirit of the moral law and every precept thereof. Where is the man, who is not under grace, who loves the Sabbath, as a day of sacred rest, holy unto the Lord? Where is the carnal mind that hesitates to covet whatever it desires? 5. If men did not hate God, they would not hate his people as they do. A child of God knows that he has passed from death unto life because he loves the brethren. But from the days of Cain to this hour, the people of God have been hated, hunted, hounded, misjudged, misrepresented and murdered, till the earth almost everywhere is ready to disclose her blood. Since Christ ascended to glory, fifty millions have been martyred for their professed subjection to him. 6. Men hate the attributes of God, in particular such as are mild and merciful. The pious everywhere exult in God's almightiness, his omniscience, his omnipresence ; but the wicked have no hallelujahs for any such perfections. The cry of the carnal heart everywhere is : " Cause the Holy One of Israel to cease from before us," Isa. 13 : 11. And when God displays his saving mercy and rich grace in the salvation of many sinners, how does the carnal mind (unless divinely restrained) rise up in opposition to so glorious a work. 7. The ingratitude of men for God's mercies (which they cannot deny are great and numerous) shows the same enmity. Now then if any man would have true piety he must avail himself of some means of slaying this enmity ; and if he would do effectual good to the souls of his fellow-men, he must not disguise, but proclaim the truth that the carnal mind is enmity against God, and must be slain.

25. In the light of the clear teachings of scripture, what becomes of the boasted ability of men to keep the commandments? The carnal mind .is not even subject to the law of God, neither indeed can be, v. 7. After regeneration Paul says; " I know that in me (that is, in my flesh) dwelleth no good thing," Rom. 7 : 18. How can a man turn to God, when no good thing dwells in him? Compare Gal. 5 : 17 ; John 8 : 43 ; Rom. 14 ; 23 ; Heb. 11 : 6; Eph. 2 : 12 and many other places. Calvin: " Paul here affirms, in ex-

press words, what the Sophists who carry high the power of free-will, openly detest." Chalmers: "There is nothing more unde-niable, than the antipathy of nature to the peculiar doctrines of the gospel." He then at length applies his remark to the great matter of the utter helplessness of men to save themselves.

26. What dismal prospects are before all men, who from the very state of their hearts and minds cannot please God, v. 8. Every hope built on human merit or human strength is delusive. Scott: "No unregenerate man can delight in God's holy law, or be subject to it; and how can it be expected that God should be pleased with the formal services of enemies and rebels?"

27. The same man cannot at one and the same time be both in the flesh and in the Spirit, v. 9. No man can at the same time work righteousness and be a worker of iniquity. There is no pos-sible way of dissolving the connection between incurable obstinacy and death. Nor let any man suppose himself safe because his are the sins of devils and not of beasts. Spiritual pride, or an evil covetousness are as fatal as debauchery or theft. Chalmers: "It is not necessary that you mind all the things of the flesh in order to constitute you a carnal man. It is enough to fasten this char-acter upon you, that you have given yourself over to the indul-gence or the pursuit, even of so few as one of these things."

28. In good men God's Spirit *dwells*, v. 9. This is the uniform doctrine of scripture, 1 Cor. 3:16; 2 Cor. 6:16; Eph. 2:22; 2 Tim. 1:14, compared with John 14:16, 17, 26; 16:7–11; Gal. 4:6. Calvin: "The reign of the Spirit is the abolition of the flesh." Nothing else secures that great end. Evans: "To be Christ's, to be a Christian indeed, one of his children, his servants, his friends, in union with him, is a privilege and honor which many pretend to, that have no part nor lot in the matter. None are his but those that have his Spirit." Without the Holy Spirit man is vain and vile. All professions, all works, all mental exercises without the Spirit of Christ are no better than a beautiful corpse. If a man is without the Spirit of Christ he is none of his, has no saving interest in Christ, is not like him, is no member of his mystical body.

29. Let us acknowledge the justice of the sentence of death upon our bodies, v. 10. They are *dead*, that is they are dying, are under the sentence of death, are liable to death at any moment. This should not, need not disturb us. Jesus has conquered death. Though death is naturally the king of terrors, yet Jesus has tri-umphed over him and taught his people to do the same. To the believer death is no longer a judicial infliction. It is the conse-crated way to his Father's house on high. But were the death

of believers even something more painful and terrible than it is, the resurrection will make all right. Christ's resurrection makes sure the resurrection of all who are his, 1 Cor. 15 : 20; Col. 1 : 18; Rev. 1 : 5. Christ and his people are one. All that sleep in Jesus will God bring with him. The resurrection of believers will be a very different thing from that of the wicked, Luke 14 : 14; 20 : 36.

30. Christian, if thou hope for such things, possess thy vessel in sanctification and honor, 1 Thess. 4 : 4. Remember that if any man defile the temple of God, him will God destroy, 1 Cor. 3 : 17. Go on. Perfect holiness in the fear of the Lord. Lay out all your strength in the cause of your Master. Keep back nothing. Give him all.

Chapter 18

ROMANS 8
VERSES 12–18

EXHORTATION TO HOLINESS. THE SPIRIT OF
ADOPTION. ITS CONSEQUENCES. AFFLICTIONS
NOT FATAL.

12 Therefore, brethren, we are debtors, not to the flesh, to live after the
flesh.

13 For if ye live after the flesh, ye shall die: but if ye through the Spirit do
mortify the deeds of the body, ye shall live.

14 For as many as are led by the Spirit of God, they are the sons of
God.

15 For ye have not received the spirit of bondage again to fear; but ye have
received the Spirit of adoption, whereby we cry, Abba, Father.

16 The Spirit itself beareth witness with our spirit, that we are the children of
God:

17 And if children, then heirs; heirs of God, and joint heirs with Christ; if
so be that we suffer with *him,* that we may be also glorified together.

18 For I reckon that the sufferings of this present time *are* not worthy *to be
compared* with the glory which shall be revealed in us.

12. *THEREFORE, brethren, we are debtors, not to the flesh, to
live after the flesh.* *Therefore* marks an inference from the
ten or eleven preceding verses. *Debtors,* the same word so rendered in the Lord's Prayer, Matt. 6:12. We met it in Rom.
1:14, on which see above. It occurs also in Rom. 15:27 where
it is explained as expressing an obligation of *duty.* So here the
apostle says, We are under the strong and solemn obligations of
duty, but they bind us not to live after the flesh. Locke's paraphrase is very good: "We are not under any obligation to the
flesh, to obey the lusts of it." The *flesh* clearly means the fallen
depraved nature of man. See above on Rom. 3:20. Chrysostom
says, the meaning is that we are debtors to the Spirit, to live after
the Spirit. This is no doubt so. Pareus says Paul did not state
the other side, "because it was so evident." It is a figure of speech
peculiar to no one language to say less than one means. Paul

uses it it in Rom. 1 : 16. The Apostle of the circumcision uses it,
1 Pet. 4 : 3. Tholuck: "Where there is an ungodly walk, the
blessing which is the fruit of the redemption cannot be taken
in."

13. *For if ye live after the flesh, ye shall die: but if ye through
the Spirit do mortify the deeds of the body, ye shall live.* The three
phrases, walk after the flesh, vs. 1, 4, are after the flesh, v. 5, and
live after the flesh, v. 13, all have the same import, and designate
an unrenewed man leading a wicked life. In this clause *ye shall
die* is the opposite of *ye shall live* in the next. The former points
to the second death; the latter, to the life everlasting. To *mortify*
is not, according to a modern use of the word, to humble, or vex,
but, as the word formerly meant, to put to death. In v. 36 in the
passive it is rendered, we *are killed.* To mortify the *deeds* of the
body is to put to death by the cross of Christ the *workings* or *actings* of the sinful nature. The use of the word *body* in this place
has given the chief support to the idea that in v. 10 the same word
means the mass of corruption in our fallen nature. But Paul often
uses words in very different senses in the same context. Besides,
some in this place for *body* read *flesh;* so the Vulgate and Doway.
Griesbach admits we may so read it. But it is not necessary to
change the text. The sense is clear. By body Beza understands
the whole man, though considered as unregenerate. That body
is used in the sense of the whole man, regenerate or unregenerate,
according to the connection perhaps none will deny, see Rom.
12 : 1. The whole verse is a repetition with some enlargement of
what the apostle had said in v. 6. The victory to be gained can
be had only through the power of the Holy Spirit.

14. *For as many as are led by the Spirit of God, they are the sons of
God. As many,* literally whosoever, often rendered as here, see
John 1 : 12; Acts 2 : 39; 4 : 34; Rom. 2 : 12; 6 : 3. *Are led,* the
same verb rendered *was led* in Luke 4 : 1; Acts 8 : 32. In the
active form we have it in Rom. 2 : 4. The goodness of God *leadeth* thee to repentance. It is a very suitable word to describe the
work of the Holy Spirit on the hearts of believers. He leads them
away from destruction. He guides them into all truth. He is the
unction that teacheth them all things. He opens the blind eyes.
He reveals Christ unto them. All their discoveries of the nature
of sin and of the way of life are from him. We have the same
precise idea presented in Gal. 5 : 18. Chrysostom: "He would
have him use such power over our life as a pilot does over a ship,
or a charioteer over a pair of horses." In previous verses of this
chapter we have had much about the influence of the Spirit. Here
he is said to lead the people of God. It is only thus that their sal-

vation is made certain. All, who are thus led by the Spirit of God, *they are the sons of God.* All men are by creation the sons of God, Acts 17 : 28, 29. But God's people are his children by a new creation and by a gracious adoption. Tholuck: " At the bottom of this figure [of sonship] lies this profound sense, that the regenerated man, by virtue of his direct entrance upon the life of God, is really become of divine extraction, and a being after his own kind." In vs. 1, 4 Paul had spoken of believers *walking after the Spirit ;* in v. 5 he had said they *were after the Spirit ;* in v. 9 he had said they were in the Spirit ; in v. 13 he had spoken of their *mortifying the deeds of the body through the Spirit.* Here he speaks of their being *led by the Spirit.* All these phrases taken together show how extensive and mighty is the work of the Spirit on the hearts of God's people. Stuart: " That a *special* divine influence is implied in their *being led* would seem to be plain." Persons thus led by the Holy Ghost are real Christians— they are the *sons of God.* The sonship of believers includes moral likeness. All of them are " partakers of the divine nature," 2 Pet. 1 : 4. When they love their enemies, bless them that curse them, do good to them that hate them, and pray for them who despitefully use them and persecute them, then they are the children of their Father which is in heaven, Matt. 5 : 44, 45. Godly is an abbreviation of godlike. If we are not like God, we are none of his. If we are like him, he will never deny his own image in us. Then sons have claims for care, protection, discipline, and the privilege of telling their sorrows to their father and appealing to him for aid and for redress of all their grievances. Nor is this all. Sons are heirs. They are heirs at law. No will or testament is necessary to give them the inheritance. But if a will and testament be made, leaving all things to them, surely none can longer doubt their title. To be called the sons and daughters of the Almighty (2 Cor. 6: 18) is to have the strongest terms of endearment applied to us.

15. *For ye have not received the spirit of bondage again to fear ; but ye have received the spirit of adoption, whereby we cry, Abba, Father.* Stuart's translation is expository : " Ye have not received a servile spirit, that ye should again be in fear." For *again* Tyndale, Cranmer and Genevan have *any more.* Before the renewing of the Holy Ghost, the spirit of servility had complete possession. Whenever men without right views of the Gospel solemnly think of God, their hearts are full of terror. In regeneration the Holy Spirit does not confirm or deepen this spirit of servility, but takes it away. If it returns at all, it is only when men fall into spiritual darkness, or declension, and lose sight, more or less, of the liberty, wherewith Christ makes his people free. Thus the Galatians

erred and suffered. Just so far as men are led by the Spirit of
God, he is to them the Spirit of adoption, and they in their hearts
own him as their Father. *Abba* is the Syro-Chaldaic word for Father. It was the name, by which a devout Hebrew would address
God. But as Paul was writing to the Romans, who understood
not his mother tongue, he gives the Greek also, thus translating
Abba. Theodoret thinks the use of the name father in two languages gives intensity. Such a view is at least harmless. Compare Mark 14: 36; Gal. 4: 6. But it seems doubtful whether in
any case more than a translation of a word in a language foreign
to that in which the evangelist or apostle is writing was intended.
Surely the idea of Calvin that the two words point to the indiscriminate offer of mercy to men derives no countenance from
Mark 14: 36; nor from our verse, where Paul is addressing Latins.
Cry, a strong word well translated. In their devotions God's
children *cry, cry out.* Compare Matt. 9: 27; Mark 9: 24; Luke 9:
39; John 7: 37; Gal. 4: 6; Jas. 5: 4, and many other places.

16. *The Spirit itself beareth witness with our spirit, that we are
the children of God.* The pronoun *itself* is used because in gender,
number and person it agrees with the word rendered Spirit. But
the masculine pronoun is also applied to the Holy Ghost, John
14: 26; 15: 26; 16: 8, 13, 14; and elsewhere. So that the scripture clearly teaches that the Spirit is not an influence but a person, of whom it is proper to say he, his, him. Several things the
Spirit of God certainly effects in the hearts of his people. He
convinces them of sin, of righteousness and of judgment, John 16:
8–11. He reveals to them the way of salvation by a Redeemer,
John 15: 26; 16: 14; Gal. 1: 16. He works in them all the Christian graces, Gal. 5: 22, 23. He strengthens all the good principles
which he implants, Eph. 3: 16; Col. 1: 11. Having done all this,
it would be marvellous if he gave to the soul no testimony of his
presence and of its own gracious state. Many, perhaps with an
unwise curiosity, ask how can the Spirit testify to us our acceptance with God? And some have said he never gives his witness
except through the word. But we know not the way of the Spirit
in any of his operations, natural or spiritual, Ecc. 11 : 5; John 3: 8.
He is a sovereign, and divides his gifts severally as he wills, 1 Cor.
12: 11. To deny the work of the Spirit because we know not the
manner of it is as unwise as to deny that the wind blows because
we cannot explain the phenomena attending it. It is freely admitted that God's Spirit honors his word in all his work in us, and
that he never witnesses contrary to his word; but no man can
prove that the Holy Spirit does not directly and immediately comfort, enlighten and animate the people of God, giving them good

hopes, bright prospects and delightful persuasions of their interest in Christ. Experienced Christians know that he does wonderful things for them, and that his presence converts night into day, dungeons into palaces, and racks and tortures into harmless things. This witness of the Spirit is not by voices from heaven, nor by dreams, nor by senseless impulses, nor by a fanatical delight in some words of scripture ; but by his testimony concurring with the clear and honest convictions of our own minds and hearts. The Spirit, by whom we have been born again, shines on his own blessed work within us, and we see the infallible tokens of our newness of life. True this doctrine may be abused, but if we deny every doctrine that is abused, we shall have a very short creed. Scott: " This ' witness of the Spirit' is borne along with that of our own consciences, not without it, nor against it ; and it coincides with the testimony of the Holy Spirit, in the scripture, and must be proved and assayed by it." God's Spirit never contradicts himself, as he would do, if he were to persuade a bad man that he was a child of God, or a good man that he was a child of the wicked one. Such a persuasion comes from the father of lies. If the foregoing be not true, how can a believer ever attain to assurance of faith or of hope? Compare 1 John 5 : 10.

17. *And if children, then heirs ; heirs of God, and joint heirs with Christ ; if so be that we suffer with him, that we may also be glorified together.* On heirs and heirship see above on Rom. 4 : 13, 14. Inspired writers often represent to us spiritual blessings, under the figure of an inheritance, Gal. 3 : 29; 4 : 1, 7, 30: Eph. 3 : 6 ; Tit. 3 : 7 : Heb. 1 : 14; 6 : 17; 11 : 7 ; Jas. 2 : 5 ; 1 Pet. 3 : 7 ; Rev. 21 : 7 ; and many other places. Brown of Haddington : " Saints are heirs of the promise ; heirs of righteousness ; heirs of salvation ; heirs of the grace of life ; heirs of the kingdom ; heirs of the world, heirs of God, and joint heirs with Jesus Christ. . . They inherit the earth, inherit promises, inherit all things." In considering our heirship we may regard God as our Father giving us our inheritance incorruptible, undefiled and unfading through Christ, or we may consider Christ as our elder brother, dying and by will and testament making us his heirs, Heb. 9 : 11–21. In our verse we are represented as inheriting from God through and with Christ. See Matt. 25 : 21 ; Luke 22 : 30; Rev. 3 : 21. There is no better title than that by inheritance. A large part of the wealth, power and honors of the world are or have been held by inheritance. But joint heirship with Christ implies a participation in the fellowship of his sufferings. This thought is often presented in scripture, Phil. 3 : 10 ; 2 Tim. 2 : 12. This is always an attendant upon our being called to the fellowship of God's Son.

18. *For I reckon that the sufferings of this present time* are *not worthy* to be compared *with the glory which shall be revealed in us.* Reckon, count, regard, compute, estimate, Wiclif: deem; Tyndale and Cranmer: suppose; Rheims: think; Stuart: count; Peshito and Doway: reckon. What *the sufferings of this present time* were may be learned from this epistle itself, even from this chapter, vs. 35–39. Compare 2 Cor. 4 : 8–10; 6:4–10; 11 : 23–30. These sufferings are not meet *to be compared with the glory that shall be revealed in us* or unto us. They cannot be compared in point of duration. The suffering is for a season, a moment, a little moment; the glory shall be enduring, shall outlive the sun, shall last world without end. Then the glory is absolutely unspeakable. Tholuck quotes R. Jacob as saying: " One hour's refreshment in the world to come is better than the whole of life on this side the grave." Lazarus had not been in Abraham's bosom for a moment till all painful impression of his earthly sufferings was gone for ever. Now we see through a glass darkly, but it shall not be so always. The verb *be revealed* is cognate to the noun from which the last book of scripture takes its name. For revealed, several of the old versions have showed; Peshito: developed. *To us* is perhaps better than *in us*, yet the latter rendering gives a good sense, coincident with the teachings of other scriptures, Eph. 3 : 10; 2 Thess. 1 : 10. Christians will be vessels of honor, fitted for the Master's use.

DOCTRINAL AND PRACTICAL REMARKS

1. We live and act under solemn and awful responsibilities, v. 12. Nothing can release us from their binding force. Go where we may, do what we will, we are *debtors;* we are under obligations of duty. The gospel does not release us from them; it does not relax them; it rather makes them the more solemn and tender. No obligations are stronger than those which have the sanctions of gratitude supperadded to those of authority and excellent majesty.

2. None of our obligations are to wrong, v. 12. Liberty to sin has never been granted to any creature. Of two natural evils we may choose the least. Of two moral evils we may choose neither. Nor is an upright man ever so situated by providence that he must violate the law of his being. In every temptation there is provided a way of escape, 1 Cor. 10: 13.

3. Particular duties devolve on particular persons, as the aged, the young, parents, children, husbands, wives, teachers, taught, strong and weak; but a large class of duties rest on all classes of

Christians, such as resisting the flesh, advancing in holiness, glorifying God in our bodies and spirits which are his. We are in
duty solemnly bound to deny all ungodliness and wordly lusts and
to live soberly, righteously and godly in this present evil world.
Nor can high station in any wise exempt us from our duty in anything. Paul was an apostle, yet includes himself among the
debtors. Chalmers : " There cannot be a more gross misunder-
standing of the gospel economy, than that it is destitute of as
plain and direct and intelligible sanctions against moral evil, as
those which were devised for upholding the legal economy."
Scott : " All that we owe to the flesh, is a holy revenge for the
injuries already done, and the hindrances already given us ; and
instead of rendering our state doubtful, by living after it in any
degree, we should, by the Spirit, continually endeavor, more and
more entirely, to mortify it, and repress all its actings."

4. The gospel is as powerless as the law to save him who lives
in sin and loves to have it so, v. 13. Christ is not the minister of
sin. He, who would make him so, grossly wrests the scriptures.
It never was more true than it is under the full blaze of gospel
light, that if men live after the flesh, they shall die. Men may
loudly boast of free grace and of their reliance on redemption;
but he, who perfects not holiness, accepts not the atonement.
Calvin : " There is no confidence in God, where there is no love
of righteousness." " Without holiness no man shall see the Lord"
is the evangelical rule, from which there is no departure.

5. But in order to any approved conformity to God we must
be partakers of the Holy Spirit, vs. 13, 15. Chrysostom : " There is
no way of mortifying the deeds of wickedness save through the
Spirit." He alone is able to subdue us unto righteousness. Good
motives are not wanting ; but they are found powerless, where the
Holy Ghost does not operate. Chalmers : " If the Holy Ghost
indeed be the agent of mortifying the deeds of the body, then he
will not select a few of our carnal tendencies for extermination
by his power ; but he will enter into hostility with all of them—
He will check the sensuality of our nature, and he will mortify its
pride, and he will check its impetuous anger, and he will wean it
from its now clinging avarice." In his blessed operations the
Spirit directs his energies against master sins and parent sins. Of
these none is more formidable than unbelief. To this he turns our
attention and against this he directs his power from the first, nor
does he ever cease to assault it till it is slain, John 16:9. All
good men have not equal degrees of light, of faith, or of holiness.
But they are habitually advancing in holiness, unless they are in
a state of spiritual declension. No Christian is satisfied with any

attainments he has made, until he awakes in God's likeness. The best of mere men receive the Spirit by measure. Blessed is he, who is filled with the Spirit, and who constantly cries for an increase of faith. But if one is sensual, having not the Spirit, he is dead in trespasses and in sins, and is no habitation of God. He that is joined to the Lord is one Spirit.

6. It is possible to mortify sin, v. 13. It can be done. It must be done. Unless it is done, iniquity will be our ruin. True, this cannot be done in human strength, or by human endeavors, unaided by divine grace. It is God that works in us both to will and to do of his good pleasure, Phil. 2 : 13. If we shall ever be saved, it must be by our God fulfilling all the good pleasure of his goodness, and the work of faith with power, 2 Thess. 1 : 11. If our faith is ever to give us the victory, it must be a faith which is of the operation of God, Col. 2 : 12. This is the ancient belief and joy of the saints: "Lord, thou wilt ordain peace for us: for thou also hast wrought all our works in us," Isa. 26 : 12. This work of putting sin to death in believers is very diverse from those checks to reigning wickedness which sometimes appear to be given by the wicked. Their warfare with sin is conducted in a feeble way, by arraying one sin against another, as covetousness against intemperance ; by drawing motives from earthly considerations, as a regard to public opinion ; or by the remorse of conscience ; or by an appeal to the natural sense of justice or amiability ; or to avoid some kind of temporal trouble. They never do actually make war on sin as such. They often resolve on some amendment ; but their purposes relying on human strength and wisdom readily yield to strong temptation. The great defects of their endeavors are these : 1. they are not directed against all sin; 2. they are not really hearty and determined ; 3. they are in human strength, without the Spirit ; 4. they are occasional or fitful, not steady and persevering. Their goodness is like the morning cloud and the early dew.

7. The mortification, to which we are called, is not will-worship, nor voluntary humility, nor neglecting the wants and necessities of the body, Col. 2 : 18, 23 ; but it consists in warring against the sinful actings of our corrupt nature. Chrysostom ; "You see that it is not the essence of the body whereof he is discoursing, but the deeds of the flesh. . . What sort of deeds then does he mean us to mortify? Those which tend toward wickedness, those which go after vice, which there is no other way of mortifying save through the Spirit."

8. Holy men shall be saved, not for the merit of their holiness, but because they are prepared unto glory. Yes, they shall live,

v. 13; live before God, live in eternal glory, enjoying the life ever-lasting, and none others shall.   As death is the sum of all penal misery, so life is the sum of all good things to the redeemed.

9. Let us never forget our dependence on the Spirit of God for guidance and support, v. 14.   And let us not perplex ourselves with questions to no profit.   Chalmers: " His work is visible, but his working is not so.   It is not of his operation that we are conscious, but of the result of that operation."   If we but see in us a godlike character, if the Christian graces flourish in our hearts, if we hate sin more and more, if we hunger and thirst after right-eousness, we may infallibly know that we are the subjects of the Spirit's operation.   The guidance of the Holy Spirit is first for illumination.   It was after they were illuminated, that the Hebrews endured a great fight of affliction, Heb. 10 : 32.   Had the affliction come first, they would not have been ready for it.   Men are never brought savingly to trust in Christ, till the eyes of their under-standing are enlightened by the Holy Spirit of promise, Eph. 1 : 13, 18.   This enlightening shows us the truth as it is in Jesus. It embraces so much truth as is necessary to our salvation ; in par-ticular it embraces the essential truths respecting the person, work and glory of Christ, as a Redeemer.   Then the Spirit purifies the hearts of believers by the truth, John 17 : 17; and is in them a well-spring of spiritual good and virtue springing up into ever-lasting life, John 4 : 14.   He is the author of every Christian grace, Gal. 5 ; 22, 23.   It is by the Spirit that sin is subdued, v. 13.   It is by the same Spirit that we have any humble and good hope through grace, v. 15.   He is the great author of all right prayer, v. 26. Without him we can do nothing.   To him let us therefore look, and whatever of temporal good we may fail to pray for, let us not fail to ask for large measures of the Holy Spirit, Luke 11 : 13.

10. It seems impossible for us fairly to avoid the doctrine of the special influences of the Holy Ghost, or the doctrine of special grace, v. 14.   Stuart, who often seems to have difficulties concern-ing the doctrines of grace, on this verse admits the truth in a very pleasant and unanswerable way : " If nothing but the simple means of moral suasion is employed in guiding the children of God, how do they differ from others, who enjoy the same means?   If you say, ' The difference is that the former *obey* the suasion, while the latter *resist* it ;' I answer: The fact is true; but then it does not reach the point of difficulty.   How comes the one to *obey* the sua-sion, and the other to *resist* it? . . . What was the efficient cause why one obeys and the other disobeys?   The passage before us (v. 14,) ascribes it to the influence of the Spirit of God."   If he operated on all equally and sufficiently with his almighty energies,

all would surely embrace Christ. But some resist to the last, having not the Spirit.   It looks like base ingratitude in one, who receives special mercies not to say so, openly, unequivocally and on
all fit occasions.

11. The pious need not fear any reproach or dishonor to which
men may subject them here. They are the sons of God, who is a
great king, and that is honor enough, v. 14. The poorest, feeblest,
most despised child of God is more honorable than the greatest,
most famous and powerful man of the world, who has not the love
of Christ in his heart. All this will soon be confessed by all men
and all angels.

12. The spirit of bondage, the principle of tormenting fear,
could never make men better, could never produce happy effects,
v. 15.   It never did so.   Chalmers: " This spirit of bondage,
which is unto fear, can only be exchanged for the Spirit of adoption, by our believing the gospel.   Every legal attempt to extricate ourselves from the misery of the former spirit, will only
aggravate it the more." This is true. Jesus Christ meets all the
wants of the poor trembling, helpless soul. Oh that men would
flee to Christ. Haldane: " All who are not dead to the law, and
know of no way to escape divine wrath but by obeying it, must
be under the spirit of bondage. For so far from fulfilling the demands of the law, they fail in satisfying themselves."   There is no
way for a sinful man ever to engage with alacrity in God's service,
except through Jesus Christ, John 14 : 6.   Anything that leads or
drives a sinner out of himself and away from the law as a means
of salvation is an unspeakable mercy.

13. By how rich a variety of appropriate terms and phrases
God has conveyed to us an idea of the certainty of his people
sharing in his everlasting favor and blessings. Here we have the
matter illustrated by *adoption*, v. 15. This was no doubt well understood, as a civil regulation, by those to whom Paul wrote.
Adoption was known in Roman law and carried with it all the
legal advantages of a birthright to honor and wealth. Haldane:
" Adoption is not a work of grace in us, but an act of God's grace
without us.   It is taking those who were by nature children of
wrath from the family of Satan, to which they originally belonged,
into the family of God."   Oftentimes adoption, as a civil institution, led to misery, the parties not being congenial. But that no
such unhappiness may arise in the case of his children, the Lord
sends into their hearts the spirit of adoption, Crying, Abba, Father.
This makes all delightful. Chrysostom: " Since it is not all children that are heirs, the Apostle shews that we are both children
and heirs; next, as it is not all heirs that are heirs to any great

amount, he shews that we have this point with us too, as we are
heirs of God. Again, since it were possible to be God's heirs,
but in no sense *joint heirs with* the Only-begotten, he shews that
we have this also." Was there ever such heirship? Was there
ever such adoption? Let not the saints grieve at their present
low estate, Gal. 4 : 1, 2. Ere long all will come right.

14. We must hold fast the doctrine of the witness of the Spirit, v.
16. It is a sheet anchor of Christian consolation. There are three
that bear record [or witness] in heaven, the Father, the Word, and
the Holy Ghost, and there are three that bear witness [or record]
in earth, the Spirit, and the water, and the blood; and these three
agree in one. Without this doctrine how can we know that we
are of the truth? Hodge: "Assurance of hope is not fanatical,
but is an attainment which every Christian should make. If the
witness of men is received, the witness of God is greater." Are
not the heirs of life sealed with the spirit of promise?" Calvin:
" The import of the whole is this—' All those are the sons of God
who are led by the Spirit of God; all the sons of God are heirs
of eternal life; then all who are led by God's Spirit ought to feel
assured of eternal life. " Olshausen: " The [Roman] Catholic
Church, with which all sects that proceed from Pelagian principles agree, deters from the certainty of the state of grace, and desires uncertainty towards God. Such uncertainty of *hearts* is then
a convenient means to keep men in the leading-strings of the
priesthood or ambitious founders of sects; for since they are not
allowed to have any certainty themselves respecting their relation
to God, they can only rest upon the judgments of their leaders
about it, who thus rule souls with absolute dominion; the true
evangelic doctrine makes free from such slavery to man."

15. What Christians are, they are by the grace of God; and
all the grace of God to sinners is by and through Jesus Christ, v.
17.. If Christians are heirs of God, it is only because they are
joint heirs with Christ. Were it possible that their relation to
him could be dissolved, all their pleasing expectations of an inheritance undefiled would perish forever. Severed from Christ,
the best man would be a withered branch, fit only to be burned.

16. United to Christ all is well with believers. They shall be
glorified together with him, v. 17. What that means we cannot
now tell. Inspiration itself admits that mortals cannot comprehend so glorious a theme, John 3 : 12. " Beloved, now are we the
sons of God, and it doth not yet appear what we shall be: but we
know that when he shall appear, we shall be like him; for we shall
see him as he is," 1 John 3 : 2.

17. Let not the people of God be dismayed at the prospect of

suffering, nor even be startled when it is foretold. What are all the sufferings of this life compared with the glory which shall soon be revealed in all the sons of God? So far from afflictions proving that a believer is not in favor with God, the opposite is most true. "As many as I love, I rebuke and chasten." "He scourgeth every son whom he receiveth." Even in this life the testimony of all the humble is, "It is good for me that I have been afflicted." "Before I was afflicted, I went astray; but now have I kept thy word." O how does sanctified affliction strip earth of its delusive charms, write vanity of vanities on all that perishes with the using, bring down high looks and proud imaginations, and make the devout long for their home in the skies, where the wicked cease from troubling, and the weary are at rest! There is a general, perhaps a universal impression among Christians of any considerable experience that they could not have made even their present attainments, inconsiderable as they may be, without the chastisements which have come upon them. It is common for them to sing,

I bless thee for all, but most for the severe.

Chapter 19

ROMANS 8

VERSES 19-23

THE CREATURE SUBJECT TO VANITY. REDEMP-
TION COMING.

19 For the earnest expectation of the creature waiteth for the manifestation of the sons of God.

20 For the creature was made subject to vanity, not willingly, but by reason of him who hath subjected *the same* in hope ;

21 Because the creature itself also shall be delivered from the bondage of corruption into the glorious liberty of the children of God.

22 For we know that the whole creation groaneth and travaileth in pain together until now.

23 And not only *they*, but ourselves also, which have the first fruits of the Spirit, even we ourselves groan within ourselves, waiting for the adoption, *to wit,* the redemption of our body.

THE history of interpretation shows great diversity attending the exposition of this passage. Stuart enumerates as many as eleven different explanations of the word *creature* found in these verses. A more recent writer has added a twelfth. Yet two things may properly be said : 1. Several of these expositions are wild and fanciful, and deserve no extended consideration. Stuart himself regards a number of them as "too improbable to need discussion." 2. The great mass of sound and sober expositors are perhaps as united in their exposition of this as of any other portion of scripture, in understanding which there is any considerable difficulty. And it is pleasant to see how opinions seem to be settling down more and more in the right direction. In v. 18 the apostle had stated that great glory was to be revealed in God's people. He now proceeds to notice an apparent discouragement to such an expectation, arising from the vanity to which the creature was subjected.

It is generally admitted that the interpretation turns upon the meaning given to the word thrice rendered creature, and once,

creation in these verses. To the English reader the difficulty is
rather increased by rendering the same word in the same connection both *creature* and *creation*, although in each case the word
clearly has precisely the same meaning. Both Bretschneider and
Robinson state that the word sometimes means the act of creating,
and both properly cite Rom. 1 : 20 in proof. Bretschneider also
cites Mark. 10 : 6; 13 : 19; 2 Pet. 3 : 4 in proof of the same thing.
In each of those places we have the phrase—from the beginning
of the creation—which may mean from the beginning of the existence of created things or from the time when God began to make
them. So that these verses are not cited by Robinson in proof
that the word means the act of creating. Again the word sometimes means anything created, the creature, the product of creative power. Clearly this is its meaning in Rom. 1 : 25 ; 8 : 39 ;
" They worshipped and served the *creature* more than the Creator ;"
" Nor any other *creature* shall be able to separate us from the love
of God." It has the same meaning in Col. 1 : 15 ; Heb. 4 : 13. In
Heb. 9 : 11 the same word is rendered *building* in contrast with the
tabernacle or temple. In 1 Pet. 2 : 13 it is rendered *ordinance* of
man. This gives a good sense and is generally accepted, but
Stuart prefers to read every human being, or every man. In Rev.
3 : 14 Christ is called the beginning [or head] of the *creation* of
God. This includes all worlds—all creatures. When preaching
is spoken of the word is limited to mankind, Mark 16 : 15 ; Col.
1 : 23 ; " Preach the gospel to every creature ;" " The gospel was
preached to every creature which is under heaven." Again, the
word *new* is put before it, as in 2 Cor. 5 : 17 ; Gal. 6 : 15 ; " If any
man be in Christ, he is a new *creature ;*" " In Christ Jesus neither
circumcision nor uncircumcision availeth anything but a new creature." Here *new creature* is equivalent to regeneration or the product of regeneration. Again, we have the word *whole* or *every* put
with creature, Mark 16 : 15 ; Rom. 8 : 23 ; " Preach the gospel to
every creature ;" " We know that the *whole creation* [or all the crea-
tion] groaneth." From all this it is evident that the word with or
without qualifying adjectives is used to denote men indiscriminately, Christians, the universe, anything made, the irrational creation, any result of creative power.

Without paying attention to wild and fanciful notions not
worthy of consideration, it may be stated that in these verses the
word creature cannot mean the universe ; for the best, the heavenly
part of the universe, has never been subject to vanity, and never
groans nor is in pain. It does not need any deliverance from the
bondage of corruption, but already enjoys the liberty of the children of God. It is manifest therefore that all creation is not spoken

of. Heaven is excepted. The same line of remark excludes the angels. Nor can it mean the fallen angels. They are not waiting *in hope*, nor shall they be delivered into the liberty of God's sons. Nor can the *creature* mean Christians, for: 1. Though they are called *new creatures*, they are never denominated simply creatures; 2. They are expressly spoken of by themselves in contrast with the creature, v. 22: "And not only they, but ourselves also, which have the first fruits of the Spirit," etc. Nor can the *creature* mean the world of mankind taken indiscriminately. For 1. men generally are eager after wealth, and honor, and pleasure, but it is not true that they earnestly expect the manifestation of the sons of God; 2. nor is it true that men were made subject to vanity not willingly. What is more clear from God's word than that wicked men willingly stay away from Christ and are willingly ignorant of the truths of the gospel? John 5 : 40; 2 Pet. 3 : 5. John Newton: "It is so far from being the concurrent desire of all mankind, or indeed the desire of any single person, to obtain freedom from the bondage of sin, that we are naturally pleased with it, and yield a willing subjection to it." All the wicked sin freely, and willingly. 3. Nor is it true that mankind indiscriminately shall be "delivered from the bondage of corruption." It is only those who believe with the heart on the Lord Jesus and love him, that shall have "the glorious liberty of the children of God." These objections are not fanciful, nor frivolous. They are drawn from these verses themselves. One can but wonder therefore to find Locke paraphrasing them and applying them to "the whole race of mankind;" and Macknight, to "mankind" and "all mankind;" and Whitby, to "all the world;" and Stuart, to "unconverted men in general," or "mankind in general."

The only other exposition, which claims attention, and which has not been virtually or formally excluded by the foregoing remarks, is that by the creature we shall understand the irrational creation, whether animate or inanimate. This is very different from that exposition which confines the word creature to brutes. That would very much limit the thought, and impair the beauty of the matter here represented. In applying it to the irrational creation it is of course necessary to suppose a bold use of that figure of speech called PERSONIFICATION. That this is a lawful mode of speaking none will deny. The Bible abounds in it. Some have made large collections of such places. If any wish fully to satisfy their minds, let them examine even a few of the following passages, Gen. 3 : 17; "Cursed is the ground for thy sake;" Gen. 4 : 11; Lev. 26 : 3-8; Ps. 19 : 1-4; 77 : 16; 97 : 4, 5; 98 : 4, 7, 8; 114 : 3-6; Isa. 1 : 2, 11; 4 : 6-8; 24 : 4-7; 55 : 12; Jer. 12 : 4;

Hab. 3 : 10 ; Luke 19 : 40.   That the Bible employs this figure, and in its boldest forms is therefore undeniable.   Ammon thinks for the plain, didactic style of Paul, personification here would be too sublime ; and Stuart thinks it would be an instance of the use of that figure even beyond what we find in Hebrew poetry.   An examination of half the places just pointed out will show that there is here nothing beyond the style of several of the prophets.   Nor do other parts of this epistle, or even of this chapter make the impression that the apostle is employing a style at all free from figures.   He has already personified sin, death, the law and the carnal mind.   The seventh and eighth chapters abound in very bold figures.   All this only proves that he may be using personification, not that he is employing it.   But that there is nothing extravagant in so understanding the apostle will be admitted when it is known that Chrysostom, Theodoret, Theophylact, Jerome, Ambrose, Beausobre, Luther, Calvin, Ferme, Brown, John Newton, Doddridge, Rosenmuller, Koppe, Flatt, Tholuck, Scott, President Hopkins, Hodge, Haldane and others have so explained the passage.   Some of these give to the figure a more comprehensive scope than others, but all agree that we have here personification. Chrysostom : " His discourse becomes more emphatic and he personifies this whole world as the prophets also do, when they introduce the floods clapping their hands, and little hills leaping, and mountains skipping."   Calvin : " I understand the passage to have this meaning—that there is no element and no part of the world, which, being touched, as it were, with a sense of its present misery, does not intensely hope for a resurrection."   Brown : " In these verses he brings in the creature, that is, the fabric of the world, heaven and earth, and the rest of the insensible and irrational creatures, and makes use of them in a figurative manner, and speaketh of them in borrowed expressions, that hereby he might incite believers the more, both to expect certainly that glory which is to be revealed, and to wait for it patiently under crosses."   Many others might be cited to the same effect.   These quotations are made not to prove a personification here, but to show the exact conception in the minds of this class of expositors.   Whether this mode of explaining these verses is correct or not can only appear by this method suiting the whole passage, and by no other method suiting it at all, or so well.   It has already been shown by reference to many parts of scripture that the irrational creation has suffered from sin.   Man's poverty and covetousness and cruelty make many brutes wretched.   The fourth commandment forbids overworking beasts of burden and of draft.   The wisest of mere men says, " A righteous man regardeth the life of his beast," Pr. 12 : 10.   There

are many, who are cruel to brutes. And the earth itself is cursed,
bringing forth briers and thorns and noxious weeds instead of
precious grains and fruits as it did before sin entered. Compare
Gen. 2 : 5, 6; 3 : 17–19. There is then nothing unnatural or unusual in the conception of the apostle here, if he does represent
the whole world as affected by sin. Nor does the apostle say, nor
do other scriptures teach that the marks of sin and the tokens of
wrath shall ever be found on the face of nature or in irrational
creatures. Far from it. Verses 19, 20, 21 and 23 teach just the
contrary. Some of these thoughts will present themselves in new
forms, and others kindred to them will arise as we proceed in the
exposition.

19. *For the earnest expectation of the creature waiteth for the manifestation of the sons of God. Earnest expectation,* in the Greek one
word, here only and in Phil. 1 : 20, well rendered there as here.
Tyndale, Cranmer and Genevan have fervent desire. Chrysostom : " Earnest expectation implies expecting intensely." Owen
of Oxford : " An intent and earnest expectation, expressing itself
by putting forth the head, and looking round about with earnestness and diligence." John Newton : " The word is very emphat-
ical ; it imports a raising up or thrusting forward the head, as
persons who are in suspense for the return of a messenger, or the
issue of some interesting event." *Waiteth,* found also in vs. 23, 25
and always rendered as here or look for. Calvin : " The expression,
expectation expects, or waits for, though somewhat unusual, yet has
a most suitable meaning ; for he meant to intimate, that all creatures, seized with great anxiety, and held in suspense with great
desire, look for that day which shall openly exhibit the glory of
the children of God." The word rendered manifestation is the
same as the name of the last book of scripture, and in Rom. 2 : 5 ;
16 : 25 is rendered revelation. We had the cognate verb in v. 18.
Throughout this epistle it is rendered revealed. This verse naturally suggests 1 John 3 : 2, " Beloved, now are we the sons of God,
and it doth not yet appear what we shall be : but we know that
when he shall appear, we shall be like him ; for we shall see him
as he is." At present things are not right ; the good are depressed ;
bad men are exalted ; Lazarus is a beggar ; Dives fares sumptu-
ously every day ; Naboth is slain ; Ahab holds the vineyard ; from
the way men fare, it is impossible to tell who is a saint and who is
a sinner ; one event happeneth to all alike ; or, if there is any difference, the vile often seem to have the advantage : they flourish
like a green bay tree ; they have more than heart could wish ;
their eyes stand out with fatness ; virtue is unrequited ; vice is
rampant. But it shall not be so always ; God has so purposed ;

righteousness so requires; nature would lift up her hands in horror at the thought of this state of things being perpetual. The creature expects that a time is rapidly approaching when things will be adjusted, and all shall discern between the righteous and the wicked, between him that serveth God and him that serveth him not.

20. *For the creature was made subject to vanity, not willingly, but by reason of him who hath subjected* the same *in hope.* Peshito: For the creation was subjected to vanity, not by its own choice, but because of him who hath subjected it, etc. Was made subject and hath subjected are different forms of the same verb. We met it in Rom. 8 : 7 with a negative, is not subject; in Rom. 10 : 2 it is with a negative rendered have not submitted; and in Rom 13 : 1 Let every soul be subject. The subjection may be reluctant or voluntary, the context determining that matter. In this case it was *not willingly*, that is it was by constraint. See 1 Pet. 5 : 2. This subjection was to *vanity*, a word with its cognates uniformly rendered. See Eph, 4 : 17; 2 Pet. 2 : 18. The life of a wicked man is called a vain conversation, 1 Pet. 1 : 18. When one with special care examines the scriptures on this point he is surprised to find how much is said of the vanity of an earthly existence even in man, who is supposed to have some dominion over the creatures. Pages might be filled with lamentations of both good and bad men over the utter vanity of all human pursuits. The words of Ethan the Ezrahite and of Solomon can never be forgotten. "Wherefore hast thou made all men in vain?" and "Vanity of vanities; all is vanity," Ps. 89 : 47; Ecc. 1 : 2. If man, with all his foresight, sagacity and contrivance, and living under a mediatorial system— a scheme of grace—is still so subject to vanity, how wretched must be the existence of the lower orders of animals? So foul has been human wickedness that on one occasion the sun literally hid his face and refused to behold the atrocity. The stars once felt such sympathy with the right and such abhorrence of the wrong, that they fought against Sisera, Luke 23 : 44; Judges 5 : 20. Yea the earth has quaked and the rocks have rent at the vileness of man, Matt. 27 : 51. The creature feels insulted and abused, degraded and wretched by being subjected to witness such sights, bear such monsters of wickedness and groan under such wanton wrongs. By *him that hath subjected* some have understood Satan, the tempter of our first parents; others, Adam our federal head, whose disobedience brought down the curse; and others, Nero who ruled in great cruelty for awhile. But the better and more common opinion is that we are to understand the Lord himself. John Newton: " God, the righteous judge, subjected the creature

to vanity, as the just consequence and desert of man's disobedience. But he has subjected it *in hope;* with a reserve in favor of his own people, by which, though they are liable to trouble, they are secured from the penal desert of sin, and the vanity of the creature is by his wisdom overruled to wise and gracious purposes. The earth, and all in it, was made for the sake of man : for his sin it was cursed, and afterwards destroyed by water; and sin at last shall set it on fire. But God, who is rich in mercy, appointed a people to himself out of the fallen race : for their sakes, and as a theatre whereon to display the wonders of his providence and grace, it was renewed after the flood and still continues; but not in its original state : there are marks of the evil of sin, and of God's displeasure against it wherever we turn our eyes." But this state of things shall not last always. There is *hope* of deliverance. That deliverance shall surely come. The subjection to vanity is not everlasting. Some make the words "by him who hath subjected it" parenthetical, and connect the words "in hope" with what comes after. There is no objection to this change; but the sense is much the same either way. This hope, which animates, is a hope that cannot fail.

21. *Because the creature itself also shall be delivered from the bondage of corruption into the glorious liberty of the children of God.* The sun, moon and stars shall not always be compelled to look down on a world offering hourly insults to their Maker. The earth shall cease to groan in the whole line of her longitude under the burden of man's sins. The winds shall not always be liable to be called on to waft vessels on errands of piracy and of blood. Wicked men shall not always wantonly wield their weapons against innocent beasts, and birds, and fishes; guilt shall be driven from the earth; death and hell shall be cast into the lake of fire ; there shall be a new heaven and a new earth, wherein dwelleth righteousness. There shall be no more curse. Sin and Satan shall no longer seduce ; and sorrow and sighing shall flee away. Calvin : "All creatures, according to their nature, shall be participators of a better condition." Guyse; "While we observe the present unnatural situation of the sensitive and inanimate parts of the world, we seem to see them looking forward in hope, that they also, at the restitution of all things (Acts 3 : 21), shall be delivered from all the oppression and confusion, which, by the sin of man, they have been subjected to; and that they shall be restored to their primitive liberty and order." Man, as the head of creation in this world, led the way to sin, and misery. As the redeemed of the Lord, pious men shall lead the way to peace, and love, and joy. Their perfect liberty, wondrous enlargement and

glorious rest shall bring to an end the curse that has fallen on the world, its fabric, and its creatures. Some think that *corruption* in this verse and vanity in the preceding verse mean the same thing, and are synonymous with sin. Such an opinion may be harmless in the minds of some : and no doubt each of those words does sometimes point directly to sin, 1 Pet. 1 : 18 ; 2 Pet. 2 : 19. But generally *vanity* seems rather to denote the unprofitableness and unsatisfactory nature of a thing or of a course of conduct than its guilt or its depravity. *Corruption* also often points to the fruits and consequences of sin rather than to sin itself, Gal. 6 : 8 ; 1 Cor. 15 : 42, 50. The creature has not been made sinful, but it sees and feels, in its measure, many of the sad effects of sin, as vanity, corruption and death. In due time it shall feel them no longer.

22. *For we know that the whole creation groaneth and travaileth in pain together until now.* The force of *we know*, says Stuart, is, " No one can have any doubt, we are all assured, no one will call in question." *Whole creation*, all the creation, or every creature. *Groaneth together*, found here only in the New Testament, well translated. *Travaileth in pain together*, one word in Greek found here only and well rendered. This verse repeats in other words what had been said before. Calvin says the similitude here used " shows that the groaning of which he speaks will not be in vain and without effect ; for it will at length bring forth a joyful and blessed fruit." *Together* is involved in both the verbs of this verse, and may mean that one part of creation sympathizes with other parts, or that all creation sympathizes with the children of God. The former is better sustained by the grammar. But either idea is sustained by scripture usage, Job 5 : 24 ; Jer. 44 : 44 ; Amos 5 : 19 ; Mark 16 : 18 ; Acts 28 : 4-6. The pain and sorrow are *until now*, from the fall of man to this time. It will last till the " manifestation of the sons of God."

23. *And not only* they [the whole creation], *but ourselves also, which have the first fruits of the Spirit, even we ourselves groan within ourselves, waiting for the adoption,* to wit, *the redemption of our body. Ourselves and we ourselves*, the Lord's regenerated people, proven to be on their way to everlasting happiness by the fact that they have the Spirit, who is the pledge of salvation. Owen of Oxford : " The first fruits of the Spirit must be either what he first worketh in us, or all his fruits in us with respect unto the full harvest that is to come ; or the Spirit himself, as the beginning and pledge of future glory. And the latter of these is intended in this place." See Rom. 11 : 16 ; 16 : 5 ; 1 Cor. 15 : 20, 23 ; 16 : 15 ; Jas. 1 : 18 ; Rev. 14 : 4. These are the only places in the New Testament where the word rendered first fruits occurs. But the idea of first fruits was

very familiar to the Jewish mind. That the first fruits were regarded as a sample and pledge of the harvest seems certain. So
the Holy Spirit dwelling in us is a pledge of the glorious inheritance above. This is taught not only by the term first fruits, but
by another word, a commercial term borrowed from the Pheni-
cians, which means pledge, and is always rendered *earnest*. Twice
do we read of the earnest of the Spirit, and once he is said to be
the earnest of our inheritance, 2 Cor. 1 : 22; 5 : 5; Eph. 1 : 14. No
voice from heaven, no vision of angels could so clearly declare
and determine our title to heaven and our being in a course of
preparation for it as the indwelling of the Holy Ghost. That
earnest is infallible. Yet those who have it do *groan*, groan within themselves. The same word is so rendered on the same subject in 2 Cor. 5 : 2; in Mark 7 : 34 it is rendered sighed. Stuart's
paraphrase is: "We suppress the rising sigh; we bow with submission to the will of God which afflicts us; we receive his chastisement as children; our frail nature feels it, and we sigh or
groan inwardly; but no murmuring word escapes us; we suppress the outward demonstration of pain, lest we should even
seem to complain." *Waiting for* the adoption, expecting it. *Adoption*, always so rendered, Rom. 8 : 15; 9 : 4; Gal. 4 : 5; Eph. 1 : 5.
Redemption, always so rendered but once, Heb. 11 : 35, where it is
deliverance. Adoption is richer, and comprehends more than redemption of the body. Hodge: "The latter event is to be coincident with the former, and is included in it, as one of its prominent
parts. Both expressions therefore designate the same period." In
the manuscript discourse of the lamented Hoge already referred
to are these pleasing sentences: "Among the Romans there were
two kinds of adoption into families of the great—private and public. The Christian has already been received into the family of
God. He is a *child*. But he is yet in obscurity. His character
is often mistaken—his sonship doubted—his title denied. But the
Spirit of adoption still abides in his heart. He calls God his
Father, and waits with longing heart for his clear manifestation,
among all the sons of God—his holy brethren—amid the glories
of his Father's throne. His adoption is, indeed, three-fold. In the
eternal purpose of God he was chosen to be a Son;—in time he
is sealed as the peculiar treasure of God, unto the day of redemption; and shall finally be welcomed, with great rejoicing, to his
Father's house. That it is this future, public and glorious adoption that is here referred to is clear from the very words of the
apostle—'waiting for the adoption, to wit, the redemption of the
body.' The resurrection of the body, which is but part of the believer's adoption, is yet, here, called his adoption, because it is the

last crowning act, which renders it complete and illustrious. His body has long lain in corruption. It has been buried in the grave as unworthy of entrance with him into his Father's house. But now it is raised incorruptible, and fashioned to the likeness of Christ's glorious body : and now, body and soul, both bought with blood by the Eternal Son—both washed and glorified by the Eternal Spirit—both accepted and openly acknowledged by the Father—enter together, inseparably united, the New Jerusalem— the palace of the King of kings and Lord of lords."

DOCTRINAL AND PRACTICAL REMARKS

1. Let not God's people be dejected at their present obscurity, v. 19. It is all right. The Saviour himself was not recognized by the great mass of men in his day. John Newton: "The sons of God are now hidden, unknown, unnoticed, and misrepresented for the most part. Their life is in many respects hidden from themselves, and their privileges altogether hidden from the world. But ere long they will be manifested, their God will openly acknowledge them ; every cloud by which they are now obscured shall be removed, and they shall shine like the sun in the kingdom of their Father."

2. While a real sense of the vanity of earthly things without any just views of the truths of religion will make no man better, yet where men are duly enlightened concerning spiritual things, it is a great matter to be assured of the unsatisfying nature of all things that perish, v. 20. Let every good man remember how short his time is, and how perishable are all things below the skies. Every thing is subject to vanity and the bondage of corruption. " Surely our fathers have inherited lies, vanity, and things wherein there is no profit," Jer. 16 : 19. Can anything be more foolish than to set our hearts on the things that perish, expecting from them solid blessedness? One thus explains such conduct : " It is because they are estranged from God, have no sense of his excellency, no regard for his glory, no knowledge of their own proper good. Fire and hail, wind and storm fulfil the word of God, though poor mortals dare to disobey."

3. How necessary is divine revelation, vs. 19–23. Who can solve the mystery of nature? The heathen have seen it and deplored it. Philosophy and human wit cast no light on the subject. None have cried out with more eloquence on this subject than Voltaire himself : " Who can, without horror, consider the whole world as an empire of destruction? It abounds with wonders; it abounds also with victims. It is a vast field of carnage and contagion.

Every species is without pity pursued and torn to pieces through
the air and earth and water.   In man there is more wretchedness
than in all the other animals put together."   Much more does he
say to the same effect, yet not one ray of light does he cast on the
subject, but concludes his dreadful picture with these sullen words:
" *I wish I had never been born.*"   Great masses of men have for
ages been sunk in idolatry.   The creatures given to man for his
good and God's glory are perverted to purposes of vanity and
shame; and until the Bible comes and says, 'Death entered by
sin,' we get no light whatever.   If the creation groans under bondage, man's offences against his Maker are in Scripture assigned as
the cause.   This scripture explains the great mystery of physical
evil.   Hume: "The whole is a riddle, an enigma, an inexplicable
mystery.   Doubt, uncertainty, suspense of judgment appear the
result of our most accurate scrutiny concerning this subject."
But if the creature is made subject to vanity and brought under
the bondage of corruption, and made to groan and travail in pain
on account of human guilt, the whole is plain enough.   Hoge:
" *Physical evil is the dark expression of the wrath of a holy God against
sin.*"

4. Well may it reconcile good men to an humble lot, and lead
them lightly to esteem the honors, pleasures and riches of earth to
remember that God gives these things chiefly to his enemies,
v. 25.   John Newton: "The earth is the Lord's and the fulness
thereof; yet the chief parts and possessions of it are in the hands
of those who hate him; yea, his enemies employ his creatures
against his own friends."

5. But things shall not be thus always.   Better days are coming.
The creature is subjected *in hope*, v. 20.   Chrysostom: "If the
creation which was made entirely for thee is in hope, much more
oughtest thou to be, through whom the creation is to come to the
enjoyment of all these good things."   Yes, glory be to God, the
night is far spent.   The day is at hand: AND SUCH A DAY!

6. Sin is indeed an inconceivably dreadful evil, vs. 20–22.   Calvin: "It is indeed meet for us to consider what a dreadful curse
we have deserved, since all created things in themselves blameless, both on earth and in the visible heaven undergo punishment
for our sins; for it has not happened through their own fault, that
they are liable to corruption.   Thus the condemnation of mankind is imprinted on the heavens, and on the earth, and on all creatures."   Haldane: "It would be derogatory to the glory of God
to suppose that his works are now in the same condition in which
they were at first formed, or that they will always continue as at
present. . . The righteous judge who subjected them to vanity

in consequence of the disobedience of man has made provision for their final restoration.

7. How very blind, stupid and insensible are the great mass of ungodly men, who seem to live without any just conception of the evil of sin, or of the intolerable miseries inseparably connected with it. The irrational creature feels the effects of sin and groans, vs. 20–22. But poor, hardened, depraved men, except when under some sore judgment, or some unusual visitations of compunction, lament but little their fallen state or deplorable guilt.

8. If irrational creatures are already subjected to vanity and corruption for the sin of man, let us beware how we needlessly add to the wretchedness of dumb brutes by overwork, by indulging passion towards them, or by denying them needed care, vs. 19–22. No wise man would be willing to be in the power of one who would be cruel to a brute. God once gave a tongue to an ass to reprove the madness of a prophet.

9. The children of God shall yet have a glorious liberty, v. 21. The chains of bondage shall be broken. We know in fact very little respecting the particulars of that great change. Our knowl- is rather negative than positive. But when a God of all and infinite perfections addresses himself to the business of emancipating, exalting and glorifying any of his creatures, we know there can be no failure. The very pangs of creation in sympathy with the sons of God demonstrate that some glorious renovation shall take place—a restitution every way worthy of God, its glorious Author. Calvin: "The excellency of our glory is of such importance, even to the very elements, which are destitute of mind and reason, that they turn with a certain kind of desire for it." Nor shall that desire be disappointed. Hodge: "The future glory of the saints must be inconceivably great, if the whole creation, from the beginning of the world, groans and longs for its manifestation."

10. If these things are so, ought not Christians to look with the tenderest concern on the nations that know not God and are ignorant of the gospel of his Son? Have Christians no pity? Are their compassions all gone? Dare they any longer keep among themselves the great mystery of God and of Christ, and do nothing for the nations that sit in the region and shadow of death? "Where no vision is, the people perish." We cannot plead the want of authority; for there stands our great commission: "Go ye into all the world and preach the gospel to every creature."

11. Let no professed follower of Christ sink down into inertness

and inaction, but let him do his duty and patiently wait for the result, v. 23. Stuart: "Let them not regard the present world as their home. It is not the Canaan in which they are to rest. They must 'seek a city which hath foundations, whose builder and maker is God.' Then the agitated breast, the heaving sigh, the groaning within will no more annoy or distress them. Let not the child of God complain, then, that his final reward is not anticipated and distributed to him here, in the present world, while he is in a state of trial. He must wait until he comes to the goal, before he can wear the crown of a victor in the race. He must defer his expected laurels until the combat is over. Then he shall receive a crown of glory which fadeth not away."

12. Surely if no other chapter in the Scriptures declared it, this abundantly shows the great importance of the true doctrine concerning the nature, personality and work of the Holy Spirit, v. 23. Without him we can do nothing. All solid peace, all holy joy, all personal righteousness are obtained in and by the Holy Ghost. The christian graces are indispensable to christian character and comfort. Nothing of more value does God ever bestow on men in this world than the gift of the Holy Ghost. He that lacks this has no earnest from God that he shall ever be saved. How else can the poor, carnal soul of man be raised above the vanities of this world, or made to long for heavenly glory? And unless one does this, how does he differ from the merest wordling? The children of the kingdom love to think of the kingdom, speak of the kingdom, and hasten into the kingdom. But if they do these things they do them by the power of the Holy Ghost.

13. Let us be very careful not to murmur or cry out in an unchristian temper, 'My Lord delayeth his coming;' but quietly wait for his salvation, v. 23. We may groan under our burdens; we may lament indwelling sin and our infirmities of soul, body and spirit. But still let us 'look for that blessed hope, even the glorious appearing of the great God our Saviour.'

14. It is impossible to administer to others or take to ourselves the full consolations of the Gospel without a clear view and a strong faith concerning the resurrection of the just, v. 23. Indeed if that doctrine be surrendered, we have no gospel. Paul himself admits as much: "If Christ be not raised your faith is vain; ye are yet in your sins," 1 Cor. 15 : 17. To what can you point the poor, afflicted, dying child of God, if you cannot show him a life beyond the tomb? Calvin: "The sacrifice of the death of Christ would be in vain and fruitless, except its fruit appeared in our heavenly renovation." Glory be to God, there

is a ' resurrection of life,' 'a resurrection of the just,' in which death shall be swallowed up in victory, when Christ shall fulfil his promise made to the evangelical prophet : " Thy dead men shall live, together with my dead body shall they arise. Awake and sing, ye that dwell in dust : for thy dew is as the dew of herbs and the earth shall cast out the dead." Then indeed the countless throng before the throne may exultingly shout, " O death, where is thy sting ? O grave, where is thy victory?" Brown : " Though now our bodies be subject to much misery, pain, sickness and the like, and must at length corrupt and rot away so that after our death worms shall destroy them, Job. 19 : 26 ; yet these very bodies of ours shall be fully delivered in the great day from all sin and misery, death and corruption, and that by virtue of the death and purchase of Christ." Wonderful change ! Wonderful grace, that shall produce it.

15. O the glory that shall be revealed in the saints at last, v. 23. Here through Christ they receive remission of sins, the accept- ance of their persons, the renewal of their hearts by the Holy Ghost, considerable measures of grace to sustain, to restrain and to comfort them ; indeed they have all the graces of the Spirit in some measure in their hearts. But these things are the mere pledges and earnests of what shall be. Eye hath not seen, ear hath not heard, the heart of man hath not conceived the things which God hath prepared for them that love him.

16. Will not the reader, who is yet without hope and without God in the world, listen to a kindly word of exhortation drawn from this theme ? Poor, dying man, shall the whole creation groan for thee and for thy sin, and wilt not thou groan also? Listen to the words of one from whom already a paragraph and several sentences have been quoted. Hoge : " For the careless sinner this subject has a rebuke and a warning.

" A rebuke : You are told that nature has been and is cursed by your existence. To it you are an oppressor and a defiler ; a burden and a loathing. The air is polluted by your words, the light by your deeds of shame, yea, all the elements by your cor- ruption, ingratitude, effrontery, rebellion. You will not praise God, as the high priest of nature, and the stones are ready to cry out ! Yours is a deeper bondage, but while creation struggles and travails, you are careless and indifferent. Aye, you cling to your chain, you sport yourself with your own deceivings, you act as if there was music in the groans of creation. This is the rebuke.

" A warning : It cannot be always so. Guilt cannot triumph for ever. Innocence will be made victorious, though it be but the innocence of mute, irrational nature. If you will not submit your heart to the tide of influence pouring up from struggling creation, it will be a power to overwhelm you. What elements of terror and wrath are around you, within you, beneath you, above you! How has God hedged and hampered you! How he thwarts you! How does violated nature sometimes recoil against you! How puny is man, and how powerful is God! Who knoweth the power of his anger? Man is an insect, caught by some terrible enginery, whirled around and borne on; yet he plays and is proud; he sins and perishes." O sinner, turn and live! If you die in your iniquities, the sighs of earth will be followed by sighs in hell, and the groans of earth by the screams of the damned.

Chapter 20

ROMANS 8

VERSES 24-30

DELIVERANCE IS SURE TO COME.   LET US WAIT.
THE SPIRIT HELPS US, ESPECIALLY IN PRAYER.
ALL IS WORKING WELL BY A PLAN WHICH IN-
VOLVES THE GLORY OF CHRIST.

24 For we are saved by hope: but hope that is seen is not hope: for what a
man seeth, why doth he yet hope for?

25 But if we hope for that we see not *then* do we with patience wait
for *it*.

26 Likewise the Spirit also helpeth our infirmities: for we know not what we
should pray for as we ought: but the Spirit itself maketh intercession for us with
groanings which cannot be uttered.

27 And he that searcheth the hearts knoweth what *is* the mind of the Spirit,
because he maketh intercession for the saints according to *the will of* God.

28 And we know that all things work together for good to them that love God,
to them who are the called according to *his* purpose.

29 For whom he did foreknow, he also did predestinate *to be* conformed to the
image of his Son, that he might be the firstborn among many brethren.

30 Moreover, whom he did predestinate, them he also called: and whom he
called, them he also justified: and whom he justified, them he also glorified.

24. *FOR we are saved by hope : but hope that is seen is not hope:*
for what a man seeth, why doth he yet hope for ?   Wiclif,
Tyndale, Cranmer, Genevan, Rheims, Doway, Chrysostom, Doddridge, and others read the verse as the authorized version—*by*
hope.   But Coverdale and Peshito read, *in hope.*   Calvin explains
it as if it read, in hope.   Bp. Hall's paraphrase is, in assured hope,
we are saved; Locke's, we have hitherto been saved but in hope
and expectation; Macknight's, we are saved only in hope; Stuart's
translation is, we are saved [only] in hope; Conybeare and Howson's, our salvation lies in hope.   Scott's comment is, "True believers are saved 'by' or in 'hope;' they have been actually
brought into a state of safety; but their comfort consists 'in
hope,' rather than fruition."   It is true Grotius says, "we have not

eternal salvation as yet, but we hope for it." Yet it will not do to
say that believers have not eternal life, even here. Our Saviour
expressly said, "Whosoever drinketh of the water I shall give
him shall never thirst; but the water that I shall give him shall
be in him a well of water springing up into everlasting life;" "He
that believeth on me hath everlasting life;" "Whoso eateth my
flesh and drinketh my blood, hath eternal life." John 4 : 14; 6 : 47,
54. His bosom friend says: "Whosoever hateth his brother is a
murderer: and ye know that no murderer hath eternal life abiding in him," 1 John 3 : 15. If eternal life is not possessed here,
then what is here said of the murderer is as true of the believer.
Is not the believer as fully pardoned and accepted as he ever shall
be? The first verse of this chapter says, There is no condemnation on him. To others Paul says: "But ye are washed, but
ye are sanctified, but ye are justified in the name of the Lord
Jesus, and by the Spirit of our God," 1 Cor. 6 : 11. There are
many passages parallel to these. Our verse itself is at war with
such an idea. The verb literally rendered is, *We were saved* and
not we are saved, meaning that when they were converted, they
were saved. If any object and say that believers have not yet got
their crown of glory, the answer is, that is so, but they have as
indefeisible a title to it as they ever shall have, Rev. 22 : 14. If it
be said, that our bodies must yet die, and lie in the grave and
be raised before all the blessings of salvation will be actually in
our possession, the reply is, that is true, but is any one prepared
to say that the penitent thief, and Paul, and Stephen, and Peter
are not saved, and will not be saved till after the resurrection?
for their bodies are still in the dust. If any say with Tholuck
that faith is the instrument whereby we receive salvation, that is
true also; but can any one prove, or will any good man attempt
to show that because faith is the bond that unites believers to
Christ, therefore the Christian grace of hope bears no important
part in accomplishing man's salvation? If so, let him read his
Bible with a little care and candor, and he will change his mind.
The fact is that hope is as necessary as faith. Leighton: "The
difference of these two graces, *faith* and *hope*, is so small, that the
one is often taken for the other in scripture; it is but a different
aspect of the same confidence, *faith* apprehending the infallible
truth of those divine promises of which *hope* doth assuredly expect
the accomplishment, and that is their truth; so that this immediately results from the other. This is the anchor fixed within the veil
which keeps the soul firm against all the tossings on these swelling
seas, and the winds and tempests that arise upon them. The
firmest thing in this inferior world is a believing soul." And what

is faith but the substance of things hoped for, and the evidence of things not seen? Heb. 11 : 1. Is it then going too far to invite men to believe that salvation is a blessing received and enjoyed in this life, and that hope is an important means of effecting it? If any say that great things are to be done for the saved, in the future, that is gloriously true, and ever will be; but it does not prove that great things in the way of actual salvation are not done in this world for all that hope in God's mercy. *But hope that is seen is not hope.* The word *hope*, as found in this clause, may be taken in the concrete—for the object of hope. Then the sense would be that things, which if future might be objects of hope, are not so when we behold them at hand. Or if we take the word in the abstract, then Guyse gives the sense: " Hope of things that are already enjoyed, is not properly speaking, hope, which is a comfortable persuasion of some future good." The explanation offered by some is that the word *seen* in this place means enjoyed, and they refer to Matt. 5 : 8; John 3 : 36, in proof. But the word rendered *seen* in this place is not the same as in those places cited. Calvin says, Paul means simply to teach us, that since hope regards some future and not present good it can never be connected with what we have in possession. *For what a man seeth, why doth he yet hope for ?* This is very much a repetition of what he had already said. One may impatiently expect a messenger, but when he arrives, whether he bring good or bad tidings, we cease to look for him.

25. *But if we hope for that we see not*, then *do we with patience wait for it*. It is good that a man should both hope and quietly wait for the salvation of the Lord, Lam. 3 : 26. As in our verse, so here and in many other places, hoping and patient waiting are connected. Were this not so, waiting would be turned into the sullenness of despair, or entirely given up in a vain attempt to find satisfaction in things that perish. An examination of the Old Testament scriptures and especially of the devotional parts thereof will satisfy any one that patient waiting is in God's esteem a great grace, indispensable to the comfort of the poor, suffering child of God. And as all christians under the Gospel, especially in early times, experienced the sorest tribulations which malice and cruelty could bring upon them, this exercise was of paramount importance. Calvin: " When we console ourselves with the hope of a better condition, the feeling of our present miseries is softened and mitigated."

26. *Likewise the Spirit also helpeth our infirmities : for we know not what we should pray for as we ought : but the Spirit itself maketh intercession for us with groanings which cannot be uttered.* The word

rendered *helpeth* is very strong, and might be rendered helpeth together.   Calvin renders it, co-assists, and Beza, lifts up together. Schleusner: " It means to succor those whose strength is unequal to carry their burden alone."   It is found in but one other place, Luke 10 : 40, where Martha petitions Christ to bid Mary that she *help* me.   This is the precise idea in this place.   *Infirmities*, commonly so rendered, a few times weakness, once sickness, and once diseases.   In 1 Tim. 5 : 23, it refers to bodily infirmities alone.   In Matt. 8 : 17 and Heb. 4 : 15, it means such infirmities of our nature as were innocent and could be borne by the Holy Saviour. It is the word used by Paul when he says, I glory in my infirmities, and I take pleasure in infirmities, 2 Cor. 12 : 9, 10.   The infirmities of the Christian are many.   They are bodily and mental. They are natural and spiritual.   His understanding is feeble and greatly needs enlightening.   His graces are weak and constantly require strengthening.   Paul now mentions a particular weakness in relation to prayer : *We know not what we should pray for as we ought*.   We are so 'ignorant, forgetful, or unbelieving, that we know not what to ask for, or how to ask for any thing in a proper manner, and with proper affections.'   This indeed is a sad case, a terrible infirmity.   Left to ourselves, what could we do?   In a thousand respects, a good, though imperfect man may be in doubt both as to the matter and manner of prayer.   Hodge: " We cannot tell what is really best for us.   Heathen philosophers gave this as a reason why men ought not to pray!"   No doubt the wicked one often tempts good men to restrain prayer because of their uncertainty whether it is best or not to ask for a given thing.   But God leaves not his children alone in their trials.   The Spirit itself comes to our relief.   *Maketh intercession for*, a word found nowhere else in the New Testament, though its leading compound is found in vs. 27, 34 of this chapter and rendered maketh intercession.   It is also found elsewhere.   This word differs from that in having a prefix, which may be rendered abundantly.   He not only pleads God's cause with us, but pleads our cause with God, by awakening proper desires within us and teaching us to pray as John could not teach his disciples.   Thus he becomes to us what the prophet calls him, " the spirit of grace and of supplications," Zech. 12 : 10. He does his work effectually.   The prayer he indites is inwrought in the soul of believers, and so it is " with groanings which cannot be uttered," or which are not uttered, for the Greek may be rendered either way.   Thus when Hannah prayed, her pious soul was mightily stirred, yet she spake in her heart ; only her lips moved, but her voice was not heard : therefore Eli thought she had been drunken, and so charged it upon her.   But she answered and said, "No, my lord, I am a woman of a sorrowful spirit: I have drunk neither wine nor strong drink, but have poured out my soul before the Lord. Count not thine handmaid for a daughter of Belial; for out of the abundance of my complaint and grief have I spoken hitherto," 1 Sam. 1 : 13–16. Thus David prayed in broken sentences: "O Lord, how long?" The same good man said: "Lord, all my desire is before thee, and my groaning is not hid from thee," Ps. 38 : 9; thus showing that praying and groaning have long been associated.

27. *And he that searcheth the hearts knoweth what* is *the mind of the Spirit, because he maketh intercession for the saints according to* the will of *God.* The particle rendered *and* is more commonly rendered *but*, and should be so here. *He that searcheth the hearts* is a periphrasis for God, and may be applied to either person of the Trinity, 1 Chron. 28 : 9; 1 Cor. 2 : 10; Rev. 2 : 23. Here it seems to have special reference to the Father, as receiving the petitions indited by the Spirit, but then they are all offered through Christ. We sigh, we groan, '*but* though we are not able to speak these desires, they are not concealed from God,' nor is he at a loss to know what they mean. *Knoweth*, has perfect intelligence and understanding, a word used very often and rendered as here, also see, behold, be sure, perceive, &c., Matt. 2 : 16; 13 : 14; Luke 19 : 41; 1 Cor. 2 : 11, etc. It is not the word *know*, which we use in the sense of approve, allow, recognize as friends, Matt. 7 : 23; Rom. 7 : 15; 2 Tim. 2 : 19. Although the *word* does not teach it, yet the very nature of God and the relations of the persons in the Godhead make it certain that every petition indited by the Spirit is approved in heaven, *because he maketh intercession for the saints according to* the will of *God*, literally *according to God*, i. e. according to the plan arranged by God for man's salvation, according to his will, according to his nature, his grace and mercy, his wisdom and sufficiency. Compare John 14 : 13; 1 John 3 : 22; 5 : 14. God's Spirit never stirs up in us approved desires for any thing, that we do not receive it, or something better; often the very thing itself and much more besides, 1 Kings 3 : 11–14; Mal. 3 : 10; Matt. 6 : 33; 2 Cor. 12 : 8–10.

28. *And we know that all things work together for good to them that love God, to them who are the called according to* his *purpose. Know*, the same word so rendered in v. 26, we are sure, we perceive; it is clear to us. It is made sure to believers in many ways. 1. God's gracious design is to that effect, Isa. 48 : 10; Heb. 12 : 10. 2. The experience of childhood under parental discipline teaches the same lesson, Heb. 12 : 10. 3. God may let a reprobate go through life with com-

paratively little trial, but he loves his own children too well to exempt them from affliction, Luke 16 : 25 ; Heb. 12 : 7, 8 ; Rev. 3 : 19. 4. The recorded experience of good men confirms this truth, Ps. 119 : 67, 71. 5. Every child of God, who has made any progress in the divine life, knows the same thing by his own blessed experience. He has found things the most cross to his plans turning to his advantage. If adverse and afflictive occurrences produce happy results, so also doubtless do the mercies of God manifested in the common events of life, in remarkable providences, and in the wise and holy arrangements and provisions of the entire plan of salvation. So that *all things*, that is, all things relating to the matter in hand, *work together*. We have the same verb in Mark 16 : 20, " The Lord *working with* them ;" in 1 Cor. 16: 16, " Every one that *helpeth with* us." The cognate noun is rendered helpers, work-fellows, fellow-laborers, fellow-helpers, 2 Cor. 1 : 24 ; Rom. 16 : 21 ; Phil. 4 : 3 ; 3 John 8. All things co-operate with each other, yes and with God too, 1 Cor. 3 : 9 ; 2 Cor. 6 : 1. The result cannot be doubtful. Who is he that will harm you, if ye be followers of that which is good? 1 Pet. 3 : 13. They work together *for good*, not for evil, not for any doubtful nor for a mere negative result. The *good* resulting is of three kinds: 1. To the christian himself. He thus becomes a partaker of God's holiness, Heb. 12 : 10 ; his temper thus becomes sweet, gentle, subdued, Ps. 131 : 2 ; affliction weans him from the world and makes him long for heaven, Phil. 1 : 23 ; he is thus assured of his being in Christ, when he has the fellowship of his sufferings, Phil. 3 : 10 ; he thus learns the certainty of his final and eternal triumph, 2 Tim. 2 : 12 ; Rev. 3: 21 ; Luke 6 : 22, 23 and parallel passages. 2. To others who see or hear of the meekness, patience, constancy and thankfulness of a christian, the example is truly edifying, Jas. 5 : 10 ; 1 Pet. 2 : 12 ; 3: 2, 3 ; 4: 2. 3. By all the exemplary suffering of his people God is glorified, and if he is glorified, all is well, cost what it may to us, Matt. 5: 16 ; John 15 : 8. But all this occurs, not to the proud, hardened and unbelieving, but only to real christians, *to them that love God*. Calvin: " In the love of God he includes the whole of religion, as on it depends the whole practice of righteousness." When it can truly be said of a man that he has not the love of God in him, we know that he has no piety, and no good hope through grace, John 5 : 42. When true piety takes complete possession of all the soul, then is the love of God perfected, 1 John 2 : 5. Nor can any one ever prove that he loves God, unless he has pity on the poor and keeps God's commandments, 1 John 3 : 17 ; 5 : 3. All who love God are also *the called according to his purpose*. On the word *called* see above on Rom. 1 :

1, 6, 7. It means not merely invited, but effectually called ; and
that not according to one's own will, counsel or merit, Isa. 48 : 11 ;
Ezek. 36 : 22, 32 ; Rom. 9 : 16 ; but *according to* and in fulfilment
of God's *purpose*. From other parts of scripture it appears that
this purpose is 1. according to election, Rom. 9 : 11 ; 2. that it will
surely be executed, Rom. 9 : 11 ; Eph. 1 : 11 ; 3. that it is eternal,
Eph. 3 : 11 ; 2 Tim. 1 : 9 ; 4. that it is all in and by Jesus Christ our
Lord, Eph. 3 : 11 ; 5. that it is wholly gracious, 2 Tim. 1 : 9. Adam
Clarke explains it as meaning " affectionate purpose," and afterwards a " gracious purpose." No doubt it is very pitiful, kind,
benevolent, else it could not result in salvation to such sinners as
we are.

29. *For whom he did foreknow, he also did predestinate* to be *conformed to the image of his Son, that he might be the first-born among
many brethren*. *Foreknew*, the same word occurs in Rom. 11 : 2,
" God hath not cast away his people which he *foreknew ;* and in 1
Pet. 1 : 20, where the apostle speaking of Christ says, " Who
verily was *foreordained* before the foundation of the world." The
cognate noun occurs twice, and is both times rendered foreknowledge, Acts 2 : 23 ; 1 Pet. 1 : 2. Three ideas are connected with
foreknowledge. One is *prescience*, simple intelligence of the future.
That God possesses this prescience the scriptures do surely teach :
" Known unto God are all his works from the beginning of the
world," Acts 15 : 18. Compare Isa. 41 : 22, 23 ; 44 : 7 ; 46 : 9, 10.
Simon Peter said to Jesus, " Lord, thou knowest all things,"
John 21 : 17 ; and the same is true of the Father and of the Spirit.
Does not every devout man adore God as knowing the end from
the beginning ? Isa. 46 : 10. The second idea connected with foreknowledge is that of foreordination. So our translation gives it
in 1 Pet. 1 : 20. So it must be understood in several places. So
Clarke explains it on Acts 2 : 23, " Him being delivered by the
determinate counsel and foreknowledge of God, ye have taken,
and with wicked hands have crucified and slain." He explains
the " determinate counsel" as " that counsel of God which *defined*
the *time, place* and *circumstance*, according to his foreknowledge, which always saw what was the most proper *time* and
place for the manifestation and crucifixion of his Son ; so
that there was nothing *casual* in these things, God having determined that the salvation of a lost world should be brought about
in this way : and neither the Jews nor Romans had any power
here, but what was given them from above." The third idea connected with foreknowledge is that of foreknowing as friends,
choosing beforehand, selecting of old, setting his love on them.
According to the scriptures the conversion of men and all that

flows from it are owing to the everlasting love set upon them. So God himself says : " I have loved thee with an everlasting love : therefore with loving kindness have I drawn thee," Jer. 31 : 3. So taught the beloved disciple : " We love him because he first loved us," 1 John 4 : 19. Indeed this is the doctrine of scripture from the days of Moses. See Deut. 7 : 7–9 ; 10 : 15 ; 33 : 3. Compare Hos. 11 : 1 ; Mal. 1 : 2. Concerning this foreknowledge of God the scriptures clearly show 1. That it is eternal, not of modern date, Jer. 31 : 3 ; Eph. 3 : 11 ; 1 Pet. 1 : 20. 2. That it is unchangeable, not unsettled, not mutable, not contingent, even when it relates to things contingent to us, Isa. 46 : 10 ; Mal. 3 : 6 ; Rom. 9 : 11. 3. That it is wholly gracious and sovereign. there being nothing in us to merit God's favor, Rom. 9 : 11. 4. That it results in the conversion of all who are embraced in its grasp, Acts 13 : 48. 5. That it will assuredly compass the sanctification of all the elect, 2 Thess. 2 : 13 ; Rom. 8 : 29. 6. That it is all wholly to the honor and glory of God, Eph. 1 : 3–6. Well, whom he did foreknow, *he also did predestinate.* The verb rendered predestinate is in sacred history thus rendered : " Of a truth against thy holy child Jesus, whom thou hast anointed, both Herod, and Pontius Pilate, with the Gentiles and the people of Israel, were gathered together, for to do whatsoever thy hand and thy counsel *determined before* to be done, Acts 4 : 27, 28. To *determine before* and to *predestinate* are the same thing. It is the same Greek word in both cases. Other scriptures tell us that God's ordination is of the greatest antiquity : " We speak the wisdom of God in a mystery, even the hidden wisdom which God ordained before the world unto our glory," 1 Cor. 2 : 7. The word rendered *ordained* is the same everywhere else rendered predestinated, or determined before. Then again Paul say : " Blessed be the God and Father of our Lord Jesus Christ, who hath blessed us with all spiritual blessings in heavenly places in Christ Jesus : according as he hath chosen us in him, before the foundation of the world, that we should be holy and without blame before him in love ; having predestinated us unto the adoption of children by Jesus Christ to himself, according to the good pleasure of his will to the praise of the glory of his grace, wherein he hath made us accepted in the Beloved," Eph. 1 : 3–6. This passage is more full on the subject of predestination than any we have in the Bible. 1. It declares that as predestination is revealed in scripture it is matter of praise and thanksgiving, " Blessed be God," etc. 2. It teaches that all spiritual blessings coming to us are connected with this purpose of God. 3. It shows that election and predestination are united in the same scheme of grace. 4. Election is from eternity and consequently predestination must have as great an antiquity. 5. Election is unto holiness and aims at making men without blame: of course, predestination can have no less glorious aim. 6. Predestination is unto adoption, of course is friendly to salvation. 7. Predestination is not from anything in us but wholly according to the good pleasure of the divine will. 8. Both election and predestination are honorable to God—" to the praise of the glory of his grace." Our verse says that those whom God chose he predestinated to be *conformed* [or fashioned] *to the image of his Son.* It is unto holiness. This all tends to the glory of Christ, *that he might be the first-born among many brethren. First-born and first begotten* in the New Testament are translations of the same word, which occurs nine times. The cognate noun is rendered *birthright,* Heb. 12 : 16. No doubt the reference is to the rights of primogeniture, and points out the pre-eminence which the Saviour has over all the sons of men redeemed by his blood. In Col. 1 : 18 it is said " he is the beginning [head], the first-born from the dead, that in all things he might have the pre-eminence." If Christ brings no sons unto glory, he can have no reward, no pre-eminence, no brethren among whom he would be the first born.

30. *Moreover, whom he did predestinate, them he also called : and whom he called, them he also justified : and whom he justified, them he also glorified.* The preterite form of the verb does not teach that all the elect are yet glorified, or justified, or even called. It simply declares that election and predestination are in every case and ever shall be followed by effectual calling, pardon, acceptance and glory. This form of the verb may be after the Hebrew, and indicate the certainty of the things declared. The preterite is the usual form of prediction. That the calling here spoken of is not a mere invitation to the gospel feast, but an effectual persuasion and enabling of the soul to embrace Christ is clear from the connection and from the ordinary use of the word. See above on v. 28. *Justified* is no doubt to be taken in the sense in which it is generally used in this epistle, the receiving of gratuitous imputation of righteousness. *Glorified* points to the blessed state, where the redeemed have all and boundless blessings, being made perfect in holiness and happiness for ever.

DOCTRINAL AND PRACTICAL REMARKS

1. WE ARE SAVED ! v. 24. Are not these amazing words? *Saved,* from wrath, and guilt, and sin, its pollution and its power; saved by an almighty hand and by amazing grace; saved when the most just and terrible destruction was impending; saved when

others no more guilty were left in their blindness and hardness of heart. Nor is this salvation all future, but it is in all its great elements a present salvation, so that while some texts say that the believers *shall be* saved, our verse says, we *are* saved. If we put the emphasis on the first word, the sense is no less striking, *we* are saved; we, who merit no good thing; we, who are by nature the children of wrath even as others; we, who were dead in trespasses and sins, we, yes even we are saved! Surely our song will ever be of salvation!

2. And we are saved by *hope*, v. 24. Despair may work some prodigy of a *feat*, but despair never did any great *work*. Nor did despondency ever raise a crop, or make a scholar, or achieve a wonder. A hopeless man is a heartless man. What is a Christian soldier in the wars of the Lamb without the helmet of the hope of salvation? 1 Thess. 5 : 8. Without it will he not be ashamed and flee in battle? When did God ever send any one on a mission of mercy, or of duty until he had first begotten him again unto a lively hope? 1 Pet. 1 : 3. True, hope's treasures are above, but its duties are all below. The fruition is in the future, but the glad expectation is in the present. Take from any good man the successes and the victories he has achieved by hope, and what has he left? Owen of Oxford: "The height of the actings of all grace issues in a well-grounded hope; nor can it rise any higher."

3. Thus may we attain to that great grace patient waiting on God and for God, v. 25. Much is said of it in both Testaments. It is illustrated by a reference to the farmer, who hath long patience and waiteth for the precious fruits of the earth; to the watchman who waits and longs for the day; to the hireling who toils on in hope as he sees the shadows lengthening and is persuaded his toils will end as the light of day disappears. Pareus: "Patience is needful for three reasons—the good expected is absent—there is delay, and many difficulties intervene."

4. How dare men undertake any great thing, particularly any thing in the form of a spiritual enterprize without seeking the special aid of God's Holy Spirit? v. 26. He is the author of all saving illumination, of all spiritual renewals and revivings, of all holy triumphs and victories. Without him we can win no battle, bear no burden, conquer no evil habit, make no progress in the divine life. He *helpeth* our infirmities. Good old Rutherford caught the true spirit of the scripture when he said of his affliction: "Jesus and I will bear it." The blessed Saviour by his Spirit carries the heavy end of every cross. God leaves our infirmities, but he *helps* them. He makes us conscious of our weakness, but he holds us up. Left to ourselves our prayers are poor and un-

worthy, like those mentioned in Hos. 7 : 14, " They have not cried unto me with their heart, when they howled upon their beds." We can do nothing to purpose without help from heaven. But the help we need in nowise sets aside our free agency. God deals with us as with rational creatures. We must bear our burdens, but we do not bear them alone. Brown: " Albeit the saints of God cannot stand if they be left to themselves, but will certainly succumb and faint in the day of adversity, but must be helped and assisted by the Spirit of God; yet this assistance and aid yielded by the Spirit doth not make them mere stocks and stones, nor loose them from a patient suffering of the same."

5. The aid of the Spirit in prayer is specially and continually necessary to two great ends; first, to preserve us from asking for that which we ought not, and secondly, to enable us to ask in a right manner for that, which we ought to ask for. The latter is commonly considered much the more difficult, but the former cannot be done without divine assistance. The scripture gives us examples of even good men making sad mistakes in asking what was wholly contrary to God's will, Job 6 : 8, 9 ; Jonah 4 : 3 ; Mark 10 : 38 ; 2 Cor. 12 : 8. The Holy Spirit not only pleads God's cause within us, but pleads our cause with God by putting right thoughts and tempers within us. How he does these things we may not be able to explain. That he does them for us all God's people know. Tholuck and others quote a beautiful sentence from St. Martin on this subject: " As the mother does to the child, so does the Holy Spirit repeat before us the supplications, which we must seek to lisp after him." Yet even this does but faintly present the truth ; for " we know not the way of the Spirit." Leighton: " The work of the Spirit is in exciting the heart at times of prayer, to break forth in ardent desires to God, whatsoever the words be, whether new or old, yea, possibly without words; and then most powerful when it *words it* least, but vents in sighs and groans that cannot be expressed. Our Lord understands the language of these perfectly, and likes it best ; he knows and approves the meaning of his own Spirit ; he looks not to the outward appearance, the shell of words, as men do." Chalmers: " Let us cease to wonder, that prayer should appear among the foremost indications of the Spirit of God being at work with us ; or that it takes the precedency of other blessings, or that it has happened so frequently in the church, that a season of supplication went before the season either of a gracious deliverance or of a gracious revival." Bp. Hall : " The Spirit of God aids us by his gracious work in us ; stirring up our drowsy and dull hearts to make powerful supplications to God, with sighs and groans that cannot be expressed."

In prayer the state of the heart is everything. A heart without words may bring down the blessing, Ex. 14 : 15. Moses had not uttered one audible word. But words without the heart God abhors.

6. Let us not be afraid of being too much moved in prayer, v. 26. The scripture warrants great earnestness and longings of soul. It condemns neither sighing, nor crying, nor groaning, Ezek. 9 : 4; Ps. 12 : 5; Luke 18 : 7; Ex. 6 : 5; Ps. 33 : 9; 102 : 20. Our prayers must move us else they will not move God. Poor Hezekiah seems to have been moved to behaviour hardly becoming, yet in the main his heart was right and God heard and saved him: " Like a crane or a swallow, so did I chatter: I did mourn as a dove: mine eyes fail with looking upward: O Lord, I am oppressed ; undertake for me," Isa. 38 14. But no groanings are more pleasing to God, than those which are too big for utterance. Tholuck : " Silent prayers, like silent grief itself, are wont to be the deepest."

7. The subtilty of Satan in tempting the people of God is often very great. He says, How can groans which are not understood profit any one or bring aid to our infirmities ? v. 26. The correct answer is, They are understood both by God's people and by God himself. Hannah knew full well what it was that lay as a mighty burden on her heart. She never acted more intelligently in her life than then. And does not the Most High know our downsitting and our uprising, and understand our thoughts afar off ? Ps. 139 : 2. So that the temptation is hardly specious ; at least it has no solid foundation.

8. Indeed it would be most wonderful if God understood not or approved not the petitions indited by his own Spirit, for he searcheth the hearts, and he searcheth all things, v. 27. Accordingly it is truly said: " He will fulfil the desire of them that fear him," Ps. 145 : 19. " The prayer of the upright is his delight," Pr. 15 : 8. For good cause the people of God have confidence in him as one that hears and answers prayer. How could it be otherwise ? Every one of them has been to the throne of grace with a burden of sin on his conscience sinking him into the depths of wo, and has found mercy. He went guilty ; he came away pardoned. He went crying for mercy ; he came away glorifying God. All things are naked and opened unto the eyes of him, with whom we have to do. Brown : " The omniscience of God, and his perfect knowledge of everything within our hearts, as it should teach us to address him alone in prayer, because he only is able to hear ; so it should strengthen our faith and hope of a hearing of our desires and groans, when we cannot get words to express our mind to God."

9. It is impossible that the people of God should perish, v. 27. They have God for their Father. They have a glorious Advocate and Intercessor above. They have a blessed Comforter and Intercessor within. The Holy Spirit takes not the office of the interceding High Priest above. But he takes of the things of Christ and shows them to us, and stirs us up to prayer and effort. Augustine : " The divine Spirit does not groan or intercede in and by himself, as God and belonging to the Trinity ; but he intercedes by his influence upon us, and by leading us to aspirations which language cannot express." Chalmers : " The Saviour intercedes for us in heaven. The Spirit intercedes for us in our own breast. The one intercession is pure and altogether unmixed with the dross of earthliness. The other passes through a corrupt medium, and finds its way among the adverse impediments of an earthly nature ; and by the time that it cometh forth in expression, has had to encounter the elements of darkness and of carnality that are within us." Here atoning blood comes in, and our imperfect prayers are perfumed with the incense in the censer of the great High Priest above, and so meet with divine acceptance.

10. Are our prayers in the main right, and for things agreeable to God's will ? v. 27. Or are we like those described by the Apostle ? " Ye lust and have not : ye kill, and desire to have, and cannot obtain : ye fight and war, yet ye have not, because ye ask not. Ye ask, and receive not ; because ye ask amiss, that ye may consume it upon your lusts," James 4 : 2, 3. There are many hindrances to the success of prayer. Let us guard against them all. It is possible, but it is not probable that any man spends too large a portion of his time and energy in scrutinizing his own motives, or in keeping his own heart ; for out of it are the issues of life.

11. Great lessons are learned in the school of affliction, v. 28. Amazing results are brought about by causes, all of which seemed adverse. Anything is good for a good man·that strips the world of its charms, that abases his pride, that teaches him the meaning of Scripture, that exercises his faith and patience, and that makes him love and long for his home in the heavens.

12. Let us not be cast down if we see not one thing producing all the good effects we could desire. God may add a second, a third, a tenth or a hundredth, in order to finish his work. The Bible does not say that each thing works separately, but that all things *work together*, v. 28. Two of the bitterest substances known in nature, when chemically combined, make a very sweet product.

13. Are you a child of sorrow? Are you perplexed? Are you cast down? Verse 28 covers all your case. Not a point is omitted. Chrysostom: "The Lord employs adversity itself in advancing the glory of those who are beset with snares, which is much greater than it would be to hinder adversity from coming at all. . . . For should even tribulation, or poverty, or imprisonment, or famines, or deaths, or anything else whatsoever come upon us, God is able to change all these things into the opposite." Doddridge gives us a sentence from Plato, shewing that to considerate heathen, some benefit seemed to arise from some forms of adversity: "Whether a righteous man be in poverty, sickness, or any other calamity, we must conclude that it will turn to his advantage, either in life or death." How necessary therefore is the doctrine of a particular and special Providence. Chalmers: "Is not the historical fact, that what is most minute often gives rise to what is most momentous, an argument for the theological doctrine of a Providence that reaches even to the slightest and most unnoticeable vanities?" But we are not left to mere logic even though it be sound. Revelation says, that the very hairs of your head are all numbered; that the lot which is cast into the lap is wholly disposed of by the Lord; and that not a sparrow falls to the ground without his notice.

14. If none can legitimately draw comfort from the leading truths of this chapter, and particularly from verse 28, unless they *love* God, how important it is to know what are the infallible signs of that holy affection. Nor do we search the scriptures in vain. The love that God demands must be sincere, not feigned, not in pretence; it must be supreme, putting Jehovah before and above all others; it must regard all God's character, laws and judgments; it must be stable, not fitful. He who loves God will love God's children, God's house, God's worship and all his ordinances. Haldane: "Love to God is given as a peculiar characteristic of a Christian. It imports that all believers love God, and that none but believers love him. Philosophers, falsely so called, and men of various descriptions, may boast of loving God, but the decision of God himself is, that to love him is the peculiar characteristic of a Christian. No man can love God till he hath shined into his heart to give him the light of the knowledge of his glory in the face of Jesus Christ. It is, therefore, only through faith in the blood of Christ that we can love God."

15. Masters of logic delight to give us specimens of strong reasoning; but where will any find more irrefragable argument than in the fundamental truths of the Gospel? Was there ever

a more glorious form of reasoning than that found in vs. 28–30?
Bishop Hall: "There is a strong and indissoluble chain of mercy
and grace in God towards his elect, the links whereof can never
be either broken or severed." We have first the glorious, eternal purpose of God; then we have his sure, infallible foreknowledge; then his adorable predestination of a conformity to the
image of his Son; then that blessed effectual calling, the same
as a spiritual regeneration; united with this, is always an irreversible justification; and following all is everlasting glorification with God in heaven. Let us not stand and cavil at these
blessed truths, but rather like our Saviour, adoringly say, ' I
thank thee, O Father, Lord of heaven and earth, because thou
hast hid these things from the wise and prudent, and hast revealed them unto babes; even so, Father, for so it seemed good
in thy sight.' Or let us, like Paul, admiringly say, ' O the
depth of the riches both of the wisdom and knowledge of God,'
etc. Let none be offended at such themes. Chalmers: "There
is an ambition on the part of some to be wise above that which
is written; but that is no reason why, in avoiding this, we should
not attempt at least to be wise up to that which is written." It is
not prudence, it is not modesty, it is not humility, it is something
bad which makes us hesitate to receive implicitly all the truths
which God has revealed in his word. At first view, they may
seem to contradict other truths of Scripture; but let us believe
all that God has spoken. Very often an annunciation may flatly
contradict our preconceived opinions and firmest prejudices; but
that only shows that God is wiser than man.

15. Could the doctrine of God's foreknowledge, as it has been
explained in the comment on these verses, be more clearly taught
than it is? v. 29. We have the very words *foreknow* and *foreknowledge*. No notice is given us that they are to be taken in any but
their usual sense. To get rid of it, even great and good men have
made such assertions as these: 1. That with God nothing is past
and nothing is future; but that he lives in an eternal *now*. It is
indeed true that the past and the future are in no sense hid or
absent from God's omniscience. In that sense, they are both forever present with him. But there is no such thing as an eternal
now; for now is a very small point in duration, and has no such
connection with the past and the future as at all to embrace them.
It surely is wiser simply to say, God inhabiteth eternity than to
say that he merely exists now, although you precede it with the
adjunct eternal. This is confounding terms. 2. Another endeavor
has been made to set aside the clear teaching of the scripture by
saying that in the divine mind, there is a distinction between things

certain and things contingent.   Suppose we admit that to us many things are contingent in the sense that they depend upon other things outside of themselves, this cannot make them uncertain to the divine mind.   On how many contingencies depended the death of Jesus Christ! Judas, Pilate, Herod, Caiaphas, the fidelity of the Roman soldiers, the malignity of the witnesses, the diabolical malice of the chief priests, and the violence of the populace were all necessary to compass that great event in the counsels of God.   And yet what good man would dare to say that that event in all its attendant circumstances was not minutely. foretold? Nor could the Scripture be broken.   And what is a prophecy but a purpose of God made known?   3. Dr. Adam Clarke has shocked the reverence of the Christian world by intimating a possibility, perhaps a probability that God does not know all things, though he might know them if he chose.   His language is: " As God's omnipotence implies his *power to do all things;* so God's omniscience implies his *power to know all things;* but we must take heed that we meddle not with the infinite free agency of this Eternal Being.   Though God *can* do all things, he *does* not all things.   Infinite judgment directs the operations of his power, so that though he *can,* yet he *does not* do all things, but only such things as are proper to be done. . . I conclude that God, although omniscient, is not obliged in consequence of this *to know all that he can know;* no more than he is obliged, because he is *omnipotent to do all that he can do."*   But does omniscience consist in mere capability of knowing all things? Surely the Bible employs no such language.   It says expressly, " Known unto God are all his works from the beginning."   But it nowhere says that God has done all things that could be done.   Besides knowledge is not a matter of choice.   Can any man at will forget his mother tongue?   Can any man classify all he knows, and say henceforth I will know this and that ; but the greater part I have known, I will know no more forever?   Charnock :. " Seeing God knows things possible in his power, and things future in his will, if his power and resolves were from eternity, his knowledge must be so too ; or else we must make him ignorant of his own power, and ignorant of his own will from eternity, and consequently not from eternity blessed and perfect."   " A God who cannot tell whether peace will be concluded, or war continue to ravage the world; whether religion will be received in a certain kingdom, or whether it will be banished ; whether the right heir will succeed to the crown, or whether the crown will be set on the head of an usurper ;" is this the God that we are called on to trust, to trust forever, to trust though he slay us ?

16. A similar line of remark may be made respecting predestination, vs. 29, 30. God's purpose and counsel can be no rule of
duty to us. Our rule of conduct is his revealed will; but he
surely has secrets that he has never revealed to us, Deut. 29: 29.
Chalmers: " If the doctrine of predestination be true, as I believe
it to be, then it extends to all the processes of human life; and in
virtue of it, every career of human exertion hath its sure result,
and must terminate in one certain fulfilment that is absolute and
irreversible." Brown: " The decree of predestination, as it is absolute and complete, so is it definite." God's predestination includes not only the end but the means whereby that end shall be
accomplished. Why shall every intelligent man be allowed to
govern his life by a plan, to build his house and conduct his business on a model formed, and why shall we deny to the Most High
equal liberty ?

17. The same gracious Lord who has ordained his people to
eternal life does in his own sovereign wisdom and good pleasure
call them by his grace, subdue them to himself, and implant holy
principles within them, vs. 28, 30. The calling that saves is the
calling that brings men to love God, that is always connected with
justification, and always followed by glorification. This is a great
change. It is bringing men out of darkness into light, out of the
kingdom of Satan into the kingdom of God's dear Son; a passing
from death unto life, from a state of alienation and enmity to a
state of love and holiness; from a state of vice and ignorance to a
state of glory and virtue ; and all this without the least violence
done to the freedom of the human will. " My people shall be
willing in the day of *my* power." " It is God that worketh in us
both to will and to do of his good pleasure."

18. How fitting that they who are thus foreknown, predestinated and called should be also *justified* freely by his grace, v. 30.
God does account and treat as righteous all who have fled for
refuge to lay hold on Jesus Christ. Luther: " Justification takes
place when, in the just judgment of God, our sins, and the eternal
punishment due to them, are remitted, and when clothed with the
righteousness of Christ, which is freely imputed to us, and reconciled to God, we are made his beloved children and heirs of eternal life."

19. Blessed is the truth that they who are thus predestinated,
called and justified, should be forever *glorified*, v. 30. Here they
are indeed often under a cloud, sometimes brought over them by
their own imprudence, by the malice of enemies, or by the course
of Providence. But in due time Jehovah will bring forth their
righteousness as the light, and their judgment as the noon day.

Saints are kept by the power of God through faith unto salvation, ready to be revealed in the last time. The intercession of Christ, the indwelling of the Spirit, the purpose of God and the promises of the covenant of grace make it certain that glory shall follow the patience of the saints.

20. Let no one therefore be offended at the doctrine of election. It is the doctrine that makes known to us the purpose and plan of God. There is nothing in it beyond what our blessed Lord taught in that great sermon which offended so many, who had seemed to be pleased with his divine mission: "All that the Father giveth me, shall come to me; and him that cometh to me, I will in no wise cast out . . . No man can come to me, except the Father which hath sent me draw him," John 6: 37, 44. Let us not be like Christ's captious hearers, who when they heard these things from that time went back and walked no more with him, John 6: 66.

21. Instead of wasting our time in quarrelling with God, or finding fault with his mode of governing the world and especially his sovereign election of men to eternal life, let us give all diligence to make our own calling and election sure, 1 Pet. 1 : 10. So averse have some been to the doctrine of Scripture on this subject that they have even maintained that the *purpose* mentioned in verse 28, was the purpose of them that loved God. Tholuck well says: "Nothing but a spirit of controversy, choosing amidst the means of warfare, could ever have brought expositors to fancy that the purpose there spoken of denotes the bias of the will in man." Our blessed Lord taught the doctrine of God's sovereignty in the choice of whom he would, and it caused the same rage and violence that it often produces now: "I tell you of a truth, many widows were in Israel in the days of Elias, when the heaven was shut up three years and six months, when great famine was throughout all the land; but unto none of them was Elias sent, save unto Sarepta, a city of Sidon, unto a woman that was a widow. And many lepers were in Israel in the time of Eliseus, the prophet; and none of them was cleansed, saving Naaman the Syrian. And all they in the synagogue, when they heard these things, were filled with wrath, and rose up, and thrust him out of the city, and led him unto the brow of the hill (whereon their city was built) that they might cast him down headlong," Luke 4: 25–29. When we remember the Scripture doctrine that nothing but a holy life can prove any one to be a child of God, where is the danger that this doctrine will lead pious men to any looseness or immorality? We are Christ's disciples, if we do whatsoever he commands us; nor is it possible for any man to have

evidence of his being elect, but by the indwelling of the Holy Ghost.

22. It is a glorious truth, never to be forgotten, that Jesus Christ is the first-born among many brethren. God's plan is, first, that Christ might have many brethren, and secondly, that he might be the first-born among them. Haldane: " Under the law, the first-born had authority over his brethren, and to him belonged a double portion, as well as the honor of acting as priest." Not only the act of God the Father hath given the pre-eminence to Jesus the Son, but all his brethren rejoice in it, and as far as it is in their power give him the pre-eminence also. They crown him in each of their songs.

Chapter 21

ROMANS 8

VERSES 31–39

THE TRIUMPHANT CONCLUSION OF THE WHOLE ARGUMENT. THE RIGHTEOUS FOREVER SAFE.

31 What shall we then say to these things? If God *be* for us, who *can be* against us?

32 He that spared not his own Son, but delivered him up for us all, how shall he not with him also freely give us all things?

33 Who shall lay any thing to the charge of God's elect? *It is* God that justifieth.

34 Who *is* he that condemneth? *It is* Christ that died, yea rather, that is risen again, who is even at the right hand of God, who also maketh intercession for us.

35 Who shall separate us from the love of Christ? *shall* tribulation, or distress, or persecution, or famine, or nakedness, or peril, or sword?

36 As it is written, For thy sake we are killed all the day long; we are accounted as sheep for the slaughter.

37 Nay, in all these things we are more than conquerors through him that loved us.

38 For I am persuaded, that neither death, nor life, nor angels, nor principalities, nor powers, nor things present, nor things to come,

39 Nor height, nor depth, nor any other creature, shall be able to separate us from the love of God, which is in Christ Jesus our Lord.

31. *WHAT shall we then say to these things? If God* be *for us, who* can be *against us? What shall we then say to these things?* Can we say anything against them? Can we deny them? Dare we impugn them? Will any one speak lightly of them? Shall we not highly prize them and hold them fast? Do they not furnish a blessed foundation for all the confidence of the boldest believer—the most intrepid follower of Jesus? Do they not prove and establish great and glorious principles? *These things* may refer not only to things said in the verses immediately preceding, but to all that the apostle had before presented as ground of hope

in God. *If God be for us,* Tyndale, Cranmer and Genevan : If God
be on our side. This is the sense of the phrase. It has been
proven that he was on the side of all whom he foreknew, predes-
tined, called and justified. He is their Friend, their Father, their
God. He has given them the earnest of his Spirit. They love
him. They have the Christian graces. *If* does not express any
doubt as to whether God is for his people. It has the force of
seeing that, or inasmuch as in other places as well as here. See
Matt. 22 : 45 ; Luke 11 : 13 ; John 10 : 35 ; Acts 11 : 17 and often
elsewhere. Seeing God is for us, *who can be against us ?* or, who
is against us ? The verb is not expressed in either clause. Nor is
there any better mode of supplying it than that adopted in the
authorized version. Who can be against us ? i. e. who can successfully oppose us ? who can hinder our salvation ? who can
defeat the gracious purpose of God respecting us ? True, we war
against the world, the flesh and the devil, we wrestle with principalities and powers, and contend against the rulers of the darkness of this world. But what of that, *inasmuch* as God is for us ?
One almighty is more mighty than all his foes. One all-wise has
more wisdom than all the wise, whose wisdom is derived and borrowed, and so is merely by measure. One infinite can sweep away
all finites with a breath, or crush them with a nod. Men have attempted to thwart God's gracious purposes, but they have never
succeeded.

32. *He that spared not his own Son, but delivered him up for us all,*
how shall he not with him also freely give us all things ? There is no
stronger kind of reasoning than that called the argument *a fortiori.*
It reasons from the greater to the less. We have it here. *God*
spared not his own Son, that is, he spared him not any humiliation,
suffering or shame, necessary to make a full and complete satisfaction to divine justice. The whole life of Christ on earth till he lay
in the sepulchre of Joseph was one of abasement and anguish. He
died, as it were, a thousand times, for he distinctly knew all that
was before him, Luke 12 : 50. Was ever sorrow like his sorrow ?
And it was all voluntary. And then he was God's *own Son*—his
dear Son. On Christ's Sonship see above on Rom. 1 : 4 ; 8 : 3.
The pertinence of this matter in this connection arises from the
fact that God's people are sore pressed by their sins and by their
sorrows. To relieve the anguish arising from the former, the
apostle points them to an atoning Saviour. To relieve them from
the latter he points them to a suffering Redeemer. If Christ our
Lord was afflicted, it is not surprising that we should drink the
cup of sorrow. If he sunk so low, and has risen so high, we may
hope through him to rise too. If God spared not him, but

accepted his great sacrifice for us, then we need not perish in our sins, but may be fully and eternally saved from wrath. *But delivered him up for us all.* We have had the word *delivered* before. See above on Rom. 4 : 25, where its various uses are given. He was delivered *for* us, in our place, for our sakes, in our behalf. For *us all*, not merely for Jews but for Gentiles ; for all in every nation, who are chosen, called and justified. *How shall he not with him also freely give us all things ?* Having given us his unspeakable gift, why should we not expect *with him* (never without him) victory over affliction, pardon, acceptance and eternal life ? Why should not our sins be removed from us as far as the east is from the west ? Why should not even our sorest afflictions be turned to our advantage ? Why should we not reign with Christ in glory ? If his people are not all, fully, eternally, and gloriously saved, where will be his reward for all he endured, and where will be the faithfulness of God, who said ? " He shall see his seed, he shall prolong his days, and the pleasure of the Lord shall prosper in his hand. He shall see of the travail of his soul, and shall be satisfied," Isa. 53 : 10, 11.

33. *Who shall lay any thing to the charge of God's elect ?* It is *God that justifieth.* Wiclif: Who shall accuse agens the chosun men of God? Peshito: Who will set himself against the chosen of God ? Arabic : Who will bring an action at law against the elect of God ? Stuart: Who shall accuse the elect of God ? Conybeare and Howson : What accuser can harm God's chosen ? Elsewhere the same verb is rendered implead, accuse. Our version gives the sense. Augustine, Grotius, Locke, Whitby, Bowyer, Doddridge, Pyle, Griesbach and Clarke continue the interrogatory form in the last clause : Is it God that justifieth ? That is, Will the same God justify and bring charges against his chosen ? The same commentators do the same in the next verse. But the authorized version gives the full sense of the passage. Who shall so accuse his elect to God, as to cause him to turn against them ? He has justified them, and he is in one mind, and who can turn him ? Job 23 : 13. Compare Isa. 43 : 25. God is the justifier, Rom 3 : 26. It is he, who has been sinned against, whose law has been infracted, whose majesty has been insulted. If he is reconciled so as to justify, his elect need not fear rejection. There is no reason for varying the meaning of the word *elect* in this verse. The same thing is taught elsewhere in many places : " We are bound to give thanks always to God for you, brethren beloved of the Lord, because God hath from the beginning chosen you to salvation, through sanctification of the Spirit and belief of the truth : whereunto he called you by our Gospel, to the obtaining of the glory of our

Lord Jesus Christ," 2 Thess. 2 : 13, 14. It is the same word rendered in these places : " For the elects' sake ;" " Shall deceive the very elect;" " Shall gather together his elect ;" " Elect according to the foreknowledge of God the Father," Matt. 24 : 22, 24, 31 ; 1 Pet. 1 : 22. In Rev. 17 : 14 they that are with the Lamb are said to be " called, and *chosen*, and faithful." The decree of election is as irreversible as the sentence of justification.

34. *Who* is *he that condemneth ?* It is *Christ that died, yea rather, that is risen again, who is even at the right hand of God, who also maketh intercession for us.* Peshito : Who is it that condemneth ? Messiah died, and arose, and is on the right hand of God, and maketh intercession for us. What allegation involving wrath can Satan, the accuser of the brethren, or conscience, however enlightened, or the law of God itself, in its perfect holiness, bring against a believer, when he has fled to Christ, who died for our sins according to the scriptures, and once suffered for sins the just for the unjust ; whose sacrifice was well pleasing to God, so that he released him, our Surety, from the prison of the grave, yea and hath famously exalted him, setting him at his own right hand, and admits him to a seat on his eternal throne, and never denies him anything that he asks, having accepted him as our interceding High Priest ? Where is the believer that needs any more, asks any more than he finds in Christ dying for our sins, rising for our justification, sitting at God's right hand, swaying the sceptre of universal dominion, and interceding for his people in the most glorious manner, being always heard and answered, Ps. 2 : 8 ; Luke 22 : 31, 32 ; John 11 : 42.

35. *Who shall separate us from the love of Christ ?* shall *tribulation, or distress, or nakedness, or peril, or sword ?* For *who* some read what, and the grammar allows it. The love of Christ here is the love he bears to us. Haldane : " That it is Christ's love to us, in this place there can be no question. A person could not be said to be separated from his own feelings. Besides, the object of the apostle is to assure us not so immediately of our love to God, as of his love to us, by directing our attention to his predestinating, calling, justifying, and glorifying us, and not sparing his own Son, but delivering him up for us all." *Separate*, a word used for putting asunder man and wife, Matt. 19 : 6 ; Mark 10 : 9 ; 1 Cor. 7 : 10, 11, 15. It also means any kind of separation, as when one departs from a given place, Acts 1 : 4 ; 18 : 1, 2. A form of it is used when Christ is said to have been *separate* from sinners, Heb. 7 : 26. The apostle then proceeds to enumerate a number of things, and to ask what power they can have to cause Christ to cease to love us. 1. *Tribulation*, a word that signifies vexation from without, a

pressure upon us by external grievances; not to be regarded however as separate from the effects naturally produced by such grievances. What such tribulation was to the early Christians we can
hardly conceive. All domestic, social, commercial and political
arrangements were liable and likely to bring to them vexation.
If one travelled, he found no inn, where a Christian's feelings were
not exposed to insult or outrage. If he would observe a day to
the Lord, the customs of his country were adverse to his quiet.
Some however prefer to give the word here a comprehensive
meaning, embracing affliction in general. Undoubtedly it is sometimes so used in the New Testament. 2. *Distress*, it probably
points to distress arising from the depressed state of one's mind,
or the afflicted state of one's heart. Stuart: It is applied more
especially to anxiety of mind. Robinson renders it straits, distress, anguish. 3. *Persecution*, pain or wrong brought on men for
their religion, literally it means pursuit with intent to destroy or
injure. How persecution, in every form, raged towards the early
Christians is no secret. History tells the whole story. Christ
gave his followers fair notice of such treatment, John 15 : 20.
4. *Famine*, commonly rendered as here, or *hunger*. Sometimes
it refers to general dearth, where all classes suffer, Acts 7 : 11;
but it as well describes the want of food where but one
or a few suffer hunger, 2 Cor. 11 : 37. One of the temptations arising to the early Christians arose from the fact that
they often suffered hunger when their heathen and cruel neighbors had bread enough and to spare. 5. *Nakedness*, like the last
this distress resulted not from idleness, nor from general want, but
from confiscation, robbery, violence or some form of persecution.
That bad element, human cruelty, was in it, 2 Sam. 24: 13, 14.
How can men provide food or raiment, who are driven from home
and from regular occupation, and wander in caves and dens of the
earth? Glad enough are they to get sheep skins and goat skins
for raiment, and the driest and coarsest food for diet. 6. *Peril*, a
word uniformly rendered. How many forms of it there are we
may judge from Paul's enumeration of them in 2 Cor. 11 : 26. 7.
Sword, the last resort of a good government, but often the first resort of tyrants and persecutors; and by them wielded wantonly
and wickedly. Now, why should Christ withdraw his love from
his elect because these sad things befall them? If they endure
such things, so did he. He knew they were to be thus tried when
he chose, called and justified them. From eternity his love has
been set upon them, Jer. 31 : 3. He has died for their sins, risen
for their justification, reigns in glory for their good, intercedes for
them above, is merciful and sympathizing towards them, and

never changes, for he is the same yesterday, to-day, and for ever. Surely he will never permit the sorrows of his saints to chill or change his love to them.   That be far from him.

36. *As it is written, For thy sake we are killed all the day long ; we are accounted as sheep for the slaughter.*   This verse is taken from Psalm 44: 22, and shows the extreme and constant sufferings of God's people, even at a time when they had not displeased him by any recent or visible defection.   It is pertinent to the scope of the Psalm, and pertinent to the discourse of Paul.   It does not deny that good may be brought out of our afflictions, nor that it is not better to suffer for well-doing than for evil-doing ; nor that it is not better to suffer in God's cause than our own.   But it is an appeal for mercy on the grounds of freedom from covenant-breaking with God, and of the great cruelty of persecutors, who insulted Jehovah by murdering his people.   These words have a sad fulfilment whenever God's people fall under persecution.   Calvin : " Lest the severity of the cross should dismay us, let us always have present to our view this state of the church, that as we are adopted in Christ, we are appointed to the slaughter."

37. *Nay, in all these things we are more than conquerors, through him that loved us.*   The first word may be rendered *nay* or *yea*, as the idiom of our language may require.   See above on Rom. 7 : 7. *In all these things*, and in all others like them, in scenes of the most unutterable earthly wo.   *We are more than conquerors*, if he had said we are conquerors, the language would have been strong and striking, but he says, we are more than conquerors.   Wiclif, Cranmer, Rheims and Doway read, we overcome ; Coverdale, we overcome farre ; Tyndale, we overcome strongly ; Peshito, we are victorious ; Macknight, we do more than overcome ; Schleusner, we most fully overcome ; Beza, we are much more than victors.   The verb in this form is found in the New Testament here only ; but without the prefix indicating abundantly, it occurs often, and is commonly rendered overcome, conquer, or get the victory.   It occurs often in Revelation. The contests of the righteous are with great evils, appalling to flesh and blood, the combined forces of wickedness in earth and hell, but they perish not ; nay, they carry trophies from the field of battle.   A man is not hurt till his soul is hurt ; and his soul is not hurt till his conscience is defiled with sin.   But the ample victory of the righteous is not due to their native wisdom, holiness or strength, but to *him that hath loved us*, which some understand as equivalent to this—he hath loved us—he loves us now—and he will love us for ever.   The reference is to Christ, whose love is specially spoken of in v. 35.   With such a stay and guide and Cap-

tain of salvation it would be marvellous indeed, if the saints were not more than conquerors.

38. *For I am persuaded that neither death, nor life, nor angels, nor principalities, nor powers, nor things present, nor things to come,*

39. *Nor height, nor depth, nor any other creature, shall be able to separate us from the love of God, which is in Christ Jesus our Lord.* *Am persuaded,* the same verb so rendered in Rom. 15:14; 2 Tim. 1:12; in 2 Cor. 2:3; Gal. 5:10; Phil. 3:3; 2 Thess. 3:4, have confidence. This persuasion was not of men but from God. It was not based on what Paul saw in man, but in what he knew to be in Christ and in the provisions of the covenant of grace. The schedule of adversaries begins thus: 1. *Death*, Aristotle's terrible of terribles, Bildad's king of terrors, Solomon's returning to the dust, the fear of which keeps so many in bondage all their lifetime; death coming to us in the usual way, or death made as frightful as possible by fiendish tormentors with chains, and whips, and racks, and wild beasts, and gibbets, and fires. This was the first ground of temptation, 2. *Life*, this is just the opposite. Some think it means life promised on condition of denying Christ before men. This is no doubt included, but life has many charms and seductions; it is also compassed with difficulties and temptations; nor can any well bear its burdens without the special grace of God. The love of life is natural; but it may become inordinate. In the catalogue of covenanted blessings, in 1 Cor. 3:22, Paul inserts both life and death. 3. *Angels*, whether good or bad, whether of high or of low rank. Flatt and Stuart by angels understand only evil spirits, because good angels would not be opposers of Christians. Pool suggests the same. But Haldane well points us to the language of Paul on another occasion: "If 'an angel from heaven preach any other gospel unto you than that which we have preached unto you, let him be accursed.' Could an angel from heaven be supposed a false preacher rather than a persecutor? But such suppositions are common in scripture. They do not imply the possibility of the things supposed, and it fully justifies them if the consequence would follow from the supposition, were it realized." The power of angels is prodigious; but they are not strong enough to sever the bonds of union between Christ and believers. 4. *Principalities*, a word which is applied to earthly potentates, Luke 12:11; to evil angels of great power, Eph. 6:12; Col. 2:15; to good angels of high rank, Eph. 1:21; 3:10; and sometimes unitedly to earthly and heavenly potentates, Col. 1:16. Speak of principalities ever so great, earthly, heavenly or infernal till you are amazed at their influence; but they all united could not sunder a soul from God, who loves

it.　5. *Powers*, sometimes rendered miracles, mighty works, wonderful works, Matt. 7 : 22 ; Mark 6 : 2 ; Acts 2 : 22 ; 1 Cor. 12 : 10, 28, 29 ; often rendered strength, power, might, once violence, Heb. 11 : 34.　Gather together all created powers, great and small, celestial, terrestrial and infernal, and they can do nothing to cut off the saints from the favor of God.　6 and 7. *Things present and things to come*, Grotius : Neither the evils we now feel, nor those which await us ; Owen of Thrussington : Neither things which now exist, nor things which shall be ; Haldane : Neither the trials nor afflictions in which the children of God are at any time involved, nor with which they may at any future period be exercised ; Hodge : Nothing in this life, nor in the future ; Stuart : Neither [troubles] present nor future.　8 and 9. *Height and depth*, Grotius : The *height* of honor and the *depth* of disgrace ; Mede : Prosperity and adversity ; Schleusner : Neither heaven nor earth. The first word occurs in but one other place in the New Testament, 2 Cor. 10 : 5, and is there rendered *high things*.　The second occurs nine times, and is twice applied to a deep soil, Matt. 13 : 5 ; Mark 4 : 5 ; once to deep poverty, 2 Cor. 8 : 2 ; once to deep waters, Luke 5 : 4 ; twice to the amazing love and wisdom of God in man's salvation ; once to the deep things of God ; once to the deep plots of Satan, Rev. 2 : 24.　Perhaps the sense given by Schleusner is to be preferred, unless we undersand with Theodoret, neither heaven nor hell.　10. *Nor any other creature*, that is, created thing, or creation.　All that God has made has the continuance of its existence by his will, is completely in his power and can never get beyond his grasp.　It may be rational or irrational, animate or inanimate, but it and all things else combined cannot change God's gracious purpose of love and mercy to his chosen—that *love of God, which is in Christ Jesus our Lord.*　The saving love of the Father flows out through his Son.　In creation and providence God has indeed manifested great benevolence ; but that love of God, which blesses us with all spiritual blessings is in Christ Jesus our Lord, and in none other.　Whosoever rejects Christ seals his own damnation.

DOCTRINAL AND PRACTICAL REMARKS

1. Let ministers of the gospel imitate the example of Paul in presenting fully and faithfully the doctrine of gratuitous salvation, answering objections to it, and then showing, as he does, vs. 31–39, how the believer may exult in the face of all foes.　It is sad when the embassadors of Christ first take away the grounds of a strong consolation, and then display no heroism in the face of appalling

dangers, but turn cowards, and by example teach the people to be unfaithful to Christ. But it is delightful when like Paul they stand forth bravely on the field of battle, beckon on the followers of the Lamb, in the name of Christ defy the assaults of earth and hell, and sing songs of salvation in the hottest of the battle.

2. When God propounds truth we ought to think of it, consider its bearings, and, if occasion offer, have something to say of it, v. 31. We should first embrace all that the Lord speaks, then practise it, and never relinquish it. If truth is for humiliation, let us be humbled thereby ; if it is for admonition, let us be admonished ; if it is for comfort, let us be strengthened. Troubles may roll in like the waves of the sea, but if our faith is clear and strong, we shall glory in them all. As in Christ the scourge, and crown of thorns, and cross, and cup of bitterness all turned to his greater exaltation, so shall it be with all his people, who are faithful unto death.

3. Every revealed truth has its relations to other principles of God's word, and should often be so considered ; but some things said in scripture are so simple and so clear that we may rejoice in them whenever we think of them. They come up a thousand times, in old and in new connections, or by themselves, and help us in our struggle. Such a truth have we here : " If God be for us, who can be against us ?" Pool : " Maximilian, the emperor, so admired this sentence, that he caused it to be written over the table where he used to dine and sup ; that, having it often in his eye, he might have it also in his mind." God's word abounds in like utterances. Let us learn and remember them. Let the word of God dwell in us richly in all wisdom and spiritual understanding.

4. Everything turns on this, Is God for us ? v. 31. If he is, results are not doubtful. Calvin : " This is the chief and the only support which can assist us in every temptation. For unless God favor us, though all things should smile on us, yet no sure confidence can be attained ; but on the other hand his favor alone is a sufficient solace in every sorrow, a protection sufficiently strong against all the storms of adversities." If there were any weakness or deficiency in his character, it would be different. But there is none. He is infinite, eternal and unchangeable, in his being, wisdom, power, holiness, justice, goodness and truth. Evans : " That includes all, that God is for us ; not only reconciled to us, and so not against us, but in covenant with us, and so engaged for us ; all his attributes for us, his promises for us ; all that he is, and has, and does, is for his people. He performs all things for them. He is for them, even when he seems to act against them." Alleluia, for the Lord God omnipotent reigneth.

5. Before such truth how opposition, persecution and all their horrid machinations fade away and become contemptible. Chrysostom : " It may be said, who is there that is not against us? Why the world is against us, both kings and people, both kindred and countrymen. Yet so far are they from thwarting us at all, that even they without their will become to us the causes of crowns, and procurers of countless blessings, in that God's wisdom turneth their plots into our salvation and glory. . . Against the Emperor there are abundance of barbarians that arm themselves, and of enemies that invade, and of body-guards that plot, and of subjects many that oftentimes are ever and anon rebelling, and thousands of other things. But against the faithful who taketh good heed unto God's laws, neither man, nor devil, nor aught besides can raise opposition! For if you take away his money, you have become the procurer of a reward to him. If you speak ill of him, by the evil report he gains fresh lustre in God's sight. If you cast him into starvation, the more will his glory and his reward be. If you give him over to death, you are twining a crown of martyrdom about him." Nor is this any new doctrine. It is the same old truth delivered to the saints before the coming of Messiah. See Isa. 43 : 1, 2, and many like passages.

6. If we reverse the sentence contained in the last clause of verse 31, we have a truth no less clear, but terribly alarming to all who live in sin : If God be against us, who can be for us? All the consolatory truths of Scripture have the reverse side, and if men were wise, they would look at both sides, and not allow the vanities of earth to divert their attention from eternal things. If God be against us! Awful thought! If he is against us, all his attributes, purposes, plans, works and word are against us. Who but a madman will tempt so unequal a war?

7. It is a glorious truth that Jesus Christ did not die by accident, or because he could not live any longer, or because man was too strong for the Almighty, but that God *spared* him not, and all according to his wise and eternal counsel, v. 32. True, Judas *delivered* him to the Roman band, and Pilate *delivered* him to be crucified, but they could do nothing except as it was given them of God. If his Father had not *delivered* him to death, he had not died. Scott : " If this was not too large a gift to his enemies, what can he withhold from his friends and children ?"

8. Idle is the expectation of the wicked that they shall escape with impunity, even though sin be not pardoned, when God *spared not his own Son*, even though he was personally innocent, and merely stood as the substitute of others, v. 32.

9. The doctrine of Christ's true and proper divinity is fundamental. It is so treated in the word of God. He is God's Son,
God's *own Son*, v. 32; God's well-beloved Son, who counted it not
robbery to be equal with God. How can any prove the divinity
of the Father, but by the very arguments which establish the
divinity of the Son? If the Father is called God, so is the Son,
John 1 : 1; if the Father made the world, so did the Son, John 1 :
3; if the Father rightly receives the worship of the heavenly
hosts, so does the Son, Heb. 1 : 6; if the Father is unchangeable,
so is the Son, Heb. 1 : 12; if the Father is Almighty, so is the Son,
Rev. 1 : 8; if the Father is omniscient, the Son also knoweth all
things, John 21 : 17.

10. Glorious is the truth, not only that with Christ God will
give us all things, but that he will *freely give* them—without money
and without price, without hesitation or reluctance, without stint
and without grudging, v. 32. When he says *all things*, of course
he means all things necessary, profitable to us, really promotive of
our best interests. The same idea is presented in Ps. 34 : 10; 84 : 11.
They that serve the Lord shall lack no *good thing*.

11. It is a blessed truth that Jesus Christ bore all the curse,
drank the cup of trembling to the dregs thereof, exhausted the
penalty that we had incurred, and so left nothing behind for us to
bear, or to hinder our reception of infinite blessings, v. 32.

12. But let us never forget that all good things come *with
Christ*, v. 32. He is the Mediator, the Prophet, Priest, and King,
the Surety of the sinner. Chalmers sums up in five different heads
the substance of the arguments used in this connection: " First—
God hath already given the very greatest thing to set my salvation agoing, and what security then is there that he shall give all
other things which are needful to complete that salvation? He
hath given his only and his well-beloved Son for us all. Secondly
—Take into account the deep and mysterious suffering that was
incurred at this first and greatest step in the historical process of
our salvation—and that now the suffering is over. Thirdly—Remember that all which God hath done from first to last in the
work of our redemption, has been entirely of free will. It was
not because he owed it to us, but because his own heart was set
upon it. Fourthly—It should still more be recollected, that when
he did give up his Son, it was on behalf of sinners with whom at
the time he was in a state of unreconciled variance. It was in the
very heat and soreness of the controversy. It was at the period
when his broken law had as yet obtained no reparation—when insult without a satisfaction, when disobedience without an apology
and without a compensation, had been rendered to him. Fifthly

—He gave up his Son at a time when mercy was closed in as it were by the other attributes of his nature—when it had not yet found a way through that justice and holiness and truth, which seemed to bar the exercise of it altogether." After such a gift, under such circumstances, who can wonder at anything else as great in the shape of bounty, pity or mercy?

13. God does indeed freely justify by his grace, but not without a cause, v. 33. His everlasting love and his unchangeable purpose lead him thereto. Through the infinite merits of Christ reckoned to the believer, God declares the sinner just, adorns him with glorious righteousness, takes him fully into favor, sees neither iniquity nor perverseness in him, Num. 28 : 21, and deals with him to all the ends and purposes of eternal life as tenderly and lovingly as if he had never sinned at all. All which could be supposed to be charged against him has been forgiven. The only competent judge in the case pronounces him absolved from all things justly charged against him. O that precious blood without the shedding of which there was no remission ! O that glorious obedience without flaw or defect, rendered by our Substitute, Rom. 5 : 19. After all this we should as soon expect God to unmake the world as to reverse the gracious sentence of justification.

14. Not only is Christ's character faultless, complete and glorious, but his work is finished also. He died, he rose, he is at God's right hand, he intercedes, v. 34. By his death he paid our dreadful debt. By rising he obtained God's testimony to the fulness of his satisfaction. By sitting at God's right hand, he evinces his sovereign authority over all, by interceding he shows himself our advocate on high. This is not after the manner of men. The ransom has been paid, plenteous redemption procured, eternal life made sure to all who accept the offers of the gospel. No marvel that he has a name above every name. No marvel that the virgins love him, that the angels adore him, that his Father crowns him with glory and honor.

15. When God permits them, wicked men and fallen angels can do a good deal. They can send tribulation, distress, persecution, famine, nakedness, peril and sword, v. 35. They cannot do even these things till God lengthens their chain, John 19: 11. But sometimes they are permitted to do such things. They are the sword in the hand of the Lord, Ps. 17 : 13. They are the rod of God's anger and the staff of his indignation, Isa. 10 : 5. Chrysostom: "Paul dares them all! He brings them forward in the shape of questions, as if it were incontrovertible that nothing could move a person so beloved, and who had enjoyed so much

providence over him." Hodge: "Trials and afflictions of every
kind have been the portion of the people of God in all ages; as
they cannot destroy the love of Christ towards us, they ought not
to shake our love towards him."

16. Dickson: "It is a mercy to us, that when God might punish us for our sins, he maketh our correction honorable, and our
troubles to be for a good cause: *for thy sake are we killed*," v. 36.
Reader, art thou at heart a martyr? Woulds't thou stand *fire* for
Christ?

17. It is marvellous that sinners do not see how saints gain the
victory even here. Every day they show themselves. to be more
than conquerors, v. 37. Sometimes wicked men do see that God
is with his people of a truth, even in this life. The heathen themselves ere now have had their eyes opened to the marvellous providence of God in behalf of his chosen. "Then said his wise men
and Zeresh his wife unto him, If Mordecai be of the seed of the
Jews, before whom thou hast begun to fall, thou shalt not prevail
against him, but shalt surely fall before him," Esther 6 : 13. The
day is coming when sinners will unite with saints in pronouncing
all sin to be madness, all iniquity to be the folly of fools.

18. This is the more clear as God's people are more than conquerors even here. He is the greater man, not who has the
greater wealth but the greater contempt of wealth ; not who seeks
and obtains most honors from men, but who seeks the honor that
cometh from God only. No man is so debased by sin that he
might not be overcome by a love of the world in any of its forms ;
but the true greatness of believers consists in despising, as a portion, all the things that perish. One said, I am greater and am
born to greater things than to trust to lying vanities. Losses
God's people do certainly sustain, but none of them are irrepara-
ble ; and none of them are worth a moment's thought compared
with the glory which shall be revealed in us. "We, Christians,
laugh at your cruelty, and grow the more resolute," said a no-
bleman to Julian the apostate. Whether bloody persecution is
likely ever to stalk abroad again is hardly a doubtful question.
Some have thought America would in such an event be exempt, because the blood of the martyrs has not yet flowed here.
But many among us are the descendants of persecutors, and the
spirit that is in the wicked still lusteth to envy. So let every
good man be prepared for *peril* and the *sword*. Both may come.

19. But all our victory is through him that loved us, v. 37.
How carefully we ought to cultivate the spirit of the Gospel
which never forgets to give glory to the Lamb. How often does
God's word remind us that all is in, by and through Christ, for

his sake, in his name, by his blood and to his glory. If in heaven above, they crown him in each of their songs, why should not we imitate them here below? It is no new thing for Scribes and Pharisees, formalists and hypocrites to be sore displeased when even the children in the temple cry, Hosanna to the Son of David, Matt. 21 : 15. But let not us be joined to their company.

20. It is a good thing to have right *persuasions* about great things in religion, and if they are true, the firmer they are, the better, v. 38. Mere convictions are not enough, though they lie at the foundation of just action.. One great cause of the instability of professing Christians is the want of firm persuasions—persuasions that all which God hath spoken shall surely be accomplished, that every word of God is pure, that no promise can fail, and that the final victory of the righteous is as certain as that God is on their side.

21. The love of Christ and the love of God which is in Christ Jesus our Lord shall be the theme of the redeemed forever, vs. 35, 39. Let all the pious duly celebrate them here. It was not easy for David to exaggerate the love of Jonathan to him. He declares it was wonderful—beyond the love of women, 2 Sam. 1 : 26. But what was the love of Jonathan to David compared with the love of Christ to his people, or with the love of God in Christ? It is even as nothing. The latter is from eternity, unchanging, overcoming all obstacles, making all sacrifices, giving a kingdom that cannot be moved, and having neither measure nor limit.

> O for this love let rocks and hills
>   Their lasting silence break ;
> And all harmonious human tongues
>   The Saviour's praises speak.

22. Come what will, nothing can separate the believer from the love of God which is in Christ Jesus our Lord. No, nothing! Earth and hell have often combined their forces, and racked their powers of invention to do something that should be a real damage to the undaunted believer. But they have never been able to succeed and they never shall. After they have killed the body, what remains for them to do? Thenceforth, the ransomed child of grace is as effectually beyond their power as is his glorified Redeemer.

23. Are these things so? Let the spirit of entire devotion to the person and glory of Christ animate the breast of all, who hope for any thing better than this poor world can supply. It is easy to fall into excess in the desire and pursuit of earthly things. But

no man ever loves Christ too much, or is too prompt to bear reproach or suffering for his sake.   The great error of us all is that
we are too slow to offer up our Isaacs, to say what have I to do
any more with idols? and to take up our cross and follow Christ
through evil and through good report.

24. The whole spirit of this passage leaves the just impression
on the mind of every candid reader that the doctrines here taught
are a contribution to holiness.   Scott: " None can have any ground
to think themselves predestinated, called, or justified, or to expect
to be glorified; except they love God, bear the image of Christ,
walk in his steps, and aim to obey and honor him."   Where is the
child of God, however feeble his graces, who does not know that
the end of the commandment is charity, out of a pure heart, and of
a good conscience and of faith unfeigned?   Where is the believer
so weak as to suppose that a wicked life is not fruit unto death?
Hodge: " It has been objected that if Paul had intended to teach
these doctrines, he would have said that apostasy and sin cannot
interfere with the salvation of believers.   But what is salvation,
but deliverance from the guilt and power of sin?   It is, therefore,
included in the very purpose and promise of salvation, that its objects shall be preserved from apostasy and deadly sins.   This is
the end and essence of salvation.   And, therefore, to make Paul
argue that God will save us if we do not apostatize, is to make
him say, that those shall be saved who are not lost.   According to
the apostle's doctrine, holiness is so essential and prominent a part
of salvation, that it is not so much a means to an end as the very
end itself.   It is that to which we are predestinated and called, and
therefore if the promise of salvation does not include the promise
of holiness, it includes nothing.   Hence, to ask, whether if one of
the called should apostatize and live in sin, he would still be saved,
is to ask, whether he shall be saved if he is not saved?"

25. The Scripture warrants the doctrine of assurance of salvation, vs. 31–39.   Haldane: " The full assurance of faith, in which
believers are commanded to draw near to God, stands inseparably
connected with having their hearts sprinkled from an evil conscience.   An evil conscience accuses a man as guilty, as deserving
and liable to punishment, and keeps him at a distance from God.
It causes him to regard the Almighty as an enemy and avenger,
so that the natural enmity of the mind against God is excited and
strengthened.   On the contrary, a good conscience is a conscience
discharged from guilt, by the blood of Christ.   Conscience tells a
man that the wages of sin is death, and that he has incurred the
penalty; but when the atonement made by Christ is believed in,
it is seen that our sins are no more ours, but Christ's, upon whom

God hath laid them all, and that the punishment due for sin, which is death, has been inflicted upon him; the demands of the law have been fulfilled, and its penalty suffered. On this the believer rests, and his conscience is satisfied." Leighton: " If election, effectual calling and salvation be inseparably linked together— then by any one of them a man may lay hold upon all the rest, and may know that his hold is sure; and this is the way wherein he may attain and ought to secure that comfortable assurance of the love of God . . . Find then but within thee sanctification by the Spirit; and this argues necessarily both justification by the Son, and election by God the Father."

PRAYER

O Lord God, the Father of mercies and the Father of our Lord Jesus Christ, give us grace to accept all the loving kindness manifested to us in the gift of thy dear Son. Make us conformable to his life and to his death. Put thy good Spirit within us as a Spirit of adoption, of truth, of grace and supplications, of wisdom and holiness. Bring us within the pale of that covenant which is ordered in all things and sure. Write our names in the Lamb's Book of Life. Surround us by thy gracious Providence. Enable us to believe every word which thou hast spoken and give us the victory over all our spiritual adversaries, letting nothing separate us from the love of God which is in Christ Jesus. And unto him that is able to keep us from falling and to present us faultless before the presence of his glory with exceeding joy; to the only wise God our Saviour, be glory and majesty, dominion and power, both now and ever. Amen.

Chapter 22

ROMANS 9
VERSES 1-5

PAUL'S SORROW AT THE REJECTION OF THE JEWS.
THE HIGH PRIVILEGES THEY HAVE ENJOYED.

I SAY the truth in Christ, I lie not, my conscience also bearing me witness in the Holy Ghost.

2 That I have great heaviness and continual sorrow in my heart.

3 For I could wish that myself were accursed from Christ for my brethren, my kinsmen according to the flesh :

4 Who are Israelites ; to whom *pertaineth* the adoption, and the glory, and the covenants, and the giving of the law, and the service *of God,* and the promises ;

5 Whose *are* the fathers, and of whom as concerning the flesh Christ *came,* who is over all, God blessed for ever.   Amen.

PAUL had proved that Gentiles and Jews were all sinners ; that they all needed gratuitous salvation ; that justification could not possibly be by the deeds of the law ; that there was but one way of salvation for all nations of men ; that there was no revelation of more than one method of restoration to God's favor ; that Abraham was saved just as sinners of the Gentiles are saved ; that David clearly spoke of this one method ; that Christ's humiliation opened up to us the way of life ; that we are justified through faith in Christ ; that the fruits of justification are abundant and blessed ; that the great principle of federal headship brought to our notice in the fall of Adam is the same as that involved in our representation in Christ ; that gratuitous salvation gives no license to loose living, but by a right apprehension of it men become servants of God ; that sanctification is by the gospel, not by the law ; that in the spiritual warfare of the Christian life the victory is won only through Jesus Christ ; that justification is complete in this life and inseparably joined with sanctification by the Spirit ; that nothing in the form of affliction is in the end really injurious to believers ; that God had an eternal plan concerning men's salvation; that nothing could destroy those, who were the called according to God's purpose; and that the combined powers of wickedness could not separate a believer from the love of God which is in Christ Jesus. Thus the apostle closes his discussion of the glorious way of life by a gratuitous justification, and by a scriptural sanctification, and closes it with shoutings and exultations the most animating.

But just here a sad topic is presented. It is this. If the foregoing is the only method of salvation, is not the case of many Jews sad? have they not rejected Jesus as the Messiah, the way, the truth, and the life? Notorious facts compel the apostle to admit that this is so. To this matter he now addresses himself in the most tender and solemn manner.

1. *I say the truth in Christ, I lie not, my conscience also bearing me witness in the Holy Ghost.* It is as if he had said, I have not taught the doctrines of this epistle because I was indifferent to the case of my countrymen, nor because they had cast me off and persecuted me for my love to the gospel. Far from it. *I say the truth,* I speak what I am sure is verity, On this point I am not mistaken. I say the truth *in Christ.* This phrase is variously explained. Four methods are chiefly relied on. 1. Many regard the phrase as equivalent to an oath. But there is no verb of swearing used here. Nor was there any propriety in his taking an oath. No one had called for it. The occasion did not call for it. 2. Some put *I* and *in Christ* together—*I in Christ,* I a man who claim to be in Christ, a new creature, a Christian. This form of expression, thus understood, could give no weight, among Jews, to what he was about to say. 3. Some think that *in Christ* means in a Christian manner. This too would not commend to Jews what he was about to say. Nor is this a very good sense to give the phrase, nor is it the usual signification of the words *in Christ.* 4. Others, admitting that it is not an oath, yet regard it as an asseveration. We are said to asseverate when with solemnity we positively aver. An asseveration expresses vehemence and is designed to give emphasis to our assertions. Asseverations are right or wrong according to the occasion or manner of using them. When lawful they do not materially differ from persistent declarations. Thus Rhoda the damsel *constantly affirmed* that Peter was at the gate. We may make our asseverations very strong, as Elijah did to Elisha, when he said, "As the Lord liveth, and as thy soul liveth," 2 Kings 2 : 2, 4, 6. This is not a formal oath, and yet it is an assertion hardly less solemn than an oath, but there is no swearing in it. So Paul here under a sense of his awful responsibility to the Master whom he served, in whose presence he felt himself to be,

and to whom he knew he must soon give account, solemnly asserts his sincerity and truthfulness. In 2 Cor. 2 : 17 there is a similar solemn assertion : " As of sincerity, as of God, in the sight of God speak we in Christ." *I lie not*, quite uniformly rendered, I speak not falsely. *My conscience also bearing me witness in the Holy Ghost.* How one's conscience bears witness to the truth of what he says men commonly suppose they well understand. The doubt arises respecting the last phrase, *in the Holy Ghost.* There are five opinions. 1. Some take it as an oath by the third person of the Trinity ; but for this there seems to be no reason whatever. There is no form of swearing, but there is a simple statement that his conscience testified to his veracity. 2. Others think the meaning is, my conscience testifies and the Holy Ghost also testifies with it. This makes good sense, and teaches the same truth as that taught in Rom 8 : 16. The only difficulty is in so construing the words as to get this sense out of them. 3. Others make the sense to be, My conscience in [or under the direction of] the Holy Ghost testifies. It is true that the Holy Spirit does purify and sanctify the conscience of a believer in Jesus Christ. But is this what Paul here intends to assert of himself? 4. Others think that the phrase *in the Holy Ghost*, is a simple claim of being under the in-spiration of the Holy Ghost. This is certainly the meaning of the phrase in Matt. 22 : 43; Mark 12 : 36; 1 Cor. 12 : 3, 13, etc. In each of these places we have the same preposition as in our verse. 5. The other explanation offered is that, like the first clause of the verse, this is a solemn asseveration, in the presence of the Spirit who searcheth the heart, that he uttered no falsehood. Either this or the 4th is best sustained by scripture usage, gives the best sense, and is most free from objections.

2. *That I have great heaviness and continual sorrow in my heart.* *Heaviness*, once rendered grief, twice heaviness, but commonly sorrow. *Sorrow*, found in but one other place (1 Tim. 6 : 16) and there rendered as here. The latter is the stronger word. Bret-schneider renders the former grief; the latter, violent grief. But to the former Paul adds the word *great*, and to the latter the word *continual*. His grief was great and without ceasing ; for how could he endure to see the destruction of his nation? Their re-jection of Christ caused them to be awfully rejected by God ; subjected them to the utter loss of all that had distinguished them as a people, and gave them over to the direst calamities that ever befell a city or a country. Though this epistle was written at least ten years before the destruction of Jerusalem, yet from the days of the personal ministry of Christ the doom of the holy city had been no secret among his disciples, Matt. 24 : 2–22 ; Luke

19 : 41–44. Indeed so well advised were even private Jewish Christians of the approaching catastrophe that tradition distinctly says that not one of them perished in the overthrow of their ancient city. As Jesus, beholding the city twenty-five or thirty years before, wept over it, so now his servant Paul was bowed down with sorrow on the same account, and so much the more as the awful events, made certain by prophecy and by the general rejection of Messiah, were near at hand.

3. *For I could wish that myself were accursed from Christ for my brethren, my kinsmen according to the flesh.* As might be expected the interpretations of this verse are both various and diverse. The extreme views are these : 1. Some explain the words as though the apostle meant to say that he loved his nation so that for their good he was willing to be excluded from the hope of salvation, separated from Christ, and brought under the curse impending over his unbelieving countrymen both in this and the next world. Surely Paul was not calling down on himself the eternal destruction of the wicked, nor expressing a readiness to be a cast-away and a blasphemer of Christ for ever. This is one extreme. 2. The other makes very little of the verse, supposing it expresses not what Paul now wished, but what he had wished before his conversion. But all, who knew Paul's history, needed not to be told of his former madness and bitterness against the Lord Jesus. The dislike of the Jews to him arose very much from the fact that he had so utterly renounced Judaism and changed his course. He was endeavoring to soften their prejudices, by telling them of his present sentiments respecting them. He was assuring his countrymen that he now ardently loved them. Between these extremes lie a large number of opinions, most, if not all of which depend on the misconstruction of some word in the Greek text of this verse. Thus Waterland, followed by Doddridge, thinks that the preposition rendered *from* means *after the example of* Christ. But the place relied on to establish it (2 Tim. 1 : 3) does not sustain the exposition. Another turns on the meaning of the word rendered *accursed*, in the Greek anathema. Because anything anathema, if possessed of animal life, was devoted to death, some think Paul meant that he was willing to die for his people, if that would save them. But the difficulty arises from the fact that the word denotes not merely death, but commonly death under the curse of God, and that here he adds the words *from Christ*. Surely Paul did not seriously desire to die under the curse of God, or to be banished from Christ. Nor can we suppose that by *accursed* he merely meant excommunicated from the church ; for a man could not be lawfully cut off from the church except for some great sin,

which must be repented of; and surely Paul did not wish to be, for his sins, excluded from the fellowship of the saints. Nor would the words thus understood at all commend him to the Jews. After these remarks it is proper to observe that examples are not wanting in the scriptures of very strong language expressive of desire for the good of others. Thus for Israel on occasion of their making the golden calf and the terrible waste of life that followed, Moses offered this prayer: "Yet now, if thou wilt forgive their sins: and, if not, blot me, I pray thee, out of thy book which thou hast written," Ex. 32: 32. Paul says: "Peradventure for a good man some would ·even dare to die," Rom. 5: 7. Again: "Being affectionately desirous of you, we were willing to have imparted unto you, not the gospel of God only, but also our own souls, because ye were dear unto us," 1 Thess. 2: 8. And the beloved disciple says: "Hereby perceive we the love of God, because he laid down his life for us: and we ought to lay down our lives for the brethren," 1 John 3: 16. Compare 2 Cor. 12: 15; Phil. 2: 17. These scriptures make it abundantly clear that a good man may be willing, and that some have been willing to suffer all that men can lawfully suffer, all that they can endure without sin, for the good of others, even to dying a violent and cruel death under a load of obloquy and ignominy. It may also be stated, that there is a lawful way of expressing our natural desires or personal wishes for things impossible, and thus indicating the intensity of our emotions, without our sinning against God, or being chargeable with insincerity. Thus our dear Lord himself in his dreadful agony "prayed, saying, O my Father, if it be possible, let this cup pass from me: nevertheless, not as I will, but as thou wilt," Matt. 26: 39. So in Gal. 1: 8, 9, Paul states a supposition of that which is wholly impossible. Now the very form of the verb here is such as to indicate that the apostle intended to admit that what he spoke of was impossible. On that question of grammar see Tholuck, Stuart and Hodge on this place. The tense of the verb is not the present *I wish*, nor the aorist *I did wish*, but the imperfect *I could wish*. The word anathema, rendered *accursed*, deserves further notice. The idea connected with it may be Greek and heathen, or Jewish and rabbinical. This gives it a wide range. It may mean 1. something devoted to God; 2. something very detestable; 3. something devoted to destruction. The word was used in the various forms of excommunication in the Jewish Church. Were it not for the words *from Christ*, there would be no difficulty in the case. To meet this some propose to read *from Christ's body*, or church; but this would in no sense commend Paul to a Jew. Guyse carries his paraphrase so far as to make the apostle express his willingness "to be cut off from the delights of present communion with Christ." But few if any seem ready to follow him. On a view of the whole case these conclusions are reached: 1. That Paul here expresses nothing that he or any one might not lawfully say. He utters no shocking imprecation, and calls down no curse on himself. 2. He expresses in the strongest terms known to him, his deep sorrow at the state and doom of his Jewish brethren and his desire to serve them. 3. The form of expression employed indicates that he regarded that of which he spoke as something impossible to be done; yet his longings for his countrymen were such that he knew of nothing and could conceive of nothing which it was lawful and possible for man to endure, that he would not suffer it to save his own people, whose ruin he saw coming on them like an armed man. *My brethren,* fully explained to mean the Jews by the words, *my kinsmen according to the flesh.*

4. *Who are Israelites : to whom* pertaineth *the adoption, and the glory, and the covenants, and the giving of the law, and the service* of God *and the promises.* No man had studied with more care the history of his people, or had a higher estimate of their distinguished privileges, or would have been personally more gratified at their piety and honor than the apostle to the Gentiles. He acknowledges the long line of an honored ancestry which they justly claimed. They were *Israelites,* descendants of the man who was a prince with God. They knew no more encouraging title belonging to Jehovah than that of the God of Jacob. They too had Abraham to their father, Moses for their leader and lawgiver, Aaron and Eli among their priests, Samuel, Elias and Isaiah among their prophets, Ehud and Samson among their heroes, David, Solomon and Josiah among their kings, and Miriam and Hannah among their honorable women. To them pertained *the adoption,* a word uniformly rendered. God often called the Jewish nation his children, and held himself forth as their Father, Ex. 4:23; Deut. 14:1; Jer. 31:9; Hos. 11:1; Isa. 1:2; Mal. 1:6. But this could not mean that the whole nation was in favor with God, for Paul at once proceeds to show that this was not so; but that among them was made known the way of becoming the true sons of God; or that God treated them, beyond any other people, with pity and favor. This latter is probably the idea intended. It coincides with other scriptures, Amos 3:2; Ps. 147:19, 20; Isa. 63:19. To them also pertained *the glory,* that is, God for long ages appeared among them by the visible glory, the shechinah, the brightness, Ex. 29:43; 40:34; and many other places. The ark seems once to be called the glory, 1 Sam. 4:21; but the glory

rested over it. To them too belonged *the covenants*, those made
with Abraham, Isaac, Jacob, Aaron and David, the covenant in
the plains of Moab, the covenant at Shechem, and the national
covenant. The only theocracy ever established among men was
in Israel. To them also was given *the law*, the Sinaitic covenant,
a law regulating everything, promoting, when observed, the highest domestic and national happiness, keeping them separate from
the abominations of heathenism, and making them a peculiar
nation. They also had *the service of God*, the grandest ritual ever
known on earth, with its priests, altars, sacrifices, feasts and
splendid temple. All its appointments were of the most imposing character. And to them pertained *the promises*, Rom. 15 : 8 ;
Gal. 3 : 16; Eph. 2 : 12 ; Heb. 11 : 17. The greatest of all the
promises, around which all clustered, were those relating to
Messiah.

5. *Whose* are *the fathers, and of whom as concerning the flesh
Christ* came, *who is over all, God blessed for ever. Amen. The fathers*, not merely Abraham, Isaac and Jacob, but all that long line
of worthies, some of whom are mentioned in holy writings, but
most of whom were known in Paul's day by tradition or were
found in the genealogical tables.   Fourteen or fifteen hundred
years of the history of such a people must have produced multitudes of men and women eminent for their virtues and piety. *Of
whom concerning the flesh Christ came.* As to his human nature
our Saviour was an Israelite. Let us not forget that. He was of
the tribe of Judah, his real mother and reputed father both being
of the house and lineage of David.   But then he had also a divine
nature, for he is not only truly man, but he *is over all, God blessed
for ever.*   Three things are here said respecting Christ, either of
which should settle the question of our Lord's divinity. One is
that he is called *God.*   Another is that he is supreme—he is *over
all.*   Compare Eph. 4 : 6, where the same language is used of the
Father.   The third is that he *is blessed for ever. Blessed*, not the
word so rendered in Matt. 5 : 3-11.   That means happy. But this
word, says Robinson, means adorable, worthy of all praise.   The
word is found eight times in the New Testament, and is seven
times applied to the Father, and here to the Son.   It shows the
desperate lengths to which the enemies of the supreme divinity of
our Lord will go, that they attempt to alter and pervert this text,
making it a doxology to God the Father.   But their rashness in
this behalf has opened the eyes of many, to see how men will dare
to tamper with God's word.   Hodge: " All the MSS., all the
versions and fathers give the passage precisely as in the common
text." *Amen*, a word of Hebrew origin. At the beginning of a

sentence it means verily, of a truth; at the end of a sentence it means, let it be. See above on Rom. 1 : 25.

DOCTRINAL AND PRACTICAL REMARKS

1. All Christians, and particularly all ministers of the gospel should speak the *truth*, especially respecting the great things of God, and where the life of men's souls is involved, v. 1. They should speak it fearlessly, solemnly, seasonably, humbly, plainly, with discrimination, faithfully, doctrinally, experimentally, by example and lovingly. Tenderness is the matter prominently brought to our notice here. In other places we find the same thing. For three years Paul wept over the Ephesians, Acts 20 : 19. Compare Phil. 3 : 18. We had almost as well not preach God's truth at all as to speak it in a harsh and violent way. A cold, severe and insolent manner of presenting it does caricature God's truth, and give to men erroneous conceptions of it. Many indulge prejudices against both the message and the messenger. Oftimes hatred of the preacher causes rejection of his doctrine. Sometimes malice rises into rage. Then great wisdom and forbearance are called for. Brown: "Ministers, in dealing with an exasperated people, should follow a Christian prudent way of insinuating themselves in their affections, and for this cause should wisely forbear any expression which may irritate." Harshness is not fidelity. There are hardly any maxims more false or mischievous than these: "There is no good done unless opposition is aroused;" "One's fidelity may be tested by the enmity he awakens against himself and the doctrine he preaches." The hostility of the natural heart against God and his word and people should never be wantonly or needlessly provoked. It is strong and active enough at all times to evince its deadly nature without our needlessly provoking it.

2. Where the case calls for it, we may assert and even asseverate our truthfulness, and our love for men's souls, v. 1. There are but few men so vile and debased as to deny that on the witness stand and in the sacred desk veracity is a prime, an indispensable quality. Let there be no lying there, say even many, who sometimes jest with truth on comparatively trifling themes and occasions. And we should never forget, nor let our hearers forget that in preaching we speak under awful responsibility to Christ and expect to give to him a solemn account of all we say and do. We all live and act in the sight of God, and all, who are not vain and frivolous, admit no less. So that, without an oath, we may, as in the presence of the Father, Son and Holy Ghost, declare to men

our sincere love for them even when we bring them unwelcome truths.

3. Although no one in our day speaks *in the Holy Ghost* in the sense of being by him infallibly preserved from error, or uttering only the words which he teacheth; yet we must insist on the ple. nary inspiration of the authors of the books of canonical scripture. They claimed such infallible guidance, v. 1. Plenary and verbal inspiration is now, and is likely for some time to come to be, the field where the hardest battle for the truth is to be fought. Let not the friends of truth yield any thing in this great contest. Let them be valiant for the truth. The issue is not doubtful, unless those, who should defend, betray Christ's cause. No point in the argument for Christianity is more defensible. One thing is very clear. The apostles and prophets claimed such inspiration. If they did it not truly, we have no religion left among us, clothed with divine authority.

4. A good man under the guidance of God's truth and Spirit may rely on the testimony of his conscience, and may appeal to it without danger of being deceived, v. 1. This conscience is the moral sense of each man, and is no more liable to deception than his taste, or memory. Indeed the first awards of conscience on any simple matter are remarkably clear and safe. Its decisions are no less cogent than they are peculiar, the remorse or compla- cency thereby produced having boundless influence over human happiness or misery. Our great endeavor should be to have a pure conscience, void of offence towards God and man, a good conscience, well enlightened by the Spirit of truth, and thor- oughly sprinkled with atoning blood, 1 Tim. 3 : 9; Acts 24 : 16; Acts 23 : 1; Heb. 9 : 14. Such a conscience makes the righteous as bold as a lion. It is worth all it ever costs of study, diligence, sacrifice and adherence to principle. Temporal death is a small evil, compared with a guilty conscience. Remorse is the fire of perdition often kindled before men reach Tophet.

5. It is very unfair for the wicked so to act as necessarily to bring great sorrow on the pious, awakening in their bosoms just and alarming apprehensions for the eternal well-being of their un- converted friends and kindred, and then to blame the religion of those, who fear God, as if it was the cause of unhappiness, v. 2. The godly often weep over the wicked, who deride their pious grief. Thus Paul had continual and vehement sorrow for his coun- trymen. Is it not benevolent, is it not right that one should grieve to see another rushing headlong to ruin? Is it fair, is it manly, is it just by our sins to fill with sadness our best friends, and then to accuse their piety as the cause of their sadness? O wicked man,

press not on to ruin amid the weepings of the godly, lest you take up the wail that is everlasting.

6. Nor is it unreasonable nor unusual for the people of God to be sad at the course of the wicked, v. 2. "I beheld the transgressors and was grieved;" "Horror hath taken hold of me, because of the wicked that forsake thy law;" "Rivers of water run down mine eyes, because they keep not thy law," Ps. 119: 53, 136, 158. Compare Jer. 9:1; 13:17; Ezek. 9:2. Is not this right? Cecil: "The world will allow a vehemence approaching to ecstasy on almost every subject but religion, which above all others will justify it." What enemy is so relentless that he would not lustily cry, Fire, *Fire*, FIRE, FIRE, if he saw his adversary's dwelling in flames and its inmates asleep? Why then should not the kind, benevolent child of God give the alarm and with tears beseech men to be reconciled to God? If they refuse, why should they not still be a burden to him? He must do what he can to save them, or be guilty before God. "If thou forbear to deliver them that are drawn unto death, and those that are ready to be slain; if thou sayest, Behold, we knew it not: doth not he that pondereth the heart consider it? and he that keepeth thy soul, doth not he know it? and shall not he render to every man according to his works?" Pr. 24: 11, 12. Scott: "Insensibility to the eternal condition of our fellow-creatures is contrary both to the love required by the law, and the mercy of the gospel." Hodge: "If we can view, unmoved, the perishing condition of our fellow-men, or are unwilling to make sacrifices for their benefit, we are very different from Paul, and from him who wept over Jerusalem, and died for our good upon Mount Calvary." Chalmers: "The awful sentence of condemnation—the signal of everlasting departure to all who know not God and obey not the gospel—the ceaseless moanings that ever and anon shall ascend from the lake of living agony—the grim and dreary imprisonment whose barriers are closed insuperably and for ever on the hopeless outcasts of vengeance—These, ye men who wear the form of godliness but show not the power of it in your training of your families—these are not the articles of your faith. To you they are as the imaginations of a legendary fable. Else why this apathy?"

7. The question then arises, How far may we go in our emotions, plans, prayers, labors and sacrifices for the salvation of others? On this inquiry we get some light from verses 2, 3. If we were sure that we understood this scripture and others, which have been cited, we might rest satisfied that we were in the way of knowing our duty. We may certainly feel very strongly, tenderly and continually. Our grief may be vehement and our sor-

row pungent. We may wisely and cheerfully give up ease, honor, luxury, wealth, popularity, if thus we can best promote their salvation. We may cheerfully consent to be anything or nothing, the song of the drunkard, the offscouring of the world, endure all conceivable privations, toils, losses and temporal calamities, and die the most painful, lingering and ignominious death man could inflict. We may pray without ceasing, with strong crying and tears. We may earnestly ask others to unite with us in our fastings and intercessions for the objects of our concern. We may do all this wisely even for the salvation of one—much more for the salvation of many. Hodge: "There is no limit to the sacrifice which one may make for the benefit of others, except that which his duty to God imposes." Nor is there anything unnatural in all this, if one has any lively sense of the worth of his own soul or the glory of Christ. Chalmers beautifully says: "The agony of an infant's dying-bed is not more real than the agony inflicted by it on a mother's bosom. The sufferings endured by the one have not a more stable or undoubted certainty, than the sympathy which is felt for them by the other." So if we love Christ supremely and men as we should, the perishing state of men will very thoroughly arouse us to seek their salvation. And the fact that men hate us without a cause, slander and revile us, despise and persecute us for righteousness' sake, is no reason why we should not seek their salvation with intense longings. Was not the dying prayer of Jesus answered in fifty days for the conversion of thousands of his murderers? Was not the prayer of dying Stephen answered in the conversion of Saul of Tarsus, who held the clothes of the men that stoned the first Christian martyr? Wondrous is the love and the power of the love which a good man may have for others. Of Paul Chrysostom says: "Broader than every sea, and keener than every flame, was that love, and no language is able worthily to express it. But he alone who really possesses it, knows what it is."

8. When we sincerely wish men well, weep over their sins and their state, we may say so in terms unmistakeable, vs. 1-3. When the weeping prophet told his countrymen the judgments about to come upon them, they said, "Thou fallest away to the Chaldeans." But he appealed to God for his innocence and benevolence: "Neither have I desired the woful day, thou knowest," Jer. 17 : 16.

9. Formerly it was very common for Christian assemblies to pray much for the Jews. Is this good practice as generally observed now as Paul's example would indicate it should be? vs. 1-3. Are they not according to the flesh the kinsmen of our

Lord ? Are not their history and true traditions more sublime than those of any other people ? Chalmers : " All the trophies of conquest, and of literature, and of all earthly renown make not out a crown of traditional glory for any of the states or monarchies of other days, which is at all like unto that crown of transcendental glory, that halo from heaven, which sits on the character and the fortunes of the children of Israel." This people shall yet be converted to Christ. Oh that the day of their restoration to fellowship with God may be hastened. Let us pray for it, often, earnestly.

10. The Jews had far greater privileges than any other ancient people. By perverting them, they demonstrated that no curses are so great as those arising from the abuse of exalted mercies and favors, vs. 4, 5.

11. There is a difference between an Israelite and an Israelite indeed. Compare v. 4 and John 1 : 47. This distinction must be maintained. Doeg was an Israelite ; David was an Israelite indeed. No distinction is more just or more obvious. Those are Christ's mother and brethren and sisters, who do the will of God and keep the commandments.

12. Have we what Luther calls the " exuberant charity " of Paul? Can we love, pity and commend what is commendable even in bitter opposers ? vs. 1–5. Are we unselfish ? Does our charity begin and end at home ? Much was said and written a half century or more since about " disinterested benevolence." The terms were not well chosen. All benevolence is disinterested. Have we benevolence ? Do we ever feel a " high pang of zeal and affection " for the vile, the guilty, the perishing ? " Love is apt to be bold and venturous and self-denying." Are we in any measure like Paul ?

13. National election is admitted by many who deny personal election, and is implied in vs. 4, 5. Every Arminian commentator at hand admits national election. Some ask, What is the difference ? So far as the rights of sovereignty are concerned there is none. If God has a right to choose a nation to exalted religious privileges, he has a right to choose an individual to eternal life and to appoint all the means thereto. If he may dispose of thrones and crowns and kingdoms here, why may he not bestow on whom he will crowns and kingdoms in glory? The real difference between national and personal election is that the former saves no one ; the latter saves all on whom it settles. For the former see Ezek. 16 : 3, 8–43 ; for the latter see Acts 13 : 48 ; John 10 : 16, 26 ; Rom. 8 : 30.

14. There was great *glory* in the old dispensation, of which the

shechinah was a part and of all of which it was an emblem. But the glory of the gospel is much greater. It "excelleth." The latter is as much in advance of the former, as Christ was greater than Moses. The former was the ministration of condemnation. The latter is the ministration of the Spirit, 2 Cor. 3 : 7–11. Compare John 1 : 17; Heb. 12 : 18–24, and many parallel passages.

15. Knowing the *covenant* of God will save no man, unless we personally embrace it, v. 4.

16. Scenes of terror, such as were witnessed at Sinai in the giving of the law, though they may make men exceedingly fear and quake, save no man, v. 4. Through unbelief they seem often to harden the heart. They may even become matter of boasting and vain glory.

17. There was much that was grand and striking, instructive and precious in the *service* of the temple, and he, who is spiritual, and loves to trace spiritual similitudes, will find knowledge and refreshment in this too much neglected field, v. 4. Perhaps a former generation may have carried to excess their love for this method of edification. But is not the tendency at present to the other extreme? A sound and sober spiritual use of Solomon's temple would delight the saints in our day. The temple had not the substance, as we have, but it had beautiful images of the very best things under the gospel.

18. Under every dispensation, no small part of spiritual wisdom consists in a right use of the *promises* of God, v. 4. In this matter wicked Jews always made sad mistakes. Under the gospel we are no less liable to err fatally. Our first duty respecting them is steadfastly to believe and firmly to embrace them, Heb. 11 : 13. Our next duty touching them is to be made holy by them. If we fail here, they can do us no lasting good, 2 Cor. 7 : 1; 2 Pet. 1 : 4.

19. It is a great blessing to have had a good ancestry, especially a pious ancestry, v. 5. It is but few men, who have a wise regard to their posterity, unless they can look back on honored progenitors. Of all the desperate acts of wickedness performed by men, none goes beyond the renunciation of the God of our pious forefathers.

20. In the early ages of the Christian church many heresies arose respecting the humanity of Christ, v. 5. For the last three centuries the enemies of the truth have chiefly assaulted his divinity. Of late it looks as if the doctrine of his entire manhood was to be again vigorously assaulted. All still admit that he had a true body, but it begins to be more than hinted that his divine nature took the place of a human soul in him. How

far this folly may go, the Head of the church knows; but let the friends of *Christ* be on the alert and valiant for the truth. The issue of the contest is not doubtful.   If the scriptures do not prove that Jesus Christ had a reasonable soul—human nature entire, sin only excepted—they prove nothing.

21. We must in like manner hold fast the true, proper, supreme divinity of Christ, as *over all, God blessed for ever*, v. 5. His divinity is established in God's word by the same line of argument, by which we prove the divinity of his Father.   The grammatical construction of scripture, the history of theological doctrine and the miracles performed in the name of Christ form a three-fold cord, respecting his divinity, which cannot be broken.

22. Let our praises to Jesus Christ abound, v. 5.   They were the joy of his apostles.   They constitute no small part of the worship of heaven, as John in the Apocalypse informs us.

Chapter 23

ROMANS 9

VERSES 6–24

NEITHER DESCENT FROM A PIOUS ANCESTRY, NOR PERSONAL MERIT SECURES TO ANY MAN GOD'S FAVOR. GOD IS SOVEREIGN. SO SAY THE SCRIPTURES. OBJECTION ANSWERED.

6 Not as though the word of God hath taken none effect. For they *are* not all Israel, which are of Israel:

7 Neither, because they are the seed of Abraham, *are they* all children: but, In Isaac shall thy seed be called.

8 That is, They which are the children of the flesh, these *are* not the children of God: but the children of the promise are counted for the seed.

9 For this *is* the word of promise, At this time will I come, and Sarah shall have a son.

10 And not only *this;* but when Rebecca also had conceived by one, *even* by our father Isaac,

11 (For *the children* being not yet born, neither having done any good or evil, that the purpose of God according to election might stand, not of works, but of him that calleth;)

12 It was said unto her, The elder shall serve the younger.

13 As it is written, Jacob have I loved, but Esau have I hated.

14 What shall we say then? *Is there* unrighteousness with God? God forbid.

15 For he saith to Moses, I will have mercy on whom I will have mercy, and I will have compassion on whom I will have compassion.

16 So then *it is* not of him that willeth, nor of him that runneth, but of God that sheweth mercy.

17 For the Scripture saith unto Pharaoh, Even for this same purpose have I raised thee up, that I might shew my power in thee, and that my name might be declared throughout all the earth.

18 Therefore hath he mercy on whom he will *have mercy*, and whom he will he hardeneth.

19 Thou wilt say then unto me, Why doth he yet find fault? For who hath resisted his will?

20 Nay but, O man, who art thou that repliest against God? Shall the thing formed say to him that formed *it,* Why hast thou made me thus?

21 Hath not the potter power over the clay, of the same lump to make one vessel unto honor, and another unto dishonor?

22 *What* if God, willing to shew *his* wrath, and to make his power known, endured with much longsuffering the vessels of wrath fitted to destruction:

23 And that he might make known the riches of his glory on the vessels of mercy, which he had afore prepared unto glory,

24 Even us, whom he hath called, not of the Jews only, but also of the Gentiles?

THE apostle had made known his sorrow at the unbelief and doom of his countrymen, notwithstanding the high privileges they had enjoyed. In those expressions of grief he did not embrace all Israelites. There were delightful instances of true and hearty piety among them. So he says he would not wish to be misunderstood:

6. *Not as though the word of God hath taken none effect. For they are not all Israel, which are of Israel.* By the word of God we may with some understand the promises make of old, or those promises in connection with the rest of scripture. By the first sentence he declares he was not speaking as if he thought his whole nation had perished or would perish through unbelief. Far from it. Only he would show that *all they are not Israel, which are of Israel.* Lineal descent from Abraham secured eternal life to no man. Tholuck quotes one of their own number, Abarbanel, as saying: "The disciple whose morals are corrupt, even though he belongs to the children of Israel, is still not of the disciples of Abraham, and the reason is, that he does not endeavor after his manners." So that the Jews had at least some apprehension of the distinction which Paul draws here, and which John, and our Lord in their personal ministry, fully established, Matt. 3 : 9 ; John 8 : 39. Paul asserts the same in Gal. 3 : 29. The saving promise of God was to such as embraced by faith the grace given to Abraham, whereas it was notorious that many of the descendants of Israel were unbelieving and abominable. No people were more familiar than devout students of the Old Testament with the distinction between the righteous and the wicked, between him that serveth God and him that serveth him not, between a good man and a son of Belial. In the whole of this argument Paul insists on maintaining that distinction.

7. *Neither, because they are the seed of Abraham,* are they *all children : but, In Isaac shall thy seed be called.* The import of this verse is the same as that of v. 6. *Children* means either children of God, or children of the promise, or children of Abraham, Rom. 9 : 8 ; Gal. 3 : 7–9. The sense is the same in either case, those

three phrases all being employed by Paul to mark the true chosen
people of God.   In proof of his doctrine, Paul quotes a sentence
from Gen. 21 : 12.   Compare Gen. 17 : 19, 21.   The covenant was
not with Ishmael, though he was the child of Abraham, and was
considerably older than Isaac.   Even in the family of Abraham
God showed his sovereignty by disregarding the primogeniture
of one of Abraham's sons and preferring another.   Therefore to
be a lineal descendant of Abraham no more proved that an Israelite would be saved than that an Ishmaelite would be saved, for the
latter also had Abraham to his father.   If God showed his sovereignty in preferring Isaac to Ishmael, surely he may call or pass
by the remoter descendants of his friend Abraham.   But let Paul
explain himself:

8. *That is, They which are the children of the flesh, these* are *not
the children of God : but the children of the promise are counted for
the seed.*   In this verse *flesh* is evidently to be taken in the sense
of the corporeal nature.   It is not by generation but by regeneration, not by birth but by the new birth that men become the children of God, John 1 : 12, 13 ; not by the course of nature but by
divine and marked interposition in their behalf.   Compare Rom.
4 : 11–16 ; Gal. 4 : 22–31.   Calvin: "He calls those *the children of
the flesh,* who have nothing superior to a natural descent ; as they
are *the children of the promise,* who are peculiarly selected by the
Lord."   *Counted,* looked upon by God and treated as the seed
whom he really designed in the promise.   This is further established by the Jewish scriptures :

9. *For this* is *the word of promise, At this time will I come, and
Sarah shall have a son.*   The reference is to Gen. 18 : 10, 14.   The
substance of the same matter is found in Gen. 17 : 21 ; 21 : 2.   Paul
does not quote the Septuagint version, but the substance of the
Hebrew.   The phrase "at this time," literally at the fit, seasonable, or right time, has given rise to some variety of interpretation,
perhaps unnecessary.   In Gen. 17 : 18 it is "at this set time in the
next year ;" in Gen. 18 : 14, "at the time appointed ;" and in Gen.
21 : 2, "at the set time of which God hath spoken to him."   It is
evidently from one of these that Paul quotes, and not from Gen.
18 : 10 where it is "according to the time of life."   Some make
emphatic the word " come " as indicating special favor and power.
It may sometimes have that force, but if so, it is not usual.   The
fact that the visits of God are in the fulness of his perfections, and,
when gracious, are sure to accomplish the goodness intended, may
have favored the idea.   Here then we have one clear case of the
sovereignty of God in choosing for the highest distinction the
younger son of Abraham, and not his first born.

10. *And not only* this; *but when Rebecca also had conceived by one,* even *by our father Isaac,*

11. (*For* the children *being not yet born,* neither having done any *good or evil, that the purpose of God according to election might stand, not of works, but of him that calleth ;*)

12. *It was said unto her, The elder shall serve the younger.* And *not only* this, i. e. not only so, or not only have we this case illustrating God's sovereignty, but we have another in the family of Isaac himself. The whole that was said to Rebecca was this:

Two nations are in thy womb,
And two manner of people shall be separated from thy bowels;
And the one people shall be stronger than the other people;
And the elder shall serve the younger.

See Gen. 25 : 23. Verse 11 is parenthetical, and is designed to state clearly the circumstances, in which the Lord declared that the elder [or greater] should serve the younger [or lesser]. The first of these was that the children were not yet born. The second flowed from the first—they had done neither good nor evil. The third was that God designed thus to declare his right to exalt whom he would and put down whom he would; in other words he would show that his purpose in election was unalterable. The fourth was that the divine choice was made, not in view of any works, done or to be done, but-solely of God's own will and pleasure, *of him that calleth,* that is, of him that effectually calleth whom he will to himself and to the enjoyment of his blessings. Paul does not dwell upon the well known fact that no preference could be given to either of these children, as in the case of Isaac, who had Sarah for his mother, while Ishmael had only Hagar, a bondwoman, for Jacob and Esau had both the same father and mother. Ishmael too had developed some traits of character before Isaac was declared to be preferred before him. But there was no possible ground of such preference in the case of Rebecca's sons, for they were twins. To show that this matter is settled by the word of God, Paul quotes as of divine authority this verse:

13. *As it is written, Jacob have I loved, but Esau have I hated.* These words are taken from the beginning of the prophecy of Malachi. The prophet is reproving the Jews for ingratitude and says: " I have loved you, saith the Lord. Yet ye say, Wherein hast thou loved us? Was not Esau Jacob's brother? saith the Lord: yet I loved Jacob, and I hated Esau, and laid his mountains and his heritage waste for the dragons of the wilderness." A few things should here be observed. 1. Malachi prophesied more than 1400 years after the birth of Jacob and Esau: yet in defending the character and government of God and his treatment of

the Jews against the charge of severity or want of kindness, he begins his argument away back at the birth of the progenitors of the two nations, and says that God made a difference even between them. This was done before they were born, or had done either good or evil. 2. Such was the effect of this marked favor to Jacob and comparative disfavor to Esau that up to the time of Malachi it had been manifest in the general treatment the two nations had' received in the course of divine providence. The original choice of God affected not only Jacob and Esau personally, but their descendants also. 3. Original sin is such an evil and brings so just and terrible a curse as to make it an act of mere sovereign grace and kindness in God to spare even the natural life of any one coming into the world by ordinary generation, or to bestow any comfort on any man or family. See above on Rom. 5 : 12–19. So that neither Jacob nor Esau had by nature any claims whatever on the favor of God. If the Lord had utterly rejected them both, he would have done no wrong, no injustice to either. Calvin : " They were both the children of Adam, by nature sinful, and endued with no particle of righteousness." They were " by nature the children of wrath even as others," Eph. 2 : 3. 4. God's preference of Isaac and Jacob over their brothers expressed no ill will to Ishmael or to Esau. In both cases he chose the younger, but he did the elder no wrong. None deserved any thing good. Nor was God unkind to either Ishmael or Esau. On the contrary he said, " Of the son of the bond-woman will I make a nation, because he is thy seed," Gen. 21 : 13. Compare Gen. 16 : 10; 17 : 20; 25 : 12–18. To Esau he gave great possessions and blessings, even after he had showed himself to be a " profane person," as Paul calls him, Heb. 12 : 16. Compare Gen. 36 : 1–43 ; Deut. 2 : 5, 12; Josh. 24 : 4. Our verse does indeed say " Jacob have I loved, but Esau have I hated." But what does that mean? Surely it does not teach that God dealt unkindly or unjustly with Esau ; but it does teach that God gave Jacob a decided preference. That this is a safe and sound interpretation is exceedingly manifest from the very words of our Lord : " If any man come to me, and hate not his father, and mother, and wife, and children, and brethren, and sisters, yea, and his own life also, he cannot be my disciple," Luke 14 : 26. Now that no ill will or unkindness to our kindred is obligatory or even lawful, we do certainly know from all the precepts, which enjoin filial piety and natural affection, from the fifth commandment, from the example of our Lord and from oft-repeated apostolic precepts. Women ought to love their husbands, and husbands ought to love their wives, even as Christ also loved the church. And as to any man positively hating his own life, it is impossible, for no man ever yet hated his own flesh.   See Ex. 20: 12 ; Luke 2: 51 ; Rom. 1: 31; Eph. 5: 25, 29; 1 Tim. 5: 4; Tit. 2: 4, and many other places.   What then did our Lord mean to enjoin, when he required us to hate our nearest and dearest relatives?   Another evangelist gives us in other words the real meaning of our Lord: "He that loveth father or mother more than me is not worthy of me.   And he that loveth son or daughter more than me is not worthy of me.   And he that taketh not his cross, and followeth after me, is not worthy of me.   He that findeth his life shall lose it : and he that loseth his life for my sake shall find it," Matt. 10: 37–39.   To *hate* therefore in this case is to *love less*. Love to God must exceed the love we bear to any creature.   He must have the preference.   So God gave the preference to Jacob and Esau.   He did it from the first.   He did it by purpose.   The hatred of this verse is therefore comparative hatred, not ill will, not unkindness.   This is a very old form of expression in the Hebrew, as may be seen by examining Gen. 29: 30, 31, 33, where the word "hated" is explained by the words Jacob "loved Rachel more than Leah."   Solomon uses both these words in the sense here contended for ; "He that spareth his rod hateth his son: but he that loveth him chasteneth him betimes."   The parent, who enforces strict and just authority over his child, loves him more than he, who refuses to restrain him.   He, who declines to chastise his erring son, does comparatively hate him.   Haldane is very averse to this mode of explaining the words under consideration.   He says: "Human wisdom has shown its folly, by endeavoring to soften the word hated into something less than hatred ;" "The word *hate* never means *to love less ;*" "This false gloss completely destroys the import of the passage."   Such language is not called for. The love of truth leads good men to seek to know not only the words that God has spoken, but the very meaning of those words. And it has been shown from both Testaments that the word hated has the sense here given it.   Haldane thinks that in the explanation adopted we might find an excuse for going on to say that all that is meant by the phrase "Jacob have I loved" is "Jacob have I hated less."   But there is nothing to warrant us in so construing this language.   Where is the word ever so used ?   Several cases have been given to show that the word hated has the meaning given it above.   5. The effect of this act of God's sovereignty both on Jacob and on his posterity was very happy in many ways. Jacob's piety, though not faultless, was sincere and eminent.   He had at least one vision as glorious as any granted to a patriarch, Gen. 28 : 10–22.   He was mighty in prayer, for he wrestled with God, and prevailed, Gen. 32: 9–12, 24–30; Hos. 12: 3–6.   He was

an honored prophet, Gen. 48 : 15–21 ; 49: 1–27. He died an honored and happy death, in faith and in true devotion, Heb. 11:
13, 21. Having served God and his generation he fell on sleep;
and for 3558 years (it is now A.D. 1870) has been walking the
streets of the New Jerusalem, Matt. 8: 11 ; and his happiness is
but just begun. He is awaiting the redemption of the body and
the glory thenceforward to be revealed. Would you see how his
descendants were blessed? Read their history. 6. Esau, born like
Jacob in original sin, was not like him chosen of God, but was left
under the power of his depravity, and although he received many
great blessings and became the head of a powerful nation, his
course was in the main very forlorn. We read of nothing indicating piety on his part. The restraints of Providence kept him
from the actual commission of some of the worst crimes ever plot-
ted. For a mess of pottage he sold his birthright, an act of great
contempt of God's promise and blessing. His whole course seems
to have been that of a " profane person." We have no account of
his fearing God, or keeping his commandments. More than once
he meditated the murder of his own and only brother. Of his latter end nothing is told us. He and his posterity possessed large
political power, but that has long since forsaken his descendants.
The mass of them seem to have been very wicked and malignant.
They would not allow the Israelites to pass through their terri-
tory in their journey from Egypt to Canaan. They were " a people against whom the Lord hath indignation for ever," Mal. 1 : 4
Such doctrine as this cannot be taught without awakening inquiry. It is well if the spirit it awakens is not malignant. God is
wholly and gloriously sovereign.

14. *What shall we say then ?* Is there *unrighteousness with God?
God forbid.* The first question has been asked five times already
in this epistle, Rom. 3 : 5 ; 4: 1 ; 6: 1; 7: 7; 8: 31. For the intent
of it see above on those places. *Is there unrighteousness with God?
Unrighteousness,* a word uniformly rendered in this epistle, elsewhere sometimes iniquity, sometimes wrong. Our translation is
good. The meaning is this : Does God's treatment of Isaac and
Jacob display injustice to Ishmael and Esau? This question has
no pertinency, if God treated all these persons alike, and loved
one no more than he loved another, giving no preference to either.
But if the doctrine of God's absolute sovereignty is taught here,
then the question is precisely the same that is asked in our day.
To it Paul returns an emphatic if not an indignant negative. On
God forbid see above on Rom. 3 : 4. In all their history the Jews
had gloried in the peculiar favor God had borne to Abraham,
Isaac and Jacob. Thus far Paul has maintained before the Jews

his defence of the divine sovereignty out of their own sacred books, (quoting them as of divine authority,) in particular from the first book of the pentateuch written by their great law-giver Moses and from their last prophet Malachi. Hodge: " These arguments of the apostle are founded on two assumptions. The first is, that the scriptures are the word of God; and the second, that what God actually does cannot be unrighteous." The apostle then shows that God of old claimed the right of manifesting his sovereignty, and that this claim was found in the Jewish scriptures, professedly received and revered by the whole nation :

15. *For he saith to Moses, I will have mercy on whom I will have mercy, and I will have compassion on whom I will have compassion.* This is a quotation from Ex. 33 : 19. In making it Paul literally follows the Septuagint. The whole verse in our English Bible reads thus : " And he said, I will make all my goodness pass before thee, and I will proclaim the name of the Lord before thee : and will be gracious to whom I will be gracious, and will shew mercy on whom I will shew mercy." So that the quotation derives great strength from the connection in which it is found. God says to Moses, " I will make all my goodness pass before thee and I will proclaim the name of the Lord before thee," that is, I will give thee insight into the divine nature, I will make a revelation of myself to thee, and the very first thing he utters is oui verse, thus claiming and asserting as a prominent truth of himself his complete and perfect sovereignty. The form of speech here employed on the face of it clearly expresses the entire independence of God, his freedom from all constraint or influence out of himself. It resolves his whole action into his sovereign good will. It also expresses the unalterableness of his counsel. In structure it resembles that sentence of Pilate : " What I have written I have written." Words more expressive of perfect freedom and fixedness of choice cannot be found or framed. The apostle himself so understands and explains them in the next verse.

16. *So that* it is *not of him that willeth, nor of him that runneth, but of God that sheweth mercy.* The doctrine here taught is a legitimate and necessary consequence of the broad truth laid down in the preceding verse. The meaning seems to be as obvious as that of any other sentence of God's word, and is abundantly sustained by other portions of scripture, Isa. 65 : 1 ; Matt. 11 : 25, 26 ; Luke 10 : 21 ; John 1 : 12, 13 ; 3 : 8 ; 1 Cor. 1 : 26–31 ; Phil. 2 : 13 ; 2 Thess. 2 : 13. The efficient cause of man's salvation is not found in his independence of God, nor in his being the master of his own destiny, nor in the supremacy of his own will, nor in the vigor of his own desires or efforts concerning salvation, but in the sovereigh

good will of God.   In every sense he has the keys of death and of hell, of life and of the kingdom of heaven.   He opens and none can shut; he shuts and none can open.   He kills and he makes alive.   No man is introduced into the kingdom of heaven through the strenuousness of his own efforts, the power of his own will, the virtue of his own merits.   "The salvation of the righteous is of the Lord," not of the creature.   God's sovereignty decides who shall have mercy.   None deserve any blessing from him.   Our eyes should not be evil because he is good, Matt. 20: 13–16.   There is nothing said here against the diligent and right use of the means of grace.   We are here merely taught that the divine favor and blessing are the fountain of our redemption from sin, and guilt, and wo.

17. *For the scripture saith unto Pharaoh, Even for this same purpose have I raised thee up, that I might shew my power in thee, and that my name might be declared throughout all the earth.*   These words are found in Ex. 9: 16.   Compare Ex. 10: 1, 2 ; 14: 17, 18 ; Ps. 76: 10; Pr. 16: 4.   Paul does not here exactly follow the Septuagint, but gives in part his own translation of the original Hebrew.   In the traditions of the Jews the name and history of Pharaoh were entirely familiar.   The book of Exodus, like the rest of the Pentateuch, was commonly read among them.   This statement respecting Pharaoh was as well known as any other portion of scripture.   Yet what Israelite in any generation had found fault with such doctrine when applied to Pharaoh?   All looked on him with abhorrence.   Yet in Pharaoh original sin was no more detestable than it is in any one else.   Nor was his heart given up to more obduracy than that of multitudes, who hear the pure gospel and never turn to the Lord; yea, no worse than many who have afterwards been brought to repentance.   There stands before all the world the case of Pharaoh, a man, whom God used as his sword, Ps. 17 : 13, and as the rod of his anger, Isa. 10: 5 ; leaving him without sanctifying grace to make him, for his sins and his outrages, a monument of divine power to put down all enemies, and to declare the divine glory through all the earth.   There is not and for thousands of years there has not been on earth even among men of like character one, who has stood forth to express sympathy with Pharaoh, or to complain of any wrong done to him.   The human conscience everywhere proclaims that God's throne is clear, his government right, and that there is no *unrighteousness* with him in all his dealings with the haughty and profane monarch, who dared to say, "Who is the Lord that I should obey him?"   No Christian will dare to contend that Pharaoh's destruction was unjust, or

unmerited. The penitent thief was not saved because he was less guilty than his companion in crime. Saul of Tarsus was not converted because he was a less bloody persecutor than Nero. Pharaoh had no more original sin than Moses. But through God's sovereign and amazing mercy Moses was pardoned, accepted, renewed and saved ; while through God's sovereign and adorable justice Pharaoh was given over to hardness of heart and utter ruin.

18. *Therefore hath he mercy on whom he will* have mercy, *and whom he will he hardeneth.* This is a fair logical deduction from what had just been said. God is a sovereign in the disposal of the destinies of all men, good and bad. In this verse God's dealings with men are twice resolved into his *will.* We can go no further. Our duty requires us to go no further. Our happiness requires us to go no further. It is only a daring presumption, a bold prying curiosity, and not a becoming humility, that leads us to desire to go further. " Why dost thou strive against him ? for he giveth not account of any of his matters," Job 33 : 13. Compare Deut. 29 : 29. Profound submission and entire acquiescence in the divine will, whatever it be, is wisdom, is piety. Impudence, rejudging God's justice, prying into his secrets is folly and wickedness. *Whom he will he hardeneth,* is a sentence that staggers some. Why it should do so in a doctrinal epistle and not in a historic record is not easily explained. In the Old Testament the hardening of Pharaoh's heart is spoken of in four ways. 1. It is twice said that Pharaoh hardened his own heart, Ex. 8 : 15; 9 : 34. Compare 1 Sam. 6 : 6. 2. Three times God says, " I will harden Pharaoh's heart," Ex. 4 : 21; 7 : 3; 14 : 4. 3. It is seven times said that God did harden Pharaoh's heart, Ex. 7 : 13; 9 : 12; 10 : 1, 20, 27 ; 11 : 10; 14 : 8. 4. It is four times said that Pharaoh's heart is or was hardened, Ex. 7 : 14; 8 : 19; 9 : 7, 35. Whatever is thus taught respecting Pharaoh is said to have come on his people also, he being their head and leader : " I will harden the hearts of the Egyptians, and they shall follow them ; and I will get me honor upon Pharaoh, and upon all his host, and upon his chariots, and upon his horsemen, Ex. 14 : 17. So that there is no room left for doubt respecting the assertion that God hardened the heart of Pharaoh and of the Egyptians. Whatever he did to the monarch, he did the same to his people. Another remark is no less true. God did nothing to Pharaoh and the Egyptians that he has not done in other cases. In Deut. 2 : 30 we read : " Sihon king of Heshbon would not let us pass by him : for the Lord thy God hardened his spirit, and made his heart obstinate, that he might deliver him into thy hand, as appeareth this day." So it is said of some nu-

merous and powerful tribes that "it was of the Lord to harden their hearts, that they should come against Israel in battle, that he might destroy them utterly," Josh. 11 : 20. So in the evangelical prophet we read: "O Lord, why hast thou made us to err from thy ways, and hardened our heart from thy fear?" Isa. 63 : 17. In one of the gospels we have like words: "He hath blinded their eyes, and hardened their hearts; that they should not see with their eyes, nor understand with their hearts," etc. John 12:40. Any explanation, that will suit one of these cases ought to suit them all. One thing is clear: God is not the author of sin. He cannot work iniquity in himself or others. Just and right is he, true and holy in all his ways. All are thus far agreed. Another point ought to be as generally conceded: It is one thing for Pharaoh to harden his own heart, and another thing for God to harden Pharaoh's heart. The distinction is stated in scripture. We ought not to confound what God distinguishes. The same distinction is preserved in other parts of scripture, as we have seen in part. Compare 2 Chron. 36: 13 ; Dan. 5 : 20, etc. Another remark is perhaps no less clear to most minds, viz: all that is necessary to cause the most atrocious evils to be developed in any man's character is that God sustain him in being, afford him the means and opportunities of doing good or evil according to his inclinations, and then leave him to himself, withholding from him those divine influences, which might check or restrain him, or suggest a different course to him, and so let all evil come to him without any interposing providence. How often and how alarmingly this befalls evil men both the history and the state of the world testify. We have in our language hardly any phrase more expressive of a sad state than this : He is awfully left to himself. When that is true of a man, his future is dark indeed. As sure as the Spirit of the Lord fully departs from one, an evil spirit rests upon him, and he is undone. His course is rapidly from bad to worse. This divine desertion is fearful and is often mentioned in scripture. See Ps. 81 : 12 ; Hos. 4 : 4, 17 ; Matt. 15 : 14 ; Rev. 22 : 11. If it is final, one's doom is sealed. All the hardness of heart displayed by any man is sufficiently accounted for, if God has thus forsaken him. The human heart led on by Satan, without divine restraint, will soon develope wickedness as atrocious as that of Pharaoh, or of any one else. Haldane: "When a man is entirely left to himself, the judgments, the warnings, the deliverances, and all the truths of scripture become causes of hardness, of insensibility, of pride, and presumption." God does not harden men's hearts, as he makes them tender and penitent, by putting his Holy Spirit into them. He does not infuse into them wickedness, as he infuses grace into the hearts of his people. The only other thought necessary to be presented to complete this view is that God hardens no man's heart capriciously—God does nothing capriciously—but always righteously. He would have done us no injustice, if he had left us all to perish in our original sin. If for his own glory he sees fit to give one up to his own heart's lusts, or to believe a lie, or to work wickedness with all greediness, and utterly perish, who are we to call him to an account?

19. *Thou wilt say then unto me, Why doth he yet find fault? For who hath resisted his will?* Piety requires that there be some limit to human presumption. Human wickedness says, it will rush in and demand satisfactory answers to all its cavils. The only fit answer to some forms of wickedness is stern rebuke, and this even when many unite in urging the same irreverent queries, as in this case. When the blameless old friar was iniquitously and publicly accused of things, of which he was wholly innocent, he gave the only reply in his power: "Thou dost most impudently lie." So when, under the pretence of reasoning or of seeking the truth men bring forward objection after objection, it is right to give them fair and scriptural answers. But when under a show of inquiry they attack the truth with questions based in impiety, they must be met in a solemn, fearless and scriptural manner, after Paul's example:

20. *Nay but, O man, who art thou that repliest against God? Shall the thing formed say to him that formed it, Why hast thou made me thus?* There are some things that no man may think, or say or do. None may think that God is such an one as himself, or say that he is competent to judge what God may or may not do, or arraign the divine conduct in any way whatever. The substance of Paul's rebuke to the bold intruder is, O feeble sinful worm, who are you? You forget that you are both a fool and a criminal. You are not fit to judge anything, except that you are of yesterday, that your own righteousnesses are as filthy rags, that you know nothing as you ought to know it, till you learn that you are a fool, and that to you God is in no wise accountable. God has not submitted his plans or his government to you for revision or to get your judgment on them. If you would acquire a little modesty and become sober and wise, read and take home to yourself the awful reproofs given by the Almighty to the pious man of Uz, when he ventured too far in telling what were or ought to be the principles of God's government. See Job XXXVIII—XLI. By the time you have well conned those sublime chapters, perhaps you may be ready like Job to say: "I have uttered that I understood not; things too wonderful for me, which I knew not . . . I

abhor myself, and repent in dust and ashes." A little spiritual exercise of that description would do you more good than a hundred years' inquiry conducted in an arrogant and self-confident spirit. Can a man measure the azure vault of heaven with a carpenter's rule? Can one measure the waters of the ocean in a pint cup? Can a poor worm of the dust thunder in the heavens like God? If he cannot do these little things, how can he by searching find out either the nature or the ways of the Almighty unto perfection? But impudent as the question is, the apostle, though as under protest, answers it by saying that God has a perfect right to do what he will with his own. What if he does make one of his sinful creatures a monument of his mercy and another a monument of his justice, he does what he has an indefeasible right to do. To deny this truth is atheistic. The last question of our verse is very much like one noticed some centuries before our Saviour's birth: "Shall the work say of him that formed it, He made me not? or shall the thing framed say of him that framed it, He had no understanding?" Isa. 29 : 16. Haldane: "That God does all things right there is no question, but the grounds of his conduct he does not now explain to his people. Much less is it to be supposed that he would justify his conduct by explaining the grounds of it to his enemies. No man has a right to bring God to trial."

21. *Hath not the potter power over the clay, of the same lump to make one vessel unto honour, and another to dishonour?* There is no necessity for saying, as some have said, that the prerogative here claimed for God asserts his right to "make innocent creatures miserable." Blessed be his holy name, he has never done that, and never said that he would do it. Scott: "The apostle goes upon the supposition, that the sovereignty of God is that of infinite wisdom, justice, truth and goodness, and that he always decrees what is most proper to be done." So that the "lump of clay," of which the apostle speaks, is the mass of mankind in their fallen state, considered as sinners. This appears thus: 1. This is beyond dispute the state of mankind. Any doctrinal treatise respecting man, based on any other supposition, is false. 2. Throughout this epistle Paul's whole argument and the deductions from it contemplate men as guilty and perishing. 3. This view of the "lump of clay" exactly suits the argument of the apostle in this immediate context. 4. Nothing of practical importance can be gained by giving the phrase a wider range, but by so doing we should soon be involved in questions of a tormenting and inexplicable nature. Then contemplating all men as sinners, all justly condemned, all naturally evil, and all righteously exposed to everlast-

ing death, has not the holy, just and merciful God a right to make a difference, if he shall so elect, between them? If he saves one, must he save all? If he punishes one, must he punish all? May he not show mercy to whom he will, and give over to hardness whom he will? Is it not infinite love in him to save any of a race, all of whom are by nature the children of wrath? If he raises Paul to honor and glory, that does not show that Nero's condemnation is not just. *Power*, not the word so rendered in the next verse, but a word rendered right, authority, jurisdiction, Luke 23 : 7 ; John 1 : 12 ; Rev. 22 : 14. It occurs again in Rom. 13 : 1-3. It means power rightfully possessed. *Honor* and *dishonor* point to the happiness or misery, the glory or shame, that shall be finally awarded to men according as their characters shall be at last ; the former being saved through great mercy ; the latter being justly cast off and punished.

22. What *if God, willing to shew* his *wrath, and make his power known, endured with much longsuffering the vessels of wrath fitted to destruction :*

23. *And that he might make known the riches of his glory on the vessels of mercy, which he had afore prepared unto glory,*

24. *Even us, whom he hath called, not of the Jews only, but also of the Gentiles ?*

What, not in the Greek, but well inserted by our translators ; q. d. what good objection can be made? what right have you to find fault? what can you say against the divine conduct, if he shall be *willing* to let his creatures see that he is glorious in justice and power in punishing some, who have long and wantonly insulted him, and at the same time in a way of righteousness saving others, by nature no less sinful, yet by grace prepared for a glorious inheritance? This whole argument regards men as sinners. By transgression men have forfeited all claims to anything good. Their natural lives, their temporal and eternal happiness are fully and in every sense at his disposal. If all should be left to perish in their own corruption, no one would have a right to say he was unjustly dealt with. Sin deserves God's sore displeasure. Therefore God has a right to manifest his power and righteousness in the punishment of all, or of as many as he pleases. And if he shall save any from their lost estate, it is wholly due to his divine compassions, and not at all to human merits. *Wrath*, the same word so rendered in Rom. 1 : 18, 25 and often ; in Rom. 3 : 5, rendered vengeance. It is incensed justice, or indignation, as in Rev. 14 : 10. *Make his power known*, his power to subdue all enemies, to put down all opposition, to bring good out of evil, and to govern the world in defiance of the malice and machinations of his foes.

Vessels of wrath and *vessels of mercy* are phrases employed in coincidence with the figurative language of v. 21, where God is compared to a potter. How stout against God are the hearts of the wicked may be seen by the multitude and aggravation of their offences against him. How long did he *endure* Pharaoh! He lengthened his chain wonderfully. He bore with him till his rage and folly knew no bounds; till he foamed out his shame, breathed death to the chosen people, and hurled defiance against God. Was not his destruction just? Would it not have been just, if it had taken place much sooner than it did? *Longsuffering*, the same word is twice rendered patience, but commonly as here. We met it in Rom. 2 : 4. *Fitted*, by sin, by a long course of rebellion, by attempting to overreach the Almighty, who turned their devices against themselves, so that they became ready for *destruction*, or perdition, as the word is often rendered. *The riches of his glory* means his glorious riches, riches of unmerited kindness, amazing wisdom, resistless power, efficacious grace, giving them possession of the unsearchable riches of Christ. Compare Eph. 1 : 18. *Had afore prepared*, in the Greek one word, found in but one other place and there rendered *hath before ordained*, Eph. 2 : 10. Whatever God does for his people is in execution of his gracious purposes respecting them. Even when he brings them to a saving knowledge of himself, it is because he graciously planned to do so, Acts 13 : 48. Nor is the destruction of the wicked a surprise to God, 1 Pet. 2 : 8; Jude 4. *Called*, i. e. effectualy called, so called as to make them vessels of mercy. This he did, whether they were by birth and nation Jews or Gentiles. God has a right to do what he will with his own, and to show his sovereignity by choosing from among men whom he would, and by leaving Jews under the power of their unbelief. This truth he proceeds to establish by citations from the scriptures received by the Jews themselves.

DOCTRINAL AND PRACTICAL REMARKS

1. The scripture cannot be broken, v. 6. God has said nothing in vain. His counsels are of old faithfulness and truth. Compare John, 10 : 35; Isa. 55 : 10, 11.

2. If we would avoid error, we must not misinterpret scripture; and if we would not misinterpret scripture, we must not be rash and hasty, but patient and candid, vs. 6, 7. We must take time and look at truths in all their connections.

3. One of the sad features of human wickedness is that men do not see when they are illustrating the most awful truths of scrip-

ture and that their whole course and character are portrayed in God's word. The very people, who had by unbelief most sadly cut themselves off from the saving mercies of God are the most persistent in declaring themselves in covenant with God. Such cases require detailed expositions of scripture that they may be undeceived, vs. 6–8.

4. The scripture should be fully and clearly explained; that, if men will not understand it, they may not lay the blame on the expounders of God's word, vs. 6–8.

5. It is in vain to plead birth or blood, lineage or earthly relations to save men's souls, v. 8. Hopes built on such grounds must perish. Scott: " The whole scripture shows the difference between the professed Christian, and the real believer. Outward privileges are bestowed on many, who are not the children of God. These are born of the Spirit, according to the promise and purpose of him, who worketh all things after the counsel of his own will." Clarke: " Not the children who descend from Abraham's loins, nor those who were circumcised as he was, nor even those whom he might expect and desire, are *therefore* the church and people of God ; but those who are made children by the good pleasure and promise of God, as Isaac was, are alone to be accounted for the seed with whom the covenant was established." " The remnant shall return, even the remnant of Jacob, unto the mighty God." Doddridge: " Let us learn to depend on no privilege of birth, on no relation to the greatest and best of men. May we seek to be inserted into the family of God, by his adopting love in Christ Jesus." None but truly converted souls are the children of God.

6. God has ever made and will ever make good all his promises in the true intent and spirit thereof, v. 9. The defection of some by unbelief never invalidates his covenant with those who truly believe his word. The real heirs of the promise never complain of any unfaithfulness in God.

7. How hard it is to banish from the human mind the conception that in some way men are justified, or in some way saved by their works, or chosen for their works done or foreseen. So urgent is Paul on this matter that he brings it up again, v. 11, though he had virtually or formally stated it often before. Pool: " Paul means, that the difference between Jacob and Esau was made through the good pleasure of God, not through their wills or works, existing or foreseen." There is evidence that Jacob loved and feared God. There is not evidence that Esau had any genuine piety ; " yet there is so much palpable imperfection and evil in Jacob, as to manifest that God did not choose him for the excellency of his foreseen works."

8. God is sovereign and his sovereignty is perfect, v. 11.   He is a King, the great King; a Judge, the Judge of all the earth ; a Governor, the Governor among the nations.   Chrysostom : " All the Israelites worshipped the calf; yet some had mercy shown them, and others had not."   God is so perfect and supreme a Judge that he is fit to decide in his own cause.   He has always exercised his own sovereignty.   Did not Jesse make all his sons pass before Samuel, and did not Samuel say, The Lord hath not chosen these, until the youngest, David, appeared? 1 Sam. 16:6–13. God asserts such sovereignty in its most absolute form in several parts of this chapter, particularly vs. 15, 18.   Calvin: " In his gratuitous election the Lord is free and exempt from the necessity of imparting equally the same grace to all; but, on the contrary, he passes by whom he wills, and whom he wills he chooses." How independently God acts of human plans, desires and efforts is well stated by Clarke : " Abraham judged that the blessing ought, and he *willed*, desired, that it might be given to Ishmael ; and Isaac also *willed,* designed it for his first-born, Esau : and Esau *wishing* and hoping that it might be his *readily* went, *ran* a hunting for venison, that he might have it regularly conveyed to him : but they were all disappointed : Abraham and Isaac who *willed* and Esau who ran."   Every day we see God's sovereignty displayed in a thousand ways.   He not only does his will in the armies of heaven, but also among the inhabitants of the earth.   He kills and he makes alive.   He exalts one and abases another.

9. As some worthy and pious people have real difficulties on this subject, it may be well to state that in the scriptural doctrine of God's sovereignty there is nothing impairing or impugning the following clear principles : a. The Lord is no seducer.   He tempts no man, Jas. 1 : 13.   b. The Lord is sincere in all his calls, offers, warnings and expostulations.   He mocks no one with delusory proposals, Ezek. 18 : 23, 32 ; 33 : 11.   c. Though God sees nothing in man's will, worth, or endeavors to decide his choice of one rather than another, and though he has not revealed to us and may never reveal to us why he does some things, yet he acts not capriciously, but in all cases has good cause for whatever he purposes, says and does.   In a future world we shall understand much that is dark to us here ; but neither our happiness nor our duty will require us to know all that is now mysterious.   In heaven they adore on account of mysteries, Rev. 15 :.3.   d. To understand God's treatment of men aright, we must never forget that they are sinners by nature ; that his wrath is kindled against them as transgressors, not as men ; that his sovereign choice of any of them to eternal life is wholly of mere love, grace and pity

Beza: "Mercy presupposes misery and sin, or the voluntary corruption of the human race; and this corruption presupposes a creation in purity and uprightness." e. Some ask, Is God's sovereignty arbitrary? The word arbitrary is used in two senses very different. Originally it meant voluntary. In this sense God's whole government is of course according to the counsel of his own will, or his good pleasure. So say the scriptures, Eph. 1 : 5, 11 ; Phil. 2 : 13. But in popular use the word arbitrary has come to be equivalent to harsh, unjust or cruel. God's soveregnty is at the greatest possible remove from any such attribute. f. Like remarks may be made concerning the word absolute. If by it is meant free, certain, complete, positive, without restriction or limitation; then God's sovereignty is beyond doubt free, certain, complete, positive, and without any other restriction or limitation than that which arises from the infinite perfection and glory of his nature, such as this, he cannot lie, he cannot deceive, he cannot do any wrong. g. God's sovereignty is universal, extending over all causes, all creatures, all effects, all agents, all results, all worlds, Ps. 103 : 19. Chalmers: "It seems hard to deny him, either a prescience over all the futurities, or a sovereignty over all the events of that universe which himself did create; or that, sitting as we conceive him to do on a throne of omnipotence, there should be so much as one department of his vast empire, where his power does not fix all, and his intelligence does not foresee all. It greatly enhances this argument when the department in question happens to be far the highest and noblest in creation." If mind cannot be governed, it matters little whether matter is controlled or not. h. It is but a decent modesty to admit that in God's sovereignty are many things inscrutable. The unwillingness to admit much to be unknowable has led to many painful thoughts, and fruitless exertions. This difficulty is not confined to the simple plebian. It has vastly exercised those, who thought themselves wise and great. To Erasmus Luther said: "Mere human reason can never comprehend how God is good and merciful, and, therefore, you make to yourself a god of your own fancy, who hardens nobody, condemns nobody, pities everybody. You cannot comprehend how a just God can condemn those who are born in sin, and cannot help themselves, but must, by a necessity of their natural constitution, continue in sin, and remain children of wrath. The answer is, God is incomprehensible throughout, and, therefore, his justice, as well as his other attributes, must be incomprehensible." i. There is nothing in the scriptural doctrine of the divine sovereignty to weaken the strength of motives to exertion. The essential freedom of the will, without which there is no moral agency, is unimpaired by it, yea is established by it.   For if God is not sovereign, man cannot be free, but must be the subject of a blind fortuity, or of the sway of devils, or of some cause or causes not understood, perhaps not even named among men.   Chalmers: " Although God is the primary, the overruling cause of every one event, whether in the world of mind or of matter, this does not supersede the proximate and the instrumental causes which come immediately before it.   Although he worketh all in all, yet if it be by means that he worketh, the application of these means is still indispensable."   Therefore the whole doctrine and matter of second causes is left precisely where scripture and reason have left them, whether we accept or reject the sovereignty of God. j. Nor does ever so firm a belief in the scriptural doctrine of God's sovereignty in the slightest degree modify the awards of conscience respecting the moral acts of ourselves or of our fellow-men.   Remorse for personal sins and displacency for turpitude in others cannot be stronger in any case than they are in those who believe that God's kingdom ruleth over all.   Witness the convictions of the converts on the day of pentecost.   Peter demonstrated to them that they had fulfilled the divine purposes in the death of Christ, and that in so doing they were heinously guilty, Acts 2 : 23. They admitted the fairness of his argument, and cried out, " Men and brethren, what shall we do?"   As long as one is free from constraint and violence, his moral sense gives him prompt and infallible evidence of his responsibility (unless his conscience is seared) and this no less when he is persuaded that the Lord God omnipotent reigneth, than when his views are quite erratic on this point.   k. In all the examples of known and terrible judgments on individuals or communities, fully stated in scripture, it is clear that God long displayed forbearance and patience — even the patience of a God.   Neither man nor angel would have so long forborne to strike the stroke, when insult was so perversely and heinously multiplied.   With a breath or a nod God could ease himself of his adversaries, and cut short their power in a moment; but see how he bore with Pharaoh, with the old world, with Sodom and Gomorroh.   See how he bears with the wicked in our day.   Some of them have heard the gospel for thirty, forty or fifty years, yet how hardened they still are, how they forget God, reject his Son and grieve his Spirit.   l. But this long-suffering is not connivance at sin.   O no!   Some persuade themselves that God's sovereignty is controlled by an easy good nature, which differs not materially from indifference to moral character.   But the scripture makes a very different impression. " Vengeance is mine ; I will repay saith the Lord," Rom. 12 : 19.

Men may say that they have too good an opinion of God to suppose that he will damn them for anything, but if they die without repentance they will find that "he that made them will not have mercy on them, and he that formed them will shew them no favor," Isa. 27 : 11.   Such will find the truth of what God here declares "that he has endured sin in the world for the very purpose of glorifying himself in its punishment."   m. Nor is there anything in the divine sovereignty, nor in the scriptural doctrine thereof that should cause one moment's delay or hesitation in any man in accepting the gracious offers of mercy. That is a prime and pressing duty.   It is obvious and indispensable.   If men would begin here at a plain and known duty, many difficulties would give way before them.   The offers made are from heaven, and in heaven's kindest and most urgent tones they are pressed on men's acceptance.   Blessed is he, who has wisdom to give them a cordial welcome.   n. We should be very careful lest in making but a feeble adherence to the doctrine of God's glorious sovereignty, we but feebly adhere to the other doctrines of scripture, especially such as have commonly been regarded as intimately connected therewith, especially depravity, the work of Christ, and the work of the Spirit.   History sounds notes of alarm on that subject.   o. Nor is it possible for us to adhere too closely to the word of God in the statement and defence of this and kindred doctrines.   If they cannot be defended on solid grounds, let them be given up altogether.   Mere abstract reasoning on such matters will lead no one safely, if God's word give not the clue and the gist of thought.   Let us humbly implore divine guidance, and submit our understandings as we do our hearts and lives to the all-wise and all-good control of him, who never errs.

10. God's purpose in election is firm.   It must and will *stand*, v. 11.   It causes and will ever cause human counsels and plans and efforts, the rights of primogeniture, nationality, and every thing that is factitious in the structure of society, to give way before it.   The Lord he is God.   The great object of scripture doctrine is to exalt God, not man.   Joseph was a good man, a type of Christ, a great statesman, and a genuine patriot, but he could not turn the blessing from Ephraim to Manasseh, Gen. 48 : 17–20. In no sense does the Lord see as man seeth.

11. While truth requires us to admit that the Bible clearly teaches the doctrine of personal election, yet such are the weakness and blindness of the human mind, that any thing so sublime and glorious may be easily abused and perverted to the hardening of our own hearts, or to the misguiding and wretchedness of oth-

ers. We should therefore carefully study the will of God on this matter with great meekness, and humility, with fervent prayer, and a fixed determination to go as far as the Lord has given us light, and no further. Thus doing, we shall find it administering to us joy and comfort wherein we understand it, and teaching us lessons of humility and self-distrust in points we cannot comprehend.

12. Among all the truths of scripture none is more practical, none more essential to right views of God's character and government, or to our own peace and joy, than this, God is righteous in all his ways and holy in all his works, v. 14. If the human mind can once be brought to entertain serious doubts on this subject, wickedness must gain the ascendancy, or a depression bordering on desperation gain possession of our minds. However thick the clouds and darkness that are round about him, let us never doubt that righteousness and judgment are the habitation of his throne, Ps. 97: 1, 2. Firmly persuaded that the Judge of all the earth will do right, we can defy a thousand assaults of the adversary, and triumph even in the midst of tribulations.

13. In all their generations there was never an Israelite, that expressed sympathy with Pharaoh. On the contrary they always looked back on that fallen foe as an enemy to God and man, justly given over to destruction. Their inspired prophets taught them to speak and even sing in notes of triumph the victory God had granted over him and other bitter opposers of God and his people, Ps. 135: 8–12; 136: 10–30. In like manner shall the church triumphant look back on all her proud and persecuting foes, long after the heavens shall be rolled together as a scroll, and tyranny, and oppression and slander shall no longer vex the souls that tremble at God's word, Rev. 15: 1–3.

14. If men are proud and obstinate, refusing to be bound in the chains of love, God has chains and bars of omnipotence that will effectually arrest their career of crime and violence, v. 17. For thousands of years Pharaoh has not had it in his power to create an uneasy sensation or awaken the slightest apprehension in the mind of any child of God in any part of this or of any other world. Glory be to God, the day is not distant when every sorrowing disciple now on earth shall be where the wicked cease from troubling and the weary are at rest.

15. Let us carefully eschew vain reasonings and sinful questionings concerning God's nature and government, vs. 19, 20. It is a fact with many a man that he dashes his head against the strongest pillars only to damage himself. " So unreasonable is the curiosity of man, that the more perilous the examination of a sub-

ject is, the more boldly he proceeds." Sadly are men forgetful of their place and their duty when they "enter into a debate with God," and presume to tell what he ought or ought not to do in matters which he has not explained to mortals. " Wo to him that striveth with his maker! Let the potsherd strive with the pot-sherds of the earth. Shall the clay say to him that fashioneth it, What makest thou? or thy work, He hath no hands?" Isa. 45 : 9. When worms cite the Almighty to their "blasphemous bar," they may assuredly know that hell feels a raven for her prey. If men will "rush in where angels fear to tread," and prescribe to the Almighty, they must answer for their presumption.

16. The sooner men adoringly submit to the sovereignty of God in all things, and say from the heart, Thy will be done, the better for them, v. 21. God is our potter. Let us own him as such, Jer. 18 : 2–10. It is sadly to be regretted that so much time is spent in arrogantly boasting of vain conceits, and so little in adoring him whose righteousness is like the waves of the sea. Indeed one hour's deep abasement before God does more to make us wise than all the great swelling words ever uttered. Brown: " It is a dangerous matter to consult with flesh and blood, and fol-low the judgment of carnal reason in the matters of God."

17. Sinners perish only on the ground of their sins; yet such is the infinite wisdom of the Most High, that God's justice and power are glorified when men refuse to glorify his mercy and grace by accepting his Son, v. 22.

18. Salvation is and ever will be wonderful in manifesting "glorious riches" of wisdom and power, justice and mercy, truth and grace, faithfulness and righteousness, v. 23. Augustine: " According to their deserts God makes some vessels of wrath; according to his grace he makes others vessels of mercy." No creature can say which of all God's attributes is most glorified in man's redemption. The common impression is that love and mercy are most illustrious. Perhaps they are. But who can fathom the wisdom, estimate the power or gauge the justice there-in displayed?

19. The first cause and the last end of all things is God, vs. 17, 22, 23. He is honored willingly or unwillingly by all his crea-tures. Some praise him silently ; some, vocally; some, willingly ; some, reluctantly. By him, and through him, and to him, and for him are all things. "Retiring into our own ignorance and weakness, as those that are less than nothing and vanity before him," letus fear by arrogance to insult his heavenly majesty. It is easy to be proud and to perish. It is not easy to be humble and reverent as ever becomes us. Glory be to God in the highest. Amen and amen.

Chapter 24

ROMANS 9

VERSES 25–33

GOD'S SOVEREIGNTY PROVEN BY THE PROPHETS. BY UNBELIEF THE JEWS REJECT SALVATION, WHILE BY FAITH THE GENTILES ACCEPT IT.

25 As he saith also in Osee, I will call them my people, which were not my people ; and her beloved, which was not beloved.

26 And it shall come to pass, *that* in the place where it was said unto them, Ye *are* not my people ; there shall they be called the children of the living God.

27 Esaias also crieth concerning Israel, Though the number of the children of Israel be as the sand of the sea, a remnant shall be saved :

28 For he will finish the work, and cut *it* short in righteousness : because a short work will the Lord make upon the earth.

29 And as Esaias said before, Except the Lord of Sabaoth had left us a seed, we had been as Sodoma, and been make like unto Gomorrah.

30 What shall we say then ? That the Gentiles, which followed not after righteousness, have attained to righteousness, even the righteousness which is of faith.

31 But Israel, which followed after the law of righteousness, hath not attained to the law of righteousness.

32 Wherefore ? Because *they sought it* not by faith, but as it were by the works of the law. For they stumbled at that stumblingstone ;

33 As it is written, Behold, I lay in Sion a stumblingstone and rock of offence : and whosoever believeth on him shall not be ashamed.

THE apostle, having laid down his doctrine concerning God's sovereignty in choosing and saving whom he will, and having shown that God exercised that sovereignty in the very dawn of the history of the Jewish people, proceeds to show from the prophets that it was to be expected that in the latter days the Most High would continue to act according to the good pleasure of his own will.

25. *As he saith also in Osee, I will call them my people, which were not my people ; and her beloved, which was not beloved.*

26. *And it shall come to pass,* that *in the place where it was said*

unto them, Ye are *not my people ; there shall they be called the children of the living God.* The first of these verses is cited from Hosea 2 : 23 ; the last, from Hos. 1 : 9, 10, but in neither case does the apostle closely follow either the Hebrew or the Septuagint; but under the guidance of the Spirit gives a rendering of his own, following the Septuagint in chief part. The variations are not important. There is some transposition of the order of the clauses, as well as of the verses cited, but we need not dwell on that. An examination of the early part of the book of Hosea shows that the prophet is there specially speaking of the ten tribes, and not of the Gentiles. This has made some difficulty, and has led to various explanations. Perhaps the best solution is this. In showing that in calling men, whether Jews or Gentiles, God exercises his own good pleasure and is a free sovereign, he proceeds to state that in the history of Abraham's descendants, there is a comparatively modern and well known example of the exercise of his prerogative as supreme Lord of all, in the history of the ten tribes, who for a season were rent off from the theocracy, and from the temple service, and so from the throne of David, but were, very much like the Gentiles, outcasts from God. Hosea and Isaiah were in part cotemporaries as we learn from the first verse of the books that bear their names respectively. Hosea here predicts the restoration of Israel or the ten tribes, at least in part, to the true worship of God ; so that they which were for a time not a people and not beloved, shall be beloved and shall be a people. More than a hundred years later a like prediction is given by the weeping prophet, Jer. 50 : 4, 5. And so God displayed his sovereignty both in rejecting for a season the ten tribes, and then in bringing many of them back to his true worship. This solution is entirely pertinent to Paul's whole argument—God's right to reject at any time any man, or class of men, who had no claim on him except that derived through lineal descent from a friend of his. It in like manner shows the riches of God's grace in extending mercy to many persons in these tribes so soon after their practice of idolatry in the worship of the calves, etc. The objection that may occur to some is that in the preceding verse Paul had mentioned the Gentiles, but in the same verse he had spoken of the Jews also ; and he had named both incidentally, and not at all in logical connection with these verses. His object had been to show that God always had exercised his sovereign right to choose, call and save whom he would, whether among the descendants of Abraham or of any one else. In his sovereignty he for a season rejected ten out of the twelve tribes ; but in his mercy he gathered again many from among them and made them his people. That this is not

doing violence to any rule of sound interpretation is manifest
from the fact that in v. 27 the apostle expressly says that he is still
speaking of Israel. Now Abram himself " was a Syrian ready to
perish," Deut. 26 : 5. He was the descendant of gross idolaters
and many think he was one himself, Josh. 24 : 2, 3. Sarah was of
the same stock of vile idolaters, Gen. 11 : 29 ; 20 : 12. So vile were
the people, from whom they sprang that in Ezek. 16 : 3 Abram is
called an Amorite and his wife a Hittite. This is of course figurative language, denoting that they descended from a people as vile
as the descendants of Heth, the second son of Canaan, and of Emor,
the fourth son of Canaan, the ancestors respectively of the Hittites
and Amorites, two tribes as odious as any that could be named to
a Jew. God showed his supreme authority as Lord of all in making choice of this man and this woman, as the ancestry of the
Jews. So in Abraham's family the Lord passed by the Son of
Hagar and the six sons of Keturah, and chose Isaac. In Isaac's
family he rejected Esau and chose Jacob. In Jacob's family he
passed by Reuben the first born, and gave the sceptre to Judah,
and the richest blessing to Joseph. In Joseph's family he gave
the preference to Ephraim the younger over his elder brother
Manasseh. In all the early history of Abraham and his descendants God showed his sovereignty. So now says Paul he did the
same in the case of the ten tribes. Other explanations are
offered by commentators. Calvin says that the most successful
in interpreting these verses supposed that Paul meant to reason
thus—" What may seem to be an hinderance to the Gentiles to become partakers of salvation did also exist as to the Jewish nation ;
as then God did formerly receive the Jews, whom he had cast
away and exterminated, so also now he exercises the same kindness towards the Gentiles." Calvin offers another interpretation
of his own, viz.: that the prophet was aiming to give consolation
both to Jews and Gentiles by showing them that they were ruined
unless they turned to the kingdom of Christ. All this is doubtless
true. The difficulty is in getting it out of this verse. The apostle
of the circumcision quotes a part of these verses and applies them
to the elect of his day, some of whom were Jews, and some, Gentiles, 1 Pet. 2 : 10. So that if the words have a primary fulfilment
in the conversion of a portion of the ten tribes they have a continu-
ous fulfilment in the effectual calling of every people. In every
age God receives outcasts, and all past history shows it. The
words of these verses are generally easily understood.

27. *Esaias also crieth concerning Israel, Though the number of
the children of Israel be as the sand of the sea, a remnant shall be
saved :*

28. *For he will finish the work, and cut* it *short in righteousness : because a short work will the Lord make on the earth.* These words are quoted from Isaiah 10 : 22, 23, and very much from the Septuagint version with slight variations. Whether by Israel we understand the ten tribes, or the body of the descendants of Jacob, will not affect the interpretation of these words in application to the matter in hand ; though they pretty certainly refer to the mass of Abraham's offspring. The first of these verses is a clear declaration that many, who were descended from Jacob, were rejected of God, and but a remnant saved. What period of history is covered by this declaration, whether merely the days of Isaiah, or a much longer period, we need not inquire as to this argument. The apostle is simply proving that great numbers of the lineal descendants of Jacob were not saved, thus showing that God did not own as his those who had not faith and piety ; and that no promise he had made to the fathers bound him to save those who lived and died in sin. The second of these verses is of more difficult explication. Paul gives as good a rendering as has been offered. The rendering in the authorized version in Isa. 10 : 22, 23 is of course different, being made directly from the Hebrew. The sense is that God will *righteously* and *speedily* terminate the destruction, or *consumption*, or sentence of divine displeasure against this people. And this consumption was to be executed on descendants of Abraham. Nor is the above the only case in which the evangelical prophet declared that many of his nation were utterly rejected by the Lord :

29. *And as Esaias said before, Except the Lord of Sabaoth had left us a seed, we had been as Sodoma, and been made like unto Gomorrah.* This is a quotation from Isa. 1 : 9. The chief difference between the verses here and there is that here we have *a seed,* and in the prophet *a very small remnant.* But the idea in each case is the same, as the portion of the crop saved for seed is a very small part of the whole. Here the prophet certainly embraces the tribes of Judah and Benjamin, as is clear from Isa. 1 : 1. It is certain that here as in Isa. 10 : 22, 23 he is speaking of the descendants of Abraham without regard to their civil condition. *Sabaoth,* in Isa. 1 : 9 correctly rendered *of hosts,* is retained from the Septuagint, which Paul in this verse literally follows. It occurs in one other place in the New Testament, Jas. 5 : 4. The *hosts* or armies of Jehovah are the angels of heaven, the sun, moon and stars of heaven, the people of God of all ages, and all creation regarded as marshalled before him. In the first part of his prophecy Isaiah is speaking of the sins of his people and of the judgments that had wasted them. Hodge : " The passage strictly proves

what Paul designed to establish, viz: that the Jews, as Jews, were as much exposed to God's judgments as others, and consequently could lay no special claim to admission into the kingdom of heaven."

30. *What shall we say then? That the Gentiles which followed not after righteousness, have attained to righteousness, even the righteousness which is of faith.* This is the sixth time in this epistle, when after clearly establishing a great principle in his argument, the apostle asks, *What shall we say then?* But this interrogatory is not always propounded for the same purpose. Sometimes it is done to state an objection, that it may be answered. Here and sometimes elsewhere it is done to open the way for announcing a conclusion. In this place it means, What is the result reached? What is the fair conclusion from these statements? He then states it, That the blessings of the gospel might be extended to the Gentiles. The form of announcing this truth is both frank and guarded. It admits that the Gentiles merited not this favor. It even admits their gross wickedness and recklessness. They *followed not after righteousness.* They were free from righteousness. They were not under restraint from any sound principle of piety. They lived as they listed and in such corruption as is well described in the first chapter of this epistle. These undeserving, ill-deserving people, through the riches of God's grace and mercy, when they were not seeking or pursuing after righteousness in any sense of that term, heard of the gospel scheme of salvation by grace through faith, by the power of God's Spirit were enabled to believe, and thus have attained unto righteousness, not in any wise by their own merits, but solely by believing in him, who justifies the ungodly. Compare Isa. 65 : 1. Such is obviously the import of this verse.

31. *But Israel, which followed after the law of righteousness, hath not attained to the law of righteousness. Followed after,* the same word so rendered in v. 30. Peshito: ran after. Israel had avowedly and formally given much attention to matters pertaining to their good standing before God. But their efforts were wretchedly spoiled by self-righteousness. They had generally fallen into the belief that acceptance with God was through a man's own good deeds. So that when a gratuitous justification through the righteousness of Christ was offered them, so far from receiving it, they generally rejected it, and so utterly failed of righteousness. This is the evident import of the passage as interpreted by the history of these people, and by the context. The phrase *law of righteousness* has given rise to some diversity of explanation. Rosenmuller says that in the first instance it means the *law of Moses,* in the sec-

ond the *doctrine of Christ*.   That is at least a loose way of stating
the matter; so general as not to aid the mind in coming at the
truth.   Calvin and Guyse think *the law of righteousness* signifies *the
righteousness of the law*.   No doubt the doctrine thus educed is
sound.   But how can it be philologically reached?   Bp. Hall:
" Israel, which sought to attain to righteousness by the works of
the law, and affected to earn both perfect justice and God's favor
by the fulfilling thereof, have not at all attained to the state of
righteousness."   The following interpretation would give a good
sense, and would be historically true: Israel, which sought to be
saved by the rule of righteousness, fell short of the rule of righteousness, their sinful nature, not any defect in the law, producing
the failure.   Other expositions are offered, but this meets the philology of the case, is sound, and is to be preferred.

32. *Wherefore ?   Because* they sought it *not by faith, but as it
were by the works of the law.   For they stumbled at that stumbling-
stone*.   How came it to pass that Israel fell short of attaining
righteousness?   This has often been stated, but Paul again says it
was because they sought it by their own works or personal conformity to law, and not by faith in the Redeemer.   *Stumble at*, or
dash against, quite uniformly rendered.   The noun rendered
stumbling is cognate to the verb stumble.   One, who persists in
following a way in which for any reason God forbids him to walk,
must expect a failure.   As far back as the days of Abraham God
clearly taught that man's justification is by faith.   Any other
method therefore is impossible.   But what is the stone of stumbling ?
Paul answers by a quotation from the evangelical prophet :

33. *As it is written, Behold I lay in Sion a stumbling stone and rock
of offence, and whosoever believeth on him shall not be ashamed*.   This
is a quotation from parts of two verses in different chapters, Isa.
8 : 14; 28 : 16.   Both these verses relate to the same matter, the
Saviour of men, and both employ the same figurative language
respecting him.   The phrase *make haste* found in Isa. 28 : 16 is
here explained as being ashamed.   This latter term is also substi-
tuted by being confounded.   Even in Old Testament times the
great support of the troubled was Messiah to come, as to us it is
Messiah already come.   Compare Ps. 118 : 22; Matt. 21 : 42;
Mark 12 : 10; Luke 20 : 17; Acts 4 : 11; Eph. 2 : 20; 1 Pet. 2 : 6,
7.   Though the wicked by their unbelief make the coming of
Christ a means of a deeper and more terrible destruction, yet
Christ is to all who believe the power of God unto salvation.
Christ is a sure, a tried, a precious corner stone.   Blessed be God,
Christ is a gin and a snare to none, who receive him in meek hu-
mility and in holy joy.

DOCTRINAL AND PRACTICAL REMARKS

1. The Scripture is to be studied.   One part should be compared with another, v. 25.   The two Testaments, like the cherubim over the mercy-seat, look towards each other.   The word of God contains more than appears to a careless or superficial reader. Many read Gen. 15 : 6 ; Hab. 2 : 4, and never learn therefrom the way of justification.   Many read Hosea through and never learn that God is a sovereign.   It is therefore a great mercy to have a good, competent person to expound God's word to us, as Paul does here, and as Philip did to the eunuch, Acts 8 : 30, 31.   Let us search the scriptures daily and candidly, embracing all they teach.

2. It is fair to appeal to scripture as binding on all who know it, v. 25.   Paul does so here.   He did so in his address before Agrippa, Acts 26 : 27.   Jesus Christ taught that infidels in all lands, who know but reject the word of God shall be judged by it, John 12 : 48.   All this is fair.   Clarke : " The apostle shows that this calling of the Gentiles was no *fortuitous* thing, but from a *firm purpose* in the Divine mind, which he had largely revealed to the prophets : and by opposing the calling of the Gentiles, the Jews, in effect, renounced their *prophets.* and fought against God." The scripture is God's word, and the denial of this fact no more makes it to be no fact than the denial of a God puts God out of the universe.

3. God's word will surely be fulfilled.   There can be no failure. Where the event requires the free agency of man, it is as freely and certainly rendered as where only inanimate creation bears a part in the fulfilling of his word.   Olshausen : " God's prophecies, being the utterances of the All-knowing and Almighty one, must needs be fulfilled, not, however, by destroying the free will of the creature, but rather through that very free will . . . Prophecies are to no purpose, unless on the presupposition of St. Paul's doctrine as to predestination : it is not man that causes their fulfilment, but God by means of man, and that precisely by his free act."

4. God's people are in covenant with him so that not only may each one of them say, Thou art my God, but God as distinctly says, Ye are my people, my beloved, my children, vs. 25, 26.   We should never forget this covenant relation between God and us. It is our life and our joy.   " The beauty of scripture is in its pronouns."

5. It is lawful for us to follow the example of Christ and his apostles, and freely use a translation of the scriptures, even though it be not inspired, as the Septuagint, which Paul quotes, was neither inspired, nor always correct.

6. The original scriptures are in the Greek and in the Hebrew, and are always to be the final resort in learning the mind of the Spirit, just as Paul follows a translation until it fails to bring out the precise idea of the original, most pertinent to his argument, then he refers to the Hebrew. True, he did this by a plenary inspiration, and so infallibly. We must do it modestly, humbly, with prayer for divine guidance, and under a solemn responsibility to God and his people for our candor in the use of all the lights we can secure.

7. How rich and free and glorious is the grace of God, which calls outcast Israelites and sinners of the Gentiles to a saving knowledge of his Son. How it overleaps all boundaries that men set up, casts into oblivion the misdeeds of a wicked life, and showers its blessings on those most justly doomed to wrath, vs. 25, 26. Brown: "How profane, naughty, and graceless soever a place hath been, and how infamous soever for wickedness and Atheism; yet that will not hinder the Lord from being gracious to that people, when the time of love dawneth." Blessed be God, who shows mercy to the chief of sinners, and brings his sons from afar.

8. If God has saved us, and made us heirs of his kingdom and grace, why should we not be greatly encouraged to pray and labor for the conversion and salvation of others. Surely if God calls us beloved, who were not long since in our sins and under wrath, he may save others, now as far from righteousness as we ever were. It seems unaccountable that really converted people should have so little zeal in saving men's souls. When first converted almost all make some spirited endeavors in that direction, but like the mild Reformer, they "find old Adam too strong for young Melancthon." Then they are in danger of falling under the power of discouragement, and thenceforth they accomplish little. Scott: "As many of us have now obtained mercy, and are the people and children of the living God, who once were far off from him; so we may pray, and hope, and take encouragement to use diligently all proper means, that this may be the case throughout the earth." In our endeavors to save others we should be mightily stirred up by gratitude for the compassion shown to us in a thousand ways. There is not a man upon earth, whose ancestors were not once abominable idolaters. Most of those who now speak the English language are descended from those who at the birth of our Saviour were as degraded and debased worshippers of devils, as the world has ever seen; and we carry about with us in the names of the days of the week the rags and shreds of that idol-worship, which our forefathers practised.

9. It is a blessed truth that our God is *the living God;* n)t dead
wood, and stone, and silver, and gold; not dead men deified by
superstition, but the living, active, moving, efficient God, full of
all energy and power, v. 26.   Let us trust him, rejoice in him, be
persuaded of his glorious perfections and his infinite faithfulness.

10. It is sad, it was so to the prophets, to Christ, and to his
apostles that among the multitudes of earth, so few from age to age
give evidence of any real love to God, v. 27.   Blessed be God for
the rich grace, by which even a *remnant* are made wise unto salvation.   It shall not be so always.   A day is coming, (Lord, hasten
it,) when the plowman shall overtake the reaper, when the light
of the moon shall be as the light of the sun, and the light of the
sun shall be sevenfold, as the light of seven days, and when the
knowledge of the Lord shall cover the earth as the waters cover
the sea, Isa. 11 : 9; 30 : 25; Amos 9 : 13.

11. Sometimes God's patience with a man or a community is
worn out, and then in anger and in righteousness he cuts short the
work, and gives them over to ruin as swift as it is just, v. 28.
When he does this he "makes quick dispatch with carnal men,"
and the flood of his wrath sweeps them away as in a moment.
They are extinguished like the fire of tow.   The suddenness and
overwhelming nature of the wrath that comes upon the incorrigible are often stated in scripture, Pr. 29 : 1; 1 Thess. 5 : 3.   Brown:
"When God is about to execute his anger against a people for
their iniquities, he can send a rod which shall make their strength
soon decay and come to a hair, and their multitudes melt like
snow before the sun, like a consumption weakening them daily."

12. There is no telling what a happy influence even one man,
and he once a wicked man, may have in saving a community.
Look at Moses in Israel, at old John Adams in Pitcairn's Island,
and at multitudes of like cases.   Ten righteous men would have
saved Sodom.   A very small remnant saved the Jewish nation
from coming to a like end in the days of Isaiah, v. 29.   If it had
not been for the elect, the world would have long since been without inhabitants, Matt. 24 : 22.   What a blessing a very few men
may be to a great nation.

13. But a terrible doom is coming on all who are finally impenitent.   Their state will soon be as doleful as that of Sodom and
Gomorrah, which suffer the vengeance of eternal fire, v. 29.   Compare Jude 7.   How is it that men can neither be won by the most
lovely things, nor aroused by the most startling things, nor alarmed
by the most terrible things, nor attracted by the most glorious
things?   O there is a mystery in iniquity that can never be solved.
Depravity is as deep as it is foul.

14. God's manner of bestowing grace on men is as sovereign and admirable, as the grace itself is rich and amazing, v. 30.   He is found of them that sought him not, Isa. 65 : 1.   What a glorious surprise of mercy was the visit of the gospel in the power of the Spirit to Rome, Corinth, Ephesus, Philippi, Samaria, and many other places.   What gladness was diffused in every place, where mercy came to heal the dying and rescue the condemned.   And then all this is bestowed in so wondrous a way—Righteousness without works!   Was there ever a kinder or more startling announcement?   Righteousness by faith!   Why it is the very thing for the lost—the only message that could cheer a sinner.   And all coming without money and without price; yea without solicitation.   Wonderful, *Wonderful*, Wonderful, WONDERFUL grace.   The like was never heard of in God's dealings with any but sinners of Adam's race.   O why will not all at once accept this grace and be saved?

15. Right views of the richness and freedom of grace are no ground of vain-glorious boasting.   All we have, we have received. And all we have received was through unmerited kindness.   God's mercy abused may be withdrawn for ever.   Let us be humble. Let us fear lest a promise being left us of entering into rest, any of us should seem to come short of it, or abuse it, and provoke the Most High to withdraw it.   We stand by faith, v. 30.   Unbelief will ruin any people whatever may have been their history.   See Matt. 21 : 43.

16. Great engagedness in some, yea, in many of the outward duties of religion, avowedly in quest of righteousness, does not secure the forgiveness of sins, and acceptance with God, until the soul turns away from every thing else to Christ Jesus, as the way, the truth, and the life, v. 31.   All is fatal error, till Christ and his righteousness are embraced—yes, fatal error.   Hodge: "Error is often a greater obstacle to the salvation of men than carelessness or vice.   Christ said that publicans and harlots would enter the kingdom of heaven before the Pharisees . . . Let no man think error in doctrine a slight practical evil.   No road to perdition has ever been more thronged than that of false doctrine. Error is a shield over the conscience, and a bandage over the eyes."   Take heed how you ever entertain even for an hour a thought counter to God's scheme of saving men by the riches of grace in Christ Jesus.   "Poison kills as well as pistol;" and the poison of error in religious doctrine is worse than the poison of asps.   Nor is this danger slight, particularly in places where the gospel has long been preached.   Brown: "There are none more ready to reject God's way of salvation by faith in Christ, and to

cleave to the way by their own works, than such as are within the
visible church, and privileged of God beyond others."

17. Want of living faith is as fatal under the gospel as under
the law. It has always been the bane of spurious piety. It believes not God's testimony respecting his Son. It rejects the Son
himself, and makes him a stumbling-stone, v. 32. This doctrine
has been no secret in the church. Whitby quotes the Chaldee
Paraphrast as saying: "If they will not obey, or receive him, [that
is Messiah,] my word shall be to them for scandal, and ruin to the
princes of the two houses of Israel." Olshausen: "As it is impossible to pour any thing into a vessel which is stopped up and full,
in like manner is a soul full of pride and devoid of love incapable
of receiving the streams of the Spirit." Chalmers: "A Christian
utterly renounces all good works, as having any value in them to
confer a legal right to heaven. And yet a Christian devotes himself to the performance of good works, as having in them that virtue of moral rightness, which is in itself the very essence of
heaven."

18. Since Jesus Christ is so meek, so holy, so loving, so glorious as all the scriptures represent him to be, how comes it to
pass that he is a stumbling-stone and rock of offence to any? vs. 32,
33. He is the joy of the meek. He is the glory of Israel. How
can any be offended in him? The reason is that his whole work
and righteousness bring honor to God in the highest, and abase
the sinner in the dust. If the Lord Jesus would demand no abasement of spiritual pride; if he would not call for the crucifixion of
the flesh with the affections and lusts; if he would not slay the
enmity; if he would not cast out the devils of uncleanness; if he
would save without a faith that works by love, purifies the heart
and overcomes the world; in short if he would save men in their
sins, not from their sins, he would be everywhere crowned with
songs. But he will never be the minister of sin. Hence his very
divinity is an offence to some, and his humanity a scandal to others.
In the heavenly race many *dash against* this stone and are broken.
Haldane: "Men cannot bear the idea of being indebted for salvation to sovereign grace, which implies that in themselves they are
guilty and ruined by sin." And yet any other scheme of acceptance with God suits none but sinless beings, and "there is no man
that sinneth not."

19. However gloomy and doleful the prospects of the incorrigibly proud and impenitent may be, let the heralds of the cross be
faithful, tender and urgent in proclaiming the offer of eternal life
to as many as shall believe in the Lord Jesus Christ. All such
shall not be ashamed or confounded, v. 33; yea, they shall be for

ever saved.   Let the vilest be persuaded to come to Christ.   Let no barrier be put in their way.   The air we breathe is not more free than salvation by Christ Jesus to all who accept it.   Such may have dark days, may see sharp trials, may endure a great fight of affliction.   But the Lord is their God ;   their defence shall be the munitions of rocks ; and a seat with Christ on his throne their everlasting reward—a reward none the less glorious, because it is all of grace.

Chapter 25

ROMANS 10
VERSES 1–13

KIND WORDS. THE FATAL ERROR OF THE JEWS. HOW MEN ARE SAVED. HOW CHRIST BE-COMES OURS.

BRETHREN, my heart's desire and prayer to God for Israel is, that they might be saved.

2 For I bear them record that they have a zeal of God, but not according to knowledge.

3 For they, being ignorant of God's righteousness, and going about to establish their own righteousness, have not submitted themselves unto the righteousness of God.

4 For Christ *is* the end of the law for righteousness to every one that believeth.

5 For Moses describeth the righteousness which is of the law, That the man which doeth those things shall live by them.

6 But the righteousness which is of faith speaketh on this wise, Say not in thine heart, Who shall ascend into heaven? (that is, to bring Christ down *from above:*)

7 Or, Who shall descend into the deep? (that is, to bring up Christ again from the dead.)

8 But what saith it? The word is nigh thee, *even* in thy mouth, and in thy heart: that is, the word of faith, which we preach ;

9 That if thou shalt confess with thy mouth the Lord Jesus, and shalt believe in thine heart that God hath raised him from the dead, thou shalt be saved.

10 For with the heart man believeth unto righteousness; and with the mouth confession is made unto salvation.

11 For the Scripture saith, Whosoever believeth on him shall not be ashamed.

12 For there is no difference between the Jew and the Greek: for the same Lord over all is rich unto all that call upon him.

13 For whosoever shall call upon the name of the Lord shall be saved.

BRETHREN, *my heart's desire and prayer to God for Israel is, that they might be saved.* Wiclif: Britheren the wille of myn herte, and my bisechynge is made to God: for hem in to helthe; Peshito: My brethren, The desire of my heart, and my intercession with God for them, is, that they might have life;

Stuart: The benevolent or kind desire of my heart; [i. e. his sincere and hearty wish] is for their salvation. The sense is very clear. *Desire*, elsewhere rendered good will, good pleasure, Luke 2 : 14; Eph. 1 : 5, 9; Phil. 1 : 15; Theophylact, earnest desire; Doddridge, affectionate desire. *Prayer*, commonly as here, a few times supplication. *That they might be saved*, literally *unto salvation*. The authorized version gives the exact sense. The occasion for this declaration is that Paul may assure them of his good will in stating to them, as he has already done, and as he is about still further to do, painful and unwelcome truths. He assures them of his best wishes, and would not have them count him an enemy because he tells them the truth. Chrysostom: "Do not then, he says, mind words or accusations, but observe that it is not in any hostile spirit that I say this. For it is not likely that the same person should desire their salvation, and not desire it only, but pray for it, and yet should also hate them, and feel aversion to them."

2. *For I bear them record that they have a zeal of God, but not according to knowledge.* *I bear record*, I bear witness, I bear testimony, I testify. *Them*, i. e. to them, in their favor. *A zeal of God.* Wiclif: love of God; Tyndale, Cranmer and Genevan: a fervent mynde to God warde; Coverdale: are zealous for God's cause. Some think a zeal of God is a Hebraism, and is equivalent to a great zeal, as the trees of God are great trees. This gives a good sense. But the meaning more probably is, that they thought and spoke and acted with a fervent mind concerning the things of God, the matters of religion. But their zeal was ignorant. It was not based on knowledge, the true knowledge of God, of his will and of the right method of securing his favor and blessing. No man can have a holy zeal in a bad cause. Owen of Thrussington quotes from Turrettin four particulars in which the necessity of knowledge as the guide of zeal is justly stated: "1. That we may distinguish truth from falsehood, as there may be zeal for error and false doctrine as well as for that which is true; 2. That we may understand the comparative importance of things, so as not to make much of what is little, and make little account of what is great; 3. That we may prosecute and defend the truth in the *right way*, with prudence, firmness, fidelity and meekness; 4. That our zeal may have the *right object*, not our own interest and reputation, but the glory of God and the salvation of men." The primary error of these Jews related to the object of their zeal. They were busied about rites and ceremonies, about forms, traditions and genealogies, and verily believed they could commend themselves to God by deeds of law. From this great error flowed

every thing else that was wrong in their zeal. Augustine "It is better to go limping in the right way than to run with all our might out of the way."

3. *For they being ignorant of God's righteousness, and going about to establish their own righteousness, have not submitted themselves unto the righteousness of God.* Scott's paraphrase of this verse is very full and just: "For they not knowing the perfect justice of the divine character, law and government; and the nature of that righteousness which God has provided for the justification of sinners consistently with his own glory, had sought by various devices to 'establish their own righteousness,' as the meritorious ground of their justification; in doing which, they had refused to submit to the justice of God in their condemnation, and to seek righteousness as his free gift by faith alone." The word *righteousness* throughout this verse is best taken in the sense so largely explained in this work. See above on Rom. 1 : 17 and other places. *Going about to establish*, literally, seeking to make stand. Their righteousness was like a house built on the sand. The rains were descending and threatening to fall faster; the winds were blowing and threatening to blow a gale; the waves were surging and showed signs of increasing. The fabric of self-righteousness was a poor affair. It shook and gave signs of falling. Meantime they were plying every pharisaic art to *make it stand*. In this mood they of course did not *submit to the righteousness of God*. The word rendered submit is elsewhere rendered be subject, or subjected. See Rom. 8 : 7, 20 ; 13 : 1, 5. They would not bow the neck and take upon them the yoke of subjection to the righteousness, which God had provided, and which he approved. Compare 1 Cor. 1 : 30 ; 2 Cor. 5 : 21 ; Phil. 3 : 9 ; 2 Pet. 1 : 1. Calvin: "The first step towards obtaining the righteousness of God is to renounce our own righteousness." This first step no man will take unless he is under the guidance of the Holy Ghost. It is the most humbling act any mortal ever performs. Divine grace alone has ever led any man to accept a gratuitous salvation. Yet this is a vital matter, essential to salvation.

4. *For Christ* is *the end of the law for righteousness to every one that believeth.* Wiclif: For the ende of the law is crist: to rightuiesnesse to eche man that belieueth ; Tyndale and Geneva: Christ is the ende of the lawe, to justifie all that beleve ; Cranmer: Christ is the fulfyllynge of the lawe, to justyfye all that beleue ; Peshito: Messiah is the aim of the law, for righteousness, unto every one that believeth in him ; Arabic: Forasmuch as Christ is the end of the law to a righteousness, whereby whosoever believeth in him is justified ; Conybeare and Howson: The end of the law is Christ,

that all may obtain righteousness who have faith in him. The word righteousness in this verse doubtless has the same meaning as in verse 3—not justification, but the righteousness by which a sinner is justified. The most difficult and perhaps the most important word in the verse is *end*. In the New Testament this word has six meanings. 1. In Rom. 13 : 7 it is twice rendered custom, meaning a tax on property. See also Matt. 17 : 25. Of course that cannot be its meaning here. 2. In 1 Pet. 3 : 8 it is rendered *finally*, in the sense of summing up all, or giving the substance of what he would say. Taking the word *law* in the sense of dispensation, we might say that Christ was the sum and substance of the law, its promises, prophecies, types, rites and sacrifices. 3. In 1 Thess. 2 : 16 it is rendered *uttermost*, meaning that there is nothing beyond it. So the law has gone to the uttermost of its punitive inflictions, and of its demands for perfect righteousness, when it reaches Christ. It asks no more than his perfect obedience, and his infinite sacrifice. 4. In Matt. 10 : 22 and often the word means the termination : "He that endureth to the end" [the termination of his trials, which will be coincident with the termination of his life] "shall be saved." Christ has forever taken away by his word all hope of salvation by the law. He has in his flesh abolished the enmity, even the law of commandments, as a scheme of justifying righteousness. He has forever blotted out the handwriting of ordinances that was against us. See Eph. 2 : 15 ; Col. 2 : 14. 5. In Luke 22 : 37 the word means fulfilment, completion ; "I say unto you that this that is written must yet be accomplished in me. And he was reckoned among the transgressors : for the things concerning me have an end." So he says : "Think not that I am come to destroy the law, or the prophets : I am not come to destroy but to fulfil," Matt. 5 : 17. 6. In Rom. 6 : 21, 22 ; Phil. 3 : 19 ; Heb. 6 : 8 and elsewhere end means that to which anything leads. Christ is that to which a right use and right views of the law lead us. The law was a schoolmaster to bring us to Christ, that we might be justified by faith, Gal. 3 : 24. Instead of detaining the reader to discuss which of the last five meanings of the word is to be here preferred, he may choose for himself either one ; or he may blend two or more of them together ; for they are all true. Calvin prefers the idea of completion. So do some others. Christ is the end of the law *for righteousness*, for a perfect righteousness, so that he is the Lord our righteousness, to *every one that believeth*, i. e. to every one that accepts him as he is freely offered, presenting nothing meritorious of his own, and putting in no plea but that of the atoning blood and spotless obedience of Jesus Christ.

    5. *For Moses describeth the righteousness which is of the law, That*

*the man which doeth those things shall live by them.   The righteousness
which is of the law* is the righteousness which is by the deeds of the
law, or by personal obedience to the law, and is everywhere the
opposite of the righteousness of God, of faith, or of Christ.   Its
great principle is, Do and live.   The particular passage in the
writings of Moses here referred to is in Levit. 18 : 5.   Compare
Neh. 9 : 29; Ezek. 20 : 11, 13, 21 ; Luke 10 : 27, 28; Gal. 3 : 12.
The obedience thus required for righteousness is, like that of unfallen angels, universal, perpetual, perfect, personal, out of love and
holy fear.   No mere man since the fall ever did so obey the law of
God.   Of course no one has attained to righteousness by works.
All have sinned, come short of the glory of God, and so are under
condemnation.   Calvin: "From the promise itself Paul proves,
that it can avail us nothing, and for this reason, because the condition is impossible."   Sinners have and can have no personal righteousness, equal to the demands of the law.

6. *But the righteousness which is of faith speaketh on this wise,
Say not in thine heart, Who shall ascend into heaven? (that is, to bring
Christ down* from above ;)

7. *Or, Who shall descend into the deep? (that is, to bring up Christ
again from the dead.)*

8. *But what saith it ?   The word is nigh thee,* even *in thy mouth,
and in thy heart : that is, the word of faith, which we preach ;*

9. *That if thou shalt confess with thy mouth the Lord Jesus, and
shalt believe in thine heart that God hath raised him from the dead,
thou shalt be saved.*

These verses are designed to tell us both negatively and positively how men may avail themselves of the righteousness which
is of faith.   In doing this great simplicity and directness of speech
are employed ; and yet not without language that has perplexed
some.   To clear these verses we may observe : 1. The apostle here
as elsewhere employs the figure of personification.   He makes the
righteousness of faith a speaker, gives it a tongue, and causes it to
instruct us in the way of life.   2. The apostle had shown that
righteousness by personal obedience to the law was impossible,
wholly out of the question.   He would now show that righteousness by faith is not impracticable.   The heavens need not to be
scaled.   The fathomless abyss need not be dived into.   In short
under the gospel nothing is required beyond what any man may
attain to, if he is willing to renounce his sins, his self-will and his
self-righteousness, and accept a gratuitous salvation offered to him
by the Lord.   3. The better to effect his object he makes use of a
passage in the writings of Moses quite familiar to his readers.   It
is found in Deut. 30 : 12–14.   In v. 11 Moses says: " This com-

mandment which I command thee this day, it is not hidden from thee, neither is it far off." The subject before him is the simplicity of the truth, the obviousness of their duty, and the fact that a perfect heart is all that is required to meet the demands, which were made on them. They need perform no miracles, nor wait till God performed miracles. He then proceeds : " It is not in heaven that thou shouldst say, Who shall go up for us to heaven, and bring it unto us, that we may hear it and do it ? Neither is it beyond the sea, that thou shouldst say, Who shall go over the sea for us, and bring it unto us that we may hear it, and do it ? But the word is very nigh unto thee, in thy mouth, and in thy heart, that thou mayest do it." The declared design and obvious intent of Moses is to state to his countrymen that they were not called to search out inscrutable things, but that their duty was obvious. He says it is not "hidden, neither is it far off;" it is not abstruse, recondite, nor hard to be understood, if the heart is right. In the words immediately following he adds : " See, I have set before thee this day life and good, and death and evil." 4. Now says the righteousness of faith speaking through Paul : The way of life under the gospel is just as clear as the way of duty under the law. You, Israelites, complain of the mysterious aspect of the gospel ; but I tell you, it is not hidden. Christ's ministers make known the way of salvation with all clearness. In all the churches one doctrine is preached. Perishing men are not sent on pilgrimages, or across seas, nor are they bidden to climb up to the stars, or have visions of the third heavens. The gospel was once a mystery hidden from ages, kept secret since the world began, but now is made manifest, and by the scriptures of the prophets, according to the commandment of the everlasting God, made known to all nations for the obedience of faith. A clearer revelation could not be made. Therefore, says the righteousness of faith, there is nothing occult or impracticable in the terms I offer. I may adopt, I do adopt very much the words of Moses, and say, ' The word is nigh thee, even in thy mouth, and in thy heart:' that is, the word of faith which is every where preached. 5. And here is that word, That if thou shalt confess with thy mouth the Lord Jesus, and shalt believe in thine heart that God raised him from the dead, thou shalt be saved. This is the positive form of the gospel offer. He, who accepts it shall never perish. And this is the whole of it. Terms could not be easier, nor better suit the condition of lost men. The message brings a gratuitous salvation, rich and free to the palace of the prince and to the cottage of the poor ; it offers mercy to the robber and to the moralist ; to old and young, bond and free, wise and unwise. 6. If these views are correct, then the words of Moses are not necessarily a quotation in proof of the doctrine of justification by faith ; nor are they used in a way of mere accommodation, as some think ; but they do directly state the clearness of the gospel offer, no less than of the teachings of Moses ; yea, if Moses spoke clearly, much more did Christ. The object of a revelation is to make things known. In the same way does Paul in the 18th verse of this chapter quote and use Ps. 19 : 4.

Let us look a little at the terms and phrases here employed. *Righteousness* is best taken in the same sense in which it was used in vs. 3, 4 and commonly in this epistle. This is made certain by the words which follow, *which is of faith*. The word rendered *deep* is in Luke 8 : 31 rendered as here, everywhere else bottomless, or bottomless pit. The meaning evidently is that we are not required to go to any place remote, or inaccessible except by miracle, or by some extraordinary measure. In v. 8 What saith it ? means what saith the righteousness which is of faith ? *The word of faith* is the message of the gospel offered to our faith and accepted by all believers, and by none others. In v. 9 confessing Christ is put before believing on him, that is, the effect is mentioned before the cause. Moses had put *mouth* before *heart* in the place referred to. But this leads to no confusion, for in the next verse the order of nature is stated. These verses (9, 10) seem to be constructed very much as Matt. 7 : 6, where the first and last clause go together, and the two intermediate clauses belong to each other. To *confess the Lord Jesus* is to confess that Jesus is Lord, and this can be done only by the Holy Ghost, 1 Cor. 12 : 3. The article of faith essential to be believed is that *God raised Christ from the dead.* This was the turning point. See above on Rom. 1 : 4. We may believe that Christ lived, and taught, and wrought miracles ; but do we believe that God so approved of his work, and so accepted it as to demonstrate to the world the divinity of his mission and the righteousness of all his claims, by raising him from the dead ? Do we in *heart* welcome and receive the Lord Jesus as *declared to be the Son of God with power by the resurrection from the dead ?* In this and the next verse *heart* is to be taken in the usual sense, involving the taste, the preference, the active powers of the soul. Calvin : " The seat of faith is not in the brain, but in the heart. Yet I would not contend about the part of the body in which faith is located : but as the word *heart* is often taken for a serious and sincere feeling, I would say that faith is a firm and effectual confidence, and not a bare notion only." If we are not persuaded as well as convinced of the truth of the gospel, our faith will not save us.

10. *For with the heart man believeth unto righteousness; and with the mouth confession is made unto salvation.* The two things here said to be essential to salvation are faith and confession. We learned the same in verse 9, though in a transposed order. Pareus: "God knows our faith; but it is made known to man by confession." Christ's kingdom is built on testimony, first on the testimony of God concerning Christ, 1 John 5 : 9–12; then on the testimony of his people to his grace and faithfulness, Luke 24 : 48; Acts 1 : 3; 5 : 32; 10 : 41; 13 : 31. If all who profess to believe in Christ were to make a secret of their supposed love to him, he would soon have no kingdom in the world. Faith is *unto righteousness*, not only in order to righteousness, but to the actual attainment of it. The righteousness here spoken of is that, which is the ground of a sinner's justification, the righteousness mentioned so often in this chapter and in this epistle. *Unto salvation;* not only is confession made in order to salvation, but when made in faith it secures salvation.

11. *For the Scripture saith, whosoever believeth on him shall not be ashamed.* These words are the same found in Rom. 9 : 3, and quoted from Isa. 28 : 16. Compare Isa. 49 : 23; 1 Pet. 2 : 6. See above on Rom. 9 : 3. *The scripture,* meaning the holy writings, of which there were many penmen, and all of which were of divine authority, because holy men spoke as they were moved by the Holy Ghost. On the truth of the doctrine taught in this quotation he sets up the gospel banner. Many Jews had refused the gracious offer, sincerely made to them. The apostle now proceeds to invite and welcome all who come to Christ, whatever their history or nationality. The indiscriminate character of the offer is clearly involved in the word *Whosoever,* each one, or every one.

12. *For there is no difference between the Jew and the Greek: for the same Lord over all is rich unto all that call upon him.* For *Greek* several versions have *Gentile.* This gives the sense. The authorized version is literal. *There is no difference;* no difference in origin, all sprang from Adam; no difference, as to the guilt of original sin or the want of original righteousness; no difference, as to their need of a salvation wholly gratuitous, by atoning blood and imputed righteousness; no difference, as to the sincerity of the offer made, nor as to the readiness, promptness, and blessedness of the reception given by God to all who accept the proffered grace; and no difference, as to the consequences of such faith, justification, adoption, renewal, sanctification and glorification invariably following a hearty reception of the Lord Jesus Christ. The rendering of the Peshito is: And in this it discriminateth

neither Jews nor Gentiles; Arabic: There is no distinction separat-
ing between the Jew and the Greek. *For the same Lord over all is
rich unto all that call upon him.* Peshito: For there is one Lord
over them all, who is rich towards every one that calleth on him;
Tyndale and Cranmer: For one is Lorde of all which is rich unto
all that call on him; Conybeare and Howson: Because the same
[Jesus] is Lord over all, and he gives richly to all who call upon
him. *Rich*, not only in kindness and wisdom, in truth and faithfulness, in power and resources, but also in blessings actually bestowed, pardon, peace, purification and all spiritual privileges.
The truth of this statement Paul knew by revelation, and so gives
it to us. But it is a truth supported by the whole tenor of scripture. He particularly cites the son of Pethuel.

13. *For whosoever shall call upon the name of the Lord shall be saved,*
Joel 2:32. Peter quotes the same words on the day of Pentecost
and gives them the same interpretation, Acts 2:21. The quotation
is most pertinent. It is taken from the Septuagint, which closely follows the Hebrew. The last verb signifies to rescue or deliver; and
is not salvation a marvellous rescue, a great deliverance? In comparison of it nothing else deserves to be called a deliverance. In
the prophet Joel the word for Lord is Jehovah, the incommunica-
ble name of the Most High; and here Paul is speaking of the
Lord Jesus, and has for several verses been speaking of no other
divine person, so that here we have proof of the supreme divinity
of our Lord Jesus Christ.

DOCTRINAL AND PRACTICAL REMARKS

1. It is no part, nor mark of true piety to harden our hearts
against our kindred, nor to disown them, however far they may
wander from Christ, or however they may oppose us, v. 1. Genuine charity suffereth long, and is kind, seeketh not her own and
is not easily provoked. Paul has set us a good example of patience
with perverse men. Let us follow it.

2. Let us cultivate benevolent desires, hearty good wishes towards all men, pitying their folly, praying for their salvation and
seeking their highest good, v. 1. The first part of most of Paul's
epistles contains such kind thoughts. Often in the midst of an
argument he turns aside to say like things, as here and in Rom.
9:1–3. Men are apt to go through the world either blessing or
cursing. The doing of one of these is a hindrance to the doing
of the other. It is to be lamented that sometimes out of the same
mouth come both blessing and cursing, Jas. 3:10. But these
things ought not so to be. We ought in all our prayers to be

careful to be honest and sincere. Chalmers: "Unless the desire of the heart goes before the prayer, it is no prayer at all. Prayer is the utterance of desire, and without desire is bereft of all its significancy. The virtue does not lie in the articulation—but altogether in the wish which precedes, or rather which prompts it. Prayer is an act of the soul; and the bodily organ is but an instrument and not the agent of this service. The soul which thinks and wills and places its hopes or its affections on any given object —this and this alone is the agent in prayer."

3. Christ's real ministers are full of pity and compassion towards even those, who injure them, and revile them, and persecute them. Even when their duty requires them to denounce the judgments of God against the wicked, they still weep between the porch and the altar, and cry that sparing mercy may, if possible, be granted.

4. Brown: "It is an old stratagem of the devil to raise jealousies and suspicions in the hearts of people at their pastors, and make them suspect their affection, and conclude their free language and inveighing against their courses, to flow from malice and ill will, and thus raise a thick mist, which may hinder them from receiving the light of truth." Ministers ought to do everything in their power to disarm such prejudices and to persuade men of their hearty good will, v. 1.

5. Unless we have good cause for believing that one has committed the sin unto death, we may and must follow men with our hearty prayers for their personal and eternal salvation, v. 1. Compare 1 John 5 : 16. Paul and the early Christians generally knew that the fall of the Jewish state was unalterably determined. We have no evidence that they ever prayed for the prolongation of their political existence. But they knew not which individual person would prove incorrigible. Many had been converted and saved. They prayed that others might be. This was right. Ordinarily while there is life there is hope. Let us not give up men, till God gives them up. Haldane: "We should never cease to pray for, and use all proper means for the conversion of those, who either oppose the gospel with violence, or from some preconceived opinion. Secret things belong to God, and none can tell whether or not they are among the number of the elect. No one among the Jews was more opposed to the gospel than Paul himself had been; and every Christian, who knows his own heart, and who recollects the state of his own mind before conversion, should consider the repugnance he once felt to the doctrine of grace."

6. It is instructive to see how the mind of Paul overleaps all

intermediate and minor matters, and concentrates its good will, its benevolent affections and its ardent prayers on the salvation of those, whose case awakened his sorrows, v. 1.   This is right.   No-thing considerable is done for any man till his salvation is secured. A sense of this great truth would cure in us many a folly.

7. We all ought promptly and cheerfully to admit any good or any appearance of good in others, even when they and we widely differ even in fundamentals, v. 2.   Paul has set us the example. Augustine followed it, admitting the good repute of Pelagius.   It is always well to remember that the wrath of man worketh not the righteousness of God.   The cause of truth is never a gainer by our bad manners, nor by our bad tempers.

8. Godly sincerity is a great excellence of character, and can-not be too diligently cultivated; and mere natural sincerity is lovely when compared with its opposites, chicanery and hypoc-risy; but there is often a malignant sincerity which makes a man all the worse for not doubting of the propriety of his course.   It would be a great mercy if many men in this world were less sin-cere than they are in their hatred, their envy, their ill will, their ingratitude to God and man, their unbelief and perverseness.   The sincerity of Paul the apostle was probably no greater than that of Saul the persecutor.   But it was of a different character.   His sincerity as a Christian was founded in a sound knowledge of God's word, in a heart full of gentleness and love, in a piety as fer-vent as it was meek.   His sincerity as a persecutor was blind, fu-rious, malignant, devilish.   Mere sincerity evinces no grace.   Hal-dane: " How often is it said that if a man be sincere in his belief, his creed is of no importance."   But there can be no greater error. Many of the heathen are sincere when they worship devils.   That does not save their idolatry from being abominable to God.

9. While every thing urges us to be candid and kind, and to say all the good things which the truth and the occasion will allow; we are never at liberty to flatter or deceive our fellow men, v. 2. If they are in the wrong, we may not say they are in the right, and if a fit occasion offers we should fearlessly warn them of their danger.   Scott: " Careless and shameless profligates, infidels, and blasphemers are not the only persons who throng the broad road to destruction, but many also who have a zeal for God and reli-gion."   Let us heal slightly no hurt.   Let us remember that God looks more at kind and quality than at degree and quantity.   A little religious emotion of the right kind is in God's eyes of greater price than all the bigoted, hateful, malignant, ignorant zeal ever felt respecting God and religion.   Men may be very serious and busy, not only about the externals of religion, but may talk much

of vital piety, bemoan indwelling sin, and express great love for Christ, and yet have no newness of spirit, no grace and no real liveliness in spiritual affairs. Let every man speak the truth in his heart. Let none handle the word of the Lord deceitfully. We may as well have no zeal in religion as a false wicked fury in serving God and promoting his cause. Stuart: " There may be *zeal without knowledge,* which is superstitious, persecuting, hostile to the peace and happiness of the community ; and there may be *knowledge without zeal,* which is cold, skeptical, unfeeling, and which devils may possess as well as men. An actual union of both is accomplished only by sincere piety ; and a high degree, only by ardent piety." Hodge : " The character of zeal is easily ascertained by noticing its effects, whether it produces self-righteousness or humility, censoriousness or charity ; whether it leads to self-denial or to self-gratulation and praise ; and whether it manifests itself in prayer and effort, or in loud talking and boasting."

10. Beware of ignorance, vs. 2, 3. It is neither the mother of devotion, nor of any thing else that is good. Men are never right, never wise unto salvation until the light of the knowledge of the glory of God in the face of Jesus Christ shines unto them. How can one do his duty when he does not know what it is? How can one go to heaven, when he has never learned the way? Why should one go to Christ, when he is so ignorant of his own sins and his lost estate, as not to know that he needs redemption by atoning blood? Where no vision is, the people perish. An ignorant zeal carries men to hell, not to heaven.

11. There are many ways of proving men alike sinful and opposed to God. One of these ways is found in their self-righteousness and their aversion to the righteousness of Christ. Here is a ruined race, of which every man, so long as left to himself, expects to commend himself to God by something he has done or expects to do; and so refuses to submit to the righteousness of God. Such conduct is as foolish as it is vile and ungrateful. It is as if the inhabitants of a city were perishing in a famine, and some good and rich man should send them abundant supplies, and offer them to the people without money and without price ; and they should say, they had need of nothing ; they were well supplied ; or at least they could not accept of his charity. Such an illustration but feebly sets forth the folly of all carnal men, touching the gospel scheme of salvation. Were men not mad upon their sins and blinded by their pride, they would never cease to admire the grace and mercy manifested in the gospel ; yea, they would certainly yield themselves to God. Olshausen : " True piety fixes its love on God not on his gifts."

12. There is no salvation but by God's plan, and righteousness, vs. 3, 4. No other scheme proposes that men shall enter heaven but by their own merits, or by the Judge of all conniving more or less at sin. No other scheme provides any adequate satisfaction to divine justice or any decent covering for the nakedness of the sinner. All penitent souls know that this is so. Brown; "Whatever course an humbled, self-condemned sinner can take for relief, when sin stareth him in the face, and is borne home upon his conscience, there is no peace to be had with God, till Christ be closed with, and laid hold on; no justification but in him; no absolution but through him; no righteousness but from him." The schemes for saving souls most popular in the world, are no more suited to that end than are filthy rags to make a beauteous robe.

13. The present and urgent duty of every man is to come to Christ, embrace him and rely solely on his finished work for salvation, vs. 3, 4. If this duty press us not, nothing does. This is the true way; it is God's appointed way; it is the only way; and it is a clear way. Our necessities declare for it. Hodge: "Christ is every thing in the religion of the true believer."

14. There is no other way of commending us to God that is not irreconcilable with the way pointed out in scripture, vs. 3, 5. Clarke: "Where the law ends, Christ begins. The law ends with representative sacrifices; Christ begins with the *real* offering. The law is our schoolmaster to bring us to Christ; it cannot save, but it leaves us at his door, where alone salvation is to be found." Haldane: "To live by the law requires, as Moses had declared, that the law be perfectly obeyed. But this to fallen man is impossible. The law knows no mercy, it knows no mitigation, it overlooks not the smallest breach, or the smallest deficiency. One guilty thought or desire would condemn forever." If salvation is by grace, it is not by works; if it is by works, it is not by grace. No two things are more opposite.

15. The very simplicity of the gospel plan of salvation is to some an offence, vs. 6-9. Chrysostom: "There is no long journey to go, no seas to sail over, no mountains to pass, to get saved. But if you be not minded to cross the threshold, you may even while you sit at home be saved." Doddridge: "Great reason have we to adore the Divine goodness, and to congratulate ourselves, and one another, upon our great happiness in this respect, that God hath given us a revelation, so obvious and intelligible in all the grand points of it." Naaman was offended with the very simplicity of the method of cure prescribed by the prophet. He wanted some great thing done. He turned away in a rage. So

to many it is a great offence to be called on simply to rest the whole weight of their salvation on the crucified Redeemer.

16. In illustrating and enforcing divine truth we may use the boldest metaphors, comparisons and personifications in order to arouse attention, and show men their danger and their remedy. We give to the law, to sin, and to righteousness a tongue, and put them to teaching, warning and exhorting men, and guiding them in the right way, vs. 6–9. Brown: "Ministers may and ought to use such a way of exhorting and dealing with people, as may be most rousing and upstirring; people being ordinarily careless and indifferent hearers even of truths of great concernment."

17. Reader, art thou a minister? Then what doctrine dost thou give the people? Dost thou *preach the word of faith!* Or dost thou give to the people old wives' fables, politics, metaphysics, thy own quiddits, or any thing else in the place of saving and necessary truth? The awful charge under which thou holdest thy commission is thus expressed: "The prophet that hath a dream, let him tell a dream, and he that hath my word, let him speak my word faithfully. What is the chaff to the wheat? saith the Lord;" "Preach the preaching that I bid thee;" "Preach the gospel;" Jer. 23:28; Jonah 3:2; Mark 16:15. Brown: "Ministers should stick close by their commission, and should not conceal any thing of it for either feud or favor; but should boldly, faithfully, and plainly, with majesty, constancy, and freedom, declare the whole counsel of God without exception; for they are *heralds,* and should behave themselves as heralds."

18. The scriptures make nothing clearer than the necessity of a real, hearty, abiding faith in the Lord Jesus Christ—a gracious persuasion that he is the only and all-sufficient Saviour, vs. 9, 10. This is every way indispensable. "Without faith it is impossible to please God." It has been so from the days of Abel. It will be so to the end of the world. Even the elect are not freed from the condemning sentence of the law till they do from the heart receive the Lord Jesus as he is freely offered in the gospel. It is always necessary that men do receive the Lord Jesus. Otherwise they are under wrath. Faith is not a condition meritorious, but it is a condition *sine qua non,* without which there is no salvation.

19. And as sure as faith is genuine and evangelical, it will show itself by corresponding fruit. In particular, it will in due time lead to an open confession of Christ and profession of subjection to him, vs. 9, 10. Joseph of Arimathea may for a while be a disciple secretly for fear of the Jews, but because the root of the matter is in him, he will on fair trial be as bold as any. At the crucifixion he could no longer conceal his love to Christ. The scriptures very

clearly insist on both a hearty and an avowed attachment to the Lord Jesus, Matt. 10 : 32–39 ; Luke 12 : 8, 9 ; 17 : 12–19 ; John 15 : 14 ; 1 John 4 : 15.   Calvin : " He rightly confesses the Lord Jesus, who adorns him with his own power, acknowledging him to be such an one as he is given of the Father, and described in the gospel." Theophylact : " The heart requires the help of the mouth, for then faith shines forth, and many are benefitted ; but the mouth also needs the heart, for there are many who profess Christ in hypocrisy."   With vain lips crying, Lord, Lord, will save no man.   " My son, give me thine heart."   Hodge : " The public profession of religion or confession of Christ is an indispensable duty."   We cannot sneak into heaven.   Christ loved us openly, and bore spitting and shame and death for us.   We must love him in our hearts. We must make no secret of our love to him.   Why should any hesitate to *own* him, in whom he *trusts ?*   Scott : " We should not trust in a faith of which we are afraid or ashamed to make an open confession : much less ought we to depend on any mere confession of faith, or assent to divine truths, which we do not believe in our hearts."   When Paul wrote, a public confession of Christ was attended by perils of every kind, even the loss of all earthly things, and it was only he that endured to the end that should be saved, Matt. 10 : 22.   Faith is necessary to our obtaining justifying righteousness.   Confession is necessary to prove that we have laid hold on Christ.   As the body without the spirit is dead, so faith without confession is dead also, being alone, fruitless and unprofitable.

20. We must steadfastly hold the doctrine of Christ's resurrection, v. 9.   If we are unsettled here, we are at sea about every thing vital, 1 Cor. 15 : 17–19.   If Christ be not risen we have no assurance of a judgment-day, or of a heaven to come, Acts 17 : 31. If Christ were still dead, we could no more safely trust him than any other dead man.   He was dead, but he is alive for evermore, Rev. 1 : 18.   Thus we must believe, or our faith is powerless.   Calvin : " Though redemption and satisfaction were effected by the death of Christ, through which we are reconciled to God, yet the victory over sin, death, and Satan was attained by his resurrection ; and hence also come righteousness, newness of life, and the hope of a blessed immortality."

21. Nothing could be more happy than the result of a genuine faith in Christ and an honest confession of his name.   They are followed by salvation, vs. 9, 10, 13.   This is the doctrine of both Testaments.

22. The offers of mercy are indiscriminately made, vs. 11, 13. What could be more general than the terms employed—" Whosoever," " Every one," " Any man," &c. ?   No language could be

more large and free and inviting. Compare Isa. 55 : 1 ; John 4 : 4 ; 7 : 37 ; Rev. 21 : 6 ; 22 : 17. Chrysostom : "The *whosoever* is put in all cases, that they might not say aught in reply." Self-emptiness is the only qualification for coming to Christ. The full soul he sendeth empty away.

23. In God's regard all the distinctions set up by national boundaries, by factitious arrangements, by social compact, position, etc., are utterly worthless, as touching acceptance with heaven, v. 12. This was all settled by Peter's vision, Acts 10 : 9–18, 28 ; 11 : 8. Indeed it was settled long before by the course of God's providence.

24. Christ's riches are unsearchable, and he is rich unto all that call upon him, v. 12. Compare Eph. 3 : 8.

25. The gospel was preached in Old Testament times, as well as in our day. Isaiah and Joel are cited here. But the same is true of all the prophets, Acts 3 : 24 ; 10 : 43.

26. Our Lord Jesus Christ is truly and supremely divine. He is Jehovah, and whosoever shall call on his name—worship him as his Lord and his God—shall be saved, v. 13. Slade : "Here then we have two arguments for the divinity of Christ : 1. That what is spoken of Jehovah is ascribed to him ; 2. That he is made the object of our religious invocation." Blessed be God, true saving faith asks no more proof of Christ's divinity than what is given us in all the scriptures. It is abundant. We need no more.

Chapter 26

ROMANS 10
VERSES 14–21

PREACHING NECESSARY. THE PROPHETS FORE-TOLD THESE THINGS.

14 How then shall they call on him in whom they have not believed? and how shall they believe in him of whom they have not heard? and how shall they hear without a preacher?

15 And how shall they preach, except they be sent? as it is written, How beautiful are the feet of them that preach the gospel of peace, and ·bring glad tidings of good things!

16 But they have not all obeyed the gospel. For Esaias saith, Lord, who hath believed our report?

17 So then faith *cometh* by hearing, and hearing by the word of God.

18 But I say, Have they not heard? Yes verily, their sound went into all the earth, and their words unto the ends of the world.

19 But I say, Did not Israel know? First Moses saith, I will provoke you to jealousy by *them that are* no people, *and* by a foolish nation I will anger you.

20 But Esaias is very bold, and saith, I was found of them that sought me not; I was made manifest unto them that asked not after me.

21 But to Israel he saith, All day long I have stretched forth my hands unto a disobedient and gainsaying ·people.

14. *HOW then shall they call on him in whom they have not believed? and how shall they believe in him of whom they have not heard? and how shall they hear without a preacher?*

15. *And how shall they preach, except they be sent? as it is written, How beautiful are the feet of them that preach the gospel of peace, and bring glad tidings of good things!* In Rom. 8 : 28, 29, Paul gives us a golden chain of several links, the first of which is the divine purpose; and the last, glorification. In these two verses he gives us the golden chain of means used for men's salvation. We have:

1. Hearty prayer offered in faith and springing from it;
2. True faith in him of whom the message speaks;
3. The report heard is not vague but by heralds;

517

4. These heralds are not upstarts, but are divinely appointed and sent ;

5. The substance of the message sent by the heralds is the gospel of peace—glad tidings of good things;

6. This arrangement must be approved, looked upon as beautiful. The glad tidings must be welcomed ;

7. All this relates to Christ, Jehovah. The prayer is to him or through him ; the faith is in him ; the report respects him ; the heralds are his messengers ; the sum of all they proclaim relates to his person, work, offices and grace; he is himself the chiefest among ten thousand and altogether lovely.

These things being so, surely the apostles and others chosen of God were not to blame for going beyond Jewry, and making known Christ wherever they went. The quotation in v..15 is from Isa. 52 : 7. Some think the prophet Isaiah had a primary reference to the release of the Jews from Babylonish captivity. This is probably true. But that great event prefigured a much greater— the redemption of men from a worse than Chaldaic bondage, even salvation by Christ Jesus; so that the passage loses none of its force or pertinency by its application to gospel times. Indeed its chief reference was to our day as any one can see by reading that part of Isaiah. Paul's inspired interpretation of it is to Christians an end of all dispute.

16. *But they have not all obeyed the Gospel. For Esaias saith, Lord, who hath believed our report?* The quotation is from Isa. 53 : 1, a passage unquestionably lying in among the most blessed evangelical prophecies. It is a remarkable fact that many of the Jews were slow to leave Babylon for their own land, even when full permission was given. Some seem never to have gone back. But much more have Jews and Gentiles been slow to welcome the Prince of peace. So Isaiah prophetically lamented. Jesus Christ deplored the unbelief of his time, Luke 19 : 42. The evangelists tell of the little success attending Christ's ministry, John 12 : 37. His apostles bewailed their want of greater success. The pertinence of this quotation is, that as the gospel was not universally or even generally hailed as glad tidings by mankind, some might object that it was not of divine origin, else it would be by all, in particular by Jews, received with joy. But Paul says that Isaiah had foretold this very unbelief. We ought not therefore to be disheartened by the fact that even many are indifferent to the most weighty and glorious tidings ever borne to mortals.

17. *So then faith* cometh *by hearing, and hearing by the word of God.* This verse seems to be closely connected with vs. 14, 15, and gives the sum of what had been there said, salvation is by

faith in the truth revealed from heaven and made known by God's ministers.   Several of these verses, especially in the Greek, clearly teach that *hearing* is the great means of believing.   A *report* has gone forth.   That report must be listened to and obeyed.

18. *But I say, Have they not heard?   Yes verily, their sound went out into all the earth, and their words unto the ends of the world.* The body of this verse is taken from Psalm 19:4.   The quotation is from the Septuagint version.   The truth thus set forth is the preaching of the gospel among the nations, so that men generally had heard of Christ Jesus.   The same is abundantly set forth in other places, see Matt. 24:14; 28:19; Mark 16:15; Col. 1:6, 23. The method and object of quoting from the Old Testament are the same as in vs. 6–8.   That is, words, which were true in reference to a matter fully set forth in the place where they are first found, are as applicable and as true in regard to the matter now in hand—the wide-spread of the report of salvation by Jesus Christ.   Chrysostom: "The whole world, and the ends of the earth have heard."   There is no need of restricting the sense so that it shall be understood that the declaration regards the Jews only.   It is as applicable to the Gentiles.   Indeed the chief reference is to the Gentiles.   The words in Ps. 19:4, taken in their original sense and intent, show that God had not left himself without witness among the nations.   He had all along taught them the lessons of natural religion.   The sun, moon and stars had shone as brightly in heathen lands as in Judea.   God had all along filled the heart of the heathen with food and gladness, Acts 14:17. It ought then to awaken no envy nor surprise that he, who had for many ages showed much providential kindness to the Gentiles, should now send them the gospel.   As the truths of natural religion had all along been widely diffused, so now were the saving truths of the gospel.

19. *But I say, Did not Israel know?   First Moses saith, I will provoke you to jealousy by them that are no people, and by a foolish nation will I anger you.* This quotation is from Deut. 32:21, which in Hebrew is poetry.   Paul puts "you" for "them;" otherwise the quotation is literally from the Septuagint, which closely follows the Hebrew.   To give the striking contrast found in the verse Owen of Thrussington gives the whole of it:

> They have made me jealous by a no-God,
> They have provoked me by their foolish idols:
> And I will make them jealous by a no-people,
> By a foolish nation will I provoke them.

This verse refers to the Jews (for Israel is named,) but refers to them to show that their great prophet foretold that the day would come when God would bring the Gentiles to a saving knowledge of himself. The provocations given by the Jews to the Almighty had been many and long continued. Often had they fallen into idolatry; often had they despised his ordinances; often had they refused to hear his reproofs. At the coming of Christ, they had disowned the true God by denying his Son, who was his express image, so that he who had seen Jesus had seen the Father, John 14 : 7, 9. He that denieth the Son, the same hath not the Father, 2 John 9. Rejecting the true God, in the brightest manifestation he had ever made of himself, is it surprising that he rejected them? The chief doubt in interpreting this verse respects the meaning of the question, Doth not Israel know? Some think it means, Doth not Israel know the Gospel? Have not the Jews had it preached among them? This would make good sense, and be pertinent also but for the connection. A better sense is obtained by making the question refer to the main matter in hand: Doth not Israel know by the teaching of their own prophets that the rejection of the Jews and the calling of the Gentiles were events to be looked for? *First*, that is the first prophet I will cite is Moses himself. Then another great prophet, who wrote several hundred years later, spoke no less distinctly on the same subject :

20. *But Esaias is very bold, and saith, I was found of them that sought me not : I was made manifest unto them that asked not after me.*

21. *But to Israel he saith, All day long have I stretched forth my hands unto a disobedient and gainsaying people.*

Esaias is *very bold*, or comes out very boldly, and plainly, speaking in a manner quite unmistakeable. The passage cited is found in Isa. 65 : 1, 2. There is a transposition of the first and second clauses, as well as other variations from both the Hebrew and Septuagint ; but the sense is clearly given. In v. 20 the quotation is made to show that the calling of the Gentiles was predicted. That in v. 21 gives the cause of the rejection of the Jews. The stretching forth of the hands is a striking figure. Conybeare and Howson think it is taken from a mother opening her arms to call back her child to her embrace. But it is not used in this way elsewhere. When Paul stretched out his hand, he beckoned to the people that he might cause silence and secure attention, Acts 21 : 40. Sometimes stretching out the hand is for rescue and deliverance, Deut. 26 : 8. Sometimes it is to offer and bestow benefits, Isa. 26 : 10, 11. Sometimes it is the gesture of threatening, chastising, displaying power as in miracles, Deut. 4 : 34. Some-

times it points to the way in which we should walk or run. No
gesture is more natural than this. Again stretching out the hand
is the posture of earnest address and imploring supplication. To
Israel God had stretched out his hand, demanding their attention,
giving them many a great deliverance, bestowing on them many
favors, chastising and punishing them, pointing out the way in
which he would have them go, and entreating them to quit their
foolish and wicked ways and lay hold on his mercies ; but after
all they were to a sad extent a disobedient, unbelieving, unconfid-
ing people. They were also a gainsaying or contradicting people, like a bad servant answering back, and speaking against God.
We have the cognate noun in Jude 11.

DOCTRINAL AND PRACTICAL REMARKS

1. Men must pray. They must call on the name of the Lord,
v. 14. This prayer must be hearty, else it is not efficacious.
Calvin : " Hypocrites pray, but not unto salvation ; for it is with
no conviction of faith. Paul assumes this as an acknowledged ax-
iom, that we cannot rightly pray unless we are surely persuaded of
success. For he does not here refer to hesitating faith, but to that
certainty which our minds entertain respecting his paternal kindness, when by the gospel he reconciles us to himself, and adopts us
for his children." Brown : " Humble depending on God, and seeking him and his help in all our straits and necessities, is necessary
unto life, by virtue of a command, so as such who scorn to call on
God, have no warrant to expect life, but do certainly exclude
themselves therefrom." Men must either pray or perish. They
must either betimes call upon the Lord Jesus, or at last call upon
the rocks and mountains to fall on them and hide them from the
face of him that sitteth upon the throne, and from the wrath of the
Lamb.

2. Men must have faith, and that faith must be lively and not
dead, genuine and not spurious, intelligent and not ignorant, vs.
14, 17. Men never act more wisely than when with a true heart
they commit their souls to Jesus Christ. Nay, they never act
wisely till they do that very thing. A poor lost sinner has the
best reason in the world for accepting the salvation offered him.

3. Nor is it reasonable to expect that men will be brought to
exercise saving faith, who refuse to listen to the calls of the gospel, vs. 14, 17. The arts of the wicked in evading the force of truth
and the dire consequences of so doing are very graphically described by one who lived more than two thousand years ago :
" They refused to hearken, and pulled away the shoulder, and

stopped their ears, that they should not hear. Yea, they made their hearts as an adamant stone, lest they should hear the law, and the words which the Lord of hosts hath sent in his Spirit by the former prophets: therefore came a great wrath from the Lord of hosts. Therefore it is come to pass, that as he cried, and they would not hear; so they cried, and I would not hear, saith the Lord of hosts," Zech. 7 : 11–13. Oh hear and your soul shall live. It is now dead, and unless you hear it will remain dead in trespasses and in sins.

4. But understand, it is not hearing the instruction that causeth to err, that will save your soul. This honor is reserved to the word of God, v. 17. Nothing but the engrafted word received with meekness is able to save your soul, Jas. 1 : 21. God's word is a fire, and a hammer, that breaketh the rock in pieces, Jer. 23 : 29. All thoughts and imaginings of human devising are as nothing compared to the word of the Lord. A writer of the XVIIIth century complains that in his time often the text was taken from Paul, and the sermon from Epictetus. In our day the sermon sometimes has a much lower origin than that, being taken from the poorest periodical literature of our times. " Sanctify them through thy truth; thy word is truth," John 17 : 17.

5. It is therefore a good thing to preach the gospel, to proclaim abroad all that God has spoken for doctrine, for reproof, for instruction, for correction in righteousness. Preaching is necessary, vs. 14, 15. Preaching and praying are the greatest things done in this world, Acts 6 : 4. They are greater than serving the poor, excellent as that work is. Paul thanked God that he had baptized but a few persons at Corinth, but he never expressed gratitude for having prayed or preached but a little. The appropriate work of the ministry is a most blessed calling. " If a man desire the office of a bishop, he desireth a good work," 1 Tim. 3 : 1. " Faith comes by hearing," not solely but chiefly. God may and does bless the reading of his word to men's salvation. Of the darkest book of Scripture it is said : " Blessed is he that readeth, and they that understand the words of this prophecy, and keep those things which are written therein," Rev. 1 : 3. When the Lord chooses he can make any part of his word quick and powerful, and sharper than any two-edged sword. Doddridge : " Blessed be God for the *preaching* of the gospel, so necessary to that *faith* without which we can have no well grounded hope of salvation. Blessed be God therefore for the *mission* of his ministers, and for his abundant goodness in sending them to us sinners of the *Gentiles.*" Brown : " Though God may sometimes bless the labors of parents in educating their children, Gen. 18 : 19 ; Eph. 6 : 4, and of

masters in instructing their scholars, and of private Christians in instructing their neighbors, yet God's ordinary way of begetting faith in souls is by the preaching of men in office, who are authorized, not only by gifts alone, but also by an authoritative mission."

6. All the ecclesiastical authorities in the world cannot impart to men the gift of preaching aright. They must have an unction to teach them all things. They must be called and *sent* by the Lord himself. There is much cause to fear that some refuse to preach who are duly called; and that others obtrude themselves into the sacred office without any divine mission. By an old prophet God says, "I have not sent these prophets, yet they ran; I have not spoken to them, yet they prophesied," Jer. 23 : 21. This is not the place to discuss at length the matter of a call to the ministry. Good treatises on that subject are not wanting. But let none forget the danger of running when one is not sent, or of refusing to run when he is sent.

7. While the scriptures make it obligatory on ministers seasonably to present all revealed truth, and to keep back nothing that is profitable for their hearers, yet they do also carefully enjoin them to give great prominence to those truths which immediately relate to their salvation. Perhaps the example of a certain man was not good, but the result of his experience is instructive. He spent nine months in a large city going from church to church. In that time he heard many fine essays on ethics, some dark texts explained, and some ingenious disquisitions; but in no case did he hear the way of salvation so explained that, if he had been a perishing sinner, he could have learned what he must do to be saved. Many sermons and hearers and preachers will perish together in the fires of the last conflagration. The great prominent theme of the gospel is Jesus Christ. His person, his natures, his obedience, his sufferings, his offices, his grace and his glory ought to have great prominence in all ministrations of the pulpit. Even the old prophets were full of that theme. Much more may it be justly expected that preachers of the gospel will dwell upon it, Acts 4 : 2, 17; 8 : 35; 1 Cor. 1 : 23; 2 : 2; Gal. 3 : 1; 6 : 14. This theme furnishes inexhaustible stores of the best thoughts. Nor do perishing men need to hear of anything so much as of salvation by grace through a Redeemer. Unless such matters are prominently before their minds, all other thoughts are barren and useless.

8. People everywhere should welcome good preaching, v. 15. The feet of them that bring the message should be beautiful, as are the feet of all who bring us good tidings, v. 15. Macknight:

" This figurative idea was not peculiar to the Hebrews. Bos tells us that Sophocles represents the hands and feet of them who came on some kind errand, as beautiful in the eyes of them who are profited thereby. The figure, as applied by Isaiah, is extremely proper. The feet of those who travel through dirty or dusty roads are a sight naturally disagreeable. But when they are thus disfigured by travelling a long journey, to bring good tidings of peace and deliverance to those who have been oppressed by their enemies, they appear beautiful." If this is true of the messengers of secular good tidings, much more is it true of them, who preach the gospel. Surely it is right to esteem them very highly in love for their works' sake, 1 Thess. 5 : 13.

9. Preachers are often discouraged by the want of success. It has long and in many a country been so. Isaiah had this trial as well as many others, v. 16. It is sad indeed when the witnesses must testify in sackcloth. Whether men will hear or whether they will forbear, God's servants must be faithful in bearing testimony to the truth. But the heart of many a good man sinks and almost dies within him, when he sees the chief apparent effect of his ministry to be that of hardening men against the truth.

10. The reason why men are not saved, is not that there are no Saviour, no message of mercy to the lost, or no heralds of glad tidings to the perishing, v. 18. If men were not vile and rebellious against God, they would at once hear and accept the pure gospel. The news would spread like other glad tidings. The winds would lend their wings to make known the good news, and all flesh would turn to the Lord.

11. There is nothing new under the sun, and in particular the opposition to the saving truth of God is old, and was spoken of by Moses and all the prophets, vs. 19–21. " Surely the Lord God will do nothing, but he revealeth it unto his servants the prophets," Amos, 3 : 7. He long since warned gospel ministers of all their trials, in particular of their want of success. Ministers should desire success and labor for it ; but if they attain it not, let them remember they are not responsible for the effect of their ministry, but only for the right use of all the appointed means.

12. How vile is the depraved heart of man, that it can be made to burn with jealousy and rage at the conversion of men to God, v. 19. How terribly the malice of the human heart breaks out against the truth is not only foretold by prophets, but recorded in history, Acts 13 : 45 ; 17 : 5, 13 ; 22 : 22, 23. Like things are occurring all the time in this wicked world. The malice of the heart against God and his truth has no holidays, and never grows obso-

lete, but burns on from age to age, unless it is extinguished by the waters of the Holy Ghost.

13. But the opposition of the carnal heart to God's truth is no reason for mincing it, or preaching it timidly ; but God's ministers should be fearless and outspoken, even as Isaiah was very bold, v. 20. It cost that great and good man his life to speak so fearlessly. Jerome says he was sawn asunder. That is a very general tradition. Some think he is specially referred to in Heb. 11 : 37. But it is better to enter into life by any means than to be faithless to the truth of God.

14. It is God's plan, in punishing the wicked, to send them retribution in kind. If men persist in loving cursing, it at last comes into their bowels like water. Israel broke covenant with God and committed horrid abominations with idols. God forsook them and he took himself mainly to the Gentiles, as his espoused people, v. 19. Israel will not have Jehovah for a God, Jehovah will not have Israel for a people. Let the wicked beware how they lay up wrath against the day of wrath, or heap treasure together for the last day.

15. The riches of divine grace are very gloriously displayed when God brings to the saving knowledge of himself a man or a people, who seem never to have sought him till he in his mercy called them to the knowledge of his Son, v. 20. In all cases it is the Lord's preventing grace that brings any soul to Christ, and the pious delight in so confessing. Where is the good man, who will not say, "What I am, I am by the grace of God?" But in some cases the change is so great and so surprising, that even careless men are almost ready to say, Behold, here is the finger of God, and there is a power in the gospel to save men's souls.

16. How obstinately and perversely some men sin and rebel against God, v. 21. There have often been cases of a very sad description, men resisting truth and their own convictions to an infatuation. In the days of the weeping prophet the Lord spake unto Israel, rising up early and speaking, but they heard not ; and he called but they answered not. Yea, he earnestly protested unto Israel from the days of Moses for a thousand years and more, yet they obeyed not, nor inclined their ear, but walked every one in the imagination of their evil heart, Jer. 7 : 13 ; 11 : 7, 8. Chrysostom : "What pardon then do they deserve, who exhibit such excessive obstinacy? None."

17. This whole section has a powerful bearing on the subject of missions. Let the candid read it over with this thought in his mind, and he will not fail to be convinced. Other scriptures teach the same. The only outline of prayer given by our Lord

to his disciples has in it seven petitions. Of these three, and those
the first three relate to a spread of the knowledge and kingdom and
worship of God in the world. What an example of zeal and
patient endurance in spreading the knowledge of God were the
apostles themselves, all of them but John actually dying a martyr's
death, and the life of John attempted to be taken away, and himself actually banished to that wretched penal colony, or rather
prison, Patmos. " Thomas seems to have travelled eastward, to
Parthia, Media, Persia and India." Some think he even went into
China. Jude long held up the banner of the cross at Edessa.
Bartholomew bore the glad tidings to Arabia. Matthew published the Gospel in modern Persia, while Paul went as far as
Spain, and, some think, as far as Britain. Wonderfully does God
honor men and communities, who honor him by spreading his
gospel. This day the fame of Bishop Heber depends more on his
missionary hymn than on all else he ever wrote. Let us stir ourselves up to this good work. Let us rejoice at even a little progress made by the gospel. No obligation resting on those, who
have received Christ, is stronger than that of making known the
glory of Immanuel.

PRAYER

Blessed and Glorious God, send forth thy light and thy truth.
Command the nations that they obey thy Son. Send forth laborers into thy harvest. Fill the whole earth with the knowledge of
God. Stir up the zeal of thy people every where in making
known the glad tidings of salvation. Hasten the time when the
Jews and the fulness of the Gentiles shall be brought in. Let
nothing obstruct the wheels of the chariot of salvation. Oh send
forth thy Spirit in large measure on all the earth, awakening
human attention and inquiry respecting the things of God. Oh
let thy word run very swiftly, and the whole earth come to the
brightness of Immanuel's rising ; and to thy name shall be all the
praise world without end. Amen.

Chapter 27

ROMANS 11
VERSES 1–10

ALL ISRAEL NOT CAST AWAY. THE SAD STATE
OF THE REJECTED.

I say then, Hath God cast away his people? God forbid. For I also am an
Israelite, of the seed of Abraham, *of* the tribe of Benjamin.

2 God hath not cast away his people which he foreknew. Wot ye not what
the Scripture saith of Elias? how he maketh intercession to God against Israel,
saying,

3 Lord, they have killed thy prophets, and digged down thine altars; and I
am left alone, and they seek my life.

4 But what saith the answer of God unto him? I have reserved to myself
seven thousand men, who have not bowed the knee to *the image of* Baal.

5 Even so then at this present time also there is a remnant according to the
election of grace.

6 And if by grace, then *is it* no more of works: otherwise grace is no more
grace. But if *it be* of works, then it is no more grace: otherwise work is no more
work.

7 What then? Israel hath not obtained that which he seeketh for; but the
election hath obtained it, and the rest were blinded

8 (According as it is written, God hath given them the spirit of slumber, eyes
that they should not see, and ears that they should not hear;) unto this day.

9 And David saith, Let their table be made a snare, and a trap, and a stumblingblock, and a recompense unto them:

10 Let their eyes be darkened, that they may not see, and bow down their
back alway.

1. *I SAY then, Hath God cast away his people? God forbid. For
I also am an Israelite, of the seed of Abraham, of the tribe of
Benjamin.* Hitherto, when an objection was to be stated, Paul did
not own it as his. But here he states it in his own name. The
import of the question seems to be this: Has God so rejected the
descendants of Abraham as to have among them no genuine children? Are they all outside of the pale of the covenant? This question is answered with an emphatic, No! On *God forbid* see above
on Rom. 3:4. The proof he offers is himself, q. d. I have **not**

527

been rejected by the Lord. He has had mercy on me. I am an illustrious example of his compassion to my nation. Any man, seeing how God has shown mercy to me, a bitter relentless persecutor, need never despair of salvation by grace. And I am an Israelite, not a proselyte to the Jews' religion, but a descendant of Abraham, and it is known to my nation that I am of the tribe of Benjamin. Compare Phil. 3 : 5. My lineage is not denied. It can be proved. So that if there were no case but mine, (blessed be God there are many other converted Jews,) none would have cause to say that God now accepts none but Gentiles. I teach no such doctrine. The hope of salvation is not taken from any Israelite, who will submit to the righteousness of God.

2. *God hath not cast away his people which he foreknew. Wot ye not what the scripture saith of Elias? how he maketh intercession to God against Israel, saying.* On *foreknew,* see above on Rom. 8 : 29, where the same word occurs. The meaning is, God does not change his plans or purposes. He never accepted all the descendants of Abraham, or even of Jacob as in a saving covenant with him. It can be shown that in the history of the Jews, they have often sadly and even generally revolted against God, but even then the Lord did not cast off all. *Wot,* a word now nearly obsolete, for know, in the past tense wist. The phrase to *make intercession against* is unusual. *In respect to* Israel would be a better rendering. It is true the prophet's appeal to God showed a state of things in his judgment utterly desperate and so what he said, so far as it was well founded, was against them. But the preposition is best rendered as above indicated. The prophet's complaint and God's answer can be seen in full in 1 Kings 19 : 9–18. The sad words are :

3. *Lord, they have killed thy prophets, and digged down thine altars ; and I am left alone, and they seek my life.* Elijah lived during the days of that bloody and beastly idolater Ahab, who was egged on by that monster of depravity Jezebel. The worship of Baal was publicly established. The land swarmed with priests of the false religion. The public and solemn worship of Jehovah had ceased. A horrible persecution against the true religion was raging. No man, nor set of men came forward to avow sympathy with Elijah either in his doctrine or in his sufferings. The error of the prophet in his statement was expressed in the words, *I am left alone.* The Hebrew is very strong—And I, I only, am left. This opinion of the prophet was incorrect.

4. *But what saith the answer of God unto him ? I have reserved to myself seven thousand men, who have not bowed the knee to* the image of *Baal.* This verse gives the sense of the original, but is

not taken from the Septuagint, nor is it a literal rendering of the Hebrew, which in the authorized version reads : " Yet I have left me seven thousand in Israel, all the knees which have not bowed unto Baal, and every mouth which hath not kissed him." The pertinence of introducing this matter is to show that even in the darkest days in Israel there were a chosen few who were under the power of the grace of God, and that by the foreordination of God. This is the use the apostle himself makes of it, as we see in the next verse, so that the suspicion that God had so wholly cast off Israel that a Jew could not be saved, was no part of Paul's doctrine, nor was it true.

5. *Even so then at this present time also there is a remnant according to the election of grace.* There were about three thousand Jews converted on the day of Pentecost, Acts 2: 41. Soon after we read that the number of the men, who believed, was about five thousand, Acts 4: 4. Still later we read: " Thou seest, brother, how many thousands of Jews there are which believe," Acts 21 : 20. In this last place the Greek word is not thousands, but myriads or tens of thousands. In most places where churches were planted among the early converts to Christ were many Israelites. So that in Paul's time there were many more of them cleaving to God in Christ, than had remained firm to the true worship of God in the days of Elijah. Some, however, think that *seven thousand* in 1 Kings 19: 18 and here also designates an indefinite though large number. This opinion is not wholly improbable as among the Jews seven was a number of perfection. Yet it is hardly safe to lay much stress upon that point. But when this epistle was written the great mass of the Jewish people stood aloof from the gospel. There was but a *remnant*, a small number, who believed in Jesus. That remnant constituted the body of elect Jews at that time, or was according to the election of grace. All of God's chosen are elected through *grace*, or unmerited favor. No man is chosen of God for any merits he has or ever shall have, but wholly and purely out of undeserved pity. This point the apostle next proves:

6. *And if by grace, then* is it *no more of works : otherwise grace is no more grace. But if* it be *of works, then is it no more grace : otherwise work is no more work,* In the early part of this epistle the apostle in various ways proved the contrariety of works and of grace in justification. Here he declares that election to salvation flows from mere kindness and pity on the part of God, and not at all from good works seen or foreseen. He says that this view must be taken; otherwise we confound grace and work, than which no two things are more opposite. Some drop the latter half of the verse from the text, and it is wanting in several manu-

scripts nor does its omission destroy Paul's argument. But in places considered parallel the apostle brings in both sides of his statement, from Rom. 4 : 4, 5. Peshito, Arabic, Tyndale, Cranmer, Genevan, Beza and Pareus retain both clauses entire.

7. *What then ?   Israel hath not obtained that which he seeketh for ; but the election hath obtained it, and the rest were blinded.   What then ?* the same question, in an abbreviated form, so often asked in this epistle, What shall we say then? What is a fair conclusion from all this?   Here is the answer : Israel, as a nation, has not succeeded in securing the divine favor ; but the election, that is the entire number, the whole mass of elect persons, who had been chosen and called through God's mere mercy, have obtained God's bless-ing.   *And the rest were blinded.*   The general tenor of remark on the hardening of Pharaoh's heart in chapter IX. is applicable to the blinding of Israel.   No doubt they blinded their own eyes and were willingly ignorant of much that they should have known.   But beyond a reasonable doubt there is a reference to a judicial act of God, by which they were blinded.   Indeed the word here ren-dered blinded is three times in the Gospels rendered hardened, Mark 6 : 52 ; 8 : 17 ; John 12 : 40.   The cognate noun is in Mark 3 : 5 rendered hardness.   God does sometimes give men over to blindness, perverseness and obstinacy.   This Paul immediately proceeds to prove :

8. (*According as it is written, God has given them the spirit of slumber, eyes that they should not see, and ears that they should not hear ;*) *unto this day.*   The last three words probably belong not to the parenthesis, but are best connected with v. 7.   The quotations embrace the substance of several places in the Old Testament, Isa. 29 : 10 ; Deut. 29 : 4 ; Isa. 6 : 9, 10.   Parallel passages are found in Jer. 5 : 21 ; Ezek. 12 : 2 ; Matt. 13 : 14, 15 ; John 12 : 39, 40 ; Acts 28 : 26, 27.   Indeed the sum of what is here said is often spoken of Israel, sometimes historically and sometimes prophetically.   There is no safe or satisfactory way of interpreting the verse unless we understand it as containing a curse brought on Israel by their un-belief and obstinacy.   This rejection was therefore just, because it was for their iniquities.   The words quoted are generally plain, being often found and sometimes explained in scripture.

9. *And David saith, Let their table be made a snare, and a trap, and a stumbling-block, and a recompense unto them :*

10. *And let their eyes be darkened, that they may not see, and bow down their back alway.*   This quotation is from Psalm 69 : 22, 23. Theodoret says that Psalm " is a prediction of the sufferings of Christ, and the final destruction of the Jews on that account." There is no doubt that it is highly Messianic and prophetic.   Au-

gustine : " These th.ngs are not said by way of wishing, but, under the form of wishing, by way of prophecy." The quotation is very much made from the Septuagint, but with considerable variations in the first of the two verses. By *table* we may understand the most ordinary and necessary enjoyments. When these are made a snare, a trap, a stumbling-block and a recompense to men, their wretchedness is complete. Olshausen : " Where they least expect it, let the snare of destruction come upon them by way of recompense." The authorized version makes the last clause in Ps. 69 : 22 very elliptical. Paul doubtless gives the sense of it here. To bow down their back alway is the Septuagint version of the Hebrew, make their loins continually to shake. The meaning of the two phrases is the same. Whoever is weak in the loins is fit for no hard service, and is sorely afflicted indeed. How the Jews have as a people been crushed and oppressed both by their sins and the judgments of God all history for eighteen hundred years declares. Paul's object in these quotations is to prove that what has befallen Israel was predicted by their own prophets, both as to the wickedness and the misery of their state ; and therefore their rejection ought to be no ground of offence to a Jew, for his own scriptures record things of the same kind in their history, and predict these very things under the reign of Messias.

DOCTRINAL AND PRACTICAL REMARKS

1. God never casts away his own people, who are his by covenant, vs. 1, 2. All reasonings, which beget the belief that God is slack concerning his promises, or changeable in his purposes, are false. Brown : " God may be avenged on a hypocritical nation, and for their contempt of the gospel may unchurch them, and take the gospel from them, and yet be as good as his word unto any true-hearted seeker of his face in that land." Let no man therefore fear that God will ever forsake one, who puts all his trust in Jehovah.

2. There is no telling, at one view, how many aspects one event may have, or how many truths one conversion may prove. One case, either of severe justice or of great clemency, may marvellously illustrate what a government, human or divine, is in its real nature, v. 1. How many truths are strikingly presented by the great change in the life of Paul. How he stood as a glorious monument of the riches, power, height, depth, length, breadth and sovereignty of divine grace. Though allusions to ourselves should be modest, yet when they are to the glory of God's grace and mercy we may make them. What has brought such matters into

disesteem has been the self-conceit and affectation with which many have spoken of themselves. If a reference to our own case will either settle or illustrate a great truth, let it in all humility be made.

3. God's true church is made up of those whom he hath loved with an everlasting love, v. 2. Compare Jer. 31 : 3. Pool: "By such as are foreknown of God, Paul means those that are elected and predestinated to eternal life." Such doctrine should not disturb us. God is wise and good and almighty. His plans are holy and infallible. Such doctrine is very humbling to the pride and offensive to the enmity of the human heart; but if God teaches it in his word, it is true; it is wise to believe it; it will have a sanctifying power. Why should it not? Hath not God chosen us in Christ, before the foundation of the world, that we should be holy and without blame before him in love? Eph. 1 : 4. Where is the danger of believing every word that God has spoken? Compare Rom. 8 : 29, 30.

4. The same wicked principles are acted out by bad men from age to age, vs. 2, 3. The manner of displaying hatred to God and his people differs somewhat at divers times; but evil men have no devices entirely new. Sometimes it is by scorn, sometimes by ridicule, sometimes by slander, sometimes by hue and cry, sometimes by murderous purposes and practices that sinful men oppose all that is good; but the root of bitterness is always there, till divine grace makes the change.

5. It is a great thing to know the scriptures, and to build all our hopes and all our doctrines upon them. Even inspired men often set us an example in this matter, v. 2. Indeed our Lord himself said to the tempter, It is written, it is written, it is written, just as Paul says here. Many a man is foiled in battle by not knowing the scripture with which to meet the enemy. Nor is any portion of God's word useless to such ends. Brown: "Acquaintance with the state of the church in former ages, recorded in scripture, is very necessary to the people of God, and will tend much to edify and comfort them in their conditions." Many a saint has revived when he found himself where Elisha, or David, or Jeremiah, or Paul had been long before him.

6. It is a great mercy to be kept from a time of persecution, v. 3. When the phrenzied demagogue, the bigoted ecclesiastic, the cunning politician, the furious sectary, the whining hypocrite, the abandoned woman, the potentate and the pauper unite to hunt good men, their lives are, but for the supports of divine grace, intolerable. No public service, no age, no sex, no old friendships, no principle of humanity have any power with men urged on by

the hatred of malice or the heat of bigotry. Brown: "So cruel and insatiable is the rage of the enemies of Christ, that if there were but one remaining to give testimony against their corruptions, they cannot be at rest till that one be made a sacrifice to their beastly savage cruelty."

7. The cries of such suffering ones enter into the ears of the Lord of hosts, and the *answer of God* is sure to come in words or deeds, in mercy or wrath to the wicked, but always in mercy to the righteous, v. 4. None can tell, as the old saint can, how wondrously God comforts such. The prison meditations of the saints form a choice library of practical divinity.

8. There are in every age some good men, perhaps even more than many suppose, v. 4. Evans: "Things are often much better with the church of God than wise and good men think they are. They are ready to conclude hardly, and to give up all for gone, when it is not so." The reason why general defections do not become universal is not that believers are in themselves, or by nature, better than others; but because the Lord *reserves them to himself*, renews, restrains, teaches and supports them in a right way. It is seldom that we escape error when we form estimates of men in the mass. Goodness is often outlawed. No doubt many, who saw Joseph led to the dungeons of Egypt, honestly thought he was a bad man. Chrysostom: "If you do not know who they are that believe, this is no wonder, for that prophet, who was so great and good a man, did not know." Let this be our rejoicing, "The Lord knoweth them that are his." That secures salvation.

9. Oftentimes the chief thing that the people of God can do is to retire from public notice, weep in secret places, or before men evince their godly principles by a refusal to conform to the sinful practices of their times, v. 4. The chief thing that could be done in the days of Elias by his pious countrymen was to refuse to bow the knee to Baal, or to kiss his image. Often "the best evidence of integrity is a freedom from the present prevailing corruptions of the times and places we live in. . . Sober singularity is commonly the badge of true sincerity." Blessed is he, who escapes the contamination of the sins of his age and generation, and refuses to go with a multitude to do evil. The most terrible monster in this world is a blind and furious set of men, given over of God to their malignant passions. No wild beast is so dangerous.

10. In all ages, in all forms and under all names idolatry is an abomination. It digs down altars; it kills God's true ministers, it degrades human nature, it sinks nations into sottishness, vs. 3, 4. All this is illustrated in every form of idolatry ever practised. It was so in the worship of Baal. This seems to have been a name

common to many idols. Brown of Haddington thinks that in the earlier ages it was a name given to the true God. A more probable opinion is that it was derived from Belus, or Bel, the great idol of Chaldea. This among the male deities held the same place as Ashtaroth among the female divinities. Sometimes we have the plural form Baalim, because there were many Baals, or at least many images of Baal. The rites used in the service of these idols were cruel, lewd, bloody and disgusting. From the feminine article found in verse 4, some good scholars, and our translators also, think the word image or statue is to be understood before Baal. If this is not so, there must be a mistake in one letter, or Baal must sometimes be used as a name of a goddess. If men in Christian lands find it so hard to resist a torrent of worldliness, what must it be to stand out against the raging violence of a popular system of devil worship? Hodge: "Those only are safe whom the Lord keeps. Those, who do not bow the knee to the image of Baal, are a remnant according to the election of grace, and not according to the firmness of their own purposes."

11. Nor is it possible for us to have clear and right views of God and of the scriptures unless we have clear and right views of the doctrine of election, of which the scriptures say much, v. 5. Macknight commenting on 2 Pet. 1 : 10 says with an air of great confidence, "How can the election of individuals to eternal life be made more sure than it is by the divine decree?" The answer is that to God nothing is more sure than his own purposes. But when we are exhorted to make our calling and election sure, it is to make them sure to ourselves. We know not the secret purpose of God. We are concerned with present personal duty, not with the hidden counsels of God. Nor can any man be rightly persuaded of his own salvation, except by having grace to perfect holiness in the fear of God. The election of God is sure to prevail. It is mighty. It secures the salvation of all whom it selects, because in its evolutions it brings such to Christ, transforms their natures, and fits them for heaven. This election is of grace, i. e. it is gratuitous. God chooses whom he will, not for their sakes, but for his own name's sake. If any say that this doctrine is a high mystery, so it is. Adoration and praise rather than a bold prying curiosity become us on many a theme of revealed truth. Let us bow in awful submission to his sovereign and adorable will and glorious majesty. Let us not cavil, nor dispute with God.

12. It is a sad mistake when we confound grace and work, human deservings and divine mercies, v. 6. And yet this is no uncommon error among men. Chrysostom: "Why are you

afraid of coming over since you have no works demanded of you?
Why are you bickering and quarrelsome, when grace is before
you, and why keep putting the law forward to no purpose whatever? For you will not be saved by that, and will mar this gift
also; since if you pertinaciously insist on being saved by it you
do away with this grace of God." Why will men set up their
will and wisdom against the counsel of God? If any man is ever
saved it must be by grace from first to last. Slade: "A claim from
works, and grace through faith is incompatible." None can stand
on two foundations so utterly opposite, so immensely remote, as
grace and works. Compare Rom. 4:4, 5; 9:11. If justification
is by grace, of course election is of undeserved kindness. And
so God has all the glory of a sinner's salvation, and boasting is
excluded. Brown: "Whoever expects anything of God for his
works, or by way of merit, quite destroys the nature of grace."

13. God's chosen shall be saved; they shall infallibly be saved,
and obtain what they seek after, glory, honor and eternal life, v. 7.
The gates of hell shall not prevail against them. No weapon
formed against them shall prosper. They shall not be hurt of the
second death. God will be their God for ever and ever. They
enjoy God's special favor, They cannot come short of heavenly
glory without a failure in God's counsel. They were not chosen
for their works. They are not justified by their works. They
overcome not by their own power and holiness. Yet they overcome,
are justified and chosen. They cannot fail of eternal glory because
the Lord changes not.

14. None can be too careful in guarding against the blinding
and hardening effects of sin, v. 7. Insensibility is as alarming a
symptom as ever appears in any case. It is wonderful that multitudes are not terror-stricken by their own stupidity. When a
wounded limb gives no more pain, it is a sign that mortification
has set in. Owen of Thrussington: "The hardening or blinding
spoken of by the prophets is uniformly stated as a punishment for
previous unbelief and impenitence." Nor has God any sorer evil
to inflict. Morison: "Judicial blindness is heaven's frequent
punishment for abused privileges." If anything should awaken
the liveliest interest and stir up all that is within us to the mightiest
activity, it is the vast concern of salvation.

15. It is mournful to think what multitudes seek to enter into
the kingdom of heaven and utterly fail, v. 7. 1. There is a
large class, who do not seek until it is too late. They defer
the whole matter till once the master of the house is risen up and
hath shut to the door. Then their cries are loud and lusty;
but they are too late. The opportunity is gone for ever. Our

Lord clearly warned such of their impending doom, Luke 13 : 24, 25. 2. There is another class, who go to work ignorantly. They know not God, nor Jesus Christ, nor the Holy Ghost. They worship they know not what. They work entirely in the dark. They grope for the wall at noon-day. They are blind and love the instruction that causeth to err. This class is not small. 3. Others seek languidly. Their hearts are not wholly in the matter, as God requires they should be, Jer. 29 : 13. They seek but not by prayer, or any real humiliation. Their every act indicates spiritual sloth. The divine life is a race. They never run. It is a conflict. They never fight. 4. Others have no perseverance in their quest of life. They do not diligently seek God. At times they seem to be in earnest, but soon they turn aside to vanity. Their goodness is like the morning cloud and the early dew. 5. Others never seek the Lord supremely. All the time something else is uppermost in their minds. 6. Others seek proudly. They have a great conceit of themselves. They do not and will not humble themselves under the mighty hand of God. They have none of the spirit of the publican. They are Pharisees. They are self-righteous. They come to God in their own names, not in the name of Christ. But to the humble, the hearty, the diligent, the instructed, who come in the name of Christ, seeking salvation, God always gives a blessing, as he has promised in many places. Compare Matt. 7 : 7; 21 : 22; John 14 : 13; 15 : 16; 16 : 24; Jas. 1 : 6; 4 : 3; Rom. 9 : 31, 32, and parallel passages.

16. It is a dreadful art that some acquire of having eyes and not seeing, of having ears and not hearing, of sleeping on when heaven, earth and hell are making their souls a battle-field, v. 8. Brown: " As there is a natural hardness, stupidity and senselessness, which lieth upon all by nature till grace remove it; so there is an acquired and habitual hardness, which is contracted through a customariness in sinning." When to these God adds the judicial blindness, which he sometimes sends in punishment for contempt of his mercies, men are undone.

17. The scriptures cut off all ground of boasting. No man has anything whereof he may glory before God, vs. 7, 8. When men set themselves against the divine plan of saving sinners, they as terribly provoke God as if they had set themselves against his holy law. Indeed he, who opposes God's method of saving sinners is opposed to both law and gospel. He is all wrong and wholly out of the way. No man sincerely obeys the law, unless he first obeys the gospel.

18 Every religious sentiment held or taught, every doctrine

believed or inculcated, every practice observed or enjoined ought
to have the sanction of the will of God, made known in his word,
either by direct teaching or by fair inference, v. 8.   If *it is written*
in the scripture, that is an end of all dispute.   If it is not written,
no human wisdom or authority can make it binding.   God's word
is the judge of all controversies, the resolver of all doubts, the
only and the unerring rule of faith and practice.

19. When the curse comes, it is neither causeless nor powerless, vs. 9, 10.   To such as provoke his anger and wear out his
patience God says, I will curse your blessings, Mal. 2 : 2.   Then
the sweetest milk at once turns sour, and the best wine becomes
the poison of dragons, the sweetest savors exhale death, and life
itself is continued only to fit the vessels of wrath for the more dire
ruin.   Blessings are blessings only while God makes them so.
When his mercy is withdrawn, all common bounties lose their
power, or vanish away.   Evans: "Of all judgments spiritual
judgments are the sorest, and most to be dreaded, though they
make the least noise."   Let every man beware how he pulls down
vengeance on his own soul.

20. If any are disturbed at the language of apparent imprecation in these verses (9, 10) he is referred for explanation to the
author's "Studies in the Book of Psalms," Introduction § 6.   They
are not imprecations, but predictions of God's righteous retribu-
tions.

21. The state of the Jews is more and more appalling, as well
as instructive from age to age.   In Babylon they suffered for their
sins seventy years; in Egypt over four hundred years; but though
they have never practised any visible form of idolatry since they
were delivered from Babylonish captivity, yet for eighteen centuries they have endured, more than any other people, the displeasure of heaven, and yet there seems to be no end.   Their temple
is gone, sacrifices have ceased, they are scattered and peeled, and
God preserves them a distinct people.   Is there not some great
sin resting at their door?   Is not that sin the rejection of Jesus of
Nazareth as Messiah?   O Israel, blindness hath happened to thee.
Wilt thou rot own thy Redeemer, the Lord Jesus Christ?

Chapter 28

ROMANS 11
VERSES 11–24

THE FALL OF ISRAEL NOT FINAL. IT BROUGHT GOOD TO US GENTILES. WE SHOULD NOT BOAST. ISRAEL SHALL BE RESTORED

11 I say then, Have they stumbled that they should fall ? God forbid : but *rather* through their fall salvation *is come* unto the Gentiles, for to provoke them to jealousy.

12 Now if the fall of them *be* the riches of the world, and the diminishing of them the riches of the Gentiles ; how much more their fulness ?

13 For I speak to you Gentiles, inasmuch as I am the apostle of the Gentiles, I magnify mine office :

14 If by any means I may provoke to emulation *them which are* my flesh, and might save some of them.

15 For if the casting away of them *be* the reconciling of the world, what *shall* the receiving *of them be*, but life from the dead ?

16 For if the first fruit *be* holy, the lump *is* also *holy :* and if the root *be* holy, so *are* the branches.

17 And if some of the branches be broken off, and thou, being a wild olive tree, wert graffed in among them, and with them partakest of the root and fatness of the olive tree ;

18 Boast not against the branches. But if thou boast, thou bearest not the root, but the root thee.

19 Thou wilt say then, The branches were broken off, that I might be graffed in.

20 Well ; because of unbelief they were broken off, and thou standest by faith. Be not high-minded, but fear :

21 For if God spared not the natural branches, *take heed* lest he also spare not thee.

22 Behold therefore the goodness and severity of God : on them which fell, severity ; but toward thee, goodness, if thou continue in *his* goodness : otherwise thou also shalt be cut off.

23 And they also, if they abide not still in unbelief, shall be graffed in : for God is able to graff them in again.

24 For if thou wert cut out of the olive tree which is wild by nature, and wert graffed contrary to nature into a good olive tree ; how much more shall these, which be the natural *branches*, be graffed into their own olive tree ?

11. *I SAY then, Have they stumbled that they should fall?   God forbid: but* rather *through their fall salvation* is come *unto the Gentiles, for to provoke them to jealousy.* *Stumbled,* nowhere else so rendered, but offend, Jas. 2 : 10; 3 : 2; or fall, 2 Pet. 1 : 10. It denotes a failure in duty or in efforts. *Fall* occurs again in v. 22; also in many places. It is very uniformly rendered as here, or fall down. It is applied to the fall of a house, of seed, of a man to worship, of the stars, of a hair, of a city. There is nothing in the word itself that is emphatic. If we take it in its usual signi- fication then Paul's question has this sense: Have they stumbled for no purpose and to no end but for their own ruin? Was there no wise and benevolent design in their fall? This makes good sense, and requires no straining of words. But if we, as many do, contrast stumbling and falling, then the latter is emphatic. Pe- shito: Have they so stumbled as to fall entirely? Cranmer: Have they therfore stombled, that they shuld vtterly fall a waye to- gether? Locke: Have they so stumbled, as to have fallen past recovery? Stuart: Have they stumbled so as utterly to fall? Grotius appeals to Rev. 18 : 2 to show that the word fall may be emphatic. Calvin, Erasmus, Scott, Haldane, Hodge and many others prefer this mode of exposition. Either method pre- sents weighty matter of thought. Each may be easily made to agree with the context. The former is the more obvious. The latter is more generally accepted, and is fully warranted. *God for- bid,* see above on Rom. 3 : 4. It is a strong form of denial. The word *fall* in the second clause of the verse is not cognate to the verb so rendered in the first clause, nor is it elsewhere rendered as here except in v. 12, but fault, offence, trespass.   See Matt. 6 : 14, 15; Rom. 5 : 15–18.   The offence of the Jews resulted in a great good to others.   Persecuting Christians and all preachers of the gospel at Jerusalem drove them out from the old mother church, and they that were scattered abroad went every where preaching the word, but confining their ministrations at first to the Jews. Compare Acts 8 : 4; 11 : 19.   It was not till God gave that great vision to Peter (Acts 10 : 9–18, 26–29) that the door seemed fairly open to preach the gospel to any but Jews.   And often, if not commonly, it was not until the Jews of a city expressed their un- willingness to receive the salvation of God, that its early preach- ers adressed themselves directly to the Gentiles.   Compare Acts 13 : 46; 18 : 6; 28 : 28.   Christ foretold this very thing, Matt. 21 : 43.   In the first of these places Paul says, "It was necessary that the word of God should first have been spoken to you." The ne- cessity here spoken of arose from the prophecies, which required that the word of the Lord should go forth from Jerusalem. The

great body of the Jews rejected the gospel themselves, and were quite averse to its being preached to others, 1 Thess. 2 : 15, 16. The acceptance of the Lord Jesus and his gospel by the Gentiles stirred up the *jealousy* of the Jews. *To provoke to jealousy* is in Greek one word, a verb, so rendered in Rom. 10 : 19; 1 Cor. 10: 22; but in Rom. 11 : 14 it is rendered provoke to emulation. In Rom. 10 : 19 it is commonly taken in a bad sense, as an awakening of the malignant passions, In 1 Cor. 10 : 22 where it is spoken of the Lord it refers to the pursuit of such a course as was suited to excite the just and sore displeasure of God. But in this place (and in v. 14) many take it in a good sense, as awakening a desire to secure, as the Gentiles had done, the blessings of the gospel. Jealousy is commonly the rage of a man or woman; but when a virtuous woman fears she has not the love and confidence of her good husband, then her jealousy may take the direction of unusual zeal and effort to deserve and to win his affections and entire approbation. This is probably the sense of the verb here and in v. 14. But how did the rejection of the gospel by the Jews promote the salvation of the Gentiles? The answer is 1. It gave the preachers of God's word great encouragement to labor among the Gentiles, who were not so utterly prejudiced. 2. It prevented the judaizers in the primitive church from having the power to bring in the law of Moses, as many were disposed to do, and require circumcision etc. to be observed by Gentile converts.

12. *Now if the fall of them* be *the riches of the world, and the diminishing of them the riches of the Gentiles : how much more their fulness. Fall*, as in v. 11. *Riches*, the same in both clauses of the verse, meaning the means of rich blessings. *World*, the word so rendered in Rom. 4 : 13, on which see above. *Diminishing*, it occurs but twice; in the other place rendered *fault*, 1 Cor. 6 : 7. That rendering would suit very well here, expressing the parallelism with fall. But if it is to be taken in opposition to *fullness*, the authorized version may as well be followed, for the word may mean an inferior state or a worse condition. *Fullness*, the common rendering of the Greek word, as the fullness of time, the fullness of God, the fullness of the blessing, Romans 15 : 29; Gal. 4 : 4; Eph. 3 : 19. In verse 25 below it is applied to the Gentiles, as, here it is to the Jews. Three explanations of the word are offered: 1. Some think it means that which fills up the intervening space. It is used in this sense in Matt. 9 : 16; Mark 2 : 21; for that *which is put in to fill up* a rent in a garment. 2. Some think it here means a great multitude, a vast number as 1 Cor. 10: 26, 28; where it means the vast number of things which are on the earth. 3. The best explanation of the word in this connection is that it means all comprehended in the

divine purpose, just as the fullness of time in Gal. 4 : 4 means all
the days embraced in the divine purpose, touching that matter.
So the time had come wherein God had determined to bring his
Son into the world. Thus when all the chosen seed of Jacob
shall be brought in, even the fullness thereof, it will be a blessing
to the Gentiles far greater than the temporary rejection of the
Jews: though even that sad event has been overruled by God and
has become the occasion of rich spiritual advantages to the world.

13. *For I speak to you Gentiles, inasmuch as I am the apostle of the
Gentiles, I magnify mine office.* Paul did not mean to say that he
had no authority or desire to preach the Gospel to his countrymen ; for he did so often. But he meant to say that he had a
special call and charge from God to carry the glad news of salvation to the nations. This was his main work, announced to him
early in his Christian life, revealed afterwards and often asserted
Compare Acts 9 : 15 ; 13 : 2, 3 ; 14 : 26 ; 22 : 21 ; Eph. 3 : 7, 8, ; 1
Tim. 2 : 7 ; 2 Tim. 1 : 11 ; Heb. 5 : 4. Paul here says that his
ministry was specially to the Gentiles, but that did in no wise
hinder the conversion of the Jews. The more Gentiles converted,
the better for well disposed Jews. The bringing in of the Gentiles
proved the divine mission of Jesus Christ, and that in two ways—
1. It showed the gospel to be the power of God unto salvation ; 2.
It fulfilled the predictions of the prophets. The conversion of the
Jews would in like manner have no bad effect on the Gentiles, but
would promote their spiritual interests. So that all animosity
between Jews and Gentiles should cease. They should rejoice at the
conversion of men, whoever they may be. *Magnify*, so rendered no
where else, several times honor, more commonly glorify. We may
exalt an office by commending it, by bestowing just praise upon
it, or by so devoting our energies to the fulfilling of its duties that
it shall become great in fact as well as in the eyes of others.
Office, so rendered here only, sometimes service, more commonly
ministry.

14. *If by any means I may provoke to emulation* them which are
my flesh, and might save some of them. On *provoking to emulation*
see above on v. 11, where the same verb is rendered provoke
to jealousy. *My flesh*, my kindred according to the flesh. All
Paul's labors aimed at the salvation of men, even of the most bitter
opposers ; and though his special call was to labor among the Gentiles, he never forgot to do what he could do for the salvation of
the Jews. The two objects were not hostile to each other. The
salvation of the Gentiles did not obstruct, but promoted the salvation of the Jews ; and the conversion of the Jews would be the
signal for the conversion of all nations.

15. *For if the casting away of them* be *the reconciling of the world,* *what* shall *the receiving* of them be, *but life from the dead?* The word rendered casting away is in Acts 27 : 22 rendered loss. The cognate verb is rendered cast away, Mark 10: 50; Heb. 10: 35. Beyond doubt it refers to that rejection which was neither total nor final, but which for a time gave the Gentiles the greatest prominence in the church. *World,* as in v. 12. *Reconciling,* the word commonly so rendered; it cannot point to *atonement,* as in Rom. 5 : 11 or the cause of reconciliation, but to the means, by which God and the Gentiles were made to be at one. *Receiving,* here only, well rendered. *Life from the dead,* a resurrection, that is a change which like a resurrection imparts life to the dead. This life from the dead is to the Gentiles. And so this verse is but a repetition in other words of what Paul had said in v. 12. From the figure of a resurrection some learn no more than that the conversion of the Jews will be a very joyful event, but there is no objection to including the idea that it will greatly illustrate the power of God in raising up those who were dead in trespasses and sins, and so making them alive unto God. Owen of Thrussington : " The restoration of the Jews unto God's favor will occasion the revival and spread of true religion through the whole world. This is clearly the meaning." Hodge : " The conversion of the Jews will be attended with the most glorious consequences for the whole world." It is but seldom that we meet a prophecy, yet unfulfilled, so clear and unmistakable as this.

16. *For if the first fruit* be *holy, the lump* is *also* holy : *and if the* *root* be *holy, so* are *the branches.* The connection of this with preceding verses is clear. The apostle had spoken of the future conversion of the Jews as an event of great importance and rightly to be expected. He now gives a reason why it was to be expected, viz : God's dealings with that people of old as well as of late. He had made many of their forefathers and in fact many of the then existing generation the subjects of his saving grace. All these were the first fruit, and no more ; the pledge and earnest of what should yet be, for the harvest of the earth should yet be gathered. Stuart and others prefer to make the first fruits refer to the portion of dough (Num. 15 : 20) which was holy unto the Lord. There is no objection to this explanation. It was a first fruit also. In 1 Cor. 5 : 6, 7 ; Gal. 5 : 9 the word rendered *lump* refers to the mass of kneaded and leavened dough. But it may be applied to the bulk of any thing. In Rom. 9 : 2 the mass of fallen men are called a lump. By the *root* some understood the early fathers of the Jewish people, and for proof refer to Paul's own exposition given in subsequent verses, especially in verse 28

where he expressly speaks of the fathers.   But every pious Israelite, whose descendants shall be alive when the latter day glory dawns, may so far be called the holy root of the people then to be gathered in, and made holy, as branches of that pious stock from which they shall have sprung.   Paul's argument is that in the ' piety and grace granted to Jews already God has given a pledge of the future conversion of the body of that people.

17. *And if some of the branches be broken off, and thou, being a wild olive tree, wert graffed in among them, and with them partakest of the root and fatness of the olive tree.*   It is not easy to interpret so highly figurative portions of scripture without over-straining them.   The general conception is clear.   If we would rest satisfied with that, there would be no difficulty.   First, certain branches are broken off—certain Jews for their sins are rejected—being wholly severed from the true church of God, which has its perpetuity in' Christ.   Then, some people, hitherto alien from the commonwealth of Israel, and wholly diverse from it, were brought into union with Christ's church, as if a wild olive were ingrafted into a good olive, and so derived sap and nourishment from it. Tholuck and others have collected some curious testimonies to shew that the law of ingrafting whereby the scion gets only life and nourishment from the stock, but continues to be barren, or productive of only the kind of fruit it had borne before, is in the case of the olive reversed, so that the scion bears the kind of fruit natural to the stock.   Were these testimonies sufficient, then indeed we could hardly press too far the figure of our apostle. But such a remarkable exception to the laws of nature, as evinced in fruit trees all over the world, needs confirmation, before building an interpretation upon it.

18. *Boast not against the branches.   But if thou boast, thou bearest not the root, but the root thee.*   Boast not against the branches, that is the branches that were broken off.   If thou hadst had thy just deserts, thou wouldst have been withered too.   God's sovereign and unmerited favor has made the difference.   The last clause of the verse is elliptical, but the ellipsis is easily supplied.   The word remember after boast would relieve it of all want of conformity to English idiom.

19. *Thou wilt say then, The branches were broken off, that I might be graffed in.*   The fact here stated is indisputable.   But the tone and connection show that it is spoken, or might be spoken in self-conceit.   There is no room for boasting exultation, but much cause for humility, gratitude and godly fear.   It was no goodness in the Gentiles, that caused them to be called and saved.

20. *Well; because of unbelief they were broken off, and thou stand-*

est by faith. Be not high-minded, but fear. Well, equivalent to this,
The fact is as thou hast stated, or It is undeniably so. The same
word is so used in Mark 12 : 32 ; John 13 : 13. Peshito : Very
true. But remember it was not thy superior merit, no, nor thy
merit at all, that caused Israel to be broken off, but only their unbelief in rejecting their own prophets, and above all in rejecting
the Lord Jesus, the Messiah. Thy own *standing,* or continued
membership in God's church, is *by faith,* not by thy own virtues
or merits. By believing in Christ thou confessest that all thy
righteousnesses are as filthy rags, and that but for God's great
love thou wouldest be for ever undone. Therefore *be not high-
minded,* the rendering is literal to an unusual degree. We have
the same verb in 1 Tim. 6 : 17. It means Be not proud, or arrogant ; but *fear.* "Happy is the man that feareth always," Pr. 28 :
14. There is a slavish fear that hath torment ; there is a salutary
fear that is a fountain of life to depart from the snares of death,
1 John 4 : 18 ; Pr. 14 : 27. Compare Heb. 3 : 12 ; 4 : 1, 13 ; 12 : 15
and parallel places.

21. *For if God spared not the natural branches,* take heed *lest he
spare not thee.* The great mass of the Gentile converts in Paul's
day had no pious ancestry to look back upon. Most of them did
not know that there had ever been a prayer lodged for them in
heaven by a pious progenitor. But the Jews could look back for
many long centuries to men whom God had publicly accepted,
and say, These were our forefathers. If the Jews were rejected,
much more may the Gentiles be ; for God's love once settling on
a people is slow to forsake them and seek new objects.

22. *Behold therefore the goodness and severity of God: on them
which fell, severity ; but toward thee, goodness, if thou continue in* hts
goodness : otherwise thou also shalt be cut off. Goodness, the same
word three times in this one verse. We met it in Rom. 2 : 4, on
which see above. Elsewhere it is once rendered gentleness, four
times kindness. It occurs in Paul's epistles only. Peshito and
Locke : benignity ; Tyndale, Cranmer, Genevan and Stuart : kindness ; *severity,* twice in this verse ; nowhere else in the New Testament ; literally a cutting off, then decisiveness, and so severity.
Wiclif : fersness ; Tyndale, Cranmer and Genevan : rigorousness ;
Locke : rigor. *On them which fell, severity,* not harshness, but a
righteous decisiveness, a just, though an awful retribution. Their
sins, especially their unbelief in rejecting Messiah, fully justified
everything God had done. Their rejection was condign. But
to the believing Gentile these acts of sovereignty marked great
goodness even a saving goodness, if he did not abuse it, but by
faith and humility continued in the enjoyment of it. Otherwise

he would be rejected as the Jew had been. *Cut off,* more exactly cut down, or hewn down, as in Matt. 3 : 10; 7 : 19; Luke 3 : 9; 13 : 7, 9. Sin, in particular unbelief will ruin any man, whatever may have been his lineage or his history.

23. *And they also, if they abide not still in unbelief, shall be graffed in : for God is able to graff them in again.* Ever since the days of Paul, whenever an Israelite has given up his wicked unbelief and taken upon him the yoke of Messiah he has been as readily accepted, as any Gentile. And at this day there are living thousands of Israelites, who believe in Jesus and are accepted of God. *Able,* this word is often used to express ability and to suggest readiness to do a thing ; see Rom. 4 : 21 ; 14 : 4 ; 2 Cor. 9 : 8 ; 2 Tim. 1 : 12.

24. *For if thou wert cut out of the olive tree which is wild by nature, and wert graffed contrary to nature into a good olive tree ; how much more shall these, which be the natural branches, be graffed into their own olive tree?* This is a summing up of the argument he had been conducting for several verses. There is no new matter in it. Stuart : " If God had mercy on Gentiles, who were outcasts from his favor and strangers to the covenant of his promise, shall he not have mercy on the people whom he has always distinguished as being peculiarly his own, by the bestowment of many important privileges and advantages upon them ? "

DOCTRINAL AND PRACTICAL REMARKS

1. Ministers should not state the doctrines and facts of the gospel with needless harshness ; but, in announcing the most awful truths and judgments, should show the holy, just and wise ends of God in sending wrath upon any of the race, v. 11. Ministers have a call to answer all fair or reasonable objections to their doctrines, but let them not reprove a scorner. It is useless. It is not fidelity to state any doctrine of scripture so as to give needless offence. The human heart hates the truth very dreadfully and we ought not to present it in a distorted manner.

2. It is amazing wisdom, power and grace that bring good out of evil, salvation to some by the rejection of others, vs. 11, 14.

3. It is a great thing to have ministerial address and so to state things, that if men shall misunderstand or misuse them, the fault shall be theirs, not ours. Chalmers : " One of Paul's maxims was, that, for the sake of the gospel, he should be all things to all men ; and, more especially, that to the Jew he should be as a Jew. No one could practise with greater skill or delicacy than he did, the art of conciliating those whom he addressed—though, of

course, he only carried this so far as truth and principle would let him."

4. Blessed be God, the salvation of one man in no way hinders the salvation of others, v. 11. If sinners of the Gentiles are brought to Christ, let the Jews be stirred up to take hold of the great salvation too. For a long time the Jews retained and preserved the true religion for the benefit of mankind. Now of a long time the Gentiles only, in large numbers, have possessed the true faith for the good of their own posterity, and for the final conversion of the Jews.

5. We have hitherto looked at Paul in various characters. Here we are called to contemplate him as a prophet, vs. 12, 15. Nor is this the only place where he has predicted great events, 2 Thess. 2 : 3–5. His prophetical teachings respecting the resurrection and the judgment-day are also very clear.

6. A facility for direct and earnest personal address to individuals and classes is a great talent, and ought to be earnestly sought after, v. 13 compared with Acts 26 : 2–29 and many other places. Platitudes and generalities impress no one. " Deceit lies in generals." Let us arouse men by the most solemn, direct and tender appeals. When everlasting things depend on our course here, and may depend on a word fitly spoken, let us constantly pray for gifts and graces to make us wise in winning souls.

7. Do we make our office in the church to be respected by men ? do we magnify our calling ? v. 13. Many have a great desire to obtain a high office in the church, and after they get it, they do not honor their office, nor does it honor them. It is better to hold the humblest station and adorn it, than to fill the highest and disgrace it. High station is not essential to extensive usefulness.

8. It is a great honor to be the means of saving even one soul. Paul was willing to use *any means*, if he might *save some*, v. 14. In this matter his judgment and his heart were both right. He is the best fisherman who catches the most fish. He is the best hunter who brings in the most game. He is the wisest preacher who wins the most souls. If all the church of God were animated with a true zeal and a right spirit surely many more souls would be converted. True, the rash, fiery, ignorant zeal of some has brought great reproach on proper efforts to save men's souls; but the folly of a few cannot justify the many in their languor or indifference to the salvation of men.

9. Though the severity of God, when his patience is exhausted, is truly terrible, yet his mercy transcends all names and forms of kindness, vs. 16, 28. Though he visits the iniquities of the fathers

upon the children to the third and fourth generation, yet he shews mercy to thousands of generations of them that love him and keep his commandments.   This is not because of any merit in pious ancestors, but wholly of the constancy of God's love in keeping covenant with his chosen.   Men may with awful and daring wicked-ness renounce the God of their fathers and so bring on themselves swift destruction.   But God never casts off the descendants of those who are in covenant with him till they first reject him.   Nay oftentimes generations of wicked men intervene, and God remem-bers his covenant of old, and so brings back the long lost children, Deut. 7 : 8 ; 10 : 15 ; Acts 2 : 39.

10. None, whether Jew or Gentile, have in themselves anything whereof to glory, vs. 17, 18.   Calvin: " The Gentiles could not contend with the Jews respecting the excellency of their race without contending with Abraham himself; which would have been extremely unbecoming, since he was like a root by which they were borne and nourished.   As unreasonable as it would be for the branches to boast against the root, so unreasonable would it have been for the Gentiles to glory against the Jews."   We ought to take great pains to cultivate right views of our sinful and helpless estate and never fail to remember that if there is any dif-ference between us and others it is entirely owing to the rich and unmerited favor of God bestowed in a manner wholly sov-ereign.

11. The church of God is one and not many.   She is the same in all ages and under all dispensations, vs. 17–24.   We have the same true old olive stock from Adam to the end of the world. Various indeed are her aspects and the degrees of lustre with which she shines ; but she is still the same.   Christ never had but one spouse and she was his beloved.   Uniformity is not unity nor is it essential thereto.

12. Unbelief is a dreadful sin in all its aspects and in all its con-sequences, vs. 19, 20.   It has been the bane of every good thing since the world began.   It was an element in the sin of our first parents.   It unchurched the Jewish nation and is now bringing swift destruction on great multitudes.   No plausible profession, no decent exterior, no fair morality, no costly ritual can ever save a poor soul on which unbelief has taken fast hold.   It is easy for men to be excessively afraid of poverty, of reproach or of bodily pain; but no man was ever too much afraid of unbelief.

13. No exhortation that God has ever given is more uniformly seasonable to men in every situation of life than that deduced by Paul from God's dealings with the Jews : *Be not high-minded, but fear*, v. 20.   The fear here commended is not the terror of dismay,

nor the offspring of unbelief, but that pious self-distrust which results from the knowledge of ourselves and of the Most High. Chrysostom : " The thing is not matter of nature, but of belief and unbelief. . . Haughtiness genders a contempt and listlessness." Brown : " Pride and haughtiness of spirit is altogether unbeseeming any who profess faith in Jesus Christ ; and yet the greater their profession be, if there be not a true and lively faith at the root, the greater will the pride of their heart be."

14. Very glorious and awful is the sovereignty of God in providing no glad tidings of great joy for fallen angels, but in making known a way of life to perishing men : and not to all men at once, but as he has seen fit to one nation and not another : sometimes exercising the awful prerogative of taking the truth from one people, who long have known it, and giving it to another, who had known it not, vs. 17–21. Pool : " If God proceeded with so much severity against his ancient people the Jews, you Gentiles may in reason expect as great severity, if you take not heed to yourselves, and to your standing."

15. How marvellously both in his word and in his ways hath God displayed both goodness and severity, setting one over against the other in such a way that none need despair, and none may presume, v. 22. O, how terrible is that severity ! How immense and adorable is that goodness ! But how amazingly is that severity outstripped by the goodness. Theodoret : " For if, whilst the majority disbelieved, such of them as did believe conveyed to the Gentiles the riches of the knowledge of God, it is clear, that supposing all to have believed, they would have become the authors of still greater blessings to the whole human race. For all would have more readily believed, if they, in place of denying, had preached the truth along with us."

16. No beginnings in a religious way whether among persons or communities, however bright and promising they may be, can at all supersede the necessity of persevering in faith and uprightness, v. 22. Chrysostom : " For the blessings now yours will not continue immovably so, if you are careless and indolent, just as little as their evils will to them, if they reform. For thou also, he says, shalt be cut off, unless thou continuest in the faith." Hodge : " The security of every individual Christian is suspended on his continuing in faith and holy obedience ; which is indeed rendered certain by the purpose and promise of God."

17. If ministers of the Gospel would be faithful to the souls committed to their charge, and save them from supineness and despair, they must present both rousing and consolatory truths, v. 22. It is no easy work rightly to divide the word of truth and

give to each his portion in due season. If men are not soundly troubled it is probable they will not be soundly converted. If all religious experience is of a highly cheerful character, there will pretty certainly be a lack of sobriety and humility. If we have no acquaintance with the depths to which we have sunk, it will not be easy for us to estimate the heights to which divine grace can raise us. He that humbleth himself shall be exalted.

18. It is great, yea it is infinite grace that seeks wanderers from the path of duty and brings them home to God and gives them good hope through grace, and raises them to the full and everlasting enjoyment of God in heaven, v. 23.

19. It would mightily strengthen the faith of all God's people if they would look back and survey the course of Providence towards ancient believers and nations, v. 24. Not a page of the history of God's Providence but teaches some truth instructive and salutary. Blessed is he that learns the lessons thus taught him.

20. What an amazing study is presented to us in the history of the Jews from the calling of Abraham to this day, vs. 11–24. What infinite kindnesses have been showered upon them ! What strange reverses in their national state ! How bright their star has sometimes shone ! Again, how dismal their prospects have been? Doddridge: "Let us cherish the most benevolent and tender disposition towards the house of Israel, to whose spiritual privileges we are raised ; and let us earnestly pray that they may be awakened to emulation ; especially as their fullness is to be the riches of the Gentiles, and the receiving them again, as life from the dead to the languishing and decayed church." Why is it that Jewish ' hopes of the Messiah on whom they still calculate as a Prince and Deliverer yet to come, other than Jesus Christ the only Son of God, do not every year become more languid and as all the periods of their computation run out, do not finally expire?' Oh that it might once be. This wonderful people shall yet in a body bow their necks and own Messiah ; for the mouth of the Lord hath spoken it by many prophets ; by Paul in particular in this chapter. It has brought no blessing on the Gentiles that they have despised and persecuted the Jews. Let all good men be kind to them, and compassionate their sad condition, and pray that their eyes may be opened. This great event is so abundantly predicted that no sober interpretation of prophecy will allow us to expect any thing less. Whether the Jews shall return to Palestine, and there form a body politic and a national church, is a matter, concerning which there is a wide difference of opinion, which will probably continue till the event shall decide the mat-

ter.   But it is impossible to believe the prophets, and not expect the conversion of this people to Christ.   It shall surely be.

> " The wandering sons of Heber, purged from dross,
>   With loud laments shall cluster round the cross ;
>   In deep and willing penitence bow down,
>   And to their Messiah yield the crown—
>   And o'er the joyful hills of Palestine
>   The holy light of God again shall shine."

Let Christians never cease to pray that Jewish prejudice may speedily give place to Christian hope, and peace in believing on Jesus.

Chapter 29

ROMANS 11
VERSES 25-36

SAME SUBJECT CONTINUED. ISRAEL SHALL YET BE SAVED. GOD'S PURPOSES FIXED AND HIS WAYS INSCRUTABLE.

25 For I would not, brethren, that ye should be ignorant of this mystery, lest ye should be wise in your own conceits, that blindness in part is happened to Israel, until the fulness of the Gentiles be come in.

26 And so all Israel shall be saved: as it is written, There shall come out of Sion the Deliverer, and shall turn away ungodliness from Jacob:

27 For this is my covenant unto them, when I shall take away their sins.

28 As concerning the gospel, *they are* enemies for your sakes: but as touching the election, *they are* beloved for the fathers' sakes.

29 For the gifts and calling of God *are* without repentance.

30 For as ye in times past have not believed God, yet have now obtained mercy through their unbelief:

31 Even so have these also now not believed, that through your mercy they also may obtain mercy.

32 For God hath concluded them all in unbelief, that he might have mercy upon all.

33 O the depth of the riches both of the wisdom and knowledge of God! how unsearchable *are* his judgments, and his ways past finding out!

34 For who hath known the mind of the Lord? or who hath been his counsellor?

35 Or who hath first given to him, and it shall be recompensed unto him again?

36 For of him, and through him, and to him *are* all things: to whom *be* glory for ever. Amen.

25. *FOR I would not, brethren, that ye should be ignorant of this mystery, lest ye should be wise in your own conceits, that blindness in part is happened to Israel, until the fulness of the Gentiles be come in.* Mystery, a word that occurs nearly thirty times in the New Testament and in the authorized version is rendered with

551

entire uniformity.　In this place it seems to mean something wrapped in obscurity but capable of explanation.　The rejection of the Jews was an awfully dark event, displaying in a manner suited to humble every man the severity and sovereignty of God. But it is capable of being understood, and it is so instructive that Paul would not have the Gentile converts ignorant of the lessons it teaches.　When understood aright, it is very well suited to take the self-conceit out of men, and it contains an awful warning against unbelief.　The *blindness* here spoken of is the same as that mentioned in v. 7.　The noun here is cognate to the verb there. This blindness was not to all Israel but only to a part.　In Mark 3 : 5 the same word is rendered hardness.　*Fulness*, see above on v. 12.　It seems to have the same meaning here as there.　It will not do to give it the sense of the mass or great body of the Gentiles; for verses 12, 15 clearly assert, as nearly all admit, that the conversion of the Israelites is the precursor of the conversion of all nations; so that the Gentiles brought into Christ's kingdom after the Jews shall generally turn to God will be far more numerous than before, and the great change in Israelites will be life from the dead to other nations.　The fulness of the Gentiles then means the whole number determined on by God, who were to live before the conversion of the Jews.　The learned reader is aware that this verse has been the battle field, where the great controversy of the XVI and XVII centuries respecting Millenarianism was conducted.　The Millenarians generally took the ground that the passage with the context contains a prediction of the future and general conversion of the Jews.　In this they were so far right, though they pressed this matter into wrong uses.　Their opponents took opposite ground, contending that all that was predicted was that the door of mercy should still be kept open to the Jews and that many of them should return.　Those, who wish to get a view of the course of the controversy, may consult Buddaeus.　Hodge has given a very good summary of the argument in favor of the correct interpretation.　Indeed the whole context seems conclusive.

26. *And so all Israel shall be saved: as it is written, There shall come out of Sion a Deliverer, and shall turn away ungodliness from Jacob:*

27. *For this is my covenant unto them, when I shall take away their sins.*

These verses contain a quotation from Isa. 59 : 20, 21, a very remarkable prophecy respecting the kingdom of Christ, and particularly its establishment among the descendants of Jacob.　It was exactly pertinent to the matter in hand.　Paul was proving

that the dark cloud which was hanging over the Jewish people
should, in God's own time, be dispersed, and that all Israel should
be saved. He cites proof from a prophet whom all received as
speaking by inspiration of God. There is a difference as to the
meaning of 'all Israel.' Calvin extends it to all the people of
God. If this be the correct view, we may understand the "all"
in an absolute sense. Then 'all Israel' in this verse embraces all
believers, whatever their lineage and nationality may be and that
to the end of time. "All are not Israel, which are of Israel."
"He is a Jew, which is one inwardly," Rom. 2 : 29 ; 9 : 6.   The
other view makes 'all Israel' to mean the mass of the Jewish
nation. In that case the word all must be taken in no absolute
sense, as it simply designates the great body of Jacob's descendants, who shall be living when the Jews shall turn to the Lord and
accept their Messiah. This is pretty certainly the correct view
of the passage. The quotation is chiefly in the very words of the
Septuagint, omitting one or two particles, and in v. 27 Paul quotes
with a slight change from the Septuagint the words " when I shall
take away their sins," as found in Isa. 27 : 9.   Some however think
that a part of the quotation is made to conform to Ps. 14 : 7.   The
main point is that Paul gives the sense of the prophet, when he
predicts the conversion of the Jewish people, as a body ; a conversion that should be by a kinsman-Redeemer, whose blessed
work should have the effect of removing both guilt and depravity,
sin and *ungodliness*, and that by a *covenant*, ordered in all things
and sure.

28. *As concerning the gospel* they are *enemies for your sakes ; but
as touching the election*, they are *beloved for the fathers' sakes.   As
concerning the gospel* means that so far as the gospel now preached
is concerned. *Enemies*, hostile in fact, or treated as enemies. Both
senses correspond with facts ; but the latter best suits the argument, for enemies in this clause is in antithesis to beloved in the
latter. And as they shall be brought home as the *beloved* of God,
so now are they, for their sins, treated as *enemies*. *For your sakes*,
that is to your advantage, or that the gospel might have free course
among you. The same idea is presented in vs. 12, 15. *Election*,
must be taken either for the gracious choice of God as in v. 5, or
for the body of those chosen, as in v. 7. In either way we finally
reach the same truths. The last clause of this verse presents the
same idea as that in v. 16.

29. *For the gifts and calling of God* are *without repentance*.
Gifts, a word applied to spiritual gifts, or miraculous bestowments,
and also to the saving benefits conferred by God, see Rom. 5 : 15,
16 ; 6 : 23. *Calling*, see above on *called*, Rom. 1 : 1, 6, 7 ; 8 : 28.

God granted many promises and benefits to the Jews. He called Abraham and addressed a great part of scripture to his descendants : he selected them out of all nations to be in the matter of his worship the most prominent and the most renowned nation in the world. In making and renewing his covenant with their fathers he declared it should have a long course to run, terminating only with time, Gen. 17 : 7; Ps. 105 : 8–11. The Lord is not slack concerning his promise. His counsel it shall stand. He has no *regrets* for anything he ever said or did. He is of one mind, and who can turn him? The word rendered *without repentance* indicates the absence of all change of purpose. God will yet do for Jacob's descendants all he ever promised and that in a very glorious manner. Peshito : God is not changeable in his free gift and calling.

30. *For as ye in times past have not believed God, yet have now obtained mercy through their unbelief :*

31. *Even so have these also now not believed, that through your mercy they also may obtain mercy.* Paul is still illustrating and explaining the great enigma of God's dealings with the Jews, in their rejection that he might bring in the Gentiles, and the conversion of many Gentiles as leading to the final conversion of the Jewish nation. Formerly those, who were now Gentile Christians, were atheists and infidels, were without God in the world, and unbelievers. But when the Jews rejected Messiah, God rejected them, and opened a wide and effectual door of mercy to the Gentiles. All this was occasioned by Jewish unbelief. Peshito renders v. 31 thus : So also are they now disobedient to the mercy which is upon you, that there may be mercy on them likewise. But the authorized version is better, because it more exactly gives the sense. The rejection of the Jews was the occasion of salvation coming to the Gentiles. So the mercy received by the Gentiles in their sound conversion shall ultimately lead to the salvation of the Jews. Abraham and his descendants were the depositories of the truth for long centuries till the kingdom of God came. Then the Gentiles became the conservators of the truth, and shall so continue till the Jews shall own Messiah.

32. *For God hath concluded them all in unbelief, that he might have mercy upon all.* Peshito : For God hath shut up all men in disobedience, that upon all men he might have mercy ; Tyndale and Cranmer : God hath wrapped all nacyons in unbeleve, that he might have mercie on all. *Concluded,* so rendered in Gal. 3 : 22 : but in Gal. 3 : 23 shut up. It is also found in Luke 5 : 6 and is rendered inclosed, meaning caught in a net. So all men, in a state of nature and left to themselves, are caught, are inclosed in a net

of unbelief,—a sin so offensive to God that if in every case he were
to punish it with final rejection his procedure would be just. So
then if any, Jew or Gentile, shall be saved, it will, it must be
wholly through mercy. *That he might have mercy upon all,* that is,
upon all without discrimination, whether Jews or Gentiles; not
upon all without exception; for then all would actually be saved.
But all who are saved are saved by *mercy*—by mere grace, by
the unmerited pity of God, by unbought love.

33. *O the depth of the riches both of the wisdom and knowledge of
God! how unsearchable are his judgments, and his ways past finding
out!* No language contains a better rendering of this verse than
that given above, though Stuart's is very good: O the boundless
riches and wisdom and knowledge of God! How unsearchable
are his counsels, and his ways past finding out! God's knowledge
is his perfect intelligence of all that ever is, ever was, or ever shall
be, and of all that could now be, or could heretofore have been, or
could hereafter be on any conceivable supposition. His wisdom,
being infinite leads him to choose good and proper ends, also fit
and appropriate means to accomplish his ends. *Judgments*, decisions, whether punitive or gracious. *Ways*, acts done in execution of his decisions. Adoring humility cannot better express its
pious wonder and warm gratitude than in such strains as are here
found. Passages somewhat parallel but not so full as this may be
found in Job 11: 7–9; Ps. 36: 6; 92: 5; 97: 2; Eph. 3: 17–19;
Col. 1: 27. The key to the exposition of this and the remaining
verses of this chapter is that they are the conclusion of the
argument which the apostle has been conducting from the
17th verse of the first chapter of this epistle to the close of the
32d verse of this chapter. The close logical connection of all
these great and vital truths terminating with that of the glorious sovereignty of God must be manifest to every devout and
intelligent student of God's word, and is fitly brought to an end
by an outburst of admiring and adoring gratitude. The things
thus presented are too deep to be sounded by the line of human
reason.

34. *For who hath known the mind of the Lord? or who hath been
his counsellor?* These clauses do not seem to be a formal quotation, and yet they are in spirit and form so much like two other
passages of scripture that one is ready to think that one or both of
them must have been before the mind of the apostle. These passages are Isa. 40: 13; Jer. 23: 18. The ideas presented in this
verse are thrown into the shape of a challenge; and the worm that
would sit in judgment on his maker's decisions and doings is
asked if he or any of his race has ever been admitted to read the

secret plans of the Almighty, or if he belongs to the privy council
of the King of kings.

35. *Or who hath first given to him and it shall be recompensed unto
him again?*   Where is the creature who has ever brought his Creator under any obligation?   Where is the man to whom his
Maker is a debtor?   Men, even if they were perfect in all things,
would but give to God his dues.   No creature can supererogate.
When he has done all that was commanded him, he has merely
done his duty, and so is an unprofitable servant, Luke 17 : 10.

36. *For of him, and through him, and to him* are *all things: to
whom* be *glory for ever.   Amen.*   All things are *of him.*   If they
are creatures, he made them ; if they are events, he ordered them ;
if they are causes, he overrules them ; if they are great, he is infinitely greater ; if they are minute, they cannot escape his notice
or his power.   All things are *through him,* through his power,
wisdom, justice or goodness.   Nothing comes through any power
or wisdom that are not subject to his control.   And all things are
to him and for him.   For his pleasure and to show forth his glory
all worlds and creatures were made, all causes are controlled, all
events shaped, and all things tend.   To him be *glory,* honor,
praise, thanksgiving, majesty and salvation *for ever*—to the ages
of eternity.   *Amen.*   So let it be, and let all creatures say so.

DOCTRINAL AND PRACTICAL REMARKS

1. How insidious is self-conceit!   It perverts everything, and
makes the most precious gifts of God the means of promoting
undue estimates of our own wisdom, v. 25.   How easy it is to turn
the grace of God into lasciviousness, and from the abundance of
the divine mercies to gather fuel for pride.   Hence it is obligatory
on ministers of the gospel in stating precious truths to guard them
against abuse, as Paul does here.   Haldane : " What marvellous
ignorance, folly and vanity are often displayed even in God's
people.   Nothing but the constant lessons of the Spirit of God
will teach them that all spiritual difference among men is by God's
grace."

2. Let us watch and pray most fervently against that awful
curse—*blindness,* v. 25.   Let the Lord send poverty, war, pestilence,
famine, earthquakes, anything that brings merely natural evils upon
us, but let him never in judicial wrath draw the veil of blindness
over our heart.   No curses are so killing as spiritual curses.   No
judgments are so terrible as spiritual judgments.   Nor is the judicial insensibility of men a whit the less dreadful, but even the more

to be deprecated, because it is so deep as to be unmoved by any consideration drawn from heaven or earth.

3. Though blindness has happened to Israel in part, yet not to all Israel, v. 25. The Lord knoweth them that are his, and he will save them by his grace.

4. Our great *Deliverer* is in all respects what we should wish him to be, v. 26. He is our kinsman, and his power to destroy ungodliness is supreme. He has never failed to put away transgression in any case he has undertaken. Nothing is too hard for him. He has put to flight every power ever raised against him. His resources are infinite. He shall not fail nor be discouraged. If he could not save from sin, from its power as well as from its guilt, he would not meet our wants at all.

5. All God does for us in the way of salvation, he does by a plan, a constitution, a *covenant*, v. 27. This covenant is ordered in all things and sure. There are no flaws in it, no errors or mistakes in it. It is all right, all certain. Infinite wisdom has guarded everything respecting it. It is a great thing to be within the pale of this covenant, Deut. 7 : 9. And it is one of the most fearful acts, that men can perform, to disown it and the God who established it. And it is a chief mercy to be brought within its pale. Brown : " All mankind now, since the fall, being naturally enemies to God, and out of his favor and friendship, are in a most wild and forlorn condition, till he take them within the compass of the covenant." All the sure mercies made over to believers are provisions of this covenant.

6. God overrules everything, even the unbelief of men, to his glory, and sometimes even to the good of men, vs. 28–30. If one won't, another will. If the Jews refuse to hear the apostles, God will send them to the Gentiles. If some are blinded, others have their eyes opened.

7. The manner in which God's love lingers about a city or a people, to whom it has flowed forth, is most wonderful, vs. 28–31. The Bible abounds in facts, appeals and expostulations, which show how unspeakably undesirable in God's esteem are the apostasy and ruin of any, at whose door mercy has once stood, offering her treasures of infinite riches. We have no finer specimens of expostulation and entreaty than are found in God's word on this very subject. Let the reader examine Ps. 81 : 13–16; Jer. 31 : 18–21; Hos. 11 : 8, 9; Luke 19 : 42, and judge if he ever saw more tender appeals, or words better suited to express divine compassion towards those, who seemed bent on their own ruin.

8. Let not any people, now in the enjoyment of the gospel,

imagine that God saw anything meritorious in them or in their ancestors to cause them to be called to the knowledge of his dear Son, vs. 30–32. The same is indeed true of all nations and people. Israel was not allowed to forget that a Syrian ready to perish was their ancestor. Men cannot merit anything before God. They cannot oblige God to anything. His choice and his acts are all free.

9. What a marvellous grace is faith! vs. 30, 31. It is not native to any human heart. It is an exotic in this world, and yet it is constantly accomplishing the greatest wonders. It has reared all the monuments ever intentionally erected to the glory of God in this dark world. It has reclaimed apostate men and nations, and brought them home to the bosom of God. It has performed more wonders than all martial songs and orations of ancient or modern heroism. And yet it is always modest, humble, making its boast in God, and not in man ; abasing the creature and exalting Jehovah. It is the gift of God. It is one of his best gifts. Lord, increase our faith.

10. If God overrules sin in general and unbelief in particular to the glory of his name and the promotion of his cause, how much more may we expect him to make piety and faith conducive to the same high ends, v. 31. They are naturally suited to produce these blessed results.

11. Hodge : " The web of Providence is wonderfully woven. Good and evil are made with equal certainty, under the government of infinite wisdom and benevolence, to result in the promotion of God's gracious and glorious design, v. 31."

12. As all men are by nature lost and perishing, out of the way and far from righteousness, and this uniformly until divine grace makes a change, therefore humility becomes every man ; for we are all concluded in unbelief, v. 32. Calvin : " Paul intends here to teach two things—that there is nothing in any man why he should be preferred to others, apart from the mere favor of God ; and that God, in the dispensation of his grace, is under no restraint that he should not grant it to whom he pleases." If at any time God's word seems sharp and cutting, severe and condemnatory, let us not find fault with the blessed word, but only with ourselves ; knowing that when God concludes us in unbelief and makes us feel our sad case it is often a sign that he is about to have mercy upon us. Know every one the plague of his own heart.

13. Though God's nature and ways are sadly misunderstood and misrepresented here upon earth, and though the great mass of men utterly renounce him and his blessing, yet both·he and his ways are fit objects of the highest admiration, v. 33. None but the

unwise will be offended at the inscrutableness of any of the divine
proceedings. There is more wisdom in some ignorance than there
is in some knowledge. When the unsearchable things of God are
for a study, it is not only more pious, but it is more philosophical
to stand and cry ' O, the depth !' than to say, ' We are the people
and wisdom will die with us.' Cobbin: "If we look at God's
general dealings in the world and in the church, and if our minds
are enlightened by divine grace, we shall see much to confound
our feeble wisdom, and to call forth our humility, gratitude, wonder and praise. Ourselves, as the subject of mercy, will ever be
an enigma we must be unable to solve." There is a difference
among writers respecting the extent to which the apostle would
have us look back, when he cries, ' O the depth !' etc.; but the
soundest and safest way is to let the scope reach to the first and to
all the intermediate truths of this epistle. For what is there in
any part of the doctrine of salvation by a Redeemer that is not
suited to confound human wisdom ? Stuart, having completed his
Commentary on the first eight chapters of this epistle, says, "With
the eighth chapter concludes what may be appropriately termed
the *doctrinal* part of our epistle." But when he has given us his
views on three chapters more he corrects himself by saying, "Such
is the conclusion of the *doctrinal* part of our epistle ; a powerful
expression of profound wonder, reverence and adoration, in regard to the unsearchable ways of God in his dealings with men ;
and an assertion of the highest intensity, respecting his sovereign
right to control all things so as to accomplish his own designs, inasmuch as all spring from him, live and move and have their being
in him, and are for his glory. A doctrine truly humbling to the
proud and towering hopes and claims of self-justifying men ; a
stumbling-block to haughty Jews, and foolishness to unhumbled
Greeks. I scarcely know of anything in the whole Bible, which
strikes deeper at the root of human pride than vs. 33–36." It is a
great thing to have a heart solemnly affected with divine things
so as to gaze, admire, and adore where we can do nothing else.
Brown : "When a soul once is graciously exercised with the apprehensions of the perfections of the Most High, and is dwelling
upon the spiritual thoughts of his excellency in his works and dispensations, he becomes so ravished with the sights he wins to,
that, as a man transported, he cannot get words, whereby to express his thoughts and conceptions." It is a great comfort that
our duty does not require us to comprehend Jehovah in all his
unsearchableness. We must know and we must do our duty ; but
we are not called to sway the sceptre of universal dominion.

14. Let us avoid all curious and presumptuous prying into the

secrets of the Most High. That God's nature and ways are a depth any one may see ; but how great a depth they are, none can see. When men think or speak as if they had been the counsellors, or as if, had they been consulted, they could have arranged things better than we find them to be, they are simply stark fools, v. 34.

15. Let us never forget that we have given nothing to God demanding any recompense, v. 35. What God has done for us, he has done out of his own infinite resources. No man receives any good thing at the hand of God, or can without lying say, This have I procured by my own merits.

16. As God is in his nature glorious, so in the end shall he in all things be glorified, v. 36. Pool: " All things are of him, as the efficient cause; through him, as the disposing cause; to him, as the final cause. They are of him, without any other motive ; through him, without any assistance; and to him, without any other end." Calvin: "The whole order of nature would be strangely subverted, were not God, who is the beginning of all things, the end also." Doddridge: "Oh, that it may be our eternal employment to render adoration, and blessing, and glory to him." Amen.

Chapter 30

ROMANS 12
VERSES 1–8

A SOLEMN CALL TO DUTY AND APPLICATION OF DIVINE TRUTH

I BESEECH you therefore, brethren, by the mercies of God, that ye present your bodies a living sacrifice, holy, acceptable unto God, *which is* your reasonable service.

2 And be not conformed to this world : but be ye transformed by the renewing of your mind, that ye may prove what *is* that good, and acceptable, and perfect will of God.

3 For I say, through the grace given unto me, to every man that is among you, not to think *of himself* more highly than he ought to think ; but to think soberly, according as God hath dealt to every man the measure of faith.

4 For as we have many members in one body, and all members have not the same office :

5 So we, *being* many, are one body in Christ, and every one members one of another.

6 Having then gifts differing according to the grace that is given to us, whether prophecy, *let us prophesy* according to the proportion of faith ;

7 Or ministry, *let us wait* on *our* ministering ; or he that teacheth, on teaching ;

8 Or he that exhorteth, on exhortation : he that giveth, *let him do it* with simplicity ; he that ruleth, with diligence ; he that sheweth mercy, with cheerfulness.

1. *I BESEECH you therefore, brethren, by the mercies of God, that ye present your bodies a living sacrifice, holy, acceptable unto God,* which is *your reasonable service. Therefore* marks the logical connection of this verse with all the preceding argument. Well guarded as the doctrines of the epistle have been, the apostle would further show their intimate connection with holy living. *Beseech,* in v. 8 and elsewhere rendered exhort ; in 1 Cor. 4 : 13 and often, intreat ; cognate to the noun rendered Comforter. In such

a connection as this, our translators very properly render it beseech. No word better expresses the earnestness and tenderness of entreaty. *By the mercies of God,* not merely by the infinite kindness known to dwell in the divine bosom, but by all the amazing mercies manifested in your election, calling, justification, adoption, sanctification, redemption and glorification, as already stated. Uniting this clause with the word beseech, the appeal rises to the highest kind of obtestation. *Brethren,* some would restrict the address to Gentile converts; but for this there is no reason. We ought to understand all members of the Christian church, of which he has been speaking, and not Jewish or Gentile converts exclusively. His argument has been to all of both classes. *Present,* in Rom. 6: 13, 19 thrice rendered *yield ;* but this context requires the rendering of the authorized version, as the figure is that of making oblations. By bodies some understand corporeal natures ; others, corporeal natures as put by synecdoche for the entire natures ; others, simply yourselves. That the word is sometimes used for the whole man is evident from several places of scripture. See Rom. 6 : 12, 13 and like passages. Between the second and third explanations there is no substantial difference. Paul beseeches them to present their entire natures a *sacrifice,* a word not found elsewhere in this epistle, but often in the New Testament, and uniformly rendered. This sacrifice is to be *living,* not dead. That which was lame, or torn, or sick, and so partly dead was not to be offered to God. Nor were they to be killed as were sheep and oxen, but living sacrifices. The offering was also to be *holy,* not polluted with any known and allowed sin; and wholly devoted, consecrated to God. The lamb or bullock offered under the law must be without blemish, disease, or defect, Ex. 12 : 5 ; Lev. 1 : 10; Deut. 15 : 21. The sacrifice must also be *acceptable unto God.* The word rendered acceptable means pleasing or well pleasing, Phil. 4 : 18; Col. 3 : 20; Heb. 11 : 5 ; 13 : 21. In order that any offering might be pleasing to God, it must first be something required by God ; it must be made in love, in holy fear, and in living faith, and with a just sense of one's unworthiness. All this is declared to be your reasonable service. Three explanations are given to the term reasonable. 1. Some think it means agreeable to reason. Whatever God requires of us is rightfully and most properly demanded. He has never asked more than his due. As a Father, we should honor him ; as a Master, we should fear him, Mal. 1 : 6. 2. By reasonable some understand spiritual. It is doubtful whether the word will bear this construction. 3. By reasonable others understand agreeable to the word of God. The word rendered reasonable is found only here and in 1 Pet. 2 : 2—

the sincere milk *of the word*. This is the best explanation. Every-where in the Scriptures God demands that we love and serve him with all our powers and faculties, with all our minds, and soul, and heart, and strength.

2. *And be not conformed to this world: but be ye transformed by the renewing of your mind, that ye may prove what* is *that good, and acceptable, and perfect will of God. Be conformed*, found also in 1 Pet. 1 : 14 fashioning according to. Tyndale: Fassion not youreselves lyke vnto this worlde. There is no better rendering than that of the authorized version. Be not conformed to the corrupt maxims, principles, customs and practices of this *age*. Mankind are apostate from God, they are without God in the world, enemies to God by wicked works, haters of God. Why should we fashion ourselves after them? *Be transformed*, the same word is in Matt. 17 : 2; Mark 9 : 2 rendered was transfigured, and in 2 Cor. 3 : 18 are changed: "We all, with open face beholding as in a glass the glory of the Lord, are changed into the same image from glory to glory, even as by the Spirit of the Lord." The change we are called upon to make in our character and course of life will make us morally and spiritually as diverse from what we were by nature as was the appearance of Jesus Christ when transfigured, from that of his ordinary life. This transforma-tion however is not in apparel, nor in sanctimonious grimace, nor in voluntary humility, nor in anything merely external, but is effected by the *renewing of the mind;* Tyndale: "By the renuynge of youre wittes;" Peshito: "By the renovation of your minds;" Doway: "In the newness of your mind." The same word occurs in Titus 3 : 5, and is rendered as here. In Heb. 6 : 6 the cognate verb is rendered renew. There is no better rendering, it is literal. Prove, also rendered try, allow, approve, examine, like and discern, 1 John 4 : 1; 1 Thess. 2 : 4; Phil. 1 : 10; 1 Cor. 11 : 28; Rom. 1 : 28; Luke 12 : 56. *Discerning* is perhaps the best here, but there is no objection to including the idea of allowing and approv-ing. *The will of God*, as made known to us for our guidance, embraces only that which is *good*, a word uniformly rendered. God's will is good in itself and in all its bearings, and conduces to the advantage of all who obey it, *Acceptable*, on this word see above on v. 1. Pool's explanation is, "By obedience to the will of God we shall be accepted." Perhaps the word here is emphatic and means pleasing to God in every sense. *Perfect* has the usual signification. Compare Eph. 5 : 10, 17; Phil. 4 : 8; 1 Thess. 4 : 3.

3. *For I say, through the grace given unto me, to every man that is among you, not to think* of himself *more highly than he ought to think; but to think soberly, according as God hath dealt to every man the*

measure of faith. *For* in this case points to the introduction of additional matter, designed farther to explain and confirm the general precepts thus given. *The grace* here spoken of is doubtless apostolic authority, which Paul uniformly speaks of as bestowed upon him without any merit on his part, Rom. 15 : 15 ; Gal. 1 : 16 ; Eph. 3 : 8. *Every man that is among you* designates not only the officers of the church, but all the members. There is doubtless special reference to spiritual gifts both ordinary and extraordinary, but there is no cause for confining the exhortation to such as had miraculous endowments. Lowliness becomes all in the church of God. True religion does not require us to think more lowly of ourselves, as it does not allow us to think more highly of ourselves, than we ought to think. But the truth will put any man in a low place. What the word of God requires is an estimate of ourselves according to sobriety, discreetness, sanity of mind. Compare Mark 5 : 15 ; 1 Tim. 2 : 9; Titus 2 : 5. We should know and understand what our endowments are and what they are not. *Faith* in this place may mean the grace of faith or the knowledge which is believed, or it may embrace both these. *Measure,* degree, a word uniformly rendered.

4. *For as we have many members in one body, and all members have not the same office :*

5. *So we,* being *many, are one body in Christ, and every one members one of another.* The figure of these two verses is a favorite with Paul, 1 Cor. 12 : 14–20. *Office,* work, deed, or function. The illustration of the apostle is exceedingly beautiful because it is just and appropriate. As a man has as truly need of a foot as of a hand, of eyes as of ears, so in the church of God there is need of all sorts of edifying gifts. If God has not granted us the highest, let us thank him for what he has given us, and remember that it is as much as any one can do to give a good account of the talents God has bestowed upon him.

6. *Having then gifts differing according to the grace that is given to us, whether prophecy,* let us prophesy *according to the proportion of faith.* *Grace,* any gift from God bestowed on us undeserving creatures. On some God bestowed more than on others. The *gifts* were for the edifying of the body of Christ. There have been great disputings respecting the gift of *prophecy,* mentioned in this and other parts of the New Testament. Without entering at length into the discussion, the reader is referred to a very lucid statement found in J. A. Alexander on Isaiah, Introduction, pp. IX–XII. It is entirely clear from other parts of the New Testament that *prophecy* was a gift not confined in the primitive Church to apostles, and that it was for the edification of the body of

believers, Acts 11 : 27, 28 ; 1 Cor. 14 : 3-5.   It is also evident that
the word as used in the New Testament does not necessarily
imply inspiration, for Paul applies it to a heathen poet, Tit. 1 : 12.
It appears also that all those, who claimed to be prophets in the
primitive Church, were liable to be tested by the inspired teachings of the apostles, 1 Cor. 14 : 37 ; 1 John 4 : 1, 6.   If a man
therefore had a gift for edifying, comforting or strengthening the
Church of God by speech, it seems at least sometimes to have been
called prophesying.   *Proportion*, (literally analogy) is not the word
rendered measure in v. 3.   It probably here means the standard
of faith.   This is the best interpretation.   In the days of Paul that
standard consisted of all the scriptures then written, and of the
infallible teachings of the apostles themselves.   The *faith* here
spoken of is the doctrine believed by the Church of God.   There
are other expositions of this latter clause, but none of them are so
satisfactory as that just given.

7. *Or ministry,* let us wait *on our ministering; or he that teacheth
on teaching.*

Some plausible theories respecting the division of the work in
the primitive church have been given to mankind.   But when we
remember the exceedingly rich variety of edifying gifts necessary,
and graciously granted to the primitive church ; and when we
remember that all these gifts, so far as miraculous, are no longer
granted to the church, it is not surprising that we are not able
exactly to define the limit of one or the other of these endowments.   Thus the term ministry may mean any general service
rendered to the church of God by the apostles or any one else ;
or, it may mean any special service, to which one is appointed,
touching the necessities of the poor, the care of the sick, of
strangers and of orphans.   *Teaching,* rendered doctrine, Matt.
15 : 9 ; Mark 7 : 7 ; Col. 2 : 22 ; 1 Tim. 1 : 10 and often ; in Rom.
15 : 4, rendered *learning,* or instruction.   The grade of the teaching was according to the capacity first of the teacher, and then of
the learner ; it might be a teacher of babes, who were to be
nourished with the sincere milk of the word, or of strong men
who required strong meat.   It was entirely unbecoming a teacher
to assume the office of a prophet.   He was to mind his own
business.

8. *Or he that exhorteth, on exhortation : he that giveth,* let him do
it *with simplicity ; he that ruleth, with diligence ; he that showeth
mercy, with cheerfulness.*   *Exhortation,* cognate to the verb beseech
in v. 1.   It is a very general term and embraces almost every
variety of comfort, encouragement and urgency to duty.   This is
a great gift.   *Giving* has the usual signification, referring to the be-

stowment of needed favors. *Simplicity,* so rendered in 2 Cor. 1 : 12 ; 11 : 3 ; in Eph. 6 : 5 ; Col. 3 : 22, *singleness* of heart ; but in 2 Cor. 8 : 2 ; 9 : 11, 13 it is rendered liberality, bountifulness, and liberal. Perhaps this is the better meaning. If any prefer the word simplicity in the sense of freedom from selfish and covert designs, there is no objection to such a rendering, The *ruling* here spoken of doubtless relates to the discipline of the church, which God has ordained for edification. This duty so important to the honor of true religion is to be performed with *diligence,* or carefulness, or earnest care, as the word is variously rendered. In verse 11 the same word is rendered business. *Showing mercy* is a phrase that may include the care of the poor, of the sick, of strangers and of orphans, which was often entrusted to particular persons of either sex. It was also a personal duty to be performed by every private Christian. *Cheerfulness,* found no where else in the New Testament, but we have its cognate adjective in 2 Cor. 9 : 7. It expresses the opposite of grudging, of niggardliness and narrow mindedness. We have here a most needful injunction.

DOCTRINAL AND PRACTICAL REMARKS

1. Truth is in order to godliness. This is shown by the whole connection of this chapter with the preceding discussion. Sound instruction is the basis of holy living. Calvin : " As philosophers, before they lay down laws respecting morals, discourse first of the end of what is good, and inquire into the sources of virtues, from which afterwards they draw and derive all duties ; so Paul lays down here the principle from which all the duties of holiness flow, even this,—that we are redeemed by the Lord for this end, that we may consecrate to him ourselves and all our members." Scott : " Surely they strangely misunderstand the doctrines which the apostle teaches, who suppose them inconsistent with exhortations, and instruction in all the several duties of Christianity ; or as inimical to the practice of them ! The same inspired writer, who most fully establishes, and most earnestly argues for the doctrines of grace, is also most exact and particular in exhorting Christians to their various duties." The same will be found true of the best writers of every age of the Christian church.

2. Experience and observation fully confirm what the Scriptures often teach, that all thorough, consistent morality is based upon the principles of true piety, v. 1. Nothing so arouses the whole nature of man to that which is good, as the very principles of grace, wherein we learn, more than any where else, the nature and extent of the mercies of God. Under the law, which was a

dark dispensation, they offered beasts ; under the gospel, we offer ourselves.   It is therefore a binding duty on us to study, not only the practice but the theory of religion. All those powerful springs and motives to a holy life, which have been found efficient, are wrapped up in the mystery of God and of Christ.

3. Nor does the history of the world furnish a solitary instance of a man or a community being brought to lead a life of vital piety, except by the truth as it is in Jesus.   Read history and see. Compare the early and the later ministry of Chalmers, and Scott, and see what a lesson is there learned.

4. So great and urgent is the business of salvation ; and so necessary is Scriptural holiness, that we may solemnly adjure and obtest men, that they give earnest heed to these things.   The more tender our appeals shall be, the more will they conform to inspired example, and the more likely will they be to bring men to uprightness of life.   Evans: " Many are soonest wrought upon, if they be accosted kindly ; are more easily led than driven." The example of Paul in this place is full of instruction.   Calvin : " Paul, that he might bind us to God not by servile fear, but by the voluntary and cheerful love of righteousness, allures us by the sweetness of that favor, by which our salvation is effected."

5. When we are called upon to offer our bodies a sacrifice unto God, we must remember that the atoning, propitiatory sacrifice is finished, and that it is awful wickedness to act as if it were incomplete.   The great impetratory and propitiatory offering of Calvary was absolutely sufficient unto all the ends of the remission of sins.   But the sacrifice we are called to make is spiritual and eucharistic.   This class of offerings peculiarly befits the gospel dispensation.   Our oblation should be a whole burnt-offering. Chrysostom : " If when Elijah offered the visible sacrifice, a flame that came down from above consumed the whole, water, wood and stones, much more will this be done upon thee.   And if thou hast aught in thee relaxed and secular, and yet offerest the sacrifice with a good intention, the fire of the Spirit will come down, and both wear away that worldliness, and carry up the whole sacrifice."   Whoever does not wish to be wholly consecrated to God, is no devotee of the true religion.   Calvin : " We must cease to live to ourselves, in order that we may devote all the actions of our life to his service."

6. All that is scriptural is reasonable, vs. 1, 2.   The sooner our judgments reach this conclusion, the better for us.   What man enjoins in the way of piety is folly and blasphemy.   What God requires is right and perfect.   Haldane : " Nothing can be added to it, nothing can be taken from it, yet that monstrous system of

Anti-christianity, which has so long, in the name of Christ, lorded it over the world, has added innumerable commands to those of Christ, and even taken taken away many of his laws." Brown: "The consideration that this law of God is good, full, complete and showeth what way we shall please our Lord, should stir up all his people to a conscionable studying, proving and approving what this will of God is."

7. We cannot be too guarded against conformity to this vain and fleeting world, v. 2. Chrysostom: "It hath no durability or fixedness, but all in it is but for a season; and so he calls it this age, hereby to indicate its liableness to misfortune, and by the word *fashion* its unsubstantialness. For speak of riches, or of glory, or beauty of person, or of luxury, or of whatever other of its seemingly great things you will, it is a fashion only, not reality, a show and a mask, not any abiding substance." If Caleb would obtain God's testimony in his favor, he must wholly dissent from the body of the spies. No man may hope to be approved unto God who is not willing to be found in a minority of one against the world, if the world turns away from Jehovah. Brown: "There is an inevitable necessity that God's children must dwell and abide amongst worldly ones, or such as have their portion in this world, and by reason thereof are still in hazard of being ensnared by their evil example; and such is the force and strength of the corrupt conversation of bad company, that even the best of God's children have reason to be walking circumspectly and warily, lest they be drawn aside and tainted by their coarse carriage."

8. True piety makes a great change, v. 2. It transforms, transfigures the moral character. Its chief work is in the inmost soul; but then it will work its way out. The heart of an unregenerate man is worse than his life, however wicked that may be. But the heart of a renewed man is the best thing about him. If he had his way, he never would sin again. Chalmers: "In order to our being not conformed, we must be transformed—and that not by a superficial amendment, but by a renewal, and, more decisive still, a renewal in the very interior of our system—a change not merely of the outward walk, but a change in the central parts of our moral nature, or at the place of command or presiding authority, and where the mainspring of every deed and every movement lies." It is this great moral transformation, giving a new nature, which imparts to christian character all its stability.

9. The first great lesson of the christian life is humility, consisting in a true estimate of ourselves, v. 3. No man's piety goes beyond his humility. Chrysostom: "Pray why dost thou stiffen

up thy neck? or why walk on tiptoe? why knit up thy brows? why stick out thy breast? Thou canst not make one hair white or black, and thou goest with as lofty gait as if thou couldest command every thing. No doubt thou wouldest like to have wings, and not go upon the earth at all! No doubt thou wouldest wish to be a prodigy! For hast thou not made thyself prodigious now, when thou art a man and triest to fly? or rather flying from within, and bloated in every limb? What shall I call thee to quit thee of thy recklessness? If I call thee ashes, and dust, and smoke, and pother, I should have described thy worthlessness to be sure, but still I should not have laid hold of the exact image I wanted." It is possible indeed that through melancholy or temptation even habitual dejection may come over a man; and cause him to write bitter things against himself, and to take such views of himself as must be depressing. Such a state of mind ought not to be cultivated, and yet it is safer than that which consists in self-conceit. Olshausen : "Through humility it is that each man acknowledges the place and the gift allotted to him, and thus makes possible a joint operation." Hodge : "Self-conceit and ambition are the besetting sins of men entrusted with power, or highly gifted in any respect, as discontent and envy are those to which persons of inferior station or gifts are most exposed."

10. A great thing it would be to the church of God if her rulers would see to it that there was a place for every man, and that every man was in his place, vs. 4, 5. A member not in his place is as useless as a foot out of joint. How little organization is there in many of our churches. A small band of earnest workers would be worth a cohort of undisciplined members.

11. The church is one, one body, one spouse of Christ, v. 5. All the efforts of infidels, schismatics and heretics to tear limb from limb shall in the end be found wholly ineffectual. It no more destroys the unity of the church of God that her members should, in nationality and in religious forms, widely differ from each other, than it destroys the unity of the human body that the foot is wholly unlike the hand, or the tongue different from the ear. In so great a body as the church some must be old and some young, some strong and some weak, some governing and some governed; but all this impairs not her unity.

12. Admirable indeed is the variety of excellent gifts which God has granted to his church for her edification, vs. 6–8. Although miraculous endowments are no longer granted to the church, yet still in the ordinary pastors, teachers and evangelists we find such a rich variety as suits all virtuous tastes and characters. One is a son of thunder. Another is a son of consolation.

One is mighty in the Scriptures. Another is impressive in exhortation. One warns of coming wrath as if he saw the flames of Tophet. Another by tenderness wins the soul to the contemplation of heavenly realities. One cries aloud and spares not. Another is gentle like a nurse among her children. Sometimes the hoary head, found in the way of righteousness like Paul the aged, beseeches. Again the young and spirited pour forth strains of sprightly eloquence. Blessed is he who enjoys the benefits of a gospel ministry! Hodge: " Real honor consists in doing well what God calls us to do, and not in the possession of high offices or great talents."

13. What is the rule of faith? is a vital question in religion, v. 6. There is but one infallible standard. " The Bible—the Bible is the religion of Protestants," and in the end will be found to be the religion of all that are saved. We may reason to the contrary of all this. We may argue so plausibly as to deceive even ourselves. But the Judge himself has told us the principle that will guide his decisions: " He that rejecteth me, and receiveth not my words, hath one that judgeth him : the word that I have spoken, the same shall judge him in the last day," John 12 : 48. If we believe not and practice not 'according to that form of faith or wholesome doctrine, by which every one who is sent out to preach the gospel is appointed to regulate his preaching according to those heads or principles of faith and good life' which are taught in the Holy Scripture, then all is in vain.

14. Reader, what is thy place in the church? Art thou a preacher? a teacher? a servant? an exhorter? a distributer of alms? a ruler? a dispenser of kindness to the needy? Stand in thy lot. Do thy whole duty. One who has lived long and noticed the history of many men lately declared that he had never seen any man, who always did his best at the post where Providence placed him, who did not at last rise to honor and command respect. Whatever thy station is, cultivate that spirit of humility, diligence, perseverance, simplicity and cheerfulness which will make thy duties pleasant to thyself and profitable to thy brethren. Chalmers: " The goodly equipment of offices in the ancient church for all sorts and varieties of well-doing, carries with it a severe reproach on the meagre, stinted and parsimonious apparatus of modern times."

15. The author here records his testimony concerning the unhappy effects of declining to perform any service to which God and his church call pious men. Scarcely anything seems more sadly to dwarf religious character.

Chapter 31

ROMANS 12
VERSES 9–21

HOLY LIVING. GOOD RULES FOR ALL THE BRETHREN

9 *Let* love be without dissimulation. Abhor that which is evil; cleave to that which is good.

10 *Be* kindly affectioned one to another with brotherly love; in honour preferring one another:

11 Not slothful in business; fervent in spirit; serving the Lord;

12 Rejoicing in hope; patient in tribulation; continuing instant in prayer;

13 Distributing to the necessity of saints; given to hospitality.

14 Bless them which persecute you: bless, and curse not.

15 Rejoice with them that do rejoice, and weep with them that weep.

16 *Be* of the same mind one toward another. Mind not high things, but condescend to men of low estate. Be not wise in your own conceits.

17 Recompense to no man evil for evil. Provide things honest in the sight of all men.

18 If it be possible, as much as lieth in you, live peaceably with all men.

19. Dearly beloved, avenge not yourselves, but *rather* give place unto wrath: for it is written, Vengeance *is* mine; I will repay, saith the Lord.

20 Therefore if thine enemy hunger, feed him; if he thirst, give him drink; for in so doing thou shalt heap coals of fire on his head.

21 Be not overcome of evil, but overcome evil with good.

9. LET *love be without dissimulation,* etc. *Love,* often also also rendered charity, see 1 Cor. 13 throughout. It embraces the entire principle of love to God and man, though the connection shows that here love to man is specially intended. It is a grace common to saints below and saints in heaven. It shall last for ever. There is a good deal of profession of love in the world. The trouble is that much of it is feigned. The word rendered *without dissimulation* is once rendered without hypocrisy, but more commonly unfeigned. *Abhor that which is evil. Abhor,* found here only. Abhorrence consists of detestation and fear. No word expresses stronger aversion. The Greek is well rendered. No man ever hated or feared sin too much. *Evil,* of course it means moral

evil, particularly that which directly injures others. *Cleave to that which is good ;* Wiclif: Drawynge to good; Peshito: Be adherers to good things. The word rendered cleave to expresses the closest adhesion—the union of concord. It is very much like the old English stick to, so happily used in our translation of Ps. 119: 31, "I have stuck unto thy testimonies." *Good,* that is moral good, that which is right, particularly that which is profitable to man, useful to our neighbor. In many languages the words rendered good and evil relate both to natural and moral good. This produces no confusion as the context determines which is meant.

10. Be *kindly affectioned one to another with brotherly love,* etc. *Kindly affectioned,* here only, very expressive of yearning kindness. Yet the love called for is not natural affection, but it is brotherly kindness. Wiclif's rendering is very striking : Louynge to gidre bi the charite of britherede. Hodge: "No doubt, the idea is, that Christians should love each other with the same sincerity and tenderness as if they were the nearest relatives." *In honor preferring one another ;* Tyndale: In gevynge honoure, goo one before another; Peshito: Be foremost in honoring one another ; Stuart: As to honor, give to each other the preference. The general law of morals requires us to love our neighbor as ourselves. In matters of courtesy and civility our brother is to have the precedence over ourselves. There are many cases in which it is impossible the same distinction should be conferred on two or more. Then, let the strife be who shall decline, not who shall win. Somewhere in his Book of Martyrs Fox says "It is a greater honor to make a king than to become a king." This witness is true.

11. *Not slothful in business,* etc. *Slothful,* there is no better rendering, see Matt. 25 : 26. *Business,* commonly rendered haste, diligence, carefulness, earnest care, forwardness. Here it seems to be taken for the care we have in our lawful calling, though some give it the signification of diligence in all things good. But the usual interpretation is to be preferred. Nor is the industry thus enjoined contrary to the warmest piety ; accordingly he adds : *Fervent in Spirit,* the word rendered fervent, applied to natural things, is used to express the boiling of water. The Scriptures never repress holy ardor. Some think *spirit* here means the Holy Spirit; but we obtain a good sense by understanding the phrase as warm-hearted, full of life, as in Acts 18 : 25. *Serving the Lord,* that is being governed in all things by pure, religious motives, being desirous in the commonest affairs of life as well as in great matters to glorify God, 1 Cor. 10 : 31. It is a poor rendering of some, serving the time.

12. *Rejoicing in hope*, etc.   In many cases Christians are not able to rejoice in their present circumstances.   They are troubled on every side; they are perplexed; they are persecuted; they are cast down; but every one of them has a fair prospect before him, of which he has a blessed assurance in the word of God, where he has set his hope.   In that he can rejoice.   *Patient in tribulation*, that is maintaining constancy of mind and an unshaken purpose even in the darkest hour.   Christ gave his followers fair notice that in the world they should have tribulation.   It is a great thing to be able, when we can do no more, at least by silent and patient endurance to honor God.   To bear all things for Christ's sake and for the elects' sake is often the height of true greatness of soul. *Continuing instant in prayer*.   Continuing instant, in Greek one word, also rendered waiting, continuing steadfastly, giving oneself continually, and attending continually, Mark 3 : 9; Acts 2 : 42; 6 : 4; Romans 13 : 6.

13. *Distributing to the necessity of saints*.   Peshito: Be communicators to the wants of the saints.   The first clause of the verse reminds us of that saying of our Lord, " The poor ye have always with you."   The necessities of saints are always very great in times of persecution.   The richest often become the poorest, and the poorest have none to look to that are much better off than themselves.   A community of goods was not enjoined at any time as a law of the church, but if a man seeth his brother have need and shutteth up his compassions from him, how dwelleth the love of God in him?   *Given to hospitality*, this indicates much more than an occasional act of entertaining a stranger.   We must *follow* up this business as a great duty of life.   In primitive times when Christians travelled in the Roman Empire they could not find inns and hotels, where they might be comfortable, and free from insult concerning their religion.   To have avowed their attachment to the Crucified would have immediately inflamed the populace against them.   There was therefore then a double necessity for hospitality, or love of strangers as the word signifies.   Let none imagine that the duty of Christian hospitality will cease while the world stands, Tit. 1 : 8.

14. *Bless them which persecute you : bless, and curse not*.   The *blessing* here required does not signify praising or commending, but showing kindness, speaking good words, and praying for enemies, revilers and persecutors.   Inspired men, under the teaching of the Holy Ghost, were often called prophetically to denounce God's judgments against the wicked; and in the way of kindly and solemn warning good men may now do the same; but every thing like bitterness, *cursing* and imprecation is contrary to the

Christian temper and to the teachings of both the Old and New Testaments, Ps. 35 : 13, 14 ; Matt. 5 : 44.

15. *Rejoice with them that do rejoice, and weep with them that weep.* A fellow-feeling with our neighbors and particularly with our Christian brethren is the duty enjoined. Some seem to perform half the duty here enjoined, They express sympathy with their neighbors in their joys ; but they eschew them when adversity rolls in her dark waters. Others are always found in families, where affliction is casting her dark pall ; but they rejoice not with the woman who has found her lost groat. They attend sickness, deaths and burials, but have no greetings for times of health, birth and marriage. If one loses his estate, they condole with him ; but if he honestly improves his estate, they do not express delight. The right way is to do both. As to that class, who care not for others' joys or sorrows, so that they succeed in their own schemes, they are neither to be admired nor imitated.

16. Be *of the same mind one toward another,* etc. Through a spirit of gainsaying and contradiction, from an affectation of singularity, or from a vain persuasion of superior wisdom some seem to endeavor to be always in the opposition. There is a class of otherwise respectable minds, that at first look at every thing from the point of objection, unless it is something of their own proposing. A like class, when outvoted, never cease their opposition ; at least they are surly, and snarl at all that is done without their sanction. They occasion continual jarrings. Wiclif's rendering is, Fele ye the same thing to gidre. The Peshito gives another turn to the thought : What estimation ye make of yourselves, make also of your brethren. Beza has it : Be entirely united in your regards for each other. Some moderns follow this rendering ; but neither of these is an improvement on the common interpretation. *Mind not high things, but condescend to men of low estate ;* Tyndale, Cranmer and Genevan : Be not hye minded : but make yourselves equall to them of the lower sorte ; Peshito : And indulge not high thoughts ; but unite yourselves with the lowly minded ; Doway : Not high minded, but condescending to the humble. *High things,* such as the vain, the ambitious, the luxurious and the covetous seek after ; leading men to flatter the great, to court the rich and be servile to the mighty. There is no better rendering of the latter clause than that of the authorized version. The difficulty in performing the duty with some is that when they condescend they continually remind you that on their part it is condescension. No duty more certainly requires faith than this. It is but few, and they are taught from heaven, who believe that the soul of the peasant or of the beggar is worth as

much as that of the prince or the king.   Yet without such faith
we shall continually err.   It is agreeable to the experience of the
most zealous and successful laborers for Christ that their efforts to
do good among the lowly are seldom repulsed, while from the
mansion of the rich they often receive scorn or coldness. *Be not
wise in your own conceits.* Doddridge says: Christ inculcates no
lesson so often as that of humility.   Certainly we require no precept to be oftener repeated.   Self-conceit is very pleasing to the
flesh.   Many complain of bad memories; few complain of bad
judgments or of feeble minds.   If this high opinion of self led us
merely to differ from some great and good men, it would be comparatively harmless.   But alas! it leads us to reject the decisions
of God, or to cavil at the precepts and doctrines of his blessed
word.

17. *Recompense to no man evil for evil,* etc.   Peshito: Repay to
no man evil for evil; Doway: Render to no man evil for evil.
The sense is very clear.   The thing prohibited is the spirit and
practice of vindictiveness.   If a wicked man injures you, surely
his sad condition should awaken your tender compassions.   If a
Christian has wronged you, you have without passion a method
of redress pointed out to you by Christ himself, Matt. 18 : 15–17.
Perhaps, too, you think yourself injured, when others have merely
claimed their just rights, or when they had no intention of wronging you at all. *Provide things honest in the sight of all men ;*
Peshito: But let it be your study to do good, before all men ;
Wiclif: But puruey ye good thingis not oonli bifor God: but also
bifor alle men ; Tyndale: Provyde afore hande thinges honest in
the syght of all men ; Doway: Provide things good not only in the
sight of God, but also in the sight of all men ; Stuart: Seek after
that which is good in the sight of all.   Guyse's paraphrase is:
"Whatever others do, let it be your conscientious care and concern, by divine assistance, to contrive and go into such measures
of conduct, as shall be good, generous, and honorable in themselves, and every way becoming your Christian characters, not
only in the sight of the Lord, but in the judgment of all the un-
prejudiced part of mankind, that none, no not the worst of your
enemies, may ever be able to upbraid you with having done an
unworthy or indecent thing."   Doddridge's is: "Act in such a
cautious and circumspect manner, that it may evidently appear
you provide against the malignity which will lead many to put the
worst constructions upon your actions.   And do only those things
which may be above the need of excuse, and may appear, at the
first view, fair and reputable in the sight of all men."   The duty
enjoined embraces proper attention to our secular affairs; but it

extends much further, relating to all our deportment towards men. *Provide*, a good and uniform rendering, meaning, have foresight. *Honest*, elsewhere worthy, more commonly good. Two things are essential to the idea of worthy or honest conduct. One is that it be strictly just, equitable, even-handed. The other is that it be of good report, not mean, but fair and honorable. It is perfectly right and reputable for an officer, whose duty it is, to execute a criminal, but it is a shame for a Christian to hire himself out as a hangman. Deut. 23 : 18.

18. *If it be possible, as much as lieth in you, live peaceably with all men.* Peshito : And if possible, so far as it dependeth on you, live in peace with every man ; Wiclif : If it mai be don, that is of you ; haue ye pees with alle men. The renderings are very uniform. The scripture requires nothing impossible. It says not that we must live in peace with all men, because that is sometimes impossible. The verse admits as much. But as far as things are in our power, we must live in peace. There is a class of men, who are not satisfied when they have all their rights, nor even when you make many concessions. What they seek is strife, a broil, a contest, a law suit. Nor is the number of such very small. When thrown with them you can only guard against partaking of their evil spirit and hateful ways.

19. *Dearly beloved, avenge not yourselves, but* rather *give place unto wrath :* for *it is written, Vengeance* is *mine; I will repay, saith the Lord.*

20. *Therefore if thine enemy hunger, feed him; if he thirst, give him drink : for in so doing thou shalt heap coals of fire on his head.*

21. *Be not overcome of evil, but overcome evil with good.* These three verses relate to the same thing—the proper treatment of those who wrong us. In v. 19 we are forbidden to avenge or revenge insults and wrongs against ourselves. A reason assigned is that *that* is the work of God, Deut. 32 : 35 ; Ps. 94 : 1–3 ; Heb. 10 : 30. A man has no right, and a pure minded Christian has no disposition to take either the law of the land or the law of God into his own hands. *To give place to wrath* is a very literal rendering of the Greek. It might signify to give a lodgment to wrath, or to give room to it in our hearts. But this would be directly contrary to the scope of the apostle's teaching. Some have thought that it means retreat before wrath, yield to the violence of others; but an example of such a construction is not found. The better exposition is that of Calvin: "To give place to wrath is to commit to the Lord the right of judging, which they take away from him who attempt revenge." Verse 20 is a quotation from Prov. 25 : 21, 22. The same thing is required in the

law of Moses, Ex. 23 : 4, 5; and in the sermon on the Mount, Matt. 5 : 44. The figure of heaping coals of fire is no doubt taken from the process of melting precious metals, where the fire is put upon the top of the metals in the crucible, and thus they are melted down. So we are to overcome the ill-will of others. Other explanations are offered but they are unsatisfactory. This is every way the best, agreeing with the scope of the passage and with the succeeding verse. *Overcome*, v. 20, in Rom. 3 : 4; once or twice rendered conquer. If anything that man can do will disarm hostility and fill our enemies with kindness and pity, it will be such a course as the apostle here recommends.

DOCTRINAL AND PRACTICAL REMARKS

1. Have you unfeigned love? v. 9, or does mere complaisance supplant the nobler endowment? We must "exceed in *evident* benevolence, kindness and courteousness, all those appearances, which polite selfishness assumes; and be *really* as ready to oblige and be serviceable, as polite worldly people *profess* to be." The loving disciple tells us how this duty is to be performed: "My little children, let us not love in word, neither in tongue; but in deed and in truth," 1 John 3 : 18. One of the real excellences of love is that it counts the cost of no service, but "gives, like a thoughtless prodigal, its all." "Jacob served seven years for Rachel; and they seemed unto him but a few days for the love he had to her," Gen. 29 : 20. Love is the fulfilling of the law, Rom. 13 : 10.

2. How much do you hate and fear sin? v. 9. Is your abhorrence of it growing? Do you dally with temptation? Do you parley with iniquity?

3. Is your adherence to God, to duty and to holiness close? v. 9. Is it daily becoming more close? Are you *glued* to good things? as the word signifies. Increasing attachment to holiness, of which the moral law is the standard, is infallible proof of a regenerate state. The want of it makes all religious profession null.

4. Civility is good; bland manners are pleasant; but nothing is a substitute for *kind affection*, v. 10. I once saw a hired nurse, not destitute of moral principle, employed in the care of a venerable stranger. By and by the sick man's daughter appeared, when a new order of services began. There is no substitute for a warm heart.

5. Do you love to honor others? v. 10. Chrysostom: "Nothing tends so much to make friends, as endeavoring to overcome one's neighbor in doing him honor." It is not long since a noble

son of a noble sire contrived by an artifice of love to bring down
the highest honors of a college on one of his friends, when he
himself doubly merited them.   Thus he earned higher laurels
than any college could have conferred.

6. Nowhere does the Scripture give the least countenance to
idleness, but constantly enjoins industry, v. 11 : " Whatsoever thy
hand findeth to do, do it with thy might," Eccles. 9 : 10.   Brown :
" Christianity doth not loose folk from following their lawful and
necessary callings in the world."   It has sometimes been stated
that while the Bible tells us of the conversion of kings, and
treasurers, and jailors, and sellers of purple, and centurions, and
publicans, and harlots, and thieves, it nowhere records the conversion of a lazy man.   Yet Paul himself once addressed an au-
dience of idlers.   His success was such as might have been expected : "Some mocked : and others said, We will hear thee
again of this matter."   There never was a more wholesome law
than that of the Christian household, " If any will not work, neither shall he eat," 2 Thess. 3 : 10.   How carefully does the apostle
enjoin on his converts that they study to be quiet, and to do their
own business, and to work with their own hands ; that they might
walk honestly toward them that are without, and that they might
have lack of nothing, 1 Thess. 4 : 11, 12.   It is both a sin and a
shame for a man to cultivate the arts of a soft effeminacy.   Labor
is the law of our present fallen existence.   The wise will not rebel
against it.

7. The very same law, which enjoins diligence in our calling,
justly demands fervent piety, v. 11.   Paul expressly desires that
Jewish converts be not slothful but followers of them who through
faith and patience inherit the promises, Heb. 6 : 12.   To undertake
to serve God with a cold and divided heart must render any life
wretched unless moral sensibility is entirely destroyed.

8. Endeavor continually to be governed by high religious
motives and considerations.   In the humblest affairs of life serve
the Lord, v. 11.   It is a great thing to have our acts right in the
matter of them ; but it is a much greater thing to have them right
both in matter and motive.

9. Dear Christian brother, is thy soul vexed ?   Art thou cast
down with manifold sorrows and temptations?   Look up to God's
eternal and propitious throne and *rejoice in hope*, v, 12.   Doddridge :
"Surely if anything consistent with the burdens and sorrows of
mortal life can inspire constant joy, it must be the Christian hope."
The martyrs have kissed the chains that bound them to the stake
and washed their hands in the flames that destroyed their natural
lives.

10. If you can do no more, at least bear with quietness and patience whatever the Lord shall lay upon you, v. 12. If possible say like the patriarch, " All the days of my appointed time will I wait till my change come."

> Is resignation's lesson hard?
> Examine, you shall find,
> That duty calls for little more
> Than anguish of the mind.

11. But if you would do all these great things, you must possess the secret of importunate prayer, v. 12. Hodge: " The source of our life is in God; without intercourse with him therefore we cannot derive those supplies of grace which are requisite to preserve the spirit of piety in our hearts, and to send a vital influence through the various duties and avocations of life." Prayer is as truly the element of a new-born soul, as water is the element of fishes. As soon as divine grace reached the heart of Saul of Tarsus, it was said of him, Behold he prayeth. Prayer is a chief method of exercising faith. But prayer is not an end. He, who rests in his prayers, might as well not pray. " It is the general tendency of human nature to substitute the *means* of grace for the *fruits* of grace."

12. Do you pity and help the necessitous? That is right, v. 13. But what is your motive? Is it that you may be seen of men, called a benefactor, and receive praise of dying worms? You give, yes, but on what scale? Have your benefactions ever gone so far as to require of you any self-denial? Or, have you merely of your abundance cast into the treasury? When you give, to whom do you give? to those from whom you may expect as much again? " When thou makest a feast, call the poor, the maimed, the lame, the blind: and thou shalt be blessed: for they cannot recompense thee: for thou shalt be recompensed at the resurrection of the just," Luke 14: 13, 14. You give, but do you really believe " it is more blessed to give than to receive?" " The Lord loveth a cheerful giver." Do you give grudgingly? Few men in early life learn what a power for good there is in bountiful liberality. Francke and Whitefield had each his Orphan House. Wesley's right arm was his systematic benevolence. Paul never forgot the " poor saints."

13. Are you a needy follower of Christ? is your raiment plain? is your fare coarse and sometimes scant? Remember there were such before you, v. 13. For the strengthening of your faith, read the promises, read the history of persecutions, remember that your Saviour was poor, and during his public ministry subsisted very

much on the charity of some women, none of whom seem to have been rich. Cultivate contentment. Practise industry and economy. Avoid an envious or murmuring spirit. Put the best possible construction on the treatment you receive. Help yourself as long and as far as you can. Then when compelled to depend on others, be not distressed at it. Poverty, sent on us by God's providence, is a great trial, but it is no crime. In your straits contrive, if possible, to help your poorer brethren and neighbors.

14. Are you given to hospitality? It is a universal duty, v. 13. It has been obligatory on all classes of persons under all dispensations, Deut. 10:18, 19; Isa. 58:7; 1 Tim. 3:2; 1 Pet. 4:9. To many in the last day the Judge will say: "I was a stranger and ye took me in," Matt. 25:35. It is peculiarly incumbent on us to "show hospitality without grudging." The reluctance with which some exercise it is sadly manifest. They are glad when the stranger is gone. They are little like Abraham and Lot, Gen. 18:3–8; Gen. 19:1–3.

15. What is your temper towards enemies? Does your spirit towards them conform to the requisitions of this chapter? vs. 14, 17, 19–21. Tholuck: "Anger and malice constitute a state of slavery." Are you in that hard bondage? A wise man would rather carry a millstone around his neck than a grudge in his heart. To the unregenerate "revenge is sweet." Is it so to you? Do you cherish the memory of wrongs? It was said of Cranmer that he had so excellent a memory that he never forgot anything but injuries. A good memory indeed was that. Is yours like it? Do you love to retaliate? Are you vindictive? Are you irreconcilable? or are you easy to be intreated? Some say they are ready to forgive all but their national or sectional enemies? But why should they form an exception? Do they not need your good will? Will malice against a whole people be less damning than against a man? Several things ought to lead us utterly to cast out the spirit of revenge. 1. To punish is God's work and prerogative. He is Lord of all; he is Judge of all. 2. If our enemy repents not of his evil deeds, his doom will be so dreadful that the bare contemplation of it will fill any benevolent mind with most fearful dread. Chrysostom: "If any one abuseth thee, he has not hurt thee at all, but himself severely. And if he wrong thee, the harm will be to the person who does thee wrong." 3. It is human to do wrong; it is Godlike to forgive, Matt. 5:48. It is the glory of a man to pass over a transgression. 4. He, who is kind to those whom he regards as friends, has a code of morals no higher than the heathen or the Pharisees. An eastern sage commends

the system of education among the ancient Persians because it
so thoroughly prepared a man to serve his friends and to punish
his enemies. And Cicero, in some respects the best of the heathen moralists, says a man ought to feel kindly towards every
one except his enemies. Are you willing to rest satisfied with
so low a grade of moral sentiment? 5. There is a much more
effectual method of gaining superiority over an enemy than by
hating or killing him, and that is to melt him down by kindness. It was said of Cranmer that he never ceased to follow
with kindness one who had done him a disservice. The power
of love to disarm enmity is beautifully illustrated in the conduct
of Joseph towards his brethren, in David's treatment of Saul
and in Elisha's behaviour towards the hosts of Syria. 6. We
have the example of Christ, who when reviled reviled not again;
when he suffered, he threatened not. If we would reign with
Christ in heaven, we must cherish a like spirit of meekness and
love. To all this some say, I would forgive, if my enemies could
express any sorrow for their injurious conduct. Yet neither Christ
nor Stephen waited for such relentings; but implored heaven's
mercies on persecutors and murderers, whose violence was still
pouring out its utmost cruelty. M'Cosh: " The cruelty inflicted
in times of political convulsion becomes so great just because it
has taken the name of justice, and seems to be the avenger of the
trampled rights of men, whether princes or people. Besides feelings of personal revenge, there has been an idea of supporting the
rights of sovereigns, and the cause of good government in those
dreadful injuries which tyrants have inflicted on their subjects
who, in fact or appearance, were disposed to rebellion. . . Oppression, whether exercised by the many or the few, has never
been intensely severe till it has assumed the name, and professes
to assert and avenge the rights of justice ; and it now becomes so
unrelenting, just because it does everything in the name of law
and conscience." But we may not indulge malice even against
such monsters of cruelty. The history of modern missions tells
us of a negro in the West Indies, who asked his master to buy an
old sickly man from a slave ship, carried him to his own hut, gave
him his own bed, cooked his food and nursed him till he died.
When asked the reason of his conduct he said, " I am trying to be
a Christian ; that was the man that stole me from my mother in
Africa and sold me into slavery." Are you that sort of a Christian?

16. Extend your sympathies to all around you in their innocent
joys and sorrows, v. 15. Especially let your heart go out warmly
towards the poor, afflicted people of God. Elsewhere Paul ex-

pressly teaches that "the members should have the same care one for another. And whether one member suffer, all the members suffer with it; or one member be honored, all the members rejoice with it. Now ye are the body of Christ, and members in particular," 1 Cor. 12 : 25–27. Compare Heb. 13 : 3. Often sympathy is all that we can give. Sometimes it is all our afflicted brethren ask. The suffering Saviour sought no more.

17. Be not contrary and stubborn but yielding and compliant as far as duty will permit, v. 16. " Now I beseech you, brethren, by the name of our Lord Jesus Christ, that ye all speak the same thing, and that there be no divisions among you ; but that ye be perfectly joined together in the same mind and in the same judgment, 1 Cor. 1 : 10. Compare Phil. 2 : 2 ; 3 : 16 ; 4 : 2.

18. Seekest thou great things? Seek them not, v. 16. Waste not your time in courting the ungodly great, in aiming at things impossible, or, if possible, injurious. Compare Jer. 45 : 5.

19. Are you humble and modest? v. 16. Prove this to be your character by your readiness to mingle with the humble. " When evil men combine, the good must associate." Chrysostom: " Bring thyself down to the condition of men of low estate, ride or walk with them, do not be humble in mind only, but help them also, and reach forth thy hand to them, not by means of others, but in thine own person, as a father taking care of a child, as the head taking care of the body."

20. Be very careful what opinion you form of yourself, your worth, your talents and your principles, v. 16. Hodge: " A wrong estimate of ourselves is a fruitful source of evil. Viewed in relation to God, and in our own absolute insignificance, we have little reason to be wise or important in our own conceits. A proper self-knowledge will preserve us from pride, ambition and contempt of others." It may be as sinful to deny good qualities which we have received, as to deny our bad qualities ; but mankind will generally agree that the latter error is far the more common.

21. Are your ways and conduct just? v. 17. It is possible to preserve the peace of neighborhoods, when all the people are strictly upright, though some may be narrow-minded. Justice is one of the great pillars of society ; it is one of the pillars of the throne of God. " Most men are admirers of justice,—when justice happens to be on their side." " Men are not always *right* in the use of their rights."

22. Are you honorable? v. 17. Is your conduct above just reproach? Do you put to silence by fair dealing the ignorance of foolish men? Has he who is of the contrary part no evil thing, that he can truly say of you?

23. Do you love a quiet life? v. 18. Seek peace and pursue
it. Blessed are the peace-makers. God hath called us to peace.
It was a good saying of a great man recently dead : "I would not
give an hour of brotherly love for a whole eternity of contention."
Sacrifice all you may lawfully do for peace, but never sacrifice
truth, honor, or conscience, even for the sake of life itself. Chrysostom : "Do thine own part, and to none give occasion of war or
fighting, neither to Jew nor Gentile. But if you see the cause.of
religion suffering anywhere, do not prize concord above truth, but
make a noble stand even to death." If anything is our duty, it is
that we be valiant for the truth. The life of truth is more important than the life of any man.

24. This whole chapter shows that it is a slander that the doctrines of grace, when correctly expounded, favor licentiousness or
Antinomianism. "Evangelical doctrines lead to evangelical practice." Hodge : "It is not more important to believe what God
has revealed than to do what he has commanded."

Chapter 32

ROMANS 13
VERSES 1–7

OUR DUTIES TO CIVIL RULERS

LET every soul be subject unto the higher powers. For there is no power but of God : the powers that be are ordained of God.

2 Whosoever therefore resisteth the power, resisteth the ordinance of God: and. they that resist shall receive to themselves damnation.

3 For rulers are not a terror to good works, but to the evil. Wilt thou then not be afraid of the power ? do that which is good, and thou shalt have praise of the same :

4 For he is the minister of God to thee for good. But if thou do that which is evil, be afraid ; for he beareth not the sword in vain : for he is the minister of God, a revenger to *execute* wrath upon him that doeth evil.

5 Wherefore *ye* must needs be subject, not only for wrath, but also for conscience' sake.

6 For, for this cause pay ye tribute also : for they are God's ministers, attending continually upon this very thing.

7 Render therefore to all their dues : tribute to whom tribute *is due ;* custom to whom custom ; fear to whom fear; honour to whom honour.

THE most extended parallel passage is found in 1 Pet. 2 : 13–17 : " Submit yourselves to every ordinance of man for the Lord's sake : whether it be to the king, as supreme ; or unto governors, as unto them that are sent by him for the punishment of evil doers, and for the praise of them that do well. For so is the will of God, that with well doing ye may put to silence the ignorance of foolish men. As free, and not using your liberty for a cloak of maliciousness, but as the servants of God. Honour all men. Love the brotherhood. Fear God. Honour the king."

It may save time and enable us to get a clearer view of the important matter here brought to our notice, if we take a general view of the duties of rulers and ruled, thus eliminating all the principles involved in this passage. The names here given to civil magistrates are the powers, the higher powers, rulers, ministers of God, and revengers. In scriptural and theological language, officers of civil government are often called magistrates, whatever may be the department of government they fill, whether supreme or subordinate; whether legislative, judicial or executive; or whether the government, of which they are functionaries, be free or despotic, elective or hereditary. Paul lived and wrote and suffered under Nero, and yet by precept and example he taught submission to our civil rulers. It is a great privilege to live under a free government, and obedience to its good laws should be rendered with the most cheerful alacrity; but even under a despotic government there ought to be no factious opposition and no hesitancy to obey right laws. Magistrates sometimes err through mistake, sometimes through prejudice, sometimes through bad passions, and sometimes through bad counsel, but wise men will bear with these errors as long as they can. As the passage under consideration suggests the duties both of those who govern and of those who are governed; let us take a summary view of the duties of both.

1. A magistrate ought to understand the duties of his office. "Woe to thee, O land, when thy king is a child;" "The prince that wanteth understanding is also a great oppressor," Ecc. 10 : 16; Prov. 28 : 16. A sound mind and correct information are essential to the magistrate. The best that ignorance can do is to commit folly.

2. Some, who have good minds and are intelligent, are sordid, selfish, and have contracted views, and thus are unfit for office. Rulers should be magnanimous, should avoid the little arts and meannesses resorted to by many to retain office and serve themselves. How can a miser, a sharper, a buffoon, a jester, a glutton or a drunkard carry on a government? "It is not for kings, O Lemuel, it is not for kings to drink wine; nor for princes strong drink: lest they drink, and forget the law, and pervert the judgment of any of the afflicted," Prov. 31 : 4, 5. A civil ruler should be eyes to the blind, feet to the lame, and strength to the feeble. He ought to have a just regard for widows, orphans, the stranger, the poor, the abused, the oppressed.

3. Civil rulers should be men of firmness and fortitude. If timid, they will be overawed by clamor, or led away by the violence of others. Without courage and intrepidity a public functionary is a public curse.

4. A magistrate must be a man of integrity and fidelity, beyond the power of bribery or flattery. He must have no favorites in the orders of society. Towards rich and poor, high and low, he must be impartial.

5. A magistrate must set a good example. In vain will he sit

in judgment on gamblers, if he is a gambler himself. How can he enforce good morals, who tramples them under his own feet?

A general summary of the duties of rulers is the enactment and execution of good laws, 2 Chron. 19 : 5–7 ; Zech. 8 : 16 ; the maintenance of authority with wisdom, justice and clemency, 2 Chron. 1 : 10 ; the punishment of evil doers, and the encouragement of them that do well ; the protection of the people and providing for the common safety, seeking their prosperity and doing all that is right to keep them from oppression, 1 Tim. 2 : 2 ; Prov. 28 : 16. Thus shall rulers be a blessing, a terror to evil men, but not a terror to good works. They will praise the virtuous ; they will be to us the ministers of God for good ; they will not bear the sword in vain. A government so conducted shall be as the light of the morning, when the sun riseth, even a morning without clouds ; as the tender grass springing out of the earth by clear shining after rain, 2 Sam. 23 : 4.

Let us look at a summary of the duties of the governed. The form of government under which men live will somewhat modify their duty to their rulers. In a well-regulated limited monarchy, or in a free commonwealth, men are citizens, and more liberty is granted, and more rights are guaranteed. In a despotic form of government, the people are subjects, and the will of the prince is the supreme law. But the form of government can never absolve any one from the duties he owes to his rulers.

1. As a general thing we are to recognize the actual incumbent of an office as having been thereto appointed by providence. " Promotion cometh neither from the east, nor from the west, nor from the south. But God is the judge : he putteth down one and setteth up another," Ps. 75 : 6, 7. When our Lord was on earth, it was much debated whether the Roman power in Judea was lawful. The question was submitted to him. He made no decision of the matter, further than this ; that it was lawful to pay tribute, and to submit to the magistrate in the exercise of actual authority. "Infidelity, or difference in religion, doth not make void a magistrate's just and legal authority."

2. It is our duty to treat all the officers of government of every grade with respect, giving to each the honor that is his due, and never using contemptuous language or deportment towards any of them. See Ex. 22 : 28 ; 1 Sam. 26 : 19 ; Ecc. 10 : 20 ; Acts 23 : 5 ; Rom. 13 : 7 ; 1 Pet. 2 : 17 ; Jude 8, 9. Beyond his place and out of it, an officer is to be treated, like other men, according to his merits. But in his official duty he must be honored.

3. We must earnestly and fervently pray for all who have au-

thority over us, whatever their rank or character may be. This is a reasonable and clearly commanded duty. The right end of these prayers is not to flatter rulers, nor to express approbation or disapprobation of their course; but that "rulers may have grace, wisdom, and understanding to execute justice, and to maintain truth ; and that the people may lead quiet and peaceful lives in all godliness and honesty." It is not possible that Paul approved of the enormities and cruelties of Nero; yet he prayed for him, and charged others to do the same.

4. We ought to pay all the taxes of every kind legally demanded of us by the government, whether it be what the Apostle here calls *tribute*, a poll-tax, or *custom*, a tax on property. This payment ought to be honest, prompt, cheerful. Matt. 18 : 27 ; 22 : 21 ; Mark 12 : 16, 17; Luke 20 : 24—26. It is as truly wicked to defraud the government as it is to rob the poor.

5. We ought to give a prompt, cheerful and conscientious obedience to all the lawful commands of our government. This is very clear from verses 1—5 of this chapter ; from Titus 3 : 1; 1 Pet. 2 : 13—17. This obedience is not to be rendered from the spirit of servile fear, but from religious principle—'for conscience' sake.' When a government issues wicked commands, which it is not lawful for us to obey, we must passively submit to the consequence of disobedience, as did Daniel and the three faithful young men, until God gives deliverance.

6. All the acts and measures of our rulers are entitled to a just and candid construction. We are no more at liberty to misjudge or misrepresent them than other people. Blind submission and fond admiration are not required of us. But "thou shalt not speak evil of the ruler of thy people."

7. When our good rulers die, we should express our sorrow in some becoming manner, as the children of Israel wept for Moses, and as all Judah and Jerusalem mourned for Josiah, Deut. 34 : 8 ; 2 Chron. 35 : 24, 25. "When the wicked perish there is shouting," Prov. 11 : 10; but when good men die, there should be weeping.

The duties of magistrates and people are enforced in very solemn terms. If the ruled have their duties, so have the rulers. If the one, by misconduct, exposes himself to reprehension, so by misrule does the other. If the oath of fidelity and allegiance binds the one, the oath of office in the other cannot be unheeded without moral perjury. If the thief and the robber, the murderer and the assassin shall not escape condemnation, shall tyrants and licentious rulers, who have every where a Doeg, be innocent? History tells us of the miserable end of wicked Shimei, who cursed the Lord's anointed. It no less warns us by the terrible judgments of God on Saul, once the Lord's anointed, but an envious, cruel creature, who took or sought the lives of his best subjects. The apostle here says that if a Christian violates the laws he shall receive *damnation*, meaning punishment from the civil authority, and from God also. Wicked rulers, too, often receive damnation, that is, punishment from the injured people; or if not from them, surely from God at last. See Isa. 14:4—21. Hodge: "There was a peculiar necessity, during the Apostolic age, for inculcating the duty of obedience to civil magistrates. This necessity arose in part from the fact that a large portion of the converts to Christianity had been Jews, and were peculiarly indisposed to submit to the heathen authorities." And there has been great reproach brought on the Christian religion by ecclesiastical persons claiming absolute exemption from the authority of temporal rulers—a thing utterly unknown to apostles and apostolic men.

DOCTRINAL AND PRACTICAL REMARKS

1. Christianity does not abolish civil government. It teaches the great to be condescending and kind. It teaches the poor to be quiet and cheerful. It declares a brotherhood in the church and abolishes the distinction of Jew and Greek, Barbarian and Scythian, bond and free. It declares that all are one in Christ Jesus. But it takes men in every civil status, just as it finds them, and fits them for their places. It requires that every thing be done decently and in order. It is an enemy of discord and confusion.

2. Government is of God and is expressly so declared to be, vs. 1—4. In like manner, marriage is of God. But there is this great difference between the two: men and women may, without sin in many cases, decline marriage; but no one can decline submission to government. Chalmers: "It is not the kind of character of any government, but the existence of it, which invests it with its claim on our obedience, or at least which determines for us the duty of yielding subjection thereunto. Its mandates should be submitted to, not because either law or justice or respect for the good of humanity presided over the formation of it, but simply because it exists." True it is a great comfort to live under a government which had its origin in truth and justice; but it is doubtful whether there are many such on earth. Meanwhile submission to all laws that are not wicked is clearly a duty.

3. Hodge: "While 'government is of God, the form is of men.' God has never made any one form obligatory on all communities; but has simply laid down certain principles, applicable

to rulers and subjects under every form in which governments exist." It is not uncommon to meet in America persons reared under monarchical governments, who believe that the only form of government which fully has the divine sanction is that of kings. Many such seem to be truly conscientious; nor in the conduct of public worship should such language be used as to wound their consciences. Yet they are certainly mistaken, although it is freely admitted that allusions in scripture are chiefly to kingly governments. Such seem to forget that God was not pleased with the Israelites for desiring a king, 1 Sam. 8: 7–9; yea, that he gave them a king in his anger and took him away in his wrath, Hos. 13:11.

4. Macknight: "It deserves both notice and praise, that in explaining to the inhabitants of Rome their duty as citizens, the apostle hath shewn the finest address. For while he seemed only to plead the cause of the magistrate with the people, he tacitly conveyed the most wholesome instruction to the heathen rulers, who he knew were too proud to receive advice from teachers of his character and nation. For by telling rulers, that they are the *servants of God for good to the people*, he taught them the purpose of their office, and shewed them that their sole aim in executing it ought to be, to promote the happiness of their people; and that as soon as they lose sight of this, their government degenerates into tyranny." It were well, if at all times, and peculiarly in times of political convulsions, men in power were constantly reminded of the same truths.

5. The rights of conscience are sacred and may never be infringed by the civil magistrate. God alone is Lord of conscience. Absolute religious freedom is the true doctrine under which alone men may expect exemption from persecution. For a long time, much was said of toleration; but the very idea supposes that governments have a right to judge of one's conscientious convictions. If any indeed shall make a plea of conscience a cloak of maliciousness, or covetousness, or perverseness, civil rulers are not bound to regard it. But when it is made in good faith, not for an occasion, but from solemn conviction, there is no higher act of presumption than to step, as it were, upon the throne of the Almighty, and assume his awful prerogative. Calvin: "This whole discourse is concerning civil government; and it is therefore to no purpose if they who would exercise dominion over consciences do here attempt to establish their sacrilegious tyranny." Hodge: "The obedience which the scriptures command us to render to our rulers is not unlimited; there are cases in which disobedience is a duty. This is evident from the very nature of

the case." That this is the true doctrine of scripture is evident
from the example of Daniel, of Shadrach, Meshech and Abed-
nego, and of the apostles themselves, who openly proclaimed,
" We ought to obey God rather than men," Acts. 5 : 29.

6. Let us love and cherish government.   It is a good gift of
God to man. Without it society is impossible. When Commodore
Cocke went, in the name of his government, to buy out the pirate
Lafitte, and thus make the navigation of the Gulf of Mexico safe,
he found near the residence of the bold buccaneer a man gibbetted.
On inquiry the great pirate informed him that the dead man had
violated some of the necessary laws of their combination.   It is
probable that the very worst regular government on earth is
better than a state of anarchy.   On this point Calvin goes very
far : " Princes do never so far abuse their power by harassing the
good and innocent, that they do not retain in their tyranny some
kind of just government : there can then be no tyranny which
does not in some respects assist in consolidating the society of
men."   Cobbin : " Where there is no magistracy there must be
anarchy.   We should be subject to the higher powers, for a more
awful state of things cannot exist than for every man to do ' that
which is right in his own eyes '."   Evans : " Never did sovereign
prince pervert the ends of government as Nero did, and yet to
him Paul appealed, and under him had the protection of the law
and the inferior magistrates more than once.   Better bad government than none at all."   Chalmers too does not hesitate to say :
" We believe that in every land, the institution of government,
even when administered by the most hateful of tyrants, is productive of good upon the whole."

7. But if civil government is in itself such a good that even mal-
administration cannot take from it all its benefits, how terrible is
the responsibility of those rulers and parties, who make it a terror
to those who do well, and seize, imprison, fine and murder those
who have been faithful to their civil obligations. When magistrates make good men groan under their systems of espionage,
inquisition and lordly cruelty, they must remember that there is
a God in heaven.   Even where rulers are sent by God to scourge
a guilty people for their sins, yet if they do it wantonly and cruelly,
not discriminating between the guilty and the innocent, and gloat-
ing over the miseries they bring upon others, the Most High has
a rod, a sword, a day of recompense and a prison for them, if they
die without repentance.   When the Assyrian had wantonly punished Israel for their sins, God said, Now I will punish you ; and
the retribution was condign and awful.   When by threats, uttered
in words or deeds, magistrates excite rebellion and work the

people up to frenzy and thus lose the respect which they would otherwise secure, it is in vain for them to attempt to shirk the fearful responsibility under which they have acted.

8. Kingdoms are not for kings, and governments are not for governors, but for the people whom they rule, v. 6. This rulers often forget and deal with men in caprice and haughtiness. They are appointed as *God's ministers for good.* Calvin : " Magistrates may hence learn what their vocation is, for them not to rule for their own interest, but for the public good ; nor are they endued with unbridled power, but what is restricted to the well-being of their subjects ; in short, they are responsible to God and to men in the exercise of their power." Hodge : " The design of civil government is not to promote the advantage of rulers but of the ruled. They are ordained and invested with authority to be a terror to evil doers, and a praise to them that do well. They are the ministers of God for this end, and are appointed 'for this very thing.' On this ground our obligation to obedience rests, and the obligation ceases when this design is systematically, constantly and notoriously disregarded." Let men in power remember that if God's curse is on the authors of anarchy and confusion, his face is awfully set against the authors of misrule and tyranny.

9. Any fair interpretation of this passage, particularly of verse 4, settles the question of the lawfulness of capital punishment for those crimes which destroy society. The sword was the instrument of beheading and, if never used for that purpose upon murderers and the like wrong-doers, it was surely borne in vain.

10. Let us set an example of cheerfulness and uprightness in paying to the government under which we live all its just dues of tribute or custom, v. 7. It is said that under some of the old governments of Europe, men otherwise respectable consider it a clever thing to defraud the government, especially in the matter of customs. Scott and Chalmers admit as much in their comments on this passage. Rumor states that like practices have gained a footing in our own land. Whether this be so or not, let every one, who has any fear of God before his eyes, eschew a practice so alien to the morals of the Bible.

11. Are you in private life, holding no post of profit, trust or honor ? Grieve not at your privacy. Every office brings with it a great weight of responsibility. If God in his wisdom and mercy relieves you of that load, thank him for his kindness. Among the very poorest occupations of men is that of office-seeking and office-holding. Many have a different judgment. But it is erroneous. The greatest man of his day in his nation, when dying, said : " If

I had served my God, as I have served my monarch, I should not have been left in this sad plight."

12. Let us never flatter tyrants, nor favor misrule, under any plea whatever. For this employment, some have such a *penchant*, that while they seem to. pretermit the living, they go back to former days, and praise dead tyrants. It would not be more ignoble to praise dead dogs. Let us be the stanch, unflinching friends of sound, sober, constitutional, civil and religious freedom. Let us rejoice in every advance that is made towards the universal enjoyment of such a blessing.

13. Let us always favor good, wholesome and permanent laws, without which all claims and pretensions to liberty are vain. It is a great thing when the stable institutions of a country extend their power to the ocean, the prairie, the wilderness, the retired hamlet and the great city. Hooker: " Of the law there can be no less acknowledged than that her seat is the bosom of God, her voice the harmony of the world. All things in heaven and earth do her homage, the very least as feeling her care, the greatest as not exempted from her power. Both angels, and men, and creatures of what condition soever, though each in different sort and measure, yet all with uniform consent, admitting her as the mother of their peace and joy."

14. It is sad when a government by any of its acts forces its good citizens to assume an attitude of apparent hostility to its course. Such was the case in the days of bloody Mary and of the ignoble Charles II. Chalmers: " And thus too at this moment, the church of Scotland—submitting to the civil power in all that is civil; and only refusing her obedience when that power assumes an authority over things sacred. Many are not able, perhaps not willing, to discriminate in this matter; and so, at their hand she suffers the obloquy of being a rebel against the laws." And so it often happens.

15. Let magistrates never forget that they will be judged by God himself, and perhaps punished in this world, and, if they die without repentance, surely in the world to come. Let them not forget that with God there is no respect of persons. Soon he will say, " Give an account of thy stewardship, for thou mayest be no longer steward." O! how will the abused, the wronged, the robbed, the whipped, the insulted and the persecuted rise before the Eternal Judge, and clank their chains to the shame and everlasting contempt and confusion of tyrants and persecutors, who once bore a sceptre or a whip in the dominions of this world.

16. One of the most difficult questions, touching the ethics of political institutions, regards the right of revolution—a right

which all men, unless they be tyrants, or their myrmidons, or fools, believe in—whatever may be their professions to the contrary.   The *Settlement* of 1688, which for ever cast out the execrable line of monarchs that had trifled with the rights of the people, was a great revolution in England.   The establishment of American Independence was by revolution.   Hodge : " When rulers become a terror to the good, and a praise to them that do evil, they may still be tolerated and obeyed, not however, of right, but because the remedy may be worse than the disease."   There are but few governments that set up any claim to liberality which do not admit the right of memorial, petition and remonstrance ; but sometimes even these fail.   Mr. Burke seems to think that when revolution is justifiable, the path of duty to good citizens is very clear.   Perhaps it may be.   Yet mankind have made so many mistakes on this great subject that the prudent will be extremely cautious in taking one step in that direction.

17. God governs this world, vs. 1–4.   By him kings reign, and princes decree justice.   By him princes rule, and nobles, even all the judges of the earth, Prov. 8 : 15, 16.   Of him and through him and to him are all things, to whom be glory in the highest forever. Amen.

Chapter 33

ROMANS 13

VERSES 8–14

SEVERAL PRINCIPLES OF MORALS STATED, AND RIGHT MOTIVES URGED

8 Owe no man any thing, but to love one another : for he that loveth another hath fulfilled the law.

9 For this, Thou shalt not commit adultery, Thou shalt not kill, Thou shalt not steal, Thou shalt not bear false witness, Thou shalt not covet; and if *there be* any other commandment, it is briefly comprehended in this saying, namely, Thou shalt love thy neighbor as thyself.

10 Love worketh no ill to his neighbor : therefore love *is* the fulfilling of the law.

11 And that, knowing the time, that now *it is* high time to awake out of sleep : for now *is* our salvation nearer than when we believed.

12 The night is far spent, the day is at hand : let us therefore cast off the works of darkness, and let us put on the armour of light.

13 Let us walk honestly, as in the day ; not in rioting and drunkenness, not in chambering and wantonness, not in strife and envying :

14 But put ye on the Lord Jesus Christ, and make not provision for the flesh, to *fulfil* the lusts *thereof.*

8. *OWE no man any thing but to love one another : for he that loveth another hath fulfilled the law.* Having defined and enforced men's duties respecting civil government, the Apostle now proceeds to call attention to some general principles. *Owe no man any thing*, the verb is cognate to the word rendered debtor in Rom. 1 : 14 ; 8 : 12 ; 15 : 27. In Matt. 18 : 28 ; Luke 16 : 5, 7 ; Philem. 18, it is rendered as here ; in Luke 11 : 14 it is rendered in the passive, is indebted ; very often it is rendered we *ought* or *are bound*. Three interpretations are offered ; 1. Meet all your obligations social, civil, pecuniary, moral. This of course covers the whole ground. The objection to adopting it arises from what follows ; q. d. meet all your obligations but love, when the whole reasoning of the apostle shows that *that* is a principal duty. 2. Erasmus, Scott and others construe the verb as in the indicative,

594

Ye owe no man any thing but love, for that includes all. The
original admits this construction, but the sense obtained is not the
best. 3. The better interpretation is the more common—Contract
not pecuniary liabilities which you are not able to meet, or, Avoid
as far as possible a system of indebtedness. Engage not in hazardous speculations except where they involve no more than you are
able to lose without injury to your family or your creditors.
Avoid all suretyships, which exceed the amount you are able and
willing to lose. Never buy any thing because it is cheap. What
you do not need is dear at any price. Never go in debt for a luxury
nor for a comfort. If you must ask credit for a necessary thing,
state fairly and precisely your prospect of payment. Sacrifice
everything but truth, honor and a good conscience to meet your
pecuniary liabilities. Yet when you have done all this, at all times
acknowledge your obligations to love all men and to do them
good. That is a bond from which a good man never seeks to be
released. The renderings of the clause are very uniform. The
love here enjoined goes quite beyond pecuniary engagements, personal promises, or the strict demands of justice. When justice has
held an even balance, and duty has paid over all thus weighed out,
love like a princely matron comes forth with her treasures, and
pours them out into the lap of want. The law said to be fulfilled
by love to man is the second table of the law, as the context shows.
Christ himself has told us that this is the second commandment
and like unto the first, Matt. 22 : 39 ; Mark 12 : 31. The exact
meaning is, he that loveth another as he loves himself has fulfilled
the law to that man.

9. *For this, Thou shalt not commit adultery, Thou shalt not kill, Thou
shalt not steal, Thou shalt not bear false witness, Thou shalt not covet ; and
if there be any other commandment, it is briefly comprehended in this
saying, namely, Thou shalt love thy neighbour as thyself.* The five precepts first alluded to are the last five of the decalogue. The last
precept is repeated in Hebrew and Greek, by Moses, Christ, Paul
and James, in all nine times, without variation, and in very plain
terms. It is a summary of the duties of the second table of the
law. It clearly teaches the duty of equal love to our neighbor.
The main object of this verse is to show the nature and the indispensable obligation of the love enjoined in v. 8. He further explains :

10. *Love worketh no ill to his neighbour : therefore love is the fulfilling of the law.* *Ill*, elsewhere harm, evil, anything bad,
noisome, or injurious. *Fulfilling*, the same word rendered fulness
in Rom. 11 : 12, 25 ; 15 : 29 and often. The meaning is that when
one loves his neighbor as he loves himself, the law calls for no

more, its demands being *fully* met in this behalf; there being no reference at all in the context to the first table of the law, which relates to our duty to God. James the Less, brother of our Lord, makes a similar allusion to the precepts of the second table; but it is not so full, Jas. 2 : 8-11.

11. *And that, knowing the time, that now* it is *high time to awake out of sleep : for now* is *our salvation nearer than when we believed.* Here we have a new topic introduced, apparently for the purpose of giving weight and solemnity to all the preceding exhortations. It is a call to shake off everything like *sleep,* a word uniformly rendered in the New Testament, here taken metaphorically for sloth, torpor, inaction. The latter clause of the verse is rendered by the Peshito: " For now our life hath come nearer to us, than when we believed." The consideration of the increasing nearness of the full deliverance promised to believers, as a motive to exertion, is presented by the apostle elsewhere, Heb. 10 : 25 ; and is one of the most awakening that can be presented. The Judge standeth before the door. Eternity is at hand.

12. *The night is far spent, the day is at hand: let us therefore cast off the works of darkness, and let us put on the armor of light.* Night, a word variously used in the Scriptures, sometimes describing the daily recurrence of darkness; sometimes, a season of mental distress ; sometimes, a season of great affliction; sometimes, a state of great ignorance. In this place it seems to be taken for the trying period of our earthly life, for it is added, *the day is at hand,* meaning the day of deliverance or *salvation,* as it is called in v. 11. If this is the correct view of the passage there is no need of detaining the reader with a notice of all the conceits and conjectures presented by various writers. That this is the correct interpretation is evident from the fact that it gives a good sense, is coincident with the scope of the context, is agreeable to the grammatical construction of the words and opposes no other clear teachings of Scripture. The inference is that we are therefore bound to cast off the works of darkness ; that is, works consistent with a state of spiritual ignorance and estrangement from God ; and that we must put on the armor of light, that is, the panoply of God granted to those who are the children of the light. See Eph. 6 : 11, 18.

13. *Let us walk honestly, as in the day ; not in rioting and drunkenness, not in chambering and wantonness, not in strife and envying. Honestly,* 1 Cor. 14 : 40 decently, that is becomingly. The cognate adjective is rendered honorable, comely, Mark 15 : 43; Acts 13 : 50; 17: 12 ; 1 Cor. 7 : 35 ; 12 : 24. As ordinarily men perform their honorable deeds in open day, and those of a base sort in the dark ;

so it is here. *Rioting*, elsewhere revellings, Gal. 5 : 21 ; 1 Pet. 4 : 3. *Drunkenness*, uniformly rendered and to be taken in the usual literal sense. *Chambering*, literally a lying down, here meaning lewdness. *Wantonness*, literally excess, immoderateness, here apparently referring to debauchery. *Strife*, contention, wrangling, a word of very uniform import. *Envying*, the Greek word is sometimes taken in a good sense for zeal, fervor, Rom. 10: 2 ; but here evidently in the sense of heartburning, or malice on account of the real or supposed excellence of others, as in 1 Cor. 3 : 3 ; 2 Cor. 12 : 20. All these are works of darkness. This verse and the next were the means of the conversion of St. Augustine. They banished every doubt. " Jesus had conquered."

14. *But put ye on the Lord Jesus Christ, and make not provision for the flesh, to* fulfil *the lusts* thereof. Peshito: " Clothe yourselves with our Lord Jesus Messiah." Wiclif: " Be ye clothid in the lord ihesus crist." But the Doway, Tyndale, Cranmer, Genevan and Stuart agree with the authorized version. Conybeare and Howson : Clothe yourselves with Jesus Christ your Lord. All believers are clothed with Christ's righteousness. Let them wear his image and follow his example, walking as he walked. No less than this is implied in a Christian profession. To *make provision for the flesh*, to *fulfil its lusts* is to seek and study to gratify our vicious inclinations, our worldly affections, the lust of the flesh, the lust of the eye, and the pride of life. It is to walk like hypocrites and unbelievers.

DOCTRINAL AND PRACTICAL REMARKS

1. The right management of our temporal affairs is not beneath the notice of the most devout, v. 8. One may live for days and weeks on crusts of bread, and yet have a peaceful mind and a good conscience, and may walk the streets without any suspicion of slight from men. But if as he turns corner after corner, he meets injured creditor after creditor, he must either be a bad man, or lead a very wretched life. This is true of all. It is peculiarly true of ministers of the gospel. The comfort and usefulness of pastors are often destroyed by the state of their worldly affairs. In secular business one of the greatest sources of evil is overtrading. Nor do the wrecked hopes and reputations of those, who have ventured on the waters of this dangerous sea, appear to have any power to warn others from the hazardous voyage. Chalmers : " The adventurer who, in the walks of merchandise, trades beyond his means, is often actuated by a passion as intense, and we fear too as criminal, as is the gamester, who in the haunts of fash-

ionable dissipation, stakes beyond his fortune. . . The frenzy of men hasting to be rich, like fever in the body natural, is a truly sore distemper in the body politic." Another great·error in worldly affairs consists in living beyond one's means. This proceeds from a foolish vanity, from luxurious habits, from a refusal to submit to the law of self-denial, or from a delusive expectation that in the future something extraordinary will occur. Chalmers: "Perhaps they who buy on credit certain of their inability to pay, as compared with those who borrow on speculation, and though uncertain of its proceeds, yet count on the favorable chances of success, so as that they shall be able to pay all—perhaps the former are distinctly the more inexcusable of the two." Much misery is also brought on mankind by borrowing. "The borrower is servant to the lender." What is generally wanted is a spirit of contentment, industry and frugality.

2. But if one is now in debt, what shall he do? Let him make up his mind that, cost what it will, he will do right. Let him retrench his usual expenses. Let him scorn luxury, while he is unable to pay his debts. Let him find out exactly what his indebtedness is. Let him not shun his creditors, but deal with them in a fair and manly way. Let him not under the plea of charity give away what really belongs to others. Let him avoid usury, practise rigid economy, resist melancholy, sacredly observe the Lord's day, maintain habits of lively devotion and cry to God for help. He has said, "Call upon me in the day of trouble: I will deliver thee, and thou shalt glorify me."

3. Is your love to man genuine? vs. 8–10. Will it bear the test found in the second table of the law? Are you guilty of sinful anger, of hatred, envy, the desire of revenge, excessive passions, distracting cares, sinful indulgences? Do you hate peevish or provoking words? Are your thoughts, feelings and actions kind, meek, gentle, charitable, courteous, forgiving? Do you cherish all chaste and pure thoughts, purposes and imaginations? Are your actions virtuous? Is your apparel modest? Is your behaviour light or impudent? Do you abhor all that is unchaste in songs, books, pictures and thoughts? Do you practise oppression, usury, idleness, law-suits, deception? Is your calling lawful? Ought you not to make restitution in some case? Do you never ask unconscionable prices? Do you promote truth and the good name of all men as you can? Do you hate reviling, scoffing, whispering, flattery, censoriousness, slander, exaggeration? Do you grieve at the good name of any? Do you needlessly mention the faults of any? Do you love to show kindness to all? Are you fair in making bargains? Do you plead your rank, condition or

former standing, as a reason why you should not love your poor neighbor?

4. A state of sin is a state of torpor, v. 11. Accordingly we see in the world amazing exhibitions of folly. The men, who have most need to be concerned and distressed about their spiritual condition, seem to have no more emotion than a statue; while those, who have made peace with God and have a good title to eternal life through grace, often fear lest, after all, they should come short of the heavenly rest. Is it not the duty of Christians, more than ever, to attempt to arouse mankind? I have seen a town of five thousand inhabitants awaked at two o'clock in the morning to search for a sick man, who in his delirium had wandered from his room. None complained of the disturbance of their slumbers. He was found. Yet in a few hours he died. And shall it be thought strange if we bestir ourselves a little to *awake* men *out of sleep?* Oh that they could be aroused! Even the best Christians often seem to be but half awake.

5. Pious reader, dear child of God, thou knowest not how near thou mayest be to thy heavenly home. Certainly thou art coming nearer to it every day, vs. 11, 12. Does this thought properly arouse thee? Chrysostom: " Since it was not unlikely, that in the beginning of their early endeavors they would be most earnest, in that their desire was then at its full vigor, but that as the time went on, the whole of their earnestness would wither down to nothing; he says that they ought however to be doing the reverse, not to get relaxed as time went on, but to be the more full of vigor. For the nearer the King may be at hand, the more ought they to get themselves in readiness. . . Let us put off imaginings, let us get clear of the dreams of this life present, let us lay aside its deep slumber and be clad in virtue for garments."

6. What unspeakable glories await the righteous in a future world, v. 12. Even in this present life, they are, as compared with men of the world, the children of light; and yet, as compared with the future world, they are still in darkness. The day-star hath already visited them. Soon the Sun of Righteousness shall pour a flood of glory ineffable upon their exultant spirits. But here they are sometimes borne down with manifold temptations; and there is a constant necessity for their 'recurring to the exercises of their first faith, their first love and their first obedience.' Chalmers: " It is the charge of the Apostle, that we should open our eyes to the realities of that unseen world, to which we every day are coming nearer. Let us by well-doing, not only put to silence the ignorance of foolish men, but the clamors of a disturbed conscience also." If we would make

our calling and election sure, it cannot be done without giving all diligence.

7. Holiness consists in hating and shunning sin, and in loving and seeking purity, in hating darkness and loving light, v. 12. These holy dispositions must manifest themselves in every department of thought, speech and behaviour. Many, who towards God at times seem to be quite pious, are towards men so lax and unlovely that many a non-professor is less disagreeable in the ordinary intercourse of life. Nor is it possible for ministers to exhort their people, or for Christians to exhort one another too tenderly or earnestly to perfect holiness in the fear of God. A failure here is fatal to all pleasing hopes of future happiness.

8. Let all our course and conduct be honorable, becoming, *honest*, v. 13. There is a region of twilight between the bounds of universally acknowledged baseness on the one side, and of universally accepted purity on the other, in which too many are inclined to walk. Let it be our aim not to see how near we can come to sinning without the actual stain of moral pollution, but rather how we may most effectually avoid the very appearance of evil. Brown: "The life of a Christian is nothing but a continual motion, there is no standing still for him here, he is upon his march, yea, his life is a race."

9. The wicked might easily know that their course is wrong, and will finally bring pain and wrath, because in this world it loves darkness, vs. 12, 13. Job describes the wicked of his day as "those that rebel against the light; they know not the ways thereof, nor abide in the paths thereof. The murderer rising with the light killeth the poor and needy, and in the night is as a thief. The eye also of the adulterer waiteth for the twilight, saying, No eye shall see me: and disguiseth his face. In the dark they dig through houses, which they had marked for themselves in the daytime: they know not the light. For the morning is to them even as the shadow of death: if one know them, they are in the terrors of the shadow of death," Job 24 : 13–17. It is of the nature of sin to be smitten with shame. Everlasting confusion will be a portion of the cup put into the hands of the wicked. Many things which men now practise openly and without concealment will in the light of eternity be seen to be covered with the foulest iniquity.

10. Let believers never forget that they have put on the Lord Jesus Christ, v. 14. Their relations to him constitute them Christians. As they have received him, so they should walk in him. As they have relied on his righteousness, so let them rely on his grace for sanctification. As they have professed to love him, so

let them prove it by a holy life.   He is their fulness, their teacher, their father, their brother, the Apostle and High Priest of their profession, their Advocate, their foundation, their corner-stone, their husband, their bridegroom, their meat, their drink, their life. Severed from him, they are nothing but poor, withered branches. Let them never spare their sins, but crucify the flesh with the affections and lusts.   Chalmers: " It is not the object of Christianity to conceal evil but to exterminate it—not to give its disciples but the face and appearance of virtue, but to give them virtue in substance and reality—and so as that they shall glorify the Lord with their soul and spirit, as well as with their bodies."   Brown : " It is not enough for people to close a bargain with Christ at the first, and by faith get his righteousness put on, that thereby guilt may be hid, and they put into a justified state."   The required holiness of life is not however for the justification of our persons, but for the justification of our professions.

11. Whatever you do, pamper not your sins.   Make not provision for the flesh to fulfil the lusts thereof, v. 14.   We are not indeed prohibited from caring for our bodies.   No man ever yet hated his own flesh.   But we are forbidden to study or practise the arts of luxury, effeminacy, idleness or wantonness.   " Peace is too dearly purchased by slavery of any kind, especially by spiritual slavery."

Chapter 34

ROMANS 14

VERSES 1–12

THE DUTIES OF CHRISTIANS TO EACH OTHER. AVOID CENSORIOUSNESS. REMEMBER THE SOLEMN ACCOUNT YOU MUST GIVE.

Him that is weak in the faith receive ye, *but* not to doubtful disputations.

2 For one believeth that he may eat all things: another, who is weak, eateth herbs.

3 Let not him that eateth despise him that eateth not; and let not him which eateth not judge him that eateth: for God hath received him.

4 Who art thou that judgest another man's servant? to his own master he standeth or falleth; yea, he shall be holden up: for God is able to make him stand.

5. One man esteemeth one day above another: another esteemeth every day *alike.* Let every man be fully persuaded in his own mind.

6 He that regardeth the day, regardeth *it* unto the Lord; and he that regardeth not the day, to the Lord he doth not regard *it.* He that eateth, eateth to the Lord, for he giveth God thanks; and he that eateth not, to the Lord he eateth not, and giveth God thanks.

7 For none of us liveth to himself and no man dieth to himself.

8 For whether we live, we live unto the Lord; and whether we die, we die unto the Lord; whether we live therefore, or die, we are the Lord's.

9 For this end Christ both died, and rose, and revived, that he might be Lord both of the dead and living.

10 But why dost thou judge thy brother? or why dost thou set 'at nought thy brother? for we shall all stand before the judgment seat of Christ.

11. For it is written, *As* I live, saith the Lord, every knee shall bow to me, and every tongue shall confess to God.

12 So then every one of us shall give account of himself to God.

THE apostle, having laid down the principles of conduct that should govern church officers in the discharge of their duties, given a summary of Christian conduct in general, explained men's duties in their civil and political relations, stated the duties we owe our neighbors, and urged upon our attention very solemn and weighty considerations enforcing these precepts, proceeds to consider the obligations, which Christians owe to each other, and in particular to such as labor under *weaknesses*, arising from prejudice, ignorance, a scrupulous conscience or other cause. Tholuck thinks the admonitions are addressed to the Gentile converts not to behave haughtily, but with affectionate forbearance towards their brethren of Jewish extraction. No doubt Jewish converts did often give trouble to their brethren. But there is nothing limiting the admonitions to persons of any nationality.

1. *Him that is weak in the faith receive ye,* but *not to doubtful disputations ;* Peshito: To him who is feeble in the faith, reach forth the hand ; Wiclif: But take ye sike man in bileue ; Doway: Now him, that is weak in faith, take unto you ; Stuart: Him that is weak in faith, receive with kindness. *Weak,* commonly so rendered, elsewhere sick, impotent, diseased. We had the same phrase in Rom. 4 : 19, on which see above. *The faith* may mean either the grace of faith, which sometimes lays vigorous hold of some truths and but a feeble hold of others ; or it may mean one's creed, the system of truth believed, concerning some things in which even some good people have sadly imperfect and confused notions. *Receive,* a word used to denote the taking of food for nourishment, the hospitable entertainment of strangers and the reception which God gives to the penitent, Acts 27 : 33, 34, 36 ; 28 : 2 ; Rom. 14 : 3. The same word is twice used in Rom. 15 : 7 : "*Receive* ye one another, as Christ also hath *received* us." The meaning is, Own and treat him as a brother in Christ. *But not to doubtful disputations ;* Peshito: And be not divided in your thoughts ; Wiclif: Not in demengis (judgings) of thougtis ; Tyndale: Not in disputynge and troublynge his conscience ; Genevan: Not to enter into doubtful disputations of controversies ; Doway: Not in disputes about thoughts ; Calvin: Not for the debatings of questions ; Stuart: Not so as to increase his scrupulous surmising. Weak brethren are to be received not to increase wrangling, not to make one man a judge of another, but in the exercise of Christian forbearance. Paul at once states a case :

2. *For one believeth that he may eat all things : another, who is weak, eateth herbs.* Disputes about dietetics were by no means confined to the primitive church. Perhaps in every age, men have arisen who have declared animal food to be unlawful, or who have taught that men's sanctification greatly depended upon the kind of food they ate. It is probable that the persons here spoken of as using only vegetable diet were led to their course by the

fear of countenancing idolatry by buying the flesh of animals, whose
blood and fat had been offered in sacrifice to devils; or that the
manner of butchering was contrary to their notions of abstinence
from blood, or who found swine's flesh mingled with many things
on Roman tables. Josephus tells of some priests, who for a time
fed only on dates and figs. In Dan. 1 : 8–17 we have a like instance.
Compare Acts 15 : 19, 20. At the same time the whimseys of even
good men are endless, and the early history of the church shows
that there was much trouble introduced by the subject of diet.

3. *Let not him that eateth, despise him that eateth not; and let not
him which eateth not, judge him that eateth; for God hath received
him.* The errors of the two classes of Christians were of an
opposite nature. The strong were in danger of contemning
others, while the weak were in danger of judging others. The
strong might regard the weak as scrupulous, troublesome, or
ridiculous; while the weak were ready to say of the strong that
they were hardened or heathenish. The reason given for avoiding
each of these errors is that God hath received both classes, and that
we may not treat a child of God insolently or censoriously.

4. *Who art thou that judgest another man's servant? to his own
master he standeth or falleth; yea, he shall be holden up: for God is
able to make him stand.* Calvin: " As you would act uncourteously,
yea, and presumptuously among men, were you to bring another
man's servant under your own rules, and try all his acts by the
rule of your own will; so you assume too much, if you condemn
any thing in God's servant, because it does not please you; for it
belongs not to you to prescribe to him what to do, and what not
to do, nor is it necessary for him to live according to your law."
The whole connection here shows that the matter concerning
which there was diversity was not an article of faith or a rule of
morals clearly made known; but one of those points raised by
scrupulosity on the one side, and leading to estrangement on one
or both sides. *Servant,* not before found in this epistle, literally a
domestic. *Master,* the word usually rendered Lord. *Stand,*
stand approved in judgment, or stand firm in profession : in
another form the same word is in this verse rendered *shall be
holden up,* so as not to perish or be condemned. So far as the
Jews were concerned, these troublesome questions arose from the
well known distinction of clean and unclean beasts, and from the
peculiar notions of the Essenes, some of whom were doubtless converted to Christianity. But in the proneness of the human mind
both Jewish and Gentile to make laws for the conscience, where
God hath left it free, may be found a cause sufficient for all these
troublesome questions.

5. *One man esteemeth one day above another : another esteemeth every day* alike. *Let every man be fully persuaded in his own mind.* There is no evidence that the observance of days here referred to relates to the Christian Sabbath. The argument for its universal observance in the primitive church is clear, decisive, and independent of the enactments of Moses respecting the observance of new moons, feast days, etc. Quite early in the Christian era too there began to be observed by Gentile churches days in commemoration of events of great interest to Christians, such as martyrdoms, etc. In the course of time there was much said respecting the holy days, whether observed by Jewish or Gentile converts.' The man, who observed them, perhaps thought them obligatory on himself. Soon he began to think them binding on others. While those, who observed them not, not being satisfied with their own liberty, were in danger of regarding their brethren as superstitious, scrupulous, or weak-minded. In this state of case the apostle enjoins that each one shall enjoy full Christian liberty—*Let every man be fully persuaded in his own mind;* Peshito: Let every one be sure, in regard to his knowledge ; Wiclif: Eche man encres in his witte ; Tyndale : Se that no man waver in his awne meanynge ; Cranmer: Let every man's mynde satisfye him selfe ; Doway : Let every man abound in his own sense. Other translations generally agree with the authorized version. Locke's paraphrase is, " Let every one take care to be satisfied in his own mind, touching the matter. But let him not censure another in what he does." The meaning is in such matters of conscience let not any go contrary to his own moral convictions ; but let not any man impose his sense of what is right on the consciences of others. The great reason for this course is next given:

6. *He that regardeth the day regardeth* it *unto the Lord; and he that regardeth not the day, to the Lord he doth not regard it. He that eateth, eateth to the Lord, for he giveth God thanks ; and he that eateth not, to the Lord he eateth not, and giveth God thanks.* The meaning of all this is that both the weak and the strong are alike the servants of God, are both seeking to glorify him, and have not attained to equal degrees of knowledge ; but each being conscientious in his own course is responsible to his Lord and not to his brother ; and so the bond of peace must not be broken. The proof of the pious character of each is found in the fact that he gives God thanks. Where God has left us free, let no man desire to make his own conscience a rule for the guidance of his brother. On the other hand let him not surrender his clear convictions to the moral sentiments of another.

7. *For none of us liveth to himself, and no man dieth to himself.*

8. *For whether we live, we live unto the Lord; and whether we die, we die unto the Lord; whether we live therefore, or die, we are the Lord's.* These verses contain a repetition and an amplification of the sentiment of v. 6. We belong to God, our life and our death are ordered by him; we are accountable to him for the use we make of our liberty, in things uncommanded; and if we make a right use of that liberty, we do glorify God living or dying, and are the property of the Lord, not of one another. The Lord here means the Lord Christ.

9. *For to this end Christ both died, and rose, and revived, that he might be Lord both of the dead and living.* There is some variation in the Greek reading in this place, but none which materially affects the doctrine, or even the sense. The object of this verse is to show the foundation of the doctrine asserted in preceding verses, that all Christians whether weak or strong are the Lord's; that Jesus Christ bought them by paying the price of his most precious blood; and that his resurrection was on the part of his Father an acknowledgment of the perfection of the work of the Redeemer and of his absolute title to all his saints. *Revived*, perhaps better rendered lives again. *Dead*, in this place evidently used in a sense different from that, in which Christ used it in Matt. 22 : 32. Here it means those who have departed this life; there it means those who have ceased to exist. The same is true of the word living. Here it means those who still enjoy their natural life; there it means those who still exist under the favor of God though their temporal life is ended.

10. *But why dost thou judge thy brother? or why dost thou set at naught thy brother? for we shall all stand before the judgment seat of Christ.* The first question contains a reproof to him who, doing more than is in express terms required of him, thinks others ought to follow his example. The second question is a reproof of him, who uses his Christian liberty to decline every service not positively enjoined or to refuse to make any distinction in his food, and despises others who are weak. The edge of the reproof to each is in the fact that both are alike amenable at the bar of Christ, the same Lord who was mentioned above. We are not each other's judges. The Lord Jesus is the common Master of all his people.

11. *For it is written,* As *I live, saith the Lord, every knee shall bow to me, and every tongue shall confess to God.* This verse is cited from Isa. 45 : 23:

I have sworn by myself,
The word is gone out of my mouth in righteousness,
And shall not return,

That unto me every knee shall bow,
Every tongue shall swear.

The quotation is neither literal from the Hebrew, nor entirely from the Septuagint, but gives the sense. Isaiah says, I have sworn by myself, Paul says, As I live. The two phrases mean exactly the same thing. *To swear by* one and *to confess to* one are, in Scripture phrase, acts of worship, whether sincere or reluctant. When these things are done they are an acknowledgment of the supremacy of another over us. The passage cited from Isaiah is given in proof of the truth of what is said in v. 10. The use of names and titles applied to the Father and the Son in this verse and the context does clearly evince that Paul regarded Jesus Christ as truly God.

12. *So then every one of us shall give account of himself to God;* Peshito: So then, every one of us must give account of himself to God; Wiclif: therfor eche of us schal yilde resoun to god for hym self.; Tyndale, Cranmer and Genevan: So shall every one of vs geve accomptes of him selfe to God. Doway: So, then, every one of us shall render account for himself to God. The point of the statement is this: We shall not give account for each other, but we shall give account for ourselves. This is universally true, there is no exception to the statement. Instead, therefore, of judging others, we should do well to be preparing to give up our own solemn and final account.

DOCTRINAL AND PRACTICAL REMARKS

1. In the culture of Christian character there may be great use in the diversity of attainments made by believers, vs. 1, 2. Some are babes, some are young men, some are fathers, some have clear knowledge, others are doubtful on points, which to most seem very plain; and so they are very unequal. But this gives an opportunity for the strong to support the weak, the clear minded to aid those who are perplexed; while the feeble lean upon the strong, and the ignorant seek instruction from the learned. It is perverseness, not fidelity to Christ that sows discord among these classes of disciples, each of whom gives evidence of love to Christ and of a tender conscience.

2. It is not wise equally to press upon young converts and newly formed churches all the truths of Scripture. There is an order in divine instruction; milk for babes, strong meat for men. Let that order be observed. At all events, let us keep the unity of the Spirit in the bond of peace. The inspired rule is, " Let us therefore, as many as be perfect, be thus minded: and if in any-

thing ye be otherwise minded, God shall reveal even this unto you. Nevertheless, whereto we have already attained let us walk by the same rule, let us mind the same thing." Phil. 3 : 15, 16. Luther spoke a sad truth, when he said : " Every man naturally has a pope in him." Scott : " We are all prone to make our views the standard of truth, to deem things *certain*, which to others appear *doubtful;* to expect by eager disputation, to bring men to see with our eyes; to perplex new converts with topics which they cannot as yet understand ; and to expect them at once to acquiesce in all those truths, which we have been learning for years."

3. Are you weak in faith? v. 1. Pray for an increase of that gracious principle, and for clear, sound knowledge in the things of God. While the Apostle would have such tenderly dealt with, he says nothing to encourage a continuance in such a state. He admits it is not desirable. Chrysostom : " You see one blow immediately given to him. For by calling him weak, he points out that he is not healthy. Then he adds next, *receive*, and points out again that he requires much attention."

4. But whatever diversities exist, let there be no schism in the body, neither strife nor contention. Let great allowances be made for natural defects of character, for bad instruction and for feeble-mindedness. Where there is true piety and a willingness to conform to the law of Christ's house, and men have the charity that beareth all things, it would seem impossible to introduce those sad divisions which sometimes alienate brethren and rend churches.

5. Let us always discourage doubtful disputations, v. 1. *Strifes of words* in the primitive church, as well as in modern times, have been great evils. Every age has furnished sad examples on this point. Chalmers : " Instead of contentious argumentation and vexatious controversies, at once endless and unfruitful, Paul inculcates a discreet silence, and meanwhile a respectful toleration—in the confidence, we have no doubt, that with mild and patient forbearance, all will come right at the last."

6. There will ever be diversities in this world. There were such in apostolic times, v. 2. Two things make this certain. One is the exceeding great scope and amazing sublimity of the divine truths submitted to our apprehension. The other is the great feebleness of the human mind, even when regenerated by the Spirit of God. It is only in that future blessed state for which we hope, and to which we hasten that we shall " all come in the unity of the faith, and of the knowledge of the Son of God, unto a perfect man, unto the measure of the stature of the fulness of Christ."

7. Let every member of Christ's church, whether weak or

strong, carefully avoid the sin of despising others, vs. 3, 10. It is a very dangerous sin to set at naught one of those little ones that has believed in Jesus. It is the duty of the parents and elder children in a family to be specially careful of the young and tender among them. It is hard, if not impossible to find any case in which contempt is a virtue. Perhaps it always partakes more or less of haughtiness. Compassion would in every case perhaps be a much more becoming sentiment. Let not contempt be indulged.

8. Let us carefully avoid all rash, harsh, severe and denunciatory judgments of our fellow-men, vs. 3, 4, 10. Doddridge: " Let us not add, to all the offences which may justly cause us to tremble before his tribunal, the criminal arrogance of usurping the place and prerogative of our Judge." Hodge: " A denunciatory or censorious spirit is hostile to the spirit of the gospel."

9. Human inventions in religion, however presented, are troublesome, even when not forced on our brethren, vs. 2, 5. They may be what Calvin somewhere calls "tolerable fooleries " —marks of weakness to be endured for a while ; but we ought carefully to abstain from pressing our conceits upon the attention of others. The history of persecution shows that immense sufferings have been brought on large classes of men, because they did not see the propriety or necessity of attention to some trifle, of which the Bible never once makes mention.

10. That our Apostle did not intend, in speaking of days, v. 5, to weaken our sense of obligation to observe the Christian Sabbath, is clear from other portions of Scripture. On the first day of the week, Jesus arose and was worshipped. On the first day of the second week after his resurrection, he assembled his disciples and said, " Peace be unto you," and confirmed their faith. The first day of the eighth week after his death was the day of Pentecost, a glorious Christian Sabbath. There are several declarations that the disciples specially observed the first day of the week as a season of religious assemblies. It is expressly stated that the churches of Galatia and of Corinth were enjoined upon the first day of the week to make their contributions for charitable purposes, 1 Cor. 16 : 1, 2. More than sixty years after Christ's ascension, John writes: " I was in the Spirit on the Lord's day," Rev. 1 : 10 ; showing that then the Christian Sabbath was as well understood in the church to be a divine appointment as the Lord's Supper. The resurrection of Christ was a very glorious event and is fitly commemorated every week. Apostolic example is as safe and correct a guide as apostolic precept.

11. Let us strive in all matters of faith and practice to be intelligent Christians, well instructed unto the kingdom of heaven,

v. 5. Let us indeed abide by our convictions so long as they adhere to us, not violating our consciences merely to please others, but let us not adhere to our own ignorance and scruples as if they were praiseworthy, refusing the proper means of enlightenment.

12. We are not our own masters, nor our own property. We are not the property nor the servants of our fellow-men. In soul, body and spirit we are the Lord's, vs. 6—8. If our views are at all right, we cheerfully admit that one is our Master, even Christ. We may not desire to *live to ourselves*, nor to *die to ourselves.* Christ's love and pity to us in our ruined condition claim an entire surrender of all to him. Olshausen: "An unreserved devotedness to the Lord is that which must ever be the essential of the Christian life ; whatever can consist with this may be willingly borne with in a brother. It is not until something is remarked in a brother, which might interfere with this devotion, that love acquires a right to be jealous."

13. Jesus Christ is divine. He is God. He is Lord both of the living and the dead. He will be the Judge at the last day. To him every knee shall bow and every tongue confess, vs. 8—12. Other Scriptures declare that he is Jehovah ; that he counted it not robbery to be equal with God ; that he is the brightness of the Father's glory, etc.

14. The fact of our approaching dissolution should never be forgotten by us, but frequently meditated on, that it may moderate all our thoughts and solicitudes about temporal things. How does the example of the heathen Philip of Macedon condemn the carelessness of many nominal Christians on this subject. That prince required a servant every morning thrice to announce to him in loud tones : " Philip, remember thou art mortal."

15. Christ's work, as an atoning High Priest and the great Founder of a kingdom on earth, is done, v. 9. Henceforth he is waiting till his enemies become his footstool. That Christ's death gave him a rightful authority over us is declared more than once in the Scripture : " If one died for all, then were all dead ; and he died for all that they which live should not henceforth live unto themselves, but unto him which died for them and rose again." His work is a finished work. His salvation is a perfect salvation.

16. The Old and New Testaments agree in teaching the same doctrines and the same duties, and particularly in subordinating every thing to Christ, vs. 9, 10. It is a great error of many that they slight some portion of God's word. All scripture is given by inspiration and is profitable. The New Testament is the key of the Old, but the Old is the lock which that key fits. The very types and shadows of the Old Testament, when explained by the

New, give us some of the clearest conceptions we have of spiritual
things.

17. No man has too solemn apprehensions of his accountability
to God, vs. 10, 12. No transaction is more fearful than that of a
creature called to reckon with his Creator. This accountability
is universal—*Every one of us,* says Paul. The account we shall
render will not be corporate but separate—every man for himself.
Nor shall anything escape the notice of the final Judge, Eccl. 12 :
14. Nor does any man know at what moment he may be called
to feel the full rigors of this responsibility. O my soul, be thou in
constant readiness to meet thy God.

18. So long as there are different Christian denominations in
the world, let the members of each set an example of courtesy,
liberality, brotherly kindness and charity. Doddridge : " Let all
the different sects and parties of Christians study to imbibe more
of the equitable and lovely temper which the apostle here expresses in so genuine a manner. The divisions of the church are
not to be healed by imposing our own sentiments, phrases and
forms, and censuring and harassing those that will not acquiesce
in them. Such a temper will only engender strife, and mutual
provocations will produce mutual increasing resentment."

Chapter 35

ROMANS 14

VERSES 13–23

SAME SUBJECT CONTINUED. THE DISTINCTION OF
MEATS NOT BINDING. TENDERNESS ENJOINED.
NATURE OF TRUE PIETY. OUR PECULIAR NO-
TIONS NOT TO BE OBTRUDED. KEEP A GOOD
CONSCIENCE.

13 Let us not therefore judge one anotner any more: but judge this rather,
that no man put a stumblingblock or an occasion to fall in *his* brother's way.

14 I know, and am persuaded by the Lord Jesus, that *there is* nothing unclean
of itself: but to him that esteemeth any thing to be unclean, to him *it is* unclean.

15 But if thy brother be grieved with *thy* meat, now walkest thou not charitably. Destroy not him with thy meat, for whom Christ died.

16 Let not then your good be evil spoken of:

17 For the kingdom of God is not meat and drink; but righteousness, and
peace, and joy in the Holy Ghost.

18 For he that in these things serveth Christ *is* acceptable to God, and approved
of men.

19 Let us therefore follow after the things which make for peace, and things
wherewith one may edify another.

20 For meat destroy not the work of God. All things indeed *are* pure; but
it is evil for that man who eateth with offence.

21 *It is* good neither to eat flesh, nor to drink wine, nor *any thing* whereby
thy brother stumbleth, or is offended, or is made weak.

22 Hast thou faith? have *it* to thyself before God. Happy *is* he that condemneth not himself in that thing which he alloweth.

23 And he that doubteth is damned if he eat, because *he eateth* not of faith:
for whatsoever *is* not of faith is sin.

13. *LET us not therefore judge one another any more: but judge
this rather, that no man put a stumblingblock or an occasion
to fall in* his *brother's way.* This verse is addressed to the strong.
The word rendered *any more* implies that hitherto there had been
improper judging. All the blame did not rest upon those who
were weak in faith. Tholuck: "Hitherto he had only wished to

persuade the two parties not mutually to condemn each other. Now, however, he asks the strong in faith, that for their weaker brethren's sake, they should not do a thing which might be in itself indifferent, even though they felt free in their own minds to do it." The play upon the word rendered *judge* is striking and characteristic of our apostle. *Stumblingblock*, always so rendered except in verse 20, where it is *offence*, literally *a stumbling*, then a cause of falling, or an occasion of sinning. *An occasion to fall*, in the Greek one word; in 1 John 2:19, rendered, an occasion of stumbling; in Rom. 11:9; Rev. 2:14, stumbling block; but commonly offence. The two words do not seem to have different significations, but are more than once rendered alike. Here one explains the other.

14. *I know, and am persuaded by the Lord Jesus, that* there is *nothing unclean of itself: but to him that esteemeth anything to be unclean, to him* it is *unclean.* It was very difficult to bring even the apostles, and much more private Christians, converts from Judaism, to believe that the distinction of meats was abolished. In the case of Peter it required a vision. Yet even he was afterwards led to dissemble on a like subject. Paul himself here informs us that he learned it by revelation from the Lord Jesus. He therefore had no conscience on the matter. But there were others, not yet well instructed, who regarded the distinction as still binding. These were the weaker brethren. How was their infirmity to be dealt with? Not harshly but tenderly. So long as they believed some kinds of food to be unclean, though they could not enforce their views on others, they were bound not to defile their own consciences by doing what they thought to be sinful.

15. *But if thy brother be grieved with* thy *meat, now walkest thou not charitably. Destroy not him with thy meat for whom Christ died.* The chief difficulty in the first clause relates to the word rendered *grieved*, a verb rendered was sorry or sorrowful, and often as here. In 2 Cor. 7:9, 11 it is rendered sorrowed or made sorry in the sense of true repentance. The best rendering in this place perhaps would be this, *brought to grief*. Wiclif: if thi brother be made sori in consciens for mete. In the second clause, the chief difficulty is with the word *destroy*, which is often so rendered; in other forms, perish or perished; in many cases it is rendered lose, Matt. 10:6, 39, 42; 18:11; Mark 8:35; 9:41: Luke 9:24, 25; 15:4, 6, 8, 9, 24, 32; 17:34; 19:10; John 12:25; 18:9; 2 Cor. 4:3; 2 John 8. Perhaps this latter is the better signification here. Lose not thy brother, that is, lose not thy hold upon his affectionate confidence and his Christian fellowship. Let him not become as a heathen man and a publican to thee. In verse 1,

Paul had commanded the strong to *receive* the weak. Now he says they must do nothing contrary to that receiving. In explaining this passage some have gone so far as absolutely to place the salvation or perdition of a weak brother in the hands of the strong But we know from many Scriptures that this is not so. Verse 4 of this chapter is decisive of the point that the weak brother no less than the strong shall be saved. Others modify the meaning by explaining the word destroy thus: Do nothing which has a tendency to destroy him. No doubt this embraces much of the spirit of the exhortation, but by adopting the word lose, as explained above, we entirely avoid the difficulty.

16. *Let not then your good be evil spoken of.* The apostle here states that on the main question the strong brother was right, that his principle was *good;* but he warns him that he may make a wrong use of even the truth itself; and that he is bound so to deport himself that his liberty shall not sow dissensions among his brethren, nor lead to the wounding of weak consciences, so bringing reproach upon truth itself.

17. *For the kingdom of God is not meat and drink; but righteousness, and peace, and joy in the Holy Ghost.* These words are spoken in confirmation of the precept of verse 16. Meat and drink are things of too little importance to be allowed to come in and disturb the church of God with vexatious questions. So far from Christ coming to regulate men's diet, he came to establish *righteousness* in every sense of that term, *and peace* in all the fulness of its blessings, *and joy in the Holy Ghost.* The kingdom of Christ is spiritual, not carnal.

18. *For he that in these things serveth Christ* is *acceptable to God, and approved of men.* *These things*, the Christian graces, particularly those he had just mentioned. He who practises them is *acceptable to God* even though he may be a weak brother, and not avail himself of all the liberty Christ has given him. Moreover his conduct is *approved of men*, that is, of just men, who take pains to inform themselves of its real nature. In Gal. 5: 22, 23, Paul enumerates eight of the Christian graces, and adds, "Against such there is no law." Bad as men are, their consciences are commonly on the side of the Christian virtues. This is so true that before the heathen persecutors could bring themselves to murder the saints, they charged them with atheism and with all manner of evil principles and practices. Indeed all persecutors habitually belie and slander their victims before torturing, killing or banishing them.

19. *Let us therefore follow after the things which make for peace, and things wherewith one may edify another.* *Follow,* a word expressing eager pursuit. The meaning is, Let us be chiefly intent

on the peace and edification of the church. Calvin: "We must indeed eat, that we may live; we ought to live, that we may serve the Lord; and he serves the Lord, who by benevolence and kindness edifies his neighbor; for in order to promote these two things, concord and edification, all the duties of love ought to be exercised." There is no danger that any man will be too intent on scriptural holiness.

20. *For meat destroy not the work of God. All things indeed are pure; but* it is *evil for that man who eateth with offence. Destroy*, not the word so rendered in verse 15; but one rendered dissolve, overthrow, bring to naught, throw down; see Mark 13 : 2; Luke 21 : 6; Acts 5 : 38, 39; 2 Cor. 5 : 1. Paul says of Christians that they are God's "workmanship, created in Christ Jesus unto good works." The *work of God* here then may mean a Christian. Again, the work of God is any good thing in the world, and so it may here mean the cause of religion, the kingdom of Christ. As a man is said to save a soul when he is the means of its salvation, so he may be said to pull down or overthrow a work or a cause when he uses the means suited to that end. *Pure*, that is not unclean. *Evil*, that is injurious.

21. It is *good neither to eat flesh, nor to drink wine, nor* anything *whereby thy brother stumbleth, or is offended, or is made weak.* The cases prominently presented here were such as these. Men brought bullocks and sheep to the heathen temples, where they were slain, and their blood sprinkled on the altar, and their fat consumed in the fire of the altar. The priests ate such portions of the flesh as they wished, and sent the rest to the market to be sold. In like manner libations of wine were offered to idols. The priests drank what they chose, and sent the rest to be sold by the wine-merchant; so that if one bought either meat in the shambles or wine in the cellar, it was probable, and in many cases certain that what he bought had been used to sanction and support idolatry. Paul said an idol was nothing in the world, and could never render unfit for use any gift of God; that he himself would as readily have a heathen priest for his butcher as any other man, and that the carrying of wine into a heathen temple could never render it an abomination. He said he and those who were strong in the faith had no conscience on these and like matters, But all this did not allow them to be reckless of the spiritual interests of the weak, so as by example or persuasion to lead him to the defiling of his own conscience. The verbs rendered *stumbleth* and *is offended* are cognate to the nouns rendered stumbling-block and occasion to fall in v. 13. *Is made weak*, the same idea as in v. 1, of this chapter.

22. *Hast thou faith ? have* it *to thyself before God.   Happy* is *he that condemneth not himself in that thing which he alloweth.* Faith here evidently means a religious conviction on a given point, yet differing from the religious convictions of some of the brethren. If such is thy case, have it to thyself before God.   " They ought to use their liberty with humility, caution, prudence, and self denial." Whatever a man's particular views on these disputed matters were, he was not at liberty to make them known ostentatiously.   The question, *Hast thou faith ?* appears in this connection to refer to the strong, whom he has been specially addressing. He does not call upon such to give up their convictions, or to hamper their consciences with the conceits of their weaker brethren ; but to behave with modesty and tenderness on the whole subject. *Blessed* [happy] *is he that condemneth not himslf in that thing which he alloweth* himself to practice. *Alloweth,* elsewhere rendered approve, meaning that which one permits himself to do.   It is a great thing to keep a conscience void of offence.

23. *And he that doubteth is damned if he eat, because* he eateth *not of faith, for whatsoever* is *not of faith is sin.* The doubting here intimated is opposed to the full persuasion of v. 5.   In Rom. 4 : 20 the same word is rendered *staggering.   Damned,* condemned or guilty ; see above on Rom. 2 : 1 ; 8 : 3, 34. The reason of his condemnation is that he violates his religious convictions.   Scott : " In general, every action must be sinful which is not done ' of faith,' as satisfied, by our views of the word of truth, that we are acting according to the command or by the allowance of God, and may therefore consider ourselves to be in the way of his promised blessings."

DOCTRINAL AND PRACTICAL REMARKS

1. If men would, in the strictest sense, mind their own business and meddle less with the affairs of others, there would soon be such a change in the world and in the church as would awaken surprising joy, v. 13. This would require a very thorough change in men's minds, speech and behaviour. The fact is, both the world and the church are in every age more or less heated with debates about things, in their own nature perplexing, and in most cases of little or no practical importance. Cobbin : " Some Christians are so rigid on some peculiar points which they adopt that, though they are minor matters, they will not admit them to be so, and spend a great part of their time in promoting their partial views on circumstantials, and causing divisions and irritable feelings, instead of promoting each other's growth in grace and mutual

edification. In too many cases they thus grasp at the shadow and lose the substance."

2. It is a great sin willingly to lead others to act contrary to their consciences, v. 13. This is sometimes done by want of tenderness on our own part, in an evil example, see Isa. 9: 16; Matt. 15 : 14; sometimes by bad advice, Rev. 2 : 14; and sometimes by an abuse of Christian liberty in general, 1 Cor. 8 : 9.

3. As there is much said in scripture and in other writings respecting scandal (using the word in an ecclesiastical sense), it may be well to give a few words of explanation respecting its nature, v. 13.   Brown : " This sin of scandalizing, or giving offence, is when any thing is done, spoken or omitted unduly, whereby our neighbor is induced, or an occasion is laid for him, to halt, stumble, or fall in his way." Pool : " Scandal, or offence, is either passive or active. Passive scandal is, where that which is good is, by reason of man's corruption, an occasion of falling to him. So Christ himself and his doctrine were a scandal to the Jews, 1 Cor. 1 : 23 ; 1 Pet. 2 : 8.   Active scandal is, when any thing is done or said, which gives occasion of offence to others, when it is an occasion of grief or of sin to them, Rom. 14 : 15, 21."   It ought not to be forgotten that our Saviour has given the most solemn warning to men to avoid every thing leading to active scandal, Matt. 18 : 7.   Paul teaches the same doctrine in 1 Cor. 8 : 12, and he carried out in practice the principles he laid down for others, 1 Cor. 9 : 19, 20. This duty is specially obligatory upon preachers of the gospel—" giving no offence in anything, that the ministry be not blamed," 2 Cor. 6: 3.

4. If the Lord has in his mercy given us a sound mind and a clear judgment on matters which perplex some of our brethren, so that we *know* and *are persuaded by the Lord,* let us be thankful for so great a mercy. But let us remember that the great adversary would pervert every thing, even so excellent a gift as this. The possession of it is no cause for haughtiness, harshness or insolence.

5. It is a great burden to any one to be left to carry about with him doubts and scruples on matters concerning which the majority of consistent and decided Christians feel well satisfied, vs. 14, 15. Chrysostom: "By nature nothing is unclean, but it becomes so by the spirit in which a man uses it."   Bp. Hall: " Nothing is, in its own nature, unclean; for God made all things good : but, in a man's conceit and opinion, some creatures seem unclean ; and, while a man is in that mind, surely that creature is unclean to him, because his conscience riseth up against the use thereof." Temptations are apt to run in classes. Feeble health, shattered nerves, natural weakness of intellect lay one peculiarly

liable to those states of uncertainty which give the adversary a peculiar advantage. Scrupulosity is no friend to grace. When men are ready to lay an undue stress upon things indifferent, making some things sinful, which God has pronounced lawful, and some things obligatory concerning which God has not expressed his will, they are in a condition peculiarly favorable to the devices of the wicked one.

6. For it cannot be denied and ought not to be forgotten that one's conscience may make to himself a thing sinful which is not so in itself, vs. 14, 20. It is therefore a great duty, binding on all Christians, not to rush on in the dark, not caring whether their course is right or wrong, but to seek light from God continually ; and that with a willingness to learn and receive the whole truth.

7. It is a great attainment, not made by all, rightly to use their talents and their liberty. One question which every man ought to ask himself concerning his course of conduct is, Is it right and lawful ? If this question is answered in the negative, he need go no further. But if in the affirmative, then let him ask, Is it edifying? is it charitable ? does it promote peace ? vs. 15, 19–21. Compare 1 Cor. 10 : 23. Calvin : "Let no cause of falling, no, nor of stumbling, no, nor of weakening be given to the brethren."

8. It is not therefore enough to do right, we must seem to do right, v. 16 The motives to this course are of the strongest kind. Stuart : " Christ died for sinners, and you are under obligation to show the spirit of similar benevolence to your fellow-men." The great object in this course of conduct is not to build up our own fame in the church, but to adorn our Christian profession and honor our blessed Master.

9. Let us never forget that our great business on earth is the cultivation of the Christian graces—even all of them, vs. 17, 18. The kingdom of God is within us, not without us. Stuart : "Spiritual life consists in holy conformity to God, peaceful and gentle demeanor, and joy such as is imparted by the influences of the Holy Spirit." When some one expressed admiration of Leighton's library, he properly said, " One devout thought is worth more than all my books." When will mankind learn and practise on the spirit of such a remark ? Even many, whose consciences approve the decisions of scripture in placing warm, living piety, full of kindness and charity, above all notions, rites and ceremonies, do yet seem to practise no better than others. How many talk much about the church, her rites, her doctrines and her worship, who yet have no joy in the Holy Ghost.

10. Let us carefully set an example of seeking the peace and edification of the whole church of God. No work is more im-

portant, v. ·19. Pool: " Christians must not only live peaceably, but profitably with one another." Brown: " In a time when offences do much abound thro' the practice of indifferent things, there useth to be much unrest, disquietness, divisions, debates, quarrels and endless, intricate, doubtful disputes, and everything tending to foster jealousies, controversies, strife and contention."

11. It is no small part of our duty to inquire into the nature and tendency of our conduct, as this whole chapter teaches us. We have no right to shut our eyes to the consequences of our own acts. Oftentimes the fruit of our own doings is so obvious that we need no other rule to indicate to us that they are right or wrong. Men have scattered arrows, firebrands and death around them, and have refused to look upon the mischief they had wrought, vindicating their own acts of wrong or recklessness.

12. Have you a strong, clear mind? Are your thoughts in advance of your generation? Do you see what is best with clearer eyes than other people? Are you one of the strong brethren? Are you certain that others will yet come to embrace your views? Or are you weak in faith, thinking some things binding, where others as conscientious as yourself see no moral obligation? In short, hast thou faith, or a full persuasion, where others have not? Then pester not the church and people of God with your notions, v. 22. Torment not others because they cannot see with your eyes. Speak not as though wisdom would die with you. Even if your views are correct, perhaps this is not the best time to adopt them. Every thing is beautiful in its season. Rain is good, but we do not want it in harvest. Snow is useful, but we do not wish it in July.

13. A good conscience is a great happiness, v. 22. It is above all price. Spare no pains to secure and maintain it. It is worth more than all the kingdoms of the world and the glory of them. Paul says, " Herein do I exercise myself to have always a conscience void of offence toward God and toward men." Never venture on a course of doubtful propriety. Avoid tortuous courses. Cultivate a continual sense of your own weakness and dependence. Above all see that your conscience is often sprinkled with the blood of Jesus. Scott: " Few are so happy, as to be quite free from self-condemnation in everything which they allow: a sound judgment, a simple heart, a tender conscience, and habitual self-denial are necessary for the enjoyment of this comfort: and most of us see frequent cause to condemn ourselves in this respect, and, by daily repentance, faith and prayer, to deprecate the merited condemnation of our God."

14. Carefully regard your doubts as long as they exist. This

is a principle in morals so clear that even Cicero states it : " If thou doubtest whether a thing be lawful or not lawful, thou shalt not do it." Paley also correctly says : " In every question of conduct, where one side is doubtful and the other safe, we are bound to take the safe side. The action concerning which we doubt, whatever it may be in itself or to another, would in *us*, while this doubt remains upon our minds, be certainly sinful." Pool : " What a man doth doubtfully, he doth sinfully." Brown : " Folks may be doing that which is lawful in itself, and yet in the doing thereof hazard their own salvation, in not heeding the right manner of going about the same." Chrysostom : " Let us then watch our own conduct on all sides, and afford to no one ever so little handle. For this life present is a race-course, and we ought to have thousands of eyes on every side, and not even to fancy that ignorance will be an adequate excuse. For there is such a thing, there certainly is, as being punished for ignorance, when the ignorance is inexcusable."

15. Mildly but determinedly maintain your Christian liberty. When Paul thought that circumcising Timothy might remove some prejudice and increase his usefulness, he circumcised him. Afterwards when certain *demanded* that Titus should be circumcised, he gave place to them by subjection, no, not for an hour. All attempts to diminish our freedom from the doctrines and commandments of men in matters of moral obligation are mischievous and should be resisted.

16. Chalmers : " There is another and we think a most legitimate inference, to be drawn from this passage. It is that Christians should either cease to differ—or if this be impossible, that then they should agree to differ. We of course exclude such differences, as, relating to what is vital and essential, imply that either one or other of the parties is not Christian, disowning, as they do, some weightier matters, whether of doctrine or of the law." Let us adopt the old rule : " In things necessary, unity ; in things indifferent, liberty ; in all things, charity."

Chapter 36

ROMANS 15

VERSES 1–13

EXHORTATIONS AND PRAYERS FOR MUTUAL LOVE AND CONCORD

WE then that are strong ought to bear the infirmities of the weak, and not to please ourselves.

2 Let every one of us please *his* neighbour for *his* good to edification.

3 For even Christ pleased not himself; but, as it is written, The reproaches of them that reproached thee fell on me.

4 For whatsoever things were written aforetime were written for our learning, that we through patience and comfort of the Scriptures might have hope.

5 Now the God of patience and consolation grant you to be likeminded one toward another according to Christ Jesus :

6 That ye may with one mind *and* one mouth glorify God, even the Father of our Lord Jesus Christ.

7 Wherefore receive ye one another, as Christ also received us, to the glory of God.

8 Now I say that Jesus Christ was a minister of the circumcision for the truth of God, to confirm the promises *made* unto the fathers :

9 And that the Gentiles might glorify God for *his* mercy ; as it is written, For this cause I will confess to thee among the Gentiles, and sing unto thy name.

10 And again he saith, Rejoice, ye Gentiles, with his people.

11 And again, Praise the Lord, all ye Gentiles ; and laud him, all ye people.

12 And again, Esaias saith, There shall be a root of Jesse, and he that shall rise to reign over the Gentiles ; in him shall the Gentiles trust.

13 Now the God of hope fill you with all joy and peace in believing, that ye may abound in hope, through the power of the Holy Ghost.

1. *WE then that are strong ought to bear the infirmities of the weak, and not to please ourselves.* This is a summing up of the argument of the preceding chapter. *Bear*, as in Rom. 11 : 18, and still more like its use in Gal. 6 : 2. It means more than to tolerate. We must help the weak to carry his burdens. *Please*, the word commonly so rendered in the New Testament. See above on Rom. 8 : 8. It occurs again in verses 2, 3 of this chapter in the same sense. We live under the law of self-denial. Both the

word of God and the example of the Saviour have placed us
there. This is the road to honor, glory and immortality. All
holy characters among men are formed in the school of self-denial. We were not made for our own glory, nor to please ourselves.

2. *Let every one of us please* his *neighbour, for* his *good to edification. Please,* as in v. 1. We may and we must be courteous,
gentle, condescending, obliging, giving no needless offence, so
that our neighbour, if well disposed, may find it easy to love us,
and that we may do him good. Thus we shall show true charity,
meekness and zeal. We must not envy his good qualities, nor are
we at liberty to lay down rules for his conscience. All this is to
be done not as courting popularity, but as seeking the edification
of our neighbour. Christians are often called God's building,
1 Cor. 3 : 9 ; 2 Cor. 5 : 1 ; Eph. 2 : 21. In carrying out the same
figure their *edification* is often spoken of. See Rom. 14 : 19 ; 1
Cor. 14 : 12 ; 2 Cor. 10 : 8 ; Eph. 4 : 12. It is delightful to see the
church of God *built up* in faith, in knowledge, and in holiness.
God is thereby so much glorified that we can do nothing more
important.

3. *For even Christ pleased not himself ; but as it is written, the
reproaches of them that reproached thee fell on me.* To a pious heart,
no argument is more cogent than that drawn from the example of
Christ. It cuts off all debate, and is an end of all strife. The connection of the last clause with the first is better understood by
quoting the whole of the verse from which it is taken : " The zeal
of thine house hath eaten me up : and the reproaches of them that
reproached thee are fallen upon me," Ps. 69 : 9. The meaning is,
that such was Christ's holy zeal for God that he pleased not himself, nor courted popularity, but willingly submitted to contumely
for the honor of God and the good of his people. That the ode
thus cited is Messianic, see the Author's " Studies on the Book of
Psalms."

4. *For whatever things were written aforetime were written for our
learning, that we through patience and comfort of the Scriptures might
have hope.* The object of this verse is to declare that the quotation
from the 69th Psalm, like all other Scriptures of the Old Testament, has its use and application in our day. *Learning,* everywhere else rendered doctrine, except in Rom. 12 : 7, where it is
teaching. Here it means sound instruction. *Patience,* endurance,
patient continuance, constancy. *Comfort,* cognate to the noun
rendered comforter ; several times rendered exhortation ; in the
next verse rendered consolation. Here it means the consolation
derived from the word of God. Some connect both *comfort* and

patience with *the Scriptures;* nor is there any objection to doing so. *Hope* is first graciously implanted in the soul by the Holy Spirit, and is nourished by his influences, taking the promises, histories and examples of Scripture, and thus strengthening the principle of holy desire and expectation. This is done that we may have hope in the darkest hour, in the most trying and perplexing circumstances.

5. *Now the God of patience and consolation grant you to be likeminded one toward another according to Christ Jesus.* This verse is a prayer that the Romans might be able, through God, who is the author of all constancy and comfort, to follow the example of Jesus Christ above stated. Those things, which in verse 4 are said to be produced by *means* of the Scripture, are here ascribed to the *power* of God.

6. *That ye may with one mind* and *one mouth glorify God, even the Father of our Lord Jesus Christ.* The word rendered *with one mind* is everywhere else rendered with one accord. *Glorify*, in Rom. 11 : 13, magnify ; but commonly as here. We are to glorify God as the Father of our Lord Jesus Christ, no less than as the Creator of the world.

7. *Wherefore receive ye one another, as Christ also received us, to the glory of God. Receive*, the same word so rendered in Rom. 14: 1, on which see above. Such reception is *to the glory of God*, because it shows the power of his grace and evinces the divine origin of Christianity, John 17: 21. And nothing lies nearer the heart of Christ and of his people than God's glory.

8. *Now I say that Jesus Christ was a minister of the circumcision for the truth of God, to confirm the promises* made *unto the fathers.*

9. *And that the Gentiles might glorify God for* his *mercy ; as it is written, For this cause I will confess to thee among the Gentiles, and sing unto thy name.* Our Saviour was a Jew, was circumcised, conformed in all things to the law of Moses, fulfilled all the righteousness required by the old dispensation and by the ministry of John ; and by his personal ministry brought the truth of God before the minds of the Jewish people, and *confirmed*, or established the promises made to the fathers, which promises related to salvation, and not merely to temporal blessings, and were by the Old Testament scriptures declared to be alike applicable to Jews and Gentiles. All Christians agree that Christ was the King of the Jews, promised to their ancestors. All should alike agree that his salvation was no less designed for other nations, though it was first offered to the Jews. On this latter point the Jewish scriptures are themselves decisive. The verse here cited is literally from the Septuagint version of Ps. 18 : 49. The manifest object of the apostle in

citing this and other verses is to show from the writings of the prophets that the Gentiles were always contemplated as a component part of Messiah's kingdom.

10. *And again he saith, Rejoice, ye Gentiles, with his people.* Some regard this verse as a quotation from Deut. 32 : 43, being an exact rendering of the Septuagint version of that place. This is better than to find it in Ps. 67 : 3, 5, where the same thing is substantially expressed in other words.

11. *And again, Praise the Lord, all ye Gentiles : and laud him, all ye people.* A literal quotation from the Septuagint version of Ps. 117 : 1, or, as that version numbers them, Ps. 116 : 1.

12. *And again, Esaias saith, There shall be a root of Jesse, and he that shall rise to reign over the Gentiles ; in him shall the Gentiles trust.* It is a literal quotation from the Septuagint version of Isa. 11 : 10 ; a clear and remarkable prediction of the certainty that the Saviour should reign over Gentiles as over Jews. Jesse was the father of David and to David it was promised that his seed should reign forever. The quotation is not literal from the Hebrew, but it sufficiently gives the sense.

13. *Now the God of hope, fill you with all joy and peace in believing, that ye may abound in hope, through the power of the Holy Ghost.* In v. 5, God is called the God of patience and consolation ; but here he is called the God of hope, not because he is the object, but because he is the author of hope. He alone can fill any heart with joy and peace in believing, or cause any to abound in hope ; and he can do all these things, *through the power of the Holy Ghost.* This benevolent prayer relates alike to Jews and Gentiles ; to strong and to weak Christians. Often in this epistle do the kind wishes of the apostle well up. His heart seems to be gushing with tender emotions towards all who love our Lord Jesus Christ.

DOCTRINAL AND PRACTICAL REMARKS

1. The same truths must often be stated over and over again, as Paul here repeats what he had as clearly stated before, vs. 1, 7. It is an old Bible rule, Line upon line ; precept upon precept. The great secret of instructing the young and the ignorant is, a little at a time and often repeated.

2. It is a great duty of the strong to help the weak, v. 1. It is so in families, it is so in armies, it is so in churches. Indeed in churches the obligations are very strong and tender ; nor can there be any exemption. Yet we often see things quite otherwise. Scott : " The powerful of this world often domineer over the weak ; but it ought not to be so in the church of Christ." Brown :

" Whoever is tenacious of his own opinion, and is bewitched with self-love and a self-pleasing humor, will walk most unchristianly when offences abound."

3. Instead of pleasing ourselves we should remember that we have far other work to do, vs. 1-3. We must please our neighbor to his edification, and please God to the glory of his name. Hodge: " The desire to please others should be wisely directed and spring from right motives." The desire to please God must be directed by the law of God itself.

4. It is our great business on earth to believe in Christ, and then to follow his blessed example, vs. 3, 5. Scott: " He is the most advanced Christian, who is most conformed to Christ, and most willing to renounce his own ease or indulgence, and to endure reproach and suffering, after his example, and in prosecution of that great design for which he shed his blood." He, who is not at all conformed to Christ, is none of his.

5. If you are reproached for the name of Christ, and in the cause of God, you are a happy man, v. 3. Compare Matt. 5 : 10–12 ; 1 Pet. 4 : 12–15. Reproach is a favorite weapon with the ungodly. It has been so in every age. It will be so as long as wickedness is left in the world. Heed it not.

6. If the Scriptures are for our learning, they can become profitable to us only by our studying them, meditating on them and practising them, with hearty prayer for the teaching of the Holy Spirit, v. 4. Jerome : " Love the Scriptures and wisdom will love thee." Chrysostom : " Is it not absurd, that, in money matters, men will not trust to others, but the counters are produced and the sum cast up ; yet, in their souls' affairs, men are led and drawn away by the opinions of others, and this when they have an exact scale and an exact rule, viz : the declaration of the divine laws ? Therefore, I entreat and beseech you all, that, not minding what this or that man may say about these things, you would consult the Holy Scriptures concerning them." Justin Martyr : " We must know, by all means, that it is not lawful or possible to learn any thing of God or of right piety, save out of the prophets, who teach us by divine inspiration." Selden : " There is no book in the universe upon which we can rest our souls, in a dying moment but the Bible." It is a great privilege to be allowed to read God's word in the original, but if we are not able to do that, the authorized English version is an excellent translation. South : " The vulgar translation of the Bible is the best standard of our language." Fisher Ames : " In no book is there so good English, so pure and so elegant. The Bible will justly remain the standard of language as well as of faith." " Buy the truth and sell it not."

Constantly cry, " Open thou mine eyes, that I may behold wondrous things out of thy law." In this life God's people have the
best reason for expecting troubles and sorrows : nor is there any
adequate provision for sustaining the pious except that which is
made known in the word of God ; and everything there revealed
may be useful to this end. Calvin : " There is nothing in Scripture
which is not useful for your instruction, and for the direction of
your life."

7. We cannot live without hope, vs. 4, 13. The reason is that
in the present life, our burdens are so heavy and our strength so
weak that if there is no bright prospect beyond the tomb, believers
must sink into despondency ; nay, they must be of all men most
miserable. It is chiefly in this way that Christians acquire constancy and have comfort in their course.

8. Let all glorify God, the Father of our Lord Jesus Christ, v.
6. He who can do that lives not in vain ; and he, who falls short
of that, falls short of the great end of his existence. He may be
learned, he may be famous, he may accumulate vast wealth, he
may be upright according to the standard of men, and yet if he
fails to glorify God, his Saviour, it had been good for him if he
had never been born.

9. Those do sadly mistake the intent of Christ's mission, who
limit it to objects narrower than those stated in Scripture, vs. 9-12.
When the Jews forbade the primitive preachers to proclaim the
Gospel to the Gentiles, it was a sign that the wrath had come upon
them to the uttermost.

10. All excellences of moral character, though enjoined by
God's Word, are never effectually wrought in us, but by the power
of the Most High, vs. 5, 13. His grace can transform the worst
moral character into the image of the heavenly Adam. We can
hope for no effectual renovation except by the Holy Ghost. Haldane : " The inward joy and peace of the Christian are the gifts of
God, and not the natural effects of anything in the mind of man.
All the promises and declarations of Scripture would fail in producing joy and peace in the mind of a sinner, were it not for the
agency of the Spirit of God." Nor is it any kindness, but real
cruelty, on the part of preachers to call on the people to work the
works of God in their own strength. In so doing they act like
the Egyptian task-masters, who required brick, but gave no
straw:

Chapter 37

ROMANS 15

VERSES 14–33

THE CONCLUSION OF HIS ARGUMENT AND EX-HORTATION, WITH FRIENDLY REMARKS, AND SOME HINTS RESPECTING HIS PLANS FOR THE FUTURE.

14 And I myself also am persuaded of you, my brethren, that ye also are full of goodness, filled with all knowledge, able also to admonish one another.

15 Nevertheless, brethren, I have written the more boldly unto you in some sort, as putting you in mind, because of the grace that is given to me of God.

16 That I should be the minister of Jesus Christ to the Gentiles, ministering the gospel of God, that the offering up of the Gentiles might be acceptable, being sanctified by the Holy Ghost.

17 I have therefore whereof I may glory through Jesus Christ in those things which pertain to God.

18 For I will not dare to speak of any of those things which Christ hath not wrought by me, to make the Gentiles obedient, by word and deed,

19 Through mighty signs and wonders, by the power of the Spirit of God ; so that from Jerusalem, and round about unto Illyricum, I have fully preached the gospel of Christ.

20 Yea, so have I strived to preach the gospel, not where Christ was named, lest I should build upon another man's foundation :

21 But as it is written, To whom he was not spoken of, they shall see: and they that have not heard shall understand.

22 For which cause also I have been much hindered from coming to you.

23 But now having no more place in these parts, and having a great desire these many years to come unto you ;

24 Whensoever I take my journey into Spain, I will come to you : for I trust to see you in my journey, and to be brought on my way thitherward by you, if first I be somewhat filled with your *company.*

25 But now I go unto Jerusalem to minister unto the saints.

26 For it hath pleased them of Macedonia and Achaia to make a certain contribution for the poor saints which are at Jerusalem.

27 It hath pleased them verily ; and their debtors they are. For if the Gentiles have been made partakers of their spiritual things, their duty is also to minister unto them in carnal things.

28 When therefore I have performed this, and have sealed to them this fruit, I will come by you into Spain.

29 And I am sure that, when I come unto you, I shall come in the fulness of the blessing of the gospel of Christ.

30 Now I beseech you, brethren, for the Lord Jesus Christ's sake, and for the love of the Spirit, that ye strive together with me in *your* prayers to God for me;

31 That I may be delivered from them that do not believe in Judea ; and that my service which *I have* for Jerusalem may be accepted of the saints ;

32 That I may come unto you with joy by the will of God; and may with you be refreshed.

33 Now the God of peace *be* with you all.   Amen.

14. *AND I myself am persuaded of you, my brethren, that ye also are full of goodness, filled with all knowledge, able also to admonish one another.*   Paul's charity towards his brethren led him to hope and believe the best things possible concerning them, whether they were at Rome or elsewhere.   He did not write as he had done, because he was filled with suspicion, but because he confided in them.   *Goodness,* a word uniformly rendered.   *Admonish,* sometimes rendered warn, Acts 20: 31 ; Col. 1 : 28 ; 1 Thess. 5 : 14, but always in the sense of admonish.   Nor was the church at Rome ignorant, for she was filled with all knowledge, that is, all knowledge necessary to mutual edification.

15. *Nevertheless, brethren, I have written the more boldly unto you in some sort, as putting you in mind, because of the grace that is given to me of God.*

16. *That I should be the minister of Jesus Christ to the Gentiles, ministering the gospel of God, that the offering up of the Gentiles might be acceptable, being sanctified by the Holy Ghost.*   The phrase *in some sort* may be rendered in part or in particular. It may qualify boldly, i. e. some things I have written are indeed bold ; or it may apply to all this epistle, as if in the whole of it there was an air of confidence.   He had not disguised anything.   This latter is perhaps the better interpretation, as the context shows.   Grace had been given him of God to do this very thing.   Besides he was the minister of Jesus Christ to the Gentiles, and it was his solemn duty to do all that he could for their edification.   The word rendered *offering up* is everywhere else rendered offering, and it here means the offering which they made to God of themselves through faith, an offering sanctified by the Holy Ghost. Some however think that the offering refers to the presenting of the Gentiles to God by the apostle.   The former is the better interpretation, though the latter is admissible.

17. *I have therefore whereof I may glory through Jesus Christ*

in those things which pertain to God.   That whereof the apostle might glory was nothing meritorious in himself, but grace that had been bestowed upon him in things pertaining to God; and in particular, the grace of the apostleship.   But all this was through Jesus Christ.

18. *For I will not dare to speak of any of those things which Christ hath not wrought by me, to make the Gentiles obedient, by word and deed,*

19. *Through mighty signs and wonders, by the power of the Spirit of God; so that from Jerusalem, and round about unto Illyricum, I have fully preached the gospel of Christ.*   The Apostle steadfastly and uniformly declines to claim for himself any credit for the work of God done by others.   Compare 2 Cor. 10 : 14–16. His sense of honor was quite too nice to allow him to do any such thing.   But God had so blessed his labors among the Gentiles *through mighty signs and wonders, by the power of the Spirit of God,* that it would have been falsehood, not modesty in him to deny his divine commission.   Two things he notices respecting his ministry. first, his faithfulness in preaching the whole truth—*I have fully preached the gospel of Christ;* secondly, the extent of his labors— *from Jerusalem, and round about unto Illyricum.*   Illyricum (or Illyria) was not always of the same size, but in Paul's days embraced a large region.   It lay on the east of the gulf of Venice, and was about one hundred and twenty miles in width, and four hundred and eighty miles in length.   Of course the countries intervening are included in Paul's statement, embracing all Asia Minor, Greece, etc.

20. *Yea, so have I strived to preach the Gospel, not where Christ was named, lest I should build upon another man's foundation;*

21. *But as it is written, To whom he was not spoken of, they shall see : and they that have not heard shall understand.*   This course of the apostle was not dictated by pride, nor ambition, but by the charge he had received of the Lord, and by the independent character of his apostleship, Gal. 1 : 12–20.   When he says, *As it is written,* he does not intend to state that the words cited receive their complete fulfilment in his ministry alone, but that his ministry was in accordance with the predictions thus uttered.   The quotation made coincides with the sense of predictions found in Isa. 52 : 15 ; 65 : 1.   But this is taken more from the former than the latter; indeed almost exactly from the Septuagint rendering of the former.

22. *For which cause also I have been much hindered from coming to you.*   This may mean either that he had been so much occupied in evangelizing other places more benighted, that he had not had

time to go to Rome ; or, it may mean that he knew others had been before him at Rome (and this was a fact), and so he would not interfere with the labors of others.   Among the converts, on the day of Pentecost were 'strangers of Rome,' Acts 2 : 10.   It is probable these were the first to carry the gospel to the imperial city.

23. *But now having no more place in these parts, and having a great desire these many years to come unto you;*

24. *Whensoever I take my journey into Spain, I will come to you: for I trust to see you in my journey, and to be brought on my way thitherward by you, if first I be somewhat filled with your* company. The word *place* may mean liberty to preach, the same word being rendered license in Acts 25 : 16 ; or, it may mean that there was no place in the region whence this epistle was written where the Gospel had not been fully made known.   The latter best agrees with the context.   The desire which Paul had long had of visiting Rome arose not only from the fact that he wished to do them good, but that he hoped to derive benefit from them, as they were famous for their faith, Rom. 1 : 8–15.   There is no scriptural account that Paul ever visited Spain, but there is nothing in Scripture against it.   Early ecclesiastical writers speak confidently of his having done so, and some moderns contend that he came as far as Britain.   It may be so.   Yet there seems to be little doubt that Paul's first visit to Rome was as a prisoner, though a prisoner having considerable liberty, dwelling in his own hired house.

25. *But now I go unto Jerusalem to minister unto the saints.*

26. *For it hath pleased them of Macedonia and Achaia to make a certain contribution for the poor saints which are at Jerusalem.*

27. *It hath pleased them verily : and their debtors they are.   For if the Gentiles have been made partakers of their spiritual things, their duty is also to minister to them in carnal things.   To minister* unto the saints was to supply their temporal necessities.   From the day of Pentecost nearly to the time of the destruction of the holy city there seems to have been a constant influx into Jerusalem of converted Jews.   Many of these were poor and for thirty or forty years there seems to have been no time when special kindness to the *poor saints* at Jerusalem was not called for.   Paul says that contributions from other churches were most reasonably called for.   The word of the Lord had gone forth from Jerusalem. This was the mother church.   Through her the gospel had been spread abroad.   If the Gentiles had received the gospel, it was a small thing that they should contribute subsistence to their poor brethren, who, for Christ's sake, were hated of their kindred the Jews, and sadly persecuted even at Jerusalem.   The statement

that the churches of Macedonia and Achaia had done no more than their duty, though they had done it very heartily, is not designed so much for the churches named as it is for a suggestion to the church at Rome. Tholuck: " Macedonia and Achaia were the two provinces into which the Romans divided the whole of Greece."

28. *When therefore I have performed this, and have sealed unto them this fruit, I will come by you into Spain.* The *fruit* was the bounty of the above-named churches, and the *sealing* of it was the safe delivery of it in person, to those who had charge of this matter in the mother church. It is probable that the sum sent was large ; compare 2 Cor. 8 : 1–4 ; 9 : 2 ; and that Paul had means of safely transmitting it not granted to every one ; for when other persons could render like service just as well as the apostles, they declined it, Acts 6 : 1–6.

29. *And I am sure that, when I come unto you, I shall come in the fulness of the blessing of the gospel of Christ.* Some manuscripts and editors omit the words *of the gospel.* This may be done without materially changing the sense. What a blessing the visit of such an one as Paul the aged must have been to a church ever so well established.

30. *Now I beseech you, brethren, for the Lord Jesus Christ's sake, and for the love of the Spirit, that ye strive together with me in* your *prayers to God for me :*

31. *That I may be delivered from them that do not believe in Judea ; and that my service which* I have *for Jerusalem may be accepted of the saints ;*

32. *That I may come unto you with joy by the will of God, and may with you be refreshed.* Paul knew too well the malice of the unconverted Jews against Christians, and against himself in particular, to suppose that he could go to Jerusalem on any errand whatever, without being an object of relentless persecution. He therefore beseeches the Romans that they would unite their prayers with his for his deliverance from ungodly men, and that he might be allowed to carry to the suffering poor the *service* or contributions of the churches, and so, having accomplished that object, to proceed speedily to Rome. His beseeching assumes the form of the most solemn obtestation. In Rom. 12 : 1 he appeals to them by the mercies of God. Here he begs them "for our Lord Jesus Christ's sake, and for the love of the Spirit ;" q. d. if you have any regard to Christ, or if the Holy Ghost has wrought in your heart any love to Christ or his people, I beseech you to pray for me. *Accepted,* in v. 16, and in 1 Pet. 2 : 5 rendered acceptable. It means more than that merely it might be received,

even that it might so reach them as to be useful, refreshing and pleasing. How the tender heart of Paul loved to receive as well as give *refreshment* is declared in several epistles, 1 Cor. 16: 18; 2 Cor. 7: 13; Philem. 7, 20. Here, as in the earlier part of the epistle, he expresses a desire that the refreshment might be mutual.

33. *Now the God of peace* be *with you all. Amen.* On *Amen* see above on Rom. 1 : 25; 9 : 5; 11 : 36. The form of benediction used in this verse is the same as that found in Phil. 4: 23; 2 Thess. 3: 18. It is Paul's pronunciation of a blessing upon the Romans in the name of the Lord.

DOCTRINAL AND PRACTICAL REMARKS

1. Whenever truth will allow, and a fit occasion shall offer, we should express favorable opinions of our Christian brethren, v. 14. Good men need encouragement as well as warning.

2. Yet the messengers of God should not speak timidly, but should use great plainness and freedom of speech, v. 15. They are not sent to deliver their own lucubrations or conceits. They have a message from God to men. It is very solemn, weighty, and full of urgency. Let them speak accordingly.

3. In worshipping God we can make no offering so pleasing, as when we heartily and wholly offer ourselves. It is sure to be acceptable through Jesus Christ, v. 16. We may bring to God all else but our hearts and ourselves, and it will be an offence to him, a smoke in his nose.

4. Ministers must so live and act that men cannot despise their youth or age, their life or their doctrine, v. 17. Compare 1 Tim. 4: 12; Tit. 2: 15. When called thereto, they may vindicate their office and calling; they may modestly show how God has honored them and blessed their labors. Nor should people be offended when ministers deal much in old and familiar truths. Of all branches of knowledge men are best informed respecting their duty ; yet of no part of truth are they so forgetful. The higher estimate an humble minister puts on his office, the deeper will be his sense of responsibility to God. Nor will he hesitate to let the people know that he is influenced by a constant remembrance of his accountability to the Judge of all.

5. What a rousing ministry was Paul's! His soul was stirred to its depths! And it stirred the souls of others! vs. 18, 19. He would spend and be spent. He would wear out, but not rust out. He set the world on fire. He knew that men, unreconciled to God, must eternally perish. We may not expect his miraculous

gifts; we may not have his great talents, but why may not the humblest man pray to be fired with his zeal, and animated with his spirit? Perhaps in nothing is the ministry more deficient than in untiring devotion to the work of saving men's souls.

6. The gospel conveys to men no saving good, until they are *obedient*, v. 18. They must receive the faith it teaches; they must practice the precepts it inculcates. Knowledge will save no man, unless it is knowledge sanctified. Professions are right, but they must be sincere, and no profession is sincere unless the truth of God controls the life. Until the truth makes us bow down our necks, and take Christ's yoke upon us, it wholly fails of its great design. Nor will any man ever thus submit to the truth until God puts his Spirit within him, and gives him a new heart and a right temper.

7. The gospel needs no more evidence than has from the first accompanied it. It has been attested by *mighty signs and wonders*, v. 19. It has withstood the rage of man and the wrath of hell. It still works as great transformations of character as it ever did. The wicked sometimes say, if one would rise from the dead, we would believe. Why, the very author of Christianity rose from the dead; yet the wicked still refuse to give their hearts to Christ. Men know that they should on proper evidence receive all truth. Accordingly they generally profess their readiness to yield to it. The very murderers of Christ did so: "If thou be the Son of God, come down from the cross, and we will believe on thee." If he had come down from the cross he would have brought down with him the unatoned sins of the world. But he did more. He died, and then burst the bars of death; and they gave *large money* to the soldiers to say that his disciples had stolen his dead body. No evidence will satisfy a wicked and perverse heart.

8. It is a great shame when one enters into the labors of another, and claims for himself the honor of all the good done in a community, where the gospel has been long and faithfully preached before he came. Yet such odious exhibitions are not very rare. Paul was careful that such folly and vanity should not be charged to him, vs. 19, 20. In an established state of the church one is constantly sowing and another reaping. It is not seemly to be contending who was the instrument of the good done. All efforts would be alike fruitless but for the power and grace of God.

9. The great matter of preaching is the gospel of Christ, vs. 19, 20. It alone is the power of God unto salvation. It is sad indeed when men put in its place their philosophy, their politics or any thing whatever. It is the deliberate judgment of a large body of

excellent men that more harm has been done to the cause of Christ by introducing into the pulpit matters foreign from the great commission than it is possible for the authors of such mischief ever to undo. Brown: "The main thing which the ministers of the gospel ought to be ever driving at, in all their deportment in the office of the ministry, is the salvation and reconciliation of their people unto God."

10. The further people are from God and righteousness, the more ignorant and destitute they are, the greater is the need of giving them the gospel, vs. 20, 21. This was evidently Paul's plan. And it well coincided with the plan of our Saviour, who commenced his ministry in Galilee of the Gentiles among a people, which sat in darkness, and in the region and shadow of death, Matt. 4 : 15, 16.

11. It is a blessed employment, greatly ministering to the personal comfort of godly preachers, to be allowed to engage in the work of planting churches, v. 20. Their trials are indeed great, but their comforts are greater. Talk with God's aged servants, who have spent at least a portion of their lives in such work, and see with what zest, even down to old age, they recount the trials and triumphs of their evangelistic labors. Brown: " As it is a matter of great difficulty to get a people brought under the gospel, who were living in atheism and idolatry before; so is it a matter of great honor to be blessed of God in laying the foundation of any good in a place." Scott: "It is honorable, when ministers, who have the opportunity, boldly face opposition and hardship in carrying the gospel to those places, where ' Christ hath not yet been named;' and when they would rather make irruptions into the uninvaded provinces of Satan's dark domain, than more securely garrison such as have already been torn from him . . . In this the genuine missionary far more resembles the apostle, than any stated pastor or ruler of the church can do." So blessed is this work, even in the midst of trials and hardships, perils and persecutions, that the author has never yet received a melancholy letter from one engaged in making known Christ to the heathen, although he has been corresponding with such men for more than forty-five years.

12. It is not in man that walketh to direct his steps, v. 22. Man proposes, God disposes. Let not the ministers of Christ despond because their course in life is directed so very differently from what they had planned. It is the prerogative of God not only to call whom he will into the ministry, but to send them whither he will. Blessed be his name. While the under-shepherds oversee the flock, the chief Shepherd oversees the pastors.

13. When God shuts one door, let us see if another is not open, v. 23. When one is sure that his work is done in a given field, why should he longer tarry there, and waste his strength?

14. It is probable that as long as the world stands, there will be calls for charitable contributions, vs. 25–28. If those, who complain of such demands upon their liberality, would but consider what an honor and blessing it is to be allowed to bear some part in spreading the knowledge of God, and in administering to the comfort of afflicted saints, they would surely express themselves far otherwise. It was a mark of an ignoble spirit in one, who was thrifty in worldly affairs, to boast that his membership in the church of Christ for twelve months had cost him but twenty-five cents. It is greatly to be lamented that the church is so afflicted with members who are narrow-minded and close-fisted, if not hard-hearted.

15. Of how little value are carnal (or temporal) things compared with spiritual, v. 27. The former are so transitory, the latter abide for ever, taking fast hold on eternity. Paul could not have argued more cogently than, when pleading for the support of the ministry, he said, "If we have sown unto you spiritual things, is it a great thing if we shall reap your carnal things?" 1 Cor. 9: 11. Some one says, "Mankind are divided into two great sects, the timists and eternists." Reader, to which sect do you belong?

16. Wherever ministers go they ought to seek to go in the fulness of the blessing of the gospel of Christ, v. 29. In the same spirit the people ought to desire them to come. The best news that ministers can carry is the glad tidings of great joy, made known in the gospel of Christ.

17. Prayer for ministers of the gospel is on many accounts a most reasonable duty, often enjoined in the sacred Scriptures, vs. 30–32. Compare 1 Thess. 5: 25; 2 Thess. 3: 1. Prayer has lost none of its efficacy. The ablest ministers the world has ever seen have greatly desired in their behalf the prayers of the godly. Brown: "The more of God's grace be in a soul, the more will one value that enriching trade of prayer; and the more earnest will he be to have the concurrence even of the weakest Christians in prayer."

18. It is an unspeakable mercy to be delivered from wicked and unreasonable men, whether by our own prayers or the prayers of others, v. 31. Compare 2 Thess. 3: 2. It is a great personal affliction and a great hindrance to usefulness to be left in the power of the enemies of God even for a short time.

19. No journey is successful but by the will of God, v. 32.

Compare Rom. 1 : 10. In the commonest affairs of life we need the constant and kindly interposition of the Most High. Without it nothing can prosper.

20. The benedictions of Scripture are among its most precious teachings and encouragements, v. 33. See above on Rom. 1 : 7. The tranquility which God alone can give is worth more than all the pomp and pageantry of earth. Evans: "The Lord of hosts, the God of battle, is the God of peace, the Author and Lover of peace." When he giveth peace, who can make disquiet? His voice calms the violence of the sea as well as the tumult of the people.

Chapter 38

ROMANS 16
VERSES 1–27

SALUTATIONS TO MANY. WARNINGS AGAINST DIVISIONS. BENEDICTIONS AND DOXOLOGIES.

I COMMEND unto you Phebe our sister, which is a servant of the church which is at Cenchrea.

2 That ye receive her in the Lord, as becometh saints, and that ye assist her in whatsoever business she hath need of you: for she hath been a succourer of many and of myself also.

3 Greet Priscilla and Aquila, my helpers in Christ Jesus:

4 Who have for my life laid down their own necks: unto whom not only I give thanks, but also all the churches of the Gentiles.

5 Likewise *greet* the church that is in their house. Salute my well beloved Epenetus, who is the first fruits of Achaia unto Christ.

6 Greet Mary, who bestowed much labour on us.

7 Salute Andronicus and Junia, my kinsmen, and my fellow-prisoners, who are of note among the apostles, who also were in Christ before me.

8 Greet Amplias, my beloved in the Lord.

9 Salute Urbane, our helper in Christ, and Stachys, my beloved.

10 Salute Apelles approved in Christ. Salute them which are cf Aristobulus' *household*.

11 Salute Herodion my kinsman. Greet them that be of the *household* of Narcissus, which are in the Lord.

12 Salute Tryphena and Tryphosa, who labour in the Lord. Salute the beloved Persis, which laboured much in the Lord.

13 Salute Rufus chosen in the Lord, and his mother and mine.

14 Salute Asyncritus, Phlegon, Hermas, Patrobas, Hermes, and the brethren which are with them.

15 Salute Philologus, and Julia, Nereus, and his sister, and Olympas, and all the saints which are with them.

16 Salute one another with a holy kiss. The churches of Christ salute you.

17 Now I beseech you, brethren, mark them which cause divisions and offences contrary to the doctrine which ye have learned; and avoid them.

18 For they that are such serve not our Lord Jesus Christ, but their own belly; and by good words and fair speeches deceive the hearts of the simple.

19 For your obedience is come abroad unto all *men*. I am glad therefore on

637

your behalf: but yet I would have you wise unto that which is good, and simple concerning evil.

20 And the God of peace shall bruise Satan under your feet shortly. The grace of our Lord Jesus Christ *be* with you. Amen.

21 Timotheus my workfellow, and Lucius, and Jason, and Sosipater, my kins .nen, salute you.

22 I Tertius, who wrote *this* epistle, salute you in the Lord.

23 Gaius mine host, and of the whole church, saluteth you. Erastus the chamberlain of the city saluteth you, and Quartus a brother.

24 The grace of our Lord Jesus Christ *be* with you all. Amen.

25 Now to him that is of power to stablish you according to my gospel, and the preaching of Jesus Christ, according to the revelation of the mystery, which was kept secret since the world began.

26 But now is made manifest, and by the Scriptures of the prophets, according to the commandment of the everlasting God, made known to all nations for the obedience of faith :

27 To God only wise, *be* glory through Jesus Christ for ever. Amen.

1. *I COMMEND unto you Phebe our sister, which is a servant of the church which is at Cenchrea.*

2. *That ye receive her in the Lord, as becometh saints, and that ye assist her in whatsoever business she hath need of you : for she hath been a succourer of many, and of myself also.* Phebe, a name not found elsewhere in Scripture. It signifies pure ; a name in this case well bestowed. She is called a sister and servant of the church. Some have attempted to show that she held the office of deaconess. This can hardly be proven. But she rendered eminent services to the church. Her membership was in the church of Cenchrea, which was the port of Corinth on the Asiatic side of that city. From this port Paul sailed for Syria with Priscilla and Aquila, Acts 18 : 18. It is mentioned in no other place in the Bible. It bears the modern name of Kikries. The port on the western side of Corinth was called Lechaeum. Some think Phebe was engaged, as Lydia was, in some branch of trade, and that in the prosecution of her business, she went to Rome. The word rendered *business* would authorize this construction. But it also means a matter, or thing of any kind whatever. The probability is that she was a person of considerable worldly possessions, and had very much given herself up to doing good ; for Paul says she was a *succourer,* helper or benefactress of many and of himself also. Under these circumstances he asks that her reception may be of the kindest sort, such as Christians only know how to give.

3. *Greet Priscilla and Aquila, my helpers in Christ Jesus ;*

4. *Who have for my life laid down their own necks : unto whom, not only I give thanks, but also all the churches of the Gentiles.* Priscilla

(or Prisca) was the wife of Aquila. They are always mentioned together and with great respect. They were tent-makers by trade, Acts 18 : 3. They were very useful to Apollos in his early ministry 'expounding unto him the way of God more perfectly,' Acts 18 : 26. They are also mentioned in 1 Cor. 16 : 19; 2 Tim. 4 : 19. At what time they risked every thing for the life of Paul is not stated in Scripture, but Paul and many Gentile churches acknowledged great obligations to them.

5. *Likewise* greet *the church that is in their house.* The church *that is in their house,* is a phrase that occurs in 1 Cor. 16 : 19. Two meanings have commonly been given it : one, the pious members of their own household ; the other, the church which habitually assembled in their house. The latter is more probably correct. *Salute my well beloved Epenetus, who is the first fruits of Achaia unto Christ.* *Epenetus* is mentioned in no other place. There is an apparent contradiction between this verse and 1 Cor. 16 : 15, where the house of Stephanas is said to be " the first fruits of Achaia unto God." Three solutions are offered. 1. One is that Epenetus may have been of the family of Stephanas. 2. Stephanas and Epenetus may have been converted at the same time and so were alike first fruits. 3. The third is, that some Greek manuscripts instead of Achaia read Asia, and so Epenetus may have been the first convert under Paul's ministry in Asia Minor. The second explanation is probably the better.

6. *Greet Mary, who bestowed much labour on us.* We have no means of determining who this Mary was. It is quite certain that it was not one of the Marys mentioned in the gospels. History pretty distinctly states that two of them lived and died in the family of John. But this Mary was known unto God and her name is here, and doubtless in the book of life also.

7. *Salute Andronicus and Junia, my kinsmen, and my fellow prisoners, who are of note among the apostles, who also were in Christ before me.* *Andronicus* and *Junia* are nowhere else mentioned in Scripture. The Greek does not determine whether Junia was the name of a man or woman. The word rendered kinsmen occurs also in vs. 11, 21, and is rendered as here, but in Luke 1 : 36, 58 the same word is rendered cousin or in the plural cousins. *Of note,* in Matt. 16 : 27, notable, that is, well known. At what time and place they were fellow prisoners of Paul we are not informed ; for Paul had been " in prisons more frequent " than the Scripture expressly states. They were also aged believers, having been in Christ before Paul.

8. *Greet Amplias, my beloved in the Lord.* Amplias is nowhere else mentioned in the Bible. But the affection of Paul towards

him was strong; the word rendered *beloved* being also rendered well-beloved and dearly beloved.

9. *Salute Urbane, our helper in Christ, and Stachys, my beloved.* The Greek determines that these were both men and not women, as the English Bible would indicate. *Helper,* work-fellow, fellow-helper, companion in labor or fellow-laborer as the word is elsewhere rendered. *Beloved,* as in v. 8.

10. *Salute Apelles approved in Christ. Salute them which are of Aristobulus'* household. *Apelles,* not elsewhere found. *Approved in Christ,* that is, approved after trial as a Christian. *Aristobulus,* not elsewhere mentioned.

11. *Salute Herodion my kinsman. Greet them that be of the* household *of Narcissus, which are in the Lord. Herodion,* not elsewhere mentioned. *Kinsman,* as in v. 7. Of *Narcissus* we know no more than we learn here.

12. *Salute Tryphena and Tryphosa, who labour in the Lord. Salute the beloved Persis, which laboured much in the Lord.* All the persons mentioned in this verse are females. They are not spoken of in any other part of Scripture. *Beloved,* as in v. 7. *Labour* and *laboured,* commonly rendered as here; once or twice toil.

13. *Salute Rufus, chosen in the Lord, and his mother and mine.* If this *Rufus* is the same mentioned in Mark 15 : 21, he was the son of the Simon who helped to bear our Saviour's cross. The woman mentioned here was probably the mother of Rufus according to the flesh, and of Paul spiritually, that is, she had been as a mother to him. *Chosen in the Lord,* by the Lord chosen unto salvation.

14. *Salute Asyncritus, Phlegon, Hermas, Patrobas, Hermes and the brethren which are with them.*

15. *Salute Philologus, and Julia, Nereus, and his sister, and Olympas and all the saints which are with them.* All the names here given are of men except that of *Julia.*

16. *Salute one another with a holy kiss. The churches of Christ salute you.* Greeting with a kiss is mentioned in 1 Cor. 16 : 20; 2 Cor. 13 : 12; 1 Thess. 5 : 26; 1 Pet. 5 : 14. The word in this chapter rendered *greet* and *salute* means literally to embrace. So expressive is this custom of embracing and kissing that it is uniformly resorted to not only in many parts of the East but also in some Western nations on a reconciliation of a difficulty between gentlemen. It is a very suitable token of friendly regard.

17. *Now I beseech you, brethren, mark them which cause divisions and offences contrary to the doctrine which ye have learned; and avoid them. Mark,* that is look after, consider, keep your eye upon, not in a malignant way, but in the way of precaution. *Divisions* so rendered in reference to the church; but in reference

to the state, seditions. *Offences*, as in Rom. 9 : 33; 11 : 9; 14 : 13,
literally scandals. *Avoid*, go out of their way, or eschew them.
See Rom. 3 : 12; 1 Pet. 3 : 11.

18. *For they that are such serve not our Lord Jesus Christ, but
their own belly; and by good words and fair speeches deceive the hearts
of the simple:* that is, they are selfish and sensual men.   These
things have marked the progress of corrupt religious opinions in
all ages: 1. Errorists propose to give great relief concerning the
theories of religion, affecting great simplicity.   2. Almost uniformly lewd practices come in among them.   3. They are never
candid, but deceitful and fond of using *good words and fair speeches.*
Arius swore to an orthodox créed before the emperor.

19. *For your obedience has come abroad unto all* men.   *I am glad
therefore on your behalf; but yet I would have you wise unto that which
is good, and simple concerning evil.*   The *obedience* here spoken
of is the obedience of faith. The clause is parallel to Rom. 1 : 8.
Paul rejoices in the good name of that church; but he begs them
not to be deceived by plausible speeches.   He would have them
wise, shrewd, discriminating concerning that which is good, but
simple or *harmless* as to that which is evil.   See Matt. 10 : 16;
Phil. 2 : 15.

20. *And the God of peace shall bruise Satan under your feet
shortly. The grace of our Lord Jesus Christ be with you. Amen.*   The
meaning is, avoid bad men, give not ear to their flatteries, keep
out of their way and out of their power, and so God shall destroy
the work of the wicked one among you.   Bruising Satan was a
figure first used in the garden of Eden.   The benediction here
used is found also in 1 Tim. and in 1 Cor.

21. *Timotheus my work-fellow, and Lucius and Jason, and Sosipater, my kinsmen, salute you.*   The history of *Timothy* is well
known for his sufferings and labors in the gospel.   *Lucius* is probably the same mentioned in Acts 13 : 1 as *a teacher at Antioch,* and
said to be of Cyrene.   *Sosipater*, in Acts 20 : 4 called Sopater,
not elsewhere mentioned.   *Kinsmen*, as in v. 7.   *Jason*, see Acts
17 : 5–7.

22. *I Tertius, who wrote* this *epistle, salute you in the Lord.*   We
are not certain that Paul wrote with his own hand more than one
of his epistles, Gal. 6 : 11, though he seems always to have written
the salutation, or something near the close, 1 Cor. 16 : 21; Col.
4 : 18; 2 Thess. 2 : 17.

23. *Gaius, mine host, and of the whole church, saluteth you,* etc.
Gaius was probably a very common name throughout the Roman
empire.   The brother here named seems to have kept ópen house
for all saints.   Learned men are undecided whether there is but

one person mentioned in Scripture bearing that name, or whether there are not several. 1. There was Gaius mentioned in Acts 19 : 29. He was a Macedonian, a companion of Paul in his journeys, and seems at one time to have been in great peril. 2. There was Gaius of Derbe mentioned in Acts 20 : 4. He travelled at least a part of the way with Paul in his last journey to Jerusalem. 3. There was a Gaius at Corinth, whom Paul baptized, 1 Cor. 1 : 14, and in whose house he was a guest when he wrote this epistle. 4. Whether the "well-beloved Gaius," to whom John addressed his third epistle, was the same as either of the above we cannot certainly tell. The character given is much the same as that of the man here spoken of. It is impossible to determine this matter. *Erastus the chamberlain of the city saluteth you, and Quartus a brother.* *Erastus* is probably the same man mentioned in Acts 19 : 22, as accompanying Timothy into Macedonia, and in 2 Tim. 4 : 20, as remaining at Corinth. It is not probable that more than one person mentioned in Scripture bears that name. The fact that he was quaestor, or treasurer of Corinth would probably indicate permanent residence in that city. *Quartus* is mentioned no where else. His name would indicate that he was a Roman.

24. *The grace of our Lord Jesus Christ be with you all. Amen.* The same as in v. 20, with the addition of the word *all.* For the import of this benediction see above on Rom. 1 : 7.

25. *Now to him that is of power to stablish you according to my gospel, and the preaching of Jesus Christ, according to the revelation of the mystery, which was kept secret since the world began.*

26. *But is now made manifest, and by the Scriptures of the prophets, according to the commandment of the everlasting God, made known to all nations for the obedience of faith :*

27. *To God only wise, be glory through Jesus Christ for ever. Amen.* This is one of the longest doxologies given in the Scriptures. With it is united a commendation of the gospel and a declaration of the object of publishing it. *Stablish,* also rendered strengthen, fix, set steadfastly, Luke 9 : 51 ; 16 : 26 ; 22 : 32 ; Rev. 3 : 2. Paul calls the Gospel his own, because he had embraced it heartily, because he had it by special revelation and because he had made it known to many. *Mystery,* see above on Rom. 11 : 25. The gospel was a mystery in this sense : that it was not known except by revelation. It was hid for ages, *kept secret since the world began,* until the time came when God would have it made known to all flesh. *Commandment,* arrangement or ordination. Jehovah is the *everlasting God,* not like many of the gods of the heathen, who were but dead men, known to have lived on earth at certain periods of

the world, and then to have passed away. *To God only wise*, that is, possessing original, infinite, eternal and unchangeable wisdom. This God is ever to be approached, whether in prayer or praise, in thanksgiving or supplication, *through Jesus Christ.* On *Amen*, see above on Rom. 1 : 25 ; 9 : 5 ; 11 : 36.

On the subscription to this epistle see Introduction § VI.

DOCTRINAL AND PRACTICAL REMARKS

1. There is a lasting and indispensable obligation on Christians to be kind to one another, and that to an unusual degree, vs. 1, 2. Such conduct *becometh saints.* God's people have very much been cast off by the world, and, by renouncing it, have incurred the hatred of the wicked. This love to the brethren is called for both by the precepts and example of Jesus Christ. To the poor, the persecuted, and the stranger among believers our attentions should be very marked, receiving them "in a holy Christian fashion." Such obligation rises very high, when those who now need our aid, have in other days and circumstances been the friends and *succourers* of the people of God. Cobbin : " Religion teaches us to be courteous and grateful. Past kindnesses should especially not be forgotten. . . It is delightful to peruse this chapter, and see the unity and fidelity of Christians so exemplified, and their kindness and affection towards each other. If such is their state on earth, when their graces are in active exercise, what will it be in heaven ! One golden chain will bind them to each other, and all to Christ ; while one song will proceed from every tongue." This kindness should proceed from pure motives, and be strong and lasting.

2. It is often well for Christians to give or obtain, as the case may be, letters of introduction and commendation, vs. 1, 2. Such notes have often been great blessings to those who bore them, and to those to whom they were presented. That this useful custom should not degenerate into mischief, it is very important that we guard it against abuse, and be careful never to give letters that are not known to be deserved.

3. In the commonwealth, in the family and in the church there is a fine sphere of usefulness for woman without her overstepping the bounds of modesty and propriety. Of the truth of this in the church of God, see vs. 1–3, 6, 12, 13. Some moderns have complained that even in Christian countries woman's sphere was too narrow. But is this so ? How often does she put to shame by her zeal and success the indolence of man. Chrysostom : " Whence is their adorning ? Let both men and women listen.

It is not from bracelets or from necklaces, nor from eunuchs either, and their maid-servants, and gold-broidered dresses, but from their toils in behalf of the truth." Conybeare and Howson · " In the case of Priscilla and Aquila it is curious to observe the wife mentioned first, contrary to ancient usage. Throughout this chapter, we observe instances of courtesy towards women sufficient to refute the calumnies of a recent infidel writer, who accuses St. Paul of speaking and feeling coarsely in reference to women." Strike out of sacred history all the instances of eminent service rendered to the church by her female members, and what a gap there would be!

4. Confessors, who did not suffer martyrdon, but who hazarded their lives in their bold avowal of love to Christ, his truth and his people, will receive a reward as glorious as if they had shed their blood, vs. 3, 4. Such were justly and greatly honored in the primitive church. They fully embraced the doctrine of the beloved disciple: " We ought to lay down our lives for the brethren," 1 John 3 : 16. Chrysostom: " What an honor to have been a succourer of Paul! at her own peril to have saved the teacher of the world! Consider how many empresses there are that no one speaks of. But the wife of the tent-maker is everywhere reported of with the tent-maker. . . Persians, Scythians, and Thracians, and they too who dwell in the uttermost parts of the earth, sing of the Christian spirit of this woman and bless it." Brown : " It is a great thing to see a husband and wife linked together in the bond of the gospel, and both giving up themselves unto the service of Christ."

5. Suitable forms and modes of Christian salutation, according to the most approved standard of morals, ought to be adopted and encouraged among us, vs. 3–23. Chalmers : " This whole chapter filled with the salutations of respect and cordiality—not only from Paul direct to his correspondents but from the friends and companions, who were with Paul, to those whom he was addressing—evinces how much Christianity is fitted to promote the interchange of such feelings between man and man." Brown : " Christianity taketh not away civility, humanity, and gentle courteousness, but rather helpeth it forward by making it run in a clear Christian channel: it is humanity and civility to be sending our respects unto our beloved friends and good willers, and Christianity putteth a noble and heavenly dye upon this."

6. It seems to be the plan of God that great changes for the better should commonly begin among the lower classes and so work their way up. Fishermen, tent-makers, publicans and others of like humble occupation were greatly honored in the early pro-

pagation of the gospel. Three centuries before Cesar bowed to the cross, they of his household sent salutations to the churches. Aristobulus mentioned in v. 10 may have been an ungodly man. Many think he was a distinguished courtier and politician of that day, but some at least of his household believed. So palaces and spacious public rooms were long closed against the preaching of the gospel; then it was preached in the house of a tent-maker and his wife and of others like minded, v. 5.

7. Some ask why the holy kiss is not retained in the church as it was once certainly practised, v. 16. Answer. 1. It was not commanded by Jesus Christ. 2. It was expressive at the time, according to Eastern ideas, and therefore suitable in many places as a token of affectionate regard. 3. But though prudently managed by pious people, yet it was liable to abuse and did at times become the 'occasion of false and scandalous reports,' and so has fallen into general disuse.

8. There have always been disturbers of the peace of churches, v. 17. In one place Paul intimates that there is a necessity for such things. 1 Cor. 11 : 19. So corrupt is human nature, so given to deceive and to be deceived, that it would be marvellous indeed if any church should escape such a trial. Not an apostle was able to live and die without confronting deceitful men. Let none therefore be cast down as though something strange had befallen them, if they are greatly annoyed by such pests.

9. How shall we treat false teachers and mischief-makers in the church? *Avoid them*, v. 17. Evans: " Shun all unnecessary communion and communication with them, lest you be leavened and infected by them. Do not strike in with any dividing interest, nor embrace any of those principles or practices which are destructive to Christian love and charity, or to the truth which is according to godliness. Their word will eat as doth a canker." Other parts of this work show that the same line of conduct is prescribed by many Scriptures.

10. Let churches and Christians ever carefully guard themselves against sensual men; against men who flatter, cajole, deceive and are ambitious, v. 18.

11. Let all Christians be harmless as doves—*simple concerning evil*, v. 19; 'so wise as not to be deceived and yet so simple as not to be deceivers.' In malice be ye children, but in understanding be men, 1 Cor. 14 : 20.

12. What a blessing it is that our God is the God of peace, v. 20. He can give a peace which earth and hell cannot destroy, as stable as the everlasting mountains. Oh that men, who are

like the troubled sea, would but come to him for rest. The peace of God passeth all understanding.

13. Let us study and receive in faith the great blessings intimated to us in the benedictions of Scripture, vs. 20, 24.

14. It is an unspeakable mercy that the gospel, which was so long hidden from the mass of mankind, is now so clearly made known to us. Doddridge: " Let us be humbly thankful, that it is now made manifest; and that we are among the nations who are called to the obedience of faith. Let us be solicitous to answer that call." " When thou said'st, Seek ye my face, my heart said, Thy face Lord will I seek."

15. We never preach the gospel aright, nor understand its true intent till we see that it is made known to us for the *obedience* which *faith* alone can render. Chrysostom: " Faith requires obedience, and not curiosity. And when God commands, one ought to be obedient, and not curious."

16. Would it not greatly add to the profit and solemnity of public worship if the ministrations of the pulpit more abounded in doxologies, vs. 25–27. They are often found in the Scriptures. They are exceedingly becoming. They are always due to God. He alone is great. He alone is wise. He alone is Almighty. He alone is infinite. He alone is eternal and unchangeable.

GLORY BE TO GOD IN THE HIGHEST; AND LET EVERY CREATURE SAY, AMEN.